BANKING LAW

WITH FORMS

BY

WILLIAM WALLACE

ADVOCATE, LATE SHERIFF-SUBSTITUTE OF ARGYLL

AUTHOR OF

"THE TRIAL OF THE CITY OF GLASGOW BANK DIRECTORS"; "A MANUAL OF THE SCOTS LAW OF BANKRUPTCY";
"THE PRACTICE OF THE SHERIFF COURT OF SCOTLAND"; AND "THE SHERIFF COURT STYLE BOOK"

AND

ALLAN M'NEIL, S.S.C., EDINBURGH

LECTURER ON BANKING IN THE UNIVERSITY OF EDINBURGH

AUTHOR OF

"THE LAW OF BILLS OF EXCHANGE, CHEQUES, AND PROMISSORY NOTES"; "A MANUAL OF COMPANY LAW
IN SCOTLAND"; JOINT AUTHOR OF "THE MERCANTILE LAW OF SCOTLAND"

FIFTH EDITION
REVISED AND ENLARGED

BY

ALLAN M'NEIL

EDINBURGH
W. GREEN & SON, LTD.
LAW PUBLISHERS
1923

PREFACE TO FIFTH EDITION

THE author records with regret the death of his esteemed colleague, Sheriff Wallace, which took place at Oban on 11th July 1922.

Since the last edition was issued many changes have taken place affecting bankers alike by Statute and Decisions of the Courts. To all these due effect has been given, and the work otherwise has been revised and brought up to date. As now issued it is hoped the book will maintain the position which has been generously accorded to it as the standard work on the subject with which it deals.

Opportunity is taken of drawing the attention of bankers to the two cases referred to in the text (p. 21), where in the one case liability was, without success, sought to be imposed upon a bank for giving advice as to an investment upon which a heavy loss was made, and in the other case where a bank was held liable by the Courts for undertaking to manage the business of a customer which was that of a farmer and maltster during his absence on military service, and in the performance of which the Court held that the bank had been negligent. These cases demonstrate the risks to which banks are liable in the conduct of their business—risks which will undoubtedly be increased if certain of the recent powers taken by banks in their Charters of Incorporation are availed of. For instance, certain of our Scottish banks have now taken power (a) to act as, and to undertake the duties of, executor and trustee of wills or settlements; (b) to guarantee or otherwise accept responsibility for the genuineness and validity of obligations, instruments, deeds, and documents of all kinds; (c) to grant indemnities against loss and risks of all kinds; (d) to guarantee or underwrite, or become liable to secure the subscription or placing of, or to agree unconditionally or subject to any conditions, to subscribe for, or procure the subscription of, any money or of the whole or any part of any issue of stock shares, loans, funds, debentures, debenture stock, mortgage debentures, or mortgage debenture stock; (e) to erect, or procure the erection of, buildings, offices, manufactories, and works of all kinds, and to construct or procure the construction of roads, railways, harbour works, and public works of all kinds, and to maintain the same;

(*f*) to take over, acquire, carry on, or procure the carrying on of, any business or undertaking in which any of the Company's debtors or customers may be engaged or interested, or the carrying on of which may be beneficial to the Company, and to enter into or perform any obligations in connection therewith. These businesses are perfectly legitimate and profitable in themselves, but under whatever classification of business they may be put they can hardly be classified as " Banking."

It may be that the extensive additional powers above referred to have been acquired for the purpose of removing limitations which in practice have been found to fetter otherwise legitimate banking transactions, but it is to be hoped that in their exercise there will be observed that proverbial caution and circumspection which have made Scottish banking what it is.

A. M'N.

EDINBURGH,
1*st November* 1923.

TABLE OF CONTENTS

PART I

THE GENERAL RELATION BETWEEN A BANK AND ITS CUSTOMER

CHAPTER I

BANKER AND CUSTOMER

CHAPTER II

THE ENTERING INTO AND EXTINCTION OF OBLIGATIONS

CHAPTER III

SPECIAL CUSTOMERS

PART II

BILLS OF EXCHANGE, CHEQUES, AND PROMISSORY NOTES

CHAPTER I

BILLS OF EXCHANGE

CHAPTER II

CHEQUES

CHAPTER III

PROMISSORY NOTES, BANK NOTES, AND I.O.U.'S

PART III

SECURITIES FOR ADVANCES

(A) HERITABLE AND MOVEABLE SECURITIES

CHAPTER I

HERITABLE SECURITIES

CHAPTER II

SECURITIES OVER MOVEABLES

CHAPTER III

SECURITIES OVER SHIPS AND SHIPPING DOCUMENTS

(B) PERSONAL SECURITIES

CHAPTER IV

1. CAUTIONARY OBLIGATIONS

2. BONDS OF CREDIT

3. GUARANTEES

PART IV

INSOLVENCY AND SEQUESTRATION

CHAPTER I

INSOLVENCY

CHAPTER II

PUBLIC INSOLVENCY OR NOTOUR BANKRUPTCY

CHAPTER III

SEQUESTRATION

CHAPTER IV

RANKING

b

CHAPTER V

DIVISION OF THE ESTATE

CHAPTER VI

DISCHARGE OF BANKRUPT AND TRUSTEE

CHAPTER VII

SUMMARY SEQUESTRATION

CHAPTER VIII

WINDING-UP OF COMPANIES INCORPORATED UNDER THE COMPANIES ACTS

CHAPTER IX

EXTRA-JUDICIAL SETTLEMENTS WITH CREDITORS

PART V

DILIGENCE

APPENDIX

INDEX OF CASES

PART I

THE GENERAL RELATION BETWEEN A BANK AND ITS CUSTOMER

CHAPTER I

BANKER AND CUSTOMER

A BANKER is under no legal obligation to open an account with any member of the public who may apply to him, and is, like a merchant, at liberty to choose those with whom he desires to have business connections. When the relationship of banker and customer is established it is substantially that of debtor and creditor, or of lender and borrower, respectively.[1] It is ordinarily established in one of two ways. Where the banker is the debtor and the customer the creditor, the banker receives from his customer a sum of money, or certain cheques, bills, or other negotiable documents, the amount of which is collected by the banker, and placed to the customer's credit either upon account current or deposit receipt. Where the money is lodged on account current, the banker is under obligation to return to his customer, or any person authorised by him, a sum equivalent in value to that lodged, either in lump or in such instalments as may be desired. Where the money, or its equivalent, is lodged on deposit and a deposit receipt given to the customer, the banker's obligation is to return an equivalent sum of money on demand, with interest from the date of lodgment to the date of payment at the advertised rate of the bank ruling in the interval. Where the banker is the lender and the customer the borrower, the relationship is established in various ways, as by the banker lending his customer a sum of money, or allowing him to overdraw his account either (a) without security ; (b) upon the security of a conveyance of his heritable property ; (c) upon the security of a cash-credit bond ; (d) upon the security of a guarantee ; or (e) upon the security of debentures, stocks, or shares of public companies, or other marketable commodities. The contract subsists only during the will of the parties to it. The customer may therefore at any time close his account and ask for the balance ; and, on the other hand, although there may be

---

[1] Joachimson v. Swiss Bank Corporation, 1921, 3 K.B. 110.

a balance at the credit of the customer, the banker may terminate the contract, in which case it becomes his duty to pay over the balance, such as it is, at the date of closure, after making provision for outstanding cheques.[1] Where the account is creditor the banker must give reasonable notice of his intention to close the account, which varies according to the circumstances of each case. In one case it was held that a month's notice was not adequate.[2]

The actual sum of money paid to a banker ceases to be the property of the customer,[3] and though in popular phraseology money deposited with a banker on deposit receipt or account current is spoken of as the customer's money, such money belongs to the banker's creditors in the event of his bankruptcy, even where it has been paid in to be applied for a specific purpose, if such specific appropriation have not taken place [4] either partially or completely [5] before that event.

Pass-Books and Current Accounts.—The entries of the receipt of money in the customer's pass-book, duly authenticated by the bank officials, are *primâ facie* evidence against the bank. It is, however, open to the bank to show by evidence *prout de jure*, that the entries contained in it are erroneous, have been made by mistake, or that, in fact, the money was never received by the bank.[6] To this rule there is the exception, that where the customer, in the belief that the entries contained in the pass-book are correct, has altered his position for the worse, the banker is bound by the entries contained in the pass-book, and cannot subsequently set off sums afterwards paid in to the customer's credit against the entries which he erroneously represented himself as having received.[7] In a recent case where a sum had been placed to the credit of a customer, and relying on the credit made the customer treated the money as his own, and in that belief had altered his position by spending it, the banker was held barred from alleging that the money was paid under a mistake.[8] In another case where there had been a wrong entry made by a bank clerk in a customer's pass-book, and the customer had issued a cheque on the faith of the balance appearing in the pass-book being available, and where the cheque was dishonoured, it was held that the customer was entitled to damages on the ground that the cheque had been granted by him in good faith to a third person.[9]

---

[1] Joachimson v. Swiss Bank Corporation, 1921, 3 K.B. 110.
[2] Prosperity Limited v. Lloyds Bank Ltd., 1923, 39 T.L.R. 372.
[3] Devaynes v. Noble (" Sleech's case "), 3 Ross's L.C. 643, at p. 652.
[4] Barned's Banking Co., 39 L.J. Ch. 635.
[5] Farley v. Turner, 26 L.J. Eq. 710.
[6] Couper's Trs. v. National Bank of Scotland Ltd., 1889, 16 R. 412.
[7] Skyring v. Greenwood, 4 B. & C. 281 ; Shaw v. Picton, 4 B. & C. 715.
[8] Holt v. Markman, 1923, 1 K.B. 504.
[9] Holland v. Manchester and Liverpool District Banking Co. Ltd., 1909, 25 T.L.R. 386.

On the other hand, entries in the pass-book of sums paid to the customer are *primâ facie* evidence against him where the pass-book has been in his possession and returned to the bank without objection.[1] The present position of the pass-book is perhaps the most uncertain of any branch of banking law. In England it seems to be the law that the mere fact of a customer's pass-book being returned to him by his bankers with entries debited therein of certain cheques passed on his account, which subsequently turn out to have been forgeries, does not preclude the customer, even after the lapse of a considerable time, from setting up the forgery, and that although the pass-book may have been returned to the banker without objection.[2] In Scotland the opinion has been expressed that there is no rule of law which requires the Court to hold that the pass-book must be taken to be an accurate record of banking transactions, or that the customer is precluded from challenging its accuracy.[3] In America, on the other hand, the decisions [4] are far more favourable to bankers. There the Courts hold that there is a duty upon customers to examine their pass-books and either sanction or repudiate the entries. Should they fail to repudiate the entries, they are held to adopt them.

It appears to be the law in England that entries in the banker's own books, other than the pass-book, are not binding on him until they have been communicated to the customer, as until this has been done the election to apply the payments in the particular manner entered in the books is not complete. " The effect of making the entries in the bankers' own private books shows only that the idea of so applying the payments had passed in their own minds ; it is much the same as if they had expressed to a stranger their intention of making such application of the payments, and had afterwards refused to carry such intention into effect." [5] It has, however, been decided in Scotland that a customer is entitled to found on the entries contained in the bank books to his credit, while the entries in such books to his debit are not admissible as evidence in favour of the bank.[6]

Bank Books as Evidence.—Where bank books, or any entries in them, are called for as productions in legal proceedings, it is provided [7]

---

[1] Commercial Bank *v.* Rhind, 1860, 3 Macq. (H.L.) 643.

[2] Chatterton *v.* London and County Bank, reported fully in The Miller, 5th May 1890, p. 100 ; 7th July 1890, p. 177 ; 3rd November 1890, p. 394 ; and 2nd February 1891 ; Kepitigalla Rubber Estates Ltd. *v.* National Bank of India Ltd., 1909, 2 K.B. 1010 ; Walker *v.* Manchester and Liverpool District Banking Co., 1913, 108 Law Times, 728.

[3] Clydesdale Bank Ltd. *v.* Continental Chocolate Co., 1917 (*per* Lord Justice-Clerk), not reported.

[4] Leather Manufacturers' Bank *v.* Morgan, 1885, 117 U.S. 96 ; Critten *v.* Chemical National Bank of New York, 1902, 171 New York Reports, 219.

[5] Simson *v.* Ingham, 2 B. & C. 65.

[6] Brit. Linen Bank *v.* Thomson, 1853, 15 D. 314.

[7] Bankers' Books Evidence Act, 1879, 42 & 43 Vict. cap. 11.

that, subject to the provisions of the Act, a copy of any entry in a banker's book—including in this expression " ledgers, day-books, cash-books, account-books, and all other books used in the ordinary business of the bank "—is in all legal proceedings received as *primâ facie* evidence of such entry and of the matters, transactions, and accounts therein recorded. A copy of an entry in a banker's book is not received in evidence unless it is first proved that the book was at the time of the making of the entry one of the ordinary books of the bank, that the entry was made in the usual and ordinary course of business, and that the book is in the custody or control of the bank.[1] Such proof may be given by a partner or officer of the bank, and may be given orally or by an affidavit sworn before any commissioner or person authorised to take affidavits.[2] A copy of an entry is not received in evidence unless it is further proved that the copy has been examined with the original entry and is correct. Where the business of one bank is taken over by another bank an affidavit by an officer of the continuing bank is sufficient.

A banker in any legal proceedings to which the bank is not a party cannot be compelled to produce any books the contents of which can be proved under the Act, or to appear as a witness to prove the matters, transactions, and accounts therein recorded, unless by order of a Judge made for special cause. On the application of any party to a legal proceeding a Court or Judge may order that such party be at liberty to inspect and take copies of any entries in a banker's book for any of the purposes of such proceedings. An order under this section may be made either with or without summoning the bank or any other party, and must be served on the bank three clear days before the same is to be obeyed, unless the Court or Judge otherwise directs.[3] The Court to whom an application is made to order an inspection of entries in a banker's books will exercise its authority in conformity with the general law as to inspection of documents before trial, in accordance with which a party to an action is entitled to refuse disclosure of entries which he swears to be irrelevant.[4] But inspection of entries in a banker's books relating to an account kept in name of a person not a party to the action, though competent under the Act, will only be granted, after notice to such person, when the Court is satisfied that those entries will be admissible in evidence against a party to the action at the trial, and

---

[1] As to construction of this section, see Asylum for Idiots *v.* Handysides & Sons, 1906, 22 T.L.R. 573.

[2] For form of affidavit, see Appendix.

[3] Act, sec. 7 ; Arnott *v.* Hayes, 36 Ch. D. 731 ; Emmott *v.* Star Newspaper Co., 62 L.J. Q.B. 77 ; Parnell *v.* Wood, 1892, P.C. 137 ; Harding *v.* Williams, 14 Ch. D. 197 ; So. Staffords. Tram. Co. *v.* Ebbsmith, 1895, L.R. 2 Q.B. 669 ; Kissam *v.* Link, 1896, L.R. 1 Q.B. 574.

[4] Duke of Hamilton's Trs. *v.* Woodside Coal Co., 1897, 24 R. 294.

when very strong grounds are shown for thinking that there are items in the account which are material to the case of the party making application.[1] When the account is that of a person who has nothing to do with the litigation, the Court will look to the effect in practice of such an order on the rights of third parties, and take care that this section of the Act is not made a means of oppression. The section refers to entries in an account which is in form or in substance the account of a party to the litigation.[2] Where, however, the bank is a party, its position is that of any other litigant, and production of its books can competently be called for. It has been held in England that a magistrate before whom criminal proceedings are being taken has power to make an order under section 7 of the Act for the prosecutor to inspect and take copies of entries in the books of a bank at which the defendant keeps an account.[3]

Banker's Duty towards Customer's Acceptances.—In the absence of any special stipulations to the contrary, an agreement on the part of the banker to pay his customer's acceptances when they fall due imports, on the one hand, an undertaking on the part of the customer to furnish or repay to the banker the funds necessary to meet his obligations as acceptor, and, on the other hand, an undertaking on the part of the banker to apply the money provided by the customer or advanced on his account, in such a manner as to extinguish the liability created by the customer's acceptances. The whole duty, consequently, of ascertaining the identity of the person to whom payment is made, with the payee whose name is upon the bill, is cast upon the banker, and though he may pay in good faith to the wrong person in circumstances by which the acceptor himself or men of ordinary prudence might have been misled, he cannot take credit for any such payment. in a question with the acceptor, since no payment made by him, which leaves the liability of his customer undischarged, can be debited to the latter. The only person who can give a valid discharge for such payment is a holder in due course. It would, however, obviously require a considerable extension of this principle in order to make it apply to documents purporting to be bills of exchange in which the drawer's signature is a forgery, the payee a person who is not intended to be a holder, and the genuine signature of the acceptor has been obtained by fraud, since the signing of such a document creates no legal obligation against the acceptor. Accordingly, in such circumstances, a banker would be entitled to debit his customer, the acceptor, with payments made to the forger or his agent, and not to a *bonâ fide* holder of the

---

[1] So. Staffords. Tram. Co. *v.* Ebbsmith, 1895, *supra.*
[2] Pollock *v.* Garle, 1898, L.R. 1 Ch. 1.
[3] Rex *v.* Kinghorn, 1908, 2 K.B. 949.

documents for value, or to any person who could sue the acceptor upon them.[1]

The acceptance, therefore, by the customer of a bill payable at his banker's is equivalent to an order to the banker to pay the amount of the bill *to the person who can give a valid discharge for it*, and as such the banker is bound to obey it if he have funds of the acceptor in his hands.[2] Where the banker has funds of the acceptor in his hands, but insufficient to meet the acceptance in full, the presentation of the bill operates as an intimated assignation of such funds to the effect of transferring them from the credit of the customer to that of the holder of the bill.[3] The efficacy of the order expressed in the words " payable at " depends upon their being authorised by the acceptor. While a banker, who pays a cheque *bonâ fide*, and without negligence, upon an indorsement, which subsequently turns out to have been forged, is protected,[4] no such protection is afforded him in the case of bills,[5] unless there are circumstances which preclude the customer from setting up the forgery, such as a direction from him to the banker to pay the bill without reference to the genuineness of the indorsement, or an admission, actual or implied, of its genuineness. Since a bank has no better means of ascertaining the genuineness of an indorsement in the case of a bill than it has in the case of a cheque, the bank should, in order to avoid the responsibility of deciding the genuineness of an indorsement, require its customers to domicile their bills at their own offices, and to honour them by cheques drawn upon their accounts.[6] When the drawer and acceptor are both customers of the bank at which the bill is domiciled, and the acceptor notifies the bank to refuse payment of it after the bank has given the drawer credit for the amount, the bank is not bound either to notify the fact to the drawer, or to apply the funds belonging to the acceptor in their hands towards the payment of the bill, but is entitled, on non-payment of it, to look to the drawer.[7] So where a banker becomes the holder of a bill accepted payable at his bank, it is sufficient to enable him to charge prior indorsers, that he has ascertained from his books that there are no funds belonging to his customer in his hands, presentation to the acceptor in such circumstances being unnecessary, since, as the banker is the holder of the bill, the ascertainment by him of the fact that there are no funds, or insufficient funds to meet the bill, constitutes both a

---

[1] *Per* Lord Watson in Vagliano *v.* B. of England, 1891, L.R. A.C. 107.
[2] Brit. Linen Bank *v.* Rainey's Trs., 1885, 12 R. 825 ; Robarts *v.* Tucker, 16 Q.B. 560 ; Forster *v.* Clements, 2 Camp. 17.
[3] See Bills, *infra*.
[4] See Cheques, *infra*.
[5] See Bills, *infra*.
[6] *Per* Parke, B., in Robarts *v.* Tucker, *supra*.
[7] Crosse *v.* Smith, 1 M. & S. 545.

sufficient demand to and refusal by the acceptor.[1] Where the banker is the indorser of such a bill, and pays it on presentation, it will depend on circumstances from which his intention may be inferred, whether he is held to have paid it as the agent of his customer or on his own behalf.[2] The Bills of Exchange Act provides in the case of cheques that the banker's authority to pay them does not cease until *notice* of the customer's death has actually reached him.[3] No such provision is made in the case of bills, from which it may, perhaps, be inferred that the banker's authority to pay them ceases at the *date* of the customer's death, and if this be so the banker who has paid his customer's acceptance after his death, but before notice of the fact has reached him, must look to the representatives of his customer to recoup him, on the ground that by paying the bill he has either become its holder in due course, or that he has done so on behalf of such representatives, and so made them holders of the bill; but he cannot, without such representatives' consent, debit the deceased's account with the amount of the acceptance.[4] The customer's bankruptcy operates as a revocation of his authority to the banker to pay his acceptances.[5] Where a banker has paid his customer's acceptance on a signature which subsequently turns out to have been forged, it appears to be a question of circumstances whether he can recover the amount from the holder. Generally speaking, a banker who pays such an acceptance negligently cannot recover the amount from the presenter, since it is his duty to know his customer's signature; nor can he recover where by his negligence in giving timely notice of the forgery he has prejudiced the rights of the holder against antecedent parties to the bill. But where the banker has not been guilty of negligence, and in addition has given such timely notice of the forgery that the situation of the parties to the bill remains unaltered, or where the presenter of the bill makes a representation of the genuineness of the signature, innocent in intention, though untrue in fact, the banker may, it is thought, recover the amount paid from the holder; but the presenter of the bill, merely by presentation, does not guarantee the genuineness of the acceptor's signature.[6]

Foreign Bills Lodged for Collection.—Bills are frequently handed to a bank by a customer to be transmitted abroad for acceptance and collection at maturity, and the bank in the ordinary course of business

---

[1] Bailey *v.* Porter, 14 M. & W. 44; Sanderson *v.* Judge, 2 H. Bl. 509.

[2] Pollard *v.* Ogden, 22 L.J. Q.B. 439.

[3] B. of E. Act, sec. 75.

[4] See Rogerson *v.* Ladbrooke, 1 Bing. 93; Newell *v.* Nat. Prov. B. of Eng., 1 C.P.D. 496.

[5] *Ex parte* Hall, *in re* Townsend, L.R. 10 Ch. D. 615.

[6] See Smith *v.* Mercer, 6 Taunt. 76; Cox *v.* Masterman, 9 B. & C. 902; Price *v.* Neal, 1 W. Bl. 390; Wilkinson *v.* Johnston, 3 B. & C. 428 (*per* Abbott, C.J.); Fuller *v.* Smith, 1 Car. & P. 197.

sends the bills to their correspondents, who receive payment of them at maturity. In the event of the foreign correspondent's bankruptcy, after having received payment of the bills, but before the remittance bills are paid, it would seem that in a question with the customer, the bank in this country would be responsible for any loss which might ensue, unless it could be shown that the customer gave the bills to the bank with instructions to employ a particular agent to collect them,[1] on the principle that the receipt of the money by the sub-agents is equivalent to receipt by the employing bank. To avoid questions on this subject, it is advisable to take a guarantee [2] from the customer to keep the bank free of any loss before the bills are sent abroad.

It is to be observed that in ranking upon the foreign bank's estate the bank in this country would only be entitled to an ordinary ranking in respect of the proceeds of the bills collected, and not to be paid in priority to the other creditors.[3]

Bank Account.—The name or heading of the account opened in a customer's name is sufficient notice to the banker of the nature of such account. Thus an account opened in the name of " John Smith, executor of William Jones," is notice to the bank that any money deposited by John Smith to the credit of that account is not his unlimited property, and falls therefore to be distinguished and treated differently from any money which he might deposit either in his own name or, e.g., as " Trustee of Robert Brown." [4]   Where, however, money is paid into a bank on a contract that it is to be drawn, out in a certain way, and payments are made in that way, the bank is free from further claims in respect of such money, no matter under what heading the account may have been opened.[5] The mere fact that an account is operated on by an individual does not of itself render him personally liable for overdrafts thereon.[6] But this rule must not be confounded with that which applies to several accounts opened in one name. Where several accounts are opened by one person, or set of persons, under various headings, with the object that the sums paid into the respective accounts may be kept separate and distinct, the various accounts may be treated by the bank, so far as the relation of debtor and creditor between it and its customer is concerned, as being one, to the effect that a debit balance in the one may be compensated

---

[1] Mackersy v. Ramsay, 9 Cl. & F. 818 ; approved of in Prince v. Oriental Bank Corporation, 1878, L.R. 3 Ap. Ca. at p. 335.

[2] For form, see Appendix.

[3] In re West of England and South Wales District Bank, L.R. 11 Ch. D. 772.

[4] Bailey v. Finch, L.R. 7 Q.B. 34, p. 41 ; ex parte Kingston, L.R. 6 Ch. Ap. 632.

[5] The Struthers Patent Diamond Rock Co. Ltd. v. Clydesdale Bank, 1886, 13 R. 434.

[6] National Bank of Scotland Ltd. v. Shaw, 1913, S.C. 133.

by a credit balance in the other.[1] In one case a partner of a firm of merchants opened three accounts with a bank under the heads " office," " deposit," and " private " accounts, intimating at the same time that the deposit account would consist mostly of clients' money. Subsequently the deposit account was closed, and the sum at its credit transferred to the office account, to which in future clients' money was to be paid. During the whole course of dealing the office account was in credit and the private account overdrawn. The bank was held entitled to set off the credit of one account against the other, on the ground that the bank could not be called on to assume that moneys standing to the credit of the office account were trust moneys, there being no suspicious circumstances calculated to put the bank upon inquiry.[2] This rule applies equally to the case where the various accounts are kept at different branches of the same bank. Thus the bank is entitled, without notice to the customer, to transfer a credit balance at one branch in reduction or satisfaction of a debit balance at another branch.[3] There is, however, no obligation on a banker at his own hand to transfer a creditor balance at one branch to meet a cheque drawn by a customer on his account at another branch where at the time of the presentation of the cheque there are insufficient funds belonging to the customer at that branch to meet the cheque so presented. There is no obligation on a bank with branches in different countries to pay in one country a debt due to a customer on current account in another country.[4]

Banker's Duty towards Customers' Cheques.—A banker is bound to honour his customer's cheque if it be presented to him within banking hours, and he have funds belonging to his customer sufficient to meet it. If he fail or refuse to do so he will be liable in damages to his customer, though not to the payee, with whom he has no privity of contract, should his customer suffer loss or damage through such failure or refusal. A banker is not entitled to retain the money of his customer in security of a claim in regard to which there is nothing more than a presumption of liability. In one case a customer having a balance to his credit in an account current drew a cheque on the 21st October. On 22nd October the bank intimated to him that they intended to retain any money at his credit pending a settlement of a claim by them, and requested him not to pass any further cheques. The claim referred to was in respect of a bill for which the bank contended they

---

[1] Pedder v. Mayor and Corporation of Preston, 31 L.J. C.P. 291 ; Kirkwood & Sons v. Clydesdale Bank Ltd., 1908, S.C. 20.

[2] T. & H. Greenwood Teale v. William Williams, Brown & Co., 1894, 11 T.L.R. 40 ; Union Bank of Australia Ltd. v. Murray-Aynsley, 1898, L.R. A.C. 693.

[3] Garnett v. MacKewan, L.R. 8 Ex. 10 ; Prince v. Oriental Bank, L.R. 3 Ap. Ca. 325.

[4] George Clare & Co. v. Dresdner Bank Ltd., 1915, 31 T.L.R. 278.

had reasonable grounds for believing the pursuer was liable to them. The bill, the bank said, was accepted in his name by his brother, who had power to sign cheques for the customer, and had admittedly a general management of his pecuniary affairs. On the other hand, the customer stated that the bill was signed by his brother without his knowledge or authority, and that he knew nothing of its existence until a demand was made for payment. On receiving the above intimation from the bank, the customer replied that he had drawn the cheque in question prior to receipt of their letter, and that if they dishonoured it his business reputation would probably be injured. The bank dishonoured the cheque, and in an action the Court held that the bank were liable in damages to the customer for injury to his credit.[1] But the banker will be excused if, between the receipt of the customer's money and the presentment of the cheque, a sufficient time have not elapsed to enable the amount received to be passed to the customer's account. Where money had been paid in at eleven o'clock it was held that a banker could not be excused for dishonouring a cheque presented at three o'clock on the afternoon of the same day, as a sufficient time had elapsed between the paying in of the money and the presentment of the cheque to enable the banker to enter the amount paid in to his customer's credit.[2]

A banker who had been in the habit of taking up his customer's bills on the security of the produce of certain consignments, and permitting his customer to draw on his current account without reference to the advances made on such consignments, was held not entitled, without express notice to his customer, to suddenly debit his customer's current account with such advances, or to dishonour his customer's cheque, when by so doing he had exhausted the funds standing to his customer's credit.[3] No action will lie against the banker for dishonouring cheques where his customer's assets have been exhausted by the payment of bills accepted by his customer and made payable at the banker's, as the acceptance of such bills is sufficient authority to the banker to pay the amounts due upon them.[4]

Trust and Fiduciary Accounts.—In order to hold a banker justified in refusing to pay a demand of his customer, the customer occupying a fiduciary position and drawing a cheque in a fiduciary capacity, there must, in the first place, be some misapplication, some breach of trust, intended by the customer, and, in the second place, proof that the

---

[1] King *v.* British Linen Co., 1899, 1 F. 928.

[2] Marzetti *v.* Williams, 1 B. & A. 415 ; Whittaker *v.* B. of England, 1 C.M. & R. 744 ; Robarts *v.* Tucker, 16 Q.B. 560 (*per* Maule, J.) ; Rollin *v.* Seward, 14 C.B. 595.

[3] Cumming *v.* Shand, 29 L.J. Ex. 129 ; *approved per* Lord President Dunedin in Kirkwood & Sons *v.* Clydesdale Bank, 1908, S.C. 20 ; Garnett *v.* MacKewan, L.R. 8 Ex. 10.

[4] Kymer *v.* Lawrie, 18 L.J. Q.B. 218.

banker is privy to the intent to make this misapplication of the trust funds. And to that may be safely added that if it be shown that any personal benefit to the bankers themselves is designed or stipulated for, that circumstance, above all others, will most readily establish the fact that the bankers are in privity with the breach of trust which is about to be committed. A banker may not, therefore, honour a cheque which is to his knowledge or reasonable belief drawn in breach of trust and for his benefit : as where an executor draws a cheque on the executry account in payment of a debt due by himself to the banker.[1] Where, however, a cheque so drawn is not for his own benefit, the banker is not bound to inquire whether the cheque be drawn in breach of trust or not.[2] Thus in one case country bankers, with whom a customer had an ordinary current account, received from their London agents a sum of money to be placed to the credit of their customer's *trust* account. The customer had, however, no trust account with the bankers, and they accordingly placed it to the credit of his current account, which at the time happened to be overdrawn upon security, and advised him of the fact. The effect of so crediting the account was to largely reduce the customer's overdraft ; but though aware of that fact, and that the money was trust money, the customer gave no instructions to his bankers, and continued to draw on his account as usual. The customer was, however, in good credit, and the bankers, without any intention of benefiting themselves, and with no suspicion of any contemplated breach of trust, continued to allow him a further and extended overdraft on further securities deposited by him. On the customer's bankruptcy, it was held that the bankers were not liable to make good to those for whom he acted in a fiduciary capacity the amount of the trust money lost.[3] A banker is not entitled to dishonour a cheque drawn upon an executry estate where the funds at the credit of the estate exceed the amount of the cheque, on the ground that the estate is insolvent, and that he intends to apply for sequestration of it.[4]

Account in Name of Person who is the Known Agent of Another.—A banker is not in safety, without satisfactory reason, in crediting the private account of the known agent of an employer with the proceeds of a cheque which on the face of it bears evidence that it is intended for the benefit of the employer and that although the agent has power to endorse cheques *per procuration* of the employer.[5]

Dishonour of Cheque when Funds Insufficient.—Where a banker has funds belonging to a customer, but insufficient in amount to meet a

---

[1] Gray v. Johnston, L.R. 3 E. & I. Ap. Ca. 1.
[2] Boddenham v. Hoskins, 21 L.J. Eq. 864; Backhouse v. Charlton, 8 Ch. D. 444; Gray v. Johnston, L.R. 3 E. & I. Ap. Ca. (*per* Ld. Westbury, p. 14).
[3] Coleman v. Bucks and Oxon. Un. Bank, 1897, L.R. 2 Ch. 243.
[4] Ireland v. North of Scot. Banking Co., 1880, 8 R. 215.
[5] Morison v. London County and Westminster Bank, 1914, K.B. 356.

cheque drawn upon the account, presentation of the cheque operates in Scotland, though not in England, as an intimated assignation on behalf of the presenter.[1] In such cases the practice is to return the cheque with the marking " insufficient funds," and to place the amount standing at the credit of the customer in a separate account bearing reference to the cheque. After this has been done, intimation of the fact is sent to the drawer, and he is also notified that the cheque must be presented again, and delivered up before the balance can be paid. The bank, however, cannot refuse payment of a cheque if the presenter offer to deliver it up. Where several cheques come in through the one clearing or by the same post, and there are not sufficient funds to meet them all, the banker cannot at his own hand select from the cheques sufficient to exhaust the creditor balance and return the others. He must return all the cheques marked " refer to drawer," and place the whole creditor balance to a separate account bearing reference to these particular cheques. But where a banker has agreed to honour his customer's cheques up to a certain amount, presentment of a cheque drawn by his customer before that limit is reached does not operate as an assignation, because there is no debt due to his customer which can be assigned.[2]

In considering whether the bank has or has not funds of the drawer in their hands, the state of affairs as between the customer and the bank at any given time must be taken to be the state of affairs upon all the accounts of the customer. If upon a balance of all these various accounts, such, e.g., as a current account, a loan account, and a cash account, the customer is in the position of being the bank's debtor, their presentation of the customer's cheque does not operate as an intimated assignation of funds to the credit of his current account, on the broad general rule, now thoroughly recognised, that in order that the rule may operate the general state of affairs between the bank and its customer must show clearly that the bank owes its customer money and not that the customer is indebted to the bank.[3]

Notice of Dishonour.—The rules as to the time when, by whom, to whom, and for whose benefit notice of dishonour must be given, will be found in the chapter on Bills.[4]

Countermand of Cheque.—The banker's authority to pay a cheque ceases on countermand of its payment by the drawer, or upon the receipt of notice of the drawer's death.[5] A cheque may be countermanded verbally, but, for obvious reasons, the drawer should be asked to put

---

[1] British Linen Co. v. Carruthers, 1883, 10 R. 923.

[2] Kirkwood & Sons v. Clydesdale Bank, 1908, S.C. 20.

[3] *Ibid.*

[4] B. of E. Act, secs. 48-50.

[5] B. of E. Act, 1882, sec. 75 ; Waterston v. City of Glas. Bank, 1874, 1 R. 470. See also Kirkwood & Sons v. Clydesdale Bank, *supra.*

his request in writing. It may also be countermanded by telegram,[1] but on receipt of a telegram a banker is justified in postponing payment pending inquiry should the cheque be presented before confirmation. It is thought that one partner of a firm can countermand payment of a cheque drawn by another partner on the firm's account. When the drawer of a cheque stops payment by a notice given only to the branch bank on which it is drawn and the payee afterwards indorses the cheque to another branch of the same bank, and the agent of that other branch advances money on the cheque in good faith and without notice that the cheque had been stopped, it has been held in England that the bank is entitled to recover against the drawer in an action on the cheque.[2] The death of the drawer does not *per se* operate as a revocation of the banker's authority, and payment of a cheque by a banker subsequent to his customer's death, but before notice of the fact has reached him, will be good.[3] Where a cheque is granted by a customer but is not presented for payment until after his death, while the banker with notice of the death is justified in declining to honour the cheque, it is thought—especially if there has been no undue delay in presenting the cheque—that in a question between the deceased's creditors and the holder of the cheque the presentation operates as a good transfer of funds in the bank in favour of the holder.[4] A cheque granted for valuable consideration cannot, in a question with a holder for value, be countermanded by the drawer,[5] unless it has been drawn on condition that it will only be used on the occurrence of a certain event, which does not happen, or in payment of goods, which have not been delivered.[6] Where the drawer of the cheque countermands payment, the holder may raise an action of multiplepoinding in the banker's name. But no direct action is competent at the instance of an onerous payee and holder of a cheque against the bank on which it is drawn, and which, having funds of the drawer sufficient to honour it, has refused to do so on presentment, on account of the drawer having countermanded payment.[7] Where the payee has paid it in to his bankers, to reduce the amount of a balance standing against him, the bankers become holders for value, and are entitled to sue the drawer for the amount,

---

[1] Curtice v. London City and Midland Bank, 1908, 1 K.B. 293 ; Reade v. Royal Bank of Ireland, 1922, 1 I.R. 22.

[2] London Provincial and South-Western Bank Ltd. v. Buzzard, 1918, 35 T.L.R. 142.

[3] See Tate v. Hilbert, 2 Ves. jun. 118.

[4] See interesting judgment by Sheriff Erskine Murray on the point in M.-P. Bank of Scotland v. Robert Reid and Royal Bank, 4th August 1886, 2 S.L. Rev. 376. The judgment was acquiesced in.

[5] Watt's Trs. v. Pinkney, 1853, 16 D. 279.

[6] Fortune v. Luke, 1831, 10 S. 115 ; Agra Bank v. Leighton, L.R. 2 Ex. 56 ; Wienholt v. Spitta, 3 Camp. 376 ; Spincer v. Spincer, 2 M. & G. 295.

[7] Waterston v. City of Glasgow Bank, 1874, 1 R. 470.

if he have countermanded payment.[1] So it has been held that if the
payee have paid a cheque, payment of which has been countermanded,
in to his bankers, with the intention that it should be placed to his
credit, it is immaterial whether a balance be standing against him or
not, and the bank, as a holder for value, can sue the drawer on
the cheque.[2]

Payment of Altered Cheques.—As between a banker and his customer
an alteration in the amount of a cheque does not necessarily void the
cheque. Thus a banker who pays the full amount upon a cheque,
the sum in which has been increased through no fault or negligence
on the part of his customer, may still debit his customer with the amount
for which it was originally drawn, but not for any excess which he has
paid over that amount.[3] Where, however, the customer has been guilty
of such neglect or carelessness as to have been the proximate cause [4]
of the banker's having been misled, as where the customer so negligently
draws the cheque as to permit an alteration to be easily made, the
banker will be entitled to debit his customer with the full amount which
he has paid upon it.[5] In a recent case [6] a clerk in the employment of
customers of a bank presented to one of the partners for signature a
cheque drawn in favour of the firm or bearer. There was no sum in
words in the space provided for the writing, but there were the figures
" 2 0 0 " in the space for figures. The partner signed the cheque.
The clerk subsequently added the words " one hundred and twenty
pounds " in the space for words, and inserted the figure " 1 " and " 0 "
respectively on either side of the figure " 2," which was so placed as to
leave room for the interpolation of the added figures. The clerk
presented the cheque for payment at the firm's bank and obtained
payment of £120, which sum was debited to the firm's account. The
clerk absconded. The firm declined to recognise the debit, but the
Court held that the account had been properly debited with the amount.
In disposing of the case in the House of Lords, Lord Finlay thus stated
the law : " It is beyond dispute that the customer is bound to exercise
reasonable care in drawing the cheque to prevent the banker being

---

[1] MacLean v. Clydesdale Bank, 1883, 11 R. (H.L.) 1.

[2] MacLean v. Clydesdale Bank, *supra* ; *ex parte* Richdale, *in re* Palmer, L.R.
19 Ch. D. 409.

[3] Hall v. Fuller, 5 B. & C. 750.

[4] Baxendale v. Bennet, *infra.*

[5] Young v. Grote, 4 Bing. 253 ; Halifax Union v. Wheelwright, L.R. 10 Ex. 183 ;
Robarts v. Tucker, L.R. 16 Q.B. 560 ; Barker v. Union Bank, 1 Macq. 513 ; Swan v.
N. B. Australasian Bank, L.J. 32 Ex. 273 ; Foster v. MacKinnon, L.R. 4 C.P. 704,
712 ; Arnold v. Cheque Bank, L.R. 1 C.P.D. 586 ; Baxendale v. Bennet, L.R. 3
Q.B.D. 525. See also B. of E. Act, sec. 64 ; Scholfield v. E. of Londesborough, 1894,
2 Q.B. 660 ; *affd.* 1896, L.R. A.C. 514 ; Marcussen v. Birkbeck Bank, 1889, 5 T.L.R.
179, 463, 646.

[6] London Joint Stock Bank v. MacMillan, 1918, A.C. 777,

misled. If he draws the cheque in a manner which facilitates fraud he is guilty of a breach of duty as between himself and the banker, and he will be responsible to the banker for any loss sustained by the banker as a natural and direct consequence of this breach of duty. . . . If the cheque is drawn in such a way as to facilitate or almost to invite an increase in the amount by forgery if the cheque should get into the hands of a dishonest person, forgery is not a remote, but a very natural consequence of negligence of this description."

A banker who negligently and without sufficient scrutiny pays a cheque which bears evidence of having been materially altered, or marks which would justifiably arouse suspicion in the mind of a careful business man, will not be allowed to debit his customer with the amount paid on it. Thus a banker is not entitled, without inquiry, to pay a cheque which has been torn in halves, the pieces of which have been pasted together, the presumption in such a case being that the drawer has destroyed it before issue.[1] Where there has been no negligence either on the part of the customer or of the banker, the general rule of law will apply, that where one of two innocent parties must suffer from the fraud of a third person, he who has given the opportunity for the commission of the fraud must bear the loss. The onus of proving that an alteration in a cheque was made in such circumstances as not to vitiate it lies upon the holder.[2]

Payment on Forged Signature of Drawer.—A banker who pays a cheque *bonâ fide* and without negligence upon an *indorsement* which subsequently turns out to have been forged, is protected.[3] But this protection does not extend to the case where the *signature* of the drawer is forged.[4] Consequently, where a banker pays a cheque, though in *bonâ fide* and without negligence, the signature to which has been forged or adhibited without the drawer's authority, he will be liable to the drawer in repetition of the amount, unless the circumstances have been such as to preclude the drawer from setting up the forgery or want of authority. And this will be so even where the drawer has directly contributed to the success of the forgery, as by losing or carelessly mislaying his cheque-book.[5] The drawer may by his actings be barred from setting up the forgery, but mere silence, after the forgery has become known to him, may not be a bar to his pleading the forgery. But silence taken in conjunction with other circumstances has been held a bar when it was the means of giving the forger time to abscond

---

[1] Scholey *v.* Ramsbottom, 2 Camp. 485 ; Ingham *v.* Primrose, 28 L.J. C.P. 295.

[2] Johnson *v.* D. of Marlborough, 2 Stark. 313 ; Henman *v.* Dickinson, 5 Bing. 183 ; Knight *v.* Clements, 8 Ad. & E. 215.

[3] See Cheques, Forged Indorsation, *infra.*

[4] *Ibid.* and Bills.

[5] *Per* Parke, B., in B. of Ireland *v.* Evan's Charities, 5 H.L.C. 389,

and so prejudice the holder.[1] Mere delay on the drawer's part in giving notice of the forgery will not necessarily imply adoption nor bar him from repudiating liability, unless the holder or others have been prejudiced by his silence.[2] If the drawer lead the bank to believe in the genuineness of his signature till the bank have lost some opportunity of recovering on the cheque, which, had the forgery been known, it might have used, such delay will effect a sufficient alteration in the bank's position to preclude the drawer setting up the forgery. But where the customer was first informed of the fact that certain entries debited against his account were in respect of cheques forged by one of the bank's servants, by the accredited agent of the bank, who requested his silence, it was held that in complying with this request honestly and with a view to what he believed to be the bank's interest, the customer had not inflicted a legal wrong upon the bank, and that he was not, therefore, prevented from relying upon the forgery.[3] Where an opportunity is afforded the drawer of denying that his signature is genuine, and he does not do so, or asks for time to see the cheque, such conduct will, if it be the means of prejudicing the holder, as by allowing the forger to abscond, afford a relevant counter issue of the adoption of his signature to the drawer's plea that his signature had been forged.[4] The mere fact of the drawer having taken no notice of a letter addressed to him informing him of the existence of a cheque with his signature attached, will not necessarily entitle the banker to a counter issue of adoption ; [5] and a person is not legally bound to answer, and incurs no liability by not answering, a letter addressed to him by a person or persons to whom he stands in no special relation. It is the right of every person who receives a letter or other document regarding a matter with which he has no concern to destroy that document at once and take no further notice of it. In accordance with these legal propositions it was held in one case that where a person received from a bank, of whom he was not personally a customer, a notice to the effect that a bill purporting to bear his signature lay at the bank under protest for non-payment, the fact that he took no steps to acquaint the bank of the fact that his signature had been forged did not in law amount to a homologation or adoption of his signature, and thus render him liable to the bank in the amount of the bill.[6] Where, however, intimation is given to the drawer that a cheque bearing his signature has been presented for payment, and thereafter an agent acting on his instructions

---

[1] Meiklem v. Walker, 1833, 12 S. 53 ; Warden v. B. L. Bank, 1863, 1 M. 402.

[2] M'Kenzie v. B. L. Bank, 1881, 8 R. (H.L.) 8.

[3] Ogilvie v. West Aust. Mort. and Agency Corp., 1896, L.R. A.C. 257.

[4] Findlay v. Currie, 1850, 13 D. 278 ; Boyd v. Union Bank, 1854, 17 D. 159.

[5] Warden v. B. L. Bank, 1863, 1 M. 402.

[6] British Linen Bank v. Cowan, 1906, 8 F. 704, following Boyd v. Union Bank, supra, and M'Kenzie, v. B. L. Bank, 1881, 8 R. (H.L.) 8.

calls on the banker, and after examining the cheque does not deny or by implication admits that the signature is genuine, the drawer will thereafter be precluded from setting up the forgery.[1] Even where the drawer knows, or has good reason to suspect, that the forger has for some years previously been in the habit of forging his signature, mere delay on his part, apart from other circumstances, in giving intimation of the forgery, will not preclude him from pleading that his signature has been forged.[2] The rule in such cases is, " that where one by his words or conduct wilfully causes another to believe in the existence of a certain state of things and induces him to act on that belief or to alter his own previous position, the former is precluded from averring against the latter a different state of things as existing at the same time." [3] By the term " wilfully," however, must be understood, if not that the party represents that to be true which he knows to be untrue, at least that he means his representation to be acted upon and that it is acted upon accordingly : and if, whatever a man's real intention may be, he so conducts himself that a reasonable man would take the representation to be true and believe that it was meant that he should act upon it and did act upon it as true, the party making the representation would be equally precluded from contesting its truth : and conduct by negligence or omission where there is a duty cast upon a person by usage of trade or otherwise to disclose a truth may often have the same effect.[4] The same principle was more broadly stated by Lord Denman, that a party who negligently or culpably stands by and allows another to contract on the faith of a fact which he can contradict cannot afterwards dispute that fact in an action against the person whom he himself has assisted in deceiving.[5] In the case of forgery under discussion, and probably in all cases of a similar description, these *dicta* must be received with the qualification that they apply only to the cases where the negligence or omission of the drawer to disclose the fact of the forgery has resulted in the holder's position being altered for the worse. Where a cheque is forged without the customer's knowledge by one who has authority to act as his agent, and where the person whose signature is thus forged obtains a benefit thereby, he is bound to repay the bank which has honoured the cheque.[6]

Overdrafts.—Where a banker has permitted his customer to overdraw his account with or without security, his having done so in the

---

[1] Brown *v.* B. L. Bank, 1863, 1 M. 793.
[2] Urquhart *v.* Bank of Scotland, 1872, 9 S.L.R. 508.
[3] Pickard *v.* Sears, 6 A. & E. 474.
[4] *Per* Parke, B., in Freeman *v.* Cooke, 2 Wel. Hurl. & G. Ex. Rep. 654.
[5] Gregg *v.* Wells, 10 A. & E. 90.
[6] Clydesdale Bank *v.* Paul, 1877, 4 R. 626. Referred to and distinguished in Sinclair, Moorhead & Co. *v.* Wallace & Co., 1880, 7 R. 874 ; *cf.* Clydesdale Bank *v.* Royal Bank, 1876, 3 R. 586.

past is no bar to his refusing to continue to do so in the future. The
banker may in such a case, without assigning any reason, intimate that
he declines to allow any further overdrafts upon the account, and call
upon the customer and his sureties (if he have any) to at once make
provision for the liquidation of the debt.[1] Where a customer has been
allowed to overdraw upon security, the banker is under no obligation
to allow his customer to continue his overdrafts until the security is
exhausted, and he may at any time, where no special period has been
stipulated for, refuse to cash his customer's cheques and call upon the
sureties for repayment. The rule is, however, modified to this extent,
that the banker must not act with undue harshness towards his customer,
and must give him reasonable notice.[2] If a customer has in the past
been allowed to overdraw his account against securities a banker is
liable in damages if in similar circumstances with the same customer
he without reasonable notice dishonours a cheque.[3]

Cheque as Obligation for Overdraft.—Where customers of a bank
desire a specific loan for an indefinite period, instead of discounting
their bill or promissory note and renewing it from time to time, the
advance may be agreed to against their cheque. The liability of the
drawers on such a cheque recently came before the Court. In that
case [4] three persons drew a cheque on a bank in favour of " . . . or
order." None of the drawers had any funds at their credit with the
bank at the time. The bank cashed the cheque, payment being made
to one of the drawers, and opened an account in name of the drawers,
to the debit of which they placed the amount of the cheque. Subsequently a question arose as to whether or not the three persons were
jointly and severally liable for the amount advanced, or each only for
one-third. The Court held that the drawers were liable to the bank
jointly and severally for the full amount. To obviate any question of
liability, the form of cheque given in the Appendix should be adopted.

Time from which Interest is Chargeable.—Interest is chargeable from
the date of the respective debits to the account, and not from the date
of the cheques drawn on the account.

Marking Cheques.—Bankers are occasionally asked to mark a cheque
to the effect that the drawer has funds at his credit sufficient to meet
it, and that the cheque will be paid on presentation. It has not yet
been decided what in Scotland is the precise legal effect of such a marking, for there is no recorded case where the holder of such a cheque was
refused payment and thereafter proceeded against a bank. The point

---

[1] Johnston *v.* Commercial Bank, 1858, 20 D. 790 ; Ritchie *v.* Clydesdale Bank,
1886, 13 R. 866.

[2] Johnston *v.* Commercial Bank, *supra* ; Smith *v.* Hughes, 1871, L.R. 6 Q.B. 597 ;
Buckingham & Co. *v.* London and Midland Bank, 1895, 12 T.L.R. 70.

[3] Forman *v.* Bank of England, 1902, 18 T.L.R. 339.

[4] Laurence Henderson, Sons & Co. Ltd. *v.* Wallace & Pennell, 1902, 5 F. 166.

has, however, been before the Privy Council on appeals from the Colonies, when the validity of such markings was recognised.[1] It is thought that a banker in Scotland would be bound to honour a cheque so marked, on the ground that the marking was equivalent to a guarantee that the cheque would be paid on due presentation.

Customer's Right to Secrecy.—A banker is bound not to disclose the state of his customer's account except on reasonable and proper grounds. The question is at present engaging the attention of the Court in England as to whether or not a banker is justified in disclosing to the employers of a customer the fact that his account is overdrawn. The judge of the first instance, in the special circumstances of the case, the bank alleging that they were unable to obtain the address of the customer for the purpose of taking steps to protect themselves with regard to his unsecured overdraft, decided the case in favour of the bank. Notwithstanding the stringent provisions contained in the Finance Act of 1918 regarding bankers collecting for their customers foreign dividends, it is specially provided that nothing therein contained shall impose on any banker the obligation to disclose any particulars relating to the affairs of any person on whose behalf he may be acting.

Bankers and bank agents are frequently asked by their correspondents and others questions as to the financial stability of their customers or their ability to meet certain liabilities, etc. In the answering of all such questions great care should be exercised. The general rule of law may be thus broadly stated :—A banker is liable to his customer in damages if he disclose facts which as a reasonably careful and prudent man of business he should not have divulged, if his customer thereby suffers damage, and to the person to whom he gives such information if he knows, or has cause to know, that such information is untrue and misleading, and such person, in reliance and acting on such information, suffers damage ; or if he imparts such information recklessly and without knowledge of the actual facts, and it subsequently turns out to be false or misleading, and the recipient, in reliance on it, suffers damage. A banker is not bound to make inquiries outside as to the solvency or otherwise of a person about whom an inquiry is made. He is not bound to do more than answer honestly the question he is asked from what he knows from the books and accounts before him. The question would be otherwise if a person who had sustained loss could show that the bank officials had been guilty of fraud in making the report.[2] A prudent banker will therefore decline to furnish any information which might either tend to the prejudice of his customer, or which he does not know or has not ample reason to believe to be true. But this general rule of

---

[1] Gaden v. Newfoundland Savings Bank, 1899, A.C. 281 ; Imperial Bank of Canada v. Bank of Hamilton, 1903, A.C. 49.

[2] Parsons v. Barclay & Co., 1910, 26 T.L.R. 628.

law is subject to this qualification, that if the representations or statements made by him are of the nature of, or amount to, a guarantee or warranty, they must, in order to render him liable in damages to the person to whom he furnishes such information, be *in writing* and *subscribed by him* or by his express authority.[1] A confidential representation as to a trader's credit is personal to the individual to whom it is made, and will not found an action of damages by another person relying on it.[2]

Liability of Bank for Acts of Manager or Agent.—A bank agent, like any other agent, will bind his principal by any act which falls within the scope of his authority in the conduct of his banking business. An agent for a bank has no implied authority to bind his principal by granting guarantees or making such representations and assurances as amount to guarantees and involve liability. Even assuming that an agent in answering questions as to a customer's financial position is acting within the scope of his delegated authority and in accordance with a general custom, any answer which he may make can only bind the bank if it be truthful and not such as would involve practically a guarantee, since the granting of a guarantee is *ultra vires* of his position as a bank agent. It may, however, be considered more than doubtful whether an agent in answering such questions even with the direct authority of the managers or directors could render the bank as a co-partnership liable, on the ground that the answering of such questions does not fall within the scope of banking business for which the bank was instituted and for the conduct of which the shareholders delegated authority to the manager and directors.[3] A doubt has been expressed as to whether or not sec. 6 of the Mercantile Law Amendment Act of 1856 requiring guarantees or representations to be made in writing applies to representations made by a bank agent to an intending guarantor of the account of a customer.[4]

When a mere inquiry is made by one banker of another, who stands in no special relation to him, in the absence of special circumstances from which a contract to be careful can be inferred, there is no duty excepting the duty of common honesty. A cautioner who had been compelled to pay the whole of a loan which he had guaranteed along with two co-cautioners who had become bankrupt brought an action against a bank of which the co-cautioners were customers to recover the amount of his loss. He averred that he had been induced to become a cautioner for the loan by reason of representations as to the financial position of

---

[1] Mercantile Law Amendment Act (Scotland), 1856, sec. 6.

[2] Salton & Co. *v.* Clydesdale Bank, 1898, 1 F. 110.

[3] Hockey *v.* Clydesdale Bank, 1898, 1 F. 119 ; Swift *v.* Dewsbury, L.R. 9 Q.B. 301 ; Derry *v.* Peek, 1889, L.R. 14 A.C. 337 ; Barwick *v.* Eng. Joint Stock Bank, L.R. 2 Ex. 259 ; Mackay *v.* Com. Bank of N. Brunswick, L.R. 5 P.C. 394 ; Western Bank *v.* Addie, 5 M. (H.L.) 80.

'Royal Bank of Scotland *v.* Greenshields, 1914, S.C. 259 (*per* Lord Dunedin).

his co-cautioners contained in a letter written by the agent of the bank to another bank in reply to inquiries as to their credit which representations he averred concealed material facts which ought to have been disclosed. This was denied by the bank. The Court held that the bank agent had not acted dishonestly, and that the bank had no special duty towards the pursuer.[1]

Within comparatively recent years attempts have been made, in one case successfully, to extend the liability of banks for the acts of their agents outside the limits of ordinary banking. Two cases may be referred to. In one case the pursuer when travelling in Canada obtained from the General Manager of the Bank of Montreal a letter addressed to the branch managers, asking them to place themselves at the pursuer's disposal if he applied to them for assistance or advice. The pursuer called at a branch bank of which he was already a customer and presented the letter. He alleged that he was advised by the branch manager to invest in a certain mortgage. He made the investment, and it turned out a heavy loss. The customer then raised an action against the bank for damages for negligence in not warning him that the investment was highly speculative. The bank maintained that no advice had been given to the customer and alternatively that the branch manager if he did give the advice alleged was acting outwith the scope of his authority. The House of Lords held that the General Manager's letter did not contemplate the creation of any such relationship as would give rise to legal liabilities on the part of the bank, that there was no evidence that the branch manager had authority to advise the customer on the investment of the money, and that the customer could not recover.[2] In the other case the ground of action principally was that the bank had contracted to supervise the business of the pursuer, which was that of a farmer and maltster during his absence on military duty, and that the bank failed to properly do so. The jury found that there was evidence to substantiate the contract founded on by the pursuer, that there was evidence of negligence on the part of the agent of the bank, and that accordingly the bank was liable in damages.[3]

In view of the extended powers now taken by Scottish banks in their Charters of Incorporation, difficult legal questions will arise as to the liability of banks for the acts of their agents outwith the limits of banking as formerly understood.

Banker as Custodier.—Bankers frequently have deposited with them for safe custody, boxes containing plate, jewels, deeds, debentures, and securities of various kinds, the depositor retaining the key of the box

---

[1] Robinson v. National Bank of Scotland Ltd., 1916, S.C. (H.L.), 154.
[2] Banbury v. Bank of Montreal, 1918, A.C. 626.
[3] Wilson v. United Counties Bank Ltd., 1920, A.C. 102.

in his possession. When the banker acts gratuitously, he is not bound to exercise more than ordinary care ; and the negligence for which alone he becomes responsible is the want of such care as an ordinarily prudent man of business would take of property of similar description belonging to himself.[1] It is not, however, necessarily sufficient to show that he has taken the same care of the articles intrusted to him as he has of his own property.[2] The banker is not responsible for a theft from such boxes committed by his servant or employee unless it can be shown that he knowingly or negligently retained a dishonest person in his service.[3] More care is required from the banker when he charges a commission.[4] The profit derived from keeping his customer's banking account is not, however, sufficient to constitute the banker an onerous custodier.[5] Property deposited with a banker for safe custody must be returned to the person who deposited it, and the banker cannot take notice of the claims of other persons over that property.[6]

As a general rule, a banker has no right of retention or lien over articles of value or securities, whether negotiable or not, deposited with him for safe custody. The mere fact, however, that a banker grants an acknowledgment of the receipt of negotiable instruments " for safe custody," unqualified by any expression indicating that the deposit is for safe custody *only* or *exclusively*, does not necessarily exclude the banker's right to retain such documents in security for a general balance due him by the depositor, if there are circumstances which show that the deposit, though ostensibly one for safe custody, was essentially and actually in security of an overdraft.[7]

Lost Documents.—Where a deposit receipt, draft, dividend warrant, or other similar document has been lost or mislaid by a customer, and application is made for the renewal thereof, or payment of the sum contained in such document, banks usually comply with the request, after the lapse of a reasonable time, on the customer and an approved person signing a letter guaranteeing the bank against any loss in respect of such payment or renewal.[8] In exceptional circumstances, and where

---

[1] See article in Journal of Institute of Bankers, vol. xvii. p. 455, following case of Langtry v. Union Bank of London in 1896, confirming the view stated. The case was settled by judgment for the plaintiff by consent for £10,000, and arose out of the delivery of certain valuables to an unauthorised person on a forged order.

[2] Doorman v. Jenkins, 2 A. & E. 256.

[3] Giblin v. M'Mullen, 1869, L.R. 2 P.C. App. 317 ; Coggs v. Bernard, Ld. Raym. 909 ; Addison on Contracts, 6th ed., p. 406.

[4] In re United Service Co., Johnston's claim, L.R. 6 Ch. 212 ; Beal v. South Devon Ry. Co., 2 H. & C. 337.

[5] Giblin v. M'Mullen, *supra*.

[6] Leese v. Martin, L.R. 17 Eq. 224-234.

[7] Horsbrugh (Robertson's Tr.) v. Royal Bank of Scotland, 1890, 18 R. 12 ; *vide* Banker's Lien.

[8] For form of such guarantee, see Appendix.

the amount is trifling, a cheque from the person making the application is taken, but in the cheque the lost document should be described and a promise to deliver it up if and when found, with a guarantee to the bank against any loss in respect of their making the payment or issuing a new document, should be inserted.

Where cheques, dividend warrants, interest coupons, or other similar documents are lost in the course of transmission through the post-office from the bank by whom they have been cashed, to the bank on whom they are drawn or the place where they are payable, the course usually adopted is for the bank cashing such documents to guarantee the bank to whom they were posted against any loss in respect of such bank refunding the money paid by the first bank, who in turn take a corresponding guarantee from their customer to keep them free from any loss in respect of their guarantee to the other bank.[1]

Lost Dividend Warrants.—If a dividend warrant is lost in course of transmission from the issuing company to the shareholder it is a question of circumstances whether the shareholder is entitled as of right to demand and receive a new warrant or not. Thus in England it has been decided that where the posting of the warrant was in accordance with the declared intention to pay the dividend, in this way contained in the report of the directors, which report was adopted by a resolution of the company, the company had discharged its duty by posting the warrant, although it was lost in the post and never reached the holder of the stock.[2] If there is no authority express or implied to post dividend warrants, the posting is not equivalent to payment.[3]

Appropriation of Payments.—In the absence of any special instructions from his customer, a banker is entitled to appropriate money paid to him in any manner he pleases, and such appropriation becomes irrevocable whenever the fact is communicated by the banker to his customer.[4] When a debtor pays money on account to his creditor and makes no appropriation to particular items, the creditor has the right of appropriation and may exercise this right up to the very last moment ; the application of the money is governed not by any rigid rule of law but by the intention of the creditor, expressed, implied, or presumed.[5] A creditor may appropriate money received from his debtor, in discharge of a debt which has prescribed, of a recent debt in preference to one of long standing, of a debt not guaranteed rather than of one which is,[6] of a debt not bearing interest rather than of one which does, or even of a

---

[1] For forms of both guarantees, see Appendix.
[2] Thairlwall v. Great Northern Ry. Co., 1910, 2 K.B. 509.
[3] See Scottish Bankers' Magazine, vol. iii. p. 263.
[4] Simson v. Ingham, 2 B. & C. 65 ; Mills v. Fowkes, 1 Bing. N.C. 455.
[5] Cory Bros. v. Owners of s.s. Mecca, 1897, L.R. A.C. 286 ; Hay & Co. v. Torbet, 1908, S.C. 781.
[6] London and County Bank v. Terry, 1884, L.R. 25 Ch. D. 692.

debt which he could not recover by action (provided there is nothing illegal in the nature of the obligation) in preference to one which he could. But the debt to which the money is appropriated must be liquid and not contingent. The banker is not entitled to appropriate a payment made by a customer *qua* executor or trustee in liquidation of a debt due by him, for example, as an individual, and *vice versâ*.

A customer has, however, a right to appropriate a payment made by him in any manner he pleases, and the banker who accepts such payment without objection to the mode in which it is to be applied, is under obligation to apply it in the manner directed. Thus a customer who has overdrawn his account is at liberty to appropriate a payment to meet a bill, or where he is indebted to the bank on two separate accounts he may appropriate a payment towards the liquidation, either whole or partial, of either account, and whether the accounts are *ejusdem generis* or not.[1] Where a customer has a current account and a loan account under an arrangement that the two accounts must be kept distinct, the effect of the arrangement is that payments to the credit of the current account are appropriated to that account and cannot be taken in reduction of the loan account.[2] The appropriation must be made at the time of payment. Appropriation of a payment need not necessarily be express, as it may be inferred from circumstances, such as the customer's conduct at the time when payment is made, the nature of the debt, the source or nature of the payment, and the position of the debtor. Where the creditor is requested to clear off a liability, a general payment by him without specific appropriation will be inferred to have been made in payment of the particular debt in respect of which application was made.[3] So interest is presumed to be paid before the principal,[4] and money paid is presumed to be in discharge of the customer's own debts rather than of those for which he is liable in a fiduciary capacity. The proceeds of the realisation of a security are presumed to be applied in extinction of the debt secured.[5] Where the security applies to several debts, the creditor may appropriate the realisation of the security towards the extinction of such of the debts and in such proportions as he thinks fit.[6] Where the debtor pays a composition or dividend upon several debts, the amount so paid is presumed to be applied rateably toward them all.[7] When the pay-

---

[1] Peters *v.* Anderson, 5 Taunt. 596.

[2] Bradford Old Bank Ltd. *v.* Sutcliffe, 1918, 34 T.L.R. 619.

[3] Peters *v.* Anderson, *supra*.

[4] Bower *v.* Marris, Cr. & Ph. 351 ; Thompson *v.* Hudson, L.R. 10 Eq. 497 ; Warrant Finance Co., L.R. 4 Ch. 643.

[5] Brett *v.* Marsh, 1 Vern. 468 ; Young *v.* English, 7 Beav. 10 ; Pearl *v.* Deacon, 26 L.J. Ch. 761.

[6] *Ex parte* Dickin, L.R. 20 Eq. 767.

[7] Thompson *v.* Hudson, L.R. 6 Ch. 320 ; Hudson *v.* Bass, *ibid.* 792.

ment of particular advances has been provided for in a particular way in the past, there is a presumption that payment of future advances will continue to be appropriated as before, in the absence of express notice to the customer of a contrary intention.[1]

The general rule for an ordinary banking account, where special appropriation is made neither by the customer nor the banker, is that the earlier items of the account are presumed to be discharged before the later, the appropriation taking place by the very act of setting the two items against each other. In other words, the first item on the credit side, whether the customer or the banker be the lender, is presumed to discharge, or reduce *pro tanto*, the first item on the debit side, and the sum first paid in is presumed to be first drawn out.[2] Lord Selborne thus stated the law : [3] " The principle of Clayton's case and of the other cases which deal with the same subject is this—that where a creditor having a right to appropriate moneys paid to him generally and not specifically appropriated by the person paying them, carries them into a particular account kept in his books, he *primâ facie* appropriates them to that account, and the effect of that is, that the payments are *de facto* appropriated according to the priority in order of the entries on the one side and on the other of that account. It is of course absolutely necessary for the application of those authorities that there should be one unbroken account, and entries made in that account by the person having a right to appropriate the payments to that account." This rule has been held not to apply to fraudulent entries,[4] nor to the case where there is no account current between the parties, nor where from an account rendered or other circumstances it appears that the creditor intended not to make any appropriation but to reserve the right.[5] (As to legal effect of closing one account and opening another in name of same customer, see Guarantees, Discharge and Relief of Guarantor.)

It has been decided in England that where a trustee or other person intrusted with money in a fiduciary capacity pays such money into his own private account and immixes it with his own money, and afterwards draws out sums by cheques in the ordinary manner, the rule in " Clayton's case " will not apply, and he is presumed to draw out his

---

[1] Cumming *v.* Shand, 29 L.J. Ex. 129.

[2] This rule is known as that of " Clayton's case " (1 Mer. 608). See also Kinnaird *v.* Webster, L.R. 10 Ch. D. 139 ; London and County Bank *v.* Radcliffe, 6 Ap. Ca. 722 ; Henniker *v.* Wigg, 4 Q.B. 792 ; Lang *v.* Brown, 1859, 22 D. 113 ; Cuthill *v.* Strachan, 1894, 21 R. 549.

[3] London and County Bank *v.* Terry, 1884, L.R. 25 Ch. D. 692 ; see also Deeley *v.* Lloyds Bank, 1912, 29 T.L.R. 1.

[4] Lacey *v.* Hill, L.R. 4 Ch. D. 537.

[5] Cory Bros. *v.* Owners of s.s. *Mecca*, 1897, L.R. A.C. 286 ; Hay & Co. *v.* Torbet, 1908, S.C. 781.

own money in preference to the trust money ; and that in the event of his death or absconding, the person for whom he held the money is entitled to a preferable claim for any money in the banker's hands.[1] In Scotland it has been decided that if a trustee pays trust money into a bank to the account of himself not in any way ear-marked to the trust, and also has private moneys of his own in the same account, the Court will disentangle the account and separate the trust moneys from the private moneys and award the former specifically to the trust beneficiaries.[2]

Annual Balance of Books.—It is the custom of bankers once in every year to bring their books to a balance, debit their customer's accounts with the interest due on them, and carry the balance brought out to the debit or credit, as the case may be, of a new account,[3] the interest thereafter becoming principal. Interest runs on an overdrawn account not from the date of the cheques on the account, but from the date of the payment of the cheques. The bank ledger should be duly docqueted by the customer, or by some one having authority from him to do so. The effect of the docquet is to shift the onus of proving payments debited prior thereto from the bank to the customer.[4] In cases where the docquet cannot be conveniently signed in the ledger, the bank for their own protection should get the customer to approve of the account by letter. Forms of the suggested communications will be found in the Appendix.

Accumulation of Principal with Interest.—The question whether the sum debited for interest remains interest throughout the account, for which the obligants in a bond of credit or guarantee would be liable under the clause in the obligation whereby they undertake to pay interest on the sums advanced from the date or dates of advance until payment, underwent careful consideration in a case decided in 1863, and the decision then given has been followed and approved in a series of cases.[5] The principle may be concisely stated thus. At the annual balance the interest accrued during the past year is added to the principal sum due, and the whole balance brought out is carried forward to the next year's account. The interest thereafter becomes principal, loses its character of interest, and is in the same position as if a cheque for the amount had been passed on the account by the holder. Although the point was raised in connection with a cash-credit bond, the rule of law as to the accumulation of interest with principal is the same

---

[1] Knatchbull *v.* Hallett, L.R. 13 Ch. D. 696.

[2] Jopp *v.* Johnston's Tr., 1904, 6 F. 1028. See also Hayman & Son *v.* Thomson M'Lintock, 1906, 13 S.L.T. 863 ; Macadam *v.* Martin's Trs., 1872, 11 M. 33.

[3] No interest is, at present, allowed on creditor current accounts. If it were, interest would fall to be added.

[4] British Linen Bank *v.* Thomson, 1853, 15 D. 314.

[5] Reddie *v.* Williamson, 1863, 1 M. 228 ; Gilmour *v.* Bank of Scotland, 1880, 7 R. 734 ; Commercial Bank *v.* Pattison's Trs., 1891, 18 R. 476.

in reference to all current accounts. " The privilege of a banker to balance the account at the end of the year and accumulate the interest with the principal is founded on this plain ground of equity, that the interest should then be paid, and because it is not paid the debtor becomes thenceforth debtor in the amount as a principal sum itself bearing interest." [1] While this is undoubtedly so, the bank is not bound to accumulate the interest with the principal on an account, the holder of which has become insolvent, whether by his estates being sequestrated, by compounding with his creditors or by granting a trust-deed for their behoof. In the event of insolvency the bank is entitled to go back to the balance immediately preceding such event and to charge interest from that date.[2] But the mere fact of a company going into voluntary liquidation does not seem to have the same effect.[3]

By sec. 37 of the Pupils Protection Act, 1849,[4] it is enacted that " from and after the passing of this Act every bank in Scotland with which any money shall have been, or shall be, deposited or lodged by any judicial factor, tutor, or curator, or under authority of any Court in Scotland, or with reference to any suit in any Court in Scotland, whether on deposit receipt, or on account current, or otherwise, shall once at least in every year accumulate the interest with the principal sum, so that both shall thereafter bear interest together as principal, and any bank failing so to do shall be liable to account as if such money had been so accumulated." The full title of the Act is " Act of Parliament for the better protection of the property of pupils, absent persons, and persons under mental incapacity in Scotland," and, although it has never been judicially determined, it is not quite clear whether the provisions of the above section are intended to apply generally to all cases of judicial consignments, or are limited to cases of deposits on behalf of the three classes of persons specified in the title of the Act. A somewhat similar point was raised under a different statute,[5] and the Court held that where provisions in an Act of Parliament are clearly expressed and leave no doubt as to the intention of the Legislature, effect must be given to them, even although they happen to be outwith the scope of the objects as to which the statute was passed.[6] Although, therefore, the Act in question does not in its general scope

---

[1] *Per* Lord Justice-Clerk Inglis in Reddie *v.* Williamson, 1863, 1 M. 228.

[2] Gilmour *v.* Bank of Scotland, 1880, 7 R. 734.

[3] Commercial Bank *v.* Pattison's Trs., 1891, 18 R. 476 (Lord Ordinary's opinion).

[4] 12 & 13 Vict. cap. 51.

[5] Titles to Land Consolidation Act, 1868, 31 & 32 Vict. cap. 101, title and preamble, and secs. 2, 139, 149.

[6] Hannay and Others, *Petrs.*, 1873, 1 R. 246. See also Kearns *v.* Cordwainers' Co., 1859, 2 L.J. C.P. 285 ; Lees *v.* Somergill, 17 Ves. jun. 508 ; Dwarris on Statutes, p. 563 ; Thoms on Judicial Factors, p. 89.

embrace any other class of officers than those acting for pupils, absent persons, and persons under mental incapacity, yet the section quoted has a more extensive application, and seems to apply to all moneys lodged under authority of any Court in Scotland, or with reference to any suit in any Court in Scotland.

Banker's Lien.—A banker has a general lien or right of retention over all unappropriated negotiable instruments belonging to, and deposited with him as a banker by, a customer for the amount of a general balance due by such customer on banking transactions, but not for debts due to the banker in any other capacity, unless there be an express contract, or circumstances which amount to an implied contract, inconsistent with such a right.[1] This right of lien is given him at common law, and must not be confounded with any right of lien which he may possess over specific subjects by virtue of an agreement between him and his customer. In England the lien is more extensive, and applies to all securities in the hands of a banker, whether negotiable or not.[2] Unlike the case where a banker has securities made over to him as cover for advances, a banker, while he may assign his debt to a third person, is not entitled, without the consent of his customer, to make over to the assignee the subjects of lien. It is competent for the owner of the subjects over which the lien extends to sell them without the consent of the bank, but the purchaser is not entitled to enforce delivery unless and until he pays the debt due to the bank. When a sale or an assignation is intimated to the banker, he cannot hold the subjects for sums advanced after the date of intimation.[3]

To enable a banker in Scotland to exercise his right of lien over the property of a customer, it is essential :

First. That the property of the customer be actually in the banker's possession, and that such possession have been legitimately obtained. Thus, there is no right of lien over securities left with a banker by mistake or accident,[4] nor over securities contained in a box, the key of which is retained in the customer's possession.[5] The right of lien ceases with loss of possession. Thus in a case where securities were delivered to the bank's customer—a bill-broker—against a cheque which was subsequently dishonoured, it was held that the bank's lien

---

[1] London Chartered Bank of Australia v. White, 1879, L.R. 4 Ap. Ca. 413 ; see Horsbrugh v. Royal Bank of Scotland, 1890, 18 R. 12, *infra* ; T. & H. Greenwood Teale v. William Williams, Brown & Co., 1894, 11 T.L.R. 56 ; Robertson v. British Linen Bank, 1891, 18 R. 1225 ; Bell's Com. ii. 115.

[2] London Chartered Bank of Australia v. White, 1879, L.R. 4 Ap. Ca. 413 ; *in re* Bower, Earl of Strathmore v. Vane, 1886, L.R. 33 Ch. D. 586.

[3] National Bank v. Union Bank, 1886, 14 R. (H.L.) 1. See also Deeley v. Lloyds Bank, 1912, 29 T.L.R. 1.

[4] Lucas v. Dorrien, 7 Taunt. 279.

[5] Leese v. Martin, 43 L.J. Ch. 193.

over the securities had been lost.[1] It is essential that the property,
over which the right of lien is sought to be exercised, belongs, or the
bank has right to assume belongs, to the customer.[2] The general
rule is, that where a person has obtained the property of another
from one who is dealing with it without the authority of the true owner,
no title is acquired against that owner, even although full value be
given, and the property be taken in the belief that an unquestionable
title thereto is being obtained, unless the person taking it can show
that the true owner has so acted as to mislead him into the belief that
the person dealing with the property had authority to do so.[3] The
banker is, however, entitled to maintain his lien over negotiable securities
deposited by his customer, even although it should afterwards turn out
that such securities belong to a third person, provided that possession
have been obtained *bonâ fide* and without knowledge that the securities
were *de facto* the property of another person.[4] If a banker refrain from
asking questions because he suspects there is something wrong he is
not a *bonâ fide* holder.

Second. That the property over which the right of lien is exercised
has not been deposited with the banker for a specific purpose, inconsistent with such right. There is, however, a presumption that the
custody of securities, belonging to a customer who is indebted to a
bank, gives the bank a right of lien over such securities, and to overcome the presumption, the terms on which the securities are deposited
must be clear and specific. Thus the terms of a receipt, which bore
that certain bonds, against which advances were concurrently made,
had been deposited " for safe keeping on your account and subject
to your order," and not for safe keeping *only* or *exclusively*, were held
not to instruct any special agreement of parties such as would exclude
the right of retention which the custody of the bonds gave the bank,
especially when supported by the actings of parties.[5] Again, a bank
agreed to continue a credit to a firm under a cash-credit bond, executed
by the firm and partners, on condition that one of the partners should
place in the hands of the bank securities of a value of twenty per cent.
in excess of the amount of the credit. In compliance with this condition one of the partners deposited the securities stipulated for, and on
the bankruptcy of the firm it was held that the bank was entitled to

---

[1] Lloyds Bank Ltd. *v.* Swiss Bankverein, 1913, 29 T.L.R. 219.
[2] Farrar & Rooth *v.* N. B. Banking Co., 1850, 12 D. 1190 ; Attwood *v.* Kinnear &
Son, 1832, 10 S. 817.
[3] London Joint Stock Bank *v.* Simmons, 1892, L.R. Ap. Ca. 201 ; Mitchell *v.*
Heys & Son, 1894, 21 R. 600.
[4] Brandao *v.* Barnett, 12 Cl. & F. 809 ; Wookey *v.* Pole, 4 B. & Ald. 1. See
Special Customers ; Stockbrokers.
[5] Horsbrugh (Robertson's Tr.) *v.* Royal Bank of Scotland, 1890, 18 R. 12 ; *vide*
Banker as Custodier.

retain the securities and apply the proceeds thereof not only in satisfaction of the amount of the cash-credit bond, but of all sums due on a separate discount account, as by the terms of the bond the bank was entitled to debit the cash-credit account with all discounted bills.[1] But this right of lien or retention does not extend over securities deposited exclusively for safe custody, nor over such as are deposited to meet a draft, or for remittance, or exchange, since if a banker choose to accept the custody of his customer's property upon specific terms, he must be held to have accepted the custody subject to such terms. But the banker appears entitled to a general lien over securities which have been deposited with him to cover a special advance.[2]

Third. That possession of the property has been obtained by the banker in his capacity of banker, and not, *e.g.* in that of custodier, as where plate is deposited with him for safe custody. The fact that a banker charges remuneration for his services is *primâ facie* evidence that the performance of the act for which such remuneration is accepted is one which does not fall properly within the scope of his business *qua* banker.[3]

Fourth. That the customer is in debt to the bank. Where the customer has more than one bank account, or where he has accounts at various branches, the right of lien cannot arise unless the general balance on all the accounts kept in his name taken together is against the customer.[4] A banker with whom a customer opens several accounts has a lien upon them all except where there is a special agreement, where specific property of a third person has been paid in, or where he has notice that a draft upon a particular account would be a fraud or breach of trust.[5]

Where a debtor is neither bankrupt nor *vergens ad inopiam*, the banker's lien does not, in the absence of special agreement, cover debts which have not yet become due. Thus, a bank has no right to retain a sum of money lying to a customer's credit on current account, as security for a bill which has not yet become due,[6] and the fact that the bank intend to apply for the sequestration of the estates of the customer does not justify a refusal to honour a cheque drawn on the account.[7]

Lien over Bills.—A banker has a general lien over all bills not specifically appropriated, and lodged by a customer for collection. He

---

[1] Alston's Tr. *v.* Royal Bank of Scotland, 1893, 20 R. 887.

[2] Jones *v.* Peppercorne, 28 L.J. Ch. 138 ; *in re* European Bank (Agra Bank claim), 1872, L.R. 8 Ch. App. 41.

[3] Brandao *v.* Barnett, 12 Cl. & F. 809.

[4] See *in re* European Bank (Agra Bank claim), *supra ;* Garnett *v.* MacKewan, L.R. 8 Ex. 10.

[5] T. & H. Greenwood Teale *v.* William Williams, Brown & Co., 1894, 11 T.L.R. 56.

[6] Paul & Thain *v.* Royal Bank of Scotland, 1869, 7 M. 361 ; Ireland *v.* North of Scotland Banking Co., 1880, 8 R. 215.

[7] Ireland, *supra.*

has no right of lien over bills which have been indorsed to him for the special purpose of negotiation. Where the acceptor of a bill, on the drawer's advice, presented the bill to a banker for discount, it was held that the banker had no right to retain the bill for a debt due by the presenter.[1] This lien being general extends to all the bills and paper of his customer, so that to entitle the customer to demand return of any one he must have paid up the whole balance due. A banker has no lien over bills deposited with him simply for safe custody [2] nor over bills left with him to be discounted but which he has refused to discount,[3] since until the bill is discounted the banker holds it as a deposit,[4] and so soon as the banker discounts it he becomes its owner and as such is entitled to sue upon it.[5] The indorsation of the customer upon a bill is *primâ facie* evidence that it has not been deposited by the customer in security of advances, but has been transferred to the banker, the test being whether the indorsement was made under such circumstances as to show that the intention of the parties was that the customer should be liable on the bill as indorser ; that is, whether the indorsement practically amounting to one without recourse and of no benefit to the indorsee, was made simply for collection of discount, or whether it was made with the intention of transferring all interest in the bill to the indorsee. In the former case the bill will be regarded as having been deposited in security and therefore subject to the banker's right of lien, while in the latter the banker becomes the owner of the bill.[6] An averment that a bill has been indorsed to a banker for discount and not by way of security can only be proved by the writ or oath of the banker.[7] So bills paid in to a banker before they are due are *primâ facie* the property of the person so paying them in, and subject, therefore, to the banker's right of lien ; [8] but such bills when indorsed become the property of the banker.[9] Bills, however, paid in to a banker at a date long prior to their coming due, and as a fund of credit on which advances on other and smaller bills are made during their currency, have been held to become the property of the banker, in respect that full value for them has been given by way of advances.[10] Bills remitted to a banker for a special purpose which has not been fulfilled remain the property of the remitter and are subject to the banker's right of

---

[1] Haig *v.* Buchanan, 1823, 2 S. 412 ; Matheson *v.* Anderson, 1822, 1 S. 486.

[2] Leese *v.* Martin, L.R. 17 Eq. 224.

[3] Borthwick *v.* Bremner, 1833, 12 S. 121 (11 S. 716).

[4] *Ex parte* Twogood, 19 Ves. 231.

[5] Carstairs *v.* Bates, 3 Camp. 301 ; Attwood *v.* Crowdie, 1 Stark, 483.

[6] Lord Eldon in *ex parte* Twogood, *supra* ; *ex parte* Schofield, L.R. 12 Ch. D. 337.

[7] Glen *v.* National Bank, 1849, 12 D. 353.

[8] Giles *v.* Perkins, 9 East, 12.

[9] *Ex parte* Bond, 1 M.D. & De G. 10 ; *ex parte* Brown, 3 Deac. 91.

[10] Glen *v.* National Bank of Scotland, *supra* ; Patten *v.* Royal Bank of Scotland, 1853, 15 D. 617.

lien.[1] So bills remitted to meet other bills which have not yet become due,[2] or which are to be retained by the banker till they fall due, the customer being meanwhile permitted to draw against them,[3] or for deposit,[4] remain the property of the customer, and are subject to the banker's right of lien.

On the other hand, where a bill has been paid in to a banker, who seeks to exercise his right of lien over it, the onus of proving the customer's intention in paying it in is upon the banker,[5] the entries in whose books may be used against him but not against the customer.[6] Where bills bear the indorsation of the customer, there may, in certain circumstances, be a presumption that the property in them has not passed to the banker but remains in the customer. In such circumstances the banker possesses a right of lien over them. Thus, where in his books the banker has entered the bills as " short " [7] or for collection,[8] and has not given credit for them, the presumption is against the property in them having passed to him. So, where in the accounts sent by the banker to his customer undue bills are described in such a way as to show that he considered them the customer's property,[9] or if there be an arrangement or understanding between the banker and his customer that the latter's bills are only to be discounted in certain contingencies, as when the customer's debit balance reaches a certain figure,[10] the presumption is against the property in the bills having passed to the banker. Where, however, the fund in the bank on which the customer draws consists wholly or mostly of bills paid in by him, the ordinary presumption that the property in the bills has passed to the banker holds, since in such circumstances the banker has of necessity the right to deal with the bills given him by the customer.[11] But where a banker enters his customer's bills paid in before they become due, in a column against which he permits his customer to draw, his conduct will be held to amount to an undertaking to answer drafts to the amount of the bills so entered, but not of a bargain that the property in the bills has passed to the banker.[12]

---

[1] *Ex parte* Dumas, 1 Atk. 232 ; Zinck *v.* Walker, 2 W. Bl. 1154 ; Tooke *v.* Hollingworth, 5 T.R. 215 ; Bent *v.* Puller, 5 T.R. 494 ; Park *v.* Eliason, 1 East, 544, 550 ; Buchanan *v.* Findlay, 9 B. & C. 738.

[2] Jombart *v.* Woollett, 2 My. & Cr. 389.

[3] *Ex parte* Edwards, 2 M.D. & De G. 625.

[4] *Ex parte* Twogood, 19 Ves. 231.

[5] *Ex parte* Sergeant, 1 Rose, 153 ; *ex parte* Barkworth, 27 L.J. Bank. 5.

[6] *Ex parte* Pease, 1 Rose, 232, 239.　See *ante*, pp. 2, 3.

[7] Zinck *v.* Walker, *supra.*

[8] *Ex parte* Schofield, L.R. 12 Ch. D. 337.

[9] *Ex parte* Pease, 1 Rose, 238.

[10] *Ex parte* Wakefield, 1 Rose, 243, 253 ; 19 Ves. 25.

[11] *Ex parte* Thomson, 1 Mount. & Mac. 113.

[12] Thomson *v.* Giles, 2 B. & C. 430.

Other Subjects of Lien.—The lien extends over all negotiable securities which have been lodged by the customer with the banker for the purpose of collecting the proceeds and crediting the customer's account therewith, and against which advances have been or are intended to be made. Thus bills of exchange indorsed in blank or payable to bearer, promissory notes, exchequer bills,[1] coupons and bearer bonds of foreign governments,[2] cheques,[3] marginal receipt notes,[4] and an order to the purchaser of bills to pay the purchase money to a banker,[5] have been held to be proper subjects of lien. Where there has been no arrangement that bearer bonds are to be held as against advances the question is still open whether a banker has a lien over bearer bonds specially deposited with him so that he may cut off and collect the coupons as they fall due. Over the coupons when cut off the banker has a right of lien and it is thought he has a right of lien over the bonds themselves in his possession. A banker has no right of lien over registered share certificates in name of his customer, as such certificates are merely representative of property otherwise vested in the customer. Where, however, shares are transferred to a banker or his nominees under an *ex facie* absolute title, and the transfer is registered in the books of the company, the banker is not bound to retransfer the shares unless and until his whole obligations are paid.[6] This rule holds good although the *ex facie* title has been qualified by a back letter or other agreement declaring that it has been granted in security of a particular debt, unless it is stated that the securities are to be held only for that debt and no other. By the terms of their constitution banking companies have usually a lien over their own stock in security of advances made to shareholders.[7] It has not been decided, but it is thought that the right of lien does not cover a deposit receipt of another bank in name of the customer. To obviate any question, the deposit receipt should be indorsed, the proceeds uplifted, and if need be lodged on deposit receipt with the bank who desire to hold it as cover for advances.

Partners.—Where a firm consisting of two or more partners has an account with a bank and the individual partners have separate accounts with the same bank, on the ground that every partner of a

---

[1] Brandao *v.* Barnett, 12 Cl. & F. 809.

[2] Jones *v.* Peppercorne, 28 L.J. Ch. 138 ; Wylde *v.* Radford, 33 L.J. Ch. 51, 53.

[3] Scott and Others *v.* Franklin, 15 East, 428.

[4] Jeffreys *v.* Agra and Masterman's Bank, L.R. 2 Ex. 674.

[5] Currie *v.* Misa, L.R. 1 Ap. Ca. 554.

[6] Hamilton *v.* Western Bank, 1856, 19 D. 152.

[7] Burns *v.* Lawrie's Trs., 1840, 2 D. 1348 ; Hague *v.* Davidson, 2 Ex. 741 ; *in re* London and Birm. Bank, 34 L.J. Ch. 418 ; Murray *v.* Pickett, 12 Cl. & F. 764 ; *in re* Stockton Mall. Iron Co., 45 L.J. Ch. 168 ; *in re* Gen. Exch. Bank (*re* Lewis), L.R. 6 Ch. 818 ; *in re* Hoylake Ry. Co. (*ex parte* Littledale), L.R. 9 Ch. 257.

firm is liable to the full extent of his means for the firm's debts, it is thought, although there is no express decision on the point, that in Scotland—it is otherwise in England [1]—a banker has a lien over the deposits or securities of a partner for the general balance due by the firm.

Care of Subjects under Lien.—The banker is bound to exercise due care of the subjects over which he claims a lien, and greater care is expected than in cases where securities are lodged with him for safe custody only.[2]

Sale of Securities over which Lien Extends.—The law of Scotland, unlike that of England, does not recognise, *in the absence of any agreement to the contrary*, an implied power on the part of a banker to sell the securities over which his lien extends. All he can do is to retain the securities until his claim is settled.[3] Where the lien extends over bills lodged for collection, the banker is bound to duly negotiate them, and is entitled to apply the proceeds in reduction or payment of any sum due to him by the person who lodged the bills.[4]

Deposit Receipts.—With the various difficult questions which arise as to what constitutes a valid donation or gift of the money contained in a deposit receipt,[5] bankers in general have no concern, their duty being to fulfil the contract they have entered into ; and so long as they pay out the money in terms of the contract under which it was deposited, such a payment is necessarily a discharge of the bank.[6] The responsibility is upon the bank to pay to the proper person. This may be illustrated by the following case. A. lodged to his credit on deposit receipt with a bank the sum of £100. He went abroad, taking the deposit receipt with him. From thence he wrote to the bank requesting them to pay to his brother £60 out of the £100 on presentation of the deposit receipt which he stated he had indorsed. At the same time A. wrote to his brother enclosing the deposit receipt and also a letter addressed to the bank in like terms to the letter sent direct to the bank. The letter to the bank was duly delivered, but the letter to the brother was stolen in transit. A person pretending to be the brother presented the indorsed receipt at the bank and received payment of the £60, and a new receipt in A.'s name for the £40. A. thereafter raised an action against the bank for payment, and it was held that the bank was responsible

---

[1] Watt *v.* Christie, 11 Beav. 546 ; *ex parte* M'Kenna, 30 L.J. Bank. 30.

[2] See Donald *v.* Suckling, 1866, L.R. 1 Q.B. 585.

[3] Horsbrugh (Robertson's Tr.) *v.* Royal Bank of Scotland, 1890, 18 R. 12.

[4] Bell's Com. ii. 23.

[5] *Vide passim* M'Cubbin *v.* Tait, 1868, 40 S.J. 158 ; M'Connell's Trs. *v.* M'Connell's Trs., 1886, 13 R. 1175 ; Penman's Trs. *v.* Penman, 4 S.L.T. 100 ; Dinwoodie's Exr. *v.* Carruther's Exr., 1895, 23 R. 234 ; Brownlee's Exr. *v.* Brownlee, 1908, S.C. 232 ; Hutchieson's Exr. *v.* Shearer, 1909, S.C. 15.

[6] Struthers Patent Diamond Co. Ltd. *v.* Clydesdale Bank, 1886, 13 R. 434.

for the loss.[1] If, however, the bank pay in terms of their contract they
are free from further responsibility. A sum forming part of a trust estate
was deposited with a bank on a consignation receipt bearing that the
money was received from the truster's executors, and was to be repayable
on the indorsation of a firm of solicitors who were the law agents in the
trust. The law firm was subsequently dissolved. Some years afterwards
B., one of the former partners, indorsed the receipt in the firm's name,
uplifted and embezzled the money. In an action against the bank at
the instance of the beneficiaries under the trust for payment of the sum
deposited, it was held that as the uplifting of the deposit was necessary
either to wind up the affairs of the partnership or to complete transactions begun but unfinished at the time of the dissolution within the
meaning of the Partnership Act, 1890, sec. 8, B. was entitled to adhibit
the firm's signature, and that the bank was justified in paying over the
money to him.[2] Interest, although not stated to be paid, is payable
according to the duly advertised rates of the banks.

Discharge of Deposit Receipts.—A deposit receipt granted to " A." is
discharged by the indorsation of A., or, on his death, of his executors,
coupled with delivery of the deposit receipt, and payment by the bank.
A receipt to " A. and B., payable to either or the survivor," is discharged
by the indorsation of A. *or* B. during their joint lives, or of the survivor
on the death of one of them, or, on the death of both, of the executors
of the last survivor. Where one of the parties only is dead, the indorsation of the survivor should be obtained. A receipt to " A. and B. "
requires the indorsation of both, and on the death of one, of the survivor and the executor of the deceased, and on the death of both, of
their respective executors. Where a deposit receipt is issued to " A.
and B.," payable to either or the survivor, the obligation thereby undertaken by the bank is, when not legally interpelled from paying, such as
by arrestment or notice from the other party to the receipt, to pay to
either of the parties the amount represented by the receipt on delivery
of it indorsed. The bank is not entitled in a question with, say, A., who
produces the receipt indorsed by him, to retain the sum due in security
of a claim against B., and that whether it is or is not the fact that the
money is the property of B. Thus in one case A. and B. deposited
money in bank, taking a deposit receipt acknowledging receipt of
the money from them payable to either or the survivor. Subsequently the
bank accepted A. as co-obligant in a bond of cash credit granted to his
brother C., relying, they alleged, *inter alia*, upon the security of the sum
contained in the deposit receipt, which they averred belonged wholly to
A. The bank therefore refused to make payment of the money to B.,
although A. consented to payment being made to him. The Court held

---

[1] Wood *v.* Clydesdale Bank Ltd., 1914, S.C. 397.
[2] Dickson *v.* National Bank of Scotland Ltd., 1917, S.C. (H.L.) 50.

that the bank was not justified in refusing payment, on the ground that they could not by a course of dealing with one of the parties altogether destroy the right of the other, but were bound by their obligation to pay either, which they had undertaken by granting the deposit receipt.[1] With that case falls to be contrasted another where, as in the previous case, a deposit receipt was granted by a bank payable to A. or B. or the survivor. C., a third party, claiming, however, that the money so lodged belonged to him, raised an action against A. to have it found that the money truly belonged to him, and on the dependence of that action arrested in the hands of the bank the sum contained in the deposit receipt. During the dependence of the action B. presented the deposit receipt to the bank duly indorsed and received payment. C. then, having obtained decree in the action against A., raised an action of damages against the bank for breach of the arrestment, and concluded for payment of the sum contained in the deposit receipt. C. averred that at the time when payment was made to B. the bank agent knew that the action against A. was pending, and that it had for its object the determination of the true ownership of the money. The Court, however, held that the bank was not precluded by the mere terms of the receipt from refusing to make payment to B. until the ownership of the money was determined, but that C.'s averments of knowledge on the part of the bank's agent (whose knowledge must be regarded as the bank's knowledge) were relevant to the question whether the bank had paid the money wrongfully to B. and in breach of the arrestment. The Court accordingly allowed a proof of these averments of knowledge on the part of the bank agent. It was pointed out that although a bank which has undertaken to pay either to A. or B. cannot refuse to make payment to A. because they have chosen to make advances to B., it does not follow they are bound to pay to A. notwithstanding that the fund has been arrested by a creditor of B. In the event of the fund being arrested on belonging to one of the parties, the bank is not bound to pay to the other party, because, for anything that appears upon the face of the deposit receipt, the fund may belong, wholly or in part, to the former, and to pay it to the latter might be to defeat the just rights of creditors. A deposit receipt is not a document of title, and no inference can be drawn from the terms in which the money is deposited as to the true ownership of the money.[2] If an arrestment is used by a third party in the hands of the bank against one of the parties, it seems clear that the arrestment may validly attach the sum in the receipt, and the bank is probably not in safety to pay until the arrestment is withdrawn. In the event of payment being insisted on by the party to the receipt other than the person against whom the arrestment is used, the bank

---

[1] Anderson v. North of Scotland Bank, 1901, 4 F. 49.
[2] Allan's Exr. v. Union Bank of Scotland, 1909, S.C. 206, and cases cited.

should, for their own protection, raise an action of multiplepoinding, and allow the Court to determine to whom the money should be paid.[1] Either party to a receipt issued in such terms may intimate to the bank that payment is not to be made without his indorsation, and such an intimation must be given effect to, even although the receipt be produced for payment bearing the other depositor's indorsation. If the depositor intimating dies before payment, the receipt must be indorsed by his executors.

The indorsement by mark of any depositor who is unable to write is invariably taken; but, to preserve evidence that the mark is really that of the depositor, it should be attested by two subscribing witnesses, who should also add their designations and addresses. Where the sum is considerable, it is preferable to have the receipt indorsed on behalf of the depositor by a notary public or justice of the peace.[2] As a bank is accountable to the depositor, it is the duty of the bank to be satisfied as to the identity and *bonâ fides* of the person to whom repayment is made. In the case of a payment to a wrongful holder the bank is liable to the depositor, unless it can show that the depositor has been guilty of fraud, or of such negligence that the responsibility for the wrongful payment is with him.[3] While payment in terms of its contract discharges the bank, the terms of a deposit receipt do not in any way determine the property in the money represented by it, nor have they any testamentary operation or effect, though they may be important elements as indicating the intention of the depositor.[4]

A bank is not bound to honour a cheque drawn on it where the only funds of the drawer in the bank's possession are those contained in a deposit receipt.

In the forms of deposit receipts at present in use there is usually a condition stated that " when money is to be drawn, this receipt must be returned with the signature of the depositor on the back," and this forms a part of the contract between the bank and its customer. When any payment, whether of principal or interest, is made, the receipt should be delivered up indorsed, and a new receipt granted for the balance continued on deposit. Unless, therefore, the deposit receipt is indorsed and delivered to the bank, the bank cannot be forced to pay except on its own terms. When the receipt is lost or mislaid, it is usual for the bank, after the lapse of a reasonable time, to pay the sum contained in it on a discharge and guarantee by the customer and an approved cautioner.[5]

---

[1] Allan's Exr. *v.* Union Bank, *supra*, commenting on and explaining Bank of Scotland *v.* Robertson, 1870, 8 M. 391.

[2] See Execution of Deeds, *infra*.

[3] Forbes' Exr. *v.* Western Bank, 1854, 16 D. 807.

[4] Crosbie's Trs. *v.* Wright, 1880, 7 R. 823 ; MacDonald *v.* MacDonald, 1889, 16 R. 758.

[5] For form of discharge and guarantee, see Appendix.

If the depositor is unable to procure a satisfactory cautioner, the bank can stipulate for any reasonable condition being complied with before paying the receipt, although in one case in the Sheriff Court, after proof as to the circumstances attending the loss, payment by the bank was ordered.[1] The point has not, however, been decided by the Supreme Court.

Negotiation of Receipts.—A deposit receipt is not in itself a negotiable document, capable of being transmitted by indorsation, either in blank or special, and with or without the addition of the words " or order," so as to confer on the indorsee by that act right to the property of the fund represented by it. There is no doubt that the debt or fund is transferable, inasmuch as it is assignable ; and an assignation of the debt or fund might be indorsed or written on the back of the document, but such assignation to be complete must in ordinary course be intimated, to the bank. Possession of an indorsed deposit receipt does not *per se* confer on the possessor any right of property in the fund represented by it. It merely implies a mandate to uplift the fund on behalf of the owner. A mandate has this peculiarity, that it falls with the death of the mandant in a question with any persons to whom the death is known.[2] Therefore, when the bank come to the knowledge of the death of a depositor, payment should not be made unless on production of confirmation. If payment be made in ignorance of the death, the bank cannot be compelled to pay a second time. The question of the negotiability of a deposit receipt was raised in one case,[3] and was decided adversely to the holder of the receipt, who had uplifted the proceeds after the death of the creditor, and who was accordingly ordered to repay the amount to his executor.

Stamp.—Deposit receipts payable (1) to the party from whom the money has been received ; (2) issued in the names of two or more persons to be drawn by any or either, or the survivor ; and (3) issued in the names of two persons in terms of the " Titles to Land (Consolidation) Act, 1868," for behoof of the party or parties having best right thereto, are not now chargeable with duty on issue. Until recently deposit receipts framed in terms of (2) and (3) were charged with a duty of one penny on issue. Every deposit receipt when paid must be discharged on a twopence stamp.

Deposit Receipt as Security.—The sum contained in a deposit receipt may be made the subject of security by the holder for a third party's indebtedness. The transaction should be carried out by the depositor

---

[1] Newlands *v.* National Bank of Scotland. Decided by Sheriff-Substitute Balfour in the Glasgow Sheriff Court on 23rd December 1891.

[2] Henderson *v.* M'Culloch, 1839, 1 D. 927 ; Heron *v.* M'Geoch, 1851, 14 D. 25 ; Barstow *v.* Inglis, 1857, 20 D. 230.

[3] Barstow *v.* Inglis, 1857, 20 D. 230.

indorsing the receipt and handing it to the bank along with a letter specifying the purposes for which the receipt has been lodged. The letter should bear a sixpenny stamp. Where the deposit receipt holder is the borrower no letter is required, for then the bank is entitled to set off the sum due on the deposit receipt against the debtor balance on the deposit account.[1]

Consignation Receipts.—The principles just explained with reference to deposit receipts apply equally to ordinary consignation receipts, as distinguished from receipts for judicial consignation. In the issuing of these receipts, care should be taken to insert a clause providing for the manner in which the receipt is to be discharged and the money repaid.

Judicial Consignations.—(1) *In Court of Session Actions.*—Such consignations are now regulated by the Court of Session Consignations (Scotland) Act, 1895.[2] The expression " consignation " as used in the Act extends and applies to any sum of money consigned or deposited in any bank under orders of the Court, or in virtue of the provisions of any Act of Parliament, and includes any sum of money, or any bank deposit receipt, security, or other voucher for a sum of money, received by the Accountant of Court, or by any of the Clerks of Court, as the case may be, for deposit or consignation in any cause or proceeding, whether by order of Court or otherwise, and any sum of money lodged by way of caution or security in corroboration of any bond, and also any unclaimed dividends or special deposits or unapplied balances in any sequestration deposited in any bank in terms of the Bankruptcy (Scotland) Act, 1913, or otherwise. Some difficulty was experienced in determining whether the Act applied to all consignations lodged in bank in virtue of any Act of Parliament, or was limited in its application to consignations of money in connection with judicial proceedings in the Court of Session. In order that an authoritative decision of the Court might be obtained as to the scope of the Act, the Accountant of Court presented a note to have it determined that the surplus money deposited by a bondholder under sec. 122 of the Titles to Land Act, 1868, should be deposited in his name, and the deposit receipt transmitted to him.[3] In deciding the point, the Court held that the Act did not apply to such consignations, but was limited in its effect to consignations of money in connection with judicial proceedings in the Court of Session, and that the wide definition of the word " consignation " as given above is merely a definition of the word as used in the Act, and has no effect except in so far as it is brought into operation by the subsequent clauses of the Act.

---

[1] See opinion of Lord M'Laren in Anderson *v.* North of Scotland Bank, *supra*, which appears to be adverse to this view.

[2] 58 & 59 Vict. cap. 19, sec. 2.

[3] Antrobus, *Petr.*, 1896, 23 R. 1032.

It is inadvisable to issue a receipt acknowledging that money has been received to await the decision in a particular action. The case may be appealed from one Court to another, and an extract decree of either of the Divisions of the Court of Session does not, under certain circumstances, preclude an appeal to the House of Lords. The proper course, therefore, is to provide in the receipt for the manner of the discharge, such as by the indorsation of certain named persons and delivery of the receipt. Where money is consigned by order of the Court to await the orders of Court, the practice is to pay on production of a certified copy of the interlocutor—the interlocutor usually providing for payment on a certified copy—and delivery of the consignation receipt.[1]

Time for Lodgment of Money and Terms of Receipt.—Within ten days after receipt of any consignation in money, the Accountant of Court must lodge the same on deposit receipt in one of the banks in Scotland established by Act of Parliament or Royal Charter ; and every deposit receipt for money lodged in any of the said banks representing a consignation, whether lodged by the Accountant, or by any party to a cause, or by any other person, must be taken in name of the Accountant of Court and his successors in office, and must bear on the face of it the name of the party or parties by whom, or on whose behalf, the consignation is made, and of the cause or proceeding or bond to which it relates.[2]

(2) *In the Sheriff Court.*—Such consignations are regulated by the Sheriff Courts Consignations (Scotland) Act, 1893.[3]   Under this Act the term " consignation " extends and applies to any sum of money received by any sheriff clerk for deposit or consignation in any cause or proceeding in the ordinary Sheriff Court, or the Small Debt Court, whether by order of Court or otherwise, and includes any sum of money lodged by way of caution or security in corroboration of any bond, civil or criminal. Within ten days after consignation is made of any sum of money amounting to not less than five pounds, the sheriff clerk must lodge the same in a bank approved by the Sheriff on deposit receipt, and the deposit receipt therefor is required to be taken in name of the sheriff clerk of the county and his successors in office, and must bear on the face of it the name of the party or parties on whose behalf it is consigned, and of the cause or proceeding or bond to which it relates. The sheriff clerk is responsible for the safe custody of all consignations, and he accounts to the King's and Lord Treasurer's Remembrancer for unclaimed consignations. The discharge to the bank is delivery of the receipt indorsed by the sheriff clerk.

---

[1] As to accumulation of interest with principal, see *supra.*

[2] Court of Session Consignations (Scotland) Act, 1895, sec. 5.   For forms of receipts, see Appendix.

[3] 56 & 57 Vict. cap. 44.

(3) *Consignation of Balance of Price of Property Sold, after Satisfying First Bondholder.*—When a property is sold under the powers contained in a bond and disposition in security, the creditor is bound to consign the surplus, if any, which may remain after deducting the debt secured, expenses, and prior incumbrances, in any bank in Scotland incorporated by Act of Parliament or Royal Charter, or in a branch of any such bank, in the joint names of the seller and purchaser, for behoof of the party or parties having best right thereto.[1] The money can be uplifted by the seller and purchaser indorsing the deposit receipt.[2] The seller and purchaser of a property are, under special circumstances, entitled to raise an action of multiplepoinding for deciding rival claims to a surplus which they have consigned. Such circumstances are not easy to figure ; for when the selling creditor has consigned, he has done his statutory duty, and so long as the money remains in bank, both he and the purchaser are quite safe. If there be a real competition, their natural course is to let the claimants settle it in their own way.[3] Any party interested may raise the action. When an action of multiple-poinding has been raised and decided, the bank pay on delivery of an extract decree of preference, having indorsed thereon a receipt for the money by the successful claimant.

Decease of Customer.—With the law of succession to the estate of a deceased person, bankers have in general little to do, their duty being confined to getting a valid discharge for the payment by them of any sum that may be standing at the credit of such deceased person. As, however, bankers are frequently asked in cases of intestacy as to the manner in which the moveable estate of a deceased person falls to be divided, it has been thought expedient to append a table [4] showing the order of succession to such estates.

The person who realises and administers the moveable estate of a deceased person is called his executor, and when no executor has been appointed by the deceased, the appointment is made by the Sheriff of the county in which the deceased died domiciled. An executor thus appointed is called an executor-dative (*i.e.* given or appointed) in distinction to an executor-nominate or one named by the deceased in his testamentary disposition. In both cases the title of the executor is completed by confirmation granted by the Sheriff of the county in which the deceased died domiciled. In the case of persons dying abroad or having no fixed place of abode, leaving funds in this country, confirmation is granted by the Sheriff of the County of Edinburgh.

---

[1] Titles to Lands Consolidation Act, 1868, sec. 122. For form of receipt, see Appendix.

[2] Antrobus, *Petr.*, 1896, 23 R. at p. 1038.

[3] Milne and Others *v.* Louttit's Tr., 1898, 5 S.L.T. 297.

[4] See Appendix.

Until confirmation is obtained the executor has no power to intromit with the estate.

Where a person dies domiciled in England or Ireland leaving funds in Scotland, probate is taken out in the Courts of England or Ireland, as the case may be, and on production of such probate in the Sheriff Court of the County of Edinburgh—no matter in what county the Scottish funds may be—a certificate is indorsed thereon by the commissary clerk that it has been so produced. The probate has then the same force, effect, and operation in Scotland as if confirmation had been originally expede in the Scottish Courts.[1]

It is not safe for a bank to pay any sum standing at the credit of a person dying domiciled in Scotland except on production of confirmation and on a receipt, indorsation, or discharge by the executors as after mentioned; and, in the case of persons dying domiciled in England or Ireland, except on production of probate expede before a competent Court having indorsed thereon the aforesaid certificate by the commissary clerk of the County of Edinburgh, and on a receipt, indorsation, or discharge by the executors.

For sums standing at the credit of the deceased on current account, the discharge usually taken is in the form[2] of a cheque by the executors on the account of the deceased; and for sums standing at the credit of the deceased on deposit receipt, an indorsation on the receipt by the executors in the form in the Appendix and delivery of the receipt. Occasionally formal discharges are taken in each case, forms of which will be found in the Appendix.

Small Estates.—Where banks are satisfied that the whole estate and effects of a deceased person do not exceed in value the sum of £100— on the inventory of which estates no duty is payable[3]—it is usual to pay any sum standing at the credit of such deceased person to his representatives or next of kin on their granting a discharge therefor, coupled with the guarantee of an approved person to keep the bank free of any claim in respect of the payment made and an undertaking to expede confirmation at any time if called upon.[4]

---

[1] 21 & 22 Vict. cap. 56, sec. 14. See also 22 & 23 Vict. cap. 30, sec. 1.
[2] See Appendix.
[3] 27 & 28 Vict. cap. 56, sec. 5.
[4] See Appendix.

CHAPTER II

THE ENTERING INTO AND EXTINCTION OF OBLIGATIONS

1. Capacity to Contract and Execution of Deeds

EVERY person, who is of full age and who is subject to no legal incapacity, may enter into contracts and render himself liable for their due performance, provided he was not induced to so contract by essential error, force, fear, or fraud. The persons who cannot so legally contract are lunatics, idiots, interdicted persons, pupils, and in some cases, minors.

Execution of Deeds.—It is not here intended to enter into minute details regulating the execution of deeds, but to state concisely the main features necessary according to the present state of the law to be kept in view in connection with deeds requiring statutory solemnities. Writings *in re mercatoria* are exempt from these requirements, and are held as legal and binding as though they complied therewith. Although not holograph, they are authentic without witnesses, and prove their own dates in ordinary mercantile transactions. Such documents include bank cheques, mandates, mercantile guarantees, bills, promissory notes, and generally all the various mandates, acknowledgments, or other like documents which the infinite occasions of trade may require. A deed may be either wholly written, printed, lithographed, engraved, or type-written,[1] or partly in one or partly another of these ways. It must be signed by the granter before two witnesses of the age of fourteen years and upwards, or they must hear him acknowledge his signature.[2] The signature may be in pencil, " as the law does not prescribe the material with which a person is to sign his name, and it is his signature equally in perishable pencil writing as in imperishable ink." By a practice, well known and recognised, transfers of stock of railways and limited liability companies are valid if authenticated by one witness to each signature. The granter must sign each sheet, but preferably each page, of the deed.[3] It does not invalidate a deed that the maker was

---

[1] Simpson *v.* MacHarg, 1902, 39 S.L.R. 562.

[2] Cumming *v.* Skeoch's Trs., 1879, 6 R. 963 ; Tener's Trs. *v.* Tener's Trs., 1879, 6 R. 1111 ; Baird's Trs. *v.* Murray, 1883, 11 R. 153.

[3] M'Laren *v.* Menzies, 1876, 3 R. 1151.

assisted in his subscription by having his hand held about the wrist, the hand not having been led in the formation of the letters.[1] The witnesses sign the last page only and add the word " witness " after their respective signatures. If two or more granters sign a deed and all sign at the same time, two witnesses are sufficient for all their signatures ; but if the signatures of the granters be adhibited at different times, although on the same day, then the witnesses must attest each signature separately, even where the same witnesses attest different signatures. The testing clause which comes at the end usually sets forth the following particulars regarding the execution of the deed : (1) the name and designation of the writer or the person who has filled in the blanks in a printed form ; (2) the place and date of subscription ; and (3) the names and designations of the witnesses. It is not, however, absolutely necessary, though it is usual, to specify—(1) the writer's name ; (2) the place or date of subscription, unless the effect of the deed depends on the date, when it must be given ; or (3) the names and designations of the witnesses, provided that where the witnesses are not so named and designed, their designations are appended to or follow their subscriptions. Such designations may be so appended or added at any time before the deed, instrument, or writing is recorded in any register for preservation or is founded on in any Court, and need not be written by the witnesses themselves.[2] In this clause any alteration, addition, or vitiation on the deed as originally written should also be declared to have been made before subscription. If it can be proved that a party's usual mode of subscribing is by initials, and that the initials to the deed are his, the deed will be held valid.[3] This, however, does not apply to the witnesses. A deed executed by the granter's mark is null, the proper course being to have it executed by a notary public or justice of the peace on his behalf.[4] A deed executed by a party who cannot write, either through never having been taught, or from physical incapacity, is executed on his behalf by a notary or justice of the peace before two witnesses, a docquet being appended, setting forth that the granter of the deed has authorised the execution thereof, and that the deed has been read over to him before signing, in the presence of the witnesses.[5] The notary's docquet must be

---

[1] Noble v. Noble, 1875, 3 R. 74.

[2] Conveyancing (Scotland) Act, 1874, sec. 38 ; Thomson's Trs. v. Easson, 1878, 6 R. 141.

[3] Erskine, iii. 2, 8 ; Speirs v. Home-Speirs, 1879, 6 R. 1359 ; Arnott v. Burt, 1872, 11 M. 62 ; Weir, 22nd June 1813, F.C.

[4] Erskine, iii. 2, 8 ; Graham v. Macleod, 1848, 11 D. 173 ; Crosbie v. Wilson, 1865, 3 Macp. 870 ; Watson v. Beveridge, 1883, 11 R. 40. See Execution of Deeds ; Deposit Receipts.

[5] Watson v. Beveridge, 1883, 11 R. 40. For form of docquet, see Appendix.

holograph.[1] The testing clause of such a deed runs in terms similar to those of a deed signed by the person granting it, and takes no cognisance of the fact that the deed was notarially executed. Execution by a stamp bearing a party's name is invalid,[2] and so is the use of a "cyclostyle."[3] Blind persons may competently execute deeds, but it is prudent and competent to have such deeds signed by a notary on their behalf.[4] A married woman may subscribe her maiden name.[5] Care should be taken to see that the testing clause is filled up as soon as possible after the deed is signed, and to see the testing clause when so filled up. It has been decided by the House of Lords that words in the testing clause unconnected with the testing of the deed have no effect in altering or adding to the provisions of the deed.[6] Further, it is necessary to see that no vitiations in the essentials of the deed, unauthenticated in the testing clause, are made, as they will be held to have been made fraudulently, or to have been made by the granter for the purpose of cancelling the deed. Vitiations, if not in essentials, will be held *pro non scriptis*, if the deed is intelligible without them and there is no room to infer fraud.[7] Deeds executed by a company registered under the Companies Acts should be signed in terms of its Memorandum and Articles of Association, or, in the absence of any express provision, by two of the ordinary directors and secretary, and sealed with the common seal of the company, such execution being effectual though not attested by witnesses.[8] Where one of the granters of a deed is a domiciled Englishman, the deed should be executed according to both Scots and English law. The deed and testing clause will be in ordinary form, but a docquet is appended.[9] Corporations sign in accordance with the provisions contained in their Act of Incorporation.

By the Conveyancing Act of 1874 it is provided that no deed, instrument, or writing subscribed by the granter or maker thereof, and bearing to be attested by two witnesses, shall be deemed invalid or

---

[1] Henry v. Reid, 1871, 9 M. 503.

[2] Stirling Stuart v. Stirling Crawfurd's Trs., 1885, 12 R. 610. See Cheques, Indorsation of, *infra*.

[3] Whyte v. Watts, 1893, 21 R. 165.

[4] Ker v. Hotchkiss, 1837, 15 S. 983 ; Reid v. Baxter, 1837, 16 S. 273 ; *affd.* 1840, 1 Rob. App. 66.

[5] Dunlop v. Greenlees' Trs., 1863, 2 M. 1.

[6] Blair v. Assets Co., 1893, 23 R. (H.L.) 36 ; but see Johnston v. Coldstream, 1843, 5 D. 1297, *per* Lord Justice-Clerk ; Dunlop v. Greenlees' Trs., 1863, 2 M. 1, 3 M. (H.L.) 46 ; Chambers' Trs. v. Smith's Trs., 5 R. 97, and 5 R. (H.L.) 151.

[7] Erskine, iii. 2, 20 ; Ross's Lect. 1, 144 ; Shepherd v. Grant's Trs., 1844, 6 D. 464 ; *affd.* 1847, 6 Bell's App. 153 ; Article in Journal of Jurisprudence, ii. 291 ; Cattenach's Trs. v. Jamieson, 1884, 11 R. 972 ; Munro v. Butler Johnston, 1868, 7 M. 250 ; Wilsons v. Taylor & Son, 1869, 7 M. 773.

[8] Companies (Consolidation) Act, 1908, sec. 76 (3), incorporating the Conveyancing (Scotland) Act, 1874, sec. 56.

[9] See Appendix.

denied effect according to its legal import because of any informality in its execution, but the burden of proving that such deed was subscribed by the granter or maker thereof, and by the witnesses by whom such deed bears to be attested, shall lie upon the party using or upholding the same ; and such proof may be led in any action or proceeding in which such deed is founded on or objected to, or in a special application to the Court of Session, or to the Sheriff within whose jurisdiction the defender in any such application resides, to have it declared that such deed was subscribed by such granter or maker and witnesses.[1] This Act, however, does not apply to deeds executed prior to the passing of the Conveyancing (Scotland) Act, 1874,[2] with the probable exception of testamentary writings which, although dated before 1st October 1874 (when the Act came into force), do not take effect until the granter's death subsequent to that time.[3] It has been decided that a deed of more than one sheet subscribed by the granter on the last page only may be validated by a proof *prout de jure*.[4]

Holograph Writings, that is, documents wholly or in the essential parts written and subscribed by the granter,[5] have special privileges attaching to them, for the reason that such writings are less liable to be forged than the mere signature of the granter, and because writing and signing a deed afford stronger evidence of intention to contract than the signing of a document written by another. A letter written and signed by one of the partners of a company in the firm's name is holograph of the firm.[6] If a deed be written by one person on behalf of himself and others named, and he and they sign it, it is only holograph of the writer.[7] The deed, however, must be signed by the granter, though a declaration by the granter to the effect that the deed should be valid without subscription will receive effect.[8] An unauthenticated holograph marginal addition cannot be competently admitted to qualify the terms of a holograph document.[9] A holograph writing, however, does not,[10] while a holograph intimation of an assignation does, prove its own date.[11]

Deeds Vitiated by Fraud, Force and Fear, and Drunkenness.—A contract induced by fraud is not void, but only voidable in the option of the party defrauded. It is therefore valid till rescinded ; and

---

[1] See also Addison, etc., 1875, 2 R. 457 ; Thomson's Trs. *v.* Easson, 1878, 6 R. 141 ; Tener's Trs. *v.* Tener's Trs., 1879, 6 R. 1111.

[2] Gardner *v.* Lucas, 1878, 5 R. (H.L.) 105.

[3] Addison, *Petr.*, 1875, 2 R. 457.

[4] M'Laren *v.* Menzies, 1876, 3 R. 1151 ; Brown, 1883, 11 R. 400.

[5] Bell's Prin., sec. 20, and cases there cited.

[6] Nisbet *v.* Neil's Tr., 1869, 7 M. 1097 ; M'Laren *v.* Law, 1871, 44 Jur. 17.

[7] Miller *v.* Farquharson, 1835, 13 S. 838 ; Sprout *v.* Wilson, 1809, Hume, 920.

[8] Robertson *v.* Ogilvie's Trs., 1844, 7 D. 236.

[9] Brown *v.* Maxwell's Ex., 1884, 11 R. 821.

[10] Erskine, iii. 2, 22.

[11] 25 & 26 Vict. cap. 85, sec. 2.

accordingly the party defrauded has in general the option when he discovers the fraud, of rescinding the contract or of affirming it. But he must do either one or the other. He cannot take the benefit of the contract so far as it is beneficial to himself, and reject it in so far as it is burdensome to him. If he affirms it, he must affirm it in all its terms. If he reduces it, he must give up any benefit he may have received before the fraud was discovered.[1] Where, however, innocent third parties have onerously acquired rights under the contract which would be injuriously affected by the rescission, the option of declaring such contract void is barred,[2] except where, owing to the fraud of one of the parties, there has been an error *in essentialibus*, and the contract is void *ab initio*, on the ground that consent cannot be said to have been given at all. It is an established principle in England, which has been held to apply to Scotland, that a person cannot avail himself of what has been obtained by the fraud of another, unless he is not only innocent of the fraud, but has given valuable consideration.[3] Besides rescission of the contract, and even where that is incompetent, the defrauded party has in his option a right to sue for damages the person actually guilty of the fraud.[4] Fraud may be either by false representation, concealment of material circumstances, underhand dealing, or by taking advantage of intoxication or imbecility.[5] " If persons take upon themselves to make assertions as to which they are ignorant, whether they are true or untrue, they must in a civil point of view be held as responsible as if they had asserted that which they knew to be untrue." [6] Fraud may be proved *prout de jure*, but the facts and circumstances must be specifically set forth.

In connection with the rescission of contracts on the ground of misrepresentation, it may not be amiss to mention, what is not infrequently only imperfectly understood, that no one has a right to expect rescission of a written contract to which he is a party on the ground that he failed to clearly understand what the terms of the contract were, or that they were not sufficiently explained to him by the other party at the time when his signature was adhibited to the contract. When contracting parties bind themselves to certain terms which are

---

[1] Smyth *v.* Muir, 1891, 19 R. 81.

[2] Graham *v.* Western Bank, 1864, 2 M. 559, 3 M. 617 ; Addie *v.* Western Bank, 1867, 5 M. (H.L.) 80 ; Tennent *v.* City of Glasgow Bank, 1879, 6 R. (H.L.) 69. See authorities in Gray *v.* Binny, 1879, 7 R. 332.

[3] Scholefield *v.* Templar, 4 De G. & J. 429 ; Clydesdale Bank *v.* Paul, 1877, 4 R. 626 (*per* Lord Shand) ; Gibbs *v.* British Linen Bank, 1875, 4 R. 630 ; Robb *v.* Gow Bros. & Gemmell, 1905, 8 F. 90.

[4] See also Agents, *infra*.

[5] Irvine, 1850, 7 Bell's App. 186 ; Broatch *v.* Jenkins, 1866, 4 M. 1030 ; Pollok *v.* Burns, 1875, 2 R. 497.

[6] *Per* Lord Cairns in Reese River Silver Mining Co. *v.* Smith, 1869, L.R. 4 E. & I. Ap. Ca. 64, at p. 79.

put in writing, that means that they are mutually bound according to the true construction of the terms of the contract as they may be expiscated by the Court if they themselves differ about them. No one who has made a written contract can escape from its obligations by the mere allegation of his own failure to understand the meaning or effect of the terms to which he has expressly assented.[1]

Force and fear are also grounds for the rescission of a contract. The degree of force and fear necessary differs according to the relation of the parties, but in general it may be said to be such as would shake a mind of ordinary firmness and resolution. A contract induced by force and fear will probably be set aside even if the rescission interferes with the rights of onerous and innocent third parties, on the ground that a forced consent is no more an actual consent than if it had been obtained by fraud *in essentialibus*.[2]

2. Extinction of Obligations

Obligations are extinguished—(1) By actual fulfilment of the engagement, payment, performance, or satisfaction made to the creditor. (2) By discharge on the part of the creditor. (3) By virtual fulfilment, compensation, novation, delegation, or confusion. (4) By abandonment or satisfaction presumed by operation of law.

1. Payment.—A creditor is not bound to accept partial payment of his debt unless by the original obligation it has been made payable in parts. Payment may be made by the debtor himself, by anyone acting on his behalf, or by a stranger, if the creditor has no interest in demanding payment by the debtor himself. The debtor cannot object to a payment made by a stranger, if the creditor is willing to accept it. The creditor may grant an assignation of the debt to a stranger who pays it, but cannot be compelled to do so without the debtor's consent. If the debtor be pressed for payment by diligence, the creditor cannot, at his request, refuse to assign the debt to one who interposes and pays it. In the absence of evidence to the contrary, payment is presumed to have been made by the proper debtor. If made by one in a representative capacity, it is presumed to have been made on the debtor's behalf, and with his funds.

To Whom.—Payment may be made to the creditor, his legal representatives, or to anyone authorised to give a discharge therefor. A messenger or officer of the law employed to do diligence for a debt, has no implied authority to discharge the debt unless he be also employed as an agent on that behalf. Payment to an agent must, in general, be

---

[1] Laing *v.* Provincial Homes Invest. Co. Ltd., 1909, S.C. 812, *per* Lord Kinnear.
[2] See Gelot *v.* Stewart, 1870, 8 M. 649 ; Stewart *v.* Gelot, 1871, 9 M. 1057.

in cash. Payment, however, of a debt made in *bonâ fide* to one who the debtor has been led or allowed by the creditor to believe has in point of fact authority to receive it, is good. Thus, payment to a factor, without notice that his factory has been recalled, or to a person in possession of the document of debt with apparently a good title to receive payment, will discharge the debtor. But payment of rent before the legal term, or of a debt before the term of payment, is not good. Where several debts are due, the creditor may, under certain limitations, appropriate a payment as he pleases.[1]

Evidence of Payment.—A debt must in general be discharged in the same way as it was constituted. A written obligation must be discharged in writing, but an obligation *in re mercatoria* may be discharged by a holograph writing, or other document valid *in re mercatoria*. Parole proof of the payment of bills has been held to be incompetent.[2] Payment is presumed where the document of debt is found in the possession of the debtor, but the presumption may be overcome by parole proof.[3] From three consecutive discharges of periodical payments, payment of all preceding is presumed. Payment may be presumed from circumstances, such as long silence on the part of the creditor.

Mode of Payment.—The creditor is not bound to accept payment in any other than legal tender. Bronze coins are legal tender to the amount of one shilling, and silver coins to the amount of forty shillings. Debts above forty shillings must, if the payee so demand and the amount is capable of being expressed in gold coinage, be paid in gold.[4] By the Currency and Bank Notes Acts, 1914,[5] Treasury notes for the sums of one pound and ten shillings are legal tender for any amount throughout the United Kingdom. Bank of England notes are not legal tender in Scotland.[6] Where payment is made in coin which afterwards turns out to be counterfeit, no liability attaches to the payer if he have made no improper representations to induce the payee to accept such coin, or if the payee voluntarily accepts such coin in satisfaction of the payment of the debt. Money once paid over the counter ceases to be the property of the banker, and he cannot revoke or recall the payment although he immediately discover that it has been made under a mistake.[7] Bank notes are not legal tender, though the creditor may agree to accept bank notes in payment, but where such notes turn out to be forged, the debtor will be liable in repetition of the amount, provided the creditor repudi-

---

[1] See Appropriation of Payments.
[2] Robertson *v.* Thomson, 1900, 3 F. 5.
[3] See Cheques as Payment.
[4] Coinage Act, 1870.
[5] 4 & 5 Geo. V. caps. 14 and 72.
[6] 8 & 9 Vict. cap. 38, sec. 15.
[7] Chambers *v.* Miller, 32 L.J. C.P. 30 ; Pollard *v.* Bank of England, L.R. 6 Q.B. 623.

4

ates them within a reasonable time,[1] " as the party negotiating them is answerable for the notes being such as they purport to be." [2]   But the mere transfer of notes does not constitute a guarantee on the part of the debtor of the solvency of the issuing bank, and if, after transfer, a note turns out to be worthless by reason of the failure of the maker, though given and accepted in perfectly good faith on each side, the transferror is not liable on the instrument to the transferee, because the transfer has been one by mere delivery and not by indorsement.[3] Though bank notes are commonly spoken of and treated, at least in Scotland, as if they were money, they are simply promissory notes, and as such are subject to the rules relating to presentation, dishonour,[4] material alteration,[5] negotiation, loss or theft,[6] etc., applicable to such documents.   The finder of a lost note is entitled, after every reasonable effort to discover the true owner has proved unavailing, to keep it or to vindicate his right to it against every one but the true owner ; [7] and it would seem that if a finder honestly believes that the true owner cannot be found, he is not guilty of theft though he appropriates it to his own use, notwithstanding the fact that he subsequently finds means of ascertaining the true owner.[8]

2. **Discharge**.—The creditor may discharge the debtor without exacting either payment or performance, but in such a case the discharge must be clear and unequivocal, and established by evidence equally as strong as the constitution of the obligation.   A creditor may discharge his debtor either of a special obligation, or of all claims competent against him.

3. **Compensation or Set-off.**—Where one person who is under obligation to another acquires against that other a right of the same kind, so that each is the obligee of the other, the respective obligations are said to compensate or extinguish each other.   The right of compensation is founded on the Statute 1592, c. 141, which provides that any liquid debt instantly verified by writ or oath of the party pleading it shall be admitted by all judges by way of exception or defence where it is proponed before the granting of decree.

The rules which govern the operation of compensation are :—

---

[1] Pooley v. Brown, 31 L.J. C.P. 134.

[2] Jones v. Ryde, 5 Taunt. 484-494 ; Woodland v. Fear, L.J. 26 Q.B. 204.

[3] See B. of E. Act, sec. 58 (2).

[4] B. of E. Act, sec. 49.

[5] B. of E. Act, sec. 64 ; Leeds Bank v. Walker, 11 Q.B.D. 84 ; Suffell v. Bank of England, 9 Q.B.D. 555.

[6] Raphael v. Bank of England, 25 L.J. C.P. 33 ; Willis v. Bank of England, 4 A. & E. 21.

[7] Bridges v. Hawkesworth, 21 L.J. Q.B. 76.

[8] See Reg. v. Clyde, L.R. 1 C.C.R. 139 ; Reg. v. Dixon, 25 L.J. M.C. 39 ; Reg. v. Moore, 30 L.J. M.C. 77.

(1) Compensation does not operate *ipso jure*. It must be pleaded by way of defence, and the plea must be sustained.

(2) The obligation in respect of which compensation is pleaded as a defence must be of the same nature and description as that sued on.

(3) The debts must be due at the time when the plea is set up. Thus a contingent or conditional debt cannot be pleaded against one due, nor one contracted subsequent to bankruptcy against one incurred prior to that event.[1] This rule applies, however, only where both parties are solvent, for if one be bankrupt, the other may plead compensation in respect of a debt not yet due. Compensation cannot be pleaded against a debt which has prescribed at the date when the plea is set up, even although at the time of concourse it has not then prescribed.

(4) The debt must, besides being actually exigible, be liquid or fixed in amount, or capable of being immediately made liquid.[2] But on equitable grounds the Court may allow a claim to be compensated by a counter-claim, where by mutual stipulation the one party cannot insist on his claim until he has satisfied the claim of the other.[3] Where, however, the stipulation is that one party has it in his option to choose one of two alternatives, the Court will be guided by circumstances. Thus in the lease of a brewery it was stipulated that in the event of any part of the premises leased becoming untenantable, it should be in the landlord's option either to repair or to allow a reasonable abatement of rent. The Court held that, notwithstanding the terms of this provision, the tenant was not entitled to retain past-due rents in respect of the alleged untenantable condition of the premises without having first constituted his claim for abatement of rent on that ground.[4] The principle of compensation is not limited to cases of express written contract, but is extended to cases where the terms of the contract fall to be interpreted according to the usage of trade.[5] Where the counter-claim pleaded by way of compensation is not actually liquid, but is in course of being made so, and there is no allegation of delay, the Court may, in the exercise of its discretion, supersede consideration of the cause for a time for the purpose of allowing the defender to make his counter-claim liquid.[6]

(5) The parties must occupy the position of debtor and creditor to each other respectively, each in his own right and at the same time.

---

[1] Taylor's Tr. *v.* Paul, 1888, 15 R. 313.

[2] Edwards *v.* Adam, 1821, 1 S. 27.

[3] Johnston *v.* Robertson, 1861, 23 D. 646 ; *cf.* Burt *v.* Bell, 1861, 24 D. 13.

[4] Dryburgh *v.* Dryburgh, 1874, 1 R. 909 ; *cf.* Davie *v.* Stark, 1876, 2 R. 1114, where the tenant's claim for damages exceeded the amount of rent due. See also MacBride *v.* Hamilton & Son, 1875, 2 R. 775.

[5] Gibson & Stewart *v.* Brown & Co., 1876, 3 R. 328.

[6] Munro *v.* M'Donald's Exrs., 1866, 4 M. 687 (*per* Lord Curriehill).

Thus a person sued for a private debt is not entitled to plead compensation in respect of any debt due to him in a representative capacity.[1] Though, since an executor, who is confirmed, is held to be the same person as the deceased so far as his debts and obligations are concerned, such an executor may competently compensate a debt due by him *proprio nomine* with one due to the deceased. So also where the customer of a bank at the date of his death was indebted to the bank, and his executors in administering his estate pay into the bank, to the credit of an account opened in their names as executors, a sum of money which practically balances the sum due by the deceased customer, it is competent for the bank, on the sequestration of the deceased debtor's estate, to compensate or set off the one sum against the other, or to retain the amount in satisfaction of their debt.[2] Where an agent as such and on behalf of a principal, whether that principal's name be disclosed or not, enters into obligations with a third person, that person is not entitled to compensate a claim by the principal in respect of such obligations by a debt due by the agent.[3] A bank agent who is debtor to a customer whose account with the bank is overdrawn, cannot, in the absence of special agreement, set off the amount due by him to the customer against the overdraft, even although he is personally responsible to the bank for the amount of the overdraft.[4] In such a case the agent should pay, and take an assignation to, the bank's debt, when the two sums may competently be compensated. A sale by a broker in his own name to persons who are cognisant that he is in the habit of selling both as a principal and as an agent, does not convey to them an assurance that he is selling on his own account, and if the intending purchasers desire to deal with the broker as a principal and not as an agent, in order to secure a right of compensation, they are put upon their inquiry. Thus, where an agent, who acts sometimes as a broker and sometimes as a principal, sells in his own name for an undisclosed principal, and the principal sues the buyer for the price, the buyer cannot compensate the debt due by the agent, unless in making the contract there were circumstances which were calculated to induce, and did induce, in the mind of the purchaser a reasonable belief that the agent was selling on his own account and not for an undisclosed principal, and that the agent was enabled to appear as the real contracting party by the conduct, or by the authority, express or implied, of the principal.[5]

(6) The debt of a partner cannot be set off against a claim by his

---

[1] Stewart *v.* Stewart, 1869, 7 M. 366.

[2] Alexander's Exr. *v.* Mackersy, 1905, 8 F. 198, overruling Gray's Trs. *v.* Royal Bank of Scotland, 1895, 23 R. 199.

[3] Lavaggie *v.* Pirie & Sons, 1872, 10 M. 312 ; Semenza *v.* Brinsley, 1869, 34 L.J. C.P. 161 ; Matthews *v.* Auld & Guild, 1874, 1 R. 1224.

[4] Tait & Co. *v.* Wallace, 1894, 2 S.L.T. 136.

[5] Cooke *v.* Eshelby, 1887, L.R. 12 A.C. 271.

firm, nor where a firm, or the trustee on a firm's bankrupt estate, sues for a debt, can the debtor set off against such claim a debt due to him by one of the partners of the firm.[1] But where a surviving and solvent partner of a dissolved and bankrupt firm is sued for a debt due by his late firm at the instance of the trustee on the firm's sequestrated estates, for behoof of the firm's creditors, it is competent for that partner to plead compensation in respect of a private debt due him by his firm.[2] On the other hand, on the principle that a creditor of a dissolved and solvent firm is entitled to claim payment of his debt from any member of the firm, a debt due to such creditor by the firm may be pleaded in compensation of a claim for a debt due by him to an individual partner.[3]

(7) The *concursus debiti et crediti* must take place at or prior to the time when either of the parties becomes bankrupt.

(8) Compensation is not pleadable by a depository against the depositor, nor can it be pleaded against a debt given or bequeathed as an alimentary fund.[4] It cannot be pleaded by the debtor to the holder of a note payable to bearer in respect of a debt due by any prior holder.

(9) Compensation cannot be pleaded in respect of a debt acquired *malâ fide*, and in order to gain an undue advantage or under circumstances in which, if the plea were sustained, the diligence of third parties would be defeated. Thus the debtor of a deceased person cannot plead compensation in respect of a debt acquired subsequent to the date of his creditor's death, nor a factor, in respect of a debt acquired after he has received his principal's rents.

(10) Compensation may be pleaded not only by the principal, but by anyone who has an interest, as, *e.g.*, a cautioner.

(11) Compensation cannot be pleaded subsequent to decree unless the decree be reduced.

4. Confusion.—Where the credit and debit in an obligation unite in the same person, the obligation is said to be extinguished *confusione*, as a person cannot be a debtor or a creditor to himself. There are, however, certain exceptions to the general principle, which must be kept in view.

(1) Where the cautioner in an obligation becomes the principal creditor, by acquiring a right to the debt by succession or otherwise, the obligation is not extinguished *confusione*, but remains effectual. (2) Where a creditor in a moveable debt succeeds to the heritage of his debtor, his right to demand payment of that debt from his debtor's executor is not lost *confusione*. So, where an executor acquires right

---

[1] Morrison *v.* Hunter, 1822, 2 S. 68.

[2] Bogle *v.* Bannantyne, 1793, M. 2581.

[3] Mitchell *v.* Canal Basin Foundry Co., 1869, 7 M. 480 ; Thomson *v.* Stevenson, 1855, 17 D. 739.

[4] Reid *v.* Bell, 1884, 12 R. 178.

to a heritable debt, he may still claim payment of that debt from the heir in heritage. (3) A debt is not extinguished *confusione* when the succession to the fund or subject liable in payment of that debt is subsequently separated from the succession to the debt itself.

5. Delegation is the substitution, with the creditor's consent, of one debtor for another, whereby the original debtor is discharged. Like novation, it will not be presumed, and must therefore be clearly expressed. Thus, where there is a change in the constitution of a firm, the fact that the creditor consents to accept the new members as his debtors, as by taking a bill from them, will not *per se* discharge the former members of the firm. To discharge them the creditor must have clearly expressed his willingness to accept the new firm as his debtors in place of the old, and have represented, either actually or impliedly, that he was willing that his former debtors should be discharged.[1]

6. Novation is the substitution, with the creditor's consent, of one obligation by the debtor for another, the second obligation taking the place of the first, and the position of the parties remaining the same. Thus the transfer of money from current account to deposit receipt constitutes a novation of the banker's obligation.[2] Novation must, to be binding, be clearly expressed, and it will not be presumed. Where the performance of an obligation or payment of a debt is guaranteed by a cautioner or a surety, the substitution of one obligation for another will in general operate to free the cautioner. Thus, in one case a creditor released his principal debtor, and accepted a third party as full debtor in his stead. The surety for the former debtor agreed to give a guarantee for the latter and to continue the guarantee until he did so, but died without giving effect to his intentions. In an action by the creditor against the surety's executors, it was held that the former debt was extinguished by the release of the principal debtor, and that therefore the creditor's remedy against the surety was gone, the novation of the debt operating as a complete release of the original debtor, and not as a mere covenant not to sue him.[3] In such cases, therefore, care must be taken to see both that the substitution has the cautioner's consent, and that the cautioner guarantees the new debtor before the old debtor is released.

7. Prescription is a means whereby rights may be either lost or acquired, or the mode of proving a claim or debt limited. By a positive prescription the right of a person in possession is protected from further

---

[1] See Pollock & Co. *v.* Murray & Spence, 1863, 2 M. 14 ; Mackintosh *v.* Ainslie, 1872, 10 M. 304 ; Pearston *v.* Wilson, 1856, 19 D. 197 ; Rolfe *v.* Flower Salting & Co., 1865, L.R. 1 P.C. App. 27.

[2] Head *v.* Head, 1894, L.R. 2 Ch. 236.

[3] Com. Bank of Tasmania *v.* Jones, 1893, L.R. A.C. (P.C.) 313.

challenge by reason of his having continued his possession for a certain period ; by a negative prescription, a person loses a right by neglecting to use it, or to follow it forth, during a certain time limited by law.

1. *The Long Positive Prescription* was introduced by the Act 1617, c. 12, which in order to remedy inconveniences arising from the loss of titles, and the danger of forgery, after the means of improbation had been lost by lapse of time, provided that where lands, annual rents, or other heritages have been possessed, peaceably and in virtue of infeftments, by any persons or their authors or predecessors, for the space of forty years continually and together from the date of the said infeftment, and without any lawful interruption during that period, such persons, their heirs and successors, should not be troubled, pursued, nor inquieted in the heritable right and property of the said heritages, by anyone pretending right to the same by prior infeftments or any other ground except forgery ; provided they are able to show a feudal title prior to the prescriptive period.

The Conveyancing Act, 1874, simplified the title necessary for prescription, by declaring that any *ex facie* irredeemable title to an estate in land recorded in the appropriate register of sasines should be sufficient foundation for prescription ; and shortened the prescriptive period by enacting that possession following on such recorded title for the space of twenty years continually and together, without legal interruption, should for all purposes be equivalent to the forty years' possession required by the Act 1617, c. 12 ; and provided that where possession is continued for thirty years no deduction is to be made on account of the minority or legal incapacity of any person against whom prescription is used or objected.[1]

2. *The Long Negative Prescription* was introduced by the Statute 1469, c. 29, which provided that the person having interest in an obligation shall follow the same within the space of forty years and take document thereupon, and if he does not follow, that it shall prescribe and be of no avail. The prescription was subsequently extended to mutual obligations, including heritable bonds and other heritable rights. Its effect is, to raise an absolute presumption which no amount of evidence can contradict or impugn, that, after a lapse of forty years during which a creditor in an obligation has remained silent, the debt has been paid or the obligation implemented by the debtor. The years of the minority of the person against whom the prescription is pleaded are not counted, and the prescription begins

---

[1] See Rankine on Land-Ownership, 23 ; Erskine, iii. 7, 2 ; Bell's Prin. 2002 ; Buchanan & Geils *v.* Ld. Advocate, 1882, 9 R. 1218 ; E. Glasgow *v.* Boyle, 1887, 14 R. 419 ; Ld. Advocate *v.* Ld. Lovat, 1880, 7 R. (H.L.) 122 ; Govs. of George Watson's Hospital *v.* Cormack, 1883, 11 R. 320 ; Glen *v.* Scale's Trs., 1881, 9 R. 317 ; Hinton *v.* Connel's Trs., 1883, 10 R. 1110 ; Black *v.* Mason, 1881, 8 R. 497.

to run from the date of payment. The prescription may be interrupted by a payment to account of the principal sum or by a payment of interest.

3. *The Vicennial Prescription* applies to retours [1] and to holograph writings. With the former, banks have no concern. All holograph writings on which an obligation can be founded [2] prescribe in twenty years after their dates. As this prescription is really a limitation, it is competent to refer to the debtor's oath in order to prove that the document founded on is holograph and that the signature is genuine. If these facts are admitted by the debtor, he must, in order to free him of his debt, prove that the debt was discharged. The prescription must be pleaded.[3] It does not run against minors.[4]

4. *The Decennial Prescription* was introduced by the Act 1696, c. 9, which declared that all actions competent to minors against their tutors and curators, or to them against the minor, shall fall if not prosecuted within ten years from the expiration of the office, whether it has terminated by the majority or by the death of the minor.[5]

5. *The Septennial Prescription* applies to cautionary obligations.[6]

6. *The Sexennial Limitation* applies to bills of exchange.[7]

7. *The Quinquennial Prescription* applies to arrears of rent in an agricultural lease, which prescribe within five years from the date of the tenant's removal from the lands, to multures, and to ministers' stipends, which both prescribe in five years after they become due, and to all bargains concerning moveables, such as sales and other consensual contracts which may be proved by witnesses and to the constitution of which writing is unnecessary, which prescribe in five years, but may then be proved by the writ or oath of the debtor. This prescription also applies to inhibitions.

8. *The Triennial Prescription.*—By the Act 1579, c. 83, it is enacted that " all actions of debt for house mails, mens' ordinars, servants' fees, merchants' compts, and other the like debts, that are not founded upon written obligations, be pursued within three years, otherwise the creditor shall have no action except he either prove by writ or by oath of his party." The Act has been held to apply to such debts as the following :—(1) To traders' accounts of the nature of shopkeepers' accounts, whether in retail or in wholesale,[8] but not to the price of goods

---

[1] See Erskine, iii. 7, 19 ; Bell's Prin. 2024.
[2] Mowat *v.* Banks, 1856, 18 D. 1093.
[3] Wyse *v.* Wyse, 1847, 9 D. 1405.
[4] See Erskine, iii. 7, 26 ; Bell's Prin. 590.
[5] See Erskine, iii. 7, 26 ; Bell's Prin. 635.
[6] Which see.
[7] Which see.
[8] Laing & Irvine *v.* Anderson, 1872, 10 M. 74.

consigned between foreign merchants,[1] nor to bargains of moveables, contracts for repairs, or accounts between master and owners of a ship. (2) To workmen's wages, whether paid by time or by the piece.[2] (3) To writers' accounts, including disbursements,[3] engineers' and surveyors' accounts for work done, but not to cash advances, travelling expenses, nor to general accountings between an agent and his principal. (4) To furnishings to a family or domestic establishment. (5) To servants' wages, each term running a separate course. (6) To house rents on a verbal lease, each term's rent running a separate course. (7) To aliment due by contract express or implied, each term's aliment running a separate course, even though payable weekly ; but not to aliment due *ex debito naturali*.

The prescription is elided by the raising of an action, or the production in an action of a counter-claim, or by showing that the debt is due under a written obligation, though for this purpose a mere written order is not sufficient, or by the pursuer's proving that his failure to sue timeously was due to the conduct of the defender. The prescription runs from the day of payment of termly debts, on the close of an account, which is the date of the last unpaid article, or of the last article preceding an interruption of three years, or of the last article preceding the day of the death of the debtor. An account is, however, continuous if it proceed without interruption, although each year's account is separately summed up and interest charged. After the three years have run, it is necessary to prove both the constitution and the subsistence of the debt by the writ or oath of the debtor or his representatives, whether the debtor have died during or after the currency of the three years. The constitution may be proved by writ, and the resting owing by oath, of the debtor. Minority or interruption is not pleadable as an exception to the prescription, and there is no deduction of the time of absence from the kingdom.

---

[1] M'Kinlay v. M'Kinlay, 1851, 14 D. 162 ; Laing & Irvine v. Anderson, *supra*.
[2] Mackay v. Carmichael & Christie, 1851, 14 D. 207.
[3] Richardson v. Merry, 1863, 1 M. 940.

CHAPTER III

SPECIAL CUSTOMERS

1. Married Women

At common law, and in the absence of special provision to the contrary contained in an ante-nuptial contract of marriage, a deed or bequest under which a married woman succeeded to property, or a post-nuptial contract of marriage—provided in this last case the rights of the husband's creditors prior to the execution of the deed were not thereby fraudulently sacrificed [1]—a husband acquired by the marriage rights over the person and property of his wife known as the *jus mariti* and right of administration. By the former of these the husband acquired a complete right to the whole moveable property of his wife belonging to her at the time of marriage, or which might be acquired by her during its subsistence, including the rents of her heritable estate, and the stock-in-trade and goodwill of any business she might then be carrying on, all of which fell into what was called the *communio bonorum*, a term signifying the combined moveable estate of the husband and wife at the time of the marriage or acquired subsequently, and of which, by virtue of the marriage, the husband became absolute owner. The right of administration gave the husband power over his wife's person and property and prevented her disposing of either her heritable or moveable estate without his consent.[2] The Legislature has, however, beginning with the Conjugal Rights Amendment Act, 1861, passed various statutes for the better protection of the estates of married women. While this is so, until the coming into operation on the 23rd December 1920 of the Married Women's Property (Scotland) Act, 1920,[3] the common law remained unaltered, in that a married woman living in family with her husband was incapable of entering into any legal obligation such as is involved in the granting or signing of personal bonds, bills, cautionary obligations, and most, if not all, the personal

---

[1] Walker *v.* Her Husband's Creditors, 1730, Mor. 5841 ; Keggie *v.* Christie, 23rd May 1815, F.C. See also the securing of earnings at common law by facts and circumstances implying renunciation of *jus mariti* ; Davidson *v.* Davidson, 1867, 5 M. 710.

[2] Brownlee *v.* Waddell, 1831, 10 S. 37.

[3] 10 & 11 Geo. V. cap. 64.

obligations known in law, so long as these were unconnected with the enjoy-
ment or management of her own estate,[1] provided she or those in her
right plead that incapacity.[2] Her husband's consent to such obligations
did not make them effectual.[3] Thus, a bill signed by a married woman
as joint acceptor with her husband did not bind her.[4] This is now altered
by the statute just mentioned, the provisions of which, bearing on the
capacity of a married woman to contract, will now be considered.

Married Women's Property (Scotland) Act, 1920.—After the 23rd
December 1920, the date when this Act came into operation, the property
—heritable or moveable—of a married woman is not subject to the right
of administration of her husband, and that right is now wholly abolished.
A married woman has with regard to her estate the same powers of disposal
as if she were unmarried. Any deed or writing executed by her with
reference to her heritable estate in Scotland or to her moveable estate
is as valid and effectual as if executed by her with consent of her husband
according to the previous law and practice. A married woman is now
capable of entering into contracts and incurring obligations to the like
extent as if she were not married. Her husband is not liable in respect
of any contract she may enter into or obligation she may incur on her
own behalf. Further, a married woman if living apart from or deserted
by her husband is, on entering into any contract for the supply of goods
or furnishings for herself or for her children, deemed to bind her own
estate in the same way as if she were unmarried, but without prejudice
to the right of the person who supplied such goods or furnishings to
recover the price thereof from such husband if he is liable therefor in
accordance with the previous law. Consequently, at present a married
woman may enter into any contract she pleases and bind her own estate
in repayment. She may sign guarantees, bonds of credit, bills or
cautionary obligations, and the creditor is entitled to enforce these
obligations against the estates both heritable and moveable of a married
woman to the like extent as if she were unmarried. She may sell her
private estate, dispone or assign that estate in security of the obligations
of herself or a third party without the consent of her husband, and as
freely as if she were not married. She may either sue or be sued in her
own name. She may enter into partnership with a third person or
even with her husband in a trading concern, and her liability as such
partner can be enforced against her separate estate.

Maintenance of Indigent Husband.—In the event of a husband
being unable to maintain himself, his wife, if she have a separate estate

---

[1] Harvey *v.* Chessels, 1785, Bell's Oct. Ca. 255 ; Erskine, i. 6, 25.

[2] *Per* Lord Fullerton in Hunter *v.* Stewart, 1840, 2 D. 564.

[3] Lennox *v.* Auchincloss, 1821, 1 S. 22.

[4] Earl of Strathmore *v.* Ewing, 1832, 6 W. & S. 56 ; Sandilands *v.* Mercer, 1833,
11 S. 665 ; M'Lean *v.* Angus, 1887, 14 R. 448.

or have a separate income more than reasonably sufficient for her own maintenance, is bound out of such separate estate to provide her husband with such maintenance as he would in similar circumstances be bound to provide for her, or out of such income to contribute such sum or sums towards such maintenance as her husband would in similar circumstances be bound to contribute towards her maintenance.

Power of Spouses to Regulate their Rights by Marriage Contract.—The power possessed by a husband and wife to settle their respective rights by Ante-nuptial Contract of Marriage is in no way affected by the Act, which specially provides that " Nothing in this Act contained shall apply to any provision made in favour of or reserved by either spouse by Ante-nuptial Contract of Marriage, whether dated before or after the passing of this Act, and all such provisions shall be as valid and irrevocable in all respects as if this Act had not been passed."

Former Statutes not Repealed.—The Act of 1920 does not in express terms repeal any of the former statutes. Certain of the provisions of these statutes may be noted.

Wife's Money Immixed with that of Husband.—Any money or estate of a wife lent or intrusted by her to her husband or immixed with his funds [1] is, on his bankruptcy, to be treated as assets of the husband subject to her right to a dividend after the claims of his other creditors have been satisfied. Under this section it has been decided that money of the wife's lodged in bank along with money of the husband's on deposit receipt payable to either or the survivor is " immixed " with the husband's funds. [2]

Husband's Rights to Share of Deceased Wife's Estate.—The husband and children have the same right of succession to the estate of a wife as at the date of the " Married Women's Property (Scotland) Act, 1881," the wife and children possessed with regard to the estate of a deceased husband, namely, a right on the husband's part to one-half of the clear residue where there are no children and one-third where there are children, and on the children's part the same right to legitim out of their mother's estate as they have in their father's estate—that is, one-half where there is no widower and one-third where there is a widower (decree of divorce against a wife is not equivalent to her death in the sense of the statute). [3]

2. Firms and Partners

In considering what follows, attention is directed to the terms of the Limited Partnerships Act of 1907, the provisions of which, so far as material, will be found on p. 70.

---

[1] Married Women's Property (Scotland) Act, 1881, sec. 1 (4).

[2] National Bank of Scotland Ltd. *v.* William Dixon Ltd. and Cowans, 1893, 21 R 4.

[3] Eddington *v.* Robertson, 1895, 22 R. 430.

It is a distinctive feature of Scots law that a partnership or firm is deemed in law to be a person, distinct from the members composing it, capable of entering into obligations and contracts, of holding personal property, and of carrying on legal proceedings, in its own distinctive name, and for its own peculiar benefit. As a consequence of this doctrine, the following points deserve notice :—(1) The funds of a partnership belong to itself (and not to the partners as joint owners). (2) Debts due by the firm must, in the first instance, be constituted against the firm itself, and not against the individual partners, although the individual partners are ultimately liable *singuli in solidum* for the debts of the partnership due to third parties. (3) If the partnership carry on business under a proper name, such as A., B. & Co., it sues, and is sued, in that name ; but if it carry on business under a descriptive name, such as the Fairfield Shipbuilding Co., it sues, and is sued, in that name along with the names of three of its partners, if there be so many.[1] (4) The firm may stand in relation of debtor and creditor to any of its partners, and may sue and be sued by them. (5) A firm may sue, or be sued, by another firm of which some or all of its members are partners. (6) A firm may be sequestrated, while the individual partners remain solvent.[2] (7) Creditors may arrest in the hands of a firm, money due to an individual partner.

Nature and Constitution of Partnership.—The law relating to partnership is now regulated by the Partnership Act, 1890. Partnership is defined as " the relation which subsists between persons carrying on a business (which includes every trade, occupation, or profession [3]) in common with a view to profit." Societies, clubs, or other organisations, not conducted with a view to profit, are not partnerships. Companies registered under the Companies Acts or incorporated by Act of Parliament, Letters-Patent, or Royal Charter, and those engaged in working mines in the Stannaries, are declared to be not partnerships under the Act. In determining whether a partnership does, or does not, exist, regard is had to the following rules :—(1) Joint tenancy, tenancy in common, joint property, common property or part ownership, does not of itself create a partnership as to anything owned, whether the tenants or owners do or do not share any profits made by the use thereof. (2) The sharing of gross returns does not of itself create a partnership, whether the persons sharing such returns

---

[1] It must, however, be borne in mind that by the provisions of rule 11 of the Sheriff Courts (Scotland) Act of 1913 " any individual or individuals, or any corporation or association, carrying on business under a firm or trading or descriptive name, may sue or be sued [in the Sheriff Court] in such name without the addition of the name or names of such individual or individuals or any of them, or of any member or official of such corporation or association."

[2] *Vide* Sequestration.

[3] Sec. 45.

have, or have not, a joint or common right or interest in any property from which, or from the use of which, the returns are derived. (3) The receipt by a person of a share of the profits of a business is *primâ facie* evidence that he is a partner in the business, but the receipt of such a share, or of a payment contingent on, or varying with, the profits of a business, does not of itself make him a partner in the business ; though a contract that a person shall receive a fixed sum " out of the profits " of a business is equivalent to a contract that he shall receive a " share of the profits." [1] And in particular, (*a*) the receipt by a person of a debt or other liquidated amount by instalments or otherwise out of the accruing profits of a business does not make him a partner in the business or liable as such ; (*b*) a contract for the remuneration of a servant or agent of a person engaged in a business by a share of the profits of the business, does not of itself make the servant or agent a partner in the business or liable as such ; (*c*) a person being the widow or child of a deceased partner, and receiving by way of annuity a portion of the profits made in the business in which the deceased person was a partner, is not by reason only of such receipt a partner in the business or liable as such ; (*d*) the advance of money by way of loan to a person engaged, or about to engage, in any business on a contract with that person, that the lender shall receive a rate of interest varying with the profits, or shall receive a share of the profits arising from carrying on the business, does not of itself make the lender a partner with the person or persons carrying on the business or liable as such, provided that the contract is in writing and signed by or on behalf of all the parties thereto ; (*e*) a person receiving by way of annuity, or otherwise, a portion of the profits of a business in consideration of the sale by him of the goodwill of the business, is not by reason only of such receipt, a partner in the business or liable as such.[2] The main rule to be observed in determining the existence of a partnership, though the principle receives no express recognition in the Act, is, that " regard must be paid to the true contract and intention of the parties as appearing from the whole facts of the case, which, if not in writing, must be ascertained from the words and conduct of the parties." But a person may be barred *personali exceptione* from pleading that he is not a partner in a firm, and every one, who by words spoken or written, or by conduct represents himself, or who knowingly suffers himself to be represented, as a partner in a particular firm, is liable as a partner to anyone who has, on the faith of any such representation, given credit to the firm, whether the representation has, or has not, been made, or communicated to the person so giving credit, by or with the knowledge of, the apparent partner making the representation or suffering it to be made.[3] Where, however, after a partner's death the partnership business is

---

[1] *In re* Young, 1896, L.R. 2 Q.B. 484.　　　[2] Sec. 2.　　　[3] Sec. 14 (1).

continued in the old firm-name, the continued use of that name or of the deceased partner's name as part thereof does not of itself make his executor's or administrator's estate or effects liable for any partnership debts contracted after his death.[1] Unless registered under the Companies Acts, not more than twenty persons, or ten in the case of a banking company, can form themselves into a partnership. All persons who have capacity to contract[2] may become partners. A partnership may now be constituted between a husband and a wife for the carrying on of a business.[3] Where no fixed term has been agreed upon for the duration of a partnership, any partner may determine the partnership at any time, on giving notice of his intention to do so to all the other partners.

Powers of Partners.—Every partner is an agent of the firm and his other partners for the purpose of the business of the partnership; and the acts of every partner who does any act for carrying on, in the usual way, business of the kind carried on by the firm of which he is a member, bind the firm and his partners, unless the partner, so acting, has in fact no authority to act for the firm in the particular matter, and the person with whom he is dealing either knows that he has no authority or does not know or believe him to be a partner.[4] But it is to be observed that all the rules that regulate the relations between a firm and persons dealing with it are matters of public law, and cannot be modified by any agreement made among the partners themselves. From the fact that each partner is the agent of the firm, it follows (1) that an admission or representation made by any partner concerning the partnership affairs, and in the ordinary course of its business, is evidence against the firm;[5] and (2) notice to any partner who habitually acts in the partnership business of any matter relating to partnership affairs, operates as notice to the firm, except in the case of a fraud on the firm committed by, or with the consent of, that partner.[6] A partner of a firm has an implied mandate to attend a meeting of creditors of one of the partnership debtors, and on behalf of his firm to enter into a composition contract with the debtor.[7]

Power to Borrow.—Each partner has an implied power to borrow money, or to overdraw, on the credit of the firm, provided that the borrowing of money is necessary or incidental to the business of the firm, as in the case of an ordinary trading firm. Where a partner has

---

[1] Sec. 14 (2).
[2] See p. 43.
[3] Married Women's (Scotland) Property Act, 1920; Raitt *v.* Raitt, 1923, 39 Sheriff C.R. 134; 1923, S.L.T. (Sher. Ct.), 66.
[4] Sec. 5.
[5] Sec. 15.
[6] Sec. 16.
[7] Mains & M'Glashan *v.* Black, 1895, 22 R. 329,

such an implied authority, a bank is not bound to inquire as to how the money is to be applied. The power to borrow money implies the power to pledge the firm's personal property in security of an advance. If the business of the partnership be not such as to require the granting of bills, no partner has an implied authority to draw or indorse bills in the firm-name. For example, the drawing and indorsing of bills does not fall within the implied power of a partner of a firm of solicitors.

Payment to a Partner.—Payment to one partner of a firm of a debt due to the firm is payment to the firm, and the receipt of a partner discharges all claims by the firm.

Partner may Assign his Interest in Firm in Security.—Any partner may, if he chooses, assign either absolutely or in security his own share in a firm to a third person, so long as that does not interfere with the conduct of the company or the respective rights and interest of the partners.[1] The assignation does not, as against the other partners, entitle the assignee, during the continuance of the partnership, to interfere in the management or administration of the partnership business or affairs, or to require any accounts of the partnership transactions, or to inspect the partnership books, but entitles the assignee only to receive the share of profits to which the assigning partner would otherwise be entitled. The assignee must accept the accounts of profit agreed to by the partners.[2] When the firm is dissolved, however, the assignee is entitled to receive the share of the partnership assets to which the assigning partner is entitled as between himself and the other partners, and, for the purpose of ascertaining that share, to an account as from the date of the dissolution.[3]

Liability of Assignee.—Where the assignation has merely been granted as a security, the assignee, although entitled to a share in the profits of the business, is not personally liable for any of the firm's debts.[4]

Liability of Firm for Wrongful Act of Partner.—Where by any wrongful act or omission of any partner acting in the ordinary course of the business of the firm, or with the authority of his co-partners, loss or injury is caused to any person not being a partner in the firm, or any penalty is incurred, the firm is liable therefor, to the same extent as the partner so acting or omitting to act.[5] Where a partner acting within the scope of his apparent authority receives the money or property of a third person and misapplies it, and where a firm in the course of its business receives money or property of a third person,

---

[1] Cassels *v.* Stewart, 1879, 6 R. 936 ; *affd.* (H.L.) 8 R. 1.
[2] Partnership Act, sec. 31 (1).
[3] Partnership Act, sec. 31 (2).
[4] Hardie *v.* Cameron, 1879, 19 S.L.R. 833 ; Partnership Act, sec. 2 (3).
[5] Sec. 10.

and the money or property so received is misapplied by one or more of the partners while it is in the custody of the firm, the firm is liable to make good the loss.[1]   But a firm is not responsible for the wrongful act of a partner, if the wrongful act have been unconnected with the business of the firm, or not within the scope of the partnership business. Nor is the firm responsible if one of the partners, while acting as a trustee, improperly employs trust-money, though such money, if still in the possession of the firm, may be recovered from it.[2]   Fraud is always personal, and though a firm may be responsible for the individual fraud of one of its partners acting within the scope of his authority, it is incompetent to charge the firm generally with fraud ; and there must, in order to make the firm liable, be specification of the individual partner or partners who have been guilty of the fraud.[3]

Liability of Firm for Known Unauthorised Acts of Partner.—Where one partner pledges the credit of the firm for a purpose apparently not connected with the firm's ordinary course of business, the firm is not bound, unless such partner is in fact specially authorised by the other partners.[4]   But where a person, who is aware that the powers conferred upon an individual partner are limited, either generally or in connection with a particular transaction, chooses to have dealings with that partner in matters outwith the scope of his authority, he cannot afterwards make the firm liable.   So also, a person who has dealings with a partner in matters outwith the scope of his firm's business, or in matters purely personal to that partner, cannot subsequently bind the firm.   Thus a partner cannot pledge his firm's goods or credit for his private debts. Where there is an agreement between the partners, that any restriction shall be placed on the power of one or more of them, no act done in contravention of the agreement is binding on the firm with respect to persons having notice of the agreement.[5]

Joint and Several Liability of Partners.—Every partner in a firm is liable, jointly and severally with the other partners, for all debts and obligations of the firm incurred while he is a partner ; and after his death his estate is also severally liable in a due course of administration for such debts and obligations, so far as they remain unsatisfied.[6]   A person admitted into a firm is not, without special stipulation to that effect, liable for any debts contracted prior to his admission.[7]   Where a person deals with a firm after a change in its constitution, he is entitled

---

[1] Sec. 11.

[2] Sec. 13.

[3] Thomson & Co. v. Pattison, Elder & Co., 1895, 22 R. 432.

[4] Sec. 7.   For interpretation of this section see opinion of Lord Johnston and Lord Mackenzie in Clydesdale Bank Ltd. v. Continental Chocolate Co., 1917 (not reported).

[5] Sec. 8.

[6] Sec. 9.

[7] Sec. 17.   See, however, Bonds of Credit, *infra.*

to treat all apparent members of the old firm as still being members until he has notice of the change.[1] Notice in the *Edinburgh Gazette* is sufficient notice to persons who have not previously had dealings with the firm. The estate of a partner who dies, or who becomes bankrupt, or of a partner who, not having been known to the person dealing with the firm to be a partner, retires from the firm, is not liable for partnership debts contracted after the date of the death, bankruptcy, or retirement respectively.[2] But after the dissolution of a partnership, the authority of a partner to bind the firm, and the other rights and obligations of the partners, continue for the purpose of winding up the affairs of the partnership, and to complete transactions begun but unfinished at the date of dissolution.[3] With regard to persons who had dealings with a firm prior to the retiral of a partner, it is only necessary to show that such persons actually had notice of the fact. Intimation in the *Gazette* or in a newspaper is sufficient, if it can be shown that the customer of the firm actually saw it or had it brought to his notice. Intimation by circular, a change in the name of a firm painted on its counting-house, general notoriety as to the change of name, an alteration in the manner of signing cheques, are each sufficient, provided it can be shown that the creditor was aware of the fact.

Liability of Retiring Partner for Past Acts.—A partner who retires from a firm does not thereby cease to be liable for partnership debts or obligations incurred before his retirement.[4] No agreement with his partners can free him—not even if he leave enough money to pay the partnership debts and take a bond from his partners that they will do so. The debts must in fact be paid. But (1) payment of a debt by one partner releases all the others, and a payment by the new firm discharges the old firm ; (2) release of one partner from a partnership debt releases all the others, subject to the rules of sequestration where such rules apply ; (3) the substitution of one debtor for another, either by agreement or implication, discharges the original debtor ; but creditors are not presumed to discharge outgoing partners, and although a creditor may discharge one or more partners while holding the other partners bound, the discharge of one partner is, except in special circumstances, a discharge of all. A retiring partner may be discharged from any existing liabilities, by an agreement to that effect between himself and the members of the firm as newly constituted and the creditors, and this agreement may be either express, or inferred as a fact from the course of dealing between the creditors and the firm as newly constituted. A creditor, by treating the continuing partners as his debtors, does not necessarily discharge a retiring partner, but he will do so by adopting the continuing partners as his debtors. Where

---

[1] Sec. 26 (1).   [2] Sec. 26 (3).   [3] Sec. 28.   [4] Sec. 17 (2).

a partner dies, a creditor who is aware of the fact does not necessarily release that partner's estate simply by continuing to deal with the firm as before, unless there be evidence that he has shown an intention to abandon his right of recourse against such partner's estate.

Dissolution of Partnership.—Subject to any agreement between the partners, a partnership is dissolved : (*a*) if entered into for a fixed term, by the expiration of that term ; (*b*) if entered into for a single adventure or undertaking, by the termination of that adventure or undertaking ; (*c*) if entered into for an undefined time, by any partner giving notice to the other or others of his intention to dissolve partnership.[1] Subject to any agreement between the partners, every partnership is dissolved as regards all the partners by the death or bankruptcy of any partner.[2] A partnership may, at the option of the other partners, be dissolved, if any partner suffers his share of the partnership property to be charged under the Act for his separate debt.[3] A partnership is, in every case, dissolved by the happening of any event which makes it unlawful for the business of the firm to be carried on, or for the members of the firm to carry it on in partnership.[4] On application by a partner, the Court may decree a dissolution of partnership : (*a*) when any partner becomes insane ; (*b*) when any partner, other than the partner suing, becomes permanently incapable of performing his part of the partnership contract ; (*c*) when any partner, other than the partner suing, has been guilty of such conduct as in the opinion of the Court, having regard to the nature of the business, is calculated to affect prejudicially the carrying on of the business ; (*d*) when any partner, other than the partner suing, wilfully or persistently commits a breach of the partnership agreement, or otherwise so conducts himself in matters relating to the partnership business as to make it unreasonably practicable for the other partners to carry on business in partnership with him ; (*e*) when the business can only be carried on at a loss ; or (*f*) when circumstances have arisen which, in the opinion of the Court, render it just and equitable that the partnership be dissolved.[5]

Firms as Customers of a Bank.—Where a partner signs his firm's name such signature is equivalent to the signature by that partner of the names of all the persons liable as partners in that firm.[6] Where an account is opened in a firm's name, the banker is, in the absence of special agreement, bound only to honour cheques drawn in the partnership name.[7] Upon the death of one partner in a firm having an account at a bank, the surviving partner has a right to draw cheques upon the partnership account.[8] Where a signature is common to an individual

---

[1] Sec. 32. [2] Sec. 33 (1). [3] Sec. 33 (2).
[4] Sec. 34. [5] Sec. 35. [6] B. of E. Act, sec. 23.
[7] Forster *v.* Mackreth, L.R. 2 Ex. 163 ; Kirk *v.* Blurton, 9 M. & W. 284 ; Emly *v.* Lye, 15 East, 7 ; Nicholson *v.* Ricketts, 29 L.J. Q.B. 55.
[8] Backhouse *v.* Charlton, L.R. 8 Ch. D. 444.

and a firm of which the individual is a member, a *bonâ fide* holder for
value, without notice whose paper it is, of a cheque with such signature
attached, has not an option to sue either the individual or the firm.
But there is a presumption that the cheque was given for the firm and
is binding upon it, at least where the individual carries on no business
separate from the business of the firm of which he is a member.   This presumption may, however, be rebutted by proof that the cheque was signed
not in the name of the partnership, but of the individual for his private
purposes, and it is immaterial that the *bonâ fide* holder takes the cheque
as that of the firm and not of the individual.[1]   Where a partner of a
firm opens an account in his own name, the banker may prove that in
so doing he was acting not on his own behalf, but as the agent of his
firm.[2]   Where money so lodged by one partner of a firm is the property
of the firm, dishonour of the firm's cheque, or of the cheque of any
partner other than that of him in whose name the account was opened,
attaches no liability to the banker.[3]

There is no implication of law, from the mere existence of a trade
partnership, that one partner has authority to bind the firm by opening
a banking account on its behalf in his own name.[4]   While a banker
is bound to honour the cheque of any partner of a firm, signed in the
firm's name, drawn upon an account opened in name of the firm, there
is no obligation on him to honour the cheque of a partner who is not
known to him as such and whose signature he does not know.[5]   Where
accounts are kept at a banker's by a firm, each partner having a right
to draw cheques, and also by the individual partners of the firm, it
is not the duty of the banker to inquire into the propriety of any transfer
of funds which may be made from and to the different accounts.[6]   Any
partner of a firm may intimate that cheques on the firm's account are
not to be honoured unless he also signs.   Effect must be given to such
an intimation.

One partner has no authority to authorise a servant of the firm to
operate on the partnership account.   The mandate to operate should
be signed by all the partners.

On the death or bankruptcy of a partner, no notice of any kind
is required to free his representatives of liability for debts contracted
subsequent to such event.   Death is a public fact, and if it is the bank's
intention to hold liable a retiring partner, or the representatives of a
deceased partner, for the obligations due as at the date of the death or

---

[1] Yorkshire Banking Co. *v.* Beatson, L.R. 4 C.P.D. 204 ; Leeds and County
Banking Co. *v.* Beatson, L.R. 5 C.P.D. 109.

[2] Cooke *v.* Seeley, 2 Ex. 746.

[3] Cooke *v.* Seeley, *supra*.

[4] Alliance Bank *v.* Kearsley, L.R. 6 C.P. 433.

[5] Cooke *v.* Seeley, *supra*.

[6] Backhouse *v.* Charlton, L.R. 8 Ch. D. 444.

retiral of that partner, their duty on receiving notice of the retiral, or on becoming cognisant of the death of the partner, is to stop operations on the account and call for a settlement. If this is not done and operations are allowed to proceed, the principle of Devaynes *v.* Nobel will apply.[1] If the partner so retiring, or who has died, has assigned property in security of the firm's obligations, he or the representatives of the deceased partner are entitled to call upon the bank to reassign the property so conveyed in security, in the event of subsequent payments into the account being sufficient to extinguish the amount at such dates. This is illustrated by the case of Christie *v.* Royal Bank.[2] In March 1832 the firm of Robert Allan & Son, of which there were three partners, including Thomas Allan, obtained from the Royal Bank a cash-credit to the extent of £20,000, and in addition to the personal obligation granted by the firm and partners as such partners and as individuals, Thomas Allan disponed to the bank certain heritable property belonging to him in security of the advances to be made to the company. Thomas Allan died in September 1833, at which time there was a sum due to the bank of £8800. The surviving partners continued the business as before, and the bank continued operations with them on the old account. In 1834 the firm became bankrupt, at which time they were largely indebted to the bank, and in a question with creditors of Thomas Allan as an individual, and of the firm of Robert Allan & Son previous to his death, it was held that by the death of Thomas Allan the firm of Robert Allan & Son was dissolved, and that the security which Thomas Allan gave to the bank for the repayment of advances made to the firm of which he was a partner was not available as a security for advances made after his death to a firm in which he was not a partner, and as the payments into the account by the surviving partners subsequent to his death exceeded the amount of the debt due to the bank at the time of Thomas Allan's death, the estates conveyed in security by him were freed from the obligations of the firm existing at the date of sequestration.

Admission of New Partner into Firm.—By the admission of a partner into a firm a new firm is thus constituted ; but the partners of a company which has contracted a trade debt, such as an overdraft with a bank, cannot relieve themselves from the obligation to pay that debt by the mere act of entering into a new co-partnery with a third person. In one case, two partners, who had carried on business under the style of Duncan & Co., and had contracted a trade debt in that name, assumed a third party as a partner, and thereafter carried on business under the style of Lancaster, Duncan & Co., the

---

[1] See p. 25, and Deeley *v.* Lloyds Bank, 1912, 29 T.L.R. 1.
[2] 1839, 1 D. 745 ; *affd.* (H.L.) 1841 ; 2 Rob. 118 ; 3 Ross's L.C. 668.

assets of the old firm being transferred to the new firm. On the failure of the new firm the Court held that the trade creditors were entitled to a ranking on the estate of the new firm, and on the individual estates of the two partners of Duncan & Co., but not on the individual estate of the new partner.[1] So, if at the time of the assumption of a partner the old firm is indebted to a bank, the bank is entitled, on the bankruptcy of the firm subsequent to the admission of the new partner, to rank on the estates of the new firm and of the old partners, even although no operations by the new firm have taken place on the account.[2] Where, however, a partner assumed into a business contributes to the capital of the business a sum of money, while the other partners contribute merely their respective shares in the concern, it is thought that special circumstances would require to be proved in order to render the new firm liable for obligations incurred prior to the date of the change.[3]

3. Limited Partnerships Act, 1907

The title of this Act, which is " An Act to Establish Limited Partnerships," is a misnomer. It is not an Act to establish limited partnerships. A condition precedent to any benefit under the statute is that there must be in the firm one or more persons, called general partners, who are liable to their last farthing for all the debts and obligations of the firm. Under the Act any lawful business, including banking and insurance, may be carried on under its provisions.

A limited partnership must not consist, in the case of a partnership carrying on the business of banking, of more than ten persons, and, in the case of any other partnership, of more than twenty persons, and " must consist of one or more persons, called general partners, who shall be liable for all debts and obligations of the firm, and one or more persons to be called limited partners, who shall at the time of entering into such partnership contribute thereto a sum or sums as capital or property valued at a stated amount, and who shall not be liable for the debts or obligations of the firm beyond the amount so contributed " (Act, sec. 4 (2)).

In the case of ordinary joint stock companies the word " limited " must form part of the company name, and those trading with the company are put upon their inquiry and made aware that there is a limitation to the liability of at least one or more of the members. No similar intimation is given in the case of limited partnerships.

The only way by which a person dealing with such a partnership

---

[1] Ridgway v. Brock, 1831, 10 S. 105.

[2] Miller v. Thorburn, 1861, 23 D. 359. See also Heddle's Exrs. v. Marwick & Hourston's Tr., 1888, 15 R. 698.

[3] Stephen's Trs. v. Macdougall & Co.'s Trs., 1889, 16 R. 779.

can ascertain that the liability of any of the partners is limited, is by application to the Registrar of Joint Stock Companies. The partnership agreement must be registered, and if it is not so registered, the partnership is deemed to be a general partnership, and every limited partner is deemed to be a general partner. The particulars required for registration are—(a) the firm name ; (b) the general nature of the business ; (c) the principal place of business ; (d) the full name of each of the partners ; (e) the term, if any, for which the partnership is entered into, and the date of its commencement ; (f) a statement that the partnership is limited, and the description of every limited partner as such ; and (g) the sum contributed by each limited partner, and whether paid in cash or how otherwise. Any partnership deed which is registered under the Act is open to inspection by the public on payment of a fee not exceeding one shilling.

A limited partner under the Act is under certain disabilities. For instance, he cannot during the continuance of the partnership either directly or indirectly draw out or receive back any part of his contribution, and if he does so draw out or receive back any such part he is liable for the debts and obligations of the firm up to the amount so drawn out or received back. Again, a limited partner has no power to take part in the management of the partnership business, and has no power to bind the firm. He may, however, by himself or his agent, at any time inspect the books of the firm, and examine into the state and prospects of the partnership business, and may advise with the partners thereon ; but if he takes part in the management of the partnership business (what degree of management is not specified) he is liable for all debts and obligations of the firm incurred while he so takes part in the management, as though he were a general partner. Further, subject to any agreement expressed or implied between the partners, (a) any difference arising as to ordinary matters connected with the partnership business may be decided by a majority of the general partners ; (b) a limited partner may, with the consent of the general partners, assign his share in the partnership, and upon such an assignment the assignee becomes a limited partner with all the rights of the assignor ; (c) the other partners are not entitled to dissolve the partnership by reason of any limited partner suffering his share to be charged for his separate debt ; (d) a person may be introduced as a partner without the consent of the existing limited partners ; and (e) a limited partner is not entitled to dissolve the partnership by notice. There is no material benefit to be derived from the Act (apart from dealings which are questionable) which could not be obtained under the law existing prior to its passing. The Act is a useless piece of legislation, and as now in operation in this country is liable to be abused and its provisions put to uses the Legislature never intended, introducing, as it does, a system whereby the position of creditors of trading companies is weakened without some public notice to them that all the partners of the firm are not severally liable for all the obligations undertaken in name of the firm.

4. Agents and Mandataries

There are various kinds of agency. A factor is an agent who buys or sells for his principal on commission, and is intrusted with the possession, management, and disposal of his principal's property. A broker is, like a factor, an agent who buys or sells for his principal, but, unlike him, is not intrusted with the custody of his principal's property. A factor cannot bind his principal without a specific mandate to do so, or possession of his principal's goods. A mandatary is one who, properly speaking, acts for another gratuitously, and is in consequence responsible to his principal in a less degree than a paid agent. A partner is an agent of his firm with power to bind his firm in doing anything which properly falls within the scope of the business of the partnership ; and so on. But so far as the relation between a banker and a person who acts on behalf of a customer is concerned, the various kinds of agent may be treated as one. The relation of principal and agent is a personal one. Generally speaking, an agent has no power to delegate his authority. Where a principal places money in a bank on the terms that a known agent should draw upon it, he retains the power if he rightly determines the agency to require the bank to return the undrawn balance to him.[1]

Constitution of Agency.—The relation of principal and agent may be constituted (*a*) in writing, (*b*) verbally, or (*c*) it may be inferred from circumstances. A person legally incapable of contracting on his own behalf may be appointed as agent for another, and enter into a contract binding as between his principal and a third party, though he cannot acquire any personal rights or incur liabilities under it. A married woman and a minor may both be appointed, and undertake the duties of an agent.

Agency may be either general or special. In the former the agent undertakes the management of his principal's entire business affairs, or of some particular branch of his business, according to the usage of trade in that business ; while in the latter his authority is limited to the performance of a particular act or class of acts, or the conduct of a particular business transaction.

General Agency.—A general agent has power to bind his principal by any act which properly comes within the scope of his authority and is sanctioned by the usage of trade ; but, without express authority,

---

[1] Société Coloniale Anversoise and Others *v.* London and Brazilian Bank Ltd., 1911, 28 T.L.R. 44.

he has no power to borrow money on his principal's credit,[1] to draw, accept, discount,[2] or indorse bills, or to grant obligations outwith the ordinary course of business, unless the drawing, accepting, discounting, or indorsing of bills is necessarily incidental to the conduct of his principal's business, or by implication necessarily falls within the scope of the business intrusted to him. But an agent, though unauthorised to draw cheques in the name of his principal, can nevertheless bind his principal by doing so, provided the drawing and indorsing of cheques is incidental to the business of the agency intrusted to him, and the person with whom he deals has no notice of the agent's disability,[3] even where there is a stipulation between the agent and his principal that he is not to do so.[4] An agent who acts for an undisclosed principal and who is believed by the person with whom he has business dealings to be a principal, may nevertheless effectually render the real principal liable for his acts. Thus in one case the manager of a brewing business, in whose name the licence was taken out and whose name appeared above the door of the business premises, ordered from a firm certain articles which he was expressly forbidden by his principal to do. The goods were supplied upon the manager's own credit, but the firm for whom he conducted the business were held liable for all the acts of their agent which were within the authority usually conferred upon an agent in that particular business, although he had never been held out as an agent and had actually exceeded the power conferred upon him.[5] So an agent who borrows money in his principal's name, but who has no authority to do so, will bind his principal to repay the sum if the money so borrowed has been applied for the benefit of his principal and not of himself.[6] The manager of a business, or of a particular branch of a business, has no power to borrow on the credit of advances due to his principal. Thus the manager of a steamship company appointed to conduct the business of the company at a particular port, including the uplifting of freights, has no power, without express authority, to borrow money, by way of advance on the credit of such freights.[7] But " the acquiescence by the principal in the performance of such acts by an agent, and the acknowledgment of the validity of obligations so undertaken, may be proved and will be held in law to amount to a mandate." [8]

---

[1] Sinclair, Moorhead & Co. *v.* Wallace & Co., 1880, 7 R. 874.

[2] Hine Bros. *v.* Steamship Insurance Syndicate, 1894, 11 T.L.R. 83.

[3] Howard *v.* Bailey, 2 H. & Bl. 618 ; Davidson *v.* Stanley, 2 M. & G. 721 ; Hogarth *v.* Wherley, L.R. 10 C.P. 630.

[4] Edmunds *v.* Bushell, 1865, L.R. 1 Q.B. 97.

[5] Watteaux *v.* Fenwick, 1893, L.R. 1 Q.B. 346.

[6] Reid *v.* Rigby, 1894, L.R. 2 Q.B. 40.

[7] Ross, Skolfield & Co. *v.* State Steamship Co., 1875, 3 R. 134.

[8] *Per* Lord Justice-Clerk in Swinburne & Co. *v.* Western Bank, 1856, 18 D. 1025. See also *infra.*

"A general agent may derive his authority (1) from the fact that business of a certain kind is intrusted to him which involves the exercise of his discretion ; or (2) from the fact that he stands in some such relation to his principal as of itself implies an authority to act in certain matters ; or (3) from the fact that the principal has habitually sanctioned acts of a particular character done by the agent on his behalf." [1] Factors, commission agents, or brokers, whose actions, if such as might be presumed to have been delegated to them, are binding on their principals, are examples of the first kind. Partners, and in certain cases shipmasters, are examples of the second, while examples of the third kind will be found in the section treating of the banker's duty towards his customer's cheques.

A general agent, who has special instructions from his principal as to the particular course he is to follow in the conduct of his business, will nevertheless effectually bind his principal for any act done in the course of such business, though contrary to his special instructions, provided that the person with whom he deals was unaware of the restrictions imposed upon him, and that the acts so done were in accordance with the usual powers intrusted to an agent and with the usage of trade. This rule applies even to the case of a wrongful or fraudulent act on the part of the agent, committed by him for purposes of his own, provided that the third party has acted with due caution. In such circumstances, where one of two innocent parties must suffer, the law holds that the loss must fall on him who has given occasion for the commission of the act by which such loss is entailed. A mandate to act as a managing clerk and to pay or discharge debts does not, according to the usage of trade, imply authority to draw or accept bills per procuration.

Dispositions by Mercantile Agents.—The law regulating the relations between principals and mercantile agents, that is, agents having in the customary course of their business as agents authority either to sell goods or to consign goods for the purposes of sale, or to buy goods or raise money on the security of goods, is now governed by the Factors Act, 1889, extended to Scotland by the Factors Act (Scotland), 1890, the provisions of which are to be construed in amplification and not in derogation of the powers possessed by agents at common law. The Act gives agents no authority, as between them and their principals, to exceed or depart from the powers conferred on them, nor exempts them from any liability, civil or criminal, for so doing, but only affects the relations which exist between agents and principals on the one hand and third parties, with whom such agents contract on behalf of their principals, on the other.[2] The Act, however, does not apply to a person

---

[1] Anson on Contract, p. 332.

[2] Secs. 12 (1), 13. See, generally, Cole v. N.W. Bank, 1879, L.R. 10 C.P. 354 ; Vickers v. Hertz, 1871, 9 M. (H.L.) 65 ; Pochin & Co. v. Robinows & Marjoribanks, 1869, 7 M. 622 ; Stewart v. Fletcher & M'Gregor, 1829, 7 S. 622 ; Johnston v. Crédit Lyonnais, 1877, L.R. 3 C.P.D. 32.

who merely pretends to be an agent. Hence in a case where a broker fraudulently obtained possession of goods from A. and sold them to B., holding himself out as the agent of A., it was decided that B. could not retain possession of the goods as against A. under the Factors Act.[1]

Where an agent is, with the consent of the owner, in possession of goods or the documents of title to goods, any sale, pledge, or other disposition of the goods, made by him when acting in the ordinary course of business of a mercantile agent, is subject to the provisions after specified, as valid as if he were expressly authorised by the owner of the goods to make the same ; provided that the person taking under the disposition acts in good faith, and has not at the time of the disposition notice that the person making the disposition has not authority to make the same.[2] A person intrusted with the custody of goods for the purpose of selling them on commission, and who pledges them with a pawnbroker who receives them in good faith and in the ordinary course of business, is not, however, a mercantile agent within the meaning of the statute.[3]

Where a mercantile agent has, with the consent of the owner, been in possession of goods or documents of title to goods, any sale, pledge, or other disposition which would have been valid if the consent had continued, is effectual notwithstanding the determination of the consent ; provided that the person taking under the disposition has not at the time thereof notice that the consent has been determined.[4]

Where such agent obtains possession of any document of title to goods by reason of his being or having been, with the consent of the owner, in possession of the goods represented thereby, or of any other documents of title to the goods, his possession of the first-mentioned documents is deemed to be with the consent of the owner.[5] Such consent is presumed in the absence of evidence to the contrary.[6]

A pledge of the documents of title to goods is deemed to be a pledge of the goods themselves.[7] So far as it applies, the language of this clause is unambiguous. It provides that to that extent a pledge of the documents of title shall, though in point of fact it is not so, be nevertheless regarded in law as equivalent to a pledge of the goods. Had the clause been embodied in a statute which contemplated an alteration of the general law with regard to contracts of pledge in Scotland, its effect would have been to make a pledge of the documents of title in *all* cases equivalent to a completed pledge of the goods themselves. But the clause is only one of a group collected under the statutory heading, " Dispositions by Mercantile Agents," and an examination of

---

[1] Gillman, Spencer & Co. *v.* Carbutt & Co., 1889, 61 L.T.R. 281.
[2] Sec. 2 (1) ; Folkes *v.* King, 1922, 39 T.L.R. 77.
[3] Hastings *v.* Pearson, 1893, L.R. 1 Q.B. 62.
[4] Sec. 2 (2).   [5] Sec. 2 (3).   [6] Sec. 2 (4).   [7] Sec. 3.

the context shows that the enactment of this clause was intended merely to define the full effect of a pledge of documents of title made by a mercantile agent under and by virtue of one or other of the subsections of the preceding clause. Accordingly, the section has no application to the case of the pledge of documents of title by any person not a mercantile agent within the meaning of the Act.[1]

Where goods are pledged in security of an antecedent debt of the agent, the pledgee acquires no further right to the goods than could have been enforced by the agent at the time of the pledge.[2]

The sale, pledge, or other disposition made by an agent, in order to be valid, must be for a valuable consideration, which may be either a payment in cash or the delivery or transfer of other goods, or of a document of title to goods, or of a negotiable security, or of anything sufficient to constitute value ; but where goods are pledged in consideration of the delivery or transfer of other goods, or of a document of title to goods, or of a negotiable security, the pledgee acquires no right or interest in the goods so pledged in excess of the value of the goods, document, or security when so delivered or transferred in exchange.[3]

An agreement made with an agent through his clerk or other person authorised in the ordinary course of business to make contracts of sale or pledge on his behalf, is deemed to be an agreement with the agent.[4]

Where the owner of goods has given possession of the goods to another person for the purpose of consignment or sale, or has shipped the goods in the name of another person, and the consignee of the goods has not had notice that such person is not the owner of the goods, the consignee has, in respect of advances made to or for the use of such person, the same lien on the goods as if such person were the owner of the goods, and may transfer any such lien to any other person.[5]

Dispositions by Sellers or Buyers of Goods.—Where a person having sold goods continues, or is, in possession of the goods or of the documents of title to the goods, the delivery or transfer by that person, or by a mercantile agent acting for him, of the goods or documents of title, under any sale, pledge, or other disposition thereof, or under any agreement for sale, pledge, or other disposition thereof, to any person receiving the same in good faith and without notice of the previous sale, has the same effect as if the person making the delivery or transfer were expressly authorised by the owner of the goods to make the same.[6]

Where a person having bought or agreed to buy goods, obtains,

---

[1] *Per* Lord Watson in Inglis *v.* Robertson & Baxter, 1898, 25 R. (H.L.) 70, L.R. A.C. 616.

[2] Sec. 4.

[3] Sec. 5 (and sec. 1 (2) of Factors (Scotland) Act).

[4] Sec. 6.   [5] Sec. 7.   [6] Sec. 8.

with the consent of the seller, possession of the goods or the documents of title to goods, the delivery or transfer by that person or by a mercantile agent acting for him, of the goods or documents of title, under any sale, pledge, or other disposition thereof, to any person receiving the same in good faith and without notice of any lien or other rights of the original seller in respect of the goods, has the same effect as if the person making the delivery or transfer were a mercantile agent in possession of the goods or documents of title with the consent of the owner.[1]

The expression " a person having agreed to buy goods " means a person who has bound himself by agreement to buy, and does not include a person who has an option to buy, the owner being bound to sell if that option is exercised.[2] Similarly, where the hirer sells to a person who buys in good faith and without notice of any lien on the part of the true owner, the delivery or transfer of the goods has the same effect as though the hirer were a mercantile agent in possession of the goods with the consent of the owner, and the purchaser accordingly acquires a complete and permanent title.[3] So also where a person who has received goods on " sale and return " pledges them, the property in the goods passes to him, and the original vendor cannot recover them from the person with whom they have been pledged.[4]

Where a document of title to goods has been lawfully transferred to a person as a buyer or owner of the goods, and that person transfers the document to a person who takes it in good faith and for valuable consideration, the last transfer has the same effect in defeating any vendor's lien or stoppage *in transitu* as the transfer of a bill of lading.[5]

The owner of goods is not prevented from recovering the goods from the agent or his trustee in bankruptcy at any time before their sale or pledge, nor, where the goods are pledged by the agent, from redeeming the goods at any time before their sale, on satisfying the claim for which the goods were pledged and paying to the agent, if by him required, any money in respect of which the agent would by law be entitled to retain the goods or the documents of title thereto, or any of them, by way of

---

[1] Sec. 9.

[2] Helby *v.* Matthews, 1895, L.R. A.C. 471.

[3] Payne *v.* Wilson, 1895, L.R. 1 Q.B. 653.

[4] Though on the entirely different principle that he has thereby " adopted " the transaction under the Sale of Goods Act, 1893, sec. 18, r. 4 (*a*), which " unhappily codified the existing law in language which is unfortunately chosen " (Kirkham *v.* Attenborough, 1897, 1 Q.B. 201). The decision is interesting as showing that anyone who may be temporarily in possession of goods with the consent of the owner under conditions of " sale and return," or probably even of " approval," may become the owner of them, and therefore capable of giving a person to whom he pledges them a valid title, by doing any act, such as pledge, which may be construed as amounting to an " adoption " of their sale.

[5] Sec. 10. See also Sale of Goods Act, 1893, sec. 25 (2), referred to in Stoppage *in transitu, infra.*

lien against the owner, or from recovering from anyone with whom the
goods have been pledged any balance of money remaining in his hands as
the produce of the sale of goods after deducting the amount of his lien.[1]
Nor is the owner of goods sold by an agent prevented from recovering
from the buyer the price agreed to be paid, or any part of that price,
subject to any right of compensation on the part of the buyer against
the agent.[2]

Special Agency.—The powers of a special agent are confined to the
particular act or class of acts authorised by the principal, and the powers
conferred upon the special agent will be rigidly construed by the Court.
A special agent cannot bind his principal for any act, power to do which
is not expressly given him by his principal. The greatest care should
therefore be taken to see that for every act which such an agent does
he has specific authority.

In the simplest form of special agency, where power to operate upon
an account current is conferred upon an agent, such power will be held
as extending only to operations on the account while a credit balance
remains, and no power can be inferred either (1) to overdraw the
account, or (2) to accept or indorse bills, or (3) to indorse deposit
receipts.

A special agent entitled to operate upon an account current has
no authority, after exhausting that account, to transfer the amount
standing at his principal's credit on deposit receipt to the current account
in order that he may make further drafts upon it ; and the bank agent
permitting such a transfer without the principal's express authority
would, in the event of fraud on the agent's part, be liable to his customer
in repetition of the amount.

A banker dealing with an agent acting under special authority has
a duty imposed on him to see that the agent is acting strictly within
the limits of the power conferred on him, and should insist, before
dealing with such an agent, on production of either a notarially-certified
copy of the document or an extract from the register in which it is
recorded.

A special agent has no implied authority to do any act which has not
been strictly delegated to him. Thus a law agent intrusted with the
custody of a deposit receipt, and in the habit of uplifting the interest
due upon it, has no authority to uplift the principal. " Where no
course of dealing is brought out, and indeed nothing averred but the
uplifting of interest, I cannot hold it a sound principle of the law of
Scotland that a party accredits an agent to receive the capital by
placing the document of debt in his hands." [3] So an agent who is

---

[1] Sec. 12 (2).   [2] Sec. 12 (3) ; *vide* Compensation.
[3] *Per* Lord Justice-Clerk, in Forbes *v.* Western Bank, 1854, 16 D. 807. See also
Stewart *v.* Central Bank, 1859, 21 D. 1180.

instructed to receive payment in cash, and who accepts the debtor's cheque, will render himself liable for the amount of the debt if the cheque be subsequently dishonoured.[1]

Procurations.[2]—Before honouring a cheque which bears to be signed per procuration of a customer, care should be taken to see that the person so signing has been authorised to do so, and the mandate itself should be in the hands of the bank. A signature by procuration operates as a notice that the agent has but a limited authority to sign, and the principal is only bound by such signature if the agent in so signing was acting within the actual limits of his authority. Where a person has been in the habit of drawing cheques on his principal's account, and has, on occasion at least, been authorised to indorse cheques and receive payment of them, there is a presumption that such person has a general authority to indorse his principal's cheques.[3]

Termination of Agency.—The agency may be terminated by notice, written or verbal, or by implication. Recall of the agency by the principal terminates its existence as between the agent and third parties from the time when they become aware of it, but where any agent or person has been intrusted with and continues in the possession of any goods or documents of title to goods, any revocation of his instrument or agency does not prejudice or affect the title or rights of any other person who, without notice of such revocation, purchases such goods, or makes advances upon the faith or security of such goods or documents.[4]

The death or bankruptcy of the principal operates *ipso jure* as a recall of the agent's authority, but notwithstanding the death or bankruptcy of the principal, transactions entered into by the agent in good faith before he becomes aware of the fact are valid and binding on the principal or his representatives. The insanity of the principal does not, however, appear to operate as a recall of the agent's authority, at least until the person so dealing with such an agent is put in *malâ fide* by becoming cognisant of the insanity.[5] But the marriage of a female principal does. The agency may also be terminated by (1) lapse of time, as when an agent has been appointed for a particular period ; (2) by the appointment of another agent in room of the first appointed ; (3) by the need for an agent ceasing to exist, as on the return of a principal from abroad, or his restoration to health, where the agent has been appointed to act during his absence or illness.

---

[1] Papé *v.* Westacott, 1893, L.R. 1 Q.B. 272.

[2] See Bills, *infra.*

[3] Prescott *v.* Flinn, 9 Bing. 19.

[4] 40 & 41 Vict. cap. 39, sec. 2.

[5] Pollock *v.* Paterson, 10th December 1811, F.C. ; Wink *v.* Mortimer, 1849, 11 D. 995 ; Drew *v.* Nunn, 1879, L.R. 4 Q.B.D. 661.

In all such cases a banker who deals with an agent in *bonâ fide* ignorance of the termination of the agency will be protected.

Where a banker has been dealing with a customer who he believed was a principal but afterwards discovers was only an agent, he cannot continue to make further advances on the faith of such principal's securities, except to the extent that such agent is interested in them. Notice that a person is only an agent may be conveyed to the banker expressly, as by receipt of a letter from such agent or his principal intimating the fact, or by implication, as where the nature and extent of the customer's business are such as to necessarily lead a prudent and careful banker to that conclusion.[1]

5. Stockbrokers

Pledge of Securities by Stockbrokers.—A stockbroker, as broker, has no right, without the consent, express or implied, of his client, to pledge the securities of his client. But in cases where a client desires to borrow a proportion of the price of stocks which he purchases and to pay only the balance, it is convenient that the loan should be negotiated through the broker, because he usually has a standing arrangement with his bankers for borrowing on the security of stocks, the titles to which are taken in his own name, and as he knows the value of stocks, he can more easily arrange with his bankers for an advance proportionate to the value of the stock, and generally at a lower rate of interest than the client could do by acting directly. As the bank contracts with the broker, it is of course necessary that the transfer of the stocks should be taken in the name of the broker in order that he may be put into the position of making a valid assignment in security to the bank, the immediate effect of this arrangement being that the broker, while he remains solvent, is entitled to a retrocession or transfer of each parcel of stock from the bank on repayment of any advances made against it, and then to hold the stock as trustee, in the first place, for repayment of his advances, and, in the second place, for the benefit of the client on whose account the purchase had been made. Now, in accordance with settled rules of law, if securities which are the absolute property of anyone, whether broker or not, are pledged by delivery, in the case of bearer securities, or made over to a banker by *ex facie* absolute transfers, in the case of non-negotiable securities, the banker is entitled to treat the stocks as security for subsequent advances as well as for the advance made at the time of transfer, on the principle that in such a case the debtor puts the creditor into possession of his

---

[1] See Locke *v.* Prescott, 32 Beav. 261 ; E. of Sheffield *v.* London Joint Stock Bank, L.R. 13 Ap. Ca. 333 ; London Joint Stock Bank *v.* Simmons, 1892, L.R. A.C. 201 ; *ex parte* Bishop, L.R. 15 Ch. D. 400.

estate on an unqualified title. But where the creditor's title is qualified in its inception, either because the transfer bears to be in security of a specific advance, or because it is so limited by a separate writing executed at the time, then the security is incapable of extension, and a second transfer must be executed if it is desired to make the subject available as a security for further advances. The fact that a broker is, by implication from a general course of business or actually to the bank's knowledge, acting on behalf of a client, does not amount to a limitation of the broker's authority as to the amount of advances to be obtained on the pledge of any particular security ; and although in point of fact a broker borrows, without having any authority, express or implied, from his client, or against his client's express instructions, an amount larger than he was authorised originally to borrow, the owners of the stock so impledged will be bound by his acts to the extent of the sums advanced by the bank on express contracts of loan, because by allowing the stocks to be taken in the agent's name, or, in the case of bonds payable to bearer, by allowing the broker to be in possession of them, they must be held, in a question with third parties, to have given him authority to dispose of the stocks either absolutely or under reversion, and thus to have given the bank a right to retain the stocks in security of the *specific* advances made against them, but not to retain them, after the repayment of such specific advances against the true owners for the personal obligations of the broker himself, for which he did not undertake to pledge them.

Bankers generally assume that where a stockbroker applies to them for an advance against stocks he is acting on behalf of a client. Therefore, while a broker's application for a loan on the security of stocks may import a representation that he has authority to pledge them for the amount he proposes to borrow and to that extent give a good security to the lender, it cannot lead to the inference that they are his own property, or that he has power to give the bank a title to retain them for other advances than those for which he actually undertakes to pledge them. Thus a stockbroker who held stock in his own name for behoof of a client transferred it to a bank in security of an advance which he obtained in his own name for a client. The broker did not lead the bank to believe, and the bank did not, in point of fact, believe, that the broker was acting as a principal in the transaction and that the stock was his own property. It was held that the bank was entitled to hold the securities so pledged only in security of the specific loan for which by contract they had been impledged, and not for the broker's general balance, as the reversion belonged, not to the broker but to his client. Now, while it is settled that a stockbroker may pledge the security of his client without his authority, or even against his express instructions, so as to give the bank a valid title to retain them against the specific advances made on their security, it is also equally settled

6

that to enable the bank to do so it must have acted in *bonâ fide* and with reasonable caution. Where there are no circumstances connected with the transaction such as to excite a reasonable suspicion or apprehension in the mind of the banker that the documents or securities sought to be pledged are being so pledged without, or contrary to, the instructions or authority of their real owner, there seems to be no reason for doubting that the bank is entitled without special inquiry to accept them as the subjects of pledge and to retain them in security of the specific advances made against them. Where, however, the circumstances connected with the pledging of documents are such as ought to excite suspicion in the mind of a reasonably prudent and careful banker, or where the banker is aware that the person pledging the documents has only a limited authority so to deal with them, or where from the very nature of the transaction he is notified that the pledger's interest in the documents is limited, he is put upon inquiry and is bound to ascertain, or at least to take reasonable means to ascertain, the actual extent of the pledger's authority to deal with the securities, whether negotiable or not, and if he fail to do so he cannot retain them against a claim by the true owner, even for the amount of the specific advances made against them.[1]

Where a broker places the proceeds of a sale of shares to the credit of his own account and that account is overdrawn, it appears that the bank is entitled, without inquiry, and even in the full knowledge that the money so paid in is the proceeds of a sale of stock, to retain the money and apply it *pro tanto* in reduction of the overdraft. The mere fact that an account is opened in the name of a broker as such does not place upon the banker any duty to inquire as to the real ownership of any money paid in to the account. If, however, the bank have actual knowledge that any money paid in to a broker's account is so paid in fraud of a third person's right, it cannot plead a right to retain the money.[2]

6. Tutors and Curators

The office of tutor relates to the guardianship of pupils, that is, of children till they reach in the case of males the age of fourteen, and in the case of females the age of twelve ; and the office of curator to minors, that is, children from the above ages till they respectively attain the age of twenty-one. Between the two offices there is a marked distinction. A tutor has control over both the person of the pupil and his estates,

---

[1] National Bank of Scotland *v.* Dickie's Tr., 1895, 22 R. 740 ; London Joint Stock Bank *v.* Simmons, 1892, L.R. A.C. 201 ; E. of Sheffield *v.* London Joint Stock Bank, 1888, L.R. 13 A.C. 333.

[2] Thomson and Others (Dunlop's Trs.) *v.* Clydesdale Bank, 1893, 20 R. (H.L.) 59, *affg.* 18 R. 751.

whereas a curator has control only over the estates of his ward. A tutor acts on his own responsibility and without the consent of the pupil, who during this period is absolutely incapable of entering into any contract. A curator, on the contrary, acts along with the minor, and validates his deeds by consent thereto, the obligation being undertaken by the minor with consent of the curator. Where a minor has curators their consent is necessary to his every act, but where he has none, the law, as gathered from various decisions of the Court, is thus stated by Professor More,[1] and quoted with approval by the Lord President : [2] " Where minors have no curators they may act by themselves, and payments made to them by their debtors will be valid and effectual. But the Court of Session will not, in every instance, compel a debtor to pay to a minor who has no curators, at least without his giving security to keep the debtor indemnified, thus indirectly compelling the minor, where this appears to be necessary for his own protection, to have curators appointed to him."

If during the four years immediately succeeding his attaining majority—the name given to this period being the *quadriennium utile*—the minor prove to the satisfaction of the Court that he was during his minority induced to enter into any contract involving lesion (that is, injury or harm) to him, it will be reduced. Lesion is presumed in the following cases :—(1) In a donation by the minor ; (2) in a cautionary obligation entered into by him ; and (3) even in a personal bond for borrowed money, unless the curator prove that the money was profitably employed for the benefit of the minor. It is proper to explain that if a minor enter into business, his curator's consent is not required to his dealings, and a mercantile obligation is as binding on him as if entered into after the attainment of majority. Considering, however, the difficulties in the way, contracts with pupils and minors are to be avoided.

To both pupils and minors their proper guardian during his life is their father ; but his power is subject to the control of the Court of Session, who have power to interfere if the child's health, morals, or life are in danger.[3] The father has power by his will to nominate tutors and curators to his children. Under the provisions of the Guardianship of Infants Act, 1886,[4] so far as regards pupils, on the death of the father, the mother, if surviving, is the guardian of such infant, either alone, when no guardian has been appointed by the father, or jointly with any guardian appointed by him. If father

---

[1] Lectures, vol. i. p. 110.
[2] Jack *v.* North British Ry. Co., 1886, 14 R. 263.
[3] Harvey *v.* Harvey, 1860, 22 D. 1198.
[4] 49 & 50 Vict. cap. 27, sec. 2. See also Jack *v.* North British Ry. Co., 1886, 14 R. 263.

and mother be both dead and no tutors have been appointed for the
pupil children, the Court will, on application, appoint a factor *loco
tutoris*. Similarly, where no curator has been appointed, the Court will,
on cause shown, appoint one.[1]   On the marriage of a female minor her
guardianship is transferred from her father to her husband.

Factors to Incapacitated Persons.—To those who are unable to manage
their own affairs, such as idiots, lunatics, and persons incapacitated
by reason of imbecility, old age, or natural weakness, the Court of
Session, or, in small estates the yearly value of which (heritable and
moveable combined) does not exceed £100, the Sheriff,[2] on the application
of the next of kin of such persons, or any near relation, and on cause
shown, may appoint a judicial factor or *curator bonis* to act for such
person.   When the Court has appointed a *curator bonis* to a person as
being of unsound mind, that person is incapacitated from dealing with
his own estate.[3]   So a factor *loco absentis* may be appointed to manage
the estates of a person absent from this country, who has not made
provision for the management of his affairs during his absence.   The
persons thus appointed are under the supervision of the Accountant
of Court, and, before entering upon their duties, they must find caution
for their intromissions to the satisfaction of the Clerk of Court.   Their
powers, duties, and responsibilities are regulated by the Pupils Protection Act, 1849, under which provision for their caution is also made.[4]
Care should be taken in all such cases, before dealings are allowed with
the funds of such persons, to have produced the factor's authority,
which is an Extract Act and Warrant from the Books of Court, as until
this is obtained he has no legal authority to act.   It has been held that
a payment to a factor *loco tutoris* before extract is unavailing, and is
made at the risk of the party who pays.[5]

7. Executors

Where an account is opened in the names of the executors of a
deceased person, if there are only two executors, cheques on the
account must be signed by them both.   If there are more than two,
the signature of a majority is sufficient.   A banker is under no obligation to ascertain more than the fact that executors have a *primâ
facie* title.

Executors have power to realise the personal estate and to pledge
specific assets, which is one mode of realising them.   But they have no

---

[1] The duties and procedure for appointments are regulated by 12 & 13 Vict.
cap. 51.

[2] 43 & 44 Vict. cap. 4 ; Act of Sederunt, 14th January 1881.

[3] Mitchell & Baxter *v.* Cheyne, 1891, 19 R. 324.

[4] 12 & 13 Vict. cap. 51 ; as to caution, 20 & 21 Vict. cap. 71, sec. 84.

[5] Donaldson *v.* Donaldson's Trs., 1833, 11 S. 740.

power, in the absence of express provision, to overdraw.[1] Where a customer at the date of his death is indebted to the bank, and his executors in administering his estate pay into the bank, to the credit of an account opened in their names as executors, a sum of money which practically balances the sum due by the deceased customer, the bank are entitled to compensate or set off the one sum against the other, or to retain the amount in satisfaction of their debt.[2]

8. Incorporated Companies [3]

Borrowing Powers.—The Companies (Consolidation) Act does not confer on all companies now regulated by it power to borrow money or issue negotiable instruments. Such a power must be conferred by the company's Act of Incorporation, either expressly or by implication, as necessarily incident to the purposes for which the company is incorporated.[4] The directors of a company formed for the purpose of trading have power to borrow money to a reasonable amount for the company's necessities,[5] but the power is confined to the directors, and does not extend to managers or agents of the company.[6] Where a society or a company has upon the face of its Act of Incorporation only a limited authority to borrow, a person dealing with such a society or company must either inquire, or run the risk of the company exceeding its powers.[7] No *ultra vires* contract or act is capable of ratification even by a majority of the members. A banker is not bound, however, to do more than acquaint himself with the constitution of the company as contained in its Memorandum and Articles of Association; and if he find in these no prohibition, but a power to borrow on condition, for example, of the power being confirmed by a resolution of the company he is entitled to assume that such resolution, if it appear on the face of a document authorising the borrowing, has been duly and properly arrived at; [8] since he has no means of knowing, if everything is *ex facie* regular, whether the internal regulations of the company have been complied

---

[1] Farhall *v.* Farhall, 1871, L.R. 7 Ch. 123.

[2] Alexander's Exr. *v.* Mackersy, 1905, 8 F. 198, overruling Gray's Trs. *v.* Royal Bank of Scotland, 1895, 23 R. 199. See also Hewitt (Clark Kennedy's factor) *v.* Symons, 1896, 3 S.L.T. No. 366.

[3] As to execution of deeds by, see *supra.*

[4] Baroness Wenlock *v.* River Dee Co., 10 Ap. Ca. 359 ; Ashbury Co. *v.* Riche, L.R. 7 H.L. 653.

[5] General Auction Estate and Monetary Co. *v.* Smith, 1891, 3 Ch. 432 ; Gibbs & West's case, 10 Eq. 312 ; *re* Hamilton's Windsor Ironworks, *ex parte* Pitman, 12 Ch. D. 712 ; English Channel Steamer Co. *v.* Rolt, 17 Ch. D. 715 ; Bryon *v.* Metropolitan Saloon Co., 3 De G. & J. 123.

[6] Hawtayne *v.* Bourne, 7 M. & W. 595.

[7] *Per* Brett, L.J., in Chaples *v.* Brunswick Building Society, 6 Q.B.D. 715.

[8] Royal British Bank *v.* Turquand, 6 E. & B. 332.

with or not.[1] A company which is not authorised by its Memorandum or Articles to borrow, and which is not a company formed for the purpose of trading, has no power to overdraw its banking account, either with or without security. A mining company, a cemetery company, a railway company, a salvage company, a gas company, and a waterworks company, have all been held to be non-trading companies.[2] Consequently, a banker who lends to such a company by way of overdraft is not the creditor of the company, though where he has taken security he may hold it for repayment of so much of the money advanced as has been applied in payment strictly of the company's debts, but the burden of proving that the money has been so expended rests upon him.[3] Where a power to borrow is contained in the Memorandum and Articles of Association, it is usually coupled with a power to grant cash-credit or other bonds or debentures, dispositions, and other conveyances, bonds and dispositions in security, bills of sale, mortgages, or other documents over the company's property or any part thereof, including the uncalled capital.[4]

Mode of Borrowing.—If a company have the power to borrow, or if the power to borrow be incidental to the conduct of its business, but the Articles of Association specially provide that certain formalities must be observed in order to bind the company, such formalities must be observed in order to constitute a valid charge upon the company's property.[5] But if the bank be informed, and *bonâ fide* believe and act upon the information furnished them by the company or its recognised officials, they will be protected. Thus in one case the articles of a company provided that cheques above a certain amount should be signed by such of the directors as might be appointed by the company. A resolution of the company appointing certain directors for this purpose was communicated to the bank, and the bank accordingly *bonâ fide* paid large sums on cheques signed by these directors. It subsequently transpired that the directors were acting as such without any legal right to do so, no appointment of directors having been made by the shareholders. It was held that the payment of these cheques was a good payment as against the company, and that a bank, having the written authority of a *de facto* secretary, were not bound to inquire whether he were the properly constituted secretary of the company, but were justified in acting upon his written authority.[6]

---

[1] Howard *v.* Patent Ivory Co., 38 Ch. D. 156.

[2] Bateman *v.* Mid Wales Railway, 1866, L.R. 1 C.P. 499.

[3] Brooks *v.* Blackburn Benefit Society, 1884, H.L. 9 Ap. Ca. 857 ; *disapproving* Waterlow *v.* Sharp, 8 Eq. 504, and Edgworth's case, 7 Eq. 90. See also Peruvian Ry. Co., 1867, 2 Ch. App. 617.

[4] *Vide* Appendix.

[5] Chaples *v.* Brunswick Building Society, 6 Q.B.D. 715 ; *In re* Gen. Prov. Assurance Co., 38 L.J. Ch. 320.

[6] Mahony *v.* East Holyford Mining Co., L.R. 7 E. & I. Appeals, 869.

Liability of Directors.—If directors assume an authority which they do not possess to borrow money, or act under an honest misapprehension of the extent of their powers or authority to borrow money, and induce a person to deal with or lend money to the company on the faith of such assumed or exceeded authority, upon representations which are unfounded in fact, they will render themselves personally responsible for any loss which may accrue.[1] The misrepresentation must, however, be one of fact and not of law. Thus the directors of a company possessing powers to borrow with the consent of a general meeting of shareholders, but not otherwise, render themselves personally liable if they obtain a loan on the representation that they have obtained authority for it, when as a matter of fact they have not.[2] But where three directors of a railway company opened, on behalf of the company, a bank account, and requested the bank by letter to honour cheques signed by any two directors and countersigned by the secretary, it was held that, assuming the letter to contain a representation that the directors had authority to overdraw the account, which in point of fact was not the case, it was not a representation in fact but in law for which the directors were not personally responsible, and that the bank was able to enforce the same remedies against the company as if the representation had been true.[3]

Power to Sign Bills and Cheques.—As regards companies formed under the Companies Acts, and now regulated by the Companies (Consolidation) Act, 1908, the form in which a bill or note is to be drawn, indorsed, or accepted so as to bind the company is regulated by the 77th section of that Act, which provides that a promissory note or bill of exchange shall be deemed to have been made, accepted, or indorsed on behalf of any company under the Act, if made, accepted, or indorsed in name of the company by any person acting under the authority of the company, or if made, accepted, or indorsed by or on behalf or on account of the company, by any person acting under the authority of the company. The authority must be in express terms. Thus a bill drawn on a limited company and accepted by one of the directors in the company's name, the bill also being signed by the director, was held not to be binding on the company, as at the time the bill was signed a resolution of the directors was in existence which provided that all bills of exchange were to be signed by one director and countersigned by the secretary.[4] A decision in the Sheriff Court at Glasgow, which was acquiesced in, is instructive. The Royal Bank became holders of

---

[1] Firbank v. Humphreys, 18 Q.B.D. 154 ; Weeks v. Propert, L.R. 8 C.P. 427 ; Collen v. Wright, 8 E. & B. 647 ; Beattie v. Lord Ebury, L.R. 7 H.L. 102.

[2] Cherry v. Colonial Bank of Australasia, 1869, L.R. 3 P.C. 24 ; Beattie v. Lord Ebury, L.R. 7 H.L. 102.

[3] Cherry v. Colonial Bank of Australasia, *supra*.

[4] Premier Industrial Bank Ltd. v. Carlton Manufacturing Co. Ltd., 1909, 1 K.B. 106.

a bill which bore to be accepted by a limited company and was signed by one of the directors and the secretary thereof as such. The Articles of Association contained the following provision : " The directors shall have power from time to time to regulate the manner in which documents to which the seal of the company does not require to be affixed shall be executed." The articles gave the company power to grant bills. On being asked for payment, the company pleaded that the acceptance was not binding on them, because the directors had not passed a resolution authorising one director and the secretary to sign such documents. It was, however, held that the bank were entitled to assume that the method of execution and the preliminaries thereto had been lawfully carried through, and that accordingly the bill was properly accepted.[1] In England it has been held in a case where a bill was drawn by the managing director of a company on behalf of the company without the authority of the directors who had power by the Articles of Association to authorise the managing director to draw bills, that a holder for value of the bill was entitled to assume that the bill was properly drawn on behalf of the company, that such holder was not bound to inquire whether the directors had formally authorised the drawing of the particular bill and that the company was liable for the amount of the bill.[2] In another case where a company had power in its Memorandum and Articles of Association to borrow money by means of bills and promissory notes, a promissory note in ordinary form beginning " I promise to pay," and signed by the managing director, the name of the company being stamped above the signature and the words " managing director " below, was held to be binding on the company.[3] In one case two directors signed a cheque as drawers, adding after their subscription the word " director." The place for the signature of the secretary was left blank. The cheque was issued in favour of A. The name of the company was printed near the top of the cheque but did not appear elsewhere thereon. In an action by A. against the two directors as individuals, it was held that they were personally liable for the amount of the cheque, on the ground that in signing the cheque they did not indicate that they did so on behalf of the company, although they added words to show their representative capacity.[4] The section above referred to does not, however, in any way authorise every company to issue or accept bills ; it merely prescribes the form which such companies as have power to issue and accept bills must adopt.[5]

---

[1] Royal Bank of Scotland v. Clyde Salvage Co. Ltd., 1908, 25 S.L.R. 91.

[2] Dey v. Pullinger Engineering Co. Ltd., 1921, 1 K.B. 77.

[3] Chapman v. Smethurst, 1909, 1 K.B. 927.

[4] Landes v. Marcus & Davids, 1909, 25 T.L.R. 478.

[5] In re Peruvian Railway Co., 1867, L.R. 2 Ch. 617 ; ex parte Overend, Gurney & Co., 1869, L.R. 4 Ch. 460.

The name of the company must appear on all bills, promissory notes, indorsements, and cheques which purport to be signed on behalf of the company, and where this is not done any person who signs on behalf of the company is liable to a fine not exceeding fifty pounds, and is further personally liable to the holder of the instrument for the amount thereof unless the same is duly paid by the company.[1]

Current Accounts.—All operations on a company's current account must be sanctioned by the directors, and the account can be operated upon only by the person or persons authorised by the directors to do so. A certified copy of the minute authorising any operation on the current account should be obtained by the bank.

9. Building Societies

Such societies are now principally regulated by the Building Societies Acts, 1874 [2] to 1894.[3] The provisions as to their borrowing powers are contained in section 15 of the 1874 Act, which enacts, in the case of permanent societies, that the maximum power of borrowing is limited to a sum equivalent to two-thirds of the amount for the time being secured to the society by mortgages from its members, and in the case of terminating societies either such two-thirds or a sum not exceeding twelve months' subscriptions on the shares for the time being in force. The Act further provides [4] that the rules of such societies shall set forth, *inter alia*, whether the society intends to avail itself of the borrowing powers contained in the Act, and if so, within what limits. So that while the Act authorises borrowing, the rules of the society alone determine the amount, if any, which can competently be borrowed.

If the society is not incorporated under the Act, the borrowing powers are regulated by the rules framed by such society.

If a borrowing power is not only consistent with but reasonably conducive to the proper objects of a benefit building society, it is competent for the members of the society to make a rule conferring such power, and unless a law prescribing and defining the conditions and limitations under which such power be given be discoverable from the statute under which the society is established, it is competent for them to define its extent and prescribe the conditions under which it is to be exercised. Thus under 6 & 7 Will. IV. c. 32, the directors of a benefit building society were authorised from time to time, as occasion might require, to borrow any sums of money, such borrowed money to be a first charge upon the funds and property of the society ; and it was held that the directors were entitled, in borrowing money, to deposit with the lenders, as security, title-deeds of properties which had been

---

[1] Companies (Consolidation) Act, 1908, sec. 63.
[2] 37 & 38 Vict. cap. 42.   [3] 57 & 58 Vict. cap. 47.   [4] Sec. 16, subsec. (2).

mortgaged to the society by advanced members, and that the lenders were entitled in the winding-up to payment out of the assets, after satisfaction of the outside creditors, in priority to the claims of all shareholders or members.[1]

Whether the society be incorporated under the Act or not, the borrowing powers contained in the rules can only be exercised for the legitimate purposes of the society and for nothing inconsistent with its objects. But if the rules authorise a course of business which necessitates, as an incident to that business, the borrowing of money, the funds of the society are liable in repayment. It must be shown that the incurring of such liabilities was justified by a reasonable regard to the interests of the society. Where a society which had no power to borrow money, and therefore no power to overdraw, was allowed by its bankers to make overdrafts on the security of certain deeds of the borrowing members, it was held that the bankers were not creditors of the society, and that they could retain the securities only for repayment of such sums advanced by them as had been actually applied in the payment of the debts and liabilities of the society properly payable.[2]

Whatever be the limit of borrowing authorised, an excess of such limit is *ultra vires* of the society and cannot be enforced as a charge on its funds. A banker, therefore, making an advance to a society must satisfy himself of the society's power to borrow, and further ascertain if the authorised limit has not already been exceeded. Although a power to borrow is given, this does not, in the absence of an express provision in the rules to that effect, imply a power to pledge specific securities.[3]

To avoid all questions, it is advisable, in connection with advances to building societies, to get the guarantee of approved persons for the due repayment of the loan.

10. Public Authorities

In dealing with such authorities, the particular Act or Acts in virtue of which they are constituted should be examined, since no powers will be inferred which are not expressly authorised by, or follow by natural implication from, the provisions of their respective Acts. It is the practice of banks to make advances to public authorities to meet their current expenses, in anticipation of the assessments levied by them,

---

[1] Murray *v.* Scott, 1884, L.R. 9 Ap. Ca. 519.

[2] Scottish Property, etc., Society *v.* Sheills' Trs., 1883, 10 R. 1198 ; 12 R. (H.L.) 14, L.R. 10 Ap. Ca. 119 ; *in re* Asiatic Banking Company, Bank of India's case, 1869, 4 Ch. App. 252 ; Mullock *v.* Jenkins, 1851, 14 Beav. 628 ; Laing *v.* Reid, 1869, L.R. 5 Ch. App. 4 ; Brooks *v.* Blackburn Benefit Society, 1884, L.R. 9 Ap. Ca. 857 ; Agnew *v.* Murray, 1884, L.R. 9 Ap. Ca. 519.

[3] Murray *v.* Scott, L.R. 9 Ap. Ca. 519.

which, although imposed for a financial year beginning on 15th May, are not payable till the November following, against minutes passed by such authorities at one of their ordinary meetings. While such a proceeding is not a satisfactory mode of constituting a legal obligation, still, if, following upon the minute, an advance is sanctioned and operations proceed on the account by drafts passed on it in the manner prescribed in the minute, there is no reason to doubt that the borrowers would be liable in the repayment of any sum due on the account thus opened up to the limit authorised. The minute should be renewed annually. The following bodies may be noticed :—

County Councils.—*Borrowing Powers.*—By the provisions of the Local Government (Scotland) Act, 1889, a County Council may, from time to time, with the consent in writing (signed by two members and the county clerk) of the standing joint committee of the Council and the Commissioners of Supply (consisting of such a number of the county councillors, not exceeding seven, and such number of Commissioners of Supply, not exceeding seven, as may be appointed at the respective annual meetings of these bodies, together with the Sheriff of the county or one of his substitutes nominated by him), borrow on the security of any rate (that is, of the particular rate to which the loan is, under the particular Act, applicable, and not on the general security of the county [1]) leviable by the Council under or in pursuance of the Act, or of any other Act, such sums as may be required for any of the following purposes :—

(*a*) For any purpose for which any authority, whose powers and duties are, by the Act, transferred to the County Council, were, at the passing of the Act, authorised to borrow. The principal borrowing powers transferred are those relating to lunatic asylums, police stations, sheriff-court houses, sewers, water supply, hospitals, prisons, new roads, and road debts.[2] (*b*) For any purpose for which the Council is expressly authorised to borrow by the Act, namely, for works involving capital expenditure, including the erection, rebuilding, or enlargement of buildings, the construction, reconstruction, or widening of roads and bridges, the construction or extension of drainage or water supply works, and the acquisition of land or of any right or interest or servitude in or over land or water for the purpose of any work involving capital expenditure ;[3] for the payment of any sum required to be paid for the purpose of any adjustment or of any award or order made by the Boundary Commissioners.[4] (*c*) For making advances to any persons

---

[1] See *infra*.
[2] 20 & 21 Vict. cap. 71, sec. 61, and cap. 72, sec. 57 ; 23 & 24 Vict. cap. 79, sec. 26 ; 30 & 31 Vict. cap. 101, secs. 86, 89 ; 34 & 35 Vict. cap. 38, sec. 2, and cap. 74 ; 40 & 41 Vict. cap. 53, secs. 20, 21, 40, 55 ; 41 & 42 Vict. cap. 78, secs. 58, 75.
[3] Sec. 18 (7).
[4] Sec. 50 (4).

or bodies of persons, corporate or unincorporate, in aid of the emigratio
or colonisation of inhabitants of the county, with a guarantee fo
repayment of such advances from any authority in the county or th
government of any colony.

A loan under this section must be repaid within thirty years, an
by equal yearly or half-yearly instalments of principal, or of principa
and interest combined, or by means of a sinking fund set apart
invested, and applied in accordance with such regulations as may b
issued by the Secretary for Scotland.

If the County Council find it necessary in any year to make pay
ments, in connection with the current annual expenditure, for th
purposes of the various Acts of Parliament administered by them
in anticipation of the rates under the said Acts applicable to th
expenditure of such year, they may, without any consent, borrow
from any incorporated or joint stock bank or other company or person
on such terms and conditions and in such form as may be agreed on
between the parties, money on the security of such part of the rates as
is still due and unreceived, but not to an amount greater than one-half
of such part of such rates ; and when any money has been so borrowed
on the security of the rates of any local financial year, it is not competent
to borrow on the security of the rates of any other year until the money
borrowed as aforesaid is paid off.

Under the County Council (Scotland) (Finance) Order, 1907, power
is conferred upon County Councils to borrow for various purposes connected
with Special Lighting Districts and Special Scavenging Districts, and by
the Military Lands Act, 1892 (55 & 56 Vict. c. 43), they may borrow for
the acquisition of land for military purposes.

Where a loan is raised for any purpose upon the security of any rate
leviable by the County Council under or in pursuance of the Act, or of
any other Act, the Council are bound to see that the sums payable in
respect of the loan are charged to the special account to which the
expenditure for that purpose is chargeable.

As Customers.—All receipts of the Council from whatever source
must be carried to a " county fund," and all payments must in the first
instance be made out of that fund. The receipts must be lodged in
bank under headings applicable to the various rates, and payments
must be made by cheques, which must be signed by two members
of the finance committee and countersigned by the county clerk or by
a deputy approved by the Council. Such accounts of the county fund
and of the sums raised by rates must be so kept as to prevent a rate
being applied to any purpose to which it is not properly applicable.
In like manner, all sums passed by the Council to the account of any
district committee must be lodged in bank and drawn upon by cheques
signed by two members of the district committee and countersigned
by the district clerk.

The form of minute in the Appendix as to Parish Councils may be
tered to suit the case of County Councils.

Parish Councils.—By the Local Government (Scotland) Act, 1894,[1]
is enacted that from and after the 15th of May 1894 every poor law
arish or combination is to have a Parish Council. This Council, while
king the place of and superseding the Parochial Board, is to be treated
s a continuance of the Parochial Board, and all the powers, duties, and
abilities of the Parochial Board pass to the Parish Council. By the
ame Act a Local Government Board was established, which super-
eded the Board of Supervision. It is foreign to the present work to
onsider the Act in detail, the object now being to deal only with that
art of the Act which immediately concerns bankers.

Borrowing Powers.—A Parish Council may, with the consent of the
ocal Government Board, borrow money for any of the following
urposes, namely, (*a*) for purchasing any land or erecting any buildings
vhich they are authorised to purchase or erect. Such loans are to be
epaid within such period, not exceeding forty years, as the Local
Jovernment Board may determine ; (*b*) for any permanent work or other
hing which they are authorised to execute or do, and the cost of which
ught, in the opinion of the Local Government Board, to be spread over
a term of years. Such loans are to be repaid within such period, not
exceeding thirty years, as the Local Government Board may determine.
Vhile the Act stipulates the time within which the loans are to be repaid,
t also provides that the loans are to be paid off by equal yearly or half-
yearly instalments of principal, or of principal and interest combined,
or by means of a sinking fund, managed in accordance with regulations
made by the Secretary for Scotland. So long as the amount of loans
lue by a Parish Council exceeds one-fifth of the annual value of the
parish as ascertained for poor law purposes, no further loans can be
raised except a temporary loan to meet current expenditure.

Temporary Loans.—If the Parish Council find it necessary in any
year or half-year to make disbursements to meet current expenditure
beyond the amount received of the assessment applicable to the
expenditure of such year or half-year, it is competent for the Council
to borrow money on the security of such part of the assessment as is
still due and unreceived to an amount not greater than one-half of such
part of such assessment. When any money has been so borrowed, it is
incompetent to borrow on the security of any future assessment until
the money borrowed as aforesaid has been paid off. This borrowing
power is exercised by the Council passing a minute [2] authorising certain
of their number to apply to a bank for permission to overdraw their
account on the security of the assessment still due and unrecovered.
The overdraft should not exceed the half of the unrecovered assessment,

---

[1] 57 & 58 Vict. cap. 58.   [2] For form of which see Appendix.

and a certificate by the clerk should be in the hands of the bank, showin
the amount of the assessment for the then current year, and the amour
due and unrecovered at the date of application.

Under the Poor Law Emergency Provisions (Scotland) Act, 192
(11 & 12 Geo. V. c. 64), Parish Councils are empowered, with th
consent of the Scottish Board of Health, to borrow in connection wit
relief to destitute able-bodied persons out of employment. The perio
of repayment is limited to five years, but in special circumstances it ma
be extended to a term not exceeding ten years. Any sum borrowed befor
the passing of the Act, with the consent of the Board, is deemed to hav
been validly borrowed even though it should have been in excess o
one-half of the amount due and unreceived.

Bank Accounts.—The Act requires that two bank accounts are to b
kept, namely, (1) a general parish fund, and (2) a special parish fund
The former has reference to the receipts and payments necessary in th
exercise of the powers vested in the Parish Council as coming in plac
of the Parochial Board, whereas the latter has reference to the receipt
and expenditure in connection with certain new powers conferred by
the Act on rural districts. Cheques on either of the accounts must b
signed by two members of the Parish Council or Landward Committee
as the case may be, and countersigned by the clerk. The account
must be so kept as to prevent the proceeds of a rate being applied to
any purpose to which it is not properly applicable. Hence a Parish
Council is not entitled to compensating interest on a sum standing at
the credit of one of the above accounts as against a debit balance on the
other, as under the Act a bank would not be entitled to transfer the
sum standing at the credit of one of the accounts to clear off or reduce
a debit balance on the other.

Education Authorities.—By the Education (Scotland) Act, 1918,[1]
School Boards were abolished and their whole powers and duties transferred to Education Authorities. School Boards had power under the
statute [2] by which they were constituted to borrow money only when
they required to incur expenses in providing or enlarging a schoolhouse.
Where this was necessary, they, with the consent of the Board of Education, might spread the payment over several years, not exceeding fifty,
and might for that purpose borrow money on the security of the school
fund and the school rate, and might charge that fund and the school
rate with the payment of the principal and interest due in respect of
the loan. They might, if they so agreed with the lender, pay the amount
borrowed, with the interest, by equal annual instalments not exceeding
fifty, and if they did not so agree, they required annually to set aside
one-fiftieth of the sum borrowed as a sinking fund. There was no
provision enabling School Boards to borrow money to meet current

---

[1] 8 & 9 Geo. V. cap. 48.   [2] Education (Scotland) Act, 1872, sec. 45.

expenses. Such advances were, however, made by banks upon minutes [1] passed by the School Boards, pledging the school fund and school rate in security of the advances, and undertaking to repay the amount out of them. This system is continued in the case of Education Authorities. The advances so made are practically safe, for the reason that if the sums are *bonâ fide* expended by the Authority for the proper educational uses of the districts under their administration in virtue of the Act, they are liable in repayment thereof.[2] In any case the members of the Authority would be personally liable in repayment as having acted beyond their powers. The minute should be renewed annually.

The account should be opened in name of the particular Education Authority, and operations should proceed on it in terms of a minute of the Authority, a certified excerpt from which should be in the hands of the bank.

Town Councils.—By section 85 of the Town Councils (Scotland) Act, 1900, the treasurer or collector is obliged to lodge all money received by him in a chartered or other bank, or in one of the branches of such bank in the burgh, to be fixed by the Council, upon an account to be opened in the name of the Council in their corporate name, thus, " The Provost, Magistrates, and Councillors of the Burgh of . . . ." The Act provides that the account is to be operated upon by the treasurer or collector respectively, with the counter signature of one or more councillors as the Council shall from time to time appoint. The Council may from time to time make regulations for the manner of keeping or operating upon such bank accounts as they think proper. A certified excerpt from the minute authorising the operations should be in the hands of the bank, and the minute should be renewed annually.

District Boards of Control.—Such Boards (which supersede District Lunacy Boards) were established in virtue of the Mental Deficiency and Lunacy (Scotland) Act, 1913, 3 & 4 Geo. V. c. 38. Power was conferred upon them to borrow for the acquisition of land, etc., but the Act did not provide for temporary borrowing in anticipation of assessments to be received. This defect was remedied by the Mental Deficiency and Lunacy (Amendment) Act, 1919, 9 & 10 Geo. V. c. 85, under which (sec. 3) power to borrow for current expenditure is conferred.

---

[1] For form, see Appendix.

[2] So decided by Lord Rutherfurd Clark (Ordinary) in Commercial Bank *v.* Lady School Board, 16th October 1878—not reported. *Cf.* The Queen *v.* Sir Charles Reed, L.R. 4 Q.B.D. 477 ; *rev.* 5 Q.B.D. 483.

PART II

BILLS OF EXCHANGE, CHEQUES, AND PROMISSORY NOTES

CHAPTER I

BILLS OF EXCHANGE

Introductory.—The origin of bills of exchange, which are perhaps the most familiar and important of all our instruments of commerce, is, like many other inventions in daily use, involved in obscurity. Hence no opinion can be expressed with any confidence in its accuracy as to when or by whom bills of exchange were first used as a circulating medium representative of money.

The law relating to bills of exchange, cheques—including dividend warrants but not drafts by one branch of a bank upon another,[1]—and promissory notes is now chiefly governed by the Bills of Exchange Act, 1882, which codified the existing law, and, with some slight exceptions, assimilated the laws of England, Scotland, and Ireland. The Act is intended to be mainly a codification of the existing law, but it is not merely a codification Act, for some alterations of the law are clearly effected by it, and it does not purport to be exhaustive, since the rules of the common law, including the law merchant, save in so far as they are inconsistent with the express provisions of the Act, continue to apply. In determining questions of liability on bills or notes, it is proper to examine the Act before turning to the cases declaratory of the common law decided before the Act, as, in considering questions affecting bills of exchange, the language of the statute must receive its natural meaning, uninfluenced by any consideration derived from the previous state of the law ; and unless the statute provides that the law existing at the date of its passing is to remain unaltered, an appeal to earlier decisions, except in so far as they are illustrative or declaratory of the meaning of the statute, can only be justified on some special ground.[2]

---

[1] Capital and Counties Bank *v.* Gordon ; London City and Midland Bank *v.* Gordon (1902), 1 K.B. 242, 273 ; *affd.* 1903, A.C. 240, 250.

[2] Lewis *v.* Clay, 1897, 14 T.L.R. 149 (*per* Lord Russell, C.J.).

As illustrative of the changes which the Act introduced, it may be noted that (1) a bill may now be made payable in the alternative to one of two, or one or some of several payees; (2) where a bill purports to be indorsed conditionally, the condition may now be disregarded by the payer, and payment to the indorsee is valid whether the condition has been fulfilled or not; and (3) the return of a dishonoured bill to the drawer or indorser is, in point of form, deemed a sufficient notice of dishonour.

As illustrative of the declaratory provision that the law existing at the date of its passing is to remain unaltered, notwithstanding any provision to the contrary contained in the Act, may be instanced (1) the rules in bankruptcy; (2) the rules of the common law, including the law merchant; and (3) the provisions of the Stamp Acts. The law merchant is a body of law, capable of indefinite expansion and enlargement, consisting of such usages and customs of 'merchants and traders in the different departments of commerce as have been ratified by judicial decision and embodied in the law of the land.

As illustrative of the differences which still exist between English and Scots law, it may be noted that, in Scotland, where the drawee of a bill (or the banker in the case of a cheque) has in his hands funds available for the payment thereof, the bill operates as an assignment of the sum for which it is drawn in favour of the holder from the time when it is presented to the drawee.

1. Form and Interpretation

3.[1] **Definition and Essentials.**—(1) A bill of exchange is an unconditional order (that is, a demand or request made as a right and not as a favour,[2] and not dependent on any act of the payee, or the occurrence of an uncertain event, such as, for example, the arrival of a certain ship),[3] expressed on paper by ink, pencil,[4] lithography, engraving, typewriting,[5] or other like means, and in any language, English or foreign,[6] addressed by one person, or body of persons, whether incorporated or not, who is called the drawer, to another, who is called the drawee (and, after giving his assent, the acceptor),[7] signed or initialled, if initialling be his usual mode of signature, by or with the

---

[1] The numbers in black type refer to the sections of the Bills of Exchange Act, 1882: those in ordinary type refer to the corresponding subsections.

[2] Little v. Slackford, 1 M. & M. 171; Hamilton v. Spottiswoode, 1849, 18 L.J. Ex. 393, 4 Exch. 200.

[3] Palmer v. Pratt, 1824, 2 Bing. 185.

[4] Geary v. Physic, 5 B. & C. 234.

[5] Simpson's Trs. v. MacHarg & Son, 1902, 39 S.L.R. 562.

[6] In re Marseilles Co., 1885, L.R. 30 Ch. D. 598.

[7] Walker's Trs. v. M'Kinlay, 1880, 7 R. (H.L.) 85.

7

authority of the person giving it,[1] requiring the person to whom it is addressed, who must be named or clearly indicated,[2] to pay, or perform an act equivalent to paying,[3] on demand,[4] or at a fixed or determinable future time,[5] a sum certain in money [6] to, or to the order of, a specified person, or to bearer. A bill may also be signed by a notary public or justice of the peace before two subscribing witnesses on behalf of any person, whether drawer, acceptor, or indorser. The docquet referred to on p. 44 would in such circumstances require to be used. (2) An instrument which does not comply with these conditions, or which orders any act to be done in addition to the payment of money, is not a bill of exchange. A writing which does not contain these essentials may yet be capable of being made a bill of exchange,[7] and, in any case, of being enforced as a document of debt, though not entitled to the privileges of a bill.[8] In one case it was held that a document in the form of a bill of exchange, which did not bear a drawer's signature, but bore the signature of the acceptor, and which was found in the repositories of the person who presumably intended to be the drawer, was not a completed bill in the sense of the Act, but was evidence of the acceptor's indebtedness to the executors of the person to whom he had delivered it.[9] In this case it was doubted,[10] notwithstanding some judicial authority to the contrary, whether the executors of the presumed drawer, in whose repositories the document was found, could have validly supplied the drawer's signature after his death. (3) An order to pay out of a particular fund, as "out of the money due from A. as soon as you receive it," or "out of the money arising from my reversion when sold," is conditional; but an unqualified order to pay, coupled with an indication of a particular fund out of which the drawee is to reimburse himself, as, "which you will please charge to my account and credit according to a registered letter I have addressed to you," [11] or a particular account to be debited with the amount, or a statement of the transaction which gives rise to the bill, is unconditional. Similarly, the addition of the words "against cheque" has been held to be

---

[1] Sec. 91 (1).

[2] Sec. 6.

[3] Swan v. Bank of Scotland, 1841, 4 D. 210.

[4] Vide sec. 10.

[5] Macfarlane v. Johnstone, 1864, 2 M. 1210.

[6] Ex parte Imeson, 2 Rose, Bank. Ca. 225; vide sec. 72 (4); M'Cormick v. Trotter, 1823, 10 S. & R. 282; re Boyse, 1886, 33 Ch. D. 612; Dixon v. Bovill, 1856, 3 Macq. (H.L.) 1.

[7] Vide secs. 18, 20.

[8] Brice v. Bannister, 1878, L.R. 3 Q.B.D. 569, C.A.; Hamilton v. Spottiswoode, 1849, 4 Exch. 200.

[9] Lawson's Exrs. v. Watson, 1907, S.C. 1353.

[10] Per Lord M'Laren.

[11] In re Boyse, 1886, 33 Ch. D. 612.

unconditional.[1] (4) A bill is not invalid (1) because it is not dated,[2] though it is irregular to issue such a bill ; (2) because it does not specify the value given or that any value was given therefor ; [3] or (3) because it does not specify the place where it is drawn or the place where it is payable.[4] It is competent to insert an alternative place of payment.

4. Inland and Foreign Bills.—An inland bill is one which is, or on the face of it purports to be, both drawn and payable within the British Isles (even although it be actually accepted abroad, or accepted payable abroad),[5] or drawn within the British Isles upon some person resident therein. Any other bill is a foreign bill. For the purposes of the statute the " British Isles " mean any part of the United Kingdom of Great Britain and Ireland, the Islands of Man, Guernsey, Jersey, Alderney and Sark, and the islands adjacent to them, being part of the dominions of His Majesty. Although a bill drawn in the Isle of Man or the other islands just specified on a person resident in the United Kingdom is for the purposes of the Bills of Exchange Act an inland bill, still as that Act does not affect the provisions of the Stamp Act, an impressed stamp is not used on such bills, the duty being denoted by an adhesive stamp.[6] A bill (though *de facto* a foreign bill) which does not expressly appear to be a foreign bill, may be treated as an inland bill or as a foreign bill in the option of the holder. A bill drawn in Liverpool on a merchant in London, accepted payable in London, but indorsed in Paris, is still an inland bill ; [7] as is a bill drawn in London upon a merchant in Brussels accepted payable in London.[8]

5. Dual Capacity.—The drawer and payee or the drawee and payee (as in a cheque in favour of the banker on whom it is drawn) may be the same person.[9] Where the drawer and drawee are the same person (as in the case of a person drawing a bill in his own name on a firm of which he is the sole partner,[10] or as in a bank post bill), or where the drawee is a fictitious person, or a person not having capacity to contract,[11] the holder, that is, the payee or indorsee in possession, or bearer, if the bill be payable to bearer, may treat the instrument either as a bill or

---

[1] Glen *v.* Semple, 1901, 3 F. 1134.

[2] *Vide* sec. 12.

[3] Law *v.* Humphreys, 1876, 3 R. 1192.   See also Hatch *v.* Trayes, 1840, 11 A. & E. 702, and sec. 27.

[4] *Vide* sec. 100.

[5] *Vide* sec. 72 (2).

[6] See Stamp Duty, *infra*.

[7] Lebel *v.* Tucker, 1867, L.R. 3 Q.B. 77.

[8] Amner *v.* Clark, 1835, 2 C.M. & R. 468.

[9] *Vide* sec. 61.

[10] Nairn *v.* Forbes & Co., 1795, referred to in Bell's Com. ii. 514.   See also Willans *v.* Ayers, 1877, 3 Ap. Ca. 133, P.C.

[11] *Vide* secs. 22, 41 (2), 46 (2), and 50 (2).

promissory note ; [1] thus, if no one is known to exist answering to the name and description of the drawee, the bill is to be treated as one payable to bearer. If, where a name and description are adopted which happen to apply to an existing person, the acceptor does not intend to pay to the actual order of the payee named, and knows that he is in that sense fictitious, the bill is also to be treated as payable to bearer.

6. The Drawee.—(1) The drawee must be named (in which case, if he be not described, the holder may prove that presentation was made to the person intended), or otherwise indicated with reasonable certainty ; as, for example, by his official title. The mere acceptance of a bill does not supply the want of a named drawee, but it is competent for any person in possession of the bill to fill in the name of the drawee. (2) A bill may be addressed to two or more drawees whether they are partners or not, but not alternatively or in succession. [2]

7. The Payee.—(1) Where a bill is not payable to bearer, the payee must be named (not necessarily with the addition of his Christian name), or otherwise indicated with reasonable certainty (though not necessarily by means of a full description). [3] A bill which when issued does not contain the payee's name, may, if a space have been left for the purpose, be converted into a bill by the person in possession filling in a name. [4] A bill made payable to " . . . order," the blank never having been filled in, must be construed as payable to "my order," that is, to the order of the drawer, and is, when indorsed by him, a valid bill of exchange, though it may be considered as at least doubtful whether a bill payable to " . . . or order " is a valid document so long as the blank remains unfilled up. [5] If a bill is made payable to the order of " J. Smythe," evidence is admissible to show that T. Smith is the person intended. [6] (2) A bill may be made payable to two or more payees jointly, or it may be made payable in the alternative to one of two, or one or some of several payees, [7] or to the holder of an office for the time being. (3) Where the payee is fictitious (that is, fictitious to the knowledge of a party sought to be charged upon the bill, [8] or inserted in the bill by way of pretence merely, without any intention that payment shall be made in conformity therewith) [8] or a non-existing person, the bill may be treated as payable to bearer, and that although the drawer believes and

---

[1] Banco de Portugal v. Waddell, 1880, L.R. 5 Ap. Ca. 161 (H.L.) ; *vide* Promissory Notes.

[2] *Vide* sec. 15.

[3] Erskine, iii. 2, 26 ; M'Cubbin v. Stephen, 1856, 18 D. 1224.

[4] *Vide* sec. 20 ; and Promissory Notes.

[5] Chamberlain v. Young, 1893, 2 Q.B. 206.

[6] Chalmers on Bills (3rd ed.), p. 18.

[7] *Altering* Thomson v. Philip, 1867, 5 M. 344 ; Holmes v. Jacques, 1866, L.R. 1 Q.B. 376.

[8] Vagliano v. Bank of England, L.R. 23 Q.B.D. 243 ; see p. 5.

intends the bill to be payable to the order of a real person. The fact
that the drawer was induced by fraud to draw the bill in favour of a
person whom he believed to exist, but who was actually non-existent,
is immaterial in a question with a *bonâ fide* holder for value.[1] A bill may
be treated as payable to bearer where the person named as payee, and
to whose order the bill is made payable on the face of it, is a real person,
but has not and never was intended by the drawer to have any right upon
it or arising out of it ; and this is so though the bill (so-called) is not in
reality a bill, but is in fact a document in the form of a bill manufactured
by a person who forges the signature of the named drawer, obtains by
fraud the signature of the acceptor, forges the signature of the named
payee, and presents the document for payment, both the named drawer
and the named payee being entirely ignorant of the circumstances.
Thus where a series of documents so manufactured were made payable
at the acceptor's bank, and the amounts were paid over the counter
to the forger or his agent by the bank *bonâ fide*, and in pursuance of letters
of advice signed by the acceptor, whose signature thereto was fraudulently
obtained by the forger, a clerk in the employment of the acceptor—it
was held that the bank was entitled to debit its customer, the acceptor,
with the amounts, although paid to the forger or his agent and not to a
bonâ fide holder of the documents for value or to any person who could
sue the acceptor upon them, on the ground that the named payee was a
fictitious or non-existent person, and that the bills might consequently
be treated as payable to bearer.[2]

8. Negotiability.—A bill is negotiable except when it contains
words clearly and unequivocally[3] prohibiting transfer or indicating
an intention that it shall not be transferable.[4] In one case where a
cheque was in the following terms, " Pay to A. B. against cheque or
order," it was held that the words " against cheque " did not affect its
negotiability.[5] An acceptance may be so qualified as to exclude claims
by indorsees against the acceptor.[6] (2) A negotiable bill may be
payable either to order or to bearer. (3) It is payable to bearer if it be
expressed to be so payable (and even if it contain, in addition, the name
of a payee, which may therefore be disregarded), or if the only or last
indorsement be an indorsement in blank (even if such indorsement be
preceded by a special indorsement, which may therefore be cancelled[7]) ;
otherwise (4, 5) it is payable to order.

9. Sum Payable.—(1) The sum payable is a sum certain within the

[1] Clutton *v.* Attenborough, 1897, L.R. A.C. 90.
[2] Bank of England *v.* Vagliano, 1891, L.R. A.C. 107.
[3] Meyer *v.* Decroix, Verley & Co., 1891, L.R. A.C. 520.
[4] *Vide* Cheques.
[5] Glen *v.* Semple, 1901, 3 F. 1134.
[6] Meyer *v.* Decroix, *supra.*
[7] *Vide* sec. 34 ; Bell's Com. i. 428.

meaning of the Act, although it may be required to be paid (a) with interest, which, in the case of inland bills, where no rate is specified (and, since the repeal of the Usury Laws, there is now no limit to the rate which parties may agree upon), is implied to be five per cent., or "legal" interest, provided the amount of interest payable is "certain" or ascertainable by numerical calculation from materials contained in the bill itself.[1] In this connection it may be mentioned that by the Money-Lenders Act, 1900, where proceedings are taken in any Court by a money-lender for the recovery of any money, or the enforcement of any agreement or security in respect of money lent, and there is evidence which satisfies the Court that the interest charged in respect of the sum actually lent is excessive, or that the amounts charged for expenses, inquiries, fines, bonus, premium, renewals, or any other charges are excessive, and that in either case the transaction is harsh and unconscionable, the Court may reopen the transaction and take an account between the money-lender and the person sued, and may, notwithstanding any statement or settlement of account, or any agreement purporting to close previous dealings and create a new obligation, reopen any account already taken between them, and relieve the person sued from payment of any sum in excess of the sum adjudged by the Court to be fairly due in respect of such principal, interest, and charges as the Court, having regard to the risk and all the circumstances, may adjudge to be reasonable. (b) By stated instalments,[2] in which case the amount of the instalments and the dates on which they are payable must be stated,[3] with or without a provision that upon default in payment of any instalment the whole shall become due. Days of grace must be added to the dates on which the instalments are payable.[4] Where a bill payable by instalments provides that if any instalment is not paid "punctually" the whole of the balance is immediately to become payable does not deprive the debtor of days of grace,[5] or (c) according to an indicated rate of exchange, or a rate ascertainable from the terms of the bill. Where no rate is indicated, the amount payable is calculated according to the rate of exchange for sight drafts at the place of payment on the day the bill is payable.[6] (2) The sum payable may be expressed in words or figures, or both, and where there is a discrepancy the sum denoted by the words is the amount payable.[7]

---

[1] Morgan v. Morgan, 1866, 4 M. 321 ; Tennent v. Crawfurd, 1878, 5 R. 435 ; Vallance v. Forbes, 1879, 6 R. 1099 ; Lamberton v. Aiken, 1899, 2 F. 189.

[2] Vide M'Farlane v. Johnstone, 1864, 2 M. 1210 ; Davies v. Wilkinson, 2 Per. & Dav. 256.

[3] Moffatt v. Edwards, 1841, Car. & M. 16 ; Worley v. Harrison, 1835, 3 A. & E. 669.

[4] Oridge v. Sherborne, 1843, 11 M. & W. 374.

[5] Schaverien v. Morris, 1921, 37 T.L.R. 366.

[6] Vide sec. 72 (4).

[7] Saunderson v. Piper, 1839, 5 Bing. N.C. 425; Garrard v. Lewis, 1882, 10 Q.B.D. 30.

The figures may be looked at to explain an ambiguity in the words,[1] but they are not an essential or operative part of a bill. A drawer who leaves a blank for the words, while filling in the sum in figures, may, on account of his negligence, be liable to the holder for the amount filled up in the vacant space, though generally he may prove that the bill as issued did not contain the words, which consequently amount to an unauthorised alteration.[2] Where a bill is expressed to be payable with interest, unless the instrument otherwise provides, interest runs from the date of the bill,[3] and, in an undated bill, from the date of issue.[4] Where there is no stipulation as to interest, interest is payable from the due date of the bill. Where an acceptor of a bill dies before its maturity, his executor, who has by law six months in which to make payment of the deceased's debts, must pay the bill with interest from the date when it fell due.

10. Time of Payment.—(1) A bill is payable *on demand* if it be expressed (*a*) to be so payable (though, if post-dated, payment cannot be demanded until after the date it bears),[5] (*b*) at sight, (*c*) on presentation, or (*d*) if no term of payment be expressed [6] and payment be demanded on a business day.[7] There are no days of grace on such bills. (2) Where a bill is accepted or indorsed when it is overdue (that is, in the case of all bills not payable on demand, on the expiry of the last day of grace),[8] it is, as regards such acceptor or indorser, deemed to be payable on demand.[9]

11. A bill is payable *at a determinable future time*,[10] which is expressed to be payable (1) at a fixed period after date or sight, or (2) on, or at a fixed period after, the occurrence of a specified event, which is certain to happen, though the time of happening be uncertain, such as " one year after my death," or " two months after demand in writing." [11] There is no limitation as to the length of time. In one case it was held that a bill, in which the month and day of the month but not the year were given, was sufficiently dated; and it was observed, " But that in any event the date on the stamp fixes the year and may be held to be a part of the date of the bill and to supply the statement of the year otherwise

---

[1] Gordon *v.* Sloss, 1848, 10 D. 1129.

[2] *Vide* secs. 64, 100.

[3] *Vide* secs. 12, 13 (2), and 20 ; Doman *v.* Dibdin, 1826, R. & M. 381.

[4] *Vide* sec. 100.

[5] Gatty *v.* Fry, 1877, 2 Ex. Div. 265.

[6] Days of grace do not attach to such bills ; see sec. 14, *post.*

[7] *Vide* sec. 45 (3).

[8] *Vide* sec. 14.

[9] *Vide* secs. 45, 54, and 97 (3).

[10] *Vide* sec. 3 (1).

[11] Roffey *v.* Greenwell, 1839, 10 A. & E. 222 ; Price *v.* Taylor, 1860, 5 H. & N. 540 ; 29 L.J. Ex. 331. See also *ex parte* Gibson, 1869, L.R. 4 Ch. 662.

omitted."[1] A bill may be made payable at a particular fair or market, although the day on which it is to be held is not known. An instrument expressed to be payable on a contingency, even though the contingency occur, such as, " when I marry," or " when I am in good circumstances," is not a bill, though it is not necessarily invalid as an obligation.

12. *Omission of Date.*—Where such a bill, or the acceptance of it, is undated, any holder may insert the true date of issue or acceptance,[2] and the bill becomes payable accordingly ; provided that the insertion of a wrong date by the holder, in good faith[3] and by mistake,[4] or, if the bill subsequently come into the hands of a holder in due course, the insertion of a wrong date, renders the bill payable on that date.[5]

13. *Ante- and Post-Dating.*—(1) The date of a bill, its acceptance, or any indorsement, are deemed to be the true dates[6] respectively, unless the contrary be proved[7] (and an averment that the date is false is relevant to a question of liability on the bill, though not in cases where the want of a date does not render the bill invalid,[8] nor in cases where there has been an unauthorised alteration which is not apparent[9]). (2) A bill is not invalid by reason only that it is ante-dated or post-dated, or dated on a Sunday.

14. Days of Grace.—For bills not payable on demand, and where the bill does not otherwise provide, three days of grace are allowed, and the bill is due and payable on the last day of grace.[10] It is competent for an acceptor to add to his acceptance of the bill the words " payable without days of grace." The acceptor has the whole of the last day of grace to make payment.[11] While the holder is entitled at any time on the last day of grace to give notice of dishonour to the drawer and the indorsers, he has no right of action against them until the expiration of that day. If the last day of grace falls on a Sunday, Christmas Day, Good Friday, or day appointed by Royal Proclamation as a public fast or thanksgiving day, the bill is, except in the case after mentioned, due and payable on the *preceding* business day : if on a bank holiday[12] (other than Christmas Day or Good Friday), or on a Sunday succeeding a bank holiday, the bill is payable on the *succeeding* business day. In cases where the last day of grace falls on Christmas Day, and that day is a

---

[1] Speirs & Knox *v.* Semple, 1901 (O.H.), 9 S.L.T. 153, *per* Lord Kincairney.
[2] *Vide* sec. 17.   [3] *Vide* sec. 90.   [4] *Vide* sec. 64.
[5] *Vide* sec. 20, limited by this section.
[6] *Vide* sec. 21.
[7] *Vide* sec. 100 ; Barker *v.* Sterne, 1854, 9 Exch. 684.
[8] *Vide* secs. 3 (4) and 12.
[9] *Vide* sec. 64.
[10] *Vide* secs. 45 (1) and 47.
[11] Kennedy *v.* Thomas, 1894, L.R. 2 Q.B. 759 ; sec. 47.
[12] In Scotland, New Year's Day, Christmas Day (and if either fall on Sunday, the Monday following), Good Friday, first Mondays of May and August.

Sunday, bills are due and payable on Saturday.[1] When in ordinary course bills fall due on Christmas Day, and that day is a Saturday, the bills are payable on the preceding business day. When the last day-of grace is upon Sunday, and the preceding day is Christmas, the bills are payable on the Monday following. With reference to New Year's Day, when that day is a Saturday, bills which in ordinary course fall due upon either the 1st or 2nd January are payable on Monday the 3rd January. As bank holidays differ in England and Scotland, the date is determined according to the place where the bill is payable.[2] Foreign bills are occasionally drawn payable at one or more usances. By " usance " is meant the customary time at which bills are made payable in a particular country—in France thirty days, Hamburg one calendar month, and Leghorn three calendar months. Double, treble, and half usance are terms implying corresponding alterations on the usual period. (2) In computing the date on which bills not payable on demand, or after sight, are due, the day from which the time begins to run is excluded, and the day of payment is included. (3) In bills payable after sight, the time begins to run from the date of acceptance if the bill be accepted, or the date of noting or protest (unnecessary in inland bills unless the holder intends to present also for payment[3]), if the bill be noted or protested for non-acceptance[4] (in which case presentment for payment is unnecessary[5]), or from the date of non-delivery, if the acceptor, who may retain the bill for the customary period before accepting or refusing to accept,[6] refuses delivery. (4) The term " month " means " calendar month." If the month in which the bill falls due has no day corresponding to that of the issue or acceptance, the last day of that month is the day from which the days of grace are reckoned. Thus a bill drawn on the 28th, 29th, 30th, or 31st January, and payable one month after date, is due on the 3rd March. If, however, a bill be drawn on the 28th January in leap-year payable one month after date, it will fall due on the 2nd March.

15. Referee in Case of Need.—The drawer or any indorser of a bill may insert the name of a person to whom the holder may resort in case the bill be dishonoured by non-acceptance[7] or non-payment.[8] Such person is called the referee in case of need. It is in the option of the holder to resort to the referee in case of need, or not, as he thinks fit. Provided that it is clear that such person is to be resorted to only in case of need, and that he is not drawn upon alternatively or in succession to the drawees, no particular form of words is necessary. The person who inserts the name of the referee should specify for whose honour the referee is to accept or pay ; as, " In case of need, apply to ·

---

[1] Bank Holidays Act, 1871, sec. 1.   [2] *Vide* sec. 72 (5).
[3] *Vide* sec. 51 (1).   [4] *Vide* sec. 51 (2), (4), (6), (7).   [5] *Vide* sec. 43.
[6] *Vide* sec. 42.   [7] *Vide* sec. 43.   [8] *Vide* sec. 47.

A. B. for C. D." The position of the reference may show by implication for whose honour it is intended ; as where it occurs below the signature of the drawer or of an indorser.[1]

16. Limitation of Liability.—The drawer and any indorser of a bill may insert in it an express stipulation negativing or limiting his own liability [2] to the holder, or waiving as regards himself some or all of the holder's duties.[3] The addition of the words " Pay D. or order without recourse to me " to the signature of a drawer or indorser, while limiting such drawer's or indorser's liability, leaves the holder free to have recourse to any other party to the bill whose liability is not so limited. A person who indorses a bill " without recourse " is in the position of a transferror by delivery.[4] In one case a person who was not a party to a cheque, at the request of the payee wrote his name at the back thereof, adding the words " sans recours," and it was held that he thereby negatived his liability as indorser.[5] The fact of the drawer or indorser waiving any of the holder's duties, such as presenting for payment, giving notice of dishonour, and protesting, while relieving any subsequent holder of the necessity of performing the duty waived in order to preserve recourse against that particular drawer or indorser, still leaves the performance of that duty necessary in order to preserve recourse against the other parties liable on the bill, whether prior or subsequent to the party waiving. The party who has waived any such duty remains liable on the bill, and he is entitled to give notice of dishonour to the parties liable on the bill prior to him, though he has not received such notice himself.[6]

17. Acceptance.—(1) The acceptance of a bill (that is, acceptance completed by delivery or notification [7]) is the signification by the drawee of his assent to the order of the drawer. " Save in the case of acceptances for honour or per procuration,[8] or in the cases provided for in the Companies (Consolidation) Act, 1908, sec. 77, by which any person acting under the authority of a company may accept or indorse bills on behalf of the company without incurring personal responsibility,[9] and even then only where such companies have power conferred on them to issue bills and notes,[10] no one can become a party to a bill *quâ acceptor* who is not a proper drawee, or, in other words, an addressee." [11] Thus, where a bill is addressed to B., and C. accepts it, C. is not liable as an acceptor ; [12] and where a bill is addressed to B., and he accepts, and C.

---

[1] *Vide* secs. 65-68.   [2] *Vide* sec. 55.   [3] *Vide* secs. 39-52.
[4] *Vide* sec. 58.   [5] Wakefield *v.* Alexander & Co., etc., 1901, 17 T.L.R. 217.
[6] *Vide* sec. 49 (1).   [7] *Vide* sec. 21.   [8] *Vide* secs. 15, 65.
[9] *Ex parte* Overend, 1869, L.R. 4 Ch. 472.
[10] *In re* Peruvian Ry. Co., 1867, L.R. 2 Ch. 617 ; Dutton *v.* Marsh, 1871, L.R. 6 Q.B. 361 ; Landes *v.* Marcus & Davids, 1909, 25 T.L.R. 478.
[11] Walker's Trs. *v.* M'Kinlay, 1880, 7 R. (H.L.) 85, and 5 L.R. Ap. Ca. 754.
[12] Davis *v.* Clark, 1844, 6 Q.B. 16.

also writes an acceptance on it, C. is not liable as an acceptor. Where a bill addressed to B. & Co. is accepted in the firm's name by C., a partner, who adds his own name, the acceptance is that of the firm and not of C.[1]

Requisites.—(2) An acceptance is invalid unless it complies with the following conditions :—(*a*) It must be written ; that is, the acceptor's signature must be in writing, though words such as " accepts," or " accepted " need not necessarily appear. The signature is necessary, and the word "accepted " without the signature does not constitute a valid acceptance. With regard, however, to a bill accepted abroad, the validity of such acceptance in point of form is determined by the law of the place where the acceptance is made.[2] (*b*) It must be on the bill itself, or on one bill of a set,[3] but not on a copy, and it may be written on the back of the bill.[4] (*c*) It must be signed, that is, it must contain the acceptor's signature (or initials if that be his usual mode of signature [5]) adhibited by himself or by his authority,[6] or, if a corporation be the acceptor, the corporate seal may be adhibited.[7] (*d*) It must not express that the drawee will perform his promise by any other means than the payment of money.[8] Thus, payable " in bills " or " in goods " is invalid. Where the bill is payable after sight, it is proper that the date of acceptance be added, though as the holder may fill in the date, it is unnecessary.[9] Where two or more persons accept a bill, their rights *inter se* may competently be determined on a proof.[10]

18. *Time for Acceptance.*—A bill may be accepted, (1) before it has been signed by the drawer, or while otherwise incomplete.[11] A foreign bill may be accepted before it is stamped.[12] A bill accepted for valuable consideration, with the drawer's name left blank, may be completed by the drawer's name being added after the acceptor's death.[13] Unless the contrary appear, a bill is *primâ facie* deemed to have been accepted before maturity and within a reasonable time after its issue, but there is no presumption as to the exact time of acceptance.[14] (2) When it is overdue,[15] or after it has been dishonoured by a previous refusal to

---

[1] *In re* Barnard, 1886, L.R. 32 Ch. D. 447, C.A.
[2] See *infra*, " Conflict of Laws."   [3] *Vide* sec. 71 (4).
[4] Walker's Trs. *v.* M'Kinlay, *supra*.
[5] *Vide* sec. 3.   [6] *Vide* sec. 91 (1).
[7] *Vide* sec. 91 (2). See as to signing bills and cheques on behalf of Public Companies, p. 87.
[8] *Ex parte* Imeson, 2 Rose, Bank. Ca. 225 ; Russell *v.* Phillips, 1850, 14 Q.B. 891.
[9] *Vide* sec. 12.
[10] Crosbie *v.* Brown, 1900, 3 F. 83 ; 8 S.L.T. 245.
[11] *Vide* sec. 20 ; London and South-Western Bank *v.* Wentworth, 1880, 5 Ex. D. 96.
[12] Stamp Act, 1891, sec. 35.
[13] Carter *v.* White, L.R. 25 Ch. D. 666.
[14] Roberts *v.* Bethell, 1852, 12 C.B.
[15] *Vide* secs. 14, 45 (1) (2).

accept[1] or by non-payment.[2] (3) When a bill payable after sight is dishonoured by non-acceptance and the drawee subsequently accepts it, the holder, in the absence of any different agreement, is entitled to have the bill accepted as of the first date of presentment to the drawee for acceptance. If on accepting at the second presentment the drawee neglect to fill in the date, the holder may fill in the date of the first presentment as that of the acceptance.[3] If on the first presentment of a bill payable after sight it be dishonoured, the drawer and prior indorsers will be discharged if without their consent the bill be accepted as of the date of its second presentment.

19. *General and Qualified Acceptances.*—(1) An acceptance is either general or qualified. (2) A general acceptance assents without qualification to the order of the drawer, and binds the acceptor to pay the sum for which the bill is drawn to the person named in the bill and his indorsers, at the date and place stated in the bill, or if no place be stated, then at the place of business or residence of the drawee. A qualified acceptance in express terms varies the effect of the bill as drawn. But the acceptance cannot vary the effect of the bill by promising the performance of anything but the payment of money,[4] nor must it engage to pay a sum larger than that for which the bill was drawn.[5] To avail the acceptor in a question with a holder in due course, the qualification must appear *ex facie* of the bill, and in such clear and unequivocal terms that any person taking the bill could not, if he acted reasonably, fail to understand that it was accepted subject to an express qualification.[6] The holder of the bill may refuse to take a qualified acceptance, and may treat the bill as dishonoured by non-acceptance. Except in the case of a partial acceptance whereof due notice has been given, if the holder desires to preserve his recourse against the drawer and indorser, unless he has their consent, actual or implied, to his taking a qualified acceptance, or they subsequently assent thereto, he must give notice thereof to prior parties.[7] But where the drawer or indorser receives notice of a qualified acceptance, and does not, within a reasonable time, express his dissent to the holder, he is deemed to have assented thereto. A qualification must truly qualify the acceptance, and not be of the nature merely of a memorandum or addition to the acceptor's signature. Thus the addition of the words " as cautioner " is not a qualification of the acceptor's engagement to pay.[8] A qualification may be (*a*) conditional, making payment by the acceptor dependent on the fulfilment of a condition stated.[9] Such an acceptance does not warrant the use of summary

---

[1] *Vide* secs. 42, 43.   [2] *Vide* sec. 47.   [3] *Vide* sec. 12.   [4] *Vide* sec. 17.
[5] Stamp Act, 1891, 54 & 55 Vict. cap. 39.
[6] Meyer *v.* Decroix, Verley & Co., 1891, L.R. A.C. 520.
[7] *Vide* sec. 44.
[8] Bell's Com. i. 424 ; Walker's Trs. *v.* M'Kinlay, 1880, 7 R. (H.L.) 85, 96.
[9] Smith *v.* Vertue, 1860, 30 L.J. C.P. 56.

diligence, since the fulfilment of the condition must be matter of proof ; (b) partial, or for part only of the sum for which the bill is drawn. Such an acceptance, unlike one that is otherwise qualified, may be taken by the holder without the assent of the drawer and prior indorsers, though to preserve recourse against them the holder must give them notice of the fact ; [1] (c) local, or to pay only at a particular specified place, though such an acceptance is general [2] unless it expressly states that the bill is to be paid there only and not elsewhere ; [3] (d) qualified as to time, as where a bill is drawn payable one month after date, but is accepted payable six months after date ; [4] or (e) the acceptance of some one or more of the drawees, but not of all. But the acceptance of one drawee, for himself and any others, will bind those for whom he signs, if he have their implied or express authority to do so.

20. Inchoate Bill.—(1) Where a simple signature on a blank stamped paper, that is, on paper bearing an impressed bill stamp specially appropriated to bills and notes, is delivered by the signer in order that it may be converted into a bill,[5] it operates as a *primâ facie* authority to fill it up as a complete bill for any amount the stamp will cover, using the signature for that of the drawer, or the acceptor,[6] or an indorser.[7] But it is essential that such stamped paper have been actually delivered and for the purpose of being converted into a bill. For if it be delivered for any other purpose, or if, instead of being delivered, it has been found or stolen and filled up and indorsed by the finder or thief, even for value, to a *bonâ fide* holder, the person who originally signed the blank paper, afterwards filled up without his consent, express or implied, will not be liable, even to a holder in due course.[8] To this rule there may, however, be an exception if the loss of the blank stamped paper be due to such negligence on the part of the person who originally signed it as to amount to the actual neglect of a duty on his part.[9] The signature on the bill is, in the first place, proof of the holder's authority to fill it up as a complete bill, but the person who signed the blank stamped paper may prove, by parole evidence, that the bill has not been filled up in accordance with his instructions.[10] And while a

---

[1] *Vide* sec. 44.

[2] Halstead *v.* Skelton, 1843, 5 Q.B. 86 Exch. Ch.

[3] Halstead *v.* Skelton, *supra.*

[4] Russell *v.* Phillips, 1850, 14 Q.B. 891 ; Fanshaw *v.* Peet, 1857, 26 L.J. Ex. 314.

[5] *Vide* secs. 3, 83 ; Baxendale *v.* Bennett, 1878, 3 Q.B.D. at p. 531, C.A.

[6] Molloy *v.* Delves, 1831, 7 Bing. 428.

[7] Foster *v.* M'Kinnon, 1869, L.R. 4 C.P. at p. 712.

[8] *Vide* Baxendale *v.* Bennett, *supra.*

[9] Swan *v.* N.B. Australasian Co., 1863, 32 L.J. Ex. 273 ; Baxendale *v.* Bennett, 1878, 3 Q.B.D., C.A.

[10] *Vide* sec. 100 ; Lyon *v.* Butter, 1841, 4 D. 178 ; Anderson *v.* Lorimer, 1857, 20 D. 74 ; Jackson *v.* M'Iver, 1875, 2 R. 882 ; Watkin Bros. Ltd. *v.* Lamb & Robertson, 1901, 17 T.L.R. 777.

bill *ex facie* complete, and no longer in the possession of the person signing it, is presumed to have been delivered,[1] no such presumption exists in the case of a bill admitted or proved to have been signed while inchoate or incomplete, and the holder must, therefore, prove that it was delivered for the purpose of being converted into a bill. While the holder has, in general, the right to use the signature on an inchoate bill as that of the drawer, acceptor, or indorser, his right is not so absolute as to entitle him to use a signature on the back of a printed form, and therefore impliedly intended as the signature of an indorser, as that of a drawer or acceptor. In one case, a person who had received a blank acceptance for his accommodation, on the understanding, though not agreement, that he should sign as drawer, was held entitled to procure another to whom he was indebted to sign as drawer and discount the bill.[2]

Primâ facie Authority to Complete Bill.—When a bill is wanting in any material particular necessary for the completion of the document[3] (that is, in any of the requisites of a bill except the signature of the drawer or maker [4]), the person in possession of it, including a transferee without indorsation of a bill payable to order [5] (who need not be the person to whom it was delivered, but may be, for example, the trustee of a creditor who has received an acceptance blank in name of the drawer, an executor,[6] or a creditor of the original holder, to whom a bill blank in the payee's name has been delivered), has *primâ facie* authority to fill up the omission in any way he thinks fit. That authority may be limited, however, to a certain extent by notes on the bill, but not forming part of it,[7] and may be revoked, and impliedly is revoked, by the sequestration of the signer. Such revocation, whether actual or implied, does not affect the rights of a holder in due course.[8]

Bill must be Completed within Reasonable Time.—(2) In order that a signature on a blank stamped paper, or a bill, which is wanting in any material particular, may be enforceable against any person who became a party thereto prior to its completion, it must be filled up within a reasonable time [9] and strictly in accordance with the authority given.[10] Reasonable time for this purpose is a question of fact, varying according

---

[1] *Vide* sec. 21 (3).

[2] Russell *v.* Banknock Coal Co., 1897, 24 R. 1009 ; *vide* sec. 29.

[3] Macdonald *v.* Shand, 1872, 10 M. 984.

[4] *Vide* secs. 3, 83.　　　　　[5] *Vide* sec. 31 (4).　　　　　[6] Bell's Com. i. 416.

[7] Cameron *v.* Morrison, 1869, 7 M. 383 ; *vide* Hogarth *v.* Latham & Co., 3 Q.B.D. 643.

[8] M'Meekin *v.* Russell and Tudhope, 1881, 8 R. 587.

[9] Temple *v.* Pullen, 1853, 8 Exch. 389 ; Montague *v.* Perkins, 1853, 22 L.J. C.P. 187.

[10] Awde *v.* Dixon, 1851, 6 Ex. 869 ; Hanbury *v.* Lovett, 1868, 18 L.T. (N.S.) 366. See Anderson *v.* Sommerville, Murray & Co., 1898, 1 F. 90 ; Herdman *v.* Wheeler, 1902, 1 K.B. 361.

to circumstances, and reckoned from the date of delivery by the signer of the blank stamped paper or incomplete bill.[1]

It was, and is, perhaps, not an unusual practice, in some parts of the country, to bring or send to bank agents bills bearing the signatures and nothing else, which are afterwards filled up by one of the officers of the bank and received in the ordinary course of business. Since a bank, as holders of a bill filled up by one of their agents after the signatures have been attached, cannot enforce payment of it against any parties who can prove that it has not been filled up strictly in accordance with the authority given by them, this practice should be avoided, and no bill should be received which is not complete.

Completed Bill in Hands of Holder in Due Course.—If any such instrument after completion is negotiated to a holder in due course, it is valid and effectual for all purposes in his hands, and he may enforce it as if it had been filled up within a reasonable time and strictly in accordance with the authority given,[2] provided he did not know at the time of taking it that it had been delivered in an incomplete state, and that it was not intended to be filled up for the amount which it bears.[3] But the holder, even with such knowledge as to deprive him of his own rights under the bill, may transfer it to another, who is not a party to the fraud, so as to invest him with all the rights of a holder in due course.[4] Thus in one case a person signed an acceptance, the amount in the body of which was then left blank, but in the margin of which were the figures £14, 0s. 6d., that being the sum for which he desired to accept, and handed the acceptance to the drawer, who subsequently filled in the blank in the body of the bill for £164, 0s. 6d., and fraudulently altered the figures in the margin to that sum. The bill was then indorsed by the drawer to a third person, who took it *bonâ fide* for value for the larger amount, and it was held that the acceptor was liable on the bill for such larger amount, on the ground that the marginal figures are not an essential part of a bill of exchange ; that one who gives an acceptance in blank, holds out the person he intrusts therewith as having authority to fill in the bill as he pleases within the limits of the stamp ; and that no alteration (even if it be fraudulent and unauthorised) of the marginal figures can vitiate the bill as a bill for the full amount inserted in the body when it reaches the hands of a holder for value, who is unaware that the marginal figures have been improperly altered.[5] A holder in due course is not deprived of his rights because the blank stamped paper is only filled up by the person in possession after the lapse of the prescrip-

---

[1] Maclean *v.* M'Ewen & Son, 1899, 1 F. 381 ; 6 S.L.T. 261.
[2] Foster *v.* Mackinnon, 1869, L.R. 4 C.P. at p. 712.
[3] *Vide* sec. 29 ; Lyon *v.* Butter, 1841, 4 D. 178.
[4] *Vide* sec. 29 (3).
[5] Garrard *v.* Lewis, 1882, 10 Q.B.D. 30.

tive period,[1] nor from the fact that between the date of the delivery of the signature and the filling up of the blank paper, the signer has been bankrupt and discharged.[2]

21. Delivery.—(1) Every contract on a bill (which may be to draw, accept, or indorse it), whether it be the drawer's, acceptor's, or indorser's, is incomplete and revocable until delivery, or the transfer of possession, actual or constructive,[3] from one person to another,[4] made by or with the authority, written or verbal, of the person drawing, accepting, or indorsing the instrument in order to give effect thereto ; that is, to transfer the existing contracts on the bills to the transferee, and thus to complete a new contract between the drawer,[5] acceptor,[6] or indorser,[7] and the holder. If an indorsee authorise the indorser to transmit the bill to him by post, the property in the bill passes to the indorsee, and the indorsement becomes complete, so soon as the letter containing the bill is posted.[8] But though, until delivery, there is no contract on the bill, and the drawee may cancel his signature and return the bill unaccepted, he may still be liable in damages for his refusal to accept.[9] It is an apparent exception to this rule that if the drawee have funds of the drawer in his hands, presentation of the bill to him operates as an intimated assignation of such funds in favour of the holder,[10] but it is explicable on the ground that the drawee's liability is not founded on the bill, but upon the fact of his indebtedness to the drawer, of his right to enforce payment of which the bill is the assignation.

But where an acceptance is written on a bill and the drawee gives notice to, or according to the directions of, the person entitled to the bill that he has accepted it, the acceptance then becomes complete and irrevocable.

By Whom.—(2) As between immediate parties (by which is meant parties who are in direct relation to each other, as the drawer and acceptor, the drawer and payee, an indorsee and his next indorsee, etc.), and as regards a remote party other than a holder in due course,[11] the delivery in order to be effectual must be made either by, or under the authority of, the party drawing, accepting, or indorsing, as the case may be.

---

[1] Montague *v.* Perkins, 22 L.J. C.P. 187.

[2] Temple *v.* Pullen, 8 Ex. 389. See also Goldsmid *v.* Hampton, 1858, 5 C.B. (N.S.) 94, 27 L.J. C.P. 286 ; *ex parte* Hayward, 1871, L.R. 6 Ch. 546.

[3] Anderson *v.* Roberson, 1867, 5 M. 507 ; Miller *v.* Miller, 1874, 1 R. 1107.

[4] Martini & Co. *v.* Steel & Craig, 1878, 6 R. 342.

[5] *Vide* sec. 55 (1).

[6] *Vide* sec. 54.

[7] *Vide* sec. 55 (2).

[8] *Ex parte* Cote, 1873, L.R. 9 Ch. 27.

[9] Prehn *v.* Royal Bank of Liverpool, 1879, L.R. 5 Ex. 92.

[10] *Vide* sec. 53 (2).

[11] *Vide* sec. 29.

Conditional Delivery.—But such delivery in a question between immediate parties and a remote party other than a holder in due course, and between such parties and even a holder in due course, if the bill bears *ex facie* to have been transferred conditionally,[1] may be shown to have been conditional [2] or for a special purpose only,[3] and not for the purpose of transferring the property in the bill. " The liability of an indorser to his immediate indorsee arises out of a contract between them, and this contract in no case consists exclusively in the writing called an indorsement, and which is necessary to the existence of the contract in question, but that contract arises out of the written indorsement itself, the delivery of the bill to the indorsee, and the intention with which that delivery was made and accepted as evinced by the words either spoken or written of the parties, and the circumstances, such as the usage at the place, the course of dealing between the parties, and their relative situations under which the delivery takes place : thus a bill with an unqualified written indorsement may be delivered and received for the purpose of enabling the indorser to raise money for his own use on the credit of the signature of the indorser, or with an express stipulation that the indorsee, though for value, is to claim against the drawer and acceptor only, and not against the indorser who agrees to sell his claim against the prior parties, but stipulates not to warrant their solvency. In all these cases the indorser is not liable to the indorsee." [3]

But if the bill be in the hands of a holder in due course, a valid delivery of the bill by all parties prior to him, so as to make them liable to him, is conclusively presumed.[4] The true owner of a bill may sue the person to whom a bill is delivered conditionally or for a special purpose, if he misappropriate it, and he may also recover from anyone who takes the bill with knowledge of the facts.[5] If the bill have been collected, the true owner may sue for the amount as money received on his behalf.[6]

2. Capacity and Authority of Parties

22. Capacity to Sign Bills.—(1) Capacity to incur liability [7] as a party to a bill is co-extensive with capacity to contract, but a corporation cannot make itself liable as drawer, acceptor, or indorser of a bill unless it is competent for it so to do under the law for the time being

---

[1] *Vide* sec. 35. [2] Wallis *v.* Lettel, 31 L.J. C.P. 100.
[3] Castrique *v.* Buttiguiez, 10 Moore, P.C. 94.
[4] *Vide* sec. 20.
[5] Alsager *v.* Close, 1842, 10 M. & W. 576.
[6] Arnold *v.* Cheque Bank, 1876, 1 C.P.D. 585.
[7] *Vide* secs. 53-58.

8

in force relating to corporations.[1] In England an infant cannot bind himself by the acceptance of a bill of exchange, even although the bill is given for the price of necessaries supplied to him during minority.[2] (2) When a bill is drawn or indorsed by a pupil, minor, or corporation having no capacity or power to incur liability on a bill, the drawing or indorsement entitles the holder (that is, the payee or indorsee in possession or the bearer) to receive payment of the bill and to enforce it against any other party thereto.[3] If such a bill be dishonoured, the holder has no recourse against the drawer, and therefore is not bound to give notice of dishonour or to protest it, and the presentment of such a bill will not operate as an intimated assignation of the drawer's assets in the hands of the drawee to the extent of the sum contained in the bill. As against a holder in due course, neither lunacy nor drunkenness is a good defence ; but complete drunkenness would seem to be a defence against an immediate party to the bill having notice.[4]

23. Signatures of Parties.—No person or body of persons, incorporated or not, is liable as a drawer,[5] indorser,[6] or acceptor [7] of a bill who has not signed it as such, and no person can be liable on a bill except in one of these three capacities.[8]

Trade or Assumed Name.—(1) Where a person signs a bill in a trade or assumed name, he is liable thereon as if he had signed it in his own name. But where the acceptor signs a different name from that of the drawee, while the holder may prove the signature to be that of the trade or assumed name of the drawee, the bill will not warrant summary diligence.

Partner.—(2) The signature of the name of a firm is equivalent to the signature by the person so signing of the names of all persons liable as partners in that firm. Such signature renders action or diligence competent against all the partners of the firm.[9] " Where a signature is common to an individual and a firm of which the individual is a member, a *bonâ fide* holder for value, without notice whose paper it is, of a bill of exchange with such signature attached, has not an option to sue either the individual or the firm. But there is a presumption that the bill was given for the firm and is binding upon it, at least where the individual carries on no business separate from the business of the firm of which he is a member ; this presumption, however, may be rebutted by proof that the bill was signed, not in the name of the partnership, but of the individual for his private purposes, and it is immaterial that the *bonâ fide*

---

[1] *Vide* p. 85.
[2] *In re* Soltykoff, 1891, L.R. 1 Q.B. 413.
[3] *Vide* sec. 54 (2).
[4] Core *v.* Gibson, 1845, 13 M. & W. 623.
[5] *Vide* sec. 55 (1).   [6] *Vide* sec. 55 (2).   [7] *Vide* sec. 54.
[8] Walker's Trs. *v.* M'Kinlay, 1880, 7 R. (H.L.) 85.
[9] Drew *v.* Lumsden, 1865, 3 M. 384.

holder took the bill as the bill of the proprietors of the business carried on by the partnership, whoever they may be, and not merely as the bill of the individual." [1] If a bill be accepted by a partner of a firm in the firm's name, the addition of that partner's own name, beneath that of the firm, does not render the partner separately liable.[2] A firm's signature on a bill of exchange, adhibited by one of the partners after the dissolution of the co-partnery, does not bind the firm or the other partners.[3] Due notice of the dissolution must be given, as until this is done the partners may bind each other by bills or other like contracts within the scope of the former partnership. Where a partner, who is precluded from signing the firm's name to bills, signs bills or notes, not in the course of the company's business, and the proceeds of which by discounting are applied, not to the firm's, but to his own pecuniary benefit, the circumstances being such as to awaken suspicion in the mind of a reasonably careful man, the loss, in discounting such bills, will not fall upon the other partners who were ignorant of the transaction and who obtained no benefit from it.[4] When all the partners of a firm carrying on business under a descriptive name grant a bill, there is a presumption that the bill was granted for the purposes of the firm (though the contrary may be proved), and the bill therefore is a good ground for diligence against the assets of the firm, if in fact it is not proved that it was not granted for the purposes of the firm. In such a case the onus of proving that the bill was not granted for the firm's benefit falls upon the partners.[5]

24. Forged Signatures.—Subject to the provisions of the Act,[6] where a signature on a bill is forged, or placed thereon without the authority of the person whose signature it purports to be, the forged or unauthorised signature is wholly inoperative, and no right to retain the bill or to give a discharge therefor, or to enforce payment thereof against any party thereto, can be acquired through or under that signature, unless the party against whom it is sought to retain, or enforce payment of the bill, is precluded from setting up the forgery or want of authority. The *onus* of proving that the signature on a bill is genuine appears to be on the holder of the bill.[7] Thus a person may, by his conduct, be barred *personali exceptione* from denying the genuineness of his signature to an innocent holder.[8] He may also be barred by negligence, if it can be

---

[1] Yorkshire Banking Co. *v.* Beatson, 4 C.P.D. 204 ; Leeds and County Banking Co. *v.* Beatson, 5 C.P.D. 109.

[2] *In re* Barnard, 1886, 32 Ch. D. 447 C.A.

[3] Goodwin *v.* Indust. and Gen. Trust Co. Ltd., 1890, 18 R. 193.

[4] Paterson Bros. *v.* Gladstone, 1891, 18 R. 403.

[5] Rosslund Cycle Co. and Others *v.* M'Creadie, 1907, S.C. 1208.

[6] Secs. 54 (2), 55 (2), 60, 80, and 82.

[7] British Linen Co. *v.* Cowan, 1906, 8 F. 704.

[8] Brook *v.* Hook, 1871, L.R. 6 Ex. 89 ; Robarts *v.* Tucker, 1851, 16 Q.B. 577.

shown that the negligence was the direct or proximate cause of the forgery being taken to be genuine.[1] The mere fact, however, that a person whose signature has been forged does not answer letters addressed to him regarding the bill does not of itself preclude him from thereafter setting up the forgery. In one case it transpired that in connection with certain bill transactions extending over a period of between twelve and thirteen years, some twenty-seven notices that certain bills were past due were sent to a person whose name appeared on them, and that he had taken no notice of the intimations. His name was forged on the bills. Subsequently the bank who held the bills sought to make the person whose name had been forged liable, on the ground that by his silence he had homologated and adopted the signature on the bills as his genuine signature, but it was decided that when a notice regarding a bill is sent to a person who has not signed it, mere silence on his part will not infer adoption of the signature, so as to make him liable for the amount of the bill.[2] It is immaterial that the holder had no notice of the forgery or want of authority, and no one can be a holder in due course who derives his title to the bill through a forged indorsation.[3] The question of negligence is one for the jury. In one case a person was induced to sign his name to promissory notes through openings in a sheet of blotting-paper made for the purpose, and which concealed the true character of the documents, under an assurance from the person who induced him to sign, who was a friend of many years' standing and against whose honour no suspicion attached, that he was signing simply as a witness to some family documents of a private nature. As a matter of fact, what he had signed were promissory notes, regularly filled up and addressed to a named payee, who subsequently, in perfectly good faith and on the strength of the signatures, advanced large sums of money to the fraudulent obtainer of them. The jury held that in the circumstances he had not been guilty of culpable negligence in signing the documents, and the Court held that the named payee had no right to recover against him.[4] But it must be remembered that it is a general principle of our law, which is in accordance with good sense and justice, that a person who proposes to put in force a written instrument which is not in itself probative (under which category bills are, of course, included) must prove it to be genuine if its genuineness is disputed. Thus if a person asserts that the signature on a bill is not his or has not been adhibited by him or with his authority, the onus of proving the genuineness of the signature lies upon the person who seeks to enforce payment of it. To this rule must be added the corollary that the onus

---

[1] Arnold v. Cheque Bank, 1846, 1 C.P.D. 585.
[2] British Linen Co. v. Cowan, 1906, 8 F. 704.
[3] Vide secs. 20, 54 (2), 59, 64 ; and Cheques, p. 179.
[4] Lewis v. Clay, 1897, 14 T.L.R. 149.

of proving the genuineness of a document may depend on the conduct of the parties with reference to it ; and it may be perfectly right at a certain stage of a particular case that the person who impugns a document should be required to disprove it, though in general one cannot be called upon or expected to prove a negative.[1]

Payment on Forged Signature.—The drawee of a bill is discharged by a payment in due course, that is, a payment made at, or after, the maturity of the bill, to the holder in good faith and without notice that his title to the bill is defective.

A merchant's clerk, by forging letters of advice, and preparing and filling in forged drafts, in which he inserted the name of a foreign correspondent of his employer as the drawer, and the names of a foreign firm who were existing persons and actual correspondents of his employer as the payees, procured his employer's acceptance of these forged instruments, and obtained payment of them across the counter from a bank. The clerk appropriated the moneys to his own use, and it was held that the loss incurred must fall upon the merchant and not upon the bank.[2] But a payment on the forged signature of the drawer is not a payment in due course, because made to a person who is not a holder in the sense of the Act, and by such a payment therefore the drawee is not discharged, but must, notwithstanding, deliver the bill to the true owner and pay it when it falls due.[3]

Forged Indorsement Abroad.—It has been decided that this section does not apply to an indorsement of a bill of exchange abroad. The section is only declaratory of the law of this country, and does not control the general rule of international law. Consequently the indorsement in a foreign country—valid in a foreign country but invalid here—of a bill of exchange would be effectual to give the indorsee a good title to the bill as against the drawer or acceptor.[4]

Ratification of Unauthorised Signature.—Nothing in the section affects the ratification of an unauthorised signature not amounting to a forgery ; that is, nothing prevents a signature, not forged, but adhibited without authority to draw or accept bills, from being subsequently ratified so as to preclude the person so ratifying from pleading that it had been adhibited without his authority. Mere silence does not necessarily amount to the adoption of an unauthorised signature.[5]

25. Procuration Signatures.—A signature by procuration operates as a notice that the agent has but a limited authority to sign, and the principal is only bound by such signature if the agent in so signing was

---

[1] M'Intyre v. National Bank of Scotland, 1910, S.C. 150, *per* Lord Kinnear.
[2] Bank of England v. Vagliano, 1891, L.R. A.C. 107 ; see sec. 7.
[3] *Vide* secs. 29 (2), 60 ; Ogden v. Benas, 1874, L.R. 9 C.P. 513.
[4] Embiricos v. Anglo-Austrian Bank, 1905, 1 K.B. 677.
[5] Mackenzie v. British Linen Co., 1881, 8 R. (H.L.) 8.

acting within the actual limits of his authority.[1] Where an agent accepts or indorses per procuration, the taker of the bill or note, so accepted or indorsed, is bound to inquire as to the extent of the agent's authority, and where an agent has such an authority, his abuse of it does not affect a *bonâ fide* holder for value.[2] A person who is authorised to sign bills per procuration in respect of his principal's private business, is not acting within the limits of his authority in accepting per procuration bills connected with his principal's partnership business.[3] A person is said to draw, accept, or indorse a bill by procuration when it is done by his agent acting under his authority. Any person having capacity to contract may authorise another to draw, accept, or indorse bills on his behalf, and the person so authorised may be anyone but a pupil or a person destitute of reason.[4] Procuration may be constituted by a verbal mandate ; by a written mandate or letter of procuration ; or by facts and circumstances which infer implied authority. Thus authority to sign per procuration will be inferred by acts of a principal, such as allowing a person to sign habitually for him, or placing him in a position, with reference to a particular business, in which power to draw or accept bills is a necessary part of the business according to the usages of that particular trade, provided that the principal can be proved to have known and acquiesced in the practice.[5] Procuration may also be conferred by a general mandate which implies authority to sign bills, but a mandate to draw bills will not confer authority to indorse them. It may also be conferred by special mandate, but a special authority to sign bills in a particular course of business does not confer authority to sign them for any other purpose.[6] A person who has authority as agent to draw or accept or indorse bills will bind his principal if he discounts bills and appropriates the proceeds, provided the bank do not act negligently and the signatures are not manifest forgeries.[7] A person signing as procurator for another must sign per procuration, or otherwise show that he is signing merely as an agent, otherwise he does not bind his principal,[8] and if the principal be not liable the agent may be, and if he sign without authority will be, held bound as a principal. If a principal subsequently

---

[1] Reid *v.* Rigby & Co., 1894, L.R. 2 Q.B. 40 ; see Cheques.

[2] Bryant *v.* Banque du Peuple, 1893, Ap. Ca. 170 ; *vide* Attwood *v.* Munnings, *infra* ; Morison *v.* London County and Westminster Bank, 1914, 3 K.B. 356.

[3] Attwood *v.* Munnings, 1827, 7 B. & C. 278 ; Stagg *v.* Elliott, *infra*.

[4] *Vide* M'Michael *v.* Barbour, 1840, 3 D. 279 ; Fraser, Husband and Wife, vol. i. p. 513 ; Thomson on Bills, 147.

[5] Edmunds *v.* Bushell & Jones, 1865, L.R. 1 Q.B. 97 ; Swinburne *v.* Western Bank, 1856, 18 D. 1025 ; Anderson *v.* Buck & Holms, 1841, 3 D. 975.

[6] Stagg *v.* Elliott, 31 L.J. C.P. 94.

[7] Union Bank *v.* Makin, 1873, 11 M. 499. See also Bryant *v.* Banque du Peuple, *supra*.

[8] North British Bank *v.* Ayrshire Iron Co., 1853, 15 D. 782.

ratify his signature, adhibited by his agent *ex facie* per procuration, but without his authority, by any act, such as the delivery of a bill so drawn, he will thereby render himself liable.[1]

26. Signature as Agent or Representative.—(1) Where a person signs a bill as a drawer, indorser, or acceptor, and adds words to his signature indicating that he signs for or on behalf of a principal, or in a representative character, he is not personally liable thereon, even if he have no authority to sign and the principal repudiates the obligation,—though in that case he will be liable to indemnify the holder for any loss,[2] unless he sign on behalf of a fictitious or non-existent principal,[3]—nor if he sign " in name of and on behalf of " a body, such as a church or congregation, which could not legally become debtors on a bill or note ; [4] but the mere addition to his signature of words describing him as an agent, or as filling a representative character, as for example that of a director,[5] trustee,[6] or executor,[7] does not exempt him from personal liability. The signatures of officials or directors, adhibited " on behalf of " the company, do not bind such individuals personally.[8] But where the officials of a company which had no authority to accept bills, accepted bills " for and on behalf of " the company, which were indorsed by the drawer to a bank for value, it was held that they were personally liable, as by their acceptance they represented that they had authority to accept on behalf of the company, which, being a false representation of a matter of fact and not of law, gave a cause of action to the holders who had acted upon it.[9] (2) In determining whether a signature on a bill is that of the principal or that of the agent by whose hand it is written, the construction most favourable to the validity of the instrument is adopted.

3. The Consideration for a Bill

27. Valuable Consideration.—To render a bill valid, in Scotland it does not require to have been granted for value,[10] nor do the words " for value received " require to form part of it, whether value have

---

[1] Miller *v.* Little, 1831, 9 S. 328.

[2] Polhill *v.* Walter, 1 L.J. K.B. 92.

[3] Nicholls *v.* Diamond, 23 L.J. Ex. 1 ; Owen *v.* Van Uster, 20 L.J. C.P. 61 ; Kelmer *v.* Baxter, L.R. 2 C.P. 174.

[4] M'Meekin *v.* Easton, 1889, 16 R. 363. See also Rew *v.* Pettet, 1834, 1 A. & E. 196.

[5] Dutton *v.* Marsh, L.R. 6 Q.B. 361 ; Landes *v.* Marcus & Davids, 1909, 25 T.L.R. 478.

[6] Brown *v.* Sutherland, 1875, 2 R. 615.

[7] Eaton, Hammond & Sons *v.* M'Gregor's Exrs., 1837, 15 S. 1012 ; Liverpool Bank *v.* Walker, 1859, 4 De G. & J. 24.

[8] Lindus *v.* Melrose, 1858, 27 L.J. Ex. 326 ; Alexander *v.* Sizer, L.R. 4 Ex. 102.

[9] West London Commercial Bank *v.* Kitson, 1884, 13 Q.B.D. 360.

[10] Law *v.* Humphreys, 1876, 3 R. 1192.

been received or not. In the cases following, however, the plea that the bill has been granted for no valuable consideration may be a relevant defence, which, if proved, will preclude an original party, and even a holder, but not a holder in due course,[1] from enforcing it :— (a) Where the bill has been signed without intention to grant an obligation, as, for example, where it has been obtained by fraud, or force and fear : (b) Where the consideration has failed, as where it has been given for a special purpose, which cannot be carried out ; to be used on the occurrence of an event which does not happen ; or in payment of goods which are not delivered : (c) Where it is an accommodation bill : (d) Where it is given for an immoral or illegal consideration, or one which the law does not recognise, or under such circumstances as to make the transaction iniquitous and tantamount to a fraud, as where a money-lender extorted from a poor woman promissory notes for very large sums in consideration of granting her twenty-four hours' delay in repaying a previous loan.[2] A bill or note given by one person to another for a gambling debt and indorsed to a third party for value is valid, and entitles the holder to recover upon it, even although he was aware at the time of taking it that it had been given for a gambling debt, as such a consideration is not illegal, but only voidable : [3] or (e) Where the bill is reducible by the granter's creditors.[4]

(1) Valuable consideration for a bill may be constituted (a) by any consideration sufficient to support a simple contract, as where it is given in security of past or future advances,[5] or by a discharged bankrupt for the amount of a debt due before sequestration ; [6] or (b) by an antecedent debt or liability, and such a debt or liability is deemed valuable consideration whether the bill be payable on demand or at a future time. The renewal of a bill or note invalid originally for want of consideration does not make it valid.[7] A mere moral obligation or a voluntary gift of money does not constitute valuable consideration.[8]

Holder for Value.—(2) Where value has at any time been given for a bill, the holder is deemed to be a holder for value as regards the

---

[1] See *infra*, p. 123.

[2] Young *v.* Gordon, 1896, 23 R. 419.

[3] Lilley *v.* Rankin, 56 L.J. Q.B. 248.

[4] See Sequestration, *infra*.

[5] Glen *v.* National Bank, 1849, 12 D. 353 ; Stott *v.* Fairlamb, 53 L.J. Q.B. 47.

[6] Clark *v.* Clark, 1869, 7 M. 335 ; Macdonald *v.* Union Bank, 1864, 2 M. 963 ; Young *v.* Sheridan, 1837, 15 S. 664 ; Gibson *v.* Rutherglen, 1842, 1 Bell's App. 519 ; Broch *v.* Newlands, 1863, 2 M. 71.

[7] Edwards *v.* Chancellor, 52 J.P. 454, *following* Forman *v.* Wright, 1851, 11 C.B. 481.

[8] Flight *v.* Reed, 1763, 32 L.J. Ex. 265 ; Hill *v.* Wilson, 1873, L.R. 8 Ch. 894.

acceptor and all parties to the bill who became parties prior to such time. (3) Where the holder of the bill has a lien on it, arising either from contract or by implication of law, he is deemed to be a holder for value to the extent of the sum for which he has a lien.[1]

28. Accommodation Party.—An accommodation *bill* is one in which the acceptor, that is, the principal debtor *ex facie* of the bill, is in substance a mere surety for some other person, who may or may not be a party to the bill; but a bill which is signed by one or more accommodation parties is not, correctly, an accommodation bill. Thus a bill drawn for the accommodation of the acceptor is not an accommodation bill, though the drawer is an accommodation party. An accommodation bill is discharged when it is paid by the person who is really, though not *ex facie*, the principal debtor,[2] or if time be given to such person.[3] An accommodation *party* to a bill is a person who has signed a bill as drawer, acceptor, or indorser, without receiving value therefor,[4] and for the purpose of lending his name to some other person. While the rights of the various parties to an accommodation bill are regulated according to the real nature of their various obligations, *prima facie* they are entitled to relief *inter se*. Accordingly the acceptor of a bill admitted or proved to have been given without valuable consideration must, to free himself of a claim for relief by a drawer or indorser who has paid the bill, prove that he accepted it for such person's accommodation.[5] Thus in one case a person received a blank acceptance for his accommodation on the understanding, though there was no actual agreement, that he should fill up the bill for a certain amount, and at a certain usance, and sign it himself as drawer. He, however, induced another, to whom he was indebted, to sign the bill as drawer and discount it, applying the proceeds towards the reduction of the debt. The person accommodated having become bankrupt and having failed to retire the bill, the acceptor was held bound to pay the bill according to his obligation.[6] Where the acceptor and indorser are both accommodation parties, there is a presumption, which may be rebutted by proof,[7] that the indorser who has retired the bill at maturity is entitled to relief from the acceptor.[8] Joint acceptors in an accommodation bill are *prima facie* entitled to rateable relief *inter se*.[9] It is the duty of a drawer

---

[1] *Vide* Banker's Lien, *supra*.

[2] *Vide* sec. 59 (3).

[3] Oriental Financial Corporation *v.* Overend, 1871, L.R. 7 Ch. 142, and L.R. 7 H.L. 358.

[4] *Vide* sec. 27.

[5] Macgregor *v.* Gibson, 1831, 9 S. 483 ; Crosbie *v.* Brown, 1900, 3 F. 83.

[6] Russell *v.* Banknock Coal Co., 1897, 24 R. 1009 ; 5 S.L.T. 73.

[7] *Vide* sec. 100.

[8] Beveridge *v.* Liddell, 1852, 14 D. 328 ; Reynolds *v.* Wheeler, 30 L.J. C.P. 326.

[9] Laing *v.* Anderson, 1827, 5 S. 851.

or indorser for whose accommodation a bill is accepted to provide funds to meet the bill at maturity, and consequently such a party cannot, as a rule, avail himself of want of due presentment for payment, notice of dishonour, or protest.[1]

(2) An accommodation party is liable on the bill to a holder for value ; and it is immaterial whether, when such holder took the bill, he knew such party to be an accommodation party or not. The fact that the holder allows time to a co-acceptor,[2] who is the real debtor, or discharges one obligant on the bill, while reserving his rights against the others,[3] does not discharge the acceptor for accommodation. The ordinary rule that payment or satisfaction by the drawer to the holder does not discharge the holder's claim against the acceptor, does not apply when the bill has been accepted for the accommodation of the drawer.[4]

Cross accommodation bills are bills which are mutually exchanged between parties, A. accepting a bill for the accommodation of B., and B. for the accommodation of A., for like amounts and of the same date and currency. It is a general rule of law that such bills are respectively good considerations for each other, and if up to the due date they have not been discharged they are then held as extinguished by compensation, the one bill being set off against the other, and neither party having a claim against the other.

Position of Parties in Event of Bankruptcy.—Where both parties become bankrupt while the bills remain undiscounted there is no ranking upon either estate in respect of the bills, since they are held to mutually extinguish each other. Where both parties are bankrupt and only one of the parties has discounted his bills, the onerous holder of the bills is entitled to rank upon both estates to the effect of recovering on the whole 20s. in the £, and the trustee on the estate of the person who has not discounted his bills is not entitled to any relief from the trustee on the other estate, since the bill-holder having already ranked in respect of the bill, no further ranking is allowed, as there would then be a double ranking upon the same estate, which is incompetent.[5] Where both parties are bankrupt and both bills have been discounted, the bill-holder is entitled to rank upon both estates for the *cumulo* amount of the two bills, and there can be no ranking of the one estate against the other on account of any excess it may have been called upon to pay. Where one of the parties alone is bankrupt and the other takes up all the bills, the person

---

[1] *Vide* secs. 46 (2), 50 (2), 51 (9).
[2] Lyon *v.* Butter, 1841, 4 D. 178.
[3] Lewis *v.* Anstruther, 1852, 15 D. 260.
[4] *Per* Stephen, J., in Solomon *v.* Davis, 1 C. & E. 83 ; *vide* sec. 59.
[5] See Sequestration (Double Ranking).

ho takes up the bills has only a ranking upon the bankrupt estate of he other party for the bills on which the bankrupt appears as the cceptor, but he has no claim upon those bills upon which the bankrupt ppears as drawer, even although the dividend received by him is much ss than the bankrupt's proper share of liability on the bills.

29. Holder in Due Course.—(1) A holder in due course is a older who has taken a bill, complete and regular on the face of it (that , not wanting, or bearing signs of alteration in, any material particular),[1] efore it was overdue,[2] and without notice that it had been previously ishonoured, if such was the fact ; provided that he took it in good ith,[3] and for value,[4] and that at the time the bill was negotiated to him e had no notice (or knowledge) of *any* [5] defect in the title of the person ho negotiated it. But if *ex facie* of the bill there is a warning conveyed, he holder, however honest, cannot acquire a better right to it than the erson from whom he took it had. Notice as here used does not ecessarily imply formal notice, but either knowledge of the facts or suspicion of something wrong combined with a wilful disregard of e means of knowledge.[6] No one can be a holder in due course of a ill the signature to which has been forged or adhibited without uthority.[7]

(2) In particular, the title of a person who negotiates [8] a bill is efective if he obtained the bill, or the acceptance of it, by fraud,[9] uress, force and fear,[10] or other unlawful means, or for an illegal onsideration,[11] or when he negotiates it in breach of faith,[12] or under ach circumstances as amount to a fraud. A person whose title is efective is to be distinguished from one who has no title at all.[13]

(3) A holder (that is, the payee or indorsee in possession, or bearer), hether for value or not, who derives his title to a bill through a holder due course, and who is not himself a party to any fraud or illegality

---

[1] *E.g.* absence of drawer's name, South Wales, etc., Coal Co. *v.* Underwood & Sons,)th January 1899, L.R. Q.B.D. ; *vide* sec. 64.

[2] *Vide* secs. 14, 36 (3).

[3] *Vide* sec. 90.

[4] *Vide* sec. 27 ; Jones *v.* Gordon, 2 Ap. Ca. 616, 632.

[5] Jones *v.* Gordon, *supra.*

[6] Raphael *v.* Bank of England, 1885, 17 C.B. at p. 174 ; Whistler *v.* Forster, 1863, 2 L.J. C.P. at p. 163 ; Currie *v.* Misa, 1875, L.R. 10 Ex. at p. 164 ; M'Lean *v.* Clydes- ale Bank, 1883, 9 Ap. Ca. at p. 114 ; Jones *v.* Gordon, 2 Ap. Ca. 616, 632.

[7] *Vide* sec. 24 ; Cheques, p. 180.

[8] *Vide* secs. 31-38.

[9] *Vide ante* ; Smith *v.* Bank of Scotland, 1829, 7 S. 244 ; Couston *v.* Miller, 1862, 4 D. 607 ; Home *v.* Hardy, 1842, 4 D. 1184.

[10] Gelot *v.* Stewart, 1870, 8 M. 649.

[11] *Vide* sec. 27.

[12] *Vide* Thomson *v.* M'Lauchline, 1823, 2 S. 497.

[13] *Vide* sec. 24.

affecting it, has all the rights of that holder in due course, as regards th
acceptor and all parties to the bill prior to that holder.[1]

30. Presumption of Value.—(1) Every party whose signature
appears on a bill is *prima facie* deemed to have become a party theret
for value.[3]

Holder Presumed to be in Due Course.—(2) Every holder of a bill
prima facie deemed to be a holder in due course, but this presumptio
may be overcome by parole evidence ; and if in an action [4] on a bi
it is admitted or proved that the acceptance, issue, or subsequer
negotiation of the bill is affected with fraud, duress, force and fear, c
illegality, the burden of proof is shifted, unless and until the holde
proves that, subsequent to the alleged fraud or illegality, value ha
in good faith been given for the bill.[5] When, however, fraud i
proved, the burden of proof is on the holder to prove both tha
value has been given and that it has been given in good faith withou
notice of the fraud.[6]

4. Negotiation of Bills

31. What Constitutes Negotiation.—(1) A bill is negotiated whe
it is transferred from one person to another in such a manner as t
constitute the transferee the holder of the bill. Thus the delivery c
unindorsed bills to a person is not negotiation of them, though th
conversion of a simple transferee into a holder is.[7] (2) A bill payabl
to bearer is negotiated by delivery.[8] (3) A bill payable to order i
negotiated by the indorsement of the holder completed by delivery
An agent having authority to do so, an executor, or a trustee i
bankruptcy, may negotiate bills for a named holder.

Transfer for Value without Indorsation.—(4) Where the holder c
a bill payable to his order transfers it for value without indorsing i₁
the transfer gives the transferee such title as the transferror had in th
bill, and the transferee in addition acquires the right to have the indorse
ment of the transferror (in which case the transfer takes effect from th
time when the indorsement is given). The delivery of a bill by th
holder to a person for value without indorsation is equivalent to a
intimated assignation of the sum contained in the bill. The transfe

---

[1] *Vide* secs. 20, 21 (2), 38, 54 (2), 55, 56, 64, 88 (2) ; *vide* May *v.* Chapman, 184'
16 M. & W. 355.

[2] *Vide* secs. 3, 17, 20, 91.

[3] *Vide* sec. 27 ; Foster *v.* Dawber, 1851, 6 Ex. at p. 853.

[4] *Vide* secs. 31-37.

[5] Jones *v.* Gordon, 1877, 2 Ap. Ca. 627 (*per* Lord Blackburn).

[6] Tatam *v.* Haslar, 58 L.J. Q.B. 432, L.R. 23 Q.B.D. 345.

[7] Day *v.* Longhurst (*per* Stirling, J.), 1893, Weekly Notes, 3.

[8] *Vide* sec. 21.

vests the transferror of all title to the bill, and invests the transferee
ith the title of the transferror, the divestiture and investiture being
oth completed by the act of transference. Henceforward the title
f the transferror is in the transferee, not in the sense that the latter
entitled to make use of a title which is still in the transferror, but in
ne sense that the title of the transferror is in the person of the trans-
eree. In other words, the transferee has a title equivalent to a duly
timated assignation. The title given by a transference differs, how-
ver, from that given by indorsation in that, while an indorser may
onfer a better title than he himself possesses, a transferee acquires his
tle subject to any exceptions and objections competent against his
ransferror's title.[1] But the transference by delivery of a promissory
ote, as a pledge to secure repayment, but without the intention to
ansfer the transferror's whole rights in it, has been held not to fall
ithin the scope of this section.[2]

(5) Where any person is under obligation to indorse a bill in a
presentative capacity, he may indorse it in such terms as to negative
ersonal liability.[3]

32. Indorsation.—*Requisites.*—An indorsement, to operate as a
egotiation, must comply with the following conditions :—

(1) It must be written [4] on the bill itself, and be signed [4] by the
dorser. An indorsement in pencil is a sufficient indorsement. Simple
ignature, even on the face of the bill,[5] without additional words is
ufficient. The fact that a person writes his name on the back of
bill and hands it to another does not necessarily constitute him an
dorser,[6] though it may render him liable as a guarantor. Thus where
person indorsed a bill, to the effect that in case of non-payment by
he acceptor the bill was to be presented to him, it was held that
lthough he could not be sued as an indorser, he was liable as a
uarantor.[7] An indorsement written on an *allonge*, that is, a slip of
aper attached to the bill, or on a " copy " of a bill issued or negotiated
n a country where " copies " are recognised, is deemed to be written on
he bill itself.

Partial Indorsement.—(2) The indorsement must be an indorse-
ent of the entire bill. A partial indorsement—that is, an indorse-
ent which purports to transfer to the indorsee a part only of the
mount payable, or which purports to transfer the bill to two or more

---

[1] Hood *v.* Stewart, 1890, 17 R. 749.
[2] Good *v.* Walker (*per* Cave, J.), 61 L.J. Q.B. 736 ; *vide* sec. 8.
[3] *Vide* secs. 16 (1) and 26.
[4] *Vide* sec. 3.
[5] Young *v.* Glover, 1857, 3 Jur. (N.S.) Q.B. 637.
[6] Westacott *v.* Smalley, 1 C. & E. 124.
[7] Stagg, Mantle & Co. *v.* Brodrick, 1895, 12 T.L.R. 12 ; *vide infra.*

indorsees severally—does not operate as a negotiation of the bill. There seems to be nothing, however, to prevent the holder, after securing a payment to account, negotiating the bill *quoad* the balance for then that is the sum payable.

Several Payees or Indorsees.—(3) Where a bill is payable to the order of two or more payees or indorsees who are not partners (and even then if the business be not one where power to indorse is presumed),[2] all must indorse, unless the one indorsing has authority to indorse for the others.

Misdescription of Payee or Indorsee.—(4) Where, in a bill payable to order, the payee or indorsee is wrongly designated, or his name mis-spelt, he may indorse the bill as therein described, adding, if he think fit, his proper signature.[3] If the proper signature is not added, summary diligence is incompetent.

Order of Indorsements.—(5) Where there are two or more indorse-ments on a bill, each indorsement is deemed to have been made in the order in which it appears on the bill, until the contrary is proved.

Kinds of Indorsements.—(6) An indorsement may be made in blank or special.[4] It may also contain terms making it restrictive or conditional.[6]

33. *Conditional Indorsation.*—Where a bill purports to be indorsed conditionally, the condition may be disregarded by the payer, and payment to the indorsee is valid whether the condition has been fulfilled or not.

34. *Blank Indorsement.*—(1) An indorsement in blank specifies no indorsee, and a bill so indorsed becomes payable to bearer. A blank indorsement may be made either by writing a simple signature on the bill or by writing above the signature the words " Pay to ——— or order," or " Pay to ——— or bearer." A blank indorsement followed by a special indorsement remains payable to bearer, but the holder must cancel the indorsements subsequent to the blank indorsement. A person taking a bill in such circumstances may be affected by notice that his transferror's title is defective.[7]

Special Indorsement.—(2) A special indorsement specifies the person to whom, or to whose order, the bill is to be payable.[8] " Pay to A. B.," " Pay to A. B. or order," or " Pay to A. B.'s order," are special indorse-ments. (3) The provisions relating to a payee apply, with the necessary modifications, to an indorsee under a special indorsement.[9]

Conversion of Blank into Special Indorsement.—(4) When a bill has

---

[1] *Vide* secs. 7 (2), 34 (3) ; Heilbut *v.* Nevill, 1869, L.R. 4 C.P. 358.
[2] Garland *v.* Jacomb, L.R. 8 Ex. 216, Ex. Ch.
[3] *Vide* Cheques, *infra.*   [4] *Vide* sec. 34.   [5] *Vide* sec. 35.
[6] *Vide* sec. 33.   [7] Crook *v.* Jadis, 5 B. & Ad. 909.
[8] *Vide* sec. 8 (4), (5).   [9] *Vide* sec. 7.

een indorsed in blank, any holder may convert the blank indorsement into a special indorsement by writing above the indorser's signature direction to pay the bill to, or to the order of, himself or some other person.

Restrictive Indorsement.—(5) Where a restrictive indorsement authorises further transfer,[1] all subsequent indorsees take the bill with the same rights, and subject to the same liabilities, as the first indorsee under the restrictive indorsement.

35. (1) An indorsement is restrictive which prohibits the further negotiation[2] of the bill, or which expresses that it is a mere authority to deal with the bill as thereby directed, and not a transfer of the ownership thereof, as, for example, if a bill be indorsed " Pay D. only," or " Pay D. for the account of X.," or " Pay D. or order for collection." " Pay to A. B. or order, value in account with C. D.," is not a restrictive indorsement, but in effect a simple indorsement " to A. B. or order." [3]

Rights and Powers of Restricted Indorsee.—(2) A restrictive indorsement gives the indorsee the right to receive payment[4] of the bill, and to sue any party thereto that his indorser could have sued, but gives him no power to transfer his rights as indorsee unless it expressly authorises him to do so. A person to whom a bill is restrictively indorsed for collection, and who pays the amount of the bill to the indorser, cannot, because of such payment, acquire rights on the bill against the acceptor, where the amount is paid to the indorser before maturity.[5] The indorsee may delegate his duty of collection to a third party, if the words " or order " are added to the indorsation, but under an indorsation such as " Pay A. B. for my account," A. B. cannot authorise a third party to collect it for him.

Negotiation of Overdue Bills.—(1) A bill which is negotiable in its origin [6] continues to be negotiable until it has been restrictively indorsed, or discharged by payment or otherwise.[7] The fact that an action has been brought on a dishonoured bill does not operate to make the bill non-negotiable. (2) An overdue bill [8] can only be negotiated subject to any defect of title [9] affecting it at its maturity, and thenceforward no person who takes it can acquire or give a better title [10] than that which the person from whom he took it had. A bill of exchange payable on demand is ordinarily given for purpose of present payment. The reasonable time allowed for presentment will necessarily vary, to a certain extent, with the circumstances. In the case of an ordinary cheque— which, of course, is a bill of exchange payable on demand, drawn on

---

[1] *Vide* sec. 35.
[3] Buckley *v.* Jackson, L.R. 3 Ex. 135.
[5] Williams *v.* Shadbolt (*per* Cave, J.), 1 C. & E. 529.
[6] *Vide* sec. 8.
[8] *Vide* secs. 11, 14.
[10] *Vide* secs. 29 (3), 38.

[2] *Vide* sec. 31.
[4] *Vide* secs. 38 and 59.
[7] *Vide* secs. 61-64.
[9] *Vide* sec. 29 (2).

a banker—the period permissible is very short, at most a matter of days
Bills of exchange payable on demand are perhaps not precisely on the
same footing as cheques ; yet it is evident that it is out of the ordinary
course to hold such documents up for a protracted period. In private
transactions, where the bills do not go into the circle, it is not uncommon
to take such bills by way of security and to hold them up indefinitely
but that is not the mode in which they are normally used in the mercantile
community. The form of instrument appropriate for use as a continuing
security is a promissory note, and the distinction between such notes
and bills has long been established and recognised in section 86 of the
Act. It has accordingly been decided that in the case of a bill drawn by
a mercantile firm or a mercantile company, both carrying on business in
Glasgow, the lapse of nine months between its issue and its negotiation
was not a reasonable time over which to hold up such a bill and that
the bill was therefore " overdue " within the meaning of this section.
(3) A bill payable on demand [2] is deemed to be overdue when it appears
on the face of it to have been in circulation for an unreasonable length
of time, which is a question of fact.[3]

Presumption as to Date of Negotiations.—(4) Except where an indorse
ment bears date after the maturity of the bill, every negotiation is
primâ facie deemed to have been effected before the bill was overdue
An undated indorsement is, in Scotland, presumed to have been made
of the same date as the bill. The date of an indorsement is presumed
to be the true date, in absence of proof to the contrary.[4]

Negotiation of Dishonoured Bills.—(5) Any person who takes a
dishonoured bill [5] which is not overdue, with notice of the dishonour
takes it subject to any defect of title attaching thereto at the time of
dishonour ; but nothing in this subsection affects the rights of a holder
in due course.[6] A bill known to be dishonoured is thus upon the same
footing as one overdue.

37. *Negotiation to Party Already Liable.*—Where a bill is negotiated
back to the drawer or to a prior indorser,[7] or to the acceptor,[8] such
party may, subject to the provisions of the Act,[9] reissue and further
negotiate the bill, but he is not entitled to enforce payment of the bill
against any intervening party to whom he was previously liable. No
action, it has been held, lies by a firm as indorsers of a bill against the
indorsers, if a member of that firm be one of the indorsers.[10] An accepto

---

[1] Easdale Slate Quarries Co. Ltd. *v.* Reid, 1910, 2 S.L.T. 295, *per* Lord Cullen
The case was decided on another ground on appeal, but the learned Judges did no
dissent from Lord Cullen's judgment.

[2] *Vide* sec. 10.

[3] *Vide* Rothschild *v.* Corney, 9 B. & C. 388 ; sec. 86 ; Cheques.

[4] *Vide* sec. 13 (1) ; Lewis *v.* Parker, 1836, 4 A. & E. 838.

[5] *Vide* sec. 43.   [6] *Vide* secs. 29, 38.   [7] *Cf.* sec. 59 (2).

[8] *Vide* sec. 59 (1).   [9] *Vide* secs. 59-64.   [10] Forster *v.* Ward, 1 C. & E. 16

who is the holder at or after maturity cannot reissue the bill,[1] nor can a drawer or indorser who is an accommodated party, if he have paid the bill in due course.[2]

5. Rights and Duties of Holder

38. Rights and Powers of Holder.—(1) He may sue on the bill in his own name, and is entitled to maintain an action on the bill in his own name against any or all of the parties liable on it, unless it can be shown that he holds the bill adversely to the interests of the true owner. He may also proceed with summary diligence or claim in a multiple-poinding [3] or found on the bill as a ground of compensation. If, however, a bill be payable to a specified person or persons, any action on the bill must be raised in the name of such person or persons. A holder, who might have sued a party to a bill, is entitled to claim against such party's estate in bankruptcy. (2) If a holder in due course, he holds the bill free from any defect of title of prior parties, as well as from mere personal defences available to prior parties among themselves, and may enforce payment against all parties liable on the bill.[4] (3) Where his title is defective (as, for example, if he be a thief, finder, or one who has obtained the bill by fraud or violence),[5] if he negotiate the bill to a holder in due course, that holder obtains a good and complete title to the bill, and if he obtain payment of the bill, the person who pays him in due course gets a valid discharge for the bill. The *right* to negotiate a bill, which is an incident of ownership, is not to be confounded with the *power* to negotiate it, which is an incident of apparent ownership. On the death of a holder his rights pass to his executors, and on his bankruptcy, if he be the beneficial owner of the bill, or if the bill be payable to a bankrupt for his own account, his rights pass to his trustee ; but if the holder be not the beneficial owner of the bill (and provided that he was not the reputed owner of it), the title does not pass to the trustee. The holder may transfer a bill as a *donatio mortis causâ*.[6]

39. General Duties of Holder.—A party to a bill who is discharged from liability by reason of the holder's omission to perform any duty is also discharged from liability on the debt or consideration for which the bill was given.

Presentment for Acceptance.—(1) Where a bill is payable after

---

[1] *Vide* sec. 61.
[2] *Vide* sec. 59 (3) ; also secs. 62-64.
[3] Agnew *v.* Whyte, 1899, 1 F. 1026.
[4] *Vide* secs. 20, 21, 29 (3), 54-56, 64, 88. See Lewis *v.* Clay, sec. 24.
[5] *Vide* sec. 29 (2).
[6] Austin *v.* Mead, 1880, 15 Ch. D. 651.

9

sight,[1] presentment for acceptance is necessary in order to fix the maturity of the instrument. An acceptor ought to date his acceptance, but the want of the date does not affect the maturity of the bill. It is competent to the holder to insert the true date. If, however, he insert a wrong date in good faith and by mistake, and the bill with such wrong date subsequently come into the hands of a holder in due course, the insertion of the wrong date renders the bill payable on that date.[2] (2) Where a bill expressly stipulates that it shall be presented for acceptance, or where a bill is drawn payable elsewhere than at the residence or place of business of the drawee, it must be presented for acceptance to the drawee, or to some one authorised to act for him, before it can be presented for payment. (3) In no other case is presentment necessary in order to render liable any party to the bill.[3] Thus a bill expressed " pay without acceptance " is valid.

Excusable Delay in Presenting.—(4) Where the holder of a bill drawn payable elsewhere than at the place of business or residence of the drawee has not time, with the exercise of reasonable diligence (which varies according to circumstances [4]), to present the bill for acceptance before presenting it for payment on the day it falls due, the delay caused by presenting the bill for acceptance before presenting it for payment is excused, and does not, as in the ordinary case, discharge the drawer and indorsers.

40. *Presentment of Bill Payable after Sight.*—(1) When a bill payable after sight is negotiated, the holder must either present it for acceptance,[5] or negotiate [6] it within a reasonable time.[7] (2) If he does not do so, the drawer and all indorsers prior to that holder are discharged. (3) In determining what is reasonable time regard is had to the nature of the bill, the usage of trade [8] with respect to similar bills, and the facts of the particular case,[9] and to the interests of the holder as well as those of the drawer and indorsers. The time will be reckoned from the date when the holder receives the bill and with reference to the time each successive holder keeps the bill.[10]

41. *Rules for Presentment for Acceptance.*—(1) A bill is duly presented for acceptance which is presented according to the following rules :—

By Whom, to Whom, and When.—(a) The presentment must be made by or on behalf of the holder, to the drawee or to some person

---

[1] *Vide* sec. 40. [2] *Vide* secs. 12, 13, 20. [3] *Vide* sec. 42.
[4] Gladwell *v.* Turner, 1870, L.R. 5 Ex. 59.
[5] *Vide* sec. 41. [6] *Vide* sec. 31.
[7] *Vide* secs. 5 (2), 38, 41 (2).
[8] *Vide* Mellish *v.* Rawdon, 9 Bing. 416.
[9] *Vide* Shute *v.* Robins, 1828, 2 C. & P. 80 ; Straker *v.* Graham, 1839, 4 M. & W. 721 ; Mullick *v.* Radakissen, 1854, 9 Moore P.C. 46.
[10] *Vide* Muilman *v.* D'Equino, 2 H. Bl. 65 ; Mullick *v.* Radakissen, *supra*.

authorised to accept or refuse acceptance on his behalf,[1] at a reasonable hour, that is, during business or bank hours, in the case of a merchant or banker,[2] on a business day,[3] and before the bill is overdue.[4] Where the drawee is not in business, it is a jury question whether the bill has been presented in reasonable hours. Where a bill is drawn on a firm whose business entitles a partner to accept bills, presentment to one of the partners is sufficient. Where a bill is drawn on a company incorporated under the Companies Acts, presentment must be. made to a person who has the authority of the company to accept bills.[5]

Two or more Drawees.—(*b*) A bill addressed to two or more drawees, who are not partners, must be presented to them all, unless one has authority to accept for all. A bill addressed to several drawees, acceptance of which is refused by one, need not be presented to the others,[6] since such an acceptance is qualified, and the taking of it, without the assent, express or implied, of the drawer and indorsers discharges them.

Drawee Dead or Bankrupt.—(*c*) Where the drawee is dead, presentment may be made to his personal representatives, and (*d*) where he is bankrupt, to him or to his trustee. (*e*) Where it is authorised by agreement or usage, presentment through the post-office is sufficient.[7]

Cases in which Presentment is Excused.—(2) Presentment in accordance with these rules is excused, and a bill may be treated as dishonoured by non-acceptance : (*a*) where the drawee is dead or bankrupt, or is a fictitious person, or a person not having capacity to contract by bill ; [8] (*b*) where, after the exercise of reasonable diligence, such presentment cannot be effected ; (*c*) where, though the presentment has been irregular, acceptance has been refused on some other ground, as, for example, where the bill has been presented on a non-business day or after hours, and refused on the ground of want of funds.

(3) The fact that the holder has reason to believe that the bill on presentment will be dishonoured does not excuse presentment. Presentment for acceptance differs from presentment for payment, in that it should be *personal* and that it is immaterial where it is made, whereas presentment for payment should be *local* and where the money is. The distinction may be material in deciding whether the holder has used reasonable diligence in presenting.

42. Non-acceptance.—When a bill is duly presented for acceptance, and is not accepted within the customary time, the person presenting

---

[1] *Vide* sec. 27 ; 25 & 26 Vict. cap. 89, sec. 47.
[2] *Vide* Neilson *v.* Leighton, 1843, 5 D. 513 ; 6 D. 622.
[3] *Vide* sec. 93.
[4] *Vide* secs. 14, 45 (2).
[5] Companies (Consolidation) Act, 1908, sec. 77.
[6] *Vide* secs. 19, 44 (1).
[7] *Vide* secs. 45 (8), 49 (15).   [8] *Vide* sec. 5 (2).

it must treat it as dishonoured by non-acceptance. If he do not, the holder loses his right of recourse against the drawer and indorsers. The drawee may require that the bill be left with him for acceptance, and he is entitled to retain it for the customary period, which is usually twenty-four hours, but varies according to the custom of the place of presentment. On the lapse of this time, however, he must deliver it, accepted or not accepted.[1]

43. Dishonour by Non-acceptance.—(1) A bill is dishonoured by non-acceptance (*a*) when it is duly presented for acceptance,[2] and such an acceptance as is prescribed by the Act[3] is refused or cannot be obtained ;[4] or (*b*) when presentment for acceptance is excused[5] and the bill is not accepted.

Consequences.—(2) Subject to the provisions of the Act,[6] when a bill is dishonoured by non-acceptance, an immediate right of recourse against the drawer and indorsers accrues to the holder, and no presentment for payment is necessary. Notice of dishonour must, however, be given and the bill protested where necessary.[7]

44. Qualified Acceptance.—(1) The holder of a bill may refuse to take a qualified acceptance,[8] and if he does not obtain an unqualified acceptance may treat the bill as dishonoured by non-acceptance. (2) Where a qualified acceptance is taken, and the drawer or an indorser has not expressly or impliedly authorised the holder to take a qualified acceptance, or does not subsequently assent thereto, such drawer or indorser is discharged from his liability on the bill. This does not apply to a partial acceptance of which due notice has been given.[9] Where a foreign bill, that is, one which appears *ex facie* to be foreign,[10] has been accepted as to part, it must be protested as to the balance.[11] The notice should be of a partial acceptance, not of dishonour. (3) When the drawer or indorser of a bill receives notice of a qualified acceptance, and does not within a reasonable time (which depends on the circumstances of each particular case) express his dissent to the holder, he is deemed to have assented thereto.

45. Presentment for Payment.—Subject to the provisions of the Act,[12] a bill must be duly presented for payment, except in the cases where presentment is excused. Presentment for payment implies a

---

[1] Bank of Van Diemen's Land *v.* Bank of Victoria, L.R. 3 P.C. 526.

[2] *Vide* sec. 41 (1).

[3] *Vide* secs. 17, 19, 44.

[4] *Vide ex parte* Commercial Bank of Sydney (*per* North, J.), 57 L.J. Ch. 131.

[5] *Vide* sec. 41 (2).

[6] *Vide* secs. 16, 22, 40, 48-51, 64, 65.

[7] Castrique *v.* Bernabo, 1844, 6 Q.B. 498.

[8] *Vide* sec. 19.

[9] *Vide* sec. 49.   [10] *Vide* secs. 4, 51 (2).   [11] *Vide* secs. 51, 73 (2).

[12] *Vide* secs. 39 (4), 43, 46, 66, and 67.

demand for payment.[1] If it be not so presented, the drawer and indorsers are discharged,[2] not only of all liability on the bill itself, but of the debt for which the bill was granted.[3] The liability of the *acceptor* is independent of presentation, and he is liable in terms of his obligation without the necessity of being charged for payment.[4]

Requisites.—A bill is duly presented for payment which is presented in accordance with the following rules :—

(1) When the bill is not payable on demand, presentment must be made on the day it falls due, that is, the last day of grace.[5] (2) When the bill is payable on demand,[6] then, subject to the provisions of the Act, presentment must be made within a reasonable time after its issue, in order to render the drawer liable, and within a reasonable time after its indorsement, in order to render the indorser liable. In determining what is a reasonable time, regard is had to the nature of the bill, the usage of trade with regard to similar bills, and the facts of the particular case.[7] (3) Presentment must be made by the holder (that is, the bearer in a bill payable to bearer, and the payee or indorsee in a bill payable to order, but not a person holding under a forged indorsement [8]), or by some person authorised to receive payment on his behalf,[9] at a reasonable hour,[10] on a business day,[11] at the proper place as after defined, either to the person designated by the bill as payer (that is, either the drawee or acceptor, or, if the bill be payable elsewhere than at the drawee's residence or place of business, the person with whom it is domiciled [12]), or to some person authorised to pay or refuse payment on his behalf, if with the exercise of reasonable diligence such person can there be found. The reasonableness of the hour depends on circumstances. If a bill is domiciled at a bank it must be presented during bank hours ; if at a trader's place of business, then within business hours ; if at a dwelling-house, presentment at any time before bedtime may be sufficient.[13] It is not necessary to present to the referee in case of need.[14] Presentment is not excused because of the acceptor's or drawee's bankruptcy, and presentment must be made to the bankrupt and not to his trustee. In the case of a company being wound up, presentment is made to the liquidator.[15]

---

[1] *Per* Lord Ordinary in Bartsch *v.* Poole & Co., 1895, 23 R. 328.

[2] *Vide* sec. 5 (2).

[3] Peacock *v.* Purssell, 1863, 32 L.J. C.P. 266.

[4] *Vide* sec. 52 ; Gordon *v.* Kerr, 1898, 25 R. 570.

[5] *Vide* sec. 14.   [6] *Vide* sec. 10.   [7] *Vide* secs. 40, 86.

[8] *Vide* sec. 24.

[9] Griffin *v.* Weatherby, 1868, L.R. 3 Q.B., at pp. 760, 761.

[10] *Vide* sec. 41.   [11] *Vide* sec. 93.

[12] Presentment to acceptor personally of a bill payable at his bankers is unnecessary.

[13] Wilkins *v.* Jadis, 1831, 2 B. & Ad. 188.   [14] *Vide* sec. 15.

[15] *In re* Agra Bank, *ex parte* Tondeur, L.R. 5 Eq. 160.

Proper Place.—(4) A bill is presented at the proper place (*a*) where a place of payment is specified in the bill, and the bill is there presented.[1] Presentment to the acceptor anywhere is not sufficient where a place of payment is specified.[2] Where a bill is addressed to the drawee at his residence, and there is no specific place of payment stated, presentment at the acceptor's place of business is not sufficient. It must be presented at the residence specified.[3] Where a bill is domiciled at a bank in a town in which there is a clearing-house, presentment through the clearing-house is deemed presentment at the bank.[4] Where there are alternative places of payment, presentment at one of these places is sufficient. Where a bill is accepted payable at a particular place, and the acceptor dies before the bill matures, presentment at the place of payment is sufficient. It is also sufficient presentation if the bill be presented at the place of payment, although the acceptor may have left there;[5] (*b*) Where no place is specified, but the address of the drawee or acceptor is given in the bill, and the bill is there presented ; (*c*) Where no place of payment is specified, and no address given, and the bill is presented at the drawee's or acceptor's place of business if known, and if not, at his ordinary residence, if known ; (*d*) In any other case if presented to the drawee or acceptor wherever he can be found, or if presented at his last known place of business or residence.

(5) Where a bill is presented at the proper place, and after the exercise of reasonable diligence no person authorised to pay or refuse payment can be found there, no further presentment to the drawee or acceptor is required.

(6) Where a bill is drawn upon, or accepted by, two or more persons who are not partners, and no place of payment is specified, presentment must be made to all of them. In all cases, therefore, in which a bank is interested, where a bill is drawn on, or a promissory note is granted by, more than one person, care should be taken to have it made payable at some particular place. A refusal to pay on the part of one does not, as in the case of presentment for acceptance, dispense with presentment to the others.

(7) Where the drawee or acceptor of a bill is dead, and no place of payment is specified, presentment must be made to a personal representative, if such there be, and, with the exercise of reasonable diligence, he can be found.

(8) Where authorised by agreement or usage, a presentment through the post-office is sufficient.

---

[1] *Vide* sec. 19.
[2] Saul *v.* Jones, 1858, 28 L.J. Q.B. 37.
[3] Neill *v.* Dobson, Molle & Co., 1902, 4 F. 625.
[4] Boddington *v.* Schlencker, 1833, 4 B. & Ad. 752.
[5] Buxton *v.* Jones, 1840, 1 M. & Gr. 83.

46. *Excusable Delay in Presenting.*—(1) Delay in making present-ment for payment is excused when the delay is caused by circumstances beyond the control of the holder, and not imputable to his default, or misconduct, or negligence, as, for example, by his sudden illness or death,[1] or in consequence of unavoidable business, or his distance from the post-office. In one case, a bill drawn in 1872 on the Bank of Eng-land was presented for payment in 1880. The drawer had no funds in bank, but owned considerable Government securities. It was held that the delay in presenting did not release the drawer's estate, as he had no reason to believe, when the bill was drawn, that it would be paid.[2] When the cause of delay ceases to operate, presentment must be made with reasonable diligence.[3]

Presentment Dispensed with.—(2) Presentment for payment is dis-pensed with (*a*) where after the exercise of reasonable diligence present-ment as required by the Act cannot be effected. But the fact that the holder has reason to believe that the bill will, on presentment, be dis-honoured, does not dispense with the necessity of presentment.[4] Thus where the drawer of a bill, after maturity, wrote the holder, accepting notice of non-payment and admitting his liability to him in every way, as though presentment had been made in the regular way, it was held that the bill *de facto* not having been presented, though the drawer was ignorant of the fact, there was no dispensation by the drawer of the consequences of non-presentment for payment.[5] Nor does the fact of the acceptor's bankruptcy dispense with presentation :[6] (*b*) where the drawee is a fictitious person ;[7] (*c*) as regards the drawer, where the drawee or acceptor is not bound, as between himself and the drawer, to accept or pay the bill, and the drawer has no reason to believe that the bill would be paid if presented—as, for example, where the acceptor is an accommodation party and the drawer is bound to put him in funds to meet the bill ;[8] (*d*) as regards an indorser, where the bill was accepted or made for the accommodation of the indorser, and he has no reason to expect that the bill would be paid if presented ; (*e*) by waiver of pre-sentment, express or implied ; as where the drawer induces the holder to delay presentment,[9] or as where the acceptor having become bankrupt before maturity, and the holder did not present for payment, the drawers waived their right to plead non-presentment by letters subsequent to

---

[1] Rothschild *v.* Currie, 1841, 1 Q.B. 47.
[2] *In re* Boyse (*per* North, J.), 56 L.J. Ch. 135.   [3] *Vide* sec. 39.
[4] *Vide in re* Agra Bank, *ex parte* Tondeur, L.R. 5 Eq. 160.
[5] Keith *v.* Burke (*per* Pollock, B.), 1 C. & E. 551.
[6] Sands *v.* Clarke, 1849, 19 L.J. C.P. 84.
[7] *Vide* sec. 5.
[8] Turner *v.* Samson, 1876, 2 Q.B.D. 23, C.A. ; *in re* Bethnell, Weekly Notes, 1887, p. 17.
[9] Cairns' Trs. *v.* Brown, 1836, 14 S. 999.

the date of maturity, in which they asked for delay and by implication acknowledged their liability.[1]

47. Dishonour by Non-payment.—(1) A bill is dishonoured by non-payment when it is duly presented for payment,[2] and payment is refused or cannot be obtained, or when presentment is excused,[3] and the bill is overdue [4] and unpaid. Since the acceptor has the whole of the last day of grace in which to pay the bill, the holder has no right of action against him until the expiry of that day, though he is entitled at any time on the last day of grace to give notice of dishonour to the drawer and indorsees.[5] (2) Subject to the provisions of the Act,[6] when a bill is dishonoured by non-payment, an immediate right of recourse against the drawer and indorsers accrues to the holder.

48. *Notice of Dishonour.*—Subject to the provisions of the Act,[7] when a bill has been dishonoured by non-acceptance or non-payment,[8] notice of dishonour (that is, formal notice [9]) must be given to the drawer and each indorser, and any drawer or indorser to whom such notice is not given is discharged,[10] and that although the omission to give notice has caused them no injury. But where a bill is dishonoured by non-acceptance and notice of dishonour is not given, the rights of a holder in due course [11] subsequent to the omission are not prejudiced by the omission ; and where a bill is dishonoured by non-acceptance and due notice of dishonour is given, it is not necessary to give notice of a subsequent dishonour by non-payment unless the bill has in the meantime been accepted.[12]

49. *Requisites.*—Notice of dishonour, in order to be valid and effectual, must be given in accordance with the following rules :—

By Whom.—(1) The notice must be given by or on behalf of the holder, or by or on behalf of an indorser, who at the time of giving it is himself liable on the bill.[13] (2) Notice of dishonour may be given by an agent, authorised to do so, either in his own name or in the name of any party entitled to give notice, whether that party be his principal or not.

Effect of Notice by Holder.—(3) Where the notice is given by or on behalf of the holder, it enures for the benefit of all subsequent holders and all prior indorsers, who have a right of recourse against the party to whom it is given.

---

[1] Allhusen & Sons *v.* Mitchell & Co., 1870, 8 M. 600.

[2] *Vide* sec. 45.   [3] *Vide* sec. 46.   [4] *Vide* secs. 14, 45.

[5] Kennedy *v.* Thomas, 1894, L.R. 2 Q.B. 759.

[6] *Vide* secs. 16, 22, 48-51, 63 (2), 64, 67 (2) (4), 68 (7).

[7] *Vide* secs. 29, 36 (3), 38 (2), 50.   [8] *Vide* secs. 43, 47.

[9] Carter *v.* Flower, 1847, 16 M. & W. 749 ; Caunt *v.* Thomson, 1849, 18 L.J. C.P. 125.

[10] Berridge *v.* Fitzgerald, 1869, L.R. 4 Q.B., at p. 642.

[11] *Vide* sec. 29.   [12] *Vide* sec. 18 (3).   [13] *Vide* secs. 16, 40, 63 (2).

Effect of Notice by Indorser.—(4) Where notice is given by or on behalf of an indorser entitled to give notice as before provided, it ensures for the benefit of the holder and all indorsers subsequent to the party to whom notice is given.[1]

Mode of Giving Notice.—(5) The notice may be given in writing or by personal communication, and may be given in any terms which sufficiently identify the bill (as by specifying its date, sum,[2] and the parties to it), and intimate that the bill has been dishonoured by non-acceptance or non-payment, as the case may be. The fact of its having been noted or protested, and that recourse is claimed against the party to whom the notice is given, should be intimated. The onus of proving notice is on the holder.[3] The identification of the bill need only be such as to leave the party notified in no doubt as to the bill referred to, and consequently notice to a person unaccustomed to deal with bills, or who has his name only to one or two, need not be so detailed as that to a person in business, who is in the habit of frequently subscribing bills, and who therefore may have difficulty in identifying a particular bill in the absence of precise details.[4]

Implied Notice of Dishonour.—(6) The return of a dishonoured bill to the drawer or indorser is, in point of form, deemed a sufficient notice of dishonour.

Unsigned Notice.—(7) A written notice need not be signed.

Insufficient Notice.—An insufficient written notice may be supplemented and validated by verbal communication.

Wrong Description in Notice.—A misdescription of the bill, as, for example, where it is described as a note,[5] where it is wrongly said to be payable at a particular bank,[6] where the drawer is described as the acceptor,[7] or generally any misdescription which could not mislead the person to whom notice is given, does not vitiate the notice, unless the party to whom notice is given is in fact misled thereby. But where the notice is one which could not reasonably mislead a drawer or indorser, a mere plea to the effect that he was, in point of fact, misled is not sufficient.

To Whom Notice may be Given.—(8) Where notice of dishonour is required to be given to any person, it may be given either to himself or to his agent in that behalf. Notice to his solicitor is not, but notice to

---

[1] Lysaght v. Bryant, 1850, 19 L.J. C.P. 160.

[2] King v. Bickley, 1842, 11 L.J. 2 Q.B. 419 ; Maxwell v. Brain, 1864, 10 L.T. (N.S.) 301.

[3] Grayson v. Smith, 3 A. & E. 499.

[4] Skelton v. Braithewaite, 10 L.J. Ex. 218 ; Cook v. French, 9 L.J. Q.B. 281 ; King v. Bickley, 11 L.J. 2 Q.B. 419 ; Everard v. Watson, 22 L.J. Q.B. 222.

[5] Stockmann v. Parr, 12 L.J. Ex. 415.

[6] Bromage v. Vaughan, 16 L.J. Q.B. 10.

[7] Millers v. Kippen, 21 L.J. Ex. 222.

a merchant's clerk given at his counting-house is, sufficient.[1] Where a person acts as secretary of two companies, a fact which comes to his knowledge as secretary of one company is not notice to him as secretary of the other company, from the mere existence of the common relationship. In order to make it notice it must be shown that it was his duty to the first company to communicate his knowledge to the second company.[2] A referee in case of need is not, for this purpose, the agent of the person inserting his name.[3] (9) Where the drawer or indorser is dead and the party giving notice knows it, the notice must be given to a personal representative, if such there be, and, with the exercise of reasonable diligence, he can be found. (10) Where the drawer or indorser is bankrupt, notice may be given either to the party himself or to his trustee. (11) Where there are two or more drawers or indorsers who are not partners, notice must be given to each of them, unless one of them has authority to receive such notice for the others.

Time for Giving Notice.—(12) The notice may be given as soon as the bill is dishonoured, and must be given within a reasonable time thereafter.[4] In the absence of special circumstances,[5] notice is not deemed to have been given within a reasonable time, unless (a) where the person giving and the person to receive notice reside in the same place, the notice be given or sent off in time to reach the latter on the day after the dishonour of the bill, non-business days being excluded ; [6] or (b) where the person giving and the person to receive notice reside in different places, the notice be sent off on the day after the dishonour of the bill, if there be a post at a convenient hour on that day, and if there be no such post on that day, then by the next post thereafter, non-business days being excluded.[6] In one case, a bill which had been received by a country bank from a customer was forwarded to the London bank, and was presented for payment and dishonoured on a Saturday, and on the following Monday notice of dishonour was given by returning it to the branch bank from which it had been sent for presentation. By inadvertence the letter was wrongly addressed, and on the day following notice of dishonour was correctly given by telegram. It was held that the letter and telegram constituted one continuing act, and that notice of dishonour had been timeously given.[7]

Notice by Agent.—(13) Where a bill when dishonoured is in the hands of an agent, he may either himself give notice to the parties liable on the bill, or he may give notice to his principal. If he give notice to his

---

[1] Viale v. Michael, 1874, 13 L.T. (N.S.) 453.

[2] *In re* Fenwick, Stobart & Co. Ltd., 1902, 1 Ch. 507.

[3] *In re* Leeds Bank Co., *ex parte* Prange, L.R. 1 Eq. 1.

[4] Hirschfield v. Smith, 1866, L.R. 1 C.P. at p. 351 ; Gladwell v. Turner, 1870, L.R. 5 Ex. 61.

[5] *Vide* Gladwell v. Turner, *supra*.   [6] *Vide* sec. 92.

[7] Fielding v. Corry, 1898, L.R. 1 Q.B. 268.

principal, he must do so within the same time as if he were the holder, and the principal, upon the receipt of such notice, has himself the same time for giving notice as if the agent had been an independent holder.[1]

Notice to Remote Parties.—(14) Where a party to a bill receives due notice of dishonour, he has, after receipt of such notice, the same period of time for giving notice to antecedent parties that the holder has after the dishonour.[2]

Miscarriage of Notice in Post.—(15) Where a notice of dishonour is duly addressed and posted, the sender is deemed to have given due notice of dishonour, notwithstanding any miscarriage by the post-office. Where a notice is not properly addressed, the party giving notice must prove that it was duly delivered.[3] If a holder does not know the address of an indorser, he is entitled to time to make inquiries.[4]

50. *Delay in Giving Notice of Dishonour Excused.*—(1) Delay in giving notice of dishonour is excused where the delay is caused by circumstances beyond the control of the party giving notice, and not imputable to his default, misconduct, or negligence.[5] When the cause of delay ceases to operate, the notice must be given with reasonable diligence.[6]

Notice of Dishonour Dispensed with.—(2) Notice of dishonour is dispensed with (*a*) when, after the exercise of reasonable diligence, notice as required by the Act[7] cannot be given to, or does not reach, the drawer or indorser sought to be charged ; but failure by the holder of a bill, after the exercise of reasonable diligence at the time the bill is dishonoured, to find the drawer of the bill at the address he has given, does not dispense with notice of dishonour if an address at which the drawer is to be found comes to the knowledge of the holder before action is brought :[8] (*b*) by waiver, expressed or implied.[9] Notice of dishonour may be waived before the time of giving notice has arrived, or after the omission to give due notice. Private knowledge on the part of the person to whom notice should be given does not imply waiver, and does not, therefore, dispense with notice ;[10] but waiver of notice by an indorser does not affect parties prior to him : (*c*) *as regards the drawer* in the following cases, namely, (1) where drawer and drawee are

---

[1] Prince *v.* Oriental Bank, 1878, 3 Ap. Ca. 332.

[2] *Vide* Horne *v.* Rouquette, 3 Q.B.D. 514.

[3] Milligan *v.* Barbour, 1829, 7 S. 489.

[4] Baldwin *v.* Richardson, 1823, 1 B. & C. 245.

[5] *Vide* sec. 46 (1).

[6] Gladwell *v.* Turner, *supra.*

[7] *Vide* sec. 49 ; Allen *v.* Edmundson, 1848, 2 Ex. 723.

[8] Studdy *v.* Beesty, 60 Law Times (N.S.) 647.

[9] *Cf.* sec. 46 (2), *supra*, and cases cited ; *vide* also Murray *v.* Morrison, 1824, 3 S. 202 ; Allan *v.* Macdonald, 1827, 6 S. 260 ; Mills *v.* Hamilton, 1830, 9 S. 111 ; Campbell *v.* Ratten, 1833, 12 S. 269 ; Cordery *v.* Colville, 1863, 32 L.J. C.P. 210.

[10] *In re* Fenwick, Stobart & Co. Ltd., 1902, 1 Ch. 507.

the same person ; (2) where the drawee is a fictitious person, or a perso
not having capacity to contract ;[1] (3) where the drawer is the perso
to whom the bill is presented for payment, or where the bill is mad
payable at his house.[2] But where the bill is signed by the drawer i
order to accommodate the acceptor, the drawer is entitled to notice ;
(4) where the drawee or acceptor is, as between himself and the drawer
under no obligation to accept or pay the bill ; (5) where the drawer ha.
countermanded payment : (*d*) *as regards the indorser* in the following
cases, namely, (1) where the drawee is a fictitious person, or a person
not having capacity to contract, and the indorser was aware of the fac
at the time he indorsed the bill ; (2) where the indorser is the person
to whom the bill is presented for payment, as where he becomes the
executor of the acceptor.[4] Where the bill is not duly stamped no notice
of dishonour need be given, as the holder must take action, not on the
bill, but for the consideration for which the bill was granted.[5] A guaranto
for the due payment of a bill by the acceptor is not entitled to notice
(3) where the bill was accepted or made for his accommodation.

51. Noting and Protest. — (1) *An inland bill* which has been
dishonoured may, if the holder think fit, be noted for non-acceptance
or non-payment, as the case may be ; but it is not necessary to note
or protest any such bill in order to preserve recourse against the
drawer or indorser. It is, however, advisable to have bills noted as
preserving evidence of their due presentment. The noting is a marking
put on the bill by the notary public recording the presentation of the
bill for acceptance or payment, and is designed to refresh the memory
of the notary when extending the protest as to the date when presentation was made. The following is the usual memorandum of noting put
upon bills :—1/12/23 pnp. (protest for non-payment), C.D., N.P. or pnac.
(protest for non-acceptance), C.D., N.P. Protest is, however, necessary
to warrant summary diligence on the bill,[6] in the case of a bill drawn
after sight, in order to fix the date of maturity,[7] and in certain cases
after specified.[8]

(2) *A foreign bill*, appearing on the face of it to be such,[9] which has
been dishonoured by non-acceptance, must be duly protested for non-
acceptance, and where such a bill, which has not been previously
dishonoured by non-acceptance, is dishonoured by non-payment, it
must be duly protested for non-payment. If it be not so protested,
the drawer and indorsers are discharged. A foreign bill payable on

---

[1] *Vide* sec. 22.   [2] Carter *v.* Flower, 1847, 16 M. & W. 743.
[3] Sleigh *v.* Sleigh, 1850, 5 Exch. 514.
[4] Caunt *v.* Thomson, 1849, 18 L.J. C.P. 125.
[5] Cundy *v.* Marriott, 1831, 1 B. & Ad. 696.
[6] *Vide* sec. 98.   [7] *Vide* sec. 14 (3).
[8] *Vide* secs. 65 (1), 67 (1) (4), 72 (3).
[9] For definition of, see sec. 4.

emand need not be protested to preserve the right of recourse of a
ælder in due course, provided it be presented for payment before it has
æen in circulation for an unreasonable length of time.[1] Where a bill
œes not appear on the face of it to be a foreign bill, protest, in case of
ishonour, is unnecessary.

Successive Protests.—(3) A bill which has been protested for non-
ǝceptance may be subsequently protested for non-payment.

Time for Noting and Protesting.—(4) Subject to the provisions of
ie Act, when a bill is noted or protested it (may be noted on the day of
s dishonour, and must be noted not later than the next succeeding
usiness day[2]). Where a bill has been duly noted, the protest may be
ubsequently extended as of the date of noting.[3] Where the extended
rotest bears that the bill was protested on a date different from that
n which the bill itself bears that the protest was noted, any diligence
ollowing thereon is inept.

Protest for Better Security.—(5) Where the acceptor of a bill becomes
ankrupt or insolvent, or suspends payment before it matures, the
older may cause the bill to be protested for better security against
he drawer and indorsers. No right of recourse accrues to him till
he date of maturity. A bill in such circumstances may be accepted
upra protest.[4] In Scotland, where during the currency of a bill a
arty liable on it becomes *vergens ad inopiam* (*i.e.* approaching insolv-
ncy), the holder may obtain diligence and use inhibitions so as to
revent the heritable property being disposed of, or use arrestments
ttaching the moveable property. The diligence is only granted on an
verment of *vergens ad inopiam* which the person applying for the
liligence must take upon himself the responsibility of averring.

Place of Protest.—(6) A bill must be protested at the place where
t is dishonoured:[5] except (*a*) when it is presented through the post-
ffice,[6] and returned by post dishonoured, it may be protested at the
lace to which it is returned, and on the day of its return if received
luring business hours, and if not received during business hours, then
tot later than the next business day; or (*b*) when a bill drawn pay-
ble at the place of business or residence of some person other than
he drawee has been dishonoured by non-acceptance, it must be pro-
ested for non-payment at the place where it is expressed to be payable,
ind no further presentment for payment to, or demand on, the drawee
s necessary.

---

[1] *Vide* secs. 8 (2), 36 (3).

[2] The words in brackets were substituted for the words " must be noted on the
lay of its dishonour " in the Act of 1882 by sec. 1 of the Bills of Exchange (Time
f Noting) Act, 1917 (7 & 8 Geo. V. cap. 48).

[3] *Vide* M'Pherson *v.* Wright, 1885, 12 R. 942.

[4] *Vide* sec. 65 (1).

[5] As to places where there is no notary, see sec. 94.   [6] *Vide* sec. 45 (8).

Requisites of Protest.—(7) A protest must contain a copy of the bil must be signed by the notary making it, and must specify (*a*) th person at whose request the bill is protested ; (*b*) the place and dat of protest, the cause or reason for protesting the bill, the demand made and the answer given, if any, or the fact that the drawee or accepto could not be found.[1] Where a bill provides that payment is to b made at the drawer's office, it is an undertaking on the part of th acceptor that he will attend there on the date specified and pay th bill, and if he fails to do so, the bill must be protested on the ground that the acceptor could not be found, and not that, the bill having been presented and there being no funds to meet it, payment wa refused.[2] Although the protest must be signed by a notary public it is not necessary that he should be present when the bill is presented. He is warranted in making the protest upon the report of his clerk o other trustworthy person. Bank messengers in Scotland usually presen bills for acceptance or payment. Further, it is not necessary that th witnesses referred to in the protest should be present at the time o presentment. They do not require to sign the protest as witnesses An extract registered protest would probably not be invalid because it did not expressly state that a demand for payment had been made but merely states that the bill has been presented and that payment has been refused, nor because certain instalments of the bill having been paid, it omits to state that the demand on presentation was limited to the balance due on the bill.[4] The protest may be issued in duplicate or triplicate, but all must be duly stamped. Where the duty on the bill or note does not exceed one shilling, the duty on the protest is the same as on the bill. In any other case the duty is one shilling.

Protest of Lost Bill.—(8) Where a bill is lost or destroyed, or is wrongly detained from the person entitled to hold it, protest may be made on a copy or written particulars thereof.

(9) *Protest is dispensed with* by any circumstance which would dispense with notice of dishonour.[5] *Delay* in noting or protesting is *excused* when the delay is caused by circumstances beyond the control of the holder and not imputable to his default, misconduct, or negligence. The want of a notary does not excuse delay in noting or protesting.[6] When the cause of delay ceases to operate, the bill must be noted or protested with reasonable diligence.[7]

52. Holder's Duty to Acceptor.—(1) When a bill is accepted

---

[1] *Vide* Appendix for forms.
[2] Bartsch *v.* Poole & Co., 1895, 23 R. 329.
[3] Cromlie *v.* Craig, 1897, 5 S.L.T. 303.
[4] *Per* Lord Kincairney in Bartsch *v.* Poole & Co.
[5] *Vide* sec. 50 (2).   [6] *Vide* sec. 94.   [7] *Vide* sec. 49.

generally, presentment for payment is not necessary in order to render the acceptor liable,[1] as he is bound at common law to find out his creditor and pay him. It is a well-established and very convenient rule that the acceptor of a bill is liable in terms of his obligation without the necessity of charging him by presentment. What are called the requisites of negotiation—presentment, protest, and notice of dishonour—are only necessary to preserve the holder's recourse against the drawer and indorsers, in order that each may be in a position without delay to enforce his recourse against those who are liable to him ; but the acceptor of a bill or the maker of a note is always liable in terms of his obligation for his signature without notice. If there be a condition that the bill is payable at a particular place, then, following a distinction that had been already established by decision, the Act made that condition as to place of payment applicable to the acceptor, because that is a condition of the contract. But as regards time there is no limit, within the prescriptive period. Presentment, therefore, of a bill or note payable at a particular place on the day when payment is due is not necessary to render the acceptor or maker liable, and presentment on a subsequent day is sufficient.[2] Altering an opinion expressed in a case decided in 1902,[3] where it was stated that presentment on the due date of a bill and at the proper place of payment was necessary in order to found summary diligence against the acceptor but reverting to the former practice on the subject,[4] it is now competent[5] as between the holder and acceptor of a bill to present the bill and proceed with summary diligence at any time within six months after the maturity of the bill. (2) When by terms of a qualified acceptance, presentment for payment is required, as where the acceptor makes presentment a condition precedent of his liability,[6] the acceptor, in the absence of an express stipulation to that effect, is not discharged by the omission to present the bill for payment on the day that it matures.[7] (3) In order to render the acceptor of a bill liable, it is not necessary to protest it, or that notice of dishonour should be given to him. (4) Where the holder of a bill presents it for payment, he must exhibit the bill to the person from whom he demands payment, and when a bill is paid, the holder must forthwith deliver it up to the party paying it. Where the payment is partial, the amount should be noted on the bill, but the holder is not bound to deliver it except for full payment. By sec. 9

---

[1] *Vide* sec. 19.
[2] Gordon *v.* Scott, 1898, 25 R. 570.
[3] Neill *v.* Dobson, Molle & Co., 1902, 4 F. 625.
[4] See opinion of Lord Wood in Bon *v.* Lord Rollo, 1850, 12 D. 1310.
[5] M'Neill & Son *v.* Innes Chambers & Co., 1917, S.C. 540.
[6] Halstead *v.* Skelton, 1843, 5 Q.B. 93, Ex. Ch.
[7] Smith *v.* Vertue, 1860, 30 L.J. C.P. 59.

of the Finance Act of 1895,[1] payments to account marked upon the back of a bill of the value of two pounds and upwards are liable in two pence of stamp duty.

6. Liabilities of Parties

53. Bill Operates as Intimated Assignation.—In Scotland, though not in England, where the drawee of a bill has in his hands funds (not goods) available for the payment thereof, the bill operates as an assignment of the sum for which it is drawn, in favour of the holder, from the time when the bill is presented to the drawee.[2] In an action against the drawee the bill is founded on as an assignation, and not solely as a bill, the holder's right to recover being dependent on the existence of a debt due by the drawee to the drawer, and on the validity of the assignation of that debt to him. A bill granted for valuable consideration cannot be countermanded by the drawer,[3] and if the drawee refuse to pay, the holder's proper course is to raise an action of multiplepoinding.[4] The acceptance of a bill payable at a banker's is authority to the banker to pay the bill, and it is the banker's duty (in the sense of legal obligation) to his customer, the acceptor, to act on the authority and pay accordingly. No doubt the authority proceeds from the customer, and the consequent duty is to the customer ; but it does not follow that the authority and duty thus created have existence only as between the banker and customer. A legal relation is created between the banker on whom the duty, or legal obligation, is imposed, and the bill-holder in whose favour it is imposed, and to whom it is prestable.[5] Where a banker has funds in his hands, but insufficient to meet the bill, the practice is to transfer the amount standing at the credit of the customer to a special account referable to the bill, and to retain the amount until the matter is judicially determined or arranged between the parties. Bills are preferable according to their respective dates of presentation to the drawee.

54. Liability of Acceptor.—The acceptor of a bill by accepting it (1) engages that he will pay it according to the tenor of his acceptance ;[6] (2) is precluded from denying to a holder in due course[7] (a) the existence of the drawer, the genuineness of his signature,[8]

---

[1] 58 Vict. cap. 16.

[2] Thomson on Bills (2nd ed.), p. 104 ; Thorburn on Bills, p. 126.

[3] *Vide* Cheques.

[4] Carter *v.* M'Intosh, 1862, 24 D. 925.

[5] *Per* Lord Young, British Linen Company Bank *v.* Rainey's Trs., 1885, 12 R. 825 ; *vide* Banker and Customer, p. 5.

[6] *Vide* sec. 19.   [7] *Vide* sec. 29.

[8] London and South-Western Bank *v.* Wentworth, 5 Ex. D. 96.

and his capacity [1] and authority [2] to draw the bill; (b) in the case of a bill payable to drawer's order, the then capacity of the drawer to indorse,[3] but not the genuineness or validity of his indorsement; [4] (c) in the case of a bill payable to the order of a third person, the existence of the payee and his then capacity to indorse, but not the genuineness or validity of his indorsement. The acceptor, therefore, may refuse to pay on the ground that the payee's signature is forged. When a bill becomes due and is presented for payment and is paid in good faith and the money is received in good faith, if subsequently, after the lapse of such an interval of time that the position of the holder may have been altered for the worse, the indorsements on the bill prove to be forgeries, the money so paid cannot be recovered from the holder.[5]

Joint Acceptors, Relief inter se.—Where a bill is accepted by two persons jointly and is at maturity paid by one of them, in a claim of relief by the person who has paid the bill against the other acceptor, it is competent to prove by parole the true nature of the transaction between the acceptors and their reciprocal obligations.[6]

55. Liability of Drawer.—(1) The drawer of a bill by drawing it (a) engages that, on due presentment,[7] it shall be accepted and paid according to its tenor,[8] and that if it be dishonoured [9] he will compensate the holder or any indorser who is compelled to pay it, provided that the requisite proceedings on dishonour be duly taken; [10] (b) is precluded from denying to a holder in due course the existence of the payee and his then capacity to indorse.

Liability of Indorser.—(2) The indorser of a bill by indorsing it (a) engages that on due presentment it shall be accepted and paid according to its tenor, and that if it be dishonoured he will compensate the holder or a subsequent indorser who is compelled to pay it, provided that the requisite proceedings on dishonour be duly taken; [11] (b) is precluded from denying to a holder in due course the genuineness and regularity in all respects of the drawer's signature and all previous indorsements; [12] (c) is precluded from denying to his immediate or a subsequent indorsee that the bill was at the time of his indorsement a valid and subsisting bill, and that he had a good title thereto.

---

[1] *Vide* sec. 22.   [2] *Vide* sec. 25.

[3] Halifax *v.* Lyle, 1849, 3 Exch. 446.

[4] Garland *v.* Jacomb, 1873, L.R. 8 Ex. 216, Ex. Ch.

[5] London and River Plate Bank *v.* Bank of Liverpool, 1896, L.R. 1 Q.B. 7 (*per* Mathew, J.).

[6] Crosbie *v.* Crosbie's Trs., 1900, 3 F. 83.

[7] *Vide* secs. 40, 41, 45.   [8] *Vide* secs. 17, 19, 44.

[9] *Vide* secs. 43, 47.   [10] *Vide* secs. 48-51.

[11] Duncan Fox & Co. *v.* North and South Wales Bank, 1880, 6 Ap. Ca. 1.

[12] M'Gregor *v.* Rhodes, 1856, 6 E. & B. 266.

10

Liability of Successive Indorsers inter se.—The liabilities *inter se* of successive indorsers of a bill or note must, in the absence of all evidence to the contrary, be determined according to the ordinary principles of the law merchant, whereby a prior indorser must indemnify a subsequent one. But the whole circumstances attendant upon the making, issue, and transference of a bill or note may be legitimately referred to for the purpose of ascertaining the true relation to each other of the parties who put their signatures upon it either as makers or indorsers ; and reasonable inferences derived from these facts and circumstances are admitted to the effect of qualifying, altering, or even inverting the relative liabilities which the law merchant would otherwise assign to them. Thus where the directors of a company mutually agreed with each other to become securities to a bank for the same debts of the company, and in pursuance of that agreement successively indorsed three promissory notes of the company, it was held they were entitled and liable to equal contributions *inter se*, and that they were not liable to indemnify each other successively according to the priority of their indorsements.[1] As regards a holder in due course, they are, however, liable jointly and severally.

56. Liability of Stranger Signing Bill.—Where a person signs a bill, otherwise than as a drawer or acceptor, he thereby incurs the liabilities of an indorser to a holder in due course. Such a signature is known as one *per aval*, and, by the law merchant, can be given only to a person who thereafter takes the bill. As no one can sign a bill as an acceptor except the drawee,[2] a referee in case of need,[3] or an acceptor for honour,[4] a stranger cannot sign as an acceptor to a bill, and if he sign as an acceptor his signature is wholly inoperative. So if a stranger subscribe his name in the place properly occupied by the acceptor's signature, his subscription is held to be *per aval* (" aval," said to be an antiquated word signifying underwriting). One who subscribed a bill *per aval* really occupies the position of a cautioner, but the addition of that or a similar word, while indicating the character in which he subscribes, does not in any way limit or alter his liability. His liability is that of an indorser, and as such liability is limited to those who succeed him, he incurs no liability to the drawer ; [5] nor has he any right of recourse against the drawer unless he has signed on the drawer's behalf. Where a stranger signed an indorsement to the effect that, in case of non-payment by the acceptor, the bill was to be presented to him, it was held that, though he was not liable as an indorser, the

---

[1] Macdonald *v.* Whitfield, 1883, L.R. 8 Ap. Ca. 733.
[2] *Vide* sec. 17.   [3] *Vide* sec. 15.   [4] *Vide* sec. 65.
[5] Walker's Trs. *v.* M‘Kinlay, 1880, 7 R. (H.L.) 85 ; Jenkins & Sons *v.* Coomber, 1898, L.R. 2 Q.B. 168.

indorsement not being part of the bill, nor as an acceptor, since he could not sign as such, his obligation was one of guarantee to the drawer, that if the acceptor failed to pay the bill he would do so.[1] A signature *per aval* is not struck at by the Act of 1856, which requires that all guarantees and cautionary obligations shall be in writing.[2]

57. Sum for which Parties are Respectively Liable.—Where a bill is dishonoured,[3] the measure of damages, which are deemed to be liquidated damages, is as follows :—

(1) (*a*) *The holder* may recover from any party liable on the bill, (*b*) *the drawer* who has been compelled to pay the bill may recover from the acceptor, (*c*) *an indorser* who has been compelled to pay the bill may recover from the acceptor or from the drawer, or from a prior indorser : (*First*) The amount of the bill. (*Second*) Interest [4] thereon from the time of presentment for payment, if the bill is payable on demand, and from the maturity of the bill in any other case. When, however, a bill has been dishonoured by non-acceptance, interest runs only from the date of the maturity of the bill. (*Third*) The expenses of noting, or when protest is necessary,[5] and the protest has been extended, the expenses of protest, including protest for non-acceptance but not for better security.[6] Expenses of commission are not included.[6] In an action on a bill which had been dishonoured, the writ was indorsed with a claim for the amount of the bill and a further sum described as " Bank charges," and it was held that the expression " Bank charges " was a sufficient description of the expenses of noting, and that the writ was therefore indorsed for a liquidated demand within the meaning of the section.[7]

Bill Dishonoured Abroad.—(2) In the case of a bill which has been dishonoured abroad, in lieu of the above damages, the holder may recover from the drawer or an indorser, and the drawer or an indorser who has been compelled to pay the bill may recover from any party liable to him, the amount of the re-exchange, with interest thereon until the time of payment. Notwithstanding this provision, the drawer of a foreign bill of exchange upon an acceptor in this country is entitled, upon the bill being dishonoured and protested, to recover from the acceptor damages in the nature of re-exchange which the drawer is, by foreign law, liable to pay to the holder.[8]

---

[1] Stagg, Mantle & Co. *v.* Brodrick, 1895, 12 T.L.R. 12.

[2] Macdonald *v.* Union Bank, 1864, 2 M. 963 ; Shaw & Co. *v.* Holland, 1913, 2 K.B. 15 ; 19 & 20 Vict. cap. 60, sec. 6.

[3] *Vide* secs. 43, 47.   [4] As to rate of interest, see *ante*, p. 102.

[5] *Vide* secs. 51 (2), 65, 67 (1), (4).

[6] *In re* English Bank of River Plate, 1893, L.R. 2 Ch. 438.

[7] Dando *v.* Boden, 1893, L.R. 1 Q.B. 318.

[8] *Ex parte* Roberts, *in re* Gillespie, 56 L.J. Q.B. 74 ; *affd.* 1886, 18 Q.B.D. 286, C.A.

Interest as Damages.—(3) Where by the Act interest may be recovered as damages, such interest may, if justice require it, be withheld wholly or in part,[1] and where a bill is expressed to be payable with interest at a given rate, interest as damages may or may not be given at the same rate as interest proper.

58. Liability of "Transferror by Delivery."—(1) Where the holder of a bill payable to bearer (which includes a bill indorsed in blank [2]) negotiates it by delivery [3] without indorsing it, he is called a "transferror by delivery." (2) A transferror by delivery is not liable on the instrument. Thus where the holder of a bill for £100 which has been indorsed in blank, discounts it with a banker for £90 without indorsing it, and the bill is subsequently dishonoured, he is not bound to repay the sum received.

Transferror's Warranty to Transferee.—(3) A transferror by delivery who negotiates a bill thereby warrants to his immediate transferee being a holder for value (*a*) that the bill is what it purports to be, that is, that the signatures to it are neither forged nor unauthorised; (*b*) that he has a right to transfer it, that is, for example, that he is neither a thief nor a finder; and (*c*) that at the time of transfer he is not aware of any fact which renders it valueless, as, for example, that the bill has been altered materially. He is liable to the transferee in compensation if in any of these considerations the warranty fails.[4]

7. Discharge of Bill

59. By Payment in Due Course.—(1) A bill is discharged by payment in due course, by or on behalf of the drawee or acceptor (and also renunciation or acceptilation,[5] by novation,[6] by compensation,[7] by delegation,[8] by confusion,[9] by cancellation,[10] or by prescription [11]). Payment in due course means payment made at or after the maturity of the bill to the holder of it (or to his authorised agent) [12] in good faith,[13] and without notice that his title to the bill is defective.[14] A bill should not

---

[1] Cameron *v.* Smith, 2 B. & A. 305; *approved*, Webster *v.* British Empire Co., 1880, 15 Ch. D. at pp. 175, 176.

[2] *Vide* sec. 34.   [3] *Vide* secs. 21, 31 (2).

[4] *Vide* Gompertz *v.* Bartlett, 23 L.J. C.P. 65; Pooley *v.* Brown, 1862, 31 L.J. C.P. 134.

[5] *Vide infra*, sec. 62.

[6] *Vide* Novation, p. 54, and Twopenny *v.* Young, 3 B. & C. 208; Allan *v.* Allan, 1831, 9 S. 529; Sandeman *v.* Thomson, 1831, 10 S. 4.

[7] *Vide* Compensation, p. 50.

[8] *Vide* Delegation, p. 54, and Shepherd & Co. *v.* Bartholomew & Co., 1868, 5 S.L.R. 595.

[9] *Vide* sec. 61, Confusion, p. 53.   [10] *Vide* sec. 63.

[11] *Vide* Prescription, p. 166.

[12] *Vide* sec. 45 (3).   [13] *Vide* sec. 90.   [14] *Vide* sec. 29 (2).

be delivered up as paid against receipt of a cheque until the cheque has been paid by the bank on which it is drawn. The giving up of bills as against cheques should be discountenanced.

(2) Subject to the provisions after specified, when a bill is paid by the drawer or an indorser it is not discharged ; but (*a*) where a bill payable to, or to the order of, a third party is paid by the drawer, the drawer may enforce payment of it against the acceptor (except, apparently, where the bill has been accepted for the accommodation of the drawer),[1] but may not reissue the bill (unless in the case where the bill has been negotiated back to the drawer before maturity) ;[2] and (*b*) where a bill is paid by an indorser, or where a bill payable to drawer's order is paid by the drawer, the party paying it is remitted to his former rights as regards the acceptor or antecedent of parties, and he may, if he think fit, strike out his own and subsequent indorsements, and again negotiate the bill. The subsequent indorsers in such a case are discharged by the payment to the drawer or prior indorsers, and consequently, even if the bill be negotiated after payment, and without cancellation of the signatures of the payer and subsequent indorsers, the indorsee can have no claim against such parties, as in these circumstances no holder can be a holder in due course.[3]

(3) Where an accommodation bill is paid in due course by the party accommodated, the bill is discharged.[4]

60,[5] 61. *By Confusion.*—When the acceptor of a bill is, or becomes, the holder of it, at or after its maturity,[6] in his own right, the bill is discharged.[7] This provision does not apply to an acceptor for honour.[8] The expression " in his own right " is not used in contradistinction to a right in a representative capacity, but indicates a right not subject to that of another person and good against all the world.[9] Where a bill is granted for an advance on loan, the mere granting of a new bill and the giving up of the old bill do not operate as a discharge of the claim for interest upon the loan.[10]

62. *By Renunciation.*—(1) When the holder of a bill at or after its maturity [11] *absolutely and unconditionally* renounces his rights against the acceptor, the bill is discharged. The renunciation may be verbal if it be at the same time accompanied by the delivery of the bill. Otherwise

---

[1] Solomon *v.* Davies (*per* Stephen, J.), 1 C. & E. 83.
[2] *Vide* sec. 37 ; Attenborough *v.* Mackenzie, 1856, 25 L.J. Ex. 244.
[3] *Vide* sec. 29.
[4] Cook *v.* Lister, 1863, 32 L.J., C.P. at p. 127 ; *in re* Oriental Bank, 1871, L.R. 7 Ch. at p. 102.
[5] *Vide* Cheques, p. 171.   [6] *Vide* secs. 10, 14.   [7] *Vide* sec. 37.
[8] *Vide* sec. 68 (5).
[9] Nash *v.* De Freville, 1900, 2 Q.B. (C.A.) 72.
[10] Hope Johnstone *v.* Hope Johnstone's Exrs., 1895, 22 R. 314.
[11] *Vide* secs. 10, 14.

the renunciation must be in writing, and it must be a record of an absolute and unconditional renunciation of the holder's rights on the bill or note ;[1] a memorandum made by or with the authority of the holder, whether signed by him or not, to the effect that he renounces his rights is not sufficient ;[1] but such a writing, or even a letter expressing intention to renounce, might go to prove that a subsequent handing of the bill to the acceptor was made with that intention. The effect of such renunciation is to release the acceptor from all liability on the bill to the holder or anyone claiming through him. A verbal renunciation by the holder of all rights under a promissory note, accompanied by delivery of the note, to a beneficiary of the maker, the heritable estate in whose hands was liable for payment of the debt, and who had for some time paid interest on it, was held not to operate as a discharge, though it would probably have done so had the delivery been made to an executor or administrator.[2]

Renunciation may be made *conditional,* and until the condition is purified there is no renunciation. Though the holder may in such circumstances be meantime barred from enforcing the bill, he may not be prevented from negotiating the bill to a new holder, who will not be affected by his disabilities, and may enforce his rights whether the condition be purified or not.[3]

(2) The liabilities [4] of any party to a bill may in like manner be renounced by the holder before, at, or after its maturity ; but nothing in the section affects the rights of a holder in due course [5] without notice of the renunciation.

63. *By Cancellation.*—(1) Where a bill is intentionally cancelled by the holder or his agent, and the cancellation is apparent, the bill is discharged.[6]

(2) In like manner any party liable on a bill may be discharged by the intentional cancellation of his signature by the holder or his agent. In such a case, any indorser, who would have had a right of recourse against the party whose signature is cancelled, is also discharged.

(3) A cancellation made *unintentionally,* or under a mistake, or without the authority of the holder, is inoperative ; but where a bill or any signature thereon appears to have been cancelled, the burden of proof lies on the party who alleges that the cancellation was made unintentionally, or under a mistake, or without authority.[7]

---

[1] *In re* George, Francis *v.* Bruce (*per* Chitty, J.), 44 Ch. D. 627 ; Crawford *v.* Muir, 1873, 1 R. 91 ; 2 R. (H.L.) 148.

[2] Edward *v.* Walters, 1896, L.R. 2 Ch. 157.

[3] Macvean *v.* Maclean, 1873, 11 M. 764.   [4] *Vide* secs. 54-56.   [5] *Vide* sec. 29.

[6] Yglesias *v.* River Plate Bank, 1877, 3 C.P.D. 60, 330.

[7] Warwick *v.* Rodgers, 1843, 5 M. & Gr. 340 ; Prince *v.* Oriental Bank, 1878, 3 Ap. Ca. 325, P.C.

In a case which came under this section, the agent of a bank offered to try to obtain payment of a bill which had been protested for non-payment, and the holders accepted the offer. The acceptors offered to pay the bill and protest charges, on the condition that they should not be called upon to pay interest and expenses. The bank's agent communicated this condition to the holders, and asked instructions, but, without waiting for authority, took payment of the bill and protest charges, marked the bill paid, and delivered it to the acceptors who deleted their names thereon. Thereafter the holders intimated their refusal to agree to the condition on which payment had been made, refused to accept the sum tendered to them by the bank agent, and received back the bill cancelled, the money being repaid to the acceptors. The holders then raised an action against the acceptors for the amount of the bill with interest and for the expenses of the action, and obtained decree; but the estates of the acceptors became bankrupt before diligence could be used against them. The holders then raised an action against the bank, concluding for the amount of the bill with interest and for the expenses of their action against the acceptors. It was held that the evidence showed that if the bill had not been cancelled through the error of the bank agent, the holders might have recovered payment by summary diligence before the acceptors became bankrupt, and that the bank was liable.[1]

The apparent cancellation of a bill renders summary diligence upon it incompetent.[2]

64. *By Alteration*—(1) *Apparent Alteration.*—[1] Where a bill or acceptance is materially altered without the assent of all parties liable on it, the bill is avoided except as against a party who has himself made, authorised, or assented to the alteration, and subsequent indorsers. The holder may sue on the original debt, though he cannot sue upon the bill. A bill may be altered *before issue*, that is, before its delivery, complete in form, to a person who takes it as a holder for value so as to be able to enforce payment thereof. An accommodation bill, it appears, is not issued within the meaning of this section until it has been delivered to some one who can sue upon it.[3]

But a material alteration made in a bill before issue, and without the consent of an acceptor who has accepted prior to the alteration, will release the acceptor from his liability.[3] Where a bill is delivered which is *awanting* in a material part, the person in possession has *primâ facie* authority to fill up the omission in any way he thinks fit.[4]

---

[1] Bank of Scotland v. Dominion Bank, 1889, 16 R. 1081 ; 1891, 18 R. (H.L.) 21.

[2] *Vide* sec. 98.

[3] Engel v. Stourton (*per* Charles, J.), 53 J.P. 535.

[4] *Vide* sec. 21.

A material alteration after issue renders a bill a new instrument requiring a fresh stamp.[1]

(2) *Non-Apparent Alteration.*—But where a bill has been materially altered, but the alteration is not apparent, and the bill is in the hands of a holder in due course, such holder may avail himself of the bill as if it had not been altered, and may enforce payment of it according to its original tenor.[2]

A person who draws a bill with such gross carelessness as not only to make it highly probable that it will be materially altered but so as to actually invite such alteration, will render himself liable for any increase in value effected by such alteration. Thus the customer of a bank signed several blank cheques and gave them to his wife to be filled up and used by her as she required. In one of these the sum of £50 was inserted, in her presence and at her request, by a clerk, to whom she then gave the cheque in order that he might get the money for her. In writing the sum the clerk had left spaces with fraudulent intent, so as to enable him to increase the amount to £350, which was paid to him by the banker, and it was held that in these circumstances the banker was entitled to debit his customer with the full amount he had paid upon the cheque, on the ground either that the customer by signing a blank cheque had given implied authority to any subsequent holder to fill it up, or that the customer, in filling up the cheque through his wife, whom he had constituted his agent for the purpose, had failed in the duty which he owed to his banker by giving facilities for fraudulent alteration. But that rule, which applies to the duty of a customer directly arising out of the contractual relation between him and his banker, who is his mandatory, does not apply to the relations between the acceptor of a bill of exchange and a holder acquiring right to it after acceptance, to whom he owes no duty and who is under no obligation, apart from express agreement or implication established by law, to take measures to prevent the commission of a crime, which he has no cause to anticipate. Persons are not to be supposed to commit forgery, and the protection against such a crime is the law of the land and not the vigilance of parties in excluding all possibility of committing it. Thus in one case the holder of a bill of exchange, purporting to be for £3500 payable three months after date, brought an action against the acceptor for payment. The bill as originally drawn and as accepted and returned to the drawer was for £500 upon a £2 stamp, and there was nothing unusual or calculated to excite attention in the fact that there were intervals between the written words and the figures of the document. The drawer then fraudulently increased its amount by an alteration of the words and figures, and it was obvious that when he wrote the bill he

---

[1] Suffell *v.* Bank of England, 1882, L.R. 9 Q.B.D. 555.
[2] *Vide* Leeds Bank *v.* Walker, 1883, L.R. 11 Q.B.D. 84.

must have had in contemplation the alterations which he subsequently made, and that he purposely used a stamp of unnecessary value and left the spaces which he afterwards filled up as described in order to facilitate his fraud. The holder subsequently acquired the bill in *bonâ fide* and for value, and it was held that the acceptor was liable only for the amount of the bill as originally drawn.[1]

Alterations which are Material.—[2] In particular, the following alterations are material, namely, any alteration of the *date*, the *sum payable*, the *time or place of payment*, the *substitution of one drawer for another*, the *alteration of the name of an indorsee*, the *erasure of the acceptor's name and the substitution of another*,[2] an alteration in the *consideration*, and where the bill has been accepted generally, the *addition of a place of payment* without the acceptor's assent.

A mere correction is not a material alteration, nor is the addition of words which do not alter the effect of the bill as issued.[3] Again, the substituting of " us " for " me " and " our " for " my " in a firm's bill are not material alterations.[4]

8. Acceptance and Payment for Honour

65. Acceptance for Honour *supra* **Protest.**[5]—(1) Where a bill has been protested for dishonour by non-acceptance,[6] or protested for better security,[7] and is not overdue,[8] any person (including the drawee before acceptance) not being a party already liable thereon, may, with the consent of the holder, intervene and accept the bill *supra* protest for the honour of any party liable thereon, or for the honour of the person for whose account the bill is drawn, but not for the honour of the drawee, as, till acceptance, he is not liable on the bill ; nor for the honour of an indorser, who has indorsed restrictively [9] or in a representative capacity [10] (though it may be for the honour of his principal) ; nor for the honour of an indorser who has negotiated the bill back to the holder ; nor for any party against whom recourse has been lost by failure to negotiate,[11] or whose obligation has been discharged by renunciation

---

[1] Scholfield *v.* Earl of Londesborough, 1896, L.R. A.C. 514, and cases there referred to ; Marcussen *v.* Birkbeck Bank, 1889, 5 T.L.R. 179, 463, 646.

[2] M'Ewan *v.* Graham, 1833, 12 S. 110.

[3] Brutt *v.* Picard, R. & M. 37 ; Aldous *v.* Cornwall, L.R. 3 Q.B. 573 ; Commercial Bank *v.* Paton, 1837, 15 S. 1202 ; London and Provincial Bank *v.* Roberts, 1874, 22 Weekly Reporter, 402.

[4] Speirs & Knox *v.* Semple, 1901, 9 S.L.T. 133.

[5] In practice such acceptances are met with but rarely. An acceptance for honour is equivalent to saying to the holder of the bill, " Keep this bill ; don't return it ; and when the time arrives at which it ought to be paid, if it be not paid by the party on whom it was originally drawn, come to me, and you shall have the money."

[6] *Vide* sec. 43.   [7] *Vide* sec. 51 (5).   [8] *Vide* secs. 14, 45 (2).

[9] *Vide* sec. 16.   [10] *Vide* sec. 26.   [11] *Vide* secs. 45, 46, 49-51.

or cancellation.[1] It is essential that the bill have been protested, as till that has been done no one but the drawee can validly accept.[2] Protest must be made on the day of dishonour by non-acceptance.[3]

Partial Acceptance.—(2) A bill may be accepted for honour for part only of the sum for which it is drawn. Without the drawer's consent, no other qualified acceptance can be taken by the holder.

Requisites.—(3) An acceptance for honour *supra* protest in order to be valid [4] must (*a*) be written on the bill, and indicate that it is an acceptance for honour. No special form of words is necessary. The acceptance need not specify for whose honour it is made. The form which is usually adopted is, "accepted for the honour of A. B. *supra* protest," or simply, "accepted S. P." (*b*) It must be signed [5] by the acceptor for honour. (4) Where an acceptance for honour does not expressly state for whose honour it is made, it is deemed to be an acceptance for the honour of the drawer.

Maturity of Bill.—(5) Where a bill payable after sight is accepted for honour, its maturity is calculated from the date of the noting for non-acceptance, and not from the date of the acceptance for honour.

66. *Liability of Acceptor for Honour.*—(1) The acceptor for honour of a bill, by accepting it, engages that he will, on due presentment, pay the bill according to the tenor of his acceptance, if it is not paid by the drawee, provided it has been duly presented [6] for payment [7] (unless excused),[8] and protested for non-payment, and that he receives notice of these facts. The notice, which should be given at or before the time of presentment for payment, need not be in writing, but must be in such terms as to sufficiently identify the bill.[9] (2) The acceptor for honour is liable to the holder and to all parties on the bill *subsequent* to the party for whose honour he has accepted. Any defence competent to an acceptor is also competent to the acceptor for honour.[10]

67. *Presentment for Payment to Acceptor for Honour.*—(1) Where a dishonoured bill has been accepted for honour *supra* protest,[11] or contains a reference in case of need,[12] it must be protested for non-payment [13] before it is presented for payment to the acceptor for honour, or referee in case of need. It is not necessary to extend the protest, noting being sufficient.

(2) *Place and Time of Presentment.*—Where the address of the acceptor for honour is in the same place where the bill is protested for non-payment, the bill must be presented to him not later than the day following its maturity ; and where the address of the acceptor for honour is in some place other than the place where it is protested for non-payment,

---

[1] *Vide* secs. 62, 63.　　[2] *Vide* sec. 17.　　　　　　　　[3] *Vide* secs. 51 (4), 57 (6)-(9), 94.
[4] *Vide* sec. 50 (7), (8).　[5] *Vide* secs. 17, 91 (1).　　[6] *Vide* secs. 52 (1), 67 (2).
[7] *Vide* sec. 45.　　　　　[8] *Vide* sec. 46.　　　　　　　[9] *Vide* sec. 49.
[10] *Vide* sec. 54.　　　　[11] *Vide* sec. 65.　　　　　　　[12] *Vide* sec. 15.
[13] *Vide* sec. 51 (4), (6)-(9).

the bill must be forwarded not later than the day following its maturity for presentment to him. Non-business days are excluded.[1]

Delay in Presentment.—(3) Delay in presentment, or non-presentment, is excused by any circumstance which would excuse delay in presentment for payment, or non-presentment for payment.[2]

Protest for Non-Payment.—(4) When a bill is dishonoured by the acceptor for honour, it must be protested for non-payment by him. Noting is sufficient.[3]

68. Payment for Honour *supra* **Protest.**—(1) Where a bill has been protested for non-payment,[4] any person may intervene and pay it *supra* protest for the honour of any party liable thereon, or for the honour of the person for whose account the bill is drawn. A person who takes up a bill *supra* protest for the benefit of a particular party succeeds to the title of the person from whom, not for whom, he receives it, and has all the title of such person to sue upon the bill, except that he discharges all the parties subsequent to the one for whose honour he accepts and that he cannot himself indorse it over.[5] The consent of the holder, as in the case of acceptance for honour, is unnecessary ; and the drawee, before acceptance, or after acceptance, if, with the assent of the drawer and indorsers,[6] the acceptance be conditional, may, if the condition be not fulfilled, pay for the honour of any party liable on the bill. The payment must be on behalf of a person already liable on the bill, and not for such a person as, for example, an indorser who has indorsed without recourse,[7] in a representative character, or as an agent [8] (though the payment may be made on behalf of the principal or person such indorser represents), nor for a person who, through any cause,[9] has ceased to be liable before such payment is made. Payment may be made on behalf of the acceptor, as in the case of a bill payable at a bank, which is dishonoured by the banker.

Preference of Payer.—(2) Where two or more persons offer to pay a bill for the honour of different parties, the person whose payment will discharge most parties to the bill is entitled to the preference. A payment for the honour of the acceptor is preferable to one for the honour of the drawer ; and a payment for the honour of the drawer to one for the honour of an indorser, and of a prior to a later indorser.

Notarial Attestment of Payment.—(3) Payment for honour *supra* protest, in order to operate as such, and not as a mere voluntary payment,

---

[1] Sec. 92. [2] *Vide* sec. 46. [3] Sec. 93.

[4] *Vide* secs. 51 (4), (6)-(9), 94. " Protest " throughout this section means protest for non-payment. *Vide in re* English Bank of River Plate, 1893, L.R. 2 Ch. 438.

[5] *Ex parte* Swan, 1868, L.R. 6 Eq. 344.

[6] *Vide* sec. 44. [7] *Vide* sec. 16. [8] *Vide* sec. 26.

[9] *Vide* secs. 45, 46, 49, 50, 51, 62, 63.

must be attested by a notarial act of honour, which may be appended to the protest, or form an extension of it.[1] (4) The notarial act of honour must be founded on a declaration made by the payer for honour, or his agent in that behalf (who, in order to pay and take the necessary steps to preserve his principal's right of recourse against the person for whose honour the payment is made, must be *specially authorised* to do so), declaring his intention to pay the bill for honour and for whose honour he pays.

Effect of Payment.—(5) Where a bill has been paid for honour, all parties subsequent to the person for whose honour it is paid are discharged ; but the payer for honour is subrogated in, and succeeds to, both the rights and duties of the holder as regards the person for whose honour he pays, and all parties liable to that party. He takes the bill subject to any exception pleadable against the holder, and he must discharge all duties incumbent on the holder, such as giving notice of dishonour by non-payment [2] to the person for whose honour he pays and any person liable to him, if that have not already been done.

Payer Entitled to Delivery of Bill.—(6) The payer for honour, on paying to the holder the amount of the bill and the notarial expenses incidental to its dishonour, is entitled to receive both the bill itself and the protest. If the holder do not on demand deliver them up, he is liable to the payer for honour in damages.

Holder Refusing Payment.—(7) Where the holder of a bill refuses to receive payment *supra* protest, he loses his right of recourse [3] against any party who would have been discharged by such payment.

9. Lost Instruments

69. Holder Entitled to Duplicate.—Where a bill has been lost or accidentally destroyed before it is overdue,[4] the person who was the holder of it may apply to, and compel the drawer to give him another bill (which, being a new contract, requires the appropriate stamp) of the same tenor, giving security to the drawer, if required, to indemnify him against all persons whatever, in case the bill alleged to have been lost is found again.[5] If the drawer, on the request as aforesaid, refuses to give such duplicate bill, he may be compelled to do so. In a question with the finder of the bill the person in right of it has a good action for recovery of the instrument ; but if it is in the possession of a holder in due course from such finder, no right of action for recovery against the holder exists. The person in right of the bill can recover from the

---

[1] *Vide* Appendix.
[2] *Vide* sec. 49.
[3] *Vide* secs. 55-57.
[4] *Vide* secs. 10, 14, 45.
[5] *Vide* Cheques, and cases there cited, substituting for " cheque," where it occurs, the word " bill." As to bills in a set, see sec. 71.

finder whatever value he has received for it. The *ad valorem* stamp duty is calculated on the value of the bill as at the date thereof, not as at the date of the maturity of the bill.[1]

70. Action on Lost Bill.—In any action upon a bill (or even upon the debt contained in it) the Court or a Judge may order that the loss or destruction of the instrument shall not be set up, provided an indemnity be given, to the satisfaction of the Court or Judge, against the claims of any other person upon the instrument in question.

Notwithstanding the loss of a bill the holder is bound to take any steps incumbent on him. Presentment for payment may be excused,[2] or dispensed with,[3] in certain cases, but the loss of the bill will not excuse delay in giving notice of dishonour nor of protesting when necessary.[4]

10. Bills in a Set [5]

71. Rules.—(1) Where a bill is drawn in a set, each part of the set being numbered, and containing a reference to the other parts, the whole of the parts constitute one bill.[6] If they be not so numbered, one part of the set becomes a separate bill in the hands of a *bonâ fide* holder for value. Where the bills bear references to each other, only one requires to be stamped. If they be not numbered, each bill requires a separate stamp. (2) Where the holder of a set indorses two or more parts to different persons, he is liable on every such part, and every indorser subsequent to him is liable on the part he has himself indorsed, as if the said parts were separate bills. (3) Where two or more parts of a set are negotiated [7] to different holders in due course,[8] the holder whose title first accrues is, as between such holders, deemed the true owner of the bill ; but nothing in this subsection affects the rights of a person who in due course accepts or pays the part first presented to him.[9] (4) The acceptance may be written on any part, and it must be written on one part only.[10] If the drawee accepts more than one part, and such accepted parts get into the hands of different holders in due course,[11] he is liable on every such part as if it were a separate bill. (5) When the acceptor of a bill drawn in a set pays it without requiring the part bearing his acceptance to be delivered up to him, and that part at maturity [12] is outstanding in the hands of a holder in due course, he is liable to the holder thereof. (6) Subject to the preceding rules, where any one part

---

[1] Stamp Act, 1891, sec. 6.
[2] *Vide* sec. 46 (1).
[3] *Vide* sec. 46 (2).
[4] *Vide* sec. 51 (8).
[5] *Vide* Appendix.
[6] *Vide* Kearney *v.* West Granada Mining Co., 1856, 26 L.J. Ex. 15.
[7] *Vide* sec. 31.
[8] *Vide* sec. 29.
[9] *Vide* sec. 59.
[10] *Vide* sec. 17.
[11] *Vide* sec. 29.
[12] *Vide* secs. 10, 14, 45 (2).

of a bill drawn in a set is discharged by payment or otherwise,[1] the whole bill is discharged.[2]

11. Conflict of Laws

72. Rules.—Where a bill drawn in one country is negotiated,[3] accepted, or payable in another, the rights, duties, and liabilities of the parties to it are determined as follows :—

Validity in Point of Form.—(1) The validity of a bill,[4] as regards requisites in form, is determined by the place of issue ;[5] and the validity as regards requisites in form of the supervening contracts, such as acceptance,[6] or indorsement,[7] or acceptance *supra* protest,[8] is determined by the law of the place where such contract is made.[9]   Thus, according to the law of Illinois, a verbal acceptance is valid, and a bill drawn in London on a town in Illinois is validly accepted if it be verbally accepted there.   But (*a*) where a bill is issued out of the United Kingdom,[10] it is not invalid by reason only that it is not stamped in accordance with the law of the place of issue ;[11] and (*b*) where a bill issued out of the United Kingdom conforms, as regards requisites in form, to the law of the United Kingdom, it may, for the purpose of enforcing payment of it, be treated as valid between all persons who negotiate, hold, or become parties to it in the United Kingdom.

Interpretation.—(2) Subject to the provisions of the Act, the interpretation of the drawing,[12] indorsement,[13] acceptance,[14] or acceptance *supra* protest[15] of a bill, is determined by the law of the place where such contract is made.[16]   But where an inland bill[17] is indorsed in a foreign country, the indorsement is, as regards the payer, interpreted according to the law of the United Kingdom.[18]

Duties of Holders.—(3) The duties of the holder with respect to presentment for acceptance[19] or payment,[20] and the necessity for, or sufficiency of, a protest[21] or notice of dishonour[22] or otherwise, are determined by the law of the place where the act is done or the bill is dishonoured.[23]

Sum Payable.—(4) Where a bill is drawn out of, but payable in the United Kingdom, and the sum payable is not expressed in the currency of the United Kingdom, the amount is, in the absence of some express stipulation, calculated according to the rate of exchange for sight drafts

---

[1] *Vide* sec. 17.　　　　[2] *Vide* secs. 59-64.　　　[3] *Vide* sec. 31.
[4] *Vide* sec. 3.　　　　　[5] *Vide* sec. 21.　　　　　[6] *Vide* secs. 17-19.
[7] *Vide* sec. 32.　　　　　[8] *Vide* sec. 65 (3).　　　[9] *Vide* sec. 21.
[10] *Vide* sec. 4.　　　　　[11] Stewart *v.* Gelot, 1871, 9 M. 1057.
[12] *Vide* sec. 55 (1).　　　[13] *Vide* sec. 55 (2).　　　[14] *Vide* sec. 54.
[15] *Vide* sec. 66.　　　　　[16] *Vide* sec. 21.　　　　　[17] *Vide* sec. 4.
[18] Lebel *v.* Tucker, L.R. 3 Q.B. 77.　　　　　　　　[19] *Vide* secs. 39, 42.
[20] *Vide* secs. 45, 46.　　　[21] *Vide* secs. 44 (2), 51.　　[22] *Vide* secs. 48-50,
[23] Horne *v.* Rouquette, 3 Q.B.D. 514, C.A.

at the place of payment on the day the bill is payable.[1]   The Postmaster-General is not responsible for any loss sustained through a bill or note having been lost or stolen from letters put into the post-office.[2]

Date of Payment.—(5) Where a bill is drawn in one country and is payable in another, the due date of it is determined according to the law of the place where it is payable.

12. Miscellaneous

90.[3] Good Faith.—A thing is deemed to be done in good faith, within the meaning of the Act, where it is in fact done honestly, whether it is done negligently or not.[4] If a person has in his possession the means of knowing that a bill for which he is asked to give value has been stolen or otherwise fraudulently obtained, and the means of knowledge in his power is wilfully disregarded, he is not acting in good faith.

91. Signature.—(1) Where by the Act any instrument or writing is required to be signed by any person, it is not necessary that he should sign it with his own hand, but it is sufficient if his signature is written thereon by some other person by or under his authority.[5] (2) In the case of a corporation, where by the Act any instrument or writing is required to be signed, it is sufficient if the instrument or writing be sealed with the corporate seal.   But nothing in this section is to be construed as requiring the bill or note of a corporation to be under seal.[6]

92. Computation of Time.—Where by the Act the time limited for doing any act or thing is less than three days, in reckoning time non-business days are excluded.[7]   Non-business days for the purpose of the Act mean (*a*) Sunday, New Year's Day (if this day fall on a Sunday then the following Monday), Good Friday, the first Mondays of May and August, Christmas Day (if this day fall on a Sunday then the Monday following); (*b*) a bank holiday under the Bank Holidays Act, 1871, or Acts amending it ; (*c*) a day appointed by Royal Proclamation as a public fast or thanksgiving day.

93. When Noting Equivalent to Protest.—For the purposes of the Act, where a bill or note is required to be protested within a specified time, or before some further proceeding is taken, it is sufficient that the bill has been noted for protest before the expiration of the specified time or the taking of the proceeding ; and the formal protest may be extended

---

[1] *Vide* sec. 57 ; Hirschfield *v.* Smith, L.R. 1 C.P. 340.

[2] Bainbridge *v.* Postmaster-General, 1906, 1 K.B. 178.

[3] For secs. 73-89, see Cheques, and Promissory Notes.

[4] May *v.* Chapman, 16 M. & W. 355 ; Raphael *v.* Bank of England, 17 Scott, C.B. 174 ; Jones *v.* Gordon, 1877, 2 Ap. Ca. 616.

[5] Lord *v.* Hall, 1849, 8 C.B. 627.   As to what is a sufficient signature, see Foster *v.* Mackinnon, 1869, L.R. 4 C.P. 704.

[6] As to powers of corporations, see p. 85.   [7] *Vide* sec. 14.

at any time thereafter as of the date of noting. Noting consists in the notary making on the bill a memorandum of the dates, usually of present-ment and refusal to accept or pay, and his initials, with the addition of the letters N. P. (notary public).

94. Protest without Notary.—Where a dishonoured bill or note is authorised or required to be protested, and the services of a notary cannot be obtained at the place where the bill is dishonoured, any householder or substantial resident of the place may, in the presence of two witnesses, give a certificate, signed by them, attesting the dishonour of the bill, and the certificate in all respects operates as if it were a formal protest of the bill. When a bill is properly presented for payment [1] and dis-honoured, the place where such presentation took place is " the place where the bill is dishonoured," and the section applies only if the services of a notary cannot be obtained at that place.[2] A form of the certificate to be used is given in the Appendix.

95,[3] 96,[4] 97. Saving Clauses.—The rules in bankruptcy,[5] and of the common law including the law merchant, or that part of the common law which is founded upon the custom of merchants, as ascertained in decided cases, or by the evidence of facts proving custom,[6] relating to bills, promissory notes, and cheques, continue to apply unless inconsistent with the express provisions of the Act. Nothing in the Act or in any repeal effected thereby affects (a) any law or enactment for the time being in force relating to the revenue ; (b) the provisions of the Companies (Consolidation) Act, 1908, or Acts amending it or any Act relating to joint-stock banks or companies ; (c) the provisions of any Act relating to or confirming the privileges of the Bank of England or the Bank of Ireland respectively ; or (d) the validity of any usage relating to dividend warrants or the indorse-ment thereof. This provision is intended not to interfere with the practice whereby certain companies pay dividend warrants drawn in favour of two or more persons on the signature of the first-named person.

98. Summary Diligence.—Nothing in the Act extends, or restricts, or in any way alters or affects the law and practice in Scotland relating to summary diligence. In order to warrant summary diligence as between the holder of a bill, and the drawer and indorsers, the bill must be presented on its due date and timeously noted. Summary diligence is, however, competent against the acceptor although the bill is not presented

---

[1] *Vide* sec. 45.

[2] Sommerville *v.* Aaronson, 1898, 25 R. 524.

[3] *Vide* Cheques, p. 171.

[4] Deals with the repeal of certain Acts, and has itself been repealed by the Statute Law Revision Act, 1898.

[5] *Vide* Sequestration, *infra*.

[6] *Vide* sec. 8, and Goodwin *v.* Roberts, L.R. 1 Ap. Ca. 476.

for payment on its due date, but is so presented within six months thereof.[1] The protest of a bill, note, or cheque, made by a notary, may be registered within six months after the date of the bill in the case of non-acceptance, and within six months of its falling due [2] in the case of non-payment, or within six months of the date of presentation for payment in the case of bills payable on demand,[3] in the Books of Council and Session, or of the Sheriff Court within the jurisdiction of which the person charged resides.[4] An extract of the registered protest containing a warrant to charge the party liable on the bill to pay the sum in the bill with interest and expenses, within six days if resident in Scotland, and fourteen days if resident furth of Scotland, may be obtained. Although a bill may be accepted payable in England where there is no such diligence, summary diligence is competent on a protest of a bill against a party liable on the instrument who is domiciled in Scotland.

By whom Competent.—The diligence is competent at the instance of any holder whose title is *ex facie* of the bill.[5] If a bill be indorsed after protest, the protest may be assigned to the indorsee to the effect of enabling him to use or proceed with diligence already begun on it.

Against whom Competent.—Summary diligence is competent, in the case of an accepted bill, against any party liable on it, provided due notice of dishonour is given to the party charged,[6] and in the case of an unaccepted bill, against the drawer and prior indorsers, but not the drawee,[7] even although he have funds in his hands sufficient to meet it. Where a firm is the drawer, diligence is competent against any member of the firm, though his name does not appear on the bill.[8]

When Incompetent.—Diligence is competent on a bill signed by a notary or justice of the peace in presence of two witnesses ; but not on one signed by the party's initials, or by mark ; nor on one in which the husband of the party liable is the debtor ; nor on an undated bill, or one awanting in any material particular ; nor on one irregular in form or *ex facie* vitiated or altered ; nor on a bill accepted conditionally ; nor on a lost bill, or one past due, found in the holder's repositories torn up ;[9] nor on an imperfect bill not completed ;[10] nor upon a bill so long as an ordinary action on it is in dependence. The provisions of section 1 of the Money-Lenders Act, 1900 (which enable the Court to reopen a money-lending transaction), do not have the effect of qualifying the obligation contained in an *ex facie* unconditional bill or note for a

---

[1] M'Neill & Son *v.* Innes Chambers & Co., 1917, S.C. 540.
[2] *Vide* secs. 10, 14.
[3] Bon *v.* Lord Rollo, 1850, 12 D. 1310.
[4] Sutherland *v.* Gunn, 1854, 16 D. 339.
[5] Fraser *v.* Bannerman, 1853, 15 D. 756 ; Summers *v.* Marianski, 1843, 6 D. 286.
[6] *Vide* sec. 49.   [7] *Vide* sec. 55 (3).
[8] Wallace *v.* Plock, 1841, 3 D. 1047.
[9] Thomson *v.* Bell, 1850, 12 D. 1184.   [10] *Vide* sec. 20.

sum certain granted in connexion with such a transaction, so as to render summary diligence on the note incompetent.[1] Summary diligence, it is thought, is competent on a householder's certificate of protest under section 94.[2] A contrary opinion has, however, been expressed.[3]

The charge must strictly conform to its warrant, and be executed against the parties named in the protest. The debtor may bring a suspension of a charge or threatened charge on a bill, but must, as a condition of having the note passed to try the question, find caution or consign the sum in the bill, unless the bill appears *ex facie* vitiated, altered, or forged, etc.

99. Construction with other Acts.—Where any Act or document refers to any enactment repealed by the Act, such Act or document is construed and operates as if it referred to the corresponding provisions of the Act.

100. Parole Evidence.—Altering the common law, and introducing an exception to the general rule that parole evidence is inadmissible to enable an obligant to contradict or modify his written obligation, the statute provides that in any judicial proceeding in Scotland, any fact relating to a bill, cheque, or promissory note, which is relevant to any question of liability thereon, may be proved by parole evidence. But this provision does not in any way affect the existing law and practice whereby the party, who is, according to the tenor of any bill, cheque, or promissory note, debtor to the holder in the amount thereof, may be required, as a condition of obtaining a sist of diligence or suspension of a charge, or threatened charge, to make such consignation, or to find such caution, as the Court or Judge before whom the cause is depending may require.

The old rule of our law, which has been displaced by the statutory provision, created a presumption of onerosity so strong that, although it might be contradicted, it was not allowed to be disproved except by the writ of the party seeking to enforce liability on the bill, or else by a reference to his deposition on oath. That rule was supposed to be supported by favour to trade, but in comparatively recent times it was seen that it might operate very unjustly, and yet the rule was so well settled that the Court could not disregard it. The main purpose of the section in question was to remedy that injustice, but it is extremely probable that the language of the clause went somewhat beyond what was required to remedy the particular mischief referred to, and it may be that it would allow parole proof being admitted with reference to other

---

[1] Inglis v. Rothfield, 1920, S.C. 650.
[2] See article in Juridical Review for October 1898 ; M'Robert v. Lindsay, 14 Sheriff Court Reports, 89.
[3] Thorburn on Bills of Exchange Act, p. 207 ; Sommerville v. Aaronson, 1898, 25 R. 524.

questions of liability than those which depend on mere presumption of onerosity. It is, however, certain, in any event, that it can apply only to cases where the alleged liability is rested exclusively upon a bill, and that it can have no application to cases where a bill is used merely as a method of carrying into effect a written contract. Where bills are granted for the purpose of working out a contract which is expressed in writing, and the terms upon which the bills are to be drawn and accepted are not therefore to be gathered from the mere terms of the bills themselves, but from the agreement which is carried into execution by their being accepted, it is contrary to perfectly well settled rules of evidence to allow the terms of the agreement to be altered or enlarged by parole evidence, and in such a case, therefore, it is not a relevant defence on the part of the acceptor to offer to prove by parole evidence that at the time the bills were accepted there was an agreement other than the written agreement which was the foundation of the obligation.[1]

This section, upon the construction of which there are two divergent currents of authority, has occasioned considerable difficulty. No authoritative decision as to its exact meaning has yet been pronounced. The section came under the notice of the First Division of the Court in one case, but the Court differed as to its interpretation. The Lord President (Inglis) and Lord M'Laren were of opinion that the section could not be construed as meaning that a written obligation *ex facie* of a bill, such as that of the drawer of a bill (who by drawing it engages that on due presentment the bill will be accepted and paid according to its tenor, and that if it be not he will compensate the holder or any indorser who is compelled to pay it [2]) might be contradicted by parole evidence—a construction which would be subversive of the fundamental principles of jurisprudence, everywhere recognised and acted on, and therefore clearly not the intention of the Legislature, whatever the actual words might seem to imply. Lord Adam, on the other hand, expressed the opinion that although it was very anomalous and against all principle that the effect of a written contract *ex facie* of a bill or any other written agreement should be altered or modified by means of parole evidence, yet as it appeared to him that this was what the Legislature had expressly done in the section, the Court must decide accordingly. Lord Kinnear guarded himself from expressing any opinion on the point, and the case was decided without reference to the section.[3] In another case, where, in defence to an action for the amount due under a promissory note, the debtor stated that, under an arrangement between him and the creditor, the promissory note was to be renewed when due,

---

[1] *Per* Lord Kinnear in Stagg & Robson Ltd. *v.* Stirling, 1908, S.C. 675. See also *infra*.

[2] Sec. 55.

[3] National Bank of Australia *v.* Turnbull & Co., 1891, 18 R. 629.

and from time to time thereafter until he should be in a position to repay it without detriment to his business engagements, and that he had been assured by the creditor that the date of repayment would be left to himself so long as interest was paid, it was held that the defender was not entitled to a proof of his averment, on the grounds that if the agreement meant that the defender was not bound to pay the principal sum, but an annuity, it contradicted his written obligation ; and that if the agreement, which was not in writing and was wholly indefinite as to time, meant a promise by the creditor not to press for payment, the loan being terminable only on the debtor's initiative, such a promise virtually imported that the debtor was not legally compellable to fulfil his obligation, and therefore contradicted the terms of his written contract.[1] In a subsequent case at the instance of the drawers against the acceptor for payment, the defender, while not denying liability, averred that the pursuers had no immediate right to enforce payment, in respect that when the bill was originally granted, a verbal agreement, which was to endure for the currency of his lease so long as his business continued to be profitable, was come to by the parties, whereby the pursuers undertook to renew the bill as it or the renewals fell due, provided the defender purchased from the pursuers all beer to be retailed by him, and that he regularly paid interest on the loan. The defender stated he had fulfilled these conditions, and that his lease had still five years to run. The Court held the defender entitled to prove his statements by parole evidence, the case being distinguishable from those decided by the First Division,[2] in that the defender did not deny the debt nor his ultimate liability to pay it, but merely averred a specific verbal agreement that payment of the bill should not be enforceable for a definite period. In accordance with the opinion of the Lord President in the first-mentioned case, to the effect that an acceptor (and therefore *ex facie* of the bill the debtor) may prove by parole that he is not the debtor but a mere accommodation party, and may therefore contradict his written obligation by parole, and of Lord Adam, already quoted, Lord Trayner expressed the opinion that the section has introduced an exception to the general rule of law, where the question is one of liability on a bill of exchange, and that therefore he saw no reason for refusing the defender a parole proof that his liability to pay his debt, which *ex facie* of the bill was to emerge at three months' date, was not to be enforceable until a more remote date.[3] This decision was followed

---

[1] Gibson's Trs. *v.* Galloway, 1896, 23 R. 414 ; see also New London Credit Syndicate *v.* Neale, 1898, L.R. 2 Q.B. 487 ; Anderson *v.* Sommerville, Murray & Co., 1898, 1 F. 90.

[2] National Bank of Australia *v.* Turnbull, 1891, 18 R. 629, and Gibson's Trs. *v.* Galloway, 1896, 23 R. 414.

[3] Dryborough & Co. Ltd. *v.* Roy, 1903, 5 F. 665 ; Harker *v.* Pottage, 1909, 1 S.L.T. 155.

(though Lord Young more than hesitated to concur in it) in a case where the *indorsee* and holder of a bill brought an action against the acceptor, who averred that the bill was accepted for the *accommodation of the indorsee*, and that the latter had agreed that in the event of the bill being in his hands at maturity he would not call on the acceptor to retire it.[1] But in a recent case the Court was, in the opinion of Lord Kyllachy, who delivered the leading judgment, asked to go a step further than it had yet gone, which his Lordship hinted was " very far " indeed, and was asked to send to proof an averment of a mere verbal agreement to the effect that under a certain bill, expressed in the usual terms, no liability of any kind should attach to the acceptor, in a question between him and an *indorsee* and holder, until the happening of an event which might never occur, and as to which the conditions attached were wholly indefinite. The case was that of a partner of a firm who drew a bill on his firm, which after its acceptance by his firm was indorsed to a company, and by them again indorsed to a bank, who claimed on the acceptors. The acceptors averred that the bank, having made advances to the company, obtained the acceptance in security of the advance on the condition that the payment of the advance was not to be demandable until " sufficient working capital " had been raised by the company, and that as " sufficient working capital " had not been raised by that company (as to the amount of which or the time within which it was to be raised the agreement was wholly indefinite), they, as the acceptors, were not liable on the bill. The Court, however, held that that was not the kind of averment which under the section could be remitted to probation.[2] The decisions, though apparently somewhat contradictory are, it is thought, reconcilable in principle. The result of the decisions appears to be that as between the parties to a bill of exchange who stood in the relation of debtor and creditor respectively as regards the original (as opposed to the ultimate) liability on the bill, parole proof is competent to the debtor of any agreement with the creditor which shows or tends to show that the liability *ex facie* of the document was modified or altered ; but that parole proof is incompetent to prove (1) as between the original parties to the bill that the debtor was relieved of his *ultimate* liability to his creditor ; and (2) as between the acceptor or the drawer and an indorsee (except an indorsee who was a party to the agreement sought to be proved by parole) any modification or alteration whatever of the liability of the acceptor or drawer to such indorsee or a holder in due course. In other words, an acceptor cannot prove by parole any agreement between himself and the drawer which entirely negatives his liability on the instrument ; nor as between himself and a third party into whose hands the bill has onerously

---

[1] Viani & Co. *v.* Gunn & Co., 1904, 6 F. 989.
[2] Manchester and Liverpool Bank Co. *v.* Ferguson & Co., 1905, 7 F. 865.

come, can he prove by parole any agreement by which his liability *ex facie* of the bill is in any way modified or altered, unless such third party have been cognisant of and a party to the agreement at the time when the bill was accepted.

In one case [1] the Lord President said that the wording of the section does not mean that there is any magic in the word " bill," and that the moment one alleges anything with regard to a bill the whole law of evidence is thereupon upset. The meaning of the provision broadly was that under it it is competent to prove what could not at common law be provable by parole—the true relations to each other of the parties to a bill. In other words, it is now possible to prove by parole evidence that the indebtedness which, *ex facie* of the bill, is upon the acceptor is not really upon him at all. But the section has really nothing to do with the general rule of law that a written agreement cannot be altered or varied by parole evidence.

It has been decided that the section under discussion does not make parole proof of payment of a bill competent. [2]

Prescription.—The section does not apply to any case where the bill, cheque, or promissory note has undergone the sexennial prescription. This prescription, introduced by 12 Geo. III. c. 72, secs. 37-40, and rendered perpetual by 23 Geo. III. c. 18, sec. 55, applies to all [3] bills and notes (except bank notes) where such bills or notes are themselves the ground of action. [4]

Terminus a quo.—The six years are reckoned, in bills payable at a future date, from the last day of grace, in bills payable on demand, at sight, or on presentation, from the date of the bill, and in bills payable so many months after notice, from the lapse of the months specified after a demand for payment has been made. [5]

Deduction of Years.—The years of the minority of creditors (that is, the actual holder, and not merely the original creditor, provided the bill has been negotiated to him, or come into his possession as representing the preceding holder, before the six years have run) are not computed in the years of prescription.

Interruption of Prescription.—Prescription can only be interrupted by raising and executing diligence, or commencing action within the six years. [6] Claiming on the bill in a multiplepoinding, presenting or concurring in a petition for sequestration, or lodging in the hands of

---

[1] Stagg & Robson Ltd. *v.* Stirling, 1908, S.C. 675.

[2] Robertson *v.* Thomson, 1900, 3 F. 5. See M'Geoch's Trs. *v.* Muir, 1903, 19 S.L.R. (Sh. Ct.) 14.

[3] Don *v.* Lippmann, 1837, 2 S. & M'L. 682.

[4] Roy *v.* Campbell, 1850, 12 D. 1028.

[5] Broddelius *v.* Grischotti, 1887, 14 R. 536.

[6] M'Lachlan *v.* Thomson, 1831, 9 S. 753 ; Denovan *v.* Cairns, 1845, 7 D. 378 ; Milne's Trs. *v.* Ormiston's Trs., 1893, 20 R. 523.

the Sheriff, Trustee, or Preses at any meeting of creditors, a claim for the sum in the bill, are each sufficient to interrupt prescription. The production of the bill in a private trust for creditors, or acceding to such a trust, is not sufficient.[1]

Effect.—The effect of prescription is to extinguish the bill or note as a document of debt, but not to extinguish the original debt itself, which may then be proved by a writing subsequent in date to the running of the prescription [2] (as, for example, a letter in which a balance of interest is acknowledged to be due,[3] or the marking of a payment of interest on the bill subsequent to the prescriptive period), or by a reference both of the constitution of the debt and the resting-owing to the debtor's oath. In order to prove the resting-owing of the debt in a bill or note which has prescribed, it is not necessary to prove that the debt existed prior to the granting of the bill or note, and if it be in the hands of the creditor it is available as an adminicle of evidence to prove the debt and that it is resting-owing. Payment of interest on a prescribed bill or debt after the period of prescription has run has frequently been sustained on proof of the existence of the debt and its resting-owing.[4] The indorsation of a prescribed bill is worth nothing, and conveys nothing.[5]

Privileges of Bills.—Bills are probative though not holograph nor granted *in re mercatoria*. They prove their dates without witnesses, and the designations of the drawer and acceptor are not essential.

Stamp Duty.—The Act does not affect the provisions of the Stamp laws.[6] Hence, for the purposes of the Stamp Acts, the Channel Islands and the Isle of Man are not within the United Kingdom; yet for all other than revenue purposes the provisions of the Bills of Exchange Act regarding inland bills apply to them. Inland notes of all kinds, and inland bills payable otherwise than on demand, or at a period not exceeding three days after date or sight, must be drawn upon paper impressed with the appropriate stamp duty, and cannot be stamped after execution.[7] Section 32 of the Stamp Act, 1891, provides that for the purposes of this Act the expression bill of exchange includes draft, order, cheque, and letter of credit and any document or writing (except a bank note) entitling, or purporting to entitle, any person, whether named therein or not, to payment by any other person of, or to draw upon any other person for, any sum of money. It is obvious that these words include documents which would not be called

---

[1] National Bank *v.* Hope, 1837, 16 S. 177 ; Lindsay *v.* E. of Buchan, 1854, 16 D. 601 ; Blair *v.* Horn, 1858, 21 D. 45.

[2] Easton *v.* Hinshaw, 1873, 1 R. 23.

[3] Wood *v.* Howden, 1843, 5 D. 507.

[4] Campbell's Trs. *v.* Hudson's Exr., 1895, 22 R. 943.

[5] Kerr's Trs. *v.* Kerr, 1883, 11 R. 108.

[6] As to stamp duties, see Appendix.

[7] Stamp Act, 1891, 54 & 55 Vict. cap. 39, sec. 37.

bills of exchange in ordinary parlance, and would not be bills of exchange at common law or under the Bills of Exchange Act. The section further provides that all documents which fall within the definition of bills of exchange and which are payable on demand shall be stamped with a penny stamp,[1] all others with an *ad valorem* stamp. So also the definition of a promissory note for revenue purposes is more comprehensive than that contained in the Bills of Exchange Act or than the common law notion of a promissory note, for the obvious reason that a document which in truth and substance is a promissory note, might, by the insertion of an unimportant condition, be taken out of the category of promissory notes with the view of evading the stamp duty, and while the Revenue Acts are conceived in phraseology of studied ambiguity,[2] that is done with the intention of preventing evasion and that the ambiguity may be cleared and a reasonable meaning ascribed to the clause by the Court.[3] As a bill is not invalid by reason only that it is post-dated or ante-dated, it would appear that a bill executed on a paper bearing an impressed stamp of a date subsequent to that on which the bill is drawn is nevertheless valid and effectual. A bill of exchange or promissory note, written on material bearing an impressed stamp of sufficient amount, but of improper denomination, may, however, be stamped with the proper stamp on payment of the duty, and a penalty of forty shillings, if the bill or note be not then payable according to its tenor, or of ten pounds if it be so payable.[4] Every person who issues, indorses, transfers, negotiates, presents for payment, or pays, any bill of exchange or promissory note liable to duty, which is not duly stamped, is liable to a fine of ten pounds ; and any person who takes or receives such a bill or note from any other person in payment, security, by purchase, or otherwise, is not entitled to recover upon it or to make it available for any purpose whatever. It has been held that an averment that a foreign promissory note when originally presented for payment in the United Kingdom was unstamped was irrelevant, since presentation without a stamp did not involve nullity.[5] The Stamp Act further provides that an instrument which is not properly stamped " shall not be given in evidence or be available for any purpose whatever." Notwithstanding this provision, an insufficiently stamped promissory note was allowed to be handed to a witness for the purpose of refreshing his memory and obtaining from him an admission of a loan.[6]

Bills Payable on Demand.—The duty on a bill of exchange payable

---

[1] Now a twopenny stamp.
[2] Welsh's Trs. *v.* Forbes, 12 R. 860, *per* Lord Moncreiff.
[3] Thomson *v.* Bell, 1894, 22 R. 16.
[4] Vallance *v.* Forbes, 1879, 6 R. 1099 ; Tennent *v.* Crawford, 1878, 5 R. 433.
[5] Broddelius *v.* Grischotti, 1887, 14 R. 536.
[6] Birchall *v.* Bullough, 1896, L.R. 1 Q.B. 325.

on demand, at sight, or on presentation, or within three days after date or sight, may be denoted by an adhesive stamp. If the bill be drawn in the United Kingdom, the stamp must be cancelled by the person who signs the bill before he delivers it out of his hands, custody, or power. If any such bill is presented for payment unstamped, the person to whom it is presented may affix thereto an adhesive stamp of one penny, and cancel the same as if he had been the drawer of the bill, and may thereupon pay the sum mentioned in the bill, and charge the duty in account against the person by whom the bill was drawn, or deduct the duty from the said sum. The bill is then, so far as respects the duty, deemed to be valid and available. This provision does not, however, relieve any person from any fine or penalty incurred by him in relation to such bill.[1]

Foreign Bills.—Every person into whose hands any bill of exchange or promissory note drawn or made out of the United Kingdom comes in the United Kingdom before it is stamped must, before he presents for payment, indorses, transfers, or in any manner negotiates or pays the bill or note, affix thereto a proper adhesive stamp or stamps of sufficient amount, and cancel every stamp so affixed thereto. But if at the time when any such bill or note comes into the hands of any *bonâ fide* holder there is affixed thereto an adhesive stamp effectually cancelled, the stamp is, as regards the holder, deemed to be duly cancelled, although it may not appear to have been affixed or cancelled by the proper person. If the stamp be not cancelled when the bill or note comes into the hands of a *bonâ fide* holder, it is competent for such holder to cancel the stamp as if he were the person by whom it was affixed, and upon his so doing, the bill or note is deemed duly stamped and as valid and available as if the stamp had been cancelled by the person by whom it was affixed. These provisions, however, do not relieve any person from any fine or penalty incurred by him for not cancelling an adhesive stamp. The *ad valorem* duties upon bills or notes drawn or made out of the United Kingdom must be denoted by an adhesive stamp.

Bills Drawn in the Channel Islands and Isle of Man.—No stamp duty is payable on purely local bills drawn and payable in these Islands. Where a bill is drawn in any of the Islands on a person resident in the United Kingdom, the stamp duty on the bill being negotiated in the United Kingdom is denoted by means of an adhesive foreign bill stamp. Bills by persons resident in the United Kingdom on persons resident in the Islands specified must be drawn on Inland Revenue impressed stamped forms.

Bills in a Set.—When a bill of exchange is drawn in a set according to the custom of merchants, and one of the set is duly stamped, the

---

[1] Stamp Act, *supra*, sec. 38.

other or others of the set are, unless issued or in some manner negotiated apart from the stamped bill, exempt from duty. Upon proof of the loss or destruction of a duly stamped bill, forming one of a set, any other bill of the set which has not been issued, or in any manner negotiated apart from the lost or destroyed bill, may, although unstamped, be admitted in evidence to prove the contents of the lost or destroyed bill.

Stamp Duty on Protest.—The stamp duty on the protest of a bill of exchange or promissory note may be denoted by an adhesive stamp, which must be cancelled by the notary.[1] Where the duty on the bill or note does not exceed one shilling, the duty on the protest is the same as on the bill or note. In any other case the duty is one shilling.

---

[1] Stamp Act, 1891, sec. 90.

CHAPTER II

CHEQUES

Definition.—A cheque (which includes coupons on Colonial stock certificates [1]) is a bill of exchange drawn on a banker, payable on demand; that is, it is an unconditional order in writing, drawn on a banker, signed by the person giving it, requiring the banker to pay on demand a sum certain in money to, or to the order of, a specified person or to bearer.[2] Any number of persons can sign as drawers of a cheque so long as the account is in their joint names. An order to pay money in the form of an ordinary cheque with a proviso in the body of the cheque that a receipt form attached should be filled up has been held not to be a cheque within the meaning of the Bills of Exchange Act.[3] If the proviso be not addressed to the banker upon whom the cheque is drawn, the cheque may be accepted as unconditional. Hence, in a case where in a footnote to the cheque it was stated " The receipt on the back hereof must be signed, which signature will be taken as an indorsement of the cheque," the Court held the cheque unconditional.[4]

Cheques differ, however, from bills of exchange payable on demand in that (a) they are not intended to be, and are not in fact, accepted by the banker on whom they are drawn; (b) they are granted not as a continuing security, but for more or less immediate payment, and consequently may become " stale " or overdue sooner; [5] (c) the drawer is not discharged by undue delay in presentment, unless he has been prejudiced by the delay; (d) the banker, who is the drawee or acceptor, is not liable for having paid on a forged or unauthorised indorsement; and (e) they may be countermanded after issue.[6]

Essentials.—The essentials of a cheque are—

1. It must be in writing.[7] Unlike bills drawn at a currency, cheques do not require to be drawn on paper specially appropriated to their use. It is sufficient if a person draw his cheque on a sheet of notepaper.

---

[1] 40 & 41 Vict. cap. 59, sec. 7.   [2] B. of E. Act, secs. 3 (1), 73.

[3] Bavins, junr., & Sims v. London and South-Western Bank, 1900, 1 Q.B. 270.

[4] Nathan v. Ogdens Ltd., 1905, 93 L.T. 553; affd. 94 L.T. 126.

[5] London and County Bank v. Groome, 8 Q.B.D. 288, 293; see infra.

[6] Vide passim, Keene v. Beard, 8 C.B. N.S. 372, 380; see infra.

[7] See Bills, sec. 3.

2. It need not be dated.[1] It is not invalid by reason only that it is post-dated, or ante-dated, or that it bears date on a Sunday. But a banker is not entitled to cash a cheque prior to the date on which it purports to be drawn, and if he does so, the payment made is at his own risk,[2] though it would appear that a post-dated cheque may validly be negotiated for value prior to the date on which it bears to be drawn.[3] An alteration of the date of a cheque will invalidate it, and a person taking a cheque with an altered date, without negligence and in ignorance of the alteration, cannot recover from the drawer.[4]

3. It must contain an unconditional order to pay. No particular form of order is necessary, but it must be so expressed as to imply a demand made by a person who has a right to make it on another who has a duty to obey. The demand may be expressed in terms of courtesy, but a mere hope that the addressee will pay is not sufficient,[5] nor is a letter, requesting the loan of money rather than ordering the payment of it, and not imposing any compulsion on the part of the payee, sufficient. So a mere authority to pay, which does not amount to a demand, is not a cheque.[6] The order must be unconditional,[7] and it must be expressed so as to imply payment. Thus, " debit my account " has been held equivalent to an order to pay,[8] and expressions such as " deliver," " credit in cash," etc., are effectual.[9] The words " against cheque " appearing upon a cheque have no effect upon its negotiability.[10]

4. It must be drawn upon a banker, that is, addressed by name to a person or body of persons, whether incorporated or not, who carry on the business of bankers.[11]

5. It must be signed by the drawer. The signature is usually, but not necessarily, adhibited in the right-hand lower corner of the cheque. It may, however, be written in any part of the cheque. The signature must be that of the person in whose name the account is kept, or of some one authorised by him to sign that name,[12] or the signature of a person who has authority, as agreed between the banker and his customer, to operate upon the account.[13] Where a customer's signature differs from that with which the banker is familiar, the banker is under no obligation to pay the cheque even on satisfactory evidence of

---

[1] See Bills, sec. 3.
[2] Da Silva v. Fuller, 7 M. & W. 178.
[3] Royal Bank of Scotland v. Tottenham, 1894, L.R. 2 Q.B. 715.
[4] Vance v. Lowther, 1876, L.R. 1 Ex. D. 176.
[5] Little v. Slackford, 1 M. & W. 171.
[6] Hamilton v. Spottiswoode, 1849, 4 Exch. 200.
[7] See Bills, sec. 3.   [8] Swan v. Bank of Scotland, 1841, 4 D. 210.
[9] See Chitty on Bills, p. 110.
[10] Glen v. Semple, 1901, 3 F. 1134.
[11] See Bills, sec. 3.
[12] Sec. 91 (1).
[13] See Banker and Customer, supra.

the authenticity of the signature. Thus, where a customer habitually signs " John Williams," a banker may, on his own responsibility, honour a cheque signed " J. Williams," if he is satisfied that his customer has so signed, but he is under no obligation to honour a cheque signed by his customer in any way different from that which he has been instructed to honour. Where a cheque is dishonoured because the signature differs from the customer's usual or specimen signature, this reason should be stated. Signature does not, however, necessarily mean subscription. It is sufficient if adequate means of the customer's identification be afforded to the banker, and a cheque which is holograph of the drawer and which contains his name is sufficient authority to the banker to honour the cheque. Thus a cheque holograph of the drawer in such terms as, " I, John Smith, desire you to pay," or " Mr. John Smith desires Messrs. —— to pay," is good. The signature may be in pencil.[1] A cheque may also be signed on behalf of any person, whether drawer or indorser, who is unable to do so, by a notary public or justice of the peace.

6. It must be payable on demand.[2]

7. It must be an order to pay a sum certain in money. An order to pay in bank notes is not a cheque. The sum payable may be expressed in words or figures, or both, and where there is a discrepancy between the two the sum denoted by the words is the sum payable.[3] Where, however, the amount is expressed in foreign currency, or in that of some British possession, the amount is payable in British currency at the customary rate of exchange.[4] Although common in practice and invariably accepted, a cheque drawn in Scotland for a less sum than twenty shillings is " absolutely void and of no effect, any law, statute, usage, or custom to the contrary thereof in any wise notwithstanding."

8. It must be made payable to a specified person or to bearer. A cheque may be made payable (a) " to bearer," " to myself or bearer," or " to A. B. or bearer," in which cases it is payable to bearer, the name of the payee being disregarded. Such a cheque is negotiated by delivery without indorsation, but it may be indorsed by A. B., or any subsequent holder. (b) " To myself," " to myself or order," or " to . . . order," in which case it is payable to the order of the drawer. The expression " to . . . order " must be construed as meaning " to my order," though it may be considered as at least doubtful whether a cheque payable " to . . . or order " is a valid document so long as the blank remains unfilled up.[5] (c) " To A. B.," " to A. B. or order," or " to the order of

---

[1] See Execution of Deeds, *ante.*
[2] See Bills, *ante*, secs. 1, 10.
[3] B. of E. Act, sec. 9 (2), *q.v.*, and cases cited.
[4] See Payment, Mode of, *ante.*
[5] Chamberlain *v.* Young, 1893, L.R. 2 Q.B. 206.

A. B.," in which cases it is payable to A. B. and is negotiated by the indorsement of A. B. completed by delivery.[1] Where the indorsement is blank it is payable to bearer. (*d*) " To A. B. *and* C. D. or order." [2] A cheque payable to two or more persons jointly must be indorsed by all to render it negotiable. A cheque payable to two or more persons jointly and severally is payable to, and is negotiable by, the indorsement of any one of them. (*e*) " To A. B. *or* C. D. or order." [3] A cheque payable in the alternative to one of two, or one or some of several payees, is (it is thought) negotiable by the indorsement of any one, or a majority or quorum, of the payees.[4] (*f*) To the holder of an office for the time being, as " to the secretary, treasurer, cashier, president, etc., of the A. B. company, association, club, etc.," or " to such person or his order," or " to the order of such person." Cheques so drawn are payable to the holder of the office for the time being,[5] but cheques payable simply to the holder of the office for the time being without the addition of the words " or order," in so far as they contain words which prohibit transfer, or indicate an intention that they should not be transferable, are not negotiable by the indorsation of the payee. Where a cheque is payable to the holder of an office for the time being, or to his order, thus negativing the idea of its non-negotiability, it may be negotiated by the indorsement of the payee. The indorsement should bear the signature of the holder of the office, and should be expressed to be signed by him *as representing his office.* Where any person is under obligation to indorse a cheque in a representative capacity, he may indorse it in such terms as to negative personal liability,[6] by the addition of words indicating that he signs merely as an agent or as filling a representative capacity. He may also negative personal liability by the addition of such words as " without recourse," but a transferee is not bound to take a cheque with such an indorsement, as it deprives him of his recourse, not merely against the indorser personally, but also against the principal whom he represents. (*g*) " To A. (*or*, to A. only) for the account of B.," or " to A. or order for collection," or " for my use," are each restrictive directions, and prohibit the negotiation of a cheque. A banker paying an indorsee of such a cheque has notice that the payee has power to deal with it only in a specified way, and he would be liable to the drawer in repetition of the amount in the event of such indorsee misapplying it. (*h*) To a fictitious or non-existing person. A cheque drawn to the order of a fictitious or non-existing person may be treated as payable to bearer, although the drawer believes and intends the cheque to be

---

[1] B. of E. Act, sec. 31 (3).   [2] See Bills, sec. 7 (2).
[3] B. of E. Act, sec. 7 (2).
[4] Thomson *v.* Philp, 1867, 5 M. 344. See *ante*, p. 100,
[5] B. of E. Act, sec. 8 (1).
[6] See Bills, sec. 31 (5).

payable to the order of a real person. The fact that the drawer was induced by fraud to draw the cheque in favour of a person whom he believed to exist, but who was actually non-existent, is immaterial in a question with a *bonâ fide* holder for value.[1]

9. It must be stamped with a twopenny stamp, which, if the cheque be drawn in the United Kingdom, may be denoted by an adhesive stamp to be cancelled by the drawer, before the cheque passes out of his hands, custody, or power. Several stamps totalling twopence may be used instead of one twopenny stamp. If the cheque be presented for payment unstamped, the banker may affix a proper adhesive stamp and cancel the same, charging the drawer with the amount of the stamp, though in that case neither the drawer, nor the payee who accepts or receives it in payment or security, is relieved from any penalty incurred in relation to the issuing of an unstamped cheque or bill of exchange payable on demand.[2] Cheques drawn on banks in the Channel Islands or Isle of Man are not liable to stamp duty in these Islands, but when negotiated in the United Kingdom there must be affixed to them and cancelled a twopenny stamp. The Stamp Act only permits the stamp to be affixed and cancelled by the drawer or the banker or other person to whom the cheque is presented for payment. If the stamp is cancelled by any other one, the cheque is not duly stamped.[3]

Holder in Due Course.[4]—Every holder of a cheque is *primâ facie* deemed to be a holder in due course. The provisions of the Act with regard to holders in due course apply to cheques.[5] But if in an action upon a cheque it is admitted or proved that the issue or subsequent negotiation of the cheque is affected with fraud, duress, force and fear, or illegality, the burden of proof is shifted, unless and until the holder proves that, subsequent to the alleged fraud or illegality, value has in good faith been given for the cheque.[6] If, therefore, it is admitted or proved that a cheque is affected with illegality (as, for example, that it has been granted for a gambling debt), the holder of it, in order to secure the privileges of a holder in due course, must prove that he has given value for it in good faith ; that is to say, he must prove both that he has given value and that he had no notice or knowledge of the illegality so proved or admitted. If his proof fails in either particular he cannot recover.[7] It is competent to prove by parole that a cheque was granted subject to certain conditions, and a holder for value who takes such a

---

[1] Sec. 7 (3). Clutton *v.* Attenborough, 1897, L.R. A.C. 90.

[2] Stamp Act, 1891 ; see Bills, Stamping, *supra*.

[3] Hobbs *v.* Cathie, 1890, 6 T.L.R. 292.

[4] See Bills, sec. 29.

[5] Semple *v.* Kyle, 1902, 4 F. 421.   [6] See Bills, sec. 30.

[7] *Per* Lord Wellwood in Tyler *v.* Maxwell, 1892, 30 S.L.R. 583. See also Pollok *v.* Burns, 1875, 2 R. 497 ; Couston *v.* Miller, 1862, 24 D. 607 ; Avner & Co. *v.* Tullis's Exrs., 1st Div., 9th June 1911.

cheque with notice of the conditions is not entitled to recover unless the conditions are implemented.[1]

Indorsation.—A cheque, being a bill of exchange payable on demand, may, like any other bill, be indorsed so as to entitle the indorsee or any subsequent holder to sue the indorser thereon, and the ordinary rules, applicable to the indorsation of bills of exchange, apply. An indorsement must transfer the whole of the cheque and not a portion of the amount. Where a cheque is indorsed in Oriental characters the paying banker is entitled to get a notarially certified translation of the indorsement or to have the indorsement guaranteed by the collecting banker. The ordinary indorsation of the payee to a banker upon whom a cheque is drawn is not such as to subject him to any liability. Such an indorsation is really of the nature of an acknowledgment of receipt of payment (though without the additional appropriate stamp it cannot operate legally as a *receipt*), and a guarantee to the drawer that the banker has paid the cheque—on the principle that when a document of debt is in the debtor's possession payment of the debt is presumed—and that he is therefore entitled to debit his account with the amount. Such indorsation is usually, though not necessarily, written on the back of the cheque.

A cheque drawn in favour of "A. B. or bearer" is negotiable by delivery without indorsation, may be passed from hand to hand like an ordinary bank note, and when presented to a banker for payment requires no indorsation. As between himself and his customer, a banker who pays such a cheque without the indorsation of the person presenting it, is protected by the rule of law that where a document of debt is in possession of the debtor payment of the debt is presumed. Such a cheque when presented to a banker for payment should, however, if possible, be indorsed by the person presenting it *ob majorem cautelam*. A cheque drawn payable to bearer, so long as it purports to be so payable, cannot be restrictively indorsed by the payee or any subsequent holder, so as to be payable to the order of the indorsee, although the payee of such a cheque is entitled to substitute the word "order" for the word "bearer" in the body of the cheque, and thus to change the cheque from one payable to bearer to one payable to order. A cheque in favour of a person "or order" is negotiable by the indorsation of that person. The indorsation may be (a) general, (b) special, or (c) restrictive.[2]

A banker is bound to pay a cheque which purports to be indorsed by the person to whom it is drawn payable, and so long as the indorsement is regular the banker is under no obligation to ascertain that it is *bonâ fide*. In the case of a crossed cheque his freedom from liability depends on his obeying the direction conveyed by the crossing.[3]

---

[1] Semple *v.* Kyle, *supra*.   [2] See Bills, Indorsation of, p. 125.

[3] Smith *v.* Union Bank of London, 1875, 1 Q.B.D. 31 ; *infra*, p. 181.

Even in the case where the banker entertains a strong suspicion, not amounting to absolute knowledge, that the indorsation, if purporting to be regular, is a forgery, he would probably not be guilty of negligence in paying the cheque. A banker who suspects on reasonable grounds an indorsation to be forged is, however, justified in taking time to inquire into its genuineness.[1]

A banker is not justified in paying a cheque payable to " John Smith " and indorsed " John Smyth," as it does not purport to be indorsed by the person to whom it is payable. But a variation in the Christian name of a payee which is obviously only one of spelling, as where " Gorge " is written for " George," will not justify the banker in refusing to honour the cheque, though a cheque payable to " Ann Smith " is not validly indorsed " Anne Smith," since Ann and Anne are not obviously different ways of spelling the same name, but may be two distinct names. Where in a cheque payable to order the payee or indorsee is wrongly designated, or his name misspelt, he may indorse the cheque as therein described, adding, if he think fit, his proper signature.[2] A cheque payable to Mrs. John Smith would not be validly indorsed " Mrs. John Smith," nor would it be so if indorsed " Mary Smith." The indorsation in such a case should be " Mary Smith, wife (or widow) of John Smith."

A cheque payable to " A. B., senior," is validly indorsed by A. B.'s signature without the addition of the word senior, which may be regarded as a superfluous designation. But a cheque payable to " A. B., junior," can only be validly indorsed " A. B., junior," the word junior in this case being necessary for A. B.'s identification. A cheque payable to A. B. is not validly indorsed " Mr. *or* Mrs. A. B.," as the addition of the prefix converts the indorsation from a signature into a mere address. But the addition of a description or designation after a person's signature, such as Knight, Esquire, M.A., LL.D., etc., has not this effect. A cheque payable to " John Jones, trustee (or executor, etc.), or order," must be indorsed " John Jones, trustee " (or executor, etc., as the case may be). A cheque payable to " Messrs. Smith " is validly indorsed " A. & B. Smith," but not " Smith & Co.," for in the former case the banker is entitled to assume that A. & B. Smith are the Messrs. Smith intended by the drawer, while in the latter case no such presumption can exist. A cheque payable to " Messrs. J. Smith & Co. or order " is not validly indorsed " Smith & Co.," and *vice versâ*, as a banker would not be justified in assuming that Messrs. Smith & Co. are Messrs. J. Smith & Co. So a cheque payable to " Messrs. Smith Brothers " is not validly indorsed by the signatures of the Messrs. Smith respectively who constitute the partnership, but should be indorsed " Smith Brothers." A cheque

---

[1] Robarts *v.* Tucker, 18 L.J. Q.B. 575.
[2] See Bills, sec. 32.

payable to " John Smith " is validly indorsed " J. Smith," as the banker is justified in assuming that the " J. Smith " who signs is the " John Smith " referred to. A cheque payable to a person is, on his decease, validly indorsed by his executor if it bear to be signed authoritatively by such executor.

A cheque payable to the order of " Mr. J. & Mrs. M. Smith " is not validly indorsed " J. & M. Smith," but should bear the indorsation of each of the payees, as where a cheque is payable to the order of two or more payees or indorsees, who are not partners, all must indorse unless the one indorsing has authority to indorse for the others. A cheque payable to Miss Smith or Miss Mary Smith should, if indorsed after her marriage to John Jones, be signed " Mary Jones (*née* Smith)." Cheques payable to the order of a limited company, or of a company trading under a descriptive name, should be indorsed " for and on behalf " or " per procuration " of the company, by one of the officials or partners of the company, with the addition of his official designation, as manager, secretary, etc. While this must be regarded as the strict law on the subject, it is right to state that according to a practice recognised by most of the Scottish banks a cheque made payable to a company is accepted as sufficiently indorsed if signed " p.p." of the company by a person in their employment, without the addition of any official designation to his signature. The bank first accepting the cheque is assumed to be satisfied of the regularity of the indorsement, and hence to guarantee the bank upon which the cheque is drawn against any claim in respect of the irregularity of the indorsement. A cheque payable to the order of a company, or the manager or secretary of a company, trading under a descriptive name, is not validly indorsed by a third person signing per procuration of the manager or an official of such company, as such person has no power to delegate his authority. But a cheque signed per procuration, or for and on behalf of such a company by a person who signs for the manager or other official of the company, is valid, as it purports to be signed by the authority of the company. So a cheque in favour of the " s.s. *Edinburgh* or order " should be indorsed by some one acting " for and on behalf of " the steamship. A cheque payable to " John Smith or order " is not validly indorsed " for John Smith, Robert Brown, trustee," as it does not purport to be indorsed by or with the authority of the payee ; but a bank, on obtaining evidence of the appointment of Robert Brown as trustee on the sequestrated estate of John Smith, would be in safety to pay the cheque on such an indorsement. An indorsement by means of an impressed stamp purporting to be a facsimile of the payee's signature would probably justify a banker in cashing a cheque, on the ground that it purports to be the signature of the payee, adhibited, if not actually by him, at least by his authority.

Forged Indorsation.—Section 19 of the Stamp Act of 1853,[1] which is
not repealed, provides that " any draft or order drawn upon a banker for
a sum of money, payable to order on demand, which shall when presented
for payment purport to be indorsed by the person to whom the same
shall be drawn payable, shall be a sufficient authority to such banker to
pay the amount of such draft or order to the bearer thereof ; and it shall
not be incumbent on such banker to prove that such indorsement, or any
subsequent indorsement, was made by or under the direction or authority
of the person to whom said draft or order was or is made payable, either
by the drawer or any indorser thereof." Section 60 of the Bills of
Exchange Act substantially repeats this provision, and enacts that it
is not incumbent on a banker, who pays in good faith and in the ordinary
course of business a cheque drawn upon him to order on demand, to show
that the indorsement of the payee or any subsequent indorsement was
made by or under the authority of the person whose indorsement it
purports to be, and that the banker in such circumstances is deemed to
have paid the cheque in due course, although such indorsement has been
forged or made without authority. In other words, a banker is justified
in paying a cheque which purports to be indorsed by the person to whom
it is drawn payable, or to be indorsed by or with his authority, as per
procuration,[2] or by his agent,[3] though it should subsequently turn out
that the indorsation is a forgery, or has been adhibited without the
payee's sanction or authority, provided that the payment have been
made without negligence, in good faith, and in the ordinary course of
business. Negligence is a question of fact which will be determined
according to the circumstances of each particular case.[4] Thus a banker
who honours a cheque drawn payable to " A. B., or order," and indorsed
" for A. B., C. D.," or " A. B. *per* C. D.," will not be protected, as such an
indorsation does not purport to be signed by A. B. or by his authority.
The protection afforded by the statute applies only to the banker on
whom the cheque is drawn, and does not extend to an indorsee, who
takes the cheque with all the latent rights and disabilities of the person
from whom he received it, or to a banker who undertakes to collect the
proceeds on behalf of a person who is not a customer of his own. Where
a cheque is presented to a banker, other than him on whom it is drawn,
by a stranger, it is the duty of such banker to satisfy himself that the
person who presents the cheque is the person in right of it. Thus in
one case a cheque was drawn by A. B. payable to C. D. or his order. It

---

[1] 16 & 17 Vict. cap. 59, sec. 19.
[2] Cookson *v.* Bank of England, 1860. Reported in " Times " newspaper of 30th
June 1860, and partially set out and approved of in Hare *v.* Copeland, 1862, 13 Irish
Common Law Reports, 426.
[3] Charles *v.* Blackwell, 1 C.P.D. 548 ; 2 C.P.D. 151.
[4] Bissell *v.* Fox, 51 L.T.R. 633 ; 53 L.T.R. 193.

was stolen from C. D. by his clerk, who, after forging his master's signature, presented it to a banker, to whom he was a stranger, for the purpose of collection. The collecting banker received the proceeds from the drawee and handed them, less commission, to the thief, who absconded. In an action by the drawer it was held that, while the banker on whom the cheque was drawn was protected, on the ground that though he was bound to know the signature of his customer the drawer, he could not be supposed to know that of the payee, and that he had paid the cheque to the order of the person to whom it purported to be payable, no such protection was afforded to the collecting banker, who took the cheque with all the disabilities attaching to the person from whom he received it, and who must be held to have received payment from the drawee, not on behalf of his principal, but of the true owner, the person who had a legal title to it prior to the forgery.[1]

A forged or unauthorised indorsement upon a cheque payable to order operates not only to annul all rights or obligations of the indorsers or indorsees subsequent to such indorsation, but also to extinguish the debt due to any such indorsee by the indorser from whom he received the cheque.[2] Each *bonâ fide* holder may, however, recover from his predecessor in title, until the author of the forged or unauthorised signature is reached.[3] A *bonâ fide* holder for value of a cheque payable to order, subsequent to the forged or unauthorised indorsation, cannot go beyond it so as to sue a party, whether as drawer or indorser, liable on the cheque prior to such indorsation.[4] Thus if A. draws a cheque on his banker, payable to B. or his order, which is lost in transmission, and falls into the hands of dishonest persons, who forge B.'s indorsement and pass it for value, the holder for value has no recourse against A. if he have stopped payment of the cheque. Nor is the holder entitled even to retain the cheque.[5]

Crossed Cheques.[6]—The crossing of a cheque operates as a direction by the drawer to the banker to pay the cheque in a particular way. Cheques may be crossed either generally or specially. It is the practice of banks to recognise as a valid crossing that made by means of a perforating machine.

1. A cheque is *crossed generally* when it bears across its face two

---

[1] Ogden *v.* Benas, L.R. 9 C.P. 513. See *infra*, Crossed Cheques.

[2] Alderson *v.* Langdale, 1832, 3 B. & A. 660 ; B. of E. Act, secs. 24, 73.

[3] Macdonald *v.* Union Bank, 1864, 2 M. 963.

[4] Bobbett *v.* Pinkett, 1876, L.R. 1 Ex. D. 368 ; Burchfield *v.* Moore, 1854, 23 L.J. Q.B. 261.

[5] Johnson *v.* Windle, 1836, 3 Bing. N.C. 225.

[6] For the origin and history of the practice of crossing cheques, see Bellamy *v.* Marjoribanks, 7 Ex. 389.

parallel transverse lines, with or without the words " and company," or an abbreviation of them, and with or without the addition of the words " not negotiable." [1] A cheque may be crossed generally or specially by the drawer ; where a cheque is uncrossed, the holder may cross it generally or specially ; and where it is crossed generally or specially, he may add the words " not negotiable." [2] The crossing of a cheque, including the words " not negotiable," is a material part of the cheque, and cannot lawfully be obliterated, added to, or altered otherwise than as authorised by the Act. By crossing a cheque generally a direction is given to the banker on whom it is drawn not to pay the cheque otherwise than to a banker ; and to the holder, an intimation that he can receive payment only through a banker. A banker who pays a cheque crossed generally otherwise than to a banker, is liable to the true owner of the cheque for any loss which he may sustain owing to the cheque having been so paid.[3] In other words, a banker who pays an *uncrossed* cheque, payable to bearer, to a thief or finder is protected, as there is no obligation on him to see that the person who presents the cheque for payment is the person who is entitled to it ; and a banker paying a cheque payable to order is protected if he pay on an indorsement which purports to be signed by, or with the authority of, the person to whom it is payable, even if the signature afterwards turn out to have been forged or adhibited without authority. But a banker who pays a cheque to a thief or finder, or upon an unauthorised or forged signature *in disregard of a crossing*, whether special or general, is in a different position, in that he is liable to the true owner, whether the drawer or a subsequent transferee, if that true owner can prove that he has suffered loss by the cheque having been so paid.[4]

It will therefore be evident that there is nothing to prevent a banker cashing a crossed cheque over the counter if he is satisfied that the presenter is the person to whom it is payable, and that if he is so satisfied the addition to the indorsement of any such words as " pay cash " is not only superfluous but useless. If, on the other hand, the banker should prove to have been mistaken in the identity of the payee, and to have paid the money to some one not entitled to it, in disregard of the crossing, the addition of any such words will afford him no protection. A banker who receives a crossed cheque through the clearing-house which bears no banker's stamp, is justified in paying it, as the payment in such a case must necessarily have been made to a banker, and therefore in obedience to the drawer's direction implied in

---

[1] B. of E. Act, sec. 76. [2] *Ibid.* sec. 77 (1)-(4).
[3] B. of E. Act, sec. 79 (2).
[4] Bobbett *v.* Pinkett, L.R. 1 Ex. D. 368 ; Smith *v.* Union Bank of London, L.R. 1 Q.B.D. 31.

the drawing. No crossed cheque drawn in favour of an incorporated or other company should be paid over the counter. If a banker, in good faith and without negligence, pay a cheque which at the time of its presentation does not appear to be crossed, or to have had a crossing which has been obliterated, or to have been added to or altered otherwise than as authorised by the Act, he will not incur any liability for disobedience to a crossing not then apparent. A banker who pays a crossed cheque otherwise than to a banker, is not entitled to debit his customer with the amount he has so paid contrary to his direction, and is liable to him in repetition of the amount if he has suffered loss by the cheque having been so paid.[1] The drawer of the cheque, however, has no right of action against the banker who honours a crossed cheque contrary to the directions given by the crossing, simply on that ground. He must prove that he has suffered loss thereby. The drawer of a cheque which has been paid contrary to his direction has a right to sue the person who has received payment of it, if such person had a bad title to it.[2]

A banker who, in good faith and without negligence, pays the amount of a cheque crossed generally to the banker presenting it, or if crossed specially, to the banker to whom it is crossed, or his agent for collection, being a banker, is entitled to debit his customer with the amount, whether the payment is made on behalf of the true owner or not. That is, if he obey the direction given by the crossing *bonâ fide* and without negligence, he is not responsible to the drawer, though it turn out that the person on whose behalf the payment is made is not the holder in due course, but a thief or a finder.[3] The drawer of the cheque in such circumstances will be discharged of his liability to the payee for payment of the debt for which the cheque is given, provided the cheque have reached the hands of the payee, and have been lost by or stolen from him. The remedy of the payee in such circumstances is against the person on whose behalf the amount of the cheque has been collected, but he has no action against the banker who in good faith and without negligence merely acts as collecting agent for his customer, and duly pays over to him the amount.[4]

Position of Collecting Banker of Crossed Cheques.—The mere receiving of payment of a cheque on behalf of a customer is not a ground of liability, and where a banker in good faith and without negligence receives payment for a customer of a cheque crossed generally or specially to himself, and the customer has no title or a defective title thereto, the banker incurs no liability to the true owner by reason only

[1] Smith *v.* Union Bank of London, *supra.*
[2] Bobbett *v.* Pinkett, L.R. 1 Ex. D. 363.
[3] See B. of E. Act, sec. 80.
[4] Mathieson *v.* London and County Bank, 1879, 5 C.P.D. 7. See Bills, sec. 82.

of having received such payment.[1] To bring a case within the protection of section 82 the three following facts must coexist, viz. :—
(1) The person for whom the cheque is collected must be a customer
of the bank ; (2) the bank must collect the proceeds of the cheque for
that customer ; and (3) the cheque must be collected and paid without
negligence, that is, without want of reasonable care in reference to the
true owner. The *onus* is on the banker to prove that he has not been
negligent, and negligence is a question of fact. The test to be applied
is whether the transaction of paying in any given cheque coupled with
the circumstances antecedent and present is so out of the ordinary course
that it ought to have aroused doubts in the banker's mind and caused
him to make inquiry.[2] In one case a cheque was drawn payable to a
limited company and crossed generally. The secretary of the company
indorsed the cheque in name of his company, subscribing his own
name as secretary. He then paid it in to the credit of his own personal
account with his bankers, and drew out the amount as he required it.
In an action by the company against the collecting bank, it was decided
that, although the bank had acted in good faith, they were liable to
the company in the amount of the cheque. The ground of the
decision was that it was apparent on the face of the transaction
that the secretary was using for himself a valuable document which
bore evidence of having been granted for the benefit of his employers ;
that the whole course of ordinary business was opposed to the idea
that the secretary of a company was likely to have been paid money
due to him as salary or otherwise by the authorisation of the indorsement by himself to himself of a cheque payable to the order of the
company, and that in accepting such a cheque so indorsed for his
private account the bank were guilty of negligence and had thus lost
the protection of the statute.[3] A like decision was given in a case where
a bank allowed a director of a limited company to pay a cheque drawn
in favour of the company into his private banking account, and that
although the director held the whole shares in the company with the
exception of one.[4] To constitute a person a customer of a bank within
the meaning of the section, there must be some sort of account between
them—either a current account or a deposit account or some similar
relation. For example, it has been held that a person was not a
customer of a bank although the bank had for some years been in the
habit of paying him cash for cheques and subsequently collecting the

---

[1] B. of E. Act, sec. 82.

[2] Morison *v.* London County and Westminster Bank, 1914, 3 K.B. 356 ; Com-
missioners of Taxation *v.* English, Scottish and Australian Bank Ltd., 1920, A.C. 683 ;
Ross *v.* London County Westminster and Parr's Bank, 1919, 1 K.B. 678 ; Hampstead
Guardians *v.* Barclay's Bank Ltd., 1923, 39 T.L.R. 229.

[3] Hannan's Lake View Central Ltd. *v.* Armstrong & Co., 16 T.L.R. 236.

[4] Underwood Ltd. *v.* Bank of Liverpool and Martin's Ltd., 1923, 39 T.L.R. 606.

amounts.[1] But the relationship would seem to begin so soon as an account is opened and the first cheque is paid in and accepted by the banker for collection.[2] Again, bankers are entitled to the protection given only in cases where they receive payment for a customer. They are not entitled to the protection where they receive a cheque under such circumstances as to constitute them holders of it on their own account. In a case [3] decided by the House of Lords in 1903, it was laid down that if a banker at once credited a customer with the value of a cheque drawn upon another bank, and allowed him to draw against the balance thus increased before the cheque was cleared, the banker became a holder for value, and collected the cheque, not on behalf of his customer, but of himself, and was therefore not within the protection afforded by the section. The Court, however, held that the banker would have been within the protection of the statute if without crediting the account of the customer with the value of the cheque before collection, he allowed him to overdraw his account in view of the anticipated credit. It is difficult to see that there is much difference between the case of a bank which at once credits a customer with the face value of a cheque paid in to his account, and allows him to draw against his credit balance thus increased, and the case of a bank which, without crediting the customer with the value of a cheque before collection, allows him to overdraw his account in view of the anticipated credit. So stood the law as decided in the case referred to. The result of the decision was so far-reaching in its effect, and so hampered the expedition of business, that the English banks at once made a strenuous effort to get an Act of Parliament passed to rectify the state of matters resulting therefrom. After various unsuccessful attempts, the following Act of Parliament was passed, entitled " The Bills of Exchange (Crossed Cheques) Act, 1906," [4] which came into force on 4th August 1906, viz., " A banker receives payment of a crossed cheque for a customer within the meaning of section 82 of the Bills of Exchange Act, 1882, notwithstanding he credits his customer's account with the amount of the cheque before receiving payment thereof." As the law now stands, a banker is entitled to the protection of the statute whether he credits his customer's account with the value of the cheque or not before it is cleared. Further, the protection only applies to cheques which are crossed before they come into the banker's possession, and the bankers cannot by afterwards crossing the

---

[1] Great Western Ry. Co. v. London and County Bank, 1901, A.C. 414 ; see also Matthews v. Brown & Co., 1894, 10 T.L.R. 386 ; Kleinwort, Sons & Co. v. Comptoir Nat. d'Escompte de Paris, 1894, L.R. 2 Q.B. 157.

[2] Commissioners of Taxation v. English, Scottish and Australian Bank, 1920, 36 T.L.R. 305.

[3] Capital and Counties Bank v. Gordon ; London City and Midland Bank v. Gordon, 1903, A.C. 240.

[4] 6 Edw. VII. cap. 17.

cheques themselves become entitled to the protection of the section.[1] Again, a banker's draft addressed by one branch of a bank to another branch of the same bank is not a cheque, and is not entitled to this statutory protection. But it is within section 19 of the Stamp Act, 1853, which protects bankers *bonâ fide* paying such drafts to holders claiming under forged indorsements.[2]

2. A cheque is *crossed specially* which bears across its face an addition of the name of a banker, either with or without the words "not negotiable." [3] A cheque which is crossed generally, with the addition of the name of a town, is not thereby crossed specially, as the name of a town is not recognised either by law or custom as part of a crossing. A cheque crossed "Bank" is not crossed specially. A cheque may be crossed specially by the drawer, by the holder of an uncrossed or generally crossed cheque, and by the banker to whom an uncrossed or generally crossed cheque is sent for collection, who may cross it specially to himself.[4] A banker to whom a cheque is crossed specially may again cross it specially to another banker for collection.[5] When a cheque is recrossed to a banker for collection, the fact should be expressed, as "the A. Bank to the B. Bank for collection," though this is not necessary. By crossing a cheque specially a direction is given to the banker on whom it is drawn to pay it only to the banker with whose name it is specially crossed, or to his agent for collection, being a banker. The consequences to the banker of disobedience to the directions contained in a special crossing are the same as those which follow disobedience to the directions given by a general crossing. A banker on whom a cheque is drawn which is crossed specially, is probably justified in paying such a cheque if he receive it through the clearing-house without the stamp of the presenting bank, since he would be justified in assuming that the cheque must have been presented by the banker to whom it was crossed. The banker on whom a cheque is drawn which is specially crossed to more than one banker, except when the second or subsequent special crossing be to a banker for collection, is bound to refuse payment of it.[6] The holder of such a cheque may, however, after presentation and dishonour, sue the drawer for the amount. In a recent case, a cheque was drawn to the order of a person and crossed to a bank where he kept an account. On receiving the cheque the bank placed it to the payee's credit and he drew upon it. The cheque was subsequently presented and payment

---

[1] Bissell *v.* Fox, 51 L.T. (N.S.) 663 ; the Gordon case, 1903, A.C. 240, *per* Lord Lindley, at p. 249.

[2] The Gordon case, *supra.*   [3] B. of E. Act, sec. 76.

[4] B. of E. Act, sec. 77 (6).

[5] *Ibid.* sec. 79.   [6] *Ibid.* sec. 79 (1).

was refused, and it was held that the crossing did not restrict the negotiability of the cheque to the bank, and that the bank were entitled as holders in due course, to sue the drawer.[1]

It is a common practice, in mercantile transactions, for the sender of an invoice for goods sold to request the buyer when transmitting the price to cross his cheque with the name of a particular bank. It is of some importance that in remitting a cheque in payment the buyer should observe the direction given, since, according to a well-known rule of law if the recipient of money directs that payment shall be made only in a certain way and the sender does not follow the direction, the loss, in the event of the money going amissing, will fall upon the sender. Thus if the seller of goods directs that, if payment of his account be made by cheque, that cheque must be crossed in the name of a bank indicated, and the purchaser in disregard of the direction transmits in payment a cheque which is not crossed in the manner indicated, the purchaser would stand a very poor chance of succeeding in an action for repayment if a clerk of the seller cashed the cheque and purloined the money.[2]

Addition of Words " Not Negotiable."—In addition to the crossing on a cheque, the drawer, or holder of it, may add the words " not negotiable." Such words, however, must not be taken to imply any limitation of the negotiability of the cheque, but a person who takes a crossed cheque which bears on it the words " not negotiable " has not and cannot give, a better title to the cheque than that of the person from whom he took it.[3] No one, therefore, can be a holder in due course of such a cheque. A person who, even *bonâ fide* and in ignorance of his transferror's want of title, takes such a cheque from a finder or a thief, is in the same position as one who takes a cheque payable to order the indorsement on which has been forged. The object of the addition is to give protection to the true owner of the cheque by preserving his right against any subsequent holder, and the addition of the words " not negotiable " imposes on the banker no liability other than that attaching to crossed cheques generally.

Addition of Words " Account Payee."—There is at present in existence a practice of adding to an ordinary crossing the words " account payee." These words have no statutory signification, and do not prohibit the ordinary negotiation of a cheque payable to order or to bearer. The words are held to be a mere direction to the banker upon whom the cheque is drawn of an intention that the account of the

---

[1] National Bank v. Silke, 1891, L.R. 1 Q.B. 435.

[2] Robb v. Gow Bros. & Gemmell, 1905, 8 F. 90, *per* Lord M'Laren. The *ratio* of the learned Judge's dictum would appear to apply equally to postal orders and other documents which may be crossed to a banker.

[3] See B. of E. Act, sec. 81.

person to whom it is made payable should be credited with the amount. Before therefore a banker is safe in crediting the account of another person with the proceeds of a cheque so crossed, he should receive a satisfactory explanation why the cheque is not being paid to the payee, otherwise he may be liable for any ensuing loss on the ground of negligence.[1]

Presentment for Payment—*How Made.*—A cheque must be presented to the banker, within bank hours, on a business day, and at his place of business, by the holder, or some person authorised by him to receive payment on his behalf.[2] A cheque payable at a branch bank must be presented there and not at the head office.[3] Where authorised by agreement or the usage of trade, a cheque may be presented for payment through the post-office,[4] a mode of presentment which has been held reasonable and customary.[5] The sender is not responsible for delay on the part of the post-office, and presentation will be held to have been duly made if the letter containing the cheque have been properly delivered to the post-office for transmission.[6]

Time for.—A cheque must be presented within a reasonable time of its issue, and a cheque is said to be issued when it is delivered complete in form to a person who takes it as a holder.[7] In determining what is a reasonable time, regard is had to the nature of the cheque, the usage of trade and of bankers, and the facts of the particular case.[8]

Somewhat different considerations arise in respect to what will be considered reasonable time, according to the relations of the parties between whom the question is raised.

(a) *As between Drawer and Payee.*—A cheque is not satisfaction of the payment of a debt until it is honoured, and unless damage have resulted from the delay, the payee of a cheque may present it any time within six years.[9] If no damage have resulted from the delay and the cheque is dishonoured, the drawer is still liable. If the cheque be not presented within a reasonable time of its issue, having regard to the usage of trade and of bankers and to the facts of the particular case, and the drawer, or the person on whose account it is drawn, had the right at the time of such presentment, as between him and the banker, to have

---

[1] House Property Co. *v.* London County and Westminster Bank, 1915, 84 L.T. Q.B. 1846 ; Ross *v.* London County and Westminster Bank, 1919, 1 K.B. 678.

[2] See Bills, sec. 45 (3).

[3] Woodland *v.* Fear, 7 E. & B. 519.

[4] See Bills, sec. 45 (8).

[5] Heywood *v.* Pickering, L.R. 9 Q.B. 428 ; Prideaux *v.* Criddle, L.R. 4 Q.B. 455.

[6] Higgins & Sons *v.* Dunlop & Co., 1847, 9 D. 1407 ; *affd.* 1848, 6 Bell, 195 ; House Fire Insurance Co. *v.* Grant, L.R. 2 Ex. D. 216.

[7] See Bills, sec. 2.

[8] B. of E. Act, sec. 74 (2).

[9] Laws *v.* Rand, 27 L.J. C.P. 76 ; see Bills, Prescription of.

the cheque paid, and suffers actual damage through the delay, he is discharged to the extent of such damage, that is, to the extent to which such drawer or person is a creditor of the banker to a larger amount than he would have been had such cheque been paid.[1] Thus, where a cheque is not presented within such reasonable time, and the banker on whom it is drawn fails in the interval, the drawer suffers no loss if in the interval he has withdrawn all his funds, and he is, therefore, in such a case liable to the payee in the full amount. But if in the meantime the fund on which the cheque is drawn is altered for the worse, the drawer is, according to circumstances, either wholly or partially discharged of his liability to the payee. Thus if in the interval the banker has failed while holding funds sufficient to meet the cheque, the drawer suffers loss to the full extent of the amount of the cheque, and his liability to the holder is completely discharged. So also if in the interval the banker has ceased to allow his customer to overdraw.[2] But if in the interval the banker has failed, and at the date of his failure had funds of the drawer's in his possession, but insufficient in amount to meet the cheque, the loss which the drawer suffers is the amount which remained in the banker's hands, and his liability to the holder, whose presentation of the cheque (in Scotland) operates as an intimated assignation in his favour, is limited to the difference between the amount in the banker's hands and that of the cheque. The payee or holder of a cheque, as to which the drawer has been discharged wholly or partially of his liability, ranks in lieu of the drawer as a creditor of the banker to the extent of the discharge, and is entitled to sue the banker for the amount of his debt to the extent of the funds in his possession.[3]

The payee of a cheque is not bound to present the cheque immediately on receipt, and if it come into his hands during banking hours the presentation will be held within reasonable time if made during banking hours on the day after its receipt.[1] If receipt of the cheque take place after banking hours, presentation will be held within reasonable time if made on the second day thereafter, i.e. on the day following that on which presentation could first be properly made. So a cheque given to an agent on behalf of his principal will be timeously presented on the day following that which ought reasonably to have been the first day on which presentation by the principal might be made. The employment of his banker to make the presentation for him does not seem to alter the position of the payee with regard to presentation. Where the presentation of the cheque is made on behalf of the payee by his banker, presentation must be made within the time available

---

[1] See B. of E. Act, sec. 74 (1).
[2] Hopkins v. Ware, L.R. 2 Ex. 268.
[3] B. of E. Act, sec. 74 (3).
[4] Boddington v. Schlencker, 4 B. & A. 752.

to the payee himself, and no extension of time is permitted to the payee because he employed another to effect the presentation for him. The fact that the payee resides in a different town from the drawee affords the former an extension of time for actual presentation, and the payee will be held to have presented the cheque within reasonable time if he forward it by post the day after receiving it, or, if there be no post on that day, by the first convenient post thereafter.[1] So, if the payee forward it to his banker, and he on the day following present it to the drawee, or forward it to his agent, who in turn presents it for payment on the day following his receipt of it, the presentation seems to be made within a reasonable time.

(b) *As between Drawer and Transferee.*—The transferee of a cheque is, as regards his right to recover from the drawer in the event of the cheque being dishonoured, in the same position as the payee, and he is therefore bound to present the cheque within the time available to the payee.

(c) *As between Payee and Transferee.*—When a cheque is transferred by indorsation, the transferee has a right of action against both the drawer and the indorser, the indorser standing in the same relation to his indorsee as the drawer does to the payee. To render an indorser liable, presentation of the cheque must be made by the indorsee within a reasonable time.[2] Reasonable time in this case has been decided to mean not later than the day after receipt of the cheque by the indorsee.

(d) *As between a Banker and his Customer.*—When a banker is intrusted with a cheque for presentation and collection by the payee or holder, he has as between himself and his customer the day after receipt of the cheque to present it, unless circumstances exist from which a contract or duty on the part of the banker to present earlier, or to defer presentment to a later period, can be inferred. If the banker employ an agent to present the cheque on his behalf, he will have the day after receipt to post it to such agent, and the agent similarly will have the day after his receipt of the cheque to present it to the drawee.[3]

Stale or Overdue Cheques.—A cheque is deemed to be stale or overdue when it appears on the face of it to have been in circulation for an unreasonable length of time. What is an unreasonable length of time is a question of fact, and varies according to circumstances.[4] Thus " it cannot be laid down that as matter of law a party taking a cheque after any fixed time from date does so at his peril, and that the mere fact of

---

[1] Heywood *v.* Pickering, L.R. 9 Q.B. 428.
[2] See Bills, sec. 45 (2).
[3] Presentment is excused in certain circumstances ; see Bills, sec. 46 (1).
[4] See Bills, sec. 36 (3).

the banker having cashed the cheque five days after it bore date, for a person who had not given value for it, did not entitle the drawer to recover from the banker." [1] By unreasonable time is meant such a length of time as ought to have excited suspicion in the mind of an ordinary careful holder. [2]

A cheque which has become stale or overdue can only be negotiated subject to any defect of title affecting it, and no person who takes it can acquire or give a better title than that which the person from whom he took it had. [3] The title of a person who negotiates a cheque is defective when he obtains the cheque by fraud, duress, force and fear, or other unlawful means, or for an illegal consideration, or when he negotiates it in breach of faith or under such circumstances as amount to a fraud. [4]

Where a cheque, which appears to have been in circulation for an unreasonable length of time, is presented to a banker for payment, he is entitled to time to consult the drawer before paying it.

Alterations on Cheque.—The alteration of a cheque in a material part, without the assent of all parties liable on it, renders such a cheque void, except as against a party who has himself made, authorised, or assented to the alteration, and subsequent indorsers. [5]

Lost and Stolen Cheques.—Where a cheque has been lost before it has been in circulation for an unreasonable length of time, the person who was the holder of it at the date of the loss may apply to and compel the drawer to give him another cheque of the same tenor, giving security to the drawer, if required, to indemnify him against all persons whatever in case the cheque alleged to have been lost shall be found again. [6] The finder of a cheque can be compelled to deliver it up to the person in right of it, or, where he has transferred it for value to another, to pay over the amount which he received for it. But a holder in due course cannot be compelled either to deliver up the cheque, or, where he has transferred it, to account for the amount he has received. A holder for value, if not in due course, is bound to deliver up a lost cheque, and if he have obtained payment of it, to account for the amount which he has received. Thus a cheque drawn payable to A., lost by, or stolen from him, and passed on to B., as a *bonâ fide* holder in due course, with A.'s indorsement forged upon it, still remains A.'s property as the true owner. In such a case the drawer may refuse to allow the banker to debit his account with the amount, if the cheque be paid by him

---

[1] *Per* Lord Tenterden in Rothschild *v.* Corney, 9 B. & C. 388.

[2] London and County Bank *v.* Groome, L.R. 8 Q.B.D. 288, 295.

[3] See Bills, sec. 36 (2).

[4] *Ibid.* sec. 29 (2).

[5] See Bills, *ante* ; Banker and Customer, *ante*, p. 14.

[6] *Ibid.* sec. 69.

contrary to the direction expressed by the crossing, and he may also recover the amount paid to B., who has acquired no title to the cheque. The person who receives payment of a cheque to which he has no title is held in law to have received it *for the true owner*.[1]

A banker, however, who acts merely as an agent for the collection of the amount, will not be compelled so to account.[2] Where a lost cheque is known to be in the hands of a holder in due course, the drawer cannot apparently be compelled to give another of the same tenor, as the person who was in right of it at the date of the loss has lost all claim both upon the cheque and the drawer of it.

The person in right of a lost cheque may bring an action of proving the tenor, in which he must prove both the tenor of the cheque and the facts relating to its loss. Mere inference will not be sufficient. In any action or proceeding upon a cheque, the Court may order that the loss of the cheque shall not be set up, provided an indemnity be given to the satisfaction of the Court against the claims of any other person upon the cheque in question.[3] The person suing on a lost bill should offer indemnity prior to bringing his action, otherwise the plea setting up the loss will not be struck out except on payment of expenses.

The former holder of a lost cheque is not by its loss relieved from the performance of his duties as a holder, and unless the loss be not imputable to his own default, misconduct, or negligence, delay in making presentment will not be excused.[4] Nor will the loss of the cheque excuse delay in giving notice of dishonour.[5]

Paid Cheques.—When a cheque is paid the holder is bound forthwith to deliver it up to the banker paying it,[6] in whose hands it is *primâ facie* evidence of the payment of the amount. A cheque on payment becomes the property of the drawer, but the banker who pays it is entitled to keep it as a voucher until his account with his customer is settled, or until the customer's account is docqueted.

A paid cheque in the drawer's possession is *primâ facie* evidence of payment as between him and the payee.[7] It is not obligatory for the banker who pays a cheque to cancel the drawer's signature.

Cheques as Payment.—The giving and taking of a cheque may operate as a payment and extinction of the debt for which it was granted. To do so, it must, however, reach the hands of the payee.

A cheque which has been delivered to the payee or his authorised agent operates as a payment of the debt for which it was granted,

---

[1] Bobbett *v.* Pinkett, L.R. 1 Ex. D. 368 ; Smith *v.* Union Bank of London, L.R. 1 Q.B.D. 31.

[2] Clydesdale Bank *v.* Royal Bank, 1876, 3 R. 586.

[3] See Bills, sec. 70.

[4] *Ibid.* sec. 46 (1).   [5] *Ibid.* secs. 50 (2), 51 (8).   [6] *Ibid.* sec. 52 (4).

[7] *Per* Cockburn, L.C.J., in Charles *v.* Blackwell, L.R. 2 C.P.D. 151, at p. 162.

subject to the condition that, if on due presentment it is not paid, the original debt revives; and if on due presentment a cheque is not paid it is immaterial whether it be because there are no assets,[1] or because payment has been stopped by the drawer.[2] If the cheque have reached the payee, and been lost by or stolen from him and cashed, before he has time, or while he delays, to give intimation of the loss or theft, the loss will fall upon him and not upon the drawer.[3]

A creditor is not bound to accept his debtor's cheque in payment of his debt, as a cheque is not money nor is it legal tender, and where a creditor receives his debtor's cheque, but refuses to accept it as payment, he may apparently sue for the original debt while retaining the cheque.[4] Even when the creditor accepts a cheque as payment, he is held to have done so only on the implied condition that the cheque will be honoured when presented, and if it be not so honoured the creditor's right to sue for the original debt is not impaired.[5] So, where a cheque has been deposited with a third person to abide the issue of a subsequent event, such person is not in breach of any duty to the drawer in cashing the cheque before the occurrence of the event.[6] The mere receipt of a cheque drawn in conditional terms does not operate as a payment. Where a person, induced by the fraud of another, or upon a condition which is not fulfilled, draws a cheque in favour of a third party, the drawer is liable on the cheque and cannot recover the amount from such third party, if he, having received it in *bonâ fide*, and for value, has cashed it.[7] The mere keeping of a cheque sent " in full of all demands " is not conclusive evidence from which accord and satisfaction are to be presumed in law; the question whether it has been kept upon the terms sent being one of fact in each particular case.[8]

The holder of a bill which the acceptor or drawee pays by cheque is entitled to retain the bill until the cheque is honoured, but a banker who receives a bill from a country correspondent for presentment will not be held guilty of negligence if he deliver up the bill on receiving a cheque in payment, even though the cheque be subsequently dishonoured.[9]

It is of some importance to notice, however, that a cheque is not legal tender, and is only a method of paying money. Payment therefore by means of a cheque payable to bearer is equivalent simply to payment

---

[1] Caine v. Coulson, 32 L.J. Ex. 97.
[2] Cohen v. Hale, L.R. 3 Q.B.D. 371.
[3] Charles v. Blackwell, L.R. 2 C.P.D. 151.
[4] Stuart v. Cawse, 28 L.J. C.P. 193.
[5] Cohen v. Hale, *supra* ; *approved* in Leggat Bros. v. Gray, 1908, S.C. 67.
[6] Wilkinson v. Godefroy, 9 A. & E. 536.
[7] Currie v. Misa, L.R. 1 Ap. Ca. 554 ; see also Watson v. Russell, 31 L.J. Q.B. 304.
[8] Day v. M'Lea, L.R. 22 Q.B.D. 610.
[9] Russell v. Hankey, 6 T.R. 12.

by bank notes. If, therefore, a person sends money in a form which makes its appropriation extremely easy—as, for instance, by means of a cheque payable to bearer—he must make sure that it ultimately reaches the hands of the person for whom it was intended, either those of the payee himself or of some one recognised as authorised to receive payment on the payee's behalf. The sending of an ordinary uncrossed cheque payable to bearer is not a remittance in the ordinary course of business. Consequently, if by any chance, whether on account of fraud or innocent accident, such a cheque sent as a payment in the ordinary course of business falls into hands for which it was not intended (such as, *e.g.* a clerk of the payee's), and is subsequently appropriated by the person into whose hands it thus falls, the payee, through whose failure or negligence the misappropriation has become possible, will not be allowed to plead against the payer that payment has been duly made, and he will consequently have to make good to the payer the amount of the cheque thus misappropriated.[1]

Cheque as Proof of Payment.—To prove that a debt has been paid, it is not sufficient to prove merely that a cheque has been drawn and delivered to the payee. It must further be shown that the circumstances were such as to make the cheque a payment by the debtor to his creditor. Thus a cheque drawn in conditional terms, as " Pay H. & Co. balance account railing," will not support a plea of payment. And though the production of a cheque which has been in circulation will afford proof of payment having been made to the payee on behalf of the drawer, the mere fact that a cheque has been cashed is not proof *per se* of the payment of a debt. To prove that a debt has been extinguished, it must be proved that at the date when the cheque was drawn the drawer was indebted to the payee, and further, either that the cheque was delivered to the payee, or that it bears his indorsement as evidencing receipt of the amount from the drawee.

Where a person pays a debt on behalf of another, and proves that a cheque for the amount drawn by him was received, and its receipt acknowledged, by the creditor, such receipt will be sufficient, without proof that the cheque was actually honoured, to enable the person so paying to recover the amount from the person on whose behalf the payment was made.[2]

Valuable Consideration.—A cheque is valid in Scotland though given for no valuable consideration. The plea of non-onerosity is, however, relevant : (1) Where there is no intention to grant an obligation, or where a cheque has been obtained from the drawer by fraud, or force and fear. In the hands of a person who has so obtained it a cheque is invalid, and if it have been passed on to a third party, such third

---

[1] Robb *v.* Gow Bros. & Gemmell, 1905, 8 F. 90.

[2] Carmarthen, etc., Ry. *v.* Manchester, etc., Ry., L.R. 8 C.P. 685.

party, to entitle him to recover from the drawer, must prove that he obtained it for valuable consideration. (2) Where a cheque has been drawn on condition that it shall only be used on the occurrence of a certain event, which does not happen, or in payment of goods, which are not delivered.[1] (3) Where it is given in consideration of the payee's delaying enforcement of an obligation which afterwards turns out to be invalid.[2] (4) Where it is given for an immoral consideration or one contrary to statute. Thus, it has been decided in England that where a cheque had been given in payment of bets upon horse-racing and indorsed by the payee to a third person for value, with notice of the consideration for which it was granted by the drawer when it was so indorsed to him, the holder could not maintain an action upon the cheque, as it must be deemed by virtue of 5 & 6 Will. IV. c. 41 to have been given for an illegal consideration. But the illegality of the gaming consideration is immaterial to a *bonâ fide* holder without notice of the consideration.[3] (5) Where it is reducible, either at common law or by statute, at the instance of the drawer's creditors.

Protest and Summary Diligence.—The Bills of Exchange Act defines a cheque as a bill of exchange drawn on a banker payable on demand. It also provides that nothing contained in it shall extend or restrict, or in any way alter or affect, the law and practice in Scotland in regard to summary diligence. It has never been decided that summary diligence upon a cheque is competent in Scotland, and the opinion of most competent writers appears to be that it is not. It therefore appears that though a cheque is a bill of exchange payable on demand, protest and summary diligence are still incompetent upon it.[4]

---

[1] Fortune v. Luke, 1831, 10 S. 115 ; Agra Bank v. Leighton, L.R. 2 Ex. 56.
[2] Macdonald v. Union Bank, 1864, 2 M. 963.
[3] Woolf v. Hamilton, 1898, L.R. 2 Q.B. 337.
[4] *Vide* M'Lean v. Clydesdale Bank Ltd., 1883, 11 R. (H.L.), at p. 5.

CHAPTER III

PROMISSORY NOTES

Definition.—A promissory note is an unconditional promise in writing made by one person to another, signed by the maker, engaging to pay on demand, or at a fixed or determinable future time, a sum certain in money to, or to the order of, a specified person, or to bearer.[1] It is apparently not invalid, however, because it contains neither the name of a specified payee nor the words " to bearer " ; if, in fact, the document contains a promise to pay and it is handed by one person to another.[2] An instrument in the form of a note payable to the maker's order is not a promissory note until it is indorsed by the maker.[3] A note is not invalid by reason only that it contains also a pledge of collateral security with authority to sell or dispose thereof,[4] which has been held to import that if a note contains anything more it would not be valid as a promissory note, although it may still be valid as an agreement.[5]

A note which is, or on the face of it purports to be, both made and payable within the British Islands, is an inland note. Any other note is a foreign note.

Essentials.—The essentials of a promissory note are—

1. It must be *in writing*. It may be, with the exception of the signature, printed, lithographed, or engraved. It may be written and subscribed in pencil.[6]

2. It must contain a *promise*. The word " promise " is not necessary, nor need a promise be actually expressed, if it be unequivocally implied.

3. It must be stamped with the appropriate stamp.

4. It must be delivered.[7]

As illustrating the principles which have guided the Courts in determining whether a document falls to be dealt with as a promissory

---

[1] B. of E. Act, sec. 83 (1).

[2] Daun v. Sherwood, 1895, 11 T.L.R. 211 (*per* Kennedy, J.) ; see B. of E. Act, sec. 20.

[3] B. of E. Act, sec. 83 (2).

[4] *Ibid.*

[5] Kirkwood v. Smith, 1896, L.R. 1 Q.B. 582.

[6] Geary v. Physic, 5 B. & C. 234.   [7] See Delivery, *infra.*

note, or merely as an acknowledgment of the receipt of money, the following cases may be cited :—

1. *Documents which have been held to be Promissory Notes.*—" I acknowledge to have this day received from you eighty pounds, which I shall pay when required." [1] " I hereby acknowledge that I have this day received from you £20, which I shall repay you when demanded." [2] " I acknowledge to be due you the sum of £10, which sum I promise to pay any time when required." [3] " Received from A. B. the sum of £30, payable on demand." [4] " At fourteen days after date I accept to pay A. B. or order the sum of £50 stg." [5] The following docquet written on the back of a cheque :—" 2nd August 1887. Received from Catherine M'Craw the sum of £104 sterling, and I agree to pay on demand." [6]

In England documents acknowledging receipt of money " to be paid on demand," or " which I will repay in two years," have been held to be promissory notes,[7] and a writing in the form of an I.O.U., but which contained the stipulation that the loan was to be repaid upon a certain date, was held to be a promissory note, as it imported an express promise to pay a sum certain on a particular date.

The addition to a joint and several promissory note in ordinary form of a clause " no time given to or security taken from or composition or arrangement entered into with either party hereto shall prejudice the rights of the holder to proceed against any other party," has been held not to invalidate the instrument as a promissory note.[8]

A debenture bond, by which a company bound themselves to pay to the bearer the principal sum contained in it on a particular date, was held to be a promissory note,[9] as was a document containing the words, " I promise to pay or cause to be paid." [10]

A writing which contains a pledge of collateral security so expressed as to be of the nature of a bond or obligation with security, does not constitute a note, though, as will be seen, a promissory note is not invalid by reason only that it contains also a pledge of collateral security with authority to sell or dispose thereof.

A letter in the terms following was held to be a promissory note

---

[1] Alexander *v.* Alexander, 1830, 8 S. 602.

[2] Pirie's Reps. *v.* Smith's Exrs., 1833, 11 S. 473.

[3] M'Intosh *v.* Stewart, 1830, 8 S. 739.

[4] M'Cubbin *v.* Stephen, 1856, 18 D. 1224.

[5] M'Kinney *v.* Van Heck & Co., 1863, 1 M. 1115. See also Vallance *v.* Forbes, 1879, 6 R. 1099 ; Blyth *v.* Forbes, 1879, 6 R. 1102.

[6] M'Craw *v.* M'Craw's Trs., 1906, 13 S.L.T. 757.

[7] Cashborne *v.* Dutton, 1 Selwyn N.P. 13th ed. 329.

[8] Kirkwood *v.* Carroll, 1903, 1 K.B. 531.

[9] *Ex parte* Colborne *v.* Strawbridge, L.R. 11 Eq. 478.

[10] Lovell *v.* Hill, 6 C. & P. 238.

and invalid for want of a stamp:—" We agree to pay you during February 1859 £100, during March 1859 £100, during April 1859 £100, in part liquidation of our debt to you of deficiency of 7s. 6d. per £ as per our settlement in December 1857." Lord President (then Lord Justice-Clerk) Inglis said : It appears to me that the use of the verb " agree " is of very little consequence ; for when a person agrees to pay a particular sum on a particular day he grants a promissory note ; for the distinction between a promise and an obligation of a different kind does not consist in the use of the word " promise." But in order that a promise to pay may be a promissory note, it must be a promise to pay a sum of money at a particular date to a particular person. It is no objection that the sum is payable at different times ; it is only necessary that each instalment should be of a definite amount payable at a fixed time and to a person named. A writing may be in part a promissory note and in part an agreement, and the law seems to be that such a document may be stamped with an agreement stamp if it has not a stamp applicable to a promissory note. This was well illustrated by a case in which there was a document like this or promise to pay in certain instalments.[1] But there were superadded certain words which were held to make the whole document an agreement within the meaning of the stamp laws and not a promissory note at all.[2]

A letter in the terms, " We beg to acknowledge receipt of yours of date covering cheque for £100 stg., which we hereby agree to pay you in say two years and six months from date, with interest at the rate of 6 per cent. *per annum* : interest payable half-yearly : in security we now enclose policies on the Life Association of Scotland on the lives of A. B. and C. D. No. ——, value £200, and No. ——, value £300 sterling, which are thus to be considered as assigned to you until repayment of the loan is made," was held to be a promissory note, and the fact of the policies of insurance being enclosed and intended to act as securities did not deprive the document of its character as a promissory note, there being no agreement entered into about them.

2. *Documents which have been Decided not to be Promissory Notes.*— " I hereby acknowledge that I have this day received from you £20 sterling, for which I shall account."[3] " Received from Mr. Thomas Watson the sum of Fifty Pounds on loan at the rate of five per cent."[4] " In consideration of your advancing to M. & H. £250 on their joint and several notes, I undertake to pay £250 on demand should their

---

[1] Davies *v.* Wilkinson, 2 Perry & Davidson, 256.
[2] M'Farlane *v.* Johnstone, 1864, 2 M. 1210.
[3] Pirie's Reps. *v.* Smith's Exrs., 1833, 11 S. 473.
[4] Watson *v.* Duncan, 1896, 4 S.L.T. 116.

note not be met at maturity." [1] A letter in these terms—Borrowed from A. £67 Pounds, July 1878, Paid back £5 Pounds, May 1885, Leaving a balance of £62 Pounds to pay still—holograph of and signed by the granter but neither dated nor stamped—was held to be neither a promissory note, not an agreement, nor a receipt. [2] A letter in the following terms :—" James M'Cracken, Esq.—Dear Sir, We beg to acknowledge having received from you the sum of £250 sterling, and we jointly and severally bind ourselves our heirs and successors to make payment of this sum, together with any interest that may accrue thereon," and signed through a penny stamp, was held not to be a promissory note, on the ground that neither the rate of interest nor the date of payment was specified on the face of the document, and that accordingly the sum payable thereunder was not " certain " in the sense of the Bills of Exchange Act. [3] A document written in the following terms on unstamped paper :—" I hereby acknowledge that I have received from you £27, which I oblige myself to pay to you at Whitsunday first, or grant you my bill with interest," was held not to be a promissory note, but a stampable obligation, being to all intents and purposes an obligation to grant a bill for a temporary loan of money if that should not be repaid before a certain day. [4] Letters in the terms, " I have borrowed from you £1000, which I hereby bind and oblige myself to repay to you at Whitsunday next, with interest at the rate which shall be paid on money lent upon first heritable security," and " I was favoured with your letter of yesterday prefixing letter of credit on A. B. for £397, which, with interest due to you, makes up £500, which I have received in loan from you, to be repaid in December next, but hope you won't be too strict as to time of payment," were held not to be promissory notes, as, though the terms of the documents somewhat differed, in neither was there contained that simple promise to pay a specific sum at a definite date necessary to constitute them promissory notes. [5] A document acknowledging the receipt of money " which is to lie for one or more years from Whitsunday next, and to bear interest at the rate of 10 per cent. per annum, payable at the usual half-yearly term as due," though accompanied by a promissory note in the ordinary form, was held not to be a promissory note itself, but nevertheless to be a document which might be used by way of evidence to prove the constitution of the debt for which the promissory note was granted, that document being inadmissible in evidence owing to its being prescribed. [6]

---

[1] Dickinson v. Bower, 1897, 14 T.L.R. 146.
[2] Todd v. Wood, 1897, 24 R. 1104.   [3] Lamberton v. Aiken, 1899, 2 F. 189.
[4] Martin v. Brash, 1833, 11 S. 782. See also ex parte Imeson, 2 Rose B.C. 225.
[5] Morgan v. Morgan, 1866, 4 M. 321. See also Tennent v. Crawford, 1878, 5 R. 433 ; and Bankier v. Robertson, 1864, 2 M. 1153.
[6] Nisbet v. Neil's Trs., 1869, 7 M. 1091.

A document acknowledging the receipt of money for which the borrower bound himself to be " accountable " with interest, was held not to be a promissory note, but an agreement, the fair and reasonable interpretation of the words " I have to be accountable," being that the person using them intended to give credit in account and pay the balance, and not that he promised to repay the amount.[1] A memorandum to the effect that a person had deposited money to be returned on demand was held to be merely an instrument recording the agreement of the parties in respect of a certain deposit of money, the consideration of which was stated in the memorandum, and to be rather an agreement than a promissory note.[2] A document containing a promise to pay a certain sum of money twelve months after date, to be held as collateral security for any moneys due to the payees by a third party, and which they might be unable to recover on realising the securities which they held, was held not to be a promissory note, as it was in substance a promise to pay if another person named in it did not, and as such it gave notice on the face of it that the promise was only conditional.[3] But a promissory note, which provides that a collateral bill of sale, payable by instalments, should be held for these instalments with interest, and that if any instalment remained unpaid the whole sum should become due, is valid.[4]

Delivery.—In order to make a promissory note complete, there must be actual or constructive transference of possession from the maker to the payee or bearer, until which the note is incomplete and revocable.[5] The transfer must be made by or with the authority of the maker.

Joint and Several Notes.—A promissory note may be made by two or more makers, and they may be liable thereon jointly, or jointly and severally, according to its tenor.[6] A note which runs, " We promise to pay," or " I promise to pay," and is signed by two or more obligants, is the joint and several obligation of all the persons who sign it,[7] any one of whom, in a question with the creditor, may be called upon to pay the full amount for which the note is granted, though entitled to relief *pro rata* from his fellow-obligants. On the other hand, in a note which is signed by two or more obligants " jointly," each person so signing is liable only for his own share.

Presentment for Payment.—Though in general not necessary in order to charge the maker, who is always liable in terms of his

---

[1] Horne *v.* Redfearn, 4 Bing. N.S. 433.

[2] Sibree *v.* Tripp, 15 M. & W. 23.

[3] Robins *v.* May, 1839, 11 Ad. & E. 213.

[4] Monetary Advance Co. *v.* Carter, 20 Q.B.D. 785.

[5] B. of E. Act, secs. 84, 21 (1).   See Martini & Co. *v.* Steel & Craig, 1878, 6 R. 342.

[6] B. of E. Act, sec. 85.   [7] 1 Bell's Com. 363.

obligation for his signature without notice, presentment must be duly made to the maker in order to render an indorser liable. When a note payable on demand has been indorsed, it must be presented for payment within a reasonable time of the indorsement, otherwise the indorser is discharged. In determining what is a reasonable time, regard is had to the nature of the instrument, the usage of trade, and the facts of the particular case.[1] In one case where a promissory note, dated the 16th of February 1864, and indorsed, the payment of which was not contemplated by the makers at any immediate or specific date, though the note was made payable on demand, was not presented to the payee for payment until the 14th of December in the same year, it was held that, as it appeared from the evidence that the note was meant to be, to a greater or less extent, a continuing security, the delay in presentation was, in the circumstances of the case, not unreasonable, and the holders of the note were entitled to recover thereon.[2]

When Overdue.—Where a note payable on demand is negotiated, it is not deemed to be overdue for the purpose of affecting the holder with defects of title of which he had no notice, by reason that it appears that a reasonable time for presenting it for payment has elapsed since its issue.[3] So far as defects of title are concerned, the holder of a note, presentation of which has been unreasonably delayed, is in the same position as a holder of a bill in due course.

Where made Payable.—Where a promissory note is in the body of it made payable at a particular place, it must be presented for payment at that place in order to render the maker liable, but in any other case presentment is not necessary to render the maker, though it is to render the indorser, liable.[4] There is, however, no limit as to time imposed by the Act, and even where, to render the maker liable, the note must be presented at a particular place, it need not be so presented on the day when payment is due, presentation on a subsequent day being sufficient.[5] When a note is in the body of it made payable at a particular place, presentment at that place is necessary to render an indorser liable. When in a note a place of payment is indicated by way of memorandum only, presentment at that place is sufficient to render the indorser liable ; but a presentment to the maker elsewhere, if sufficient in other respects, will be equally good.

Liability of the Maker and Indorser.—The position of the maker of a note corresponds to that of the acceptor of a bill, and by making it he engages that he will pay it according to its tenor, and is precluded

---

[1] B. of E. Act, sec. 86 (1) and (2).
[2] Chartered Mercantile Bank of India, etc. v. Dickson, 1871, L.R. 3 P.C. 574.
[3] B. of E. Act, sec. 86 (3).
[4] B. of E. Act, sec. 87.
[5] Gordon v. Kerr, 1898, 25 R. 570.

from denying, to a holder in due course, the existence of the payee and his then capacity to indorse.[1] The position of the first indorser of a note corresponds to that of the drawer of an accepted bill payable to drawer's order. It is doubtful whether the payee of a note can under any circumstances be the holder of it in due course.[2]

Generally, the rules of law applicable to bills of exchange apply, with the necessary modifications, to promissory notes, except those applicable to bills relating to (a) presentment for acceptance, (b) acceptance, (c) acceptance *supra* protest, and (d) bills in a set. Further, protest of a foreign note is unnecessary.

Stamp.—A promissory note must be stamped with an *ad valorem* stamp, and, unlike a bill of exchange, the duty is *ad valorem* whether the promissory note is payable on demand or at a determinable future period. The note must be stamped before execution,[3] except (1) where it is made abroad, (2) where it bears an impressed stamp of sufficient value but wrong denomination, in either of which cases it may be competently after stamped upon payment of the duty and a penalty of forty shillings if the note be not then payable according to its tenor, or of ten pounds if it be so payable. A note which is not stamped is subject to the same disabilities as an unstamped bill of exchange, and cannot therefore be received in evidence. In England, an insufficiently stamped promissory note was allowed to be handed to a witness for the purpose of refreshing his memory and obtaining from him an admission of a loan.[4]

Bank Notes.—Bank notes are promissory notes issued by bankers, payable to bearer on demand, and pass from hand to hand by delivery.[5] "Bank notes," says Lord Mansfield,[6] "are not goods, not securities nor documents for debts, nor are they so esteemed; but are treated as money, as cash in the ordinary course and transactions of business, by the general consent of mankind, which gives them the credit and currency of money, to all intents and purposes. They are as much money as guineas themselves are, or any other current coin that is used in common payments as money or cash. They pass by a will which bequeaths all the testator's money or cash, and are never considered as securities for money, but as money itself. On payment of them, whenever a receipt is required, the receipts are always given as for money, not as for securities or notes. So, on bankruptcies they cannot be followed as identical (*sic*), and distinguishable from money, but are always considered as money or cash." In Scotland the right to issue

---

[1] B. of E. Act, sec. 88.
[2] Wheeler *v.* Herdman, 1902, 1 K.B. 361.
[3] Welsh's Trs. *v.* Forbes, 1885, 12 R. 851.
[4] See, however, Birchall *v.* Bullough, 1896, L.R. 1 Q.B. 325; Bills, Stamp Duty.
[5] 17 & 18 Vict. cap. 83, sec. 11.
[6] Miller *v.* Race, 1758, 1 Smith's L.C., 12th ed. 525.

bank notes was formerly regarded as a common-law right not confined to any of the great banking corporations, but extending to individuals whose power of issuing notes was only limited by their credit with the public and their ability to maintain their notes in circulation. Some of the companies issued notes for ten shillings, five shillings, and even for lower sums. There are instances where notes have been issued for one penny. By the Act 7 & 8 Vict. c. 32, sec. 10, it is enacted " that from and after the passing of this Act, no person other than a banker, who on the sixth day of May 1844 was lawfully issuing his own bank notes, shall render or issue bank notes in any part of the United Kingdom." This was followed by the Act 8 & 9 Vict. c. 38, " to regulate the issue of bank notes in Scotland," under which and since its date the circulation of the Scottish bank notes has been conducted.   By section 5 it is enacted that all bank notes to be issued or reissued in Scotland must be expressed to be, under certain specified penalties, for payment of a sum in pounds sterling without any fractional part of a pound.   By a subsequent Act,[1] no bank other than the Bank of England can issue bank notes for more than one hundred pounds. It is not lawful for any bank in Scotland to have in circulation upon the average of a period of four weeks a greater amount of notes than the amount of its authorised issue *plus* the amount of the monthly average of gold and silver coin held by such bank at its head office or principal place of issue during the same period of four weeks. Currency notes may now be held as against the excess circulation, and the total of these is included as " coin."

Bank notes are exempt from the application of the sexennial prescription.[2] But there seems no reason for holding them exempt from the long negative prescription. A bank note is a warrant for summary diligence.[3] The question has been raised but not decided whether bank notes may be poinded.[4] Where a sum in a bank note has been fraudulently altered, the note as such is destroyed, but the issuing bank is liable to an onerous holder for its true amount.

Money Orders and Postal Orders.—There is a marked legal distinction between the position of a banker who pays a money order and a postal order to a wrongful holder. Money orders issued by the Post-Office were introduced in 1840 by the Act 3 & 4 Vict. c. 96, sec. 3, and may be issued for sums not exceeding £40.   Such documents are not negotiable, and a banker paying a wrongful holder is liable in repetition to the true owner, and that whether the order be crossed or not.[5] Postal orders were introduced in 1880 by the Post-Office (Money Orders) Act, 1880.

---

[1] Stamp Act, 1891, 54 & 55 Vict. cap. 39, sec. 29.

[2] 12 Geo. II. cap. 72, sec. 39.

[3] 5 Geo. III. cap. 49.

[4] Alexander *v.* M'Lay, 1826, 4 S. 439.

[5] Fine Art Society *v.* Union Bank, 1886, 17 Q.B.D. 705.

The law regarding such documents is now regulated by the Post-Office Act, 1908, sec. 25. Such orders are issued for varying sums not exceeding twenty-one shillings. They are all marked "not negotiable," and whether crossed or uncrossed a banker incurs no responsibility to the true owner should it turn out that he has paid to a wrongful holder.

I.O.U.'S

An I.O.U. is a writing, signed by the granter, containing the words " I owe you," or the letters " I.O.U." It need not be addressed to a specified person, nor need it be holograph nor tested. It is an admission of debt involving a promise or obligation to pay, and it is enforceable against the granter unless he can show, either by writ or oath, reason to the contrary. So, if the granter admit the genuineness of the document decree will go against him unless he can prove, either by writ or oath, that the debt has been paid or extinguished. It requires no stamp. It is not a receipt, since it need not acknowledge the receipt of any money, nor need its language necessarily imply the receipt of any money. Nor is it a bond, since it need contain no word of obligation, though the law implies obligation from its terms. Nor is it a promissory note or bill, since it contains neither a promise to pay nor a fixed date of payment. And, lastly, it is not an agreement, since it is unilateral.[1]

In a subsequent case this statement was somewhat qualified. It was laid down that an I.O.U. is nothing but an acknowledgment of debt. So long as it stands it is good against the granter to prove that he acknowledges a debt to the grantee. But it does not express the ground of debt or give any indication whatever of the kind of contract out of which the debt has arisen. It does not therefore follow that when an I.O.U. is granted it is granted for a loan or in respect of any particular contract, and it does not follow that, to get rid of it, the granter of the I.O.U. must prove payment of money. The granter accordingly always has the right to demand its restitution upon satisfaction of the obligation, whatever it may have been, in respect of which it was granted. The question whether in any case it is necessary to prove payment cannot be solved by anything which appears on the face of the I.O.U., and it depends entirely upon the circumstances under which it was granted and the intention with which it was given by one party to the other. The I.O.U. is the result of some transaction, but the kind of transaction is not disclosed. In order, therefore, to determine the rights of the parties, if there be a difference between them on the facts, it is indispensable

---

[1] Thiem's Trs. *v.* Collie, 1899, 1 F. 764, and cases there cited.

that there should be a proof of these facts. It may now be therefore taken as the law on the subject that it is competent to prove by parole evidence facts and circumstances from which it may be inferred that the obligation in an I.O.U. has been discharged, and that it is no longer a living document of debt in the hands of the holder.[1]

---

[1] Bishop *v.* Bryce, 1910, S.C. 426, commenting on Thiem's Trs. *v.* Collie, 1899, 1 F. 764.

CHAPTER IV

LETTERS OF CREDIT

Nature and Description.—Letters of credit, strictly speaking, are mandates, giving authority to the person addressed to pay money or furnish goods on the credit of the writer. They are generally made use of for facilitating the supply of money or goods required by one going to a distance or abroad, and avoiding the risk and trouble of carrying specie, or buying bills to a greater amount than may be required. The debt which arises on such a letter in its simplest form, when complied with, is between the mandatary and mandant, though it may be so conceived as to raise a debt also against the person who is supplied by the mandatary. Thus, where the relation between the mandant and the payee is really that of debtor and creditor, as, for example, when the payee purchases the letter from the mandant for a sum of money or lodges with him securities equivalent in amount, or where the letter is granted in discharge of a debt due by the mandant to the payee, the letter is, in its effect, similar to a bill of exchange drawn by the mandant on his correspondent abroad. In such cases payment of the money by the person on whom the letter is granted raises a debt or goes into account between him and the writer of the letter; but raises no debt to the person who pays on the letter against him to whom the money is paid. Where, however, the giving of the letter is truly an accommodation and meant to raise a debt against the person accommodated, the engagement generally is, to see paid any advances made to him, or to guarantee any draft accepted or bill discounted; and the compliance with the mandate in such a case raises a debt both against the writer of the letter and against the person accredited.[1] The person accommodated is the real debtor, the writer of the letter being his cautioner. Letters of credit are distinguished as being either general or special.

General Letters of Credit.—A general letter of credit is addressed to no specified person, and gives authority to anyone to whom it may be presented to give credit to the person named therein, on the guarantee that the person so paying will be indemnified by the writer. The amount of the credit to be given may be specified or it may be left unrestricted. The date on which the credit is to be given may

---

[1] Bell's Com. (M'L.'s ed.) i. 389 ; Story on Bills, sec. 463.

be specified, it may be limited to a specified period, or it may be unrestricted, in which case the letter partakes of the nature of a continuing guarantee.[1] The mode in which credit is to be given and the manner in which it is to be drawn upon may further be specified, and whatever directions the letter contains or limitations it imposes must be strictly complied with to render the writer liable.[2] The person to whom the letter is addressed has a duty to see that the credit is given to the person named in the letter and no other, and mere possession of the letter on the part of the person presenting it does not relieve the person so paying from the duty of satisfying himself that such possessor is the person named in it. So that where the letter authorises the giving of credit by honouring a person's drafts or cheques, payment on a forged order is not payment in terms of the letter, nor one which can be debited to the writer of the letter, unless, perhaps, where the forgery has been successfully accomplished owing to the negligence of the person whose name is forged.[3] General letters of credit partake of a negotiable quality to this extent, that the person who on the faith of the letter gives credit to the person named therein is entitled, as against the person signing the letter, to recover full payment of his debt without reference to any change of circumstances which may have happened in the interval between the giving of the letter and the drawing of bills under the same, of which the person advancing the money had no notice.[4] Marginal letters of credit are letters of credit, written in the margin of blank bills of exchange.[5]

Special Letters of Credit are addressed to a specified person or persons, or, as in the case of special letters of credit issued by bankers, to the correspondents of the bank, a list of whom is given in a "letter of indication" issued along with the letter of credit. Such letters are issued against a deposit of money by the bank's customer, the bank being bound to repay the amount through the medium of one of its correspondents. They can be operated on only by the person in whose favour they are drawn, and are thus not negotiable ; but it appears to be competent for the person in whose favour they are drawn to indorse and deliver them to a third person for value, and such delivery requires no intimation. Such indorsation, being the indorsation of a non-negotiable instrument, confers upon the indorsee

---

[1] See Guarantees, *infra*.

[2] Brit. Linen Co. *v.* Cal. Ins. Co., 1861, 23 D. (H.L.) 3 ; 4 Macq. 107 ; Union Bank of Canada *v.* Cole and Others, 1877, 47 L.J. C.P. 100.

[3] Orr *v.* Union Bank of Scotland, 1854, 17 D. (H.L.) 24 ; 1 Macq. (H.L.) 513-23 ; Brit. Linen Co. *v.* Cal. Ins. Co., *supra*.

[4] *In re* Agra Bank, *ex parte* Asiatic Bank Co., 1867, L.R. 2 Ch. App. 391.

[5] See Banner *v.* Johnston, 1871, L.R. 5 H.L. 157 ; Maitland *v.* Chart. Merc. Bank of India, etc., 1869, L.J. 38 Ch. 363, in which a form is given.

only such rights as the indorser himself possessed at the date of transference.[1] The bearer of the letter of credit is not bound to require the whole sum mentioned therein at the place or places indicated, and is entitled to recover the whole sum or any balance left over from the person with whom, and at the place where, the deposit was originally made, without giving any indemnity, since the letter merely gives him an option, but imposes no obligation, to cash his credit either up to the full sum or to a part of it according to his inclinations or necessities.[2]

Stamp Duty.—By the Stamp Act, 1891, the term "bill of exchange," for the purposes of the stamp duties, includes *inter alia* a letter of credit and any document or writing (except a bank note) entitling, or purporting to entitle, any person, whether named therein or not, to payment by any other person of, or to draw upon any other person for, any sum of money. By Exemption 4, a letter of credit granted in the United Kingdom authorising drafts to be drawn out of the United Kingdom, payable in the United Kingdom, is exempt from stamp duty.

Circular Notes

These are notes similar in their import to, but quite distinct from, letters of credit, and are issued by bankers to their correspondents abroad, requesting them to pay a certain amount to a person named, on production by him of a "letter of indication," showing that he is the person referred to. The notes are issued against a payment of money corresponding to their amount paid into the bank of issue, and are of convenience to travellers and others, who are thus relieved from the necessity of carrying money from place to place. The 'letter of indication" contains a list of the bank's correspondents, by any of whom the full amount contained in the circular note will be paid at the current rate of exchange on London, which, if the town where payment is required has no direct exchange with London, is arranged in accordance with that of the nearest place which has such an exchange. The letter of indication contains a blank for the signature of the payee as a precaution against forgery in the event of the notes being lost or stolen. The letter and the notes constitute practically one document, and payment of the money cannot be demanded except on production of both, though if the notes be lost or stolen, their owner is entitled, on production of the letter of indication and the grant of a satisfactory indemnity, to recover their value

---

[1] Struthers *v.* Commercial Bank, 1842, 4 D. 460 ; Orr *v.* Union Bank of Scotland, 854, 17 D. (H.L.) 24 ; 1 Macq. (H.L.) 513-23.

[2] Conflans Quarry Co. *v.* Parker, 1867, L.R. 3 C.P. 1.

from the issuing bank.[1] In cases where the circular notes and the letter of indication are both stolen or lost, and the notes are subsequently cashed in good faith by a correspondent of the issuing bank, the purchaser must bear the loss.[2] As with letters of credit, the person who pays them has a duty to see that payment is made to the proper person, and that duty is sufficiently discharged if payment is made in good faith on production of the notes and letter of indication.[3] Such notes need not necessarily be cashed, and may, upon their return to the banker, be exchanged for the amount for which they were originally issued.[1]

---

[1] See Conflans Quarry Co. *v.* Parker, 1867, L.R. 3 C.P. 1.

[2] Rhodes *v.* The London and County Bank, 1880, 1 Journal of Institute of Bankers, 770; Hume Dick *v.* Herries Farquhar & Co., 1888, 4 T.L.R. 541.

[3] Rhodes *v.* The London and County Bank, *supra*.

PART III

SECURITIES FOR ADVANCES

CHAPTER I

HERITABLE SECURITIES

THERE are three recognised modes of constituting a valid security over heritable property for sums advanced, or intended to be advanced, to a customer. These are (1) the Bond and Disposition in Security ; (2) the Bond of Credit and Disposition in Security ; and (3) the Disposition *ex facie* absolute, qualified by a back-bond or back-letter.

1. The Bond and Disposition in Security

This deed is in the form of a personal bond, to which is joined, for the creditor's further security, a conveyance in his favour of heritable property, belonging either to the debtor himself, or to some one who is willing that his heritable property should be conveyed in security of the debtor's obligations. It is the usual mode of taking a security over heritage, when the loan intended to be secured is advanced instantly and in one sum. The Bond and Disposition in Security may, however, be made available for securing advances due, or to become due, on current account. But as by the Act 1696, c. 5, dispositions and other rights granted for the relief or security of debts to be contracted in the future are not available as a security for debts contracted subsequent to the infeftment following on such disposition or right,[1] and as at common law no security can be effectually constituted over lands or other heritable subjects for debts or burdens of an indefinite or fluctuating amount,[2] a difficulty is created in making this mode of taking a security over heritage available with reference to advances on current accounts. The difficulty thus created may be, and in practice usually is, overcome by the bank opening an account in the

---

[1] See Dunbar's Crs. *v.* Abercromby, 1789, M. 1156 ; 2 Ross's L.C. 632.

[2] Pickering *v.* Smith, 1788, M. 1155 ; Stein's Trs. *v.* Newnham, 1789, M. 1158 ; Tod *v.* Dunlop, 1838, 1 D. 231 ; Smith, Sligo & Co. *v.* Dunlop & Co., 1855, 12 R. 107 ; *cf.* Bell's Trs. *v.* Bell, 1884, 12 R. 85.

debtor's name with reference to the loan, to the credit of which is placed the amount contained in the bond. A cheque is drawn on the account, withdrawing the whole sum, which is then placed to the credit of an ordinary current account, upon which operations proceed as usual. The loan account should, however, be kept inoperative, and no payment should be credited to it, since, if this be not done, any payment made will operate *pro tanto* towards reduction of the bond without the necessity of a formal discharge, while sums drawn out will not be covered by the conveyance in security. A statutory form of Bond and Disposition in Security is provided by the Titles to Land Consolidation Act, 1868.[1] Bonds are registered in the appropriate Register of Sasines, and in competition are preferred according to the date of their registration, as until registration the creditor has no real right over the land.

Rights preferable to those of Creditor in Bond.—The rights of the creditor in a Bond and Disposition in Security are postponed to the payment of (1) local rates, since all ordinary public burdens are declared by statute to be a first charge upon land, preferable to the rights of creditors, whether fortified by diligence or not; (2) the superior's feu-duty and the casualty of relief; (3) the widow's terce, the widow of the debtor, if she have been served and cognosced in her terce, being liable in payment of one-third of the interest on the bond; and (4) creditors who have attached the subjects of the security by the diligence of adjudication or inhibition.

Remedies competent to Creditor.—He may charge the debtor or his representative under the personal obligation contained in the bond and proceed thereon by summary diligence. He cannot, however, unless under a special agreement, proceed against purchasers of the property from the debtor under the bond. There is nothing to prevent him proceeding under both the personal obligation and the power of sale contained in the bond.

Realisation of Security Subjects.—The statute[1] provides for the manner in which the security is to be realised, and its provisions must be strictly adhered to. A Notarial Intimation, Requisition, and Protest is served on the debtor, requiring him to make payment within three months, with certification that, in the event of his failure to do so, he will incur the penalty in the bond, that the power of redemption will thenceforth cease and determine, and that the creditor after the expiration of the notice may sell the lands by public roup at such price as they will bring. If the debtor has ceased to be owner of the estate, intimation that the estate is to be brought to sale must be made to the present owner. After the expiration of the notice, the sale is advertised once a week for six weeks in an Edinburgh or

---

[1] 31 & 32 Vict. cap. 101, sec. 118. For import of the clauses in the bond and powers of sale, see sec. 119.

Glasgow newspaper, and also in a newspaper published in the county where the lands are situated ; or, if there be no newspaper published in that county, then in a newspaper published in the next or a neighbouring county. The sale takes place either at Edinburgh or Glasgow, or at the head burgh of the county within which the lands or the chief part thereof are situated, or at the burgh or town sending, or contributing to send, a member to Parliament, or at the burgh or town nearest to the lands which has adopted the General Police Act, whether within or without the county. If the property is sold, the creditor executes in favour of the purchaser a disposition in ordinary form. Upon receiving the purchase price, the creditor must hold count and reckoning with the debtor, or with any other party having interest, and consign the surplus, if any, in bank.[1] The creditor is entitled to retain from the purchase price the expenses of the sale. On the surplus being consigned, the disposition by the creditor to the purchaser has the effect of completely disencumbering the lands not only of the security and diligence of the creditor himself, but of all securities and diligences posterior to that security.[2] If there be no surplus, the lands are disencumbered by registration of a certificate by a notary along with the disposition by the creditor to the purchaser.[3] The creditor cannot, except in the case after mentioned, bid at the sale,[4] and in selling he must proceed with a due regard to the interests of the postponed creditors.

Provision for Security Holder becoming Absolute Proprietor of Security Subjects.—Any creditor who has exposed for sale under his security the lands held in security, at a price not exceeding the amount due under the said security, and under any prior security, and any security or securities ranking *pari passu* with the exposer's security (exclusive of the expense attending the exposure or prior exposures), or at any lower price, and has failed to find a purchaser, may apply to the Sheriff of the county in which the lands or part thereof are situate, or, where the lands are situate in more counties than one, the Sheriff of any of such counties, for decree that the debtor in the bond has forfeited the right of redemption reserved to him, and that the petitioner has right to and is vested in the lands described in the bond as absolute proprietor, but subject always to the burdens and conditions contained or referred to in the bond. The Sheriff may, after such intimation and inquiry as he may think fit, grant such application and issue decree in the said terms. On such decree being pronounced, and an extract thereof in which said lands are described at length or by reference recorded in the appropriate Register of Sasines, the right of redemption reserved

---

[1] See Consignation Receipts, *ante*, p. 39.

[2] Stewart *v.* Brown, 1882, 10 R. 192.

[3] Conveyancing Act, 1874, sec. 48.

[4] Maxwell *v.* Drummond's Trs., 1823, 2 S. 122 ; Stirling's Trs., *Petrs.*, 1865, 3 M. 851.

to the debtor is extinguished, and the creditor has right to the lands disponed in security in the same manner and to the same effect as if the disposition in security had been an irredeemable disposition as from the date of such decree. Upon registration of an extract of the decree in the appropriate register, the lands are disencumbered of all securities and diligences posterior to the security of the said creditor. Instead of granting such decree, the Sheriff may, upon any such application being made to him as aforesaid, appoint the lands held subject to the security to be re-exposed for sale at a price to be fixed by him, and in that event the creditor has right to bid for and purchase the said lands at such sale. In the event of the creditor purchasing, the Sheriff may issue decree in the form and to the effect aforesaid, or the creditor may grant a disposition of the lands to himself in the same manner as if he had been a stranger. Notwithstanding the foregoing provisions, the personal obligation of the debtor is reserved in full force and effect so far as not extinguished by the price at which the lands have been acquired.[1]

Instead of selling, the creditor may (1) enter into possession of the subjects under a decree of maills and duties, which entitles him to collect the rents and sequestrate the tenant's effects.[2] The rents are applied in payment of the interest due to the creditor, including the expenses of management, insurance, and repairs, and any surplus to the payment of the principal sum. The creditor is not bound to intromit beyond the amount of his interest, and he may pay over to the debtor any surplus without being responsible to postponed creditors, unless he has entered into possession in opposition to the diligence of such creditors and to their exclusion, in which case he must either pay the surplus to such creditors or hold it in reduction of his debt;[3] or (2) by a poinding of the ground he may attach the moveable effects on the ground belonging to the proprietor and also those of the tenants to the extent of the rents due by them.

Security Holder may Eject Proprietor if in Possession of Subjects.—Where a creditor desires to enter into possession of the lands disponed in security, and the proprietor thereof is in personal occupation of the same or any part thereof, such proprietor is deemed to be an occupant without a title, and the creditor may take proceedings to eject him in all respects in the same way as if he were such occupant. This does not apply, in any case, unless the proprietor has made default in the punctual payment of the interest due under the security, or in due payment of the principal after formal requisition.[4]

---

[1] Heritable Securities (Scotland) Act, 1894, 57 & 58 Vict. cap. 44, secs. 8, 9, 15.
[2] Railton v. Muirhead, 1834, 12 S. 757.
[3] Stewart v. Brown, 1882, 10 R. 192.
[4] Heritable Securities (Scotland) Act, 1894, 57 & 58 Vict. cap. 5.

Power of Creditor in Possession to Lease Security Subjects.—Any person in possession of lands—which extends to and includes all heritable subjects—disponed in security may let such lands held in security, or part thereof, for a period not exceeding seven years in duration. The creditor may, however, apply to the Sheriff for warrant to let the lands disponed in security, or part thereof, for a period exceeding seven years, setting forth the name of the proposed tenant or tenants, the duration and conditions of the proposed lease ; and the Sheriff may, after service on the proprietor and on the other heritable creditors, if any, and after such intimation and inquiry as he may think proper, and if satisfied that a lease for a longer period than seven years is expedient for the beneficial occupation of the lands, approve of the proposed lease on the terms and conditions proposed, or on such other terms and conditions as may appear to him expedient. The lease must, however, in no case exceed twenty-one years for heritable property and thirty-one years for minerals.

2. Bond of Credit and Disposition in Security

To remedy the inconvenience occasioned by the fact that a heritable bond, or Bond and Disposition in Security, could not be made available as a security for any sum of money to be advanced upon it, subsequent to the date of the recording of the sasine, it was provided by 54 Geo. III. c. 137, sec. 12, and re-enacted by 19 & 20 Vict. c. 91, sec. 7, after the repeal of the former statute, that heritable securities may be given for cash accounts, or for the relief of cautioners in cash accounts, on condition that the principal sum and interest to become due under the bond is limited to a certain definite sum to be specified in the security, not exceeding the amount of principal and three years' interest at five per cent. By the latter statute the heritable security subsists to the extent of the sum limited, or any less sum, until the cash account is finally closed and the balance paid up and discharged.[1] If the security subjects be realised, any surplus there may be cannot, in a question with other creditors, be applied by the bank in reduction of any other debt due to it. The deed is in the form of an ordinary bond of credit, with the addition of a disposition of certain specified subjects in security. The security may be conveyed by persons other than the holder of the credit, in which case such persons are entitled to the rights and equities of cautioners.[2] The creditor's right is completed

---

[1] Opinion *per* Lord Low (Ordinary) that a heritable bond for a principal sum with interest, the rate not being specified, did not constitute a valid security *quoad* the interest as imposing a burden of indefinite amount. Opinions in Inner House reserved. Forbes *v.* Welsh & Forbes, 1894, 21 R. 630.

[2] See Cautionary Obligations, *infra*.

by the bond being recorded in the appropriate Register of Sasines. While in terms of the Act the subjects conveyed in security can only be made available for the repayment of the specified amount of principal and three years' interest at five per cent., the personal obligation contained in the bond can be enforced for the repayment of whatever sum is due. The security subjects can be realised in the same manner as those conveyed in a Bond and Disposition in Security.[1] General Letters of Inhibition against a debtor do not affect a prior cash-credit bond granted to a bank in security of advances made subsequent to the date of the inhibition.[2]

3. Disposition *ex facie* Absolute

This mode of constituting a security over heritable property, rendered necessary, or at least very desirable, by the exigencies of commerce and the nature of the transactions between banks and their mercantile customers, is more elastic than either of the modes already considered. By its means banks are enabled with safety not only to make advances to customers on the security of their heritable property, but to continue making advances after the amount originally required by the customer, and intended to be advanced, has been exhausted, so long as a safe margin of security is left for their reimbursement. The disposition by the debtor in favour of his creditor is in absolute terms, and is qualified by a back-bond or back-letter from the latter to the former, wherein the conditions entitling the debtor to a reconveyance of his property, and the nature of the transaction, are stated. In practice, the separate obligation occasionally takes the form of an explanatory letter from the debtor to the creditor, with an acceptance by the creditor indorsed on it, a copy of which is handed to the debtor. In the two former modes of constituting securities over heritable property, the creditor is a mere incumbrancer, whose right is extinguished by a discharge, whereas in the present mode the creditor acquires a right of property which cannot be extinguished by discharge, but only by reconveyance. The back-bond or back-letter may effectually provide that the debtor shall be entitled to demand such reconveyance only on condition of his paying everything he owes the creditor at the date of the demand.[3] The absolute disposition is usually stamped with a duty of ten shillings, and the back-letter with mortgage duty to the amount intended to be secured.

The right conveyed is an absolute right of property, and imposes on the creditor the liabilities of a proprietor. As a consequence, the

---

[1] See *ante*.

[2] De Lisle's Exrs. *v.* Campbell's Trs., 1870, 9 M. 252. See Inhibitions.

[3] See Lord President's opinion in National Bank *v.* Union Bank, 1885, 13 R. at p. 409, and *infra*.

creditor is entitled to sell the subjects, to collect the rents, to grant leases, to remove tenants, and even to remove the debtor himself, from possession.[1] Where a sale is resorted to, the creditor must have a due regard to the interests of the debtor.[2] The creditor's relation to the lands being thus that of a feudal proprietor and not of a creditor, he is not entitled to use the diligence of poinding of the ground.[3] The disposition is, while the back-bond should not be, recorded in the appropriate Register of Sasines. The effect of recording the back-bond in the Register of Sasines is to render the security conveyed unavailable for any sum advanced subsequent to the date of recording.[4] The security conferred by an absolute disposition, qualified by a back-letter, may be restricted in another way. In one case,[5] a bank held a recorded absolute disposition, granted by A., of certain subjects, which by back-letter it agreed to hold " in security and until full and final payment of all sums of money now due, or which may hereafter become due." The back-letter was not recorded. Some months afterwards, A., for onerous considerations, granted to another bank a deed by which she alienated, assigned, and disponed her whole right and interest and right of reversion in the subject. Intimation of the assignation was made to the first bank. Thereafter advances were made to A. by both banks. In a question between the two banks, the first bank's security was held to be limited to advances made prior to the date when the assignation was intimated. After notice to the bank of a second mortgage by the customer the debit is struck at the date of notice, and in the ordinary case—that is to say, where an account is merely continued without alteration, or where no specific appropriation of fresh payments is made—such payments are credited to the earliest items on the debit side of the account and continue so to be credited until the balance secured under the first mortgage is extinguished.[6] It is competent to stipulate that the *ex facie* right is to be a security for certain specified obligations, and if this be clearly expressed the property cannot be held for any other debt.[7] Upon payment of his whole indebtedness, including any sum expended by the creditor while in possession of the property, to the extent to which the real owner is *lucratus* or benefited thereby, but not until then, the debtor can compel the creditor to grant a reconveyance of the property.[8]

---

[1] Rankin *v.* Russell, 1868, 7 M. 126.

[2] Shrubb *v.* Clark, July 1897, 5 S.L.T. p. 125.

[3] Scottish Heritable Security Co. *v.* Allan Campbell & Co., 1876, 3 R. 333.

[4] Bell's Com. i. 725. See also National Bank *v.* Union Bank, *supra*.

[5] National Bank *v.* Union Bank, 1886, 14 R. (H.L.) 1.

[6] *Per* Lord Shaw of Dunfermline, in Deeley *v.* Lloyd's Bank, 29 T.L.R. at p. 6.

[7] Robertson *v.* Duff, 1840, 2 D. 279 ; Nelson *v.* Gordon, 1874, 1 R. 1093.

[8] Riddel *v.* Creditors of Niblie, 16th February 1782, M. 1154 and F.C. ; Keith *v.* Maxwell, 1795, Bell's Folio Cases, 234 ; Maitland *v.* Cockerell & Trail, 1827, 6 S.

It is customary in taking an absolute disposition to include in the conveyance not only the ground and buildings thereon, but also the whole machinery and plant of every description, both heritable and moveable, in or about the premises. While this is so, the conveyance does not cover the moveable machinery upon the ground, but only the heritable, unless the creditor enter into possession, either by himself or by some one on his behalf.[1] Difficult questions arise as to what machinery and plant are heritable and what moveable, and the determination of such questions largely depends on the circumstances of each particular case. Subjects which the law regards as heritable consist of things which, although in their nature moveable, become heritable in respect of their connection with the land, and which are so attached to the ground, or to a building thereon, that they cannot be removed without injury or destroying their usefulness. Such things are held to become the property of the owner of the soil on the principle of accession, by which where two things are connected with each other the property of the principal thing draws after it that of its accessory. In deciding whether any erections, machinery, plant, or additions are to be regarded as fixtures, it has been pointed out that there are two elements to be considered : (1) the character of the erections or additions themselves as more or less of the nature of fixtures ; and (2) the intention of the parties in making erections or additions, or in consenting to their being made. As regards the character and nature of the erections, the general rule is, that the subject must be fixed in or to the ground, or in or to something fixed in the ground. If a subject, however large, is merely laid on the ground, it has not generally the character of a fixture.[2]

Creditor can never become, unless by Special Agreement, Absolute Proprietor of Subjects.—A disposition expressly in security can never become, by prescription or otherwise, a disposition in absolute property. Hence, although the debtor becomes bankrupt, and the creditor deducts from his claim the value of the subjects disponed in security, and ranks merely for the balance due to him, if any, although the trustee does not take over the property, the creditor does not acquire thereby an absolute right to the property, so as to entitle him thereafter to obtain

---

109 ; Russell *v.* Earl of Breadalbane, 1829, 7 S. 767 ; 1 Scot. Jur. 296 ; *affd.* 1831, 5 W. & S. 256 ; 3 Scot. Jur. 431 ; James *v.* Downie, 1836, 15 S. 12 ; 9 Scot. Jur. 13 ; Robertson *v.* Duff, *supra* ; Nelson *v.* Gordon, *supra.*

[1] See as to this, Securities over Moveables.

[2] See generally on the subject, Fisher *v.* Dixon, 1845, 4 Bell's App. 286 ; Brand's Trs. *v.* Brand's Trs., 1876, 3 R. (H.L.) 16 ; Syme *v.* Harvey, 1861, 24 D. 202 ; Tod's Trs. *v.* Finlay, 1872, 10 M. 422 ; Dowall *v.* Miln, 1874, 1 R. 1180 ; Marshall *v.* Tannoch Chemical Co., 1886, 13 R. 1042 ; Erskine, ii. 24 ; Bell's Prin. 1255, 1473 ; Rankine on Land-Ownership, 104.

any benefit other than payment of his debt and interest in full which may result from the creditor continuing to hold the property. If the debtor has merely granted a trust-deed, although the creditor may have discharged him it would seem that subsequently the creditor is entitled to require the debtor to accept a reconveyance of the subjects so as thereby to relieve the creditor of the incidents of ownership of the property.[1]

Where the creditor deems it advisable to hold the property, his course, should the trustee decline to take it over at the specified value, is to get the trustee to execute in his favour a renunciation of any reversionary or other right he may have to the property.

Leasehold Subjects

By the common law of Scotland, an assignation of a lease by way of security, not followed by possession on the part of the assignee, is invalid as against creditors.[2] An important modification of this rule was introduced by the Registration of Leases (Scotland) Act, 1857, in regard to leases of thirty-one years and upwards.[3] When any such lease has been duly recorded, it is lawful for the party in right of such lease, and whose right is recorded (but in accordance always with the conditions and stipulations of such lease, and not otherwise), to assign [4] the same, in whole or in part, by assignation, the recording of which vests the assignee with the right of the granter thereof in and to such lease to the extent assigned. Such assignation does not prejudice the right of hypothec or other rights of the landlord. The person in right of any recorded lease, and whose right thereto has been recorded, may (but in accordance always with the conditions and stipulations of such lease, but not otherwise) assign [5] the same, in whole or in part, in security for the payment of borrowed money, or of annuities, or of provisions to wives or children, or in security of cash-credits or other legal debts or obligations. The recording of such assignation in security completes the right thereunder, and constitutes a real security over such lease to the extent assigned. The registration of all such leases, assignations, or assignation in security, completes the right under the same, to the effect of establishing a preference in virtue thereof, as effectually as if the grantee or party in his right had entered into the actual possession

---

1 Clydesdale Bank Ltd. *v.* M'Intyre, 1909, 1 S.L.T. 501.
2 Cabbell *v.* Brock, 1828, 3 W. & S. 75.
3 20 & 21 Vict. cap. 26.
4 A form of assignation is scheduled to the Act.
5 *Ibid.*

of the subjects leased, under such writs respectively at the date of registration thereof. In competitions, rights are preferable according to the dates of recording.

The creditor, or any party in right of such assignation in security without prejudice to the exercise of any power of sale [1] therein contained is entitled, in default of payment of the capital sum for which such assignation in security has been granted, or of a term's interest thereof or of a term's annuity, for six months after such capital sum or term' interest or annuity has fallen due, to apply to the Sheriff for a warrant to enter on possession of the lands and heritages leased. The Sheriff after intimation to the lessee for the time being, and to the landlord if he see cause, grants such warrant, which is a sufficient title for such creditor or party to enter into possession of such lands and heritages to uplift the rents from any sub-tenants therein, and to sublet the same as freely and to the like effect as the lessee might have done. No creditor or party, unless and until he enter into possession as aforesaid is personally liable to the landlord in any of the obligations and prestations of the lease.

Pledge of Title-Deeds

By the law of Scotland, only such moveables as are by their nature intrinsically valuable or substantially serviceable, and which, therefore would fetch a price in open market, can be made the subjects of pledge. Title-deeds and documents of debt have no intrinsic value, and therefor cannot be impignorated so as to confer a title of possession to the estate or debt represented by them, capable of competing with the right to vindicate possession competent to the proprietor or creditor who has acquired his right by singular and onerous title from the pledger. The Court has accordingly negatived a claim to retain title-deeds in security of a loan.[2]

In England, however, a *primâ facie* equitable mortgage is created over heritable (or real) property by a deposit of the title-deeds, though where the deposit is accompanied by a written document, the terms of such document must be referred to in order to ascertain the exact nature of the charge.[3] Title-deeds may be deposited with a banker as an equitable security, during the continuance of his possession of the documents, for the payment with interest of all moneys due, or to become due, by the mortgagor to the banker.

---

[1] A creditor's rights under a lease may be sold in the same manner as under bond and disposition in security. See *ante*.

[2] Christie *v.* Ruxton, 1862, 24 D. 1182.

[3] M'Creight *v.* Foster, L.R. 5 H.L. 321.

As questions affecting heritable property are usually [1] decided in accordance with the law of the place where the property is situated, advances may competently be made in Scotland against the deposit of titles of heritable property situated in England.[2]

---

[1] See, however, Studd v. Cook, 1880, 8 R. 249 ; *affd.* 10 R. (H.L.) 53.

[2] For forms, see Appendix.

CHAPTER II

SECURITIES OVER MOVEABLES

MOVEABLES may be divided into two classes: Corporeal, or those in which the property may be transferred by actual delivery from hand to hand; and Incorporeal, or those which are incapable of being so transferred, and which require writing to effect their transference. Furniture, stock in trade, etc., may be instanced as examples of the former class, while Policies of Insurance, Stock Certificates, Debentures, a vested interest in a trust-estate, etc., are examples of the latter class.

1. Corporeal Moveables

From a consideration of the cases bearing on the transference of corporeal moveables in security of a debt,[1] the law as it at present stands may be briefly summarised thus. No security can be obtained over corporeal moveables unless the creditor or some one on his behalf gets possession of the articles. There is thus no process by which the furniture in a man's house, or the stock in his warehouse, can be effectually assigned by him in security so long as he remains in possession thereof. Nor does a mere colourable contract of sale make any difference, as for example where the pretended sale does not take immediate effect so as to give the alleged purchaser the full and complete right which a true contract of sale confers.[2] But where it can be shown that there has been a *bonâ fide* out and out sale, the purchaser can assert his right to the goods, even although they remain in the seller's possession.

The Sale of Goods Act, 1893, which repeals and substantially re-enacts sections 1 to 5 of the Mercantile Law Amendment (Scotland)

---

[1] Heritable Securities Invest. Assoc. *v.* Wingate & Co.'s Tr., 1880, 7 R. 1094; Liquidator of West Lothian Oil Co. *v.* Muir, 1892, 20 R. 64; Pattison's Tr. *v.* Liston, 1893, 20 R. 806; M'Bain *v.* Wallace, 1881, 8 R. 360; 8 R. (H.L.) 106; Cropper *v.* Donaldson, 1880, 7 R. 1108; M'All's Tr. *v.* Thomson, 1883, 10 R. 1064; Murdoch *v.* Greig, 1889, 16 R. 296; Barr *v.* Warr & Co., 1893, 20 R. 806; Clark *v.* West Calder Oil Co., 1882, 9 R. 1017.

[2] Edmond *v.* Mowat, 1868, 7 M. 59; see also Sale of Goods Act, 1893, sec. 61 (4).

ct, 1856, and, save in some minor details, assimilates the laws of England and Scotland with respect to the sale of goods, provides—

Transfer of Property in Goods.—Where there is a contract for the sale of specific or ascertained goods, the property in them is transferred to the buyer at such time as the parties to the contract intend it to be transferred. The intention to transfer the property may be gathered from the terms of the contract, the conduct of the parties, and the circumstances of the case,[1] but unless it is otherwise apparent it is ascertained in accordance with the following rules :—(1) Where there is an unconditional contract for the sale of specific goods, in a deliverable state, the property in the goods passes to the buyer when the contract is made, and it is immaterial whether the time of payment or the time of delivery, or both, be postponed. (2) Where there is a contract for the sale of specific goods, and the seller is bound to do something to the goods, for the purpose of putting them in a deliverable state, the property does not pass until such thing be done, and the buyer has notice thereof. (3) Where there is a contract for the sale of specific goods in a deliverable state, but the seller is bound to weigh, measure, test, or do some other act or thing with reference to the goods, for the purpose of ascertaining the price, the property does not pass until such act or thing be done, and the buyer has notice thereof. (4) When goods are delivered to the buyer on approval, or " on sale and return," or other similar terms, the property therein passes to the buyer (*a*) when he signifies his approval or acceptance to the seller, or does any other act adopting the transaction ; (*b*) if he does not signify his approval or acceptance to the seller, but retains the goods without giving notice of rejection, then, if a time has been fixed for the return of the goods, on the expiration of such time, and if no time has been fixed, on the expiration of a reasonable time, what is a reasonable time being a question of fact. (5) Where there is a contract for the sale of unascertained or future goods by description, and goods of that description and in a deliverable state are unconditionally appropriated to the contract, either by the seller with the assent of the buyer, or by the buyer with the assent of the seller, the property in the goods thereupon passes to the buyer. Such assent may be express or implied, and may be given either before or after the appropriation is made. Where, in pursuance of the contract, the seller delivers the goods to the buyer, or to a carrier, or other bailee or custodier (whether named by the buyer or not), for the purpose of transmission to the buyer, and does not reserve the right of disposal, he is deemed to have unconditionally appropriated the goods to the contract.[2]

---

[1] Sec. 17. See Sir James Laing & Co. Ltd. *v.* Barclay, Curle & Co. Ltd., 1908, S.C. 1 (H.L.) 82.

[2] Sec. 18.

Reservation of Right of Disposal.—Where there is a contract for the sale of specific goods, or where goods are subsequently appropriated to the contract, the seller may, by the terms of the contract or appropriation, reserve the right of disposal of the goods until certain conditions are fulfilled. In such case, notwithstanding the delivery of the goods to the buyer, or to a carrier, or other bailee or custodier, for the purpose of transmission to the buyer, the property in the goods does not pass to the buyer until the conditions imposed by the seller are fulfilled. Where goods are shipped and by the bill of lading the goods are deliverable to the order of the seller or his agent, the seller is *primâ facie* deemed to reserve the right of disposal.[1] Unless otherwise agreed, the goods remain at the seller's risk until the property therein is transferred to the buyer, but when the property therein is transferred to the buyer, the goods are at the buyer's risk, whether delivery has been made or not. Where, however, delivery has been delayed, through the fault of either buyer or seller, the goods are at the risk of the party in fault as regards any loss which might not have occurred but for such fault.[2]

Sale by Person not Owner.—Subject to certain provisions,[3] where goods are sold by a person who is not the owner thereof, and who does not sell them under the authority or with the consent of the owner, the buyer acquires no better title to the goods than the seller had, unless the owner of the goods is by his conduct precluded from denying the seller's authority to sell. The provisions of the Factors Acts,[4] or any enactment enabling the apparent owner of goods to dispose of them as if he were the true owner, and the validity of any contract of sale under any special common law, or statutory power of sale, or under the order of a Court of competent jurisdiction, are not affected.

Seller or Buyer in Possession after Sale.—Where a person, having sold goods, continues, or is in possession of the goods, or of the documents of title to the goods, the delivery or transfer by that person, or by a mercantile agent acting for him, of the goods or documents of title under any sale, pledge, or other disposition thereof, to any person receiving the same in good faith and without notice of the previous sale, has the same effect as if the person making the delivery or transfer were expressly authorised by the owner of the goods to make the same. Where a person, having bought or agreed to buy goods, obtains, with the consent of the seller, possession of the goods, or the

---

[1] Sec. 19. See also Bills of Lading, *infra.*

[2] Sec. 20. The duties or liabilities of either party as custodier of the goods of the other party are not affected.

[3] Secs. 22-25 of Act.

[4] See Special Customers ; Agents.

locuments of title to the goods, the delivery or transfer by that person, or by a mercantile agent acting for him, of the goods or documents of title under any sale, pledge, or other disposition thereof, to any person receiving the same in good faith and without notice of any lien or other right of the original seller in respect of the goods, has the same effect as if the person making the delivery or transfer were a mercantile agent in possession of the goods or documents of title with the consent of the owner.[1]

Unpaid Seller's Rights.—The seller of goods, including any person who is in the position of a seller, as for instance an agent of the seller to whom the bill of lading has been indorsed, or a consignor or agent who has himself paid, or is directly responsible for, the price, is an " unpaid seller " when the whole of the price has not been paid or tendered, or when a bill of exchange or other negotiable instrument has been received as conditional payment, and the condition on which it was received has not been fulfilled by reason of the dishonour of the instrument or otherwise.[2] Subject to provisions after mentioned,[3] notwithstanding that the property in the goods may have passed to the buyer, the unpaid seller of goods, as such, has by implication of law (*a*) a lien on the goods, or right to retain them for the price while he is in possession of them ; (*b*) in case of the insolvency of the buyer, a right of stopping the goods *in transitu* after he has parted with the possession of them ; (*c*) a right of resale, as limited by the Act. Where the property in goods has not passed to the buyer, the unpaid seller has, in addition to his other remedies, a right of withholding delivery similar to, and co-extensive with, his rights of lien and stoppage *in transitu* where the property has passed to the buyer. In Scotland, a seller of goods may attach the same, while in his own hands or possession, by arrestment or poinding ; and such arrestment or poinding has the same operation and effect in a competition or otherwise as an arrestment or poinding by a third party. Subject to the provisions of the Act, the unpaid seller of goods who is in possession of them is entitled to retain possession of them until payment or tender of the price (*a*) where the goods have been sold without any stipulation as to credit ; (*b*) where the goods have been sold on credit, but the term of credit has expired ; (*c*) where the buyer becomes insolvent. The seller may exercise his right of lien notwithstanding that he is in possession of the goods as agent or bailee or custodier for the buyer. Where an unpaid seller has made part delivery of the goods, he may exercise his right of lien or retention on the remainder, unless such part delivery has been made under such circumstances as to show an agreement to waive the lien or right of retention. The unpaid seller of goods loses

---

[1] Sec. 25. [2] See Bills of Lading, *infra.*
[3] See Stoppage *in transitu, infra,* and Special Customers, Agents, *ante.*

his lien or right of retention thereon (a) when he delivers the goods to a carrier, or other bailee or custodier, for the purpose of transmission to the buyer without reserving the right of disposal of the goods; (b) when the buyer or his agent lawfully obtains possession of the goods; (c) by waiver thereof. The unpaid seller of goods, having a lien or right of retention thereon, does not lose his lien or right of retention by reason only that he has obtained judgment or decree for the price of the goods.[1]

The Sale of Goods Act, however, does not apply to " any transaction in the form of a contract of sale which is intended to operate by way of mortgage, pledge, charge, or other security." Hence in order to the constitution of a valid security, it is still necessary for the creditor to obtain actual or constructive delivery of the goods. Where, therefore, a security over corporeal moveables is desired, it may be effected by the lender obtaining actual delivery, or that constructive delivery which the law holds as equivalent to actual delivery. Actual delivery consists in delivering actual corporeal possession of the goods into the lender's warehouse, vehicle, or vessel, or into a wharfinger's warehouse where the lender is in the habit of storing goods, or in delivering to the lender the key of the cellar or other repository where the goods are stored. Constructive delivery is effected by all those acts, which, although they do not confer on the purchaser the actual possession of the thing sold, have been held, by operation of law, equivalent to acts of real delivery. Intimating a delivery order to the custodier of goods,[2] or transferring the goods in the custodier's books from the name of the borrower to that of the lender, are examples of acts of constructive delivery. While the owner of the goods retains them in his own possession, no entry in his books will by itself operate as constructive delivery of such goods, nor will it do so even where the goods of others, as well as of the borrower, are kept in his store.

The kind of corporeal moveables with which a banker has most frequent connection is that of goods belonging to his debtor in the custody of a third person, the property in which the debtor is willing, in security of his indebtedness, to transfer to the bank. This transference is effected by means of a

Delivery Order.—A delivery order is defined by the Stamp Act [3] to be " any document or writing entitling, or intending to entitle, any person therein named, or his assigns or the holder thereof, to the delivery of any goods, wares, or merchandise of the value of forty

---

[1] Secs. 38-43. See also Stoppage *in transitu*, *infra*.

[2] *Vide* Lord President Inglis in Anderson *v.* M'Call, 1866, 4 M. 765 ; Black *v.* Incorporation of Glasgow Bakers, 1867, 6 M. 136 ; Pochin & Co. *v.* Robinows & Marjoribanks, 1869, 7 M. 622 ; Vickers *v.* Hertz, 1871, 9 M. (H.L.) 65 ; Distillers' Co. *v.* Russell's Tr., 1889, 16 R. 479.

[3] Stamp Act, 1891, 54 & 55 Vict. cap. 39, sec. 69.

shillings or upwards, lying in any dock or port, or in any warehouse in which the goods are stored or deposited on rent or hire, or upon any wharf, such document or writing being signed by or on behalf of the owner of such goods, wares, or merchandise upon the sale or transfer of the property therein." The order formerly required a penny stamp, but the duty was repealed in the Finance Act of 1905. It is usual for the storekeeper to acknowledge receipt of the order, and such an acknowledgment requires no stamp.[1] If besides simply acknowledging receipt of the document the warehouse-keeper adds to his letter words which bring the document within the statutory definition of a " warrant for goods," the letter is liable to a duty of threepence.[2] The following is the statutory definition of a " warrant for goods " :—
" Any document or writing being evidence of the title of any person therein named or his assigns or the holder thereof to the property in any goods, wares, or merchandise lying in any warehouse or dock, or upon any wharf, and signed or certified by or on behalf of the person having the custody of the goods, wares, or merchandise." [3] It does not affect the title of the bank as holders of a delivery order duly intimated, that it appears from the transaction that a mere security was intended, because when a delivery order in absolute terms is presented to a warehouse-keeper, and given effect to by him in the warehouse books, a complete transfer of the goods from their previous owner to the possessor of the delivery order takes place, and the possessor of the order is put in possession of the goods to the same effect as if he had bought them and obtained actual delivery on a contract of sale. As holders of a delivery order, the bank is entitled to sell or otherwise dispose of the goods, but the bank's right to the proceeds of the sale is limited to the amount of its customer's indebtedness, and it is bound to account to its customer for any surplus remaining over, after its debt has been satisfied. In virtue of the fact, however, that the possession of the delivery order by the bank, accompanied by notification in the storekeeper's books, constitutes a transfer of the proprietary right in the goods to the bank, the bank is entitled to hold the goods represented by the delivery order in security of a general balance due by the original owner of the goods, even where the delivery order was given as a collateral security for a specific purpose.[4] It must, however, be remembered that in order that this right may be effectually constituted, it is necessary that the goods intended to be pledged or delivered in security should be specifically ascertained and identified.

---

[1] For forms of delivery order and acknowledgment by storekeeper, see Appendix.
[2] Distillers' Co. Ltd. v. Inland Revenue, 1899, 1 F. 737.
[3] Stamp Act, 1891, sec. 111.
[4] Hamilton v. Western Bank, 1856, 19 D. 152 ; approved in Hayman & Son v. M'Lintock, 1907, S.C. 936.

15

Thus where certain sacks of flour, represented by a delivery order, were neither numbered, nor marked, nor put into receptacles, nor ascertained in such a way as to distinguish them from other flour in the storekeeper's warehouse, it was held, in accordance with the provisions of sections 16 and 29 of the Sale of Goods Act, 1893, which requires that before the property in any goods can pass to the vendor they must be ascertained or identified, that as the goods sold were unascertained no property in them had passed, and no effectual right of security had been constituted by the delivery order.[1] Where a delivery order is taken by the bank in security of past advances, there should be an express agreement to this effect entered into between it and its customer.[2] But even in the absence of an express agreement to the contrary, the bank is, it is thought, entitled to reimburse itself for its customer's whole obligations, irrespective of what may have been due at the time of the granting of the delivery order. Three independent persons are necessary to constitute constructive delivery by means of a delivery order, namely, the granter, the person in whose favour it is granted, and the storekeeper or custodier of the goods. If the custodier be identified with the granter of the order, he ceases to be an independent third person, and therefore there cannot be constructive delivery by means of such a delivery order.[3] Thus, if a merchant has goods in a store exclusively occupied by him, or in a store into which he receives the goods of others as well as his own goods, a delivery order granted by him on the storekeeper is not effectual as an instrument for pledging the property even if the storekeeper accepts liability for the goods to the transferee.[4] Mere possession of the order is not sufficient to constitute constructive delivery. There must be, over and above possession, intimation to the storekeeper, and the date of the intimation, not the date of the order, fixes the time of the change of ownership.[5] When the delivery order is indorsed to a third party, the indorsee to complete his right must intimate the same to the storekeeper. The indorsation of a delivery order requires no stamp.

Security over Moveables by Means of Bond and Disposition in Security.—A direct security may competently be constituted over moveables in the hands of a third party by means of a Bond and Disposition in Security. The bond is executed with reference to an inventory of the goods assigned, and the security is completed by intimation to the custodier of the goods.

Pledge of Title to Goods by Person in Possession thereof.—When a

---

[1] Hayman & Son v. M'Lintock, *supra*.

[2] See Robertson v. Duff, 1840, 2 D. 279.

[3] Anderson v. M'Call, 1866, 4 M. 765; Distillers' Co. v. Russell's Tr., 1889, 16 R. 479.

[4] Rhind's Trs. v. Robertson & Baxter, 1891, 18 R. 623.

[5] Robertson & Baxter v. Inglis, 1898, 25 R. (H.L.) 70.

factor or agent is accredited with the ostensible ownership of goods, not merely by being intrusted with the bare custody, but by having documents put into his hands which *ex facie* confer upon him the character of owner, such as to enable him to deceive those with whom he transacts, he may effectually pledge the property of his principals by the transference of such documents to a party making *bonâ fide* advances on the goods, such party being entitled to rely on the probative title with which the factor has been clothed, and not being bound to make restitution without repayment of his advances.[1] Where any dock warrant, warehouse-keeper's certificate, warrant or order for the delivery of goods, or any other document used in the ordinary course of business as giving proof of the possession or control of goods, is pledged or transferred as a security by indorsement or delivery, whether in consideration of an original advance or of any future advance or pecuniary liability, such pledge or transference is deemed to be a pledge of the goods thereby represented.[2]

2. Incorporeal Moveables

By the Transmission of Moveable Property (Scotland) Act, 1862,[3] a simple and effectual mode of assigning a person's right in a personal bond or conveyance of moveable estate is introduced. The Act provides that this may be done either by a separate writing or by an assignation written upon the bond or conveyance itself. While not superseding the forms in use at the passing of the Act, which may still be used, the schedules annexed to the Act contain forms.[4] Upon such assignation being duly stamped and intimated, the assignee is placed in the right of his cedent, but until intimation there is no completed transference to the assignee. So essential is intimation, that, in a competition, an assignation first intimated will be preferred to one prior in date, but posterior in intimation.[5] An assignation is validly intimated (1) by a notary public delivering a copy thereof certified as correct to the person or persons to whom intimation may in any case be requisite, or (2) by the holder of such assignation, or any person authorised by him, transmitting a copy thereof certified as correct by post to such person. Where the deed contains also other conveyances or trust purposes, a copy of the part respecting the subject-matter of the assignation is enough. In the first case a certificate by the notary public in, or as nearly as may be in, the form set forth in the schedule annexed to the Act,[6] and in the second case a written acknowledgment by the person to whom such copy may have

---

[1] Pochin & Co. *v.* Robinows & Marjoribanks, 1869, 7 M. 622.

[2] Factors (Scotland) Act, 1890, extending to Scotland the Factors Act, 1889.

[3] 25 & 26 Vict. cap. 85.

[4] For these schedules, see Appendix.

[5] Menzies' Conveyancing, 248 ; Stair, iii. 1, 6 ; Erskine's Institutes, iii. 5, 3.

[6] For which see Appendix.

been transmitted by post as aforesaid, of receipt of the copy, is sufficient evidence of such intimation having been duly made. In practice it is common to send the principal assignation along with the copy to the person entitled to receive the intimation, and get him to write his acknowledgment of receipt of the copy on the principal assignation. The words " bond " and " conveyance " in the Act extend to and include personal bonds for payment or performance, bonds of caution, bonds of guarantee, bonds of relief, bonds and assignations in security of every kind, decreets of any Court, policies of assurance of any assurance company or association in Scotland, whether held by parties resident in Scotland or elsewhere,[1] protests of bills or of promissory notes, dispositions, assignations, and other conveyances of moveable or personal property or effects, translations and retrocessions, and also probative extracts of all such deeds from the books of any competent Court. Moveable estate extends to and includes all personal debts and obligations and moveable or personal property or effects of every kind.

Besides the statutory provisions as to intimation, the following modes are still competent : (1) by the execution of a charge on letters of horning at the instance of the assignee against the common debtor ; (2) by a judicial demand, as by the raising of an action at the instance of the assignee against the common debtor, in which the assignation is founded on, or by the production of the deed in an action of multiplepoinding ; (3) by tacit acquiescence of the assignee's right of possession, as by the receipt of payment of rents or interest from the common debtor ; (4) by the common debtor being a party to the assignation ;[2] (5) by the debtor's acknowledgment on the back of the assignation or by letter ; (6) by a written promise by the common debtor to pay to the assignee as in right of the granter of the assignation ; or (7) in the case of a money debt, by a draft accepted or presented and protested.

Where there is a competition among creditors, the debtor's private knowledge of the assignation cannot be pleaded by the assignee as an equivalent to intimation, as such private knowledge does not amount to a completion of the assignation. Unless, therefore, the assignation be intimated, the assignee's right will be postponed to debts secured by arrestment or by another assignation duly intimated. Private knowledge of the assignation, however, may be a sufficient bar to the common debtor paying to the granter of the assignation. Registration of the assignation in the Books of Council and Session is not equivalent to intimation.[3] Where there are several debtors the assignation should

---

[1] See also Policies of Assurance.

[2] Charteris v. Sinclair, 27th November 1707, M. 2876 ; Turnbull v. Stewart & Inglis, 12th June 1751, M. 868 ; Paul v. Boyd's Tr., 1835, 13 S. 818.

[3] Tod's Trs. v. Wilson, 1869, 7 M. 1100.

be intimated to all of them, and where the beneficial right under a trust is assigned, the assignation should be intimated to all the acting trustees. In one case,[1] where the intimation of such an assignation was only made to A., one of two trustees, the Court held the intimation sufficient, as the funds were in A.'s hands, and he managed the whole affairs of the trust. It is, however, advisable to intimate to the whole acting trustees, although in one case the Court decided that as a general rule an assignation of rights in a trust-estate is sufficiently intimated to trustees by intimation to their law agents.[2] In the case of ordinary trading companies, intimation should be made to each of the partners, unless there is a regularly appointed manager. Intimation to one who is *de facto* the managing partner is not sufficient.[3] In the case of an incorporated joint stock bank, intimation should be made to the manager at the head office, and also, if the money is lying at a branch office, to the agent there. In the case of companies incorporated under the Companies Acts, intimation is left, or sent by post in a prepaid letter addressed to the company, at their registered office.[4] When the common debtor is out of Scotland, the intimation must be made edictally, the warrant for which is obtained at the Bill Chamber on production of the grounds of debt and assignation.

Assignations to Policies of Life Assurance.—The mere possession by a creditor of a policy of insurance over the life of his debtor, without any assignation to it, confers, under a contract entered into in Scotland, no right on the creditor to the policy or any claim arising in respect thereof. If the creditor in such circumstances pays the annual premium, he is not entitled when a claim under the policy emerges to a preferential ranking in respect of such payments, as the payments so made are held to be cash advances to the assured for which the creditor must accept an ordinary ranking.[5] It may be mentioned that if a contract is entered into in England with a domiciled Englishman for a loan against a policy, although both the debtor and the insurance company are domiciled in Scotland, an effectual preference is conferred on the creditor by the mere delivery of the policy and intimation of the fact to the insurance company.[6]

When policies are accepted as security by a bank, the assignations are usually taken absolutely without reference to any debt, the consideration being expressed as " for certain good and onerous causes and considerations." The benefit of this course, so long as the assignation

---

[1] Jameson *v.* Sharp, 1887, 14 R. 643 ; Erskine's Institutes, iii. 5, 5.

[2] Browne's Trs. *v.* Anderson, 1901, 4 F. 305.

[3] Hill *v.* Lindsay and Others, 1846, 8 D. 472.

[4] Companies' Consolidation Act, 1908, secs. 116, 285.

[5] Wylie's Exr. *v.* M'Jannet, 1901, 4 F. 195.

[6] Scottish Provident Institution *v.* Cohen & Co., 1888, 16 R. 112.

is not qualified either in the body of the deed or in a separate writing, and the assignation contains no statement that it is granted in security of a debt, is, that the bank is enabled to hold the policy assigned not only for the repayment of any sum due at the time of the granting of the assignation, but for any debt that may be subsequently incurred,[1] while, if the assignation bear to be granted for a special consideration, the bank is unable to hold it in security of any further advance.[2] The assignation to a policy of assurance carries with it—unless a contrary intention is expressed—all the bonus or other benefits whether accrued or accruing to the principal sum. If before a claim emerges under a policy the indebtedness is cleared off, the assigner of the policy is entitled to have it reassigned to him, which is effected by a deed of retrocession executed by the creditor and duly intimated to the insurance company.

Stamp.—No matter for what amount the policy may be, the assignation is sufficiently stamped with a duty of ten shillings, provided the assignation is absolute, and the cause of granting stated to be " for certain good and onerous causes and considerations." The opinion here expressed has been much discussed and questioned. In July of 1912 the Associated Scottish Life offices, following, it is understood, on representations by the Inland Revenue authorities, issued a circular declining under any circumstances to accept assignations to life policies unless adjudicated as duly stamped. A special case for the opinion of the Court was proposed, but was subsequently abandoned. The difficulty has now been arranged. Assignations to life policies stamped with a duty of ten shillings, the consideration being as above stated, are accepted without adjudication on the assignee producing at the settlement of a claim under the policy a certificate stating the highest amount advanced, stamped with mortgage duty to cover that amount. For this course there seems neither precedent nor principle.

Assignation by Partners or Third Parties.—Where the assignation is granted by a member of a firm in security of his firm's indebtedness, or by a third party on behalf of a customer, in order to enable the bank to avail themselves of the security, there must be some deed which connects the transaction with the customer's indebtedness. This deed usually takes the form of an explanatory letter, in which the nature of the transaction is set forth. In assignations of this description, various considerations as to stamp duty fall to be observed. The assignation itself, if it proceed on the narrative referred to, is sufficiently

---

[1] Nelson v. Gordon, 1874, 1 R. 1093 ; Wylie & Lochhead v. Hornsby, 16 R. 907. (See Lord Young's Opinion.)

[2] Forbes v. Robb, 1858, 21 D. 79 ; Borthwick v. Scottish Widows' Fund, 1864, 2 M. 595.

stamped with a duty of ten shillings, but the explanatory letter requires to be stamped with mortgage duty of two shillings and sixpence per cent. on the amount intended to be secured.[1] Where the amount of indebtedness to the bank is small, and it is not intended that the policy should be held as security for a larger sum, the assignation itself may be stamped with mortgage duty of two shillings and sixpence per cent. on the amount intended to be secured. In such a case, however, the cause of granting should be stated to be "in consideration of certain banking facilities allowed me by the ——— bank to an extent not exceeding £———." It will be observed that unless the sum to be secured does not exceed three hundred pounds, no saving of stamp duty is effected, and it is better to take the assignation absolutely on a ten shilling stamp.

Intimation of Assignation.—The assignation of a policy *per se* confers no right on the assignee to recover the amount due under it, until notice [2] of the assignation has been given in writing to the insurance company at their head office. It has, however, been decided that an assignation of a policy of life insurance constituted a right in the assignee which was valid against the executor of the cedent, although it had not been intimated to the insurance company prior to the cedent's death. Intimation, it was pointed out, is necessary in order to constitute a real right to the subject assigned, but as against the cedent's representatives an assignment of the policy, like any other deed purporting to give a contract right, is binding on the granter and his heirs, and therefore the executor of the cedent being under obligation to warrant the assignment cannot set up his title in opposition to that of the assignee.[3] The company, on receiving the statutory fee of five shillings, is bound to give an acknowledgment of the intimation of the assignation. The date of the notice to the company, and not that of the assignation, is declared to regulate the priority of all claims regarding the amount contained in the policy.[4] Should the assured be sequestrated before the assignation is intimated, his trustee would be preferred to the policy; and this right of the trustee requires no intimation, as the act and warrant in his favour operates as a completed title in favour of the trustee as at the date of the first deliverance.

Policies Invalidated.—Most, if not all, policies of insurance are effected on the condition that certain questions relative to the insured's habits of life, his health, his transactions with other companies, etc., put to, and answered by, the insured or some one on his behalf, have been

---

[1] Stamp Act, 1891, 54 & 55 Vict. cap. 39, sec. 86 (*d*).
[2] See Appendix. As to other modes of intimation, see *supra*.
[3] Brownlee *v.* Robb, 1907, S.C. 1302.
[4] Policies of Insurance Act, 1867, 30 & 31 Vict. cap. 144; Campbell's Trs. *v.* Whyte, 1884, 11 R. 1078.

answered truthfully, and it is provided that false answers to any such questions may have the effect of absolutely invalidating the contract. The questions put must, however, be clear and unambiguous in their terms, as the Courts will not readily declare an answer to be false, which may be only an innocent misinterpretation of an ambiguous question.[1] As a general rule, an answer is deemed to be true, if true in the *bonâ fide* belief and to the best of the knowledge of the person making it.[2] The validity of a policy may, however, in certain circumstances depend on whether an answer was true in point of fact, independently of its truth in the *bonâ fide* knowledge and belief of the person making it.[3] It is important, therefore, that this should be kept in view, as an onerous assignee of a policy holds it subject to reduction on the same grounds as those on which it might have been challenged while still in the hands of the original grantee.[4] The interest held by a debtor in a mutual insurance company under a policy payable at his death may validly be arrested during his life, and the arrestment does not fall by another termly payment of premium falling due after the date of arrestment.[5]

Policies Effected over the Lives of Third Persons.—*Insurable Interest.*—Down to the latter part of last century wagering contracts of insurances on lives prevailed to a large extent, and on the recital that "it has been found by experience that the making of insurance on lives or other events wherein the assured shall have no interest hath introduced a mischievous kind of gambling," an Act was passed which provided "that no insurance shall be made by any person or persons on the life or lives of any person or persons, or on any other event or events whatsoever wherein the person or persons for whose use, benefit, or on whose account such policy or policies shall be made, shall have no interest, or by way of gaming or wagering, and that every assurance made contrary to the true intent and meaning hereof shall be null and void to all intents and purposes."[6] By the second section of the Act it is provided that "it shall not be lawful to make any policy or policies

---

[1] Fowkes *v.* Manchester and London Life Assurance Association, 1863, 3 B. & S. 917.

[2] Hutchison *v.* National Loan Assurance Co., 1845, 7 D. 480 ; M'Laws *v.* United Kingdom Temperance Institution, 1861, 23 D. 559 ; Life Association of Scotland *v.* Foster, 1873, 11 M. 351 ; Scottish Equitable Life Assurance Society *v.* Buist, 1877, 4 R. 1076, 5 R. (H.L.) 64. See also Standard Life Assurance Co. *v.* Weems, 1884, 11 R. (H.L.) 48 L.R. 9 Ap. Ca. 671.

[3] Standard Life Assurance Co. *v.* Weems, *supra*.

[4] Anderson *v.* Fitzgerald, 1853, Clark, 4 H.L.C. 484 ; Scottish Equitable Life Assurance Society *v.* Buist, 1876, *supra*. See also in a question with insured's representatives and company, Standard Life Assurance Co. *v.* Weems, 1884, *supra*.

[5] Bankhardt's Trs. *v.* Scottish Amicable Society and Duncan, 1871, 9 M. 443.

[6] 1774, 14 Geo. III. cap. 48, sec. 1.

on the life or lives of any person or persons, or other event or events, without inserting in such policy or policies the person or persons, name or names, interested therein, or for whose use, benefit, or on whose account such policy is so made or underwrote." The third section provides that " in all cases where the insured hath interest in such life or lives, event or events, no greater sum shall be recovered or received from the insurer or insurers than the amount or value of the interest of the insured in such life or lives, or other event or events." A creditor has an insurable interest in the life of his debtor. A wife has an insurable interest in the life of her husband. The insurable interest must, however, be pecuniary apart from relationship.[1] The terms of the enactment that no greater sum shall be recoverable than the amount or value of the creditor's interest in the life gave rise to difficulties where the interest which existed at the time of effecting the policy had come to an end, or had been diminished in value prior to a claim emerging under the policy. But it has been decided that the provisions of the Act are satisfied if the person effecting the insurance has an insurable interest in the life at the time when the insurance was effected.[2] If, however, the creditor insure the same interest with several companies, he or his assignee cannot recover upon the whole more than the amount of the original creditor's insurable interest.[3]

While a creditor is entitled to insure the life of his debtor, he is not obliged to set off against the debt the sum received under the insurance minus the amount of premiums paid by him, but is entitled both to his debt and to the proceeds of the policy. The insurance company is not entitled, as a condition of their paying, to demand from the creditor an assignation to his debt. When, however, a creditor, having insured his debtor's life, debits him with the annual premiums, the debtor or his representatives are, upon payment of the debt and interest, entitled to the proceeds of the policy, since they, and not the creditor, have kept the policy in force.

The original creditor under the policy may assign his claim to a third person, and such person is entitled to recover under the policy to the extent of the insurable interest of the person from whom he received the policy. It is advisable in such circumstances to get the insurance company to indorse on the policy an admission of the insurable interest of the original creditor.

Sale or Surrender of Policy.—In the assignation, express power should be taken by the creditor to sell or surrender the policy at any time, as no statutory facilities exist in Scotland for the sale by the

---

[1] As to what constitutes interest, see Turnbull & Co. *v.* Scottish Provident Institution, 1896, 34 S.L.R. 146.

[2] Dalby *v.* The India and London Assurance Co., 1854, 15 C.B. 365.

[3] Simcock *v.* Scottish Imperial Insurance Co., 1902, 10 S.L.T. 286.

creditor at his own hand of any personal property belonging to his debtor, with the single exception of shares in ships. Before, therefore, the creditor could sell or surrender the policy without the consent of the debtor, he would require to go to the Court for authority to do so.

Married Women's Policies of Assurance (Scotland) Act, 1880.[1]— *Married Woman may Effect Policy of Assurance for her Separate Use.*[2]—A married woman may effect a policy of assurance on her own life or on the life of her husband for her separate use ; and the same and all benefit thereof, if expressed to be for her separate use, shall immediately on being so effected vest in her, and shall be payable to her and her heirs, executors, or assignees, excluding the *jus mariti* and right of administration of her husband, and shall be assignable by her either *inter vivos* or *mortis causa* without consent of her husband, and the contract in such policy shall be as valid and effectual as if made by an unmarried woman. A policy taken out under this section may be assigned by the married woman in security of advances to herself, her husband, or a third person.

Policy of Assurance may be Effected in Trust for Wife and Children.[3]— A policy of assurance effected by any married man on his own life, and expressed upon the face of it to be for the benefit of his wife or of his children, or of his wife and children, shall, together with all benefit thereof, be deemed a trust for the benefit of his wife, for her separate use, or for the benefit of his children, or for the benefit of his wife and children ; and such policy, immediately on its being so effected, shall vest in him and his legal representatives in trust for the purpose or purposes so expressed, or in any trustee nominated in the policy or appointed by separate writing, duly intimated to the insurance office, but in trust always as aforesaid, and shall not otherwise be subject to his control, or form part of his estate, or be liable to the diligence of his creditors, or be revocable as a donation, or reducible on any ground of excess or insolvency ; and the receipt of such trustee for the sums secured by the policy or for the value thereof, in whole or in part, shall be a sufficient and effectual discharge to the assurance office : Provided always, that if it shall be proved that the policy was effected and premiums thereon paid with intent to defraud creditors, or if the person upon whose life the policy is effected shall be made bankrupt within two years from the date of such policy, it shall be competent to the creditors to claim repayment of the premiums so paid from the trustee of the policy out of the proceeds thereof.[4] Policies effected under this section cannot be validly assigned by the husband and wife, or either of them, in security of a general balance due or to become due by both or either of them, or of a third

---

[1] 43 & 44 Vict. cap. 26.   [2] Act, sec. 1.   [3] Act, sec. 2.
[4] Scottish Life Assurance Co. Ltd. *v.* John Donald Ltd., 1901, 9 S.L.T. 200, 438.

person. It has been held, however, that a husband and wife were entitled to surrender a policy taken out under this section.[1]

Policy Assigned as Post-Nuptial Provision for Wife and Children.— If a policy, although not taken out in terms of the Married Women's Policies of Assurance Act, is assigned by the insured for the benefit of his wife and children in a post-nuptial contract or other similar deed, and the assignation is intimated to the insurance company, the insured is not thereafter entitled, even with the consent of his wife, the trustees under the deed, and the whole children of the marriage, although they may all have attained majority, to assign the policy in security of advances to himself.[2]

In the Appendix will be found forms for (1) assignation of policy, and containing an obligation by a third party to pay the premiums ; (2) notice to the insurance company ; (3) explanatory letter by a member of a firm or a third party assigning a policy in security of a customer's indebtedness ; and (4) deed of retrocession and relative notice to insurance company.

Securities over Shares.—Where advances are made on, or overdrafts are intended to be secured by, the transfer of shares in an incorporated or other joint stock company, the practice is to have such shares transferred to the name of the bank or their nominees. The transfer must be duly registered in the books of the company, as until registration the bank's title is not complete. Where there is no agreement to hold shares so transferred for any specific debt or account, the bank is, in general, entitled to hold the shares in security of whatever sum may be due to them by their customer, upon payment of which, but not till then, he is entitled to demand a retransfer of the shares. But to enable the bank to hold the shares, in security of advances made prior to the transfer of the shares, there must probably have been an agreement to that effect between them and their customer.[3] Where the bank have the shares transferred to them and registered, they thereby render themselves liable as contributories. For this reason it is inadvisable to take a transfer of shares in any company in which the liability of the shareholders is unlimited, or in which the whole of the capital has not been paid up. Where, however, such shares are taken, it is the duty of the bank, when they come to be retransferred, to see that the transfer is registered, since a dishonest transferee may delay registering a transfer, and so save himself from being placed on the list of contributories should the company be forced into liquidation. If the transferee delays registering the transfer, it is provided by the Companies (Consolidation) Act,

---

[1] Schumann *v.* Scottish Widows' Fund and Life Assurance Society, 1886, 13 R. 678.

[2] Barras *v.* Scottish Widows' Fund and Life Assurance Society, 1900, 2 F. 1094.

[3] *Cf.* Robertson *v.* Duff, 1840, 2 D. 279.

1908, sec. 28, that a company shall on the application of the transferror of any share or interest in the company, enter in its register of members the name of the transferee of such share or interest in the same manner and subject to the same conditions as if the application for such entry were made by the transferee.[1] In the absence of an express or an implied agreement to the contrary it is the duty of a banker who has received specific shares in security of advances to retain and retransfer the identical shares to the borrower upon repayment of the loan.[2] Following the decision just noted it is now the practice of banks in accepting shares as security to provide that they are not to be bound to retransfer the identical shares transferred, and that the customer is to be bound to accept shares for like amounts although of different numbers to those transferred.[3] Where the transfer is taken in favour of the bank's nominees, or where the transfer is made by a third party in security of a customer's advances, an explanatory letter, connecting the transfer with the account intended to be secured, should be in the bank's possession. The debtor may with the consent of the bank dispose of shares pledged to the bank in security of advances. Where he does so, and the bank at his request execute a transfer in favour of the purchaser, and thereafter receive from the debtor the purchase price in reduction *pro tanto* of his indebtedness to them, they are not, in a question with the purchaser, liable to make restitution of the price of the shares, where it is proved that the sale has been induced by fraud on the part of the true owner, so long as the bank are not parties to the fraudulent representations.[4]

Position of Bankers where Transfer of Shares in their Favour is Forged.—In view of the increasing number of shares in public companies now taken by bankers in security of advances, their responsibility for the proper execution of transfers is of the utmost importance. The question has been considered by the Courts, and has been decided by the House of Lords. The material facts of the case,[5] which are of paramount interest to bankers, were as follows :—On 11th April 1893 Barclay & Co. Ltd., bankers, forwarded to the Sheffield Corporation a transfer in their favour of Sheffield Corporation Stock purporting to be executed by two persons named Timbrell and Honnywill, who were the registered holders of the stock, with a request in ordinary form to register the transfer and issue a new certificate in favour of Barclay & Co. The Corporation did so. Barclay & Co. afterwards transferred the stock for value to third parties. The names of Barclay's

---

[1] Symons, *in re* Asiatic Banking Corporation, L.R. 5 Ch. App. at p. 298.
[2] Crerar *v.* Bank of Scotland, 1921, S.C. 737.
[3] For form of letter, see Appendix.
[4] Gibb *v.* British Linen Co., 1875, 4 R. 630 (decided by Lord Shand, Ordinary, and acquiesced in).
[5] Sheffield Corporation *v.* Barclay, 1905, A.C. 392.

transferees were registered in due course, and it was admitted at the trial that they obtained a good title against the Corporation. All the parties believed that the signatures to the transfer from Timbrell and Honnywill were genuine, but in fact Honnywill's signature had been forged by Timbrell. It was not, however, until 1899, after Timbrell's death, that Honnywill discovered the fraud. He thereupon brought an action against the Corporation for rectification of the register and other relief, and was successful in having them compelled to buy equivalent stock, register it in his name, and pay him the past due dividends with interest. The Corporation then sought to make the bank repay them the amount of loss sustained, and in this they were successful, the Court holding that the bank in sending the transfer for registration warranted that the document was genuine, and this not having been the case, although the bank were innocent of the fraud, they must suffer the loss. The Lord Chancellor (Halsbury) thus stated the law : " Now, apart from any decision on the question (it being taken for granted that all the parties were honest), I should have thought that the bank were clearly liable. They have a private bargain with a customer. Upon his assurance they take a document from him as a security for a loan which they assume to be genuine. I do not suggest that there was any negligence—perhaps business could not go on if people were suspecting forgery in every transaction—but their position was obviously very different from that of the Corporation. The Corporation is simply ministerial in registering a valid transfer and issuing fresh certificates. They cannot refuse to register, and though for their own sake they will not and ought not to register or to issue certificates to a person who is not really the holder of the stock, yet they have no machinery and they cannot inquire into the transaction out of which the transfer arises. The bank, on the other hand, is at liberty to lend their money or not. They can make any amount of inquiries they like. If they find that an intended borrower has a co-trustee, they may ask him or the co-trustee himself whether the co-trustee is a party to the loan, and a simple question to the co-trustee would have prevented the fraud. They take the risk of the transaction, and lend the money. The security given happens to be in a form that requires registration to make it available, and the bank ' demand '—as if genuine transfers are brought, they are entitled to do—that the stock shall be registered in their name or that of their nominees, and are also entitled to have fresh certificates issued to themselves or nominees. This was done, and the Corporation by acting on this ' demand ' have incurred a considerable loss. . . . I think both upon principle and authority the Corporation are entitled to recover."

It is a safe general rule, the observance of which would have prevented the fraud in the above case, to have all deeds to be granted in favour of banks signed in the presence of at least one of their own officers.

Debentures.—Advances against debentures are secured by the creditor obtaining from the holder an assignation to the debenture, which requires to be intimated to the company issuing the same. The security must be validly completed as at the date of sequestration of a private individual or firm or the liquidation of a limited company. A mere promise of security is not sufficient.[1] A company has not the right, as an incident of its incorporation, to borrow money or issue debentures, and a company which has no power to borrow, conferred upon it either expressly or by implication in its Memorandum and Articles of Association, cannot issue valid debentures. When a company has power to borrow only to a limited extent, debentures issued in excess of the limit are void. Debentures issued under authority of the Companies (Consolidation) Act, 1908, are merely personal obligations by a company for repayment of money advanced on loan, and confer on the holders, who are merely ordinary creditors of the company, no preferential right over its assets in a liquidation. A special security may, however, be constituted in favour of debenture-holders by means of a conveyance of certain subjects to trustees for their behoof, which, when the legal formalities are complied with, vests the subjects in the trustees, and gives an effectual security to the debenture-holders for repayment of their loans. Unless and until, however, the subjects are properly vested in the trustees, the debenture-holders can claim no preferential ranking over the ordinary creditors of the company. Thus, a public company limited by shares, in security of sums advanced on debentures, assigned certain leases of minerals of which they were tenants, together with the moveables and plant on the ground, to trustees for debenture-holders. The assignations were duly intimated to the landlords, but the assignees took no steps to enter into possession of the subjects. On the liquidation of the company the Court held that, as no possession had followed on the assignation, the debenture-holders had no preference, as regards the leasehold or moveable property, over the ordinary trade creditors of the company.[2] In order to be effectual, the security must be given and completed according to the law of the country where the registered office of the company is situated. Hence ordinary joint stock companies having their registered office in Scotland have not the privilege of creating securities over their moveable property or leasehold subjects of which they remain in possession. Nor can they take power in the Memorandum and Articles of Association to grant debentures secured over their moveable property while retaining its possession, which will be effectual to the debenture-holders against the ordinary creditors of the company in a winding-up.

---

[1] Bank of Scotland v. Liquidator of Hutchison Main & Co. Ltd., 1914, S.C. (H.L.).

[2] Clark v. West Calder Oil Co., 1882, 9 R. 1017.

The power of a company to borrow and to issue debentures should in all cases be examined.

There is no fixed form for the valid transfer of a debenture. Some companies have a special form, others again accept a transfer on the back of the debenture, while others again accept a transfer in the form given in the Schedule to the Transmission of Moveable Property (Scotland) Act, 1862, or in Schedule E of the Companies' Clauses Consolidation Act of 1845. In whatever form the transfer is made, the right of the creditor is not completed until intimation thereof is sent to the issuing company.

Bearer Bonds, when taken in security, should be accompanied by a letter from the customer, stating the purpose for which they are to be held.[1] If the bonds at the time of the constitution of the security are in the bank's possession for safe custody, the safe custody receipt should be delivered up. No intimation of the constitution of the security is necessary to the issuing company. In the letter pledging the securities, express power to sell should be taken, for unless this be done a banker is not entitled at his own hand to do so, but must apply to the Court for authority to sell.[2] The bonds should not be delivered against a cheque for the amount of the secured account until the cheque is honoured, for the reason that if the cheque is dishonoured and the bonds be then in the hands of a third party for value the security of the bank is defeated.[3] The letter should be stamped with a duty of sixpence.

Letters of Postponement.—Occasionally banks make advances to a customer on condition that certain prior loans made to him by third parties are postponed to the bank's claim. A form of the letter taken will be found in the Appendix. The legal effect of such documents has not been determined by the Court. So long as the customer and the third party remain solvent it seems clear that the third party could not enforce his claim in priority to that of the bank. In the event of the bankruptcy of the customer the third party would be entitled to rank on the estate of the customer, but would be bound either to assign his claim to the bank or pay to the bank the dividend received by him so far as necessary to enable the bank to receive payment of their debt in full. A difficulty would arise in the event of the bankruptcy of the postponing creditor. In such an event it is thought that the trustee on his estate would be entitled to enforce his claim against the customer irrespective of the letter granted in favour of the bank.

---

[1] For form of letter, see Appendix.
[2] Robertson's Tr. v. Royal Bank, 1890, 18 R. 12.
[3] Lloyds Bank Ltd. v. Swiss Bankverein, 1912, 28 T.L.R. 501.

CHAPTER III

SECURITIES OVER SHIPS AND SHIPPING DOCUMENTS

1. Mortgages over Ships

THE property in a ship, with the exception of a sea fishing boat, is divided into sixty-four shares, and, except with respect to joint owners or owners by transmission, not more than sixty-four individuals can be registered at the same time as owners of any one ship. A share may be held by not more than five persons jointly, who, for the purposes of holding or of conveying such share, constitute but one person in the eye of the law, though no one is entitled to be registered as the owner of a fractional part of a share in a ship. The property in a sea fishing boat [1] is divided into sixteen shares, and not more than sixteen persons can be registered at the same time as owners of any one boat. No person is entitled to be registered as the owner of a fractional part of a share in a sea fishing boat, but any number of persons not exceeding five may be registered as joint owners of one boat or of a share or shares therein. A sea fishing boat or any shares or share therein may be made a security for a loan or other valuable consideration. What follows relates to ships in general, excluding sea fishing boats. A ship or any share therein may be held by a company incorporated under the Companies Acts or under any Act of Parliament, and may be registered under such company's corporate name. [2] Private firms cannot be registered as the owners of a ship or any share therein. But where the ship or shares belong to the firm, the entry in the register is made in the name of one or more of the individual partners of the firm. No notice of any trust, whether express, implied, or constructive, can be entered in the register or received by the registrar. [3] Where trustees, as such, are vested in the property of a ship, or of any shares therein, their names must appear on the register, not *qua* trustees, but as joint owners of such ship or shares. The person, or persons, whose names appear on the register as individual or joint owners of a ship or of any share therein, have absolute power to dispose of, and to mortgage, such ship

---

[1] Sea Fishing Boats (Scotland) Act, 1886, 49 & 50 Vict. cap. 53.
[2] Merchant Shipping Act, 1894, 57 & 58 Vict. cap. 60, sec. 5.
[3] Sec. 56.

r share. Persons *bonâ fide* buying or lending on the security of such
ship or share, are indemnified and protected in so doing, notwithstanding
any defect or invalidity in the title of the person or persons selling or
transferring such ship or share, on the ground that the public are entitled
to rely on the faith of the entries as they appear in the register. A
single share may be sold or mortgaged. Mortgages over ships are
taken in security, either (a) of a sum presently due, or (b) of an account
current. They may be granted either directly in favour of the creditor,
or, as occasionally happens, in favour of the creditor's nominees, in which
case the mortgage must be accompanied by an explanatory letter from
the mortgagor, connecting the mortgage with the account to be secured.[1]
The mortgage which is exempt from stamp duty,[2] must be written
on the form prescribed by the Merchant Shipping Act of 1894, or as
near thereto as circumstances permit, and can be made in no other
manner.[3] The creditor's right is completed by the registration of the
mortgage at the ship's port of registry. The priority of mortgages is
determined, not by their dates, but by the dates of their respective
registrations, the registrar, on a mortgage being presented to him for
registration, notifying the fact by a certificate indorsed on the mortgage,
setting forth the day and hour of registration.[4] Any person, on payment of a fee not exceeding one shilling, is entitled, on application
to the registrar at a reasonable time during the hours of his official
attendance, to inspect any register book.[5]

Before taking a mortgage from a joint stock company, care should
be taken to ascertain that the company has power to borrow and to
mortgage. So far at least as a trading company is concerned, if it
possesses the power to borrow, it seems to possess by implication the
power to secure the repayment of a loan by the execution of a mortgage.[6]
The mere fact of a person being the mortgagee of a ship or share therein
does not constitute him the owner of such ship or share, nor does the
mortgagor cease to be the owner, except in so far as may be necessary
for making such ship or share available as a security for a mortgage
debt.[7] Where it is intended to make the transferee the owner of the
ship or share, the transfer is effected by means of a bill of sale duly
registered. Such transactions should, however, be entered into by
bankers with extreme caution, as by becoming the transferees under a

---

[1] For forms of current account mortgage, and explanatory letter, where mortgage
is granted in favour of creditor's nominees, see Appendix.

[2] Act, sec. 21.

[3] Liverpool Borough Bank v. Turner, 29 L.J. Ch. 827 ; 30 L.J. Ch. 379.

[4] Sec. 33.   [5] Sec. 64 (1).

[6] Australian, etc., Co. v. Mounsey, 4 K. & J. 733 ; 6 W. R. 734 ; 31 L.T. O.S. 246 ;
Bryon v. Metropolitan, etc., Co., 3 De G. & J. 123 ; Palmer's Company Precedents
5th ed.), 177.

[7] Act, sec. 34 ; see also Laming & Co. v. Seater, 1889, 16 R. 828.

16

bill of sale they may render themselves liable for risks incidental t
shipowners.

Powers of Mortgagee.—A mortgagee cannot take possession unt
there has been default on the part of the mortgagor in payment or
breach of his duty in respect of the mortgage by his unlawfully impai
ing the subject of security. Apart from this, every registered mortgage
has power absolutely to dispose of the ship or share in respect of whic
he is registered, and to grant effectual receipts for the purchase money
Where two or more persons are registered as mortgagees of the sam
ship or share, a subsequent mortgagee cannot, except under the authorit
of a competent Court, sell such ship or share without the concurrenc
of every prior mortgagee.[1] A mortgagee, who takes possession for th
purpose of sale, is bound to exercise that care and diligence which
prudent man would exercise in the conduct of his own business. Th
mortgagee so selling holds any surplus which he may have, after payin
himself, as trustee for the owner and subsequent mortgagees according t
their respective rights.[2] The mortgagee has also the power to take posses
sion of the ship and to draw the earnings,[3] though to employ the ship i
the exercise of this power he must act with prudence, and is liable fo
necessary disbursements.[4] He is entitled to the freight if he enter o
possession before it becomes payable, and is further entitled to remai
in possession until his debt is paid either by the mortgagor or from th
ship's earnings. On payment of his loan he is bound to retransfer.
The usual mode of a mortgagee taking possession of a ship is to pu
a representative on board. When the ship is at sea, notice to th
charterer to pay freight to the mortgagee is held equivalent to takin
possession. A mortgagee may competently transfer his mortgage t
another person, but only on the form prescribed by the Act, whic
requires to be registered. There is a certain amount of risk in takin
such a transfer, since, if the original mortgagor has paid the debt, o
it has been satisfied in any other competent mode, even althoug
a discharge has not been executed and registered, the mortgage i
nevertheless at an end ; and since the original mortgagee can confe
no higher right than he himself possesses, any subsequent transfe
becomes worthless.[6]

Insurance of Mortgaged Ship.—The question of insurance is on

---

[1] Sec. 35.

[2] Tanner v. Heard, 3 Jur. N.S. 427.

[3] Cato v. Irving, 5 De G. & J. 210 ; Williams v. Allsup, 30 L.J. C.P. 353 ; 10 C.
N.S. 417.

[4] Haulland, Routh & Co. v. Thomson, 1864, 3 M. 313 ; Russel v. Baird, 183
1 D. 931.

[5] Marriot v. Anchor Rev. Co., 2 Giff. 457 ; (on appeal) 3 De G. F. & J. 177 ; 3
L.J. Ch. 571 ; De Mattos v. Gibson, 28 L.J. Ch. 498 ; 7 Jur. N.S. 282.

[6] Bell's Com. (M'L.'s ed.) i. 171.

of importance to bankers. In taking a mortgage over a ship, the bank should take care that the policy of insurance on the ship is transferred to them, or that it is in their possession or under their control, for if this be not done, and the ship be lost, even although fully insured by the owner, the bank have no preferable claim over the insurance money in respect of the mortgage, although they still have a personal claim against the mortgagor for the amount due. To obviate this risk, the bank should either have the policy transferred to them, obtain a letter from the holder of the policy that he holds it on their behalf to the extent of a certain specified sum, or effect an insurance for the amount of their interest under the mortgage. The bank may, in special circumstances, deem it expedient to insure special risks through clubs, or otherwise.

Discharge of Mortgage.—On production of a mortgage deed, with a receipt for the mortgage money duly signed and attested indorsed thereon, the registrar makes an entry in the register book to the effect that the mortgage has been discharged, and on that entry being made, the estate (if any) which passed to the mortgagee vests in the person in whom, having regard to intervening acts and circumstances (if any), it would have vested, had the mortgage not been made.[1]

2. Bills of Lading

A bill of lading is the written evidence of contract for the carriage and delivery of goods sent by sea. It contains an acknowledgment by the master of the ship, or others authorised by the owners to grant it,[2] of the shipment of certain goods or merchandise, subject usually to conditions therein specified as to the perils of the sea, etc., and an obligation to deliver them at the port of discharge to the consignor or his order, or to bearer, or to a named consignee, his order or assigns, upon payment of freight.[3] It is customary for three copies of the bill of lading to be signed, one of which is retained by the consignor of the goods, one forwarded to the consignee, and the other given to the master of the ship. The three parts constitute one contract like a bill of exchange, and they each usually contain a clause " the one of which being accomplished the others to stand void." Without delivery of one of the parts of the bill of lading the shipmaster is not bound to deliver his cargo. There is no difference in law between the different parts of the instrument in conveying a title to an indorsee.

---

[1] Act, sec. 32.

[2] Jessel v. Bath, L.R. 2 Ex. 267 ; Hayn v. Culliford, 3 C.P.D. 410 ; 4 *ibid.* 182 ; 7 L.J. C.P. 755 ; 48 *ibid.* 372.

[3] Bell's Com. (M'L.'s ed.) i. 212.

Stamp.—A bill of lading requires a sixpenny stamp, and cannot be stamped after execution. Any person who makes or signs a bill of lading not duly stamped is liable to forfeit £50.[1]

Indorsation.—Formerly by the custom of merchants, and now by Act of Parliament,[2] a bill of lading represents the goods for which the shipmaster has signed, and the transference of the bill of lading transfers the ownership of the goods. A bill of lading may therefore be transferred by indorsation, and the indorsement and delivery of the bill by the shipper or owner of the goods, or mercantile agent with the consent of the owner in possession thereof, transfer the property to the indorsee, who may in turn transfer his right to a subsequent indorsee. The indorsation of a bill of lading differs in effect from that of a bill of exchange or promissory note (in respect that an indorsee of a bill of exchange engages that if the bill be dishonoured at maturity, he will compensate the holder who is compelled to pay it, and is precluded from denying to a holder in due course the genuineness and regularity in all respects of the drawer's signature and all previous indorsements, and to his immediate or a subsequent indorsee the validity of the bill or his title thereto), whereas an indorsee of a bill of lading takes it subject to the same liabilities in respect of the goods as if the contract contained in the bill of lading had been made with himself.[3] The bill of lading only represents the goods and the transfer of the symbol does not operate more than a transfer of what is represented. Hence, if it be stolen from the consignee, or transferred without his authority, a subsequent *bonâ fide* transferee for value cannot compel delivery of the goods as against the shipper. In the hands of a *bonâ fide* indorsee for value a bill of lading is equivalent to actual delivery of the goods thereby represented.[4] A bill of lading remains in force as a symbol of property until the goods have been delivered, but no longer, unless the goods have been wrongfully delivered.

Bills of lading are frequently made use of as securities for advances and the pledge of a bill of lading duly indorsed is as effectual as a pledge of the goods themselves, but the right conferred by such delivery depends upon the contract under which it is delivered. Accordingly, if one buy a cargo afloat, the indorsation and delivery of the bill of lading is equivalent to the delivery of the goods sold, and passes the property therein to the buyer. Similarly, if the goods are stored, the delivery of the bill of lading has effect in all respects, whether as a title of property

---

[1] Stamp Act, 1891.

[2] Factors Act, 1889, sec. 1 (4).

[3] Bills of Lading Act, 18 & 19 Vict. cap. 111, sec. 1 ; Craig & Rose *v.* Delargy, 1879, 6 R. 1269 ; Guerney *v.* Behrend, 23 L.J. Q.B. 265 ; Schuster *v.* M'Kellar, 2 L.J. Q.B. 281.

[4] Rodocanachi, Sons & Co. *v.* Millburn Bros., L.R. 18 Q.B.D. 67.

[5] Barber *v.* Meyerstein, 1870, L.R. 4 H.L. 317 ; Pirie & Sons *v.* Warden, 187 9 M. 523.

or whether as a security to the person to whom it has been indorsed or delivered, exactly as if the goods were on board ship, because it is now settled that the question as to the effect of a bill of lading does not depend upon the arrival, or even the unloading, of the ship, and that a bill of lading must be taken to be an effective document of title representing the goods until these have been actually delivered to the person in right of the bill.[1] If the contract, however, be pledge, not sale, then the delivery of the indorsed bill of lading completes the contract just as if the goods themselves had been deposited with the pledgee, but gives the pledgee no greater or higher right to the goods than delivery of the subject of pledge to the pledgee gives him. According to the law of England, the delivery of goods in pledge confers on the pledgee what is called a special property therein, while the general property remains in the pledgor. There is no such thing in Scots law as the term "special property," and there cannot be, according to the law of Scotland, a distinction between *the* property and a special property. But the form of security effectuated by what in the law of England is called a special property is perfectly well known in the law of Scotland,[2] and the rights of a pledgee in the subject of pledge seem to be very much the same in both countries.[3] The indorsement of a bill of lading, by way of pledge for a loan, does not therefore pass the property in the goods to the indorsee so as to transfer to him all liabilities in respect thereof.[4] The pledge of a bill of lading requires no intimation, for when the vessel is at sea the parting with the bill of lading is parting with that which is the symbol of property, and which, for the purpose of conveying a right and interest, is the property itself.[5]

But this statement must be received with caution, for it has been decided that, both according to English and Scots law, in order that a pledge may be effectual, possession need not necessarily continue in the pledgee, as he may part with possession of the pledge temporarily for a necessary purpose or for safe custody to a third person, whose right is that which the pledgee gives him, and that parting with the possession of the pledge is thus not necessarily parting with the security and with any property which the pledge gives, but what is of more importance, that a pledgee may redeliver to the pledgor, as his agent for a specific purpose, such as sale, the goods he had pledged (or, what is equivalent

---

[1] *Per* Lord M'Laren in Hayman & Son *v.* M'Lintock, *infra.*

[2] *Per* Lord President Dunedin in Hayman & Son *v.* M'Lintock, 1907, S.C. 936 ; *approving* Barber *v.* Meyerstein, 1870, L.R. 4 H.L. 317, and Sewell *v.* Burdick, *infra.*

[3] *Per* Lord Trayner in North-Western Bank Ltd. *v.* Poynter, Son & Macdonalds, 1894, 21 R. 513, 524.

[4] Sewell *v.* Burdick, 1884, 10 Ap. Ca. 74 ; Tod & Son *v.* Merchant Banking Co. of London Ltd., 1883, 10 R. 1009 ; Erskine, iii. 1, 33.

[5] Barber *v.* Meyerstein, *supra* ; Sanders *v.* Maclean, 1883, 11 Q.B.D. 327.

a document of title to them such as a bill of lading) without in the slightest degree diminishing the full force and effect of his security. Thus in one case a Liverpool firm owned and held the bills of lading of a cargo destined to the port of Glasgow. The firm obtained an advance from a Liverpool bank, to whom they, as a security, duly indorsed the bill of lading, which carried the property of the goods according to Scots as well as English law. The bank sent the bill of lading, without indorsing it, to the pledgors in Liverpool, in order that they might act as the agents of the bank in selling the cargo and receiving and accounting for the price. Upon that footing the pledgors sold the cargo, and a Scottish creditor, to whom they owed a personal debt, arrested the price in the hands of the purchaser in Scotland, and claimed a preferable right to it, upon the ground that by the law of Scotland the pledgees had lost their right of property in the cargo, which had reverted to the pledgors in consequence of their having returned the bill of lading to them for a temporary and special purpose. In these circumstances the House of Lords held that the relative rights of the pledgor and pledgee fell to be determined by the law of England, the country in which the pledge of the bill of lading was made, and in which the facts which were said to have destroyed the right of the pledgee occurred, though at the same time it declared that according to both Scots and English law the pledgee had not parted with possession of the pledge so as to extinguish his right of security.[1]

Trust Letters.—It is now the practice when produce is returned to the customer for sale to take from him a Trust Letter acknowledging that the goods or the bill of lading are received by him as agent for the bank and undertaking to hold the goods when received and their proceeds when sold in that capacity, the object being to preserve the right of the bank as secured creditors over the goods until sold, and the proceeds when sold until the debt due to the bank is paid. The validity of such letters has, in England, been challenged, but unsuccessfully.[2]

Risk Attending Advance against One Part of Bill of Lading.—There is a certain risk attending the giving of an advance against delivery of one part of a bill of lading. Where the different parts of a bill of lading are acquired by different persons *bonâ fide* and for value, the person who first gets any one of the parts acquires the property.[3] The master of a ship is justified or excused in giving delivery of his cargo according to his contract to the person appearing to be the assignee of the bill of lading which is produced to him, although there has been in point of fact a prior indorsement for value of another part, provided he acts in *bonâ fide* and without notice or knowledge of such prior indorsement

---

[1] North-Western Bank Ltd. *v.* Poynter, Son & Macdonalds, 1894, 22 R. (H.L.)
[2] *In re* David Allistair Ltd., 1922, 2 Ch. 211.
[3] Barber *v.* Meyerstein, 1870, L.R. 2 H.L. 326.

But where the master has notice, or probably even knowledge, of a prior indorsement, he must deliver to the first indorsee, and it is at his peril if he delivers to the wrong person.[1] If he is in doubt as to whom he should deliver, his duty is to raise an action of multiplepoinding and have the question judicially determined. For the preservation of the lender's security over the goods, care is necessary as to the borrower's dealings with them. Until payment of the advance, the borrowers should not be allowed to sell the goods in their own name, or otherwise than as agents for the lender, for by so allowing the borrowers to deal with the goods, and upon their delivery to the purchaser, the lenders are held to have consented to waive their security over the goods so delivered. In the event of an arrestment being used in the purchaser's hands by other creditors of the borrower, such arrestment is preferable to a demand by the lender for payment of the purchase price.

Short Shipment.—A bill of lading in the hands of a consignee or indorsee for value, representing goods to have been shipped on board a vessel, is conclusive evidence of such shipment *as against the master* or other person signing the same, notwithstanding that such goods, or some part thereof, may not have been so shipped, unless the holder when he received the bill had actual notice that the goods were not on board, or unless there was fraud on the part of the shipper or holder.[2] As *against the owner* of the vessel the bill of lading is *primâ facie* evidence that the quantity therein specified was put on board, but it is competent for the owner to prove that the quantity shipped was less than that specified ; and he is not bound for a greater quantity of goods than that actually shipped.[3] But if he is to escape liability he must prove by the clearest evidence that the goods as described in the bill of lading were not actually shipped, and in this connection it must be borne in mind that the contract expressed in the terms of the bill of lading cannot be contradicted by parole proof,[4] even where the consignee takes delivery of the goods before receiving the bill of lading.[5] The validity of a bill of lading as a negotiable instrument is not affected by its having been signed by the master blank as to the amount of cargo.[6]

Stoppage *in transitu.*—The law relating to stoppage *in transitu* is

---

[1] Glyn, Mills & Co. v. E. & W. India Dock Co., L.R. 6 Q.B.D. 475 ; L.R. 7 Ap. Ca; 591 ; 50 L.J. Q.B. 62 ; Gabarron v. Kreeft, L.R. 10 Ex. 274 ; 44 L.J. Ex. 238. Sanders v. Maclean, 1883, 11 Q.B.D. 327.

[2] 18 & 19 Vict. cap. 111, sec. 3.

[3] M'Lean & Hope v. Munch, 1867, 5 M. 893 ; *affd.* M'Lean & Hope v. Fleming, 1871, 9 M. (H.L.) 38 ; Craig & Rose v. Delargy, 1879, 6 R. 1269 ; Grieve & Co. v. König & Co., 1880, 7 R. 521 ; Horsleys v. Grimmond, 1894, 21 R. 410 ; Bedouin Steam Navigation Co. Ltd. v. Smith & Co., 1895, 22 R. 350.

[4] Knight S.S. Co. Ltd. v. Fleming, 1895, 25 R. 1070.

[5] Mossgiel S.S. Co. Ltd. v. Della Casa Granite Quarries of Italy, 1899, 1 F. 385.

[6] Cowdenbeath Coal Co. v. Clydesdale Bank, 1895, 22 R. 682.

codified by the Sale of Goods Act, 1893.[1] Subject to the provisions after specified, when the buyer of goods becomes insolvent, the unpaid seller who has parted with the possession of the goods has the right of stopping them *in transitu*, that is to say, he may resume possession of the goods as long as they are in course of transit, and may retain them until payment or tender of the price. Goods are deemed to be in course of transit from the time when they are delivered to a carrier by land or water, or other bailee or custodier, for the purpose of transmission to the buyer, until the buyer, or his agent in that behalf, takes delivery of them from such carrier or other bailee or custodier. If the buyer, or his agent in that behalf, obtains delivery of the goods before their arrival at the appointed destination, the transit is at an end. If, after the arrival of the goods at the appointed destination, the carrier, or other bailee or custodier, acknowledges to the buyer, or his agent, that he holds the goods on his behalf, and continues in possession of them as bailee or custodier for the buyer, or his agent, the transit is at an end, and it is immaterial that a further destination for the goods may have been indicated by the buyer. If the goods are rejected by the buyer, and the carrier, or other bailee or custodier, continues in possession of them, the transit is not deemed to be at an end, even if the seller has refused to receive them back. When the goods are delivered to a ship chartered by the buyer, it is a question depending on the circumstances of the particular case whether they are in the possession of the master as a carrier, or as agent of the buyer. Where the carrier, or other bailee or custodier, wrongfully refuses to deliver the goods to the buyer, or his agent in that behalf, the transit is deemed to be at an end. Where part delivery of the goods has been made to the buyer, or his agent in that behalf, the remainder of the goods may be stopped *in transitu*, unless such part delivery has been made under such circumstances as to show an agreement to give up possession of the whole of the goods.

How Stoppage in transitu is effected.—The unpaid seller may exercise his right of stoppage *in transitu* either by taking actual possession of the goods, or by giving notice of his claim to the carrier, or other bailee or custodier, in whose possession the goods are. Such notice may be given either to the person in actual possession of the goods or to his principal. In the latter case the notice, to be effectual, must be given at such time and under such circumstances that the principal, by the exercise of reasonable diligence, may communicate it to his servant or agent in time to prevent a delivery to the buyer. When notice of stoppage *in transitu* is given by the seller to the carrier, or other bailee, or custodier in possession of the goods, he must redeliver the goods to, or according to the directions of, the seller. The expenses of such redelivery must be borne by the seller. Subject to the provision that,

---

[1] 56 & 57 Vict. cap. 71, secs. 44-48 ; see Bethell *v.* Clark, 1888, L.R. 20 Q.B.D. 615.

where a person having bought or agreed to buy goods, obtains, with the consent of the seller, possession of the goods, or the documents of title to the goods, the delivery or transfer by that person, or by a mercantile agent acting for him, of the goods or documents of title under any sale, pledge, or other disposition thereof, to any person receiving the same in good faith and without notice of any lien or other right of the original seller in respect of the goods, has the same effect as if the person making the delivery or transfer were a mercantile agent in possession of the goods or documents of title with the consent of the owner,[1] the unpaid seller's right of lien or retention or stoppage *in transitu* is not affected by any sale or other disposition of the goods, which the buyer may have made, unless the seller has assented thereto. Provided that where a document of title to goods has been lawfully transferred to any person as buyer or owner of the goods, and that person transfers the document to a person who takes the document in good faith and for valuable consideration, then, if such last-mentioned transfer was by way of sale, the unpaid seller's right of lien or retention or stoppage *in transitu* is defeated, and if such last-mentioned transfer was by way of pledge or other disposition for value, the unpaid seller's right of lien or retention or stoppage *in transitu* can only be exercised subject to the rights of the transferee.[2] But where the seller of goods draws on the buyer for the price, and transmits the bill of exchange and bill of lading to the buyer together, to secure acceptance or payment of the bill of exchange, the buyer is bound to return the bill of lading if he does not honour the bill of exchange. If he wrongfully retains the bill of lading, the property in the goods does not pass to him.[3] Accordingly, it has been decided that a sale by the original buyer, without accepting the bill of exchange, to a third person, and indorsing the bill of lading to him, could transfer no right of property in the goods, in the person of the indorsee of the bill of lading.[4]

Effect of Sub-Sale or Pledge by Buyer.—Subject to the provisions following, a contract of sale is not rescinded by the mere exercise by an unpaid seller of his right of lien or retention or stoppage *in transitu*. Where an unpaid seller, who has exercised his right of lien or retention or stoppage *in transitu*, resells the goods, the buyer acquires a good title thereto as against the original buyer. Where the goods are of a perishable nature, or where the unpaid seller gives notice to the buyer of his intention to resell, and the buyer does not within a reasonable time pay or tender the price, the unpaid seller may resell the goods,

---

[1] Sec. 25 (2), reproducing, with slight modifications, sections 8 and 9 of the Factors Act, 1889 (extended to Scotland by the Factors (Scotland) Act, 1890).

[2] This section reproduces and develops section 10 of the Factors Act, 1889 (Scotland, 1890).

[3] Sale of Goods Act, 1893, 56 & 57 Vict. cap. 71, sec. 19 (3).

[4] Cahn & Mayer *v.* Pockett Bristol Channel Co. Ltd., 1898, 2 Q.B. 61.

and recover from the original buyer damages for any loss occasioned by his breach of contract. Where the seller expressly reserves a right of resale in case the buyer should make default, and, on the buyer making default, resells the goods, the original contract of sale is thereby rescinded, but without prejudice to any claim the seller may have for damages.

The right of stoppage is therefore no real burden on the rights of bankers or other persons in the position of holders of a bill of lading. In certain circumstances, however, the right may be of advantage to the banker. Thus, if the banker have acquired the bill of lading against a bill of exchange drawn on the purchaser for the price, and he delivers the bill of lading to him in return for the acceptance of the bill of exchange, it is competent to the banker, as to the original vendor, if the purchaser becomes insolvent before the bill of exchange falls due, to stop *in transitu*.

Conditional Indorsement.—Where the seller of goods draws on the buyer for the price, and transmits the bill of exchange and bill of lading to the buyer together, to secure acceptance or payment of the bill of exchange, the buyer is bound to return the bill of lading if he does not honour the bill of exchange, and if he wrongfully retains the bill of lading the property in the goods does not pass to him.[1] So when the indorsement and delivery of a bill of lading is made conditional on the acceptance of a bill of exchange, or the performance of a similar obligation, for the price of the goods shipped, the indorsee cannot retain the bill of lading and refuse to accept the bill of exchange or perform the obligation, and any transferee taking the bill of lading from him takes it subject to the condition imposed on the original indorsee.[2]

Holders for Value.—The value requisite to constitute a *bonâ fide* holder is the same as that required for a bill of exchange, so that an antecedent debt or liability is a good consideration.[3] The shipowner is not entitled to question the right of an indorsee, on the ground that he does not possess more than one copy of the bill of lading. No action, therefore, lies against the shipmaster, or the owner of the goods or ship, in respect of delivery of the goods having been made in *bonâ fide* to an indorsee of a bill of lading, though it should afterwards turn out that there was a prior indorsee whose right was preferable.[4] Where the shipmaster, after having signed a bill of lading, or the sets of a bill of lading, fraudulently or negligently grants another bill or bills of lading for the same goods, no action, even at the instance of a *bonâ fide* holder for value of the subsequent bill or set of bills, will lie against the owners

---

[1] Sale of Goods Act, 1893, sec. 19 (3).
[2] Shepherd *v.* Harrison, L.R. 5 H.L. 116
[3] Leask *v.* Scott, 1877, L.R. 2 Q.B.D. 376.
[4] Glyn, Mills & Co. *v.* E. & W. India Docks Co., L.R. 7 Ap. Ca. 591.

of the vessel, because this act of the master's, being unauthorised, does not bind his principals. The rights of a *bonâ fide* indorsee for value are not affected by the fraud of his author, provided that author was in point of fact the person *in titulo* of the bill of lading at the date of the transfer. Thus, for example, the fact that a person in possession of a bill of lading had no right to indorse it to another, in respect of agreement between him and a third party to hold it for behoof of that third party, is quite irrelevant in an action at the instance of that third party against the indorsee, unless he avers that the indorsee was a party to the fraud.

Liability of Indorsee.—The indorsee of a bill of lading is subject to the same liabilities with respect to the goods as was his indorser. The weight of this burden is diminished by the fact that, so soon as the indorsee transfers the right of property, he ceases to be under obligation to fulfil the duties imposed on the merchant under the bill of lading. It is of even less importance in the case of bankers and others who ordinarily hold bills of lading as security for advances. So long as the bill of lading is held by a banker by way of security solely, and so long as he does not proceed to take possession of the goods themselves, the property in the goods does not pass to him so as to make him liable under the Bills of Lading Act for the liabilities imposed upon the merchant.[1] Apart from the statute, but probably under it also, the holder and indorsee of a bill of lading, whether he hold it merely by way of security or not, who applies for and takes delivery of the goods, renders himself liable to fulfil the obligations imposed on the merchant in the bill of lading.

1. *Liability for Freight.*—The primary charge on the goods is the freight agreed to be paid for their carriage. The shipowner has a lien on the goods for the payment of freight, and even if he does not exercise his right of lien, he still has the right to sue the person presenting the bill of lading and taking delivery of the goods. Freight is payable to the shipowner only where the goods have been carried to the agreed-on port of destination, or where they have been taken possession of at some place short of the agreed-on port, under circumstances which imply a willingness on the part of the merchant to take delivery at that place and to pay freight *pro rata*.[2] If the ship be unable to deliver the goods at the port of destination, or to arrange for their transhipment, and the merchant refuses to take delivery elsewhere, no freight is exigible.[3] If the merchant insist on delivery at a port short of that destination, where the shipmaster is in a position to reasonably perform

---

[1] Sewell *v.* Burdick, 1884, 10 Ap. Ca. 74 ; Smurthwaite *v.* Wilkins, 1862, 31 L.J. C.P. 214 ; 11 C.B. N.S. 847.

[2] Osgood *v.* Groning, 1810, 2 Camp. 466 ; " The Newport," 1858, Swabey, 335.

[3] " The Kathleen," 1874, L.R. 4 Ad. 269 ; Hill *v.* Wilson, 4 C.P.D. 329.

the contract, full freight is exigible. The abandonment of the ship and cargo relieve the merchant of all claim for freight, and he may claim the goods at any port to which the ship may be brought, however near that may be to the original port of destination.

Freight is still exigible, although, from any cause for which the shipowners are not responsible, such as natural decay or deterioration through perils of the sea, the goods on their arrival at the port of destination are of less value than the freight payable. If the goods have suffered damage from causes for which the shipowners are responsible, the merchant may claim to deduct the loss so sustained from the amount of freight payable.[1] In such circumstances, if the shipmaster refuses to deliver the goods unless on payment of the full freight, the practice is to deposit the amount of the freight under reservation of all questions, and take delivery of the goods.

2. *Liability for Freight under Bill of Lading following on a Charter-Party.*—A charter-party is a mutual contract between the owners of a ship and a merchant, by which the latter hires the ship, or a part of it, either for a particular voyage, or for a certain specified time, at a stipulated hire or freight. Under a charter, which amounts to a demise of the ship, an indorsee for value of a bill of lading has, in general, no claim against the shipowners. And where the goods are not only shipped by, but delivered to, a merchant who has entered into a contract of affreightment with a charterer, knowing him to be a charterer and not the owner, no action, it is thought, will lie against the real owners, though there are *dicta* which might be construed as possibly indicating an opposite view.[2] When the shipper is not aware that the person with whom he contracts, and from whom he receives a bill of lading, is only a charterer and not the owner, he, or the person in his right as indorsee of the bill of lading, has a valid claim against the real owners for any damage to the cargo.[3]

The rights of the indorsee of a bill of lading may be affected by the fact that the bill contains a reference to the charter-party importing its terms in whole or in part. A mere reference in the bill of lading to a clause in the charter-party will not, in general, render the holder of the bill liable under the charter-party as a whole.[4] Where the reference includes the expression " and all other conditions of the charter-party," it has been decided that even although the charter contains the usual clause, exempting the shipowner from liability in respect of defective stowage or the negligence of the master and crew, if the bill of lading do not, the holder of the bill may sue the shipowner for damage to

[1] Taylor *v.* Forbes, 1830, 9 S. 113.
[2] *Per* Lord Kyllachy in Delaurier *v.* Wyllie, 1889, 27 S.L.R. 148.
[3] Sandeman *v.* Scurr, L.R. 2 Q.B. 86.
[4] Chappel *v.* Comfort, 31 L.J. C.P. 58 ; Smith *v.* Sieveking, 24 L.J. Q.B. 257.

the goods sustained through defective stowage or negligent seamanship.[1] .
Where the terms of the charter-party and the bill of lading differ,
the rule is that the charter-party determines the right of parties bound
by it, unless it can be shown that the terms of the charter-party were
intended to be modified by the bill of lading. By the terms of an
ordinary charter, and at common law, the charterer has a lien over the
goods shipped for the amount of the freight, and on any portion of
the cargo for the whole freight. Where the freight is payable in a
lump sum, delivery of a part of the cargo, the rest having been lost
through causes for which the shipowner is not responsible, entitles him
to the full freight ; but where the freight is at the rate of so much per
ton, freight is payable only on that portion of the cargo which is
actually delivered.

3. *Liability for Demurrage.*—Demurrage is simply a sum agreed to
be paid by the charterer or hirer to the shipowner, usually at the rate
of so much per ton per day, for each day's detention of the ship in
loading or unloading beyond a specified period. Where the bill of lading
itself contains no clause stipulating for demurrage, and contains no
clause incorporating the charter, if there is one, the indorsee of
the bill who intends taking delivery of the goods, must do so within
a reasonable time and according to the usual and customary practice
of the port at which discharge takes place, or he will render himself
liable in damages for the undue detention of the ship. To bind the
indorsee of a bill of lading to pay demurrage, there must either be an
express provision to that effect in the bill, or it must incorporate the
provisions of the charter, which almost invariably stipulates for demurrage.

The charter frequently stipulates that so many days will be allowed
for demurrage, in which case any detention beyond that period will
be payable for as damages ; but the demurrage rate will generally be
considered the rate of damage. Where the bill of lading provides that
demurrage is to be payable " as per charter-party," and the charter
stipulates that so many days are to be allowed on demurrage, the
indorsee of the bill will not be liable for any damage due by reason
of the detention of the ship beyond the time on which demurrage runs.[2]
Demurrage is payable, in cases where a specified number of days is
allowed for loading or discharge, for any detentions of the ship after she
reaches the port of discharge, whether caused by the charterer or not,
except those which are due to the shipmaster or owners. Thus the
charterer is liable for detention caused by the crowded state of the port,
which prevents the vessel reaching a loading or discharging berth,
unless it be specially provided that the ship is to reach a particular part
of the port or dock before demurrage begins to run, in which case

---

[1] Delaurier *v.* Wyllie, *ut supra.*
[2] Gray *v.* Carr, L.R. 6 Q.B. 522.

demurrage will not begin to run till after a lapse of a reasonable time.[1] But where a charter-party provided that a ship should proceed to a named dock and there load " always afloat as and where ordered by the charterers," it was held that the charterers were not bound to do that which, as was known to the shipowners, might be physically impossible, the water in the named dock being insufficient at neap tides to float a vessel of the size of the chartered vessel, and that the charterers were not responsible for delay occasioned by natural and physical causes beyond their control.[2] Where the provision is that the ship is to proceed to a particular port, " or as near thereto as she can get," demurrage will, in general, begin to run so soon as the vessel has got as near to the port as is consistent with safety.[3] When the charter stipulates that so many days are to be allowed on demurrage, the expression is held to mean running days in which Sundays and holidays are included. When such days are meant to be excluded, they must be expressly excluded by the use of such an expression as " working days only," which will not include any days on which, from force of circumstances, work cannot be done. Without express stipulation, days saved in loading cannot be used so as to compensate days spent in discharging.

Where the charter contains what is known as a " cesser clause," stipulating that the charterer's liability shall cease as soon as the cargo is loaded, and a further clause providing that the shipowner shall have a lien over the cargo for freight, dead-freight, or demurrage, the Courts have held that unless an intention to the contrary is clearly expressed, the charterer will be discharged only to the extent the lien can be enforced.

4. *For Dead-Freight.*—Dead-freight is the claim the shipowners have against the charterer who, in breach of contract, fails to load a full cargo, and so deprives the shipowner of the full freight he has a right to expect—it is, in short, an unliquidated compensation for the loss of freight, recoverable in the absence and place of freight.[4] To entitle the shipowner to exercise his right of lien over the cargo for dead-freight against an indorsee of the bill of lading, the bill must contain a special provision to that effect, or it must contain a clause incorporating the charter.

Clauses Limiting Shipowner's Liability.—The bill of lading may contain provisions qualifying the shipowner's liability so far as to leave him legally responsible for practically no damage or loss which can happen to the goods he is paid for carrying. If such conditions are

---

[1] Nelson *v.* Dahl, 12 Ch. Div. 568.
[2] Coulton S.S. Co. *v.* Castle Mail Packet Co., 1898, L.R. A.C. 486.
[3] Hillstrom *v.* Gibson & Clark, 1870, 8 M. 463.
[4] Phillips *v.* Rodie, 15 East, 547.

clearly expressed, and are not in themselves illegal or contrary to public policy, they will be binding on the charterer, and consequently on the indorsee of the bill of lading, who may find himself in possession of a valueless security and without any recourse against the shipowner. To make such stipulations binding, the meaning of the words must be clear and precise, and their import must have been clearly brought home to the knowledge of the charterer.

3. Policies of Marine Insurance over Goods

When a bill of lading is transferred to an indorsee, or to a banker in security of advances, it is usual, if the goods specified in the bill of lading have been insured, to transfer the policy of insurance along with the bill of lading as a collateral security in the event of the goods being lost, destroyed, or depreciated. As the assignee or indorsee of the policy takes it subject to the same rights and disabilities as his predecessor with regard to the recovery of the amount insured, it is necessary shortly to detail the essentials requisite to the validity of a policy.

The law relating to marine insurance has been codified by the Marine Insurance Act, 1906, which in the main is declaratory of the law as it existed prior to the date of its enactment, though certain changes in the law have been effected, to which, of course, effect must necessarily be given. The statute will be generally, and where necessary, referred to as "the Act," and its words will be used to state the law where applicable.

Stamp.—The policy requires to be duly stamped. It may be stamped after execution, but under the heavy penalty of £100.[1] Where one set of underwriters effect a policy on different ships for different sums in respect of each ship, the policy need be stamped only with one stamp in respect of the gross sum insured.[2]

Essentials.—The policy must set forth a contract of marine insurance, it must fully specify the nature and extent of the risk insured against, the name of the insurer and of the ship in which the goods are carried, and it must be subscribed by the underwriters or persons who undertake the risk. Under the qualification to be referred to, the person who insures the goods must have an insurable interest in them. In all ordinary cases the indorsee for value of a bill of lading has such an interest in the goods as to entitle him to insure them if that have not been already done. Policies over goods are either voyage or time policies. In the former the goods are insured for a certain specified voyage, while in the latter they are insured for a certain definite time, which, however, cannot exceed twelve months. By the Marine Insurance

---

[1] Stamp Act, 1891, sec. 95.
[2] Great Britain S.S. Association v. Whyte, 1891, 19 R. 109.

Gambling Policies Act, 1909, a person who effects a marine insurance without any *bonâ fide* interest, direct or indirect, or a *bonâ fide* expectation of acquiring such an interest, or a person in the employment of the owner of a ship, not being a part owner, who effects an insurance in relation to the ship, and the contract is made interest or no interest, or without further proof of interest than the policy itself, or without benefit of salvage to the insured, or subject to any other like term, is guilty of a criminal offence. Nevertheless, in practice, it is common for underwriters to issue policies containing a clause to the effect that the policy is proof of interest, and though such policies are not enforceable in a Court of law, they are not usually disputed. The insurable interest which is required by law must be something more than a mere possibility of gain, not founded on any right or liability (legal or equitable) in or in respect of, the subject-matter insured. Insurable interest, in the absence of proof to the contrary, is presumed (Act, sec. 5). The tendency of modern law is to recognise an insurable interest in all cases where a foundation exists for doing so. The master has an insurable interest in his wages as well as his effects, and seamen may now insure their wages (Act, sec. 11). A policy is assignable unless it contains terms expressly prohibiting assignment, and it may be assigned either before or after loss. The assignation may be by indorsement on the policy or in other customary manner (Act, sec. 50). Where, however, the insured has parted with or lost his interest in the subject-matter insured, and has not, before or at the time of so doing, expressly or impliedly agreed to assign the policy, any subsequent assignation of the policy is inoperative (Act, sec. 51).

Facts which Invalidate the Policy.—The contract of marine insurance is one requiring the utmost mutual good faith on the part of both parties, and the policy will be invalidated by the concealment or misrepresentation of a material fact, or by the breach of a warranty, express or implied. The misrepresentation or concealment on the part of the insured need not be fraudulent, and it is no defence to the insured to state that though a fact which he disclosed to the underwriter was untrue, it was made in *bonâ fide*, and in the belief that it was true, or that a fact which he failed to disclose to the underwriter was one which he *bonâ fide* believed to be immaterial, or was one of which he was not aware at the time when the insurance was effected, provided it be a fact which the underwriter is entitled to assume the insured ought reasonably to have known. A fact is "material" to the underwriter when it is one which might be supposed to influence a reasonably careful man in fixing the premium or determining whether he will take the risk.[1]

---

[1] Tate *v.* Hyslop, L.R. 15 Q.B.D. 368 ; Hutchison & Co. *v.* Aberdeen Sea Insurance Co., 1876, 3 R. 682 ; Proudfoot *v.* Montefiore, L.R. 2 Q.B. 511 ; Ionides *v.* Pender, L.R. 9 Q.B. 531 ; Rivaz *v.* Gerussi, L.R. 6 Q.B.D. 222.

There is, however, no duty on the insured to declare a fact which the underwriter ought to know or which he can find out for himself, as for example the fact that a ship is unclassed at Lloyds,[1] or any fact which diminishes the risk or as to which information is waived by the insurer (Act, sec. 18). The assured need not make any communication as to matters of common notoriety or knowledge, nor of matters which the insurer ought to know in the ordinary course of his business (Act, sec. 18). But the non-communication of a fact which, though known to the underwriter at one time, was not present to his mind at the time of effecting the insurance, will vitiate the policy.[2] Where the underwriters have (as by initialling a " slip ") made a contract of insurance, which, although legally invalid for want of the statutory requisites, is, in practice and according to the usage of trade, binding upon them in honour and good faith, non-disclosure of facts coming to the insured's knowledge, subsequent to the initialling of the slip, but prior to the execution of the policy, will not invalidate the policy.[3] No particular form of words is necessary to constitute a misrepresentation, and whatever the assured says or does which is reasonably calculated to lead the insurer to a particular conclusion will, if false or untrue, amount to a misrepresentation. If, however, the insured can show by the clearest evidence that the concealment or misrepresentation, as the case may be, in no way influenced the insurer, the policy will stand good. To void the policy the misrepresentation must be *material*. There is, however, this difference to be noted, that in the case of a breach of warranty, to which reference will now be made, it is immaterial whether the breach is material to the risk or not, since a breach of warranty of any kind is sufficient to void the policy (Act, sec. 33). Warranties are either implied by law or express, *i.e.* contained in the policy itself.

Among the implied warranties on which the underwriter is entitled to rely, besides those made the subject of special contract, two of the most important are, that the vessel in which the goods are carried is seaworthy, and that she will not unnecessarily deviate from the line of her voyage. There is no implied seaworthiness in a time policy.[4] The warranty of seaworthiness implies that the ship, her crew, tackle, apparel, and equipments,[5] including (in the case of a steamer) a reasonable supply

---

[1] But see Gandy v. Adelaide Insurance Co., L.R. 6 Q.B. 746 ; Asfar, 1896, 1 Q.B. 123. See also Blackburn, 21 Q.B.D. 144 ; Thames v. Mersey Marine Insurance Co. Ltd., 1911, A.C. 528.

[2] Bates v. Hewitt, L.R. 2 Q.B. 597.

[3] Cory v. Patton, L.R. 9 Q.B. 577.

[4] Dudgeon v. Pembroke, 1877, 2 Ap. Ca. 284 ; Kenneth & Co. v. Moore, 1883, 10 R. 547.

[5] Steel & Craig v. State Line Steamship Co., 1877, 4 R. (H.L.) 103 ; Seville Sulphur and Copper Co. v. Colvils, Lowden & Co., 1888, 15 R. 616 ; Cunningham v. Colvils, Lowden & Co., 1888, 16 R. 295.

of bunker coal,[1] are reasonably fit and sufficient for the intended voyage
and for the purposes of the particular subject-matter insured.[2] Seaworthiness is presumed, and it is not sufficient for the underwriter to
prove that the ship became unseaworthy after the risk began, though, if
the ship spring a leak or founder without any adequate cause, unseaworthiness will be inferred, and the onus of proving that the ship was
seaworthy will be thrown on the insured.[3] It is immaterial that the
unseaworthiness of a vessel was not known to the insured, or that it
could not have been provided against, or that it was due, *e.g.* to a latent
defect of her machinery. The warranty may differ at successive stages.
Thus a vessel which is seaworthy in harbour may be unseaworthy if she
proceeds to sea in the same state ; and a vessel, seaworthy in harbour,
may become unseaworthy from the manner in which she is loaded. If
the vessel is unseaworthy from whatever cause, the implied warranty is
broken, provided that the unseaworthiness of the vessel applied at the
commencement of the voyage insured. Of course, where damage to or
loss of the cargo results from the unseaworthiness of a vessel, the holder
of the bill of lading, though he has no action against the underwriters,
has still a ground of action against the shipowners, who are under an
implied warranty to the cargo-owners that the vessel in which the goods
are carried is seaworthy. But it is not uncommon, as already explained,
for the owners of a ship, either in the charter-party or in the bill of
lading, to contract themselves out of all liability for the unseaworthiness
of their vessel, and the assignee or indorsee of a policy ought therefore
to make sure either that the shipowner has not so exempted himself
from liability, or that the underwriter in the policy agrees to waive the
implied warranty of seaworthiness.

Deviation is an abandonment or a departure from the voyage insured
against made after the voyage has begun. Since the risk begins to run
the moment the goods are on board the vessel, and terminates whenever
she reaches her port of destination, any voluntary deviation of the
vessel, whether the insured be privy to it or not, except for the purpose
of saving life, between the occurrence of these two events, amounts to
a breach of an implied warranty, which discharges the insurer of all
subsequent liability. Thus, unreasonable delay on the part of the
vessel in setting out on her voyage, or very unusual delay, for which
the cargo-owners are responsible, in discharging at the port of destination, amounts to a breach of the implied warranty of non-deviation.
The voyage is deemed to be changed *so soon as the election to change has
been made,* and the insurer may avoid the contract as from the date of

---

[1] Greenock S.S. Co., 1903, 2 K.B. 65.

[2] See Daniels *v.* Harris, L.R. 10 C.P. 1.

[3] See observations *per* Lord Shaw of Dunfermline on onus of proof in questions
of unseaworthiness in Klein *v.* Lindsay and Others, 20th February 1911, S.C. (H.L.) 9.

election. It is therefore immaterial that the ship may not in fact have deviated from the voyage contemplated when the loss actually occurs (Act, sec. 45). If the deviation have once taken place it is immaterial that the vessel has subsequently returned to her proper course without any apparent injury or change of risk. The deviation must be voluntary, for, if made *bonâ fide*, and imperatively necessary in the interests of all concerned, as, *e.g.* to avoid danger, to make necessary repairs, to avoid an enemy, to save life, or to aid a ship in distress, the insurer is not discharged.

There is, further, an implied warranty that the adventure insured is a lawful one, and that so far as the insured can control the matter the adventure shall be carried out in a lawful manner. There is no implied warranty as to the nationality of a ship, or that her nationality shall not be changed during the risk (Act, secs. 37, 41). It has, however, been held to be concealment of material information not to disclose the fact that a British ship was having her flag changed in order to avoid the requirements of the Merchant Shipping Act.[1]

Risks Covered by the Policy.—The risks which are usually covered by the policy are those due to perils of the sea, men-of-war, fire, enemies, pirates, rovers, thieves, jettisons, letters of mart and countermart, surprisals, takings at sea, arrests, restraints and detainments of all kings, princes, and peoples, barratry of the master and crew, and generally all other perils, losses, and misfortunes, which may damage or destroy the goods. The policy contained in the First Schedule to the Act has, however, a memorandum appended to it, which declares that " corn, fish, salt, fruit, flour, and seed are warranted free from average, unless general, or the ship be stranded ; sugar, tobacco, hemp, flax, hides and skins are warranted free from average under five per cent. ; and all other goods, also the ship and freight, are warranted free from average under three per cent., unless general, or the ship be stranded." The effect of the qualification, " unless general, or the ship be stranded," has occasioned a good deal of litigation, but it is now settled that once it is held the ship has been stranded the memorandum no longer applies. A ship is stranded when, by accident or through some unforeseen event, not to be expected in ordinary circumstances from the nature of the voyage, she is rendered, even for a very short time, immoveable on the strand.[2] Where memorandum goods of the same species are shipped, whether in bulk or in packages, not expressed, by distinct valuation or otherwise in the policy, to be separately insured, and there is no general average and no stranding, the ordinary memorandum exempts the underwriters from liability for a total loss or destruction of part only, though consisting of one

---

[1] Hutchison & Co., 1876, 3 R. 682.
[2] See Thomson *v.* Murison, 1844, 6 D. 1120 ; Letchford *v.* Oldham, L.R. 5 Q.B.D. 538.

or more entire package or packages, and although such package or packages be entirely destroyed or otherwise lost by the specified perils.[1]

The risk commences in the case of time policies from the date of the policy, and under voyage policies from the time, generally speaking, when the goods are actually on board the ship, and terminates when they are landed, or placed on board another vessel for transmission to the port of discharge in the usual way. When the subject-matter is insured " at and from " or " from " a particular place, it is not necessary that the ship should be at that place when the contract is concluded, but there is an implied condition that the adventure shall be commenced within a reasonable time, and so that the risk shall not be materially varied, otherwise the insurer may avoid the contract (Act, sec. 42). In an insurance " from " a particular place the risk does not attach until the ship starts on the voyage insured (r. 2, First Schedule). Where a ship is insured " at and from " a place, either a port or it may be a district, and the ship is at the place in good safety when the contract is concluded, the risk attaches immediately ; if she be not at the place, the risk attaches immediately on her arrival, provided she is in a state of reasonable safety (r. 3). But when lighters are employed to discharge the cargo at the port of unloading, the risk still remains while the goods are on board the lighter, unless (at least in English law) the lighter belongs to the insured himself, when delivery on board his lighter is held to be delivery to him.

Claims for Loss or Damage.—The claims which the insured has against the underwriters may be for the total loss of the goods, either actual or constructive, or for their partial loss or damage. The cause of loss may be due to (1) perils of the sea, as by the ship's foundering, stranding, striking on a rock, or shipwreck ; (2) fire, even when the ship is set on fire to prevent her falling into the hands of the enemy ; (3) collision, unless due to the fault of the master or crew ; (4) capture, which may give rise to a claim for total loss, or to a partial loss when the vessel is recaptured ; (5) detention by the ruling powers of a country, unless due to the fault of the master or crew ; (6) barratry, or fraud or misconduct amounting to gross malversation, of the master or crew ; and (7) general average contributions, or contributions made by the owners of the ship, freight, or goods on board, in proportion to their respective interests, towards any particular loss or expense sustained or rendered necessary for the general safety of the ship and cargo, in order that the particular loss may be shared equally by all interested in the voyage ; as where goods are thrown overboard in a storm, or masts, etc., are cut away to lighten or preserve the ship, or where expense is incurred in salving the ship.

Total Loss.—Total loss may be either actual or constructive, and

---

[1] Ralli *v.* Janson, 6 E. & B. 422.

unless a different intention appears from the policy an insurance against total loss only includes a constructive total loss (Act, sec. 56). When the ship founders at sea and ship and cargo are lost, or, having sailed, the ship is never heard of again, there is, of course, an undoubted actual total loss (Act, sec. 58). But if the ship is wrecked and so irreparably damaged that she has ceased to be a ship and becomes only a " congeries of planks," and if the cargo is so damaged as to cease to belong to the category under which it was insured (*e.g.* hides which have putrefied), there is also an actual total loss, which needs no notice of abandonment (Act, sec. 57). No notice need be given to the underwriters if there is in point of fact at the time when notice falls to be given nothing to abandon (Act, sec. 62). There is constructive total loss when the subject insured is reasonably abandoned on account of its actual loss appearing to be unavoidable, or because it has been so far damaged by the perils insured against that the expense of repairing or recovering it would exceed its marketable value when repaired or recovered [1] (Act, sec. 60). In such a case the insured may abandon the subject to the underwriters and claim for a total loss, provided that his election to do so is made on receipt of intelligence that the subject is regarded as constructively a total loss, and that intimation is made to the underwriters within a reasonable time thereafter.[2] The intimation may be made in any form, and it must be made within reasonable time (Act, sec. 61). It may be given verbally or in writing, and in any terms which sufficiently indicate the assured's intention to abandon the subject-matter insured unconditionally to the insurers. By giving notice of abandonment the insured assigns his entire interest in the subject insured to the underwriters, according to their respective subscriptions, to the effect of surrogating them in his interest, and so enabling them to take any action which might have been competent to him had he not been insured.[3] The underwriters may, however, refuse to accept the abandonment, and in that case the rights of parties must be judged according to the date of the raising of an action on the policy.[4] Thus a loss, constructively total when notice of abandonment is given, may, by the force of circumstances, become only partial; but underwriters cannot escape liability as for a total constructive loss by gratuitously intervening and taking upon themselves, between the notice of abandon-

---

[1] Stewart *v.* Greenock Marine Insurance Co., 1848, 1 Macq. 328 ; Rankin *v.* Potter, L.R. 6 H.L. 83 ; Farnworth *v.* Hyde, L.R. 2 C.P. 204 ; see also Montreal Light, etc., Co., 1910, A.C. 598.

[2] Kaltenbach *v.* Mackenzie, L.R. 3 C.P.D. 467.

[3] Simpson *v.* Thomson, 1877, 5 R. (H.L.) 40 ; L.R. 3 Ap. Ca. 279. See Burnand *v.* Rodocanachi, L.R. 7 Ap. Ca. 333 ; Castellain *v.* Preston, L.R. 11 Q.B.D. 380 ; Scottish Marine Insurance Co. *v.* Turner, 1853, 1 Macq. 334.

[4] This is the English rule, which would probably be followed in Scotland. See Shepherd *v.* Henderson, 1881, 8 R. 518.

ment and the time when legal proceedings are commenced under the policy, the expenses of raising the insured vessel and saving her from being a constructive total loss.[1] The master of a vessel may do all in his power to prevent a loss becoming total, without affecting the insured's right to subsequently abandon, and he acts in such a case as agent of the person who may ultimately be found to have an interest in the subject insured. An insured person may abandon a portion of the subject insured to the extent to which it suffers damage, retaining, as common owner along with the underwriters, the portion not abandoned.

Valuation of Loss.—In regard to total loss, whether actual or constructive, the amount recoverable by the insured depends on whether the policy under which the goods are insured is an " open " or " valued " one. In an " open " policy no agreement is entered into as to the true value of the subject insured. In such a policy the insured must prove that the subject insured was actually on board at the time of the loss. The true value of the subject is then arrived at by adjustment. In a valued policy the value of the subject is agreed upon and stated, and upon this value the insured is entitled to recover. In the case of partial loss, the value of the subject insured is determined by adjustment, whether the policy be open or valued. Where the policy is an open one, partial losses are adjusted in the same way as total losses. Where, however, the policy is a valued one, the insured is not entitled to claim for the difference between the value of the subject insured as declared in the policy, and its value in its damaged or depreciated condition. The amount of the loss is estimated by ascertaining the difference between the price which the goods might have been expected to realise at the port of destination and their actual value in their damaged condition. The insured is entitled to recover the amount declared in the policy, in the ratio which the price that the goods might have been expected to realise at the port of destination bears to the difference in value thus ascertained. Thus suppose goods are valued in a policy at £100, and that at their port of destination they would have realised £80, while in their damaged or depreciated condition they are only worth £60. The difference between these values is £20, and as £80, the amount which the goods would have realised, is to £20, so is £100 to the amount which the insured is entitled to receive. He would thus receive from the insurer only £25, and not £40, the difference between the value in the policy and the actual price the goods realised. When the loss is adjusted, a note is indorsed on the policy by the underwriters.

---

[1] " The Blairmore," 1898, L.R. A.C. 593.

PERSONAL SECURITIES

CHAPTER IV

1. Cautionary Obligations

Nature and Essentials.—The obligation or engagement of a cautioner is a collateral one, to the effect that, in the event of the principal on whose behalf the obligation is undertaken failing to pay a debt, or perform an act, for which he is or may become liable, the cautioner will do so. Cautionary obligations were formerly gratuitous, and a cautioner could not legally stipulate for any reward as a condition of his undertaking the obligation, but it is unlikely that this would now receive effect, in view of the fact that the Legislature has, in certain cases, sanctioned the taking of bonds of guarantee associations,[1] and that the Courts have sanctioned the use of such bonds in cases where the appointment of an officer of their own fell to be made.[2] It is of the essence of a cautionary obligation that there should be some one, independently of the cautioner, primarily bound for the payment of the debt or performance of the obligation; and while in cautionary obligations undertaken by a minor without the consent of his curators the primary obligation is not enforceable against the principal obligant, the obligation is still enforceable against the cautioner. As the cautioner is presumed to know the debtor's condition, the plain language of his engagement is that if the debtor take the benefit of the law, he, the cautioner, shall make good the debt.[3] A cautioner has a right to avail himself of any defences in bar or reduction of payment competent to the principal debtor; and although *ex facie* of his obligation he may be bound for a larger sum, he cannot be compelled to pay more than is due by the principal obligant.[4] Where the principal obligation comes to an end, the liability of the cautioner ceases to exist.[5] Further, by his signing

---

[1] Pupils' Protection Act, 12 & 13 Vict. cap. 51, sec. 27.

[2] M'Kinnon, *Petr.*, 1884, 12 R. 184.

[3] Erskine, iii. 3, 64 ; Stevenson *v.* Adair, 1872, 10 M. 920.

[4] Jackson *v.* M'Iver, 1875, 2 R. 882. See also Beckervaise *v.* Lewis, 1872, L.R. 7 C.P. 372 ; Duncan, Fox & Co. *v.* N. & S. Wales Bank, 1880, L.R. 6 Ap. Ca. 1.

[5] Commercial Bank of Tasmania *v.* Jones, 1893, L.R. Ap. Ca. 313.

a blank sheet of paper and intrusting it to some one to fill up according to arrangement, the cautioner cannot be subjected to a liability greater than that which he had previously agreed to. Thus, in one case a father received a blank sheet of paper, with a sixpenny stamp upon it, from his son, with a request that he should sign across the stamp. He did so on the understanding that his son was simply to fill in a guarantee for £500. The son filled in the guarantee for £500, and added, without his father's knowledge or consent, an obligation by the father to pay certain premiums of insurance upon the son's life. It was held that as the father had given his son no authority to fill in this obligation, he was not bound to pay the premiums.[1]

Constitution.—The Mercantile Law Amendment (Scotland) Act, 1856, sec. 6, provides in terms as comprehensive as they are imperative, that " from and after the passing of this Act all guarantees, securities, or cautionary obligations, made or granted by any person for any conduct, credit, ability, trade, or dealings of any person, made or granted to the effect, or for the purpose of enabling such person to obtain credit, money, goods, etc., postponement of payment of debt or of any other obligation demandable from him, shall be in writing, and shall be subscribed by the person undertaking such guarantee, security, or cautionary obligation, or making such representations and assurances, or by some person duly authorised by him or them, otherwise the same shall have no effect." These enactments are in substance the same as the provisions of sec. 6 of 9 Geo. IV. c. 14, commonly known as Lord Tenterden's Act, which applies to England and Ireland. Under these provisions—which obviously were not intended to meet the case of truthful and honest representations, and necessarily include all representations of the character and made with the purpose specified, however false and however fraudulent—it is immaterial that the person making the representations has in view some ulterior and illegitimate purpose beyond inducing the person to whom they were made to give credit or money to a third party.[2] Every cautionary obligation must therefore be in writing, and, with the exception of those *in re mercatoria*, or those which although improbative have been perfected *rei interventu*,[3] must be holograph of the granter, or tested ; that is, executed according to the usual formalities required by law.[4] Cautionary obligations are construed strictly, and nothing will be inferred which the terms of the obligation do not warrant. An offer of guarantee in writing importing an understanding that a guarantee will be given when required, or which is contingent on the acceptance of an offer which is duly accepted

---

[1] Wylie & Lochhead *v.* Hornsby, 1889, 16 R. 907.
[2] *Per* Lord Watson in Clydesdale Bank *v.* Paton, 1896, 23 R. (H.L.) 22.
[3] Church of England Life Assurance Co. *v.* Wink, 1857, 19 D. 414 and 1079.
[4] See Execution of Deeds, p. 43, *et seq.*

on the strength of the offered guarantee, is, though not a direct, yet a good cautionary obligation.[1]

Kinds of Obligation.—Cautionary obligations are of two kinds, proper and improper. In proper cautionary obligations there must be three parties—the primary obligant, the cautioner or surety, and the creditor or obligee ; the obligation of the cautioner being *ex facie* of the deed expressly recognised as such. In an improper cautionary obligation the cautioner is taken bound along with the primary obligant as principal debtor, his rights as a cautioner being renounced *quoad* the creditor but reserved *quoad* the principal debtor. A Bond of Credit is an example of an improper cautionary obligation.

Negotiations Prior to Execution of Deed.—In entering into a cautionary obligation, the utmost good faith between a banker and a cautioner is required ; but while this is so, in the taking of such an obligation, whether by bond of credit, guarantee, or other security, a bank is under no obligation to disclose the affairs of its customer or the state of his account, it being the duty of the cautioner to make such inquiries as he may deem necessary, and to inform himself upon the various matters material to the obligation he is about to undertake. Neither is it a banker's duty unsolicited to explain to the cautioners the legal effect of a document which they can and ought to read for themselves, and a banker's silence on the subject will not be considered such undue concealment as to afford grounds for the reduction of the deed.[2] But, on the other hand, if the bank choose to disclose anything, they must disclose the whole state of matters between them and their customer, material to the obligation about to be undertaken, as the Court will protect a cautioner from fraud or undue concealment.[3] In a recent case a guarantor repudiated his obligations on the ground that when he signed the guarantee he was not informed that, besides sums due on an overdrawn account, the customer was indebted to the bank for considerable sums in respect of bills discounted. This defence the Lord Ordinary sustained, holding that the defender signed the guarantee under a material error, and that this error was induced by the failure of the bank agent to disclose the existence of the bill debts under circumstances which laid on him a duty of disclosure. On appeal the Court recalled the judgment of the Lord Ordinary and decided the case in favour of the bank on the ground that the averments of the pursuer had not been proved, and that consequently the guarantor was not in fact misled by the bank agent.[4] Since parole proof is incompetent to

---

[1] Wallace *v.* Gibson, 1895, 22 R. (H.L.) 56.

[2] Young *v.* Clydesdale Bank, 1889, 17 R. 231.

[3] Royal Bank *v.* Ranken, 1844, 6 D. 1418 ; Hamilton *v.* Watson, 1845, 4 S. Bell, 67 : *affd.* 5 D. 280 ; British Guarantee Association *v.* Western Bank, 1853, 15 D. 834.

[4] Royal Bank of Scotland *v.* Greenshields, 1914, S.C. 259.

explain the terms of an executed deed,[1] care should in every case be taken to see that no writing passes between the bank on the one hand, and the cautioner or the customer on the other, which might qualify the terms of the written obligation. Where it can be proved that the negotiations have been conducted under circumstances which show that the obligation has been obtained from the cautioner by means of false representations, not simply as an ordinary business transaction, but really as a means of obtaining from a known insolvent debtor a settlement for a part at least of a bad debt, the principles recognised in ordinary banking transactions will not receive effect. Thus in one case a bank made an arrangement with an insolvent debtor, by which they agreed that a part of the debt should be abated, that the debtor should furnish securities for the balance, and, *inter alia*, should assign a policy of insurance on his life, and find security for payment of the premiums and interest. A bond which narrated an advance of £2000 as the consideration, and which contained an assignation of the policy, was prepared by the debtor and revised on behalf of the bank. The law agent of the bank, in revising the draft, altered the terms of the consideration as stated by the debtor, and disclosed the real nature of the transaction, which was that the sum of £2000 was not to be actually advanced, but that credit was to be allowed in account for that sum, as part of an arrangement by which the bank agreed to accept the composition on their debt. On a final adjustment of the draft, the terms as they originally stood were, at the request of the debtor, restored. After the bond had been extended, the debtor, for the first time, requested one of the parties named as cautioners for the premiums to subscribe, which he accordingly did. On the cautioner repudiating liability, the Court decided that he had been induced to sign in the belief that the true consideration was an advance of money by the bank as set forth in the narrative, and in ignorance of the true nature of the transaction, and that the bank was responsible for these misrepresentations.[2] Where a person signs a guarantee to a bank for behoof of another, there is a presumption that his signature to the obligation was adhibited at the request of the debtor, and not of the bank. To entitle a cautioner to repudiate liability, it is not sufficient for him to prove that he was led to draw certain erroneous inferences from his conversations with the bank agent, but he must show that misleading statements were unequivocally made to him.[3] But if either the creditor or the debtor actively dissuades the cautioner from con-

---

[1] Macpherson *v.* Haggarts, 1881, 9 R. 306. See exception in case of bills, B. of E. Act, sec. 100.

[2] Falconer *v.* North of Scotland Banking Co., 1863, 1 M. 704. See also Hamilton *v.* Watson, 1845, 4 S. Bell, 67 ; *affd.* 5 D. 280 ; and Royal Bank *v.* Learmonth & Ranken, referred to and distinguished by L.J.-C. Inglis in this case.

[3] Bank of Scotland *v.* Dunnet, 10th May 1893.

sulting his legal adviser, and he in consequence abstains from doing so, then very little more will be necessary to warrant a reduction of the obligation.[1]

Commencement of Obligation.—No transactions should be permitted on the faith of the obligation until all the parties by whom it bears to have been granted have signed it, nor until it has been delivered to the creditor as a completed deed. In one case a charge against a co-obligant was suspended, on the ground that, while the bond bore to be granted by four parties, it was only signed by three of them.[2] Care should further be taken to see that all the obligants are alive at the date of the delivery of the deed, for it has been decided that if one of the parties who has signed it should die before delivery, his executors are not responsible for any sum advanced, the implied mandate to deliver the deed having fallen by the death.[3] It is the duty of the creditor to see that the signatures of the cautioners or co-obligants are duly adhibited to the obligation, for if a person advances money on the faith of, and in reliance upon, the signatures of certain parties named and designed in the document he takes in security for repayment, he ought to see the subscription of that document by the parties on whose obligation he relies for his safety in making the advance. If he does not do so, he runs the risk of such signatures being forged, and the result in law of any one or more of the signatures to an obligation being forged is to free, not only the person whose signature is so forged, but also all the other cautioners or co-obligants, of all liability to the bank under the deed.[4] The principal debtor, however, remains bound apart from the bond.

Liabilities of the Cautioner.—An obligation by several cautioners will not import a joint and several liability, unless such a liability be clearly expressed. Where cautioners are bound jointly and severally, the creditor is entitled to call upon any of the sureties for payment of the full amount due, and the surety so paying is entitled, as against his co-sureties, only to recover their rateable proportion of the amount paid.[5] In the event of one of the sureties being bankrupt, the solvent sureties are liable for his share or deficiency. Where the principal is unable to pay, and one of the sureties is bankrupt, it is competent for the creditor to rank upon, and recover a dividend from, the bankrupt's estate on the full amount of his claim, whereas if the creditor call upon a solvent surety to pay, such surety, if he does pay, can rank upon the estate of the bankrupt only for his share of the amount paid under the obligation. Where the creditor ranks upon the estate of an

---

[1] Sutherland v. Low & Co. Ltd., 1901, 38 S.L.R. 710.
[2] Paterson v. Bonar, 1844, 6 D. 987.
[3] Life Association of Scotland v. Douglas, 1886, 13 R. 910.
[4] Scottish Provincial Assurance Co. v. Pringle & Others, 1858, 20 D. 465.
[5] See Relief of Cautioners inter se, infra.

insolvent surety for the full amount of his debt, so long as the dividen received from him does not exceed the share which, in ordinary cours would fall to be paid by the bankrupt surety, the co-sureties cannot b called upon by the trustee to pay any part of the dividend received b the creditor on his claim as lodged.

Firms as Cautioners or Co-obligants.—A partner of a firm canno bind the firm by signing the firm's name to an obligation, such as tha contained in a Bond of Caution, Bond of Credit, or Guarantee, unles it can be shown that the granting of such obligations is necessary an incidental to the conduct of the firm's business, or provided for in th contract of co-partnery.[1] In one case, where a partner of a firm of rail way contractors had, without authority from his co-partners, grante a guarantee in the firm's name for payment of coals, to be supplied t persons who had a sub-contract with the firm, it was held that th guarantee was not binding on the other partners, there being no eviden that the granting of such guarantees was usual in the conduct of th firm's business.[2] To render a firm or company liable for obligation outwith the scope of the partnership business, not only must the firm' name be signed to the contract or obligation by one of the partners, bu the signature of each individual partner must also be adhibited. I obligations where a firm and the individual partners are taken bound, i is usual to add a personal obligation by the partners as individuals over and above their obligation as partners.[3] Thus, where A. B. & Co. and A. B. and C. D., the individual partners of the firm of A. B. & Co. become bound as sureties as such partners and as individuals, ther are three separate parties bound, namely, the firm and each o the partners. The dissolution of the firm of A. B. & Co. terminate its existence, and therefore its liability as a cautioner for any futur advances. As the relief of one cautioner without the consent of th others frees the remaining obligants, the dissolution of the firm operate to free the partners, unless in the obligation it is specially provided tha the liability of the individual partners is not to be affected by a dissolu tion of the firm. Where the obligation contains no such provision, th course to be followed, on a dissolution of a co-partnership, is either t get the surviving or remaining partners of the firm to consent to th continuance of the credit, or to have a new bond executed. Wher a partner is assumed into a firm, he is in a different position, as h cannot be held liable on a bond to which he was not a party, withou express provision to that effect in the contract of co-partnery, or th adoption by the new firm of the liability under the obligation. He is

---

[1] See Partners, p. 63.

[2] Brettle v. Williams, 4 Exch. 623.

[3] Freeth v. Wm. Hamilton & Co., 1889, 16 R. 1022 ; MacBride v. Clark, Grierson & Co., 1865, 4 M. 73 ; Mellis v. Royal Bank, 22nd June 1815, 18 F. C. 454.

owever, liable for any advances made subsequent to his admission as a
partner of the firm.[1]   Where the obligation is *granted for behoof of a firm*,
and a change takes place in the constitution of that firm, either by the
death or retiral of one or more of the partners, or the assumption of
a new partner, the obligation of the sureties is, in the absence of agreement to the contrary, thereby revoked as to future advances.   Where,
however, express provision is made that the obligation of the sureties is
to continue binding and effectual, notwithstanding any change in the
firm, the agreement thus made will receive effect, and bind the sureties
for subsequent advances.   Companies incorporated under the Companies Act or by Royal Charter cannot become bound as cautioners,
unless power to do so is contained in their respective Acts of Incorporation.

Discussion.—Prior to the passing of the Mercantile Law Amendment Act, it was necessary, before proceeding against a cautioner in
a proper cautionary obligation, to *discuss* the principal debtor ; that
is, to take action against him for recovery of the amount due, and
follow it up with legal diligence.   It is, however, no longer necessary
to do so, and a creditor may now proceed directly against the cautioner
without even having first constituted his debt against the principal
obligant,[2] or he may, if he so choose, include in the same action both
the principal debtor and cautioner, provided that no stipulation is contained in the obligation that the principal debtor shall be discussed
before calling upon the cautioner.   It has, however, been decided that,
when a plurality of persons are alleged to be bound jointly and severally,
no one of them can be separately sued for payment or performance
of the whole debt or obligation, till the debt or obligation has been
constituted by writing or by decree ; or, in other words, that where
such a debt or obligation has not been so constituted, the whole
co-obligants, subject to the jurisdiction of the Courts of this country,
must be called in any action to enforce payment of the debt or performance of the obligation.[3]   Payment of the amount due, or performance
of the obligation, may be made by anyone, and unless the creditor is
able to assign a satisfactory reason for his refusal, he has no right
to object to fulfilment by a stranger.   A stranger so paying is entitled
to an assignation of the debt, and of any securities held specially
therefor.[4]   Where the obligation is one *ad factum præstandum*, the
provisions of the Mercantile Law Amendment Act do not apply, and
in such obligations it is still necessary to discuss the principal obligant
before calling on the cautioner.

Discharge of the Cautioner.—The cautioner may be freed (1)

---

[1] See Partners.
[2] Sec. 8 of Act ; Morrison *v.* Harkness, 1870, 9 M. 35.
[3] Neilson *v.* Wilson, 1890, 17 R. 608.   See Zuill *v.* M'Murchy, 1842, 4 D. 871.
[4] Rainnie *v.* Milne, 1822, 1 S. 377.

directly, by direct discharge, the principal debtor still remaining bound or (2) *indirectly* and consequentially, as by (*a*) *satisfaction, paymen* or *extinction* of the principal obligation ; (*b*) by any *essential alteration* in the respective positions of the creditor and the principal debtor unassented to by the cautioner ; (*c*) by the *discharge of the debtor* without the cautioner's consent ; (*d*) by the *discharge of a co-cautioner* without the consent of the other cautioner ; (*e*) by the creditor's *giving time* to the principal debtor ; (*f*) by the creditor's *extreme neglect* of legal proceedings ; or (*g*) by the creditor's *relinquishing any security* over the debtor's estate without the cautioner's consent. Any essential alteration in the respective positions of the creditor and the principal debtor, either with regard to the principal obligation or in respect to the person relied on, unassented to by the cautioner during the continuance of the obligation, has the effect of freeing the cautioner. In one case three persons became bound for the conduct of a bank agent, and in the bond the agent was taken bound to have no other business of any kind. The bank afterwards entered into an agreement with the agent, whereby he became liable for one-fourth of the losses arising from discounts, but this arrangement was not communicated to the cautioners. Losses arose from the misconduct of the agent, and it was held that the cautioners were relieved by the mere fact of the agreement having been entered into.[1] In another case four persons, as cautioners for a principal, executed a joint and several bond, by the terms of which the liability of two of them was limited to £50 each, and that of the other two to £25 each. One of those whose liability was limited to £50, after the other three had executed the bond, signed it but added to his signature the words " £25 only." It was held that the effect of these words was to make a material alteration in the bond, so that the first three cautioners were thereby discharged from their obligation ; and that as the last signatory executed the bond only as a joint and several obligation, he also was not bound by it.[2] Generally, if the creditor does anything which discharges the principal debtor, or extinguishes his claim against him, without the cautioner's consent, he thereby discharges the cautioner.[3] But a discharge by the creditor of a principal debtor, either with or without the cautioner's consent, in such a manner as to clearly express an intention to reserve his claim entire against the cautioner, does not have the effect of freeing the cautioner. This principle is well illustrated by a case where the

---

[1] Bonar *v.* Macdonald, 1847, 9 D. 1537 ; *affd.* 13 D. (H.L.) 37. See also Stewart, Moir & Muir *v.* Brown, 1871, 9 M. 763 ; Philips *v.* Foxall, 1872, L.R. 7 Q.B. 666 ; Pollak *v.* Everett, L.R. 1 Q.B.D. 669 ; Sanderson *v.* Aston, L.R. 8 Ex. 73 ; Holme *v.* Brunskill, L.R. 3 Q.B.D. 495.

[2] Ellesmere Brewery Co. *v.* Cooper, 1895, L.R. 1 Q.B. 75.

[3] Murray *v.* Lee, 1882, 9 R. 1040.

holder of a bill, after it had been dishonoured and duly protested, while retaining possession of it, granted a discharge to the acceptors " of all claims and demands competent " to him against them, " reserving entire my claims against any obligants other than " the acceptors " presently bound to me along with " the acceptors. He thereafter sued the last of three indorsers of the bill for the amount in the bill, and it was held that the discharge did not extinguish the debt, but was merely an agreement not to sue the acceptors, and that the indorser was liable, his recourse against the acceptors not being prejudiced. The Lord Chancellor remarked : " There is no doubt that, by a proper and apt instrument, it is competent for the holder of a security of this kind to agree with the principal debtor not to enforce his remedies against the principal debtor, and if he does that in an instrument which at the same time reserves his rights against those who are liable in the second degree, there will be no discharge of those persons so liable." [1]

To the general rule that a discharge of the principal debtor frees the cautioner, an exception is allowed in the case of sequestration. It is provided by statute [2] that no act of the creditor in voting and drawing a dividend, or in assenting to the discharge of the bankrupt, or to a composition, discharges a co-obligant of the debtor. But it is provided that such obligant may require, and obtain at his own expense, from such creditor an assignation of the debt on payment of the amount thereof, and in virtue thereof enter a claim on the bankrupt estate, and draw dividends, if otherwise entitled so to do. Except, however, in the case of sequestrations, if the creditor consent to the receiving of a composition from his debtor, such as under a trust-deed, or offer of settlement, without the cautioner's consent, he thereby frees the cautioner. A creditor, before agreeing to any such arrangement, should get the consent, in writing,[3] of the whole other parties bound for the debt. If he has not obtained such consent, he should add to his assent the following or similar words : " Subject to the necessary consents being received," so as to leave his hands free to act otherwise if necessary. If the consent is refused, and he desires to draw a dividend, then his receipt for the composition should expressly reserve his rights against the other obligants, by the following or similar words : " Without prejudice to my rights against A. B. and C. D., which are hereby expressly reserved." It is thought that this course will success-

---

[1] Muir v. Crawford, 1873, 1 R. 91 ; affd. 2 R. (H.L.) 148. See also Smith v. Ogilvie, 1821, 1 S. 159 ; (H.L.) 1825, 1 W. & S. 315 ; Lewis v. Anstruther, 1852, 15 D. 260 ; Green v. Wynn, L.R. 7 Eq. 28, 4 Ch. 204 ; Megarth v. Gray, L.R. 9 C.P. 216 ; ex parte Jacobs, L.R. 10 Ch. 211 ; Price v. Barker, 1855, 4 E. & B. 760 ; Bateson v. Goslin, 1871, L.R. 7 C.P. 9 ; cf. Cragoe v. Jones, L.R. 8 Ex. 81.

[2] Bankruptcy (Scotland) Act, 1913, sec. 52.

[3] See Appendix.

fully enable him to recover payment of the balance from the remaining co-obligants.[1] It might be well, however, not to apply the amount received to the account, but to place it in a separate account in the agent's name with reference to the particular obligation.

Extreme Neglect.—The cautioner will also be freed by extreme neglect on the part of the creditor to enforce his rights against the principal obligant, provided the cautioner can show that his position has been thereby injured. Thus, while mere delay to institute legal proceedings will not operate to relieve the cautioner, extreme neglect of such proceedings on the part of the creditor (especially if proceedings have already been begun against the estate of the principal) [2] may, in certain circumstances, have this effect.[3] But mere inactivity on the part of the creditor is not sufficient to discharge the cautioner, unless there be such a degree of negligence as to imply connivance or fraud. There must, over and above mere neglect, be some positive act done by the creditor to the prejudice of the surety, or an omission of an act which his duty enjoins him to perform, and the omission of which proves injurious to the surety,[4] as, *e.g.* the omission to complete, or take advantage of, a security in competition,[5] or undue neglect in negotiating a bill,[6] or, as in one case, the protesting of a promissory note on the debtor's failure to pay the first instalment without intimation to the cautioner, who had stipulated in his letter of guarantee to see the amount paid back in monthly instalments, and whose position was thus materially altered for the worse.[7] Neglect on the part of the creditor to safeguard his own and the cautioner's interest, as by allowing the debt to prescribe, will have the effect of relieving the latter of his obligation. So will the omission on the part of the creditor to perform an act which, by the terms of his obligation, he was bound to perform. Thus, in one case, where a proposal to a guarantee association contained a clause stipulating that the cash of a teller, whose cash transactions it was proposed to insure, was to be checked in a particular way, it was held relevant to aver that his cash had not been checked in that way, though the bond itself did not expressly stipulate that his cash was to be so checked.[8]

---

[1] Smith *v.* Ogilvie, 1821, 1 S. 159 ; *affd.* 1825, 1 W. & S. 315.

[2] M'Millan *v.* Hamilton, 1729, M. 3390 ; Sinclair *v.* Sinclair, 1744, M. 3524 ; Anderson *v.* Wood, 1821, 1 S. 31 ; Wallace *v.* Donald, 1825, 3 S. 304.

[3] Smith *v.* Wright, 1829, 8 S. 124 ; Smith *v.* Campbell, 1829, 7 S. 789 ; Macfarlan *v.* Anstruther, 1870, 9 M. 117.

[4] Clapperton, Paton & Co. *v.* Anderson, 1881, 8 R. 1004. See also Watts *v.* Shuttleworth, 29 L.J. Ex. 229 ; Black *v.* Ottoman Bank, 8 Jur. N.S. 801.

[5] Storie *v.* Carnie, 1830, 8 S. 853 ; Fleming *v.* Thomson, 1825, 4 S. 224 ; *revd.* 1826, 2 W. & S. 277.

[6] National Bank *v.* Robertson, 1836, 14 S. 402.

[7] Murray *v.* Lee, 1882, 9 R. 1040.

[8] British Guarantee Association *v.* Western Bank, 1853, 15 D. 834.

It is well settled that in an ordinary cautionary obligation for payment of money the creditor is not bound to give intimation to the cautioner that the principal debtor has not paid the sum, or instalments of the sum, when they became due and prestable. That is a matter on which it is the cautioner's duty to inform himself. There may, however, be exceptions to the general rule. For example, if during the currency of a continuing cautionary obligation circumstances come to the knowledge of the creditor which materially affect the risk which the cautioner has undertaken, and which, if they had existed when the obligation was undertaken, would presumably have prevented the cautioner from entering into it, the creditor might very well be bound to communicate these circumstances to the cautioner.[1] There is, however, no authority for the view that it is the duty of a bank whenever it becomes aware of any circumstance seriously affecting the credit of a customer to at once communicate with any of that customer's friends who may have signed cash-credits on his behalf or guarantees for his pecuniary obligations. It might be otherwise if the bank subsequently gave fresh accommodation, so as to increase the cautioner's obligation.[2]

Giving Time.—An agreement on the part of the creditor with the principal debtor, without the cautioner's consent, to give time for payment of the obligation, is analogous in its effect to the relief of a cautioner by a change in the character of the obligation, unassented to by the cautioner. Mere forbearance on the part of the creditor to enforce payment from the principal debtor, or even a mere agreement not to sue him, provided the cautioner's right of recourse is not thereby imperilled, will not have the effect of freeing the cautioner. But if the creditor so tie up his hands as to prevent him from enforcing his obligation at any time, should he wish to do so, the cautioner will be discharged. This principle is illustrated by two cases. In one, a cautioner endeavoured to rid himself of his obligation, because the creditor had for two years delayed to enforce payment from the principal debtor, but the Court repelled this plea.[3] In the other,[4] the pursuer, a landlord, having obtained a letter from the defender guaranteeing payment of the tenant's rent, allowed the tenant to sell and remove the stock from a farm. Subsequently, without the cautioner's consent, he took two bills from the tenant, one for the

---

[1] Britannia Steamship Insurance Association Ltd. *v.* Duff, 1909, S.C. 1261, *per* Lord Low.

[2] Bank of Scotland *v.* Morrison, 1911, S.C. 593.

[3] Fleming *v.* Wilson, 1823, 2 S. 336.

[4] Richardson *v.* Harvey, 1853, 15 D. 628. See also Overend, Gurney & Co. Ltd. *v.* Oriental Financial Corporation Ltd., L.R. 7 Ch. 142 ; L.R. 7 H.L. 348 ; Swire *v.* Redman, L.R. 1 Q.B.D. 536 ; Croydon Coml. Gas Co. *v.* Dickinson, L.R. 1 C.P.D. 707 ; L.R. 2 C.P.D. 46 ; Clarke *v.* Birley, L.R. 41 Ch. D. 422.

Martinmas rent, and the other for the rent due at Whitsunday. The tenant became bankrupt, and in an action at the instance of the landlord, it was held that by taking the bills he had given time to the principal debtor and thus freed the cautioner. It must, however, be kept in view that the mere taking of a bill will not in all cases relieve a cautioner. If it can be shown that the taking of a bill is usual in the particular trade in which the principal debtor is engaged, and to which the cautioner's obligation extends, he will still be bound.[1] Wherever there is a continuing guarantee, the cautioner is not liberated by the taking of a bill, so long as it can be shown that it is not inconsistent with mercantile usage to do so.

Where two or more persons primarily indebted as principals subsequently agree that, as between themselves, one shall be a surety only, and this agreement is made known to the creditor, the rule as to the discharge of a surety by giving time to the principal debtor applies. The rule may be modified by circumstances. Thus, in one case a partner retired from a firm under a deed of dissolution, whereby he assigned his interest in the business to the remaining partners on an agreement that they should pay the partnership debts and indemnify him against them, with a proviso that so long as he was thus kept indemnified he should not be entitled to insist on the debts being discharged. Among the debts of the firm was an overdraft to a bank for £50,000. After the dissolution, the terms of which were communicated to the bank, a transaction was entered into between the new firm and the bank, whereby the firm was allowed for a limited period to increase the overdraft to £53,000. It was held that, under these circumstances, there was no agreement on the part of the bank to give time to the new firm or to alter the relations between the parties, and the bank had not released the retiring partner from his liabilities as a debtor for the amount of the overdraft.[2]

Discharge of Co-Cautioner.—The Mercantile Law Amendment Act, sec. 9, provides that where two or more parties become bound as cautioners for any debtor, any discharge granted by the creditor in such debt or obligations to any one of such cautioners, without the consent of the other cautioners, shall be deemed and taken to be a discharge granted to all the cautioners. Where, however, a bank holds two or more guarantees from different persons, the one without reference to the other, it is a question of circumstances whether the bank can competently release one of the guarantors without the consent of the

---

[1] Bowe & Christie v. Hutchison, 1868, 6 M. 642 ; Stewart, Moir & Muir v. Brown, 1871, 9 M. 763 ; Cook v. Moffat, 1827, 5 S. 774 ; Forsyth v. Wishart, 1859, 21 D. 449 ; Warne v. Lillie, 1867, 5 M. 283 ; Nicolsons v. Burt, 1882, 10 R. 121.

[2] Rouse v. Bradford Banking Co. Ltd., 1894, L.R. A.C. 586 (*affd.* 19th December 1894).

others. The separate guarantors are not co-cautioners, as there is no unity of obligation. If one of the guarantors became bound, relying on an agreement with the bank that he was a co-cautioner with other guarantors whose obligation was already held, the bank could not relieve one of such co-cautioners without the consent of all the guarantors, otherwise all the guarantors would be discharged. But although the obligations are contained in different writings, the ordinary rules will apply if the cautioners in them are bound jointly and severally. To entitle a surety to claim such relief, he must show an existing right to contribution, from the surety so relieved, which has been taken away or injuriously affected by such release.[1] Where one enters into a bond as cautioner for the performance by another of two things, which are separate and distinct, a subsequent alteration of the principal's conduct, without the surety's consent, as to one of them, does not relieve the surety from his obligation as to the other.[2]

Relief of Cautioners.—An important right which cautioners have is that of total relief against the principal debtor for the sums paid under their obligations. This right of relief arises either on actual payment of the debt by the cautioners, or on their being distressed for it by the creditor, or they may at any time, unless there is any agreement to the contrary, insist upon being relieved from their obligation.[3] Where they have actually paid the debt, they are entitled to an assignation of it, and of any securities held as against it, to the effect of enabling them to take proceedings as though they were the original creditors. Payment of a part only of the debt confers no right to demand an assignation, so that, in the case of a surety who has become bankrupt, payment of a dividend on the whole debt confers no right to an assignation in favour of the trustee.[4] But where the cautioner undertakes payment of periodical sums, and has paid up all that was due, he is entitled to an assignation to the extent of the sums paid, although his whole obligation has not been implemented.[5] When the cautioners are distressed for payment of the debt, they may at once insist on relief. Even before this, if the debtor is *vergens ad inopiam*, the Court will, on equitable grounds,[6] sustain an action of relief. If the principal obligant has assigned to the creditor certain securities, not given specially as against the debt for which the cautioners are responsible, but held generally, and there are further sums due, the

---

[1] Morgan *v.* Smart, 1872, 10 M. 610 ; Ward *v.* National Bank of New Zealand, L.R. 8 Ap. Ca. 755.

[2] Harrison *v.* Seymour, L.R. 1 C.P. 518.

[3] Doig *v.* Lawrie, 1902, 5 F. 295.

[4] Ewart *v.* Latta, 1865, 3 M. (H.L.) 36, *revg.* 1 M. 905.

[5] Lowe *v.* Greig, 1825, 3 S. 543.

[6] Kinloch *v.* M'Intosh, 1822, 1 S. 491 ; Spence *v.* Brownlee, 1834, 13 S. 199.

creditor will not be bound to assign such securities except on payment of his whole debt.

Relief of Cautioners inter se.—The principle on which the liability of cautioners *inter se* rests is that cautioners for the same principal and for the same engagement, even although bound by different instruments and for different amounts, have a common interest and a common burden ; so that if one cautioner who is directly liable to the creditor pays such creditor, he can claim contribution from his co-cautioners whose obligation to the creditor he has discharged.[1] Therefore, in a question among themselves, cautioners can always insist on mutual rateable relief, but they are each bound to communicate the benefit of any ease or deduction, as well as of any security over the estate of the principal debtor.[2] If, however, one of the obligants is in truth a cautioner for a previous surety, he is entitled to total relief as against his co-obligants. The right of relief among cautioners does not arise until one of them has paid more than his share.[3] Where one of the cautioners has paid up the whole debt, he is entitled to an assignation of the bond, to the effect of enabling him to operate his right of relief against his co-cautioners.[4] The measure of cautioners' liability *inter se* was decided by the Second Division of the Court of Session, in a case in which five persons jointly and severally guaranteed to a bank payment of all sums for which a company might become liable to the bank. The company having gone into liquidation, the bank called on two of the cautioners to pay the balance due under the guarantee. They did so, and then brought an action against another of the guarantors for relief to the extent of one-third of the sum they had paid. The pursuers averred and led evidence to prove that the two remaining guarantors were insolvent. The defender denied that the insolvency of either of the remaining guarantors had been proved, and pleaded that he was liable in relief only to the extent of a fifth of the sum paid by the pursuers ; but the Court held that whether the two remaining guarantors were insolvent or not, the pursuers were not bound to bear the whole risk of their insolvency, and therefore that the defender was liable in relief to the extent of one-third of the sum paid by the pursuers.[5] The right of relief of cautioners *inter se* cannot be impaired or discharged by the creditor, without discharging the co-cautioners.[6]

Prescription.—Cautionary obligations fall under the septennial

---

[1] Ellesmere Brewery Co. *v.* Cooper, 1895, L.R. 1 Q.B. 75.

[2] Steel *v.* Dixon, 1881, L.R. 17 Ch. D. 825 ; Berridge *v.* Berridge, L.R. 44 Ch. D. 168.

[3] Davies *v.* Humphreys, 6 M. & W. 153 ; Craythore *v.* Swinburne, 14 Ves. 160 ; *ex parte* Snowdon, L.R. 17 Ch. D. 44.

[4] See Appendix.

[5] Buchanan *v.* Main, 1900, 3 F. 215.

[6] Erskine, iii. 3, 68 ; Smith *v.* Ogilvie, 1821, 1 S. 159 ; H.L. 1825, 1 W. & S. 315.

limitation or prescription, introduced by the Act 1696, cap. 5, which provides that " no man binding, or engaging hereafter for and with another conjunctly and severally, in any bond or contract for sums of money, shall be bound for the said sum for longer than seven years after the date of the bond, but that, from and after the said seven years, the said cautioner shall be *eo ipso* free of his caution." The persons to whom the Act applies are declared to be—" whoever is bound for another, either as express cautioner, or as principal, or co-principal, shall be understood to be a cautioner, and have the benefit of this Act, provided that he have either a clause of relief in the bond, or a bond of relief apart, intimated personally to the creditor at his receiving of the bond." The seven years run from the date of the obligation. In dealing with this Act, it must be kept in view that a surety or cautioner may be, and very often is, as between himself and the party to be secured, a principal debtor, as is the case in a Bond of Credit, his undertaking being to pay the sum secured to the creditor, not on default of the real principal debtor, but in the first instance, and without reference to the creditor. In contracts of this description, the liability of the cautioner is not affected by the creditor's knowledge that the cautioner is not the real debtor. Keeping this in view, the construction of the statute seems to be relieved of much of the obscurity that is supposed to belong to it. It provides a septennial limitation (first) for those who bind, or engage for, or with, another in any bond or contract expressly as cautioners, and (second) for those who, though cautioners as between the parties who contract to pay, are principals, so far as regards the creditor, provided, however, there be a clause of relief in the bond itself, which gives the creditor notice of the character in which the party binds himself, or a separate bond of relief, of which the creditor has personal intimation at the time of receiving the bond.[1] The statute only extinguishes obligations prestable within the *septennium*. It does not apply to the obligation of a cautioner who is bound only for interest on the principal sum due under a bond.[2] The effect of the statute on those obligations which it governs is of a very sweeping description. It does not merely presume payment or satisfaction of the obligation at the end of the prescriptive period. Its effect is to free the cautioner absolutely ; and accordingly it has been decided that a cautioner paying money after the seven years was entitled to get it back.[3] The payment of interest after the seven years does not perpetuate the obligation. The following obligations do not fall within the operation of the statute :—(1) those in which the

---

[1] Scott *v.* Yuille, 5 W. & S. 436 ; Tait *v.* Wilson, 1 Rob. App. 137 ; Stocks *v.* M'Lagan, 1890, 17 R. 1122.

[2] Molleson *v.* Hutchison, 1892, 19 R. 581.

[3] Carrick *v.* Carse, 1778, Mor. 2931, *quoted with approval in* Stocks *v.* M'Lagan, *supra*.

term of payment is beyond the seven years; (2) those in marriage contracts; (3) those for payment of an annuity, or interest upon a loan, and Cash-Credit Bonds;[1] (4) bonds of corroboration, bonds of relief by one cautioner to another, and mercantile or other guarantees; (5) those *ad facta præstanda*, bonds of caution for discharge of an office, and judicial bonds; (6) bonds for a composition in bankruptcy; (7) bonds for mutual relief; (8) bonds to pay, or see paid, a sum already lent;[2] (9) bonds executed in a foreign country, since the laws of this country cannot govern those of another;[3] and (10) the statute does not apply to bills, in which one person signs as cautioner for another.[4]

Extension of Liability beyond Prescriptive Period.—The obligation of the cautioner, even when strictly of the character contemplated by the Act, does not always fall under the limitation introduced by the Act. It will be extended beyond the seven years in the following cases :—(1) where the bond is renewed, or a bond of corroboration is executed by the cautioner; (2) where a correspondence has passed between the creditor and cautioner, which bars the cautioner *personali exceptione*, from pleading the Act;[5] (3) where the creditor has raised diligence against the cautioner during the seven years;[6] and (4) where the creditor has obtained decree against the cautioner.[7] Mere service of an action before the expiry of the seven years is, however, insufficient to elide the plea.[8]

A clause in the Act further provides that " what legal diligence by inhibition, horning, arrestment, adjudication, or any other way, shall be done, within the seven years, by creditors against their cautioners, for what fell due in that time, shall stand good and have its course and effect, after the expiry of the seven years, as if this Act had not been made."

Cautioner for Bank Agent.—When a cautioner becomes surety for the due performance of a bank agent's duties, or of his intromissions in that office, the utmost good faith on the part of the bank at the time of entering into the bond is necessary to render the cautioner liable.[9] Unless the cautioner in the bond expressly stipulates as to the supervision the bank is to exercise over the agent, he will not be freed of

---

[1] Alexander *v.* Badenach, 1843, 6 D. 322.

[2] Howison *v.* Howison, 1784, M. 11030.

[3] Alexander *v.* Badenach, *supra.*

[4] Sharp *v.* Harvey, 1808, M. App. Bill of Exchange, No. 22 ; but see Bills, p. 166.

[5] Douglas, Heron & Co. *v.* Riddick, 1793, M. 11032 ; *affd.* H.L. 4 Pat. 133 ; Stocks *v.* M'Lagan, 1890, 17 R. 1122.

[6] Irving *v.* Copeland, 1752, M. 11043.

[7] Douglas, Heron & Co. *v.* Riddick, *supra.*

[8] Bell's Com. (M'L.'s ed.) i. 376.

[9] Smith *v.* Bank of Scotland, 1829, 7 S. 244 ; 4 F. 300 ; Ross's L.C. iii. 66 (Commercial Law). See also Royal Bank *v.* Rankin, 1844, 6 D. 1418 ; M'Dougall & Herbertson *v.* Northern Assurance Co., 1864, 2 M. 935.

his obligation merely by showing that the bank has been negligent in exercising its supervision, but he must be able to prove something amounting almost to fraud or actual connivance on the bank's part at the wrong-doing of its agent before he can be so freed.[1] A cautioner for a bank agent, who by the terms of his bond of caution becomes cautioner for overdrafts on cash-credits sanctioned by the agent, is not liable under his bond for overdrafts on the agent's own private account-current known to the bank, as these are truly advances by the bank to its agent, and not by the agent on behalf of a customer.[2] It is to be observed, however, that any important change in the duties or responsibilities of the agent, unassented to by the cautioner, will free the latter.[3] Like other cautioners, a cautioner for a bank agent may terminate his responsibility on giving the bank reasonable notice of his intention so to do. The cautioner's liability does not fall with his death, but remains binding on his representatives, and it is not incumbent on the bank to give such representatives notice of the existence of the bond.[4]

2. Bonds of Credit

General Description.—We are indebted to the Royal Bank for the introduction of the Bond of Credit, or Cash-Credit Bond as it is some-times called, a form of obtaining cash advances, which in its inception was peculiar to Scotland, and which has very materially aided in develop-ing the commerce of the country. The Royal Bank was founded in 1727, and soon found that " in the very contracted sphere of commerce in Scotland at that time there were not sufficient commercial bills in circulation to exhaust the credit of the banks ; they had, as it were, a superfluity of credit on hand ; and the new bank devised a scheme for getting its credit into circulation. It agreed, on receiving sufficient guarantees, to open credits to certain limited amounts in favour of respectable and trustworthy persons. A cash-credit is therefore a drawing account created in favour of a customer, upon which he may operate precisely in the same manner as upon an ordinary account ; the only difference being that, instead of receiving interest on the daily balance at his credit, he pays interest on the daily balance at his debit. It is therefore merely an inverse drawing account. Every man in business, however humble or however extensive, must necessarily keep a certain portion of his money by him to answer immediate demands for small

---

[1] British Guarantee Association v. Western Bank, 1853, 15 D. 834 ; Biggar v. Wright, 1846, 9 D. 78 ; M'Taggart v. Watson, 1835, 1 S. & M. 553.

[2] North of Scotland Banking Co. v. Fleming, 1882, 10 R. 217.

[3] Holme v. Brunskill, L.R. 3 Q.B.D. 495 ; Lewis v. Jones, 1825, 4 B. & C. 506 ; Ross's L.C. iii. 96 (Commercial Law).

[4] British Linen Co. v. Monteith, 1858, 20 D. 557.

daily expenses, wages, and other things. This could, of course, be much more profitably employed in his business, where it might produce a profit of fifteen to twenty per cent. instead of lying idle. But unless the trader knew that he could command it at a moment's notice, he would always be obliged to keep a certain portion of ready money in his own till, or he must be able to command the use of some one else's till. Now, one object of a cash-credit is to supply this convenience to the trader, to enable him to invest the whole of his capital in business, and, upon proper security being given, to furnish him with the accommodation of a till at a moment's notice, in such small sums as he may require, on his paying a moderate interest for the accommodation." [1] Although, properly speaking, the credit thus obtained is merely an overdraft on a current account, which fluctuates from day to day, it has an advantage over an ordinary unsecured overdraft, in so far as a less rate of interest, usually a half per cent., is charged upon it. It has, further, an advantage over the method of obtaining credit by the discounting of a bill, drawn or accepted for the accommodation of the customer by one or more of his friends, in so far as interest is paid only on that sum which actually stands at the debit of the customer's account, and not, as in the case of the bill, on the full amount of the advance. But perhaps the most signal advantage which can be claimed for the cash-credit is, that it directly encourages thrift and frugality in the conduct of business, since, as a customer is charged interest only on the actual sum at the debit of his account, it will necessarily be to his advantage to make as few drafts as possible on his account ; and as he is under an obligation to his friends, in respect of their becoming surety for him, to repay the amount of his overdraft, he may reasonably be expected so to conduct his business as to avoid, so far as possible, incurring any risk which might result in loss to them. In addition to which, the co-obligants, who will naturally keep a watchful eye on the proceedings of the customer, have always the right of inspecting his account with the bank, and of stopping further supplies at any time if they see fit.

Nature of the Bond.—The bond proceeds on the narrative that the whole granters thereof have obtained a credit for a specified sum with a particular bank, in name of one of their number, and that they bind and oblige themselves and their heirs, jointly and severally, to repay to the bank, up to the amount of the specified sum, such sum as may be due to the bank on the account, including interest, whether the amount have been drawn out by the holder, or be due by him in respect of bills, drafts, cheques, etc. Unless specially provided for in the bond, the holder cannot by mandate authorise any person to operate on the account.

Liability of the Obligants.—So far as liability to the bank is con-

---

[1] Macleod's Theory and Practice of Banking, i. 345.

cerned, no distinction is made between the obligants, who are severally liable as though the drafts upon the account had been signed by each of them. Where the credit is for behoof of a company or firm, or where a firm or co-partnership are the co-obligants, special provision is made that no death, retirement, substitution, or addition of any partner or partners, or no dissolution or change in the co-partnery, shall affect the obligation contained in the bond. The sums due are stated to be repayable on demand. It is provided that any account or certificate, signed by an official of the bank, shall ascertain, specify, and constitute the sums or balances of principal and interest to be due, and shall warrant all executorials of law for such sums or balances and interest, whereof no suspension shall pass but on consignation only. This does not mean that the account may be kept in any way the bank thinks fit. It must be kept in the ordinary course of business, and in the usual way in which a cash account is kept. The certificate is not conclusive evidence between the parties, rebutting evidence being competent in proceedings under a suspension.[1] The stipulation that no suspension is to pass except on consignation is not effectual, as it is an interference with the discretionary power inherent in the Court, and while, no doubt, such a stipulation will receive due weight from the Court, it will not be allowed to interfere with the principles of law and justice.[1] The co-obligants are not liable for any sum in excess of the limit of the credit with the interest thereon from the date of the last balance of the account. The person in whose name the account is kept, and who operates on it, is, in law, merely the mandatary of the others, any one of whom may at pleasure intimate to the bank that he desires to withdraw from the credit, except where such withdrawal is inconsistent with the nature of the obligation undertaken, as where the bond bears to have been granted for a specific time. On receipt of such intimation, the bank's duty is to stop further operations on the account. Should the bank, subsequent to such an intimation, continue to allow operations, the result is, that while any sum paid into the account after the date of the intimation will be held as a reduction of the amount due as at such date, any sum drawn out of the account cannot be charged against the co-obligants, as the first item on the debit side is held to be discharged or reduced by the first item on the credit side.[2] The principal obligant, however, still remains bound for any debit balance apart from the bond. The course which ought to be followed by the bank on receipt of such an intimation, is to stop further operations on the account under the credit, and call for a settlement. If so advised, they may, however, open a new account in the principal's own name and allow operations thereon. The principle just stated will not apply to such new account.

---

[1] Gilmour v. Finnie, 1831, 9 S. 907.
[2] Devaynes v. Noble (Clayton's case). See Banker and Customer, p. 25.

Where the amount of the original bond is restricted, while the original agreement subsists between the parties, the bank is entitled to hold any securities deposited, against all debts due by the obligants, even although such securities have been deposited to meet the amount so specifically restricted. Thus in one case, a sum of £10,000 was allowed a firm, consisting of three partners, on cash-credit, the bond providing that all sums for which the firm might be liable were to be placed to the debit of the account. One of the partners died, and the firm induced the bank to restrict the sum for which the remaining partners were to be liable to £5000, at the same time pledging securities to cover that sum. The firm and the individual partners were subsequently sequestrated, being due to the bank at the time the sum of £5000 on the cash-credit, and an additional sum of £3000 on bills which the bank had discounted. The trustee on the sequestrated estate of one of the partners claimed that the bank were entitled to hold the securities pledged in security only of the restricted credit of £5000, and after reimbursing themselves to this extent, were bound to hand over the surplus amount to him, as the securities had been deposited for a specific purpose. The Court held that, as the original agreement between the bank and the obligants still subsisted, the amount of the credit only being restricted, the bank was entitled to hold the securities against all debts due by the obligants, the fact that the credit was restricted to a specific sum being no bar to the obligants asking, or the bank's granting, credit to a much greater extent.[1]

Although those who are in truth cautioners subscribe as principal obligants, and the technical term "cautioner" is not used, they are, nevertheless, entitled to the equities of cautioners,[2] though not to the benefits of their legal privileges, such as the prescription applicable to cautionary obligations.[3] A co-obligant who enters into a bond on behalf of another is held to have satisfied himself of that other's financial condition.[4] Consequently it has been decided that the bank is not bound to disclose to a surety the particular application of the money which is to be advanced, even though it should be intended and applied to pay off an existing credit. If the cautioner wishes to limit the application of the money obtained under a bond, he must so stipulate with his principal, and secure himself by some private obligation or penalty against failure to comply with it; for the bank is neither bound nor entitled to inquire into the application of a draft made upon a cash-credit which they may have granted. The party is the best judge of how

---

[1] Muir (Alston's Tr.) v. Royal Bank of Scotland, 1893, 20 R. 887.

[2] Fleming v. Royal Bank, 1825, 4 S. & D. 224, 2 W. & S. 27; M'Cartney v. M'Kenzie, 5 W. & S. 504; S. & D. 862. See Discharge of Cautioners, p. 269.

[3] See p. 276; Paterson v. Bonar, 1844, 6 D. 987.

[4] See also Cautionary Obligations, supra.

he ought to apply his cash-credit, and having granted the credit the bank is bound to answer the draft without inquiry. In like manner the bank cannot be called upon to refuse payment if the holder wishes to apply it in paying a debt due to themselves. When, however, a new bond is taken to replace one then in existence, the bank are not entitled, at their own hand, to transfer from the new account a sum sufficient to clear off the amount at the debit of the old account.[1] This difficulty is, however, obviated by the person entitled to operate on the new account passing a cheque on it for the amount at the debit of the old account, and the bank are, on receiving such a cheque, entitled to debit the new and credit the old account therewith. In a case in which this principle was applied, it was held that the bank were under no obligation to disclose to a co-obligant the fact that the party in whose favour the credit had been obtained stood indebted to them in a sum similar in amount to the extent of the bond under which he was an obligant.[2] Nor is the bank bound, or even entitled, to give information of the state of any customer's account to any inquirer, and if any person should come to a bank, and state that he had been applied to by such a person to be cautioner for him to the bank, and that he wished to know how his account stood, or whether he was regular or otherwise in his dealings with the bank, the banker would not feel himself entitled to give this information without due authority from the party, and he would desire the cautioner to bring this authority to him, and he would then be bound to furnish all the information in his power, and a failure to do so correctly would unquestionably liberate the cautioner.[3]

Interposition of Surety.—A surety who interposes in a bank credit already granted will be liable for any sums advanced either before, or after, the date of the bond. But to make a surety responsible for a debt of the principal contracted prior to the surety's interposition in the bond, there must have been a fair disclosure of the state of the account, or else a distinct stipulation in the bond relating to past advances.[4]

Operations on the Account.—When the bond has been duly delivered,[5] operations proceed on the credit as on an ordinary current account, a voucher being necessary for every payment by the bank.

Debit of Bills to Account.—It was at one time doubted whether, if a banker did not enter a bill to the debit of the cash-credit at the time of discounting it, he could afterwards do so, or, if the bill was not truly for the benefit of the holder of the credit, whether this could be done

---

[1] Paterson v. Bonar, *supra.*
[2] Hamilton v. Watson, 1845, 4 Bell's App. 67.
[3] *Per* Lord Medwyn in Hamilton v. Watson, 1842, 5 D. 280.
[4] Falconer v. North of Scotland Banking Co., 1863, 1 M. 704.
[5] See Cautionary Obligations, p. 267.

at all. It has, however, been decided that a banker is entitled to debit the account with the whole obligations of the principal debtor, whether such advance has been made directly on the security of the bond, or was not at the time specifically brought into the account.[1] If, however, the bank debit the account with a discounted bill, upon which the holder of the credit is, along with others, liable, and subsequently moneys are paid in sufficient to clear off the bill after the account has been so debited, the principles of Clayton's case will apply,[2] and the bank will lose what claim they may have had on the other parties liable on the bill. If the bank desire to hold the other parties to the bill bound, the proper course is not to debit the account with the bill, but to keep it separate as an isolated transaction.

Termination of the Credit.—While the death of the principal obligant necessarily brings the credit to an end, it is otherwise in the case of individual sureties. Their obligation is held to be a continuing one, and therefore to transmit against their representatives. Thus, upon the death of an individual co-obligant, his estate is liable in repayment, not only of such sums as may be due at the time of death, but also of any sums drawn out after the surety's death, and that whether or not the deceased's representatives have notice of the existence of the bond.[3] For a bank's protection, and to obviate the risk of the estate being disposed of before the amount due upon the bond is paid up, notice of the existence of the bond should always be given to the representatives of a deceased co-obligant. In the case of death of one of the sureties, banks are occasionally asked to relieve his representatives of their obligations under the bond. If the bank is willing, this may be done with the consent of the remaining obligants. The course usually adopted is for the surviving obligants to address a letter to the bank, requesting that such relief be granted, and agreeing that, notwithstanding the relief, their obligation will remain binding and effectual. Upon receipt of this letter the bank intimates the relief.[4] In the Appendix will be found the form usually employed in such a case, with the letter from the bank granting the relief. The forms can be altered to suit the case of a surviving obligant desiring to be relieved of his obligation. A bank is entitled, provided that it does not act capriciously, and gives due notice of its intention to the principal obligant, to bring the credit to an end at any time, even though it has not been operated upon to the full extent.[5]

---

[1] Liddel v. Sir Wm. Forbes & Co., July 1820 ; Bell's Com. (M'L.'s ed.) i. 386.

[2] Devaynes v. Noble, see p. 25.

[3] British Linen Co. v. Monteith, 1858, 20 D. 557 ; Midland Ry. Co. v. Sylvester, 1895, L.R. 1 Ch. 573.

[4] See Appendix.

[5] Johnston v. Commercial Bank, 1858, 20 D. 790 ; Parkinson v. Wakefield & Co., 1889, 5 T.L.R. 562.

Effect of "Ultimate Loss Clause."—In a case decided in 1907, the bond of credit founded on, which otherwise was in the usual terms, contained the following clause : " and in general to refund to the said bank whatever loss and expense not exceeding said sum of £ of principal the said bank may sustain or incur through their transactions with the said   ; all which sums, losses, and expenses the bank may debit to the said current account, without losing any right, remedy, or claims competent against other obligants; it being the express meaning of these presents that this bond shall to the extent foresaid be a covering security to the said bank against any ultimate loss that may arise on the transactions of the said   with said bank." The principal obligant suspended payment at a time when he was indebted to the bank in sums in excess of the amount stated in the bond. The bank ranked upon the insolvent estate for the full amount due to them, and received a dividend, which after being applied to the account left a considerable sum due over and above the amount mentioned in the bond. The bank then claimed from the solvent obligants the maximum liability under the bond, on the ground that the clause above quoted was a general guarantee against all loss which the bank might sustain through their transactions with the principal debtor, the only limit being that the total loss should not exceed the amount in the bond. The solvent obligants on the other hand maintained that they were entitled to the benefit of the dividend in respect of the sum in the bond, and that their liability was limited to the deficiency. This contention was upheld, on the ground that on a construction of the bond the obligation of the parties other than the principal debtor as between them and the bank was applicable only to the debt due by the principal debtor, which was co-extensive with the amount stated in the bond. It was pointed out that had the solvent obligants (or either of them) paid the full amount stated in the bond to the bank they (or he) would have been entitled in relief to an assignation of the bank's right to rank on the principal obligant's estate for that sum.[1]

Diligence on the Bond.—In the event of its being found necessary to proceed with diligence against any of the obligants, on the bond being recorded in the books of the Lords of Council and Session, an extract thereof is obtained which grants warrant for all lawful execution thereon. On this warrant arrestments can be used at once; but if a poinding of the debtor's effects, or proceedings by way of sequestration, be deemed advisable, a charge of six free days by a Messenger at Arms must be given.

---

[1] Veitch v. National Bank of Scotland Ltd., 1907, S.C. 554.

3. Guarantees

Nature and Kinds of Guarantees.—When an advance is intended to be of a temporary nature, or when it is otherwise found desirable, it is customary for banks to take a simple guarantee from one or more approved third parties, for the due repayment of any sum, or sums, with interest, advanced or to be advanced by them, to a customer. Guarantees are distinguished as those applicable : [1] (1) to a past advance ; (2) to a specific future transaction ; (3) prospectively to a future course of dealings limited, as regards the liability of the guarantor, to a certain specified sum, or without any pecuniary limit ; or (4) to discounts.[1]

Requisites and Execution.—Guarantees must be in writing and subscribed by the granter.[2] In this connection it must be kept in view that the Act which made this provision was passed to remedy certain inconveniences, said to have been felt by persons engaged in trade, by reason of the law of Scotland differing from that of England in some particulars in regard to matters of common occurrence in the course of trade. So far as guarantees relating to mercantile transactions are concerned, the only solemnities necessary in their execution are, that they should be in writing, and subscribed by the granter or by some one duly authorised by him. The creditor in such a guarantee should be named, but it is not necessary that the guarantee should be addressed to any person named specifically, provided the creditor is indicated with reasonable certainty.[3] The provisions of the statute only apply to guarantees in, or connected with, mercantile transactions. It has not yet been decided that a guarantee to a bank falls within this category, but a consideration of a series of decisions [4] relating to documents alleged to be guarantees *in re mercatoria* points to the conclusion that, while an improbative guarantee to a bank for future advances, followed by *rei interventus*, will be held binding, not because it is a document *in re mercatoria*, but because it has been followed by *rei interventus*, there cannot be said to be satisfactory authority for the opinion either that a guarantee for past advances, which by its nature is incapable of support by *rei interventus*, or that a guarantee for future advances unsupported by evidence of *rei interventus*, will be held binding.

---

[1] Forms of all such guarantees will be found in the Appendix.

[2] Mercantile Law Amendment Act, 1856, sec. 6.

[3] Clapperton, Paton & Co. *v.* Anderson, 1881, 8 R. 1004 ; Ewing *v.* Wright, 1808, 14 F.C. 172.

[4] Goodlet Campbell *v.* Lennox, 1739, M. 16979 ; Foggo *v.* Milliken, 1746, M. 16979 ; Campbell *v.* M'Lauchlan, 1752, M. 12286 ; Henderson *v.* Murray, 1765, M. 16986 ; Paterson *v.* Wright, 31st January 1810, F.C. ; *affd.* 4th July 1814, 17 F.C. 683 ; 6 Pat. App. 38 ; Thomson *v.* Gilkison, 1831, 9 S. 520 ; Ballantyne *v.* Carter, 1842, 4 D. 419 ; Johnston *v.* Grant, 1844, 6 D. 875.

It is not necessary to give effect to an improbative guarantee by reason of *rei interventus*, to prove the guarantor's knowledge of what followed his subscription, though proof of such knowledge might be very important as giving a character to the facts following the subscription of the guarantee, different to that which they might otherwise possess. The principle of *rei interventus* in such a case is, that the person signing such a document has given it over to the creditor to be used in the way and for the purpose intended, and that if others have acted on the faith of it, he is not entitled to turn round and plead defects in point of form against those whom he has encouraged to rely on his signature. The fact that money has been advanced upon the faith of the guarantee constitutes sufficient *rei interventus* to make it obligatory on the guarantors.[1] This principle is illustrated by reference to the following case :—A bank agreed to make advances to A. on his obtaining B.'s guarantee. A formal letter of guarantee, ending with the words " in witness whereof," was then prepared by the bank and handed to A. for execution by B. A. obtained B.'s signature, and afterwards got two persons to sign as witnesses who had not seen B. subscribe nor heard him acknowledge his subscription. A. returned the document to the bank with the names and designations of the witnesses, the testing clause was filled up by the bank, and the bank made an advance to A. upon the faith of the guarantee. In an action by the bank upon the letter of guarantee against B., the defender pleaded that he was not bound, as the deed was not tested. The above facts were admitted or proved. It was decided that the defender having signed the deed and delivered it to A., who was *in hac re* the bank's agent, he had delivered it to the bank as a guarantee for advances to be made to A., and that the bank having made advances on the faith of it, the defender's imperfect obligation had been validated by *rei interventus*.[2] As guarantees, however, are frequently taken by banks for past as well as for future advances, it is advisable that such guarantees should be either holograph of the granter or tested.[3]

Guarantees to bankers are generally executed on a printed form. In the execution of such guarantees, the course usually and properly followed is to have the blanks filled up, and to have the granter's subscription tested in the usual way by two witnesses. Occasionally, however, it may happen that the granter himself fills in the blanks and subscribes the document without the presence of attesting witnesses. In such a case the question arises, Does such a document possess the advantages of a document holograph of the granter so as to constitute

---

[1] Church of England Life Assurance Co. *v.* Wink, 1857, 19 D. 1079.
[2] National Bank of Scotland Ltd. *v.* Campbell, 1892, 19 R. 885.
[3] See as to Execution of Deeds, p. 43.

it a valid guarantee ?   The parts of such a document in the granter's
handwriting are those which, taken by themselves apart from the
printed form, would neither form complete sentences nor be intelligible.
A writing is held to be holograph of the granter where large sentences,
though not necessarily the whole document, are in his handwriting, and
the test of whether a document is holograph or not is, whether in its
essentials it is holograph of its granter.[1]   In the case under consideration the document contains neither large sentences, nor at least some
of its essentials, in the handwriting of the granter.   Such a document
would probably not be held valid as a holograph writing, and a bank,
therefore, might not be safe in accepting it.   To obviate any difficulty,
it is suggested that when a document executed in this manner is presented to a bank, or when it is desirable or convenient that the document
should be filled up and signed by the granter without witnesses, the
bank should insist on the granter adding a memorandum or docquet to
the following effect : " I adopt the above," and thereafter signing in the
usual way, a proceeding which would have the effect of rendering the
guarantee free from challenge.[2]

Construction and Interpretation.—There is sometimes considerable
difficulty in distinguishing between a guarantee which, to be probative,
must be in writing, and a primary obligation which is capable of proof
by parole.   Thus, where a person undertook to see that an account was
paid, it was held that this was a primary and substituted obligation in
which the guarantor was the principal debtor.[3]   So where, to induce a
railway company to complete their line to a certain town, several of the
inhabitants by a letter of guarantee bound themselves, to the extent of
the sums written opposite their respective signatures, upon the secretary
of the railway company obtaining an allotment of shares, to guarantee
him against any loss which he might sustain if he should not be able
to dispose of the shares at par within three years after the opening of
the line, it was held that the letter of guarantee was not of the nature
of a cautionary obligation, but was really one of the reciprocal stipulations to a mutual agreement which did not entitle the guarantors to
any of the equities of cautioners.[4]

Continuing Guarantees.—A continuing guarantee is one which
relates not to a specific obligation, but to a contemplated course of
dealing for the future.   The guarantor, if there be nothing to the
contrary expressed in his obligation, is not presumed to have granted

---

[1] Stair, iv. 42, 6.

[2] Gavine's Trs. v. Lee, 1883, 10 R. 448.

[3] Morrison v. Harkness, 1870, 9 M. 35.

[4] Milne v. Kidd, 1869, 8 M. 250 ; vide Milne v. Souter, 1868, 6 M. 977 ; Birkmyr
v. Darnell, 1 Sm. L.C. 326 ; Wilson v. Tate, 1840, 1 Rob. 137, 150 ; Blackwood v.
Forbes, 1848, 10 D. 920.

it on the faith of any specific conditions, but rather to have had in view the general usage of trade and the ordinary credit given among bankers. Where one guarantees all goods which may be furnished to a trader, or all sums that may be due to, or all bills which may be discounted by, a banker, he necessarily leaves the principal debtor and creditor free to arrange the details of their transactions as they think fit, so long as these are in conformity with the ordinary custom of merchants. Under a continuing guarantee, which is usually, but not invariably, limited to a definite amount, the guarantor is liable not only for one dealing to that amount, but for successive dealings up to the amount of the guarantee.[1] Any words which imply that a guarantee is applicable, not to a series of transactions or a continuous course of dealing but as a guarantee from loss in one transaction or advance, will receive effect. Thus, a letter in the terms, " as you have become security to the Clydesdale Bank for £150 on account of J. W., I hereby guarantee you against any loss by your doing so," was construed as a guarantee from loss on one advance of £150, and not as a continuing guarantee in security of advances on a cash-credit account.[2] A letter guaranteeing an overdraft on a current account has been decided to be a continuing guarantee.[3]

In one case a surety guaranteed the bank the payment of all sums of money which then were, or might thereafter from time to time become, due or owing to the bank from their customer, but nevertheless the total amount recoverable from the surety was not to exceed a stipulated amount. The guarantee was to be a continuing security, and any dividends which the bank might receive on the bankruptcy of their customer were not to prejudice their right to recover from the surety, to the full extent of the guarantee, any sums which after the receipt of such dividends might remain owing to them by their customer. On the customer's bankruptcy, the bank, after receiving the

---

[1] Downie v. Barr, 1840, 3 D. 59 ; Tennant & Co. v. Bunten, 1859, 21 D. 631 ; Veitch v. Murray & Co., 1864, 2 M. 1098 ; Caledonian Bank v. Kennedy's Trs., 1870, 8 M. 862 ; Stewart, Moir & Muir v. Brown, 1871, 9 M. 763 ; Cook v. Moffat, 1827, 5 S. 774 ; Prest, Brown & Prest v. Hotson, 1809, Hume, 97 ; Bowe & Christie v. Hutchison, 1868, 6 M. 642 ; vide Journ. of Jur. xv. 350 ; Wood v. Priestner, L.R. 2 Ex. 66, 282 ; Heffield v. Meadows, L.R. 4 C.P. 595 ; Laurie v. Scholefield, L.R. 4 C.P. 622 ; Coles v. Pack, L.R. 5 C.P. 65 ; Leathley v. Spyer, L.R. 5 C.P. 595 ; Eedes v. Boys, L.R. 10 Eq. 467 ; Burgess v. Eve, L.R. 13 Eq. 450 ; Nottingham Hide, etc., Co. Ltd. v. Bottrill, L.R. 8 C.P. 694 ; Morrell v. Cowan, L.R. 7 Ch. D. 151.
[2] Scott v. Mitchell, 1866, 4 M. 551. See also Rennie v. Smith's Trs., 1866, 4 M. 669 ; Baird v. Corbet, 1835, 14 S. 41 ; Wilson & Corse v. Woods, 1797, Hume, 85 ; Slade & Co. v. Black & Knox, 1808, Hume, 95 ; Melville v. Hayden, 3 B. & C. 593 ; Kay v. Groves, 6 Bing. 276.
[3] Sir W. Forbes & Co. v. Dundas, 1830, 8 S. 865. See also Houston's Exrs. v. Speirs, 1834, 12 S. 879.

19

limit of the guarantee from the surety, claimed, and were held entitled, to rank for the whole debt in the customer's sequestration, without any deduction.[1]

Limited Guarantees.—Nothing will be presumed which the terms of the guarantee do not expressly warrant, so any limitation which may be imposed will be rigidly interpreted.[2] A guarantee is limited to the persons to whom it is addressed.[3] Any limitation in regard to time,[4] or the number of transactions or operations to take place on the faith of it, will receive effect. If the guarantee bear that the transactions or operations intended to be secured are to take place under an account current, or implies that such is the plain intention of parties, it will be construed as a permanent and continuing guarantee.[5] The guarantee alone must be looked to for its terms. A separate agreement between the creditor and the principal debtor, unless it form part of the obligation, cannot be looked to for the interpretation of the terms of the obligation.[6]

Del Credere Guarantees.—This is an Italian phrase, akin to our word guarantee, meaning a guarantee by an agent in this country to a foreign principal, whereby the former in respect of higher remuneration undertakes to sell the goods of his principal, and keep him free from any loss arising through the insolvency of parties with whom he deals. Bankers have little concern with such guarantees.

Discharge and Relief of Guarantor.—The obligation of a guarantor in a continuing guarantee continues until recalled, and where his heirs, executors, or representatives are taken bound, does not fall by his death,[7] and is binding upon his representatives. In the absence of express provision, a continuing guarantee is revoked as to subsequent advances by notice of the death of the guarantor.[8] Where it is intended to hold the estate of a deceased guarantor liable for any sum due at the date of his death, the banker on receiving notice of his death should stop

---

[1] *Ex parte* National Provincial Bank of England Ltd., 1896, L.R. 2 Q.B. 12. See also Logan's Sequestration, 1908, 25 S.L.R. 160.

[2] Scott *v.* Mitchell, 1866, 4 M. 551 ; Rennie *v.* Smith's Trs., 1866, 4 M. 669. See also Smith *v.* Bank of Scotland, 1813, 1 Dow, 272 ; 1829, 7 S. 244 ; Paterson *v.* Wright, 1814, 6 Pat. 38 ; Napier & Co. *v.* Bruce, 1842, 1 Bell's App. 78 ; Downie *v.* Barr, 1840, 3 D. 59 ; Glynn *v.* Hertel, 8 Taunt. 208 ; Britannia Steamship Insurance Association Ltd. *v.* Duff, 1909, S.C. 1261.

[3] Bowie *v.* Watson, 1840, 2 D. 1061 ; Raimes *v.* Alexander, 1842, 4 D. 1167 ; Stewart *v.* Scott, 1803, Hume, 91 ; Bell's Com. i. 374.

[4] M'Lagan & Co. *v.* M'Farlan, 19th November 1813, F.C. ; Douglas *v.* Gordon, 24th December 1814, F.C. ; *vide* also cases under Continuing Guarantees, *supra.*

[5] Caledonian Banking Co. *v.* Kennedy's Trs., 1870, 8 M. 862.

[6] Nicholson *v.* Burt, 1882, 10 R. 121.

[7] Harris *v.* Fawcett, L.R. 15 Eq. 311 ; Lloyds *v.* Harper, L.R. 16 Ch. D. 290.

[8] Coulthart *v.* Clementson, 1879, L.R. 5 Q.B.D. 42.

operations on the guaranteed account.[1] The bank may, if they so desire, open a new account upon which transactions can proceed, but no credit entries should be made to the guaranteed account, as, if this is done, the principles of Clayton's case will apply. Similarly, where a guarantor intimates to the bank his intention to withdraw from the obligations undertaken by him, the proper course for the bank is to stop operations on the guaranteed account, and to open a fresh account, upon which operations can proceed. This was decided in a case where five persons guaranteed the account of a limited company. Two of the guarantors intimated to the bank their desire to withdraw from the guarantee. The bank then closed the account, which was debtor in a considerable sum. Immediately thereafter the directors of the company made a call on the shareholders, payable at the bank for the unpaid amount of their shares. The sums so received were placed to the credit of an account called " No. II. call account," and this account was always kept creditor. Subsequently a third account was opened, upon which the ordinary operations of the company took place. On the company going into liquidation, a question was raised as to the amount due by the guarantors, who claimed that the call made upon the shares should have been applied to reduce the balance due on the guaranteed account, but the Court negatived this contention, and held that the bank were not bound to apply the call money to the extinction of the balance due on the guaranteed account.[2] The principles explained as to the discharge of cautioners apply to guarantees.[3] A guarantor, if he pays up the full amount, is entitled to relief from the principal debtor. Where the principal debtor becomes bankrupt, an important distinction exists between the position of a surety under a cash-credit bond and that of a guarantor under the forms of guarantee in use with bankers. The cautioner under a bond of credit may, on the bankruptcy of the principal debtor, pay up the amount due under the bond, and thereafter rank on the bankrupt estate for the amount he has so paid, even although the bank may have further claims upon the same estate. But in the case of a guarantee under similar circumstances, the bank is entitled to rank upon the bankrupt estate for the full amount of its claim of every kind, and, having drawn all it can under such ranking, thereafter to recover any deficiency from the guarantor up to the limit of his guarantee. As there can be no double ranking upon the same estate, the effect of this principle is to preclude the guarantor from participating in any benefit under the sequestration.[4] The legal principle upon which this rule is established is, that a guarantor guarantees the

---

[1] London and County Banking Co. *v.* Terry, 1884, L.R. 25 Ch. D. 692.
[2] Buchanan *v.* Main, 1900, 3 F. 215.
[3] See p. 269.
[4] See Sequestration " Double Ranking."

whole debt, but stipulates that his payment is to be restricted to a specified sum.[1] When a guarantor pays the amount of his guarantee before the sequestration of the principal debtor and receives delivery of his guarantee, although with a receipt indorsed thereon, containing a reservation in the following or like terms : " This payment is accepted under reservation of and without prejudice to our right to claim on the estate of the said . . . for the full amount of his indebtedness," and the amount so received is placed to the credit of a separate account in the books of the bank in name of the agent for the obligations of the guarantor, on the subsequent sequestration of the principal debtor the bank are bound to deduct from the amount of their claim the payment so received from the guarantor. It has been decided [2] that payments from a guarantor prior to sequestration must be deducted " whatever may have been the terms of the guarantee under which the payments were made." It is respectfully thought this decision requires reconsideration. It is as yet an undecided point, whether, if a bank demanded payment from a guarantor before exhausting the bankrupt's estate, and the guarantor paid the amount due by him and demanded an assignation to the extent of the amount so paid, the bank would be entitled to withhold such an assignation, and so to preclude the guarantor ranking on the estate and drawing a dividend in preference to the bank. It is a safe general rule for a bank first to exhaust the bankrupt estate, and then to call upon the guarantors to make good any deficiency.

Guarantor Entitled to be Relieved of his Obligation by Principal Debtor at any Time.—It has been decided that under a letter of guarantee to a bank which contained the usual clause, " this guarantee is to remain in force until recalled by me in writing," the guarantor, although he had not been called upon to pay anything, was entitled to be relieved of his obligation, on giving reasonable notice to the person on whose behalf the guarantee had been granted. The defender did not within the time specified by the Court pay the amount due to the bank, and accordingly the Court ordained him to free and relieve the pursuer by making payment to the bank of all sums due under the guarantee, and to obtain and deliver to the pursuer a discharge of his liability from the bank. Assuming the defender is unable to implement an order such as this, it is difficult to see what the guarantor could do unless to apply to the Court for a warrant to imprison the debtor.[3]

Hypothecation of Letters of Guarantee.—Letters of guarantee

---

[1] Houston's Exrs. *v.* Speirs, 1835, 13 S. 945 ; Ellis *v.* Emmanuel, L.R. 1 Ex. D. 157 ; Harvie's Trs. *v.* Bank of Scotland, 1885, 12 R. 1141.

[2] Mackinnon's Tr. *v.* Bank of Scotland, 1915, S.C. 411.

[3] Doig *v.* Lawrie, 1902, 5 F. 295.

are not negotiable instruments, and hence the hypothecation or pledge of the *ipsa corpora* of letters of guarantee creates no right or security over the funds or the letters in favour of the person in whose hands the letters may be placed.[1]

---

[1] Robertson *v.* British Linen Co. Bank, 1891, 18 R. 1225.

PART IV

INSOLVENCY AND SEQUESTRATION

CHAPTER I

INSOLVENCY

So long as a person remains solvent, his creditors, if they find it necessary to proceed against him for payment of his debts or performance of his obligations, must do so according to certain recognised processes of law. When, however, a person is so situated financially as to give his creditors reasonable grounds for averring that, though still in a position to meet his current liabilities, he is *vergens ad inopiam*, or bordering on insolvency, the law recognises a right on the creditor's part, when the debt or obligation is prestable in the future, to require from the debtor security for the due payment of the debt or the performance of the obligation, and in certain cases to take proceedings for the purpose of securing his claims, which would otherwise be inadmissible and oppressive. Thus, for example, a person who sells goods to another on credit may, if the buyer be *vergens ad inopiam*, refuse to deliver the goods without security for the due payment of the price.[1]

When a debtor comes to a point at which he can no longer pay his way, according to the obligations he has undertaken, he is insolvent, and it is immaterial whether the cause of his insolvency have arisen from actual want of funds or from the fact that his assets are unrealisable.[2] So soon as the state of insolvency has arisen, the law assigns to the debtor a definite position, and gives his creditors certain rights with regard to his property. Insolvency, unlike bankruptcy, is not a *status* fixed by any public legal criterion, but depends on the circumstances of each individual case. When a person becomes insolvent, he becomes to all intents and purposes a mere trustee of his property for behoof of the general body of his creditors, and any

---

[1] For further illustrations, see Stoppage *in transitu*, *supra* ; Arrestment in Security and Inhibitions, *infra*.

[2] Teenan's Trs. *v.* Teenan, 1886, 13 R. 833.

fraudulent alienation of his estate which he may make in prejudice of his creditors is reducible, either at common law or by statute. A person who is insolvent, and who is contemplating bankruptcy, whether he knows that he is on the verge of insolvency, or is really in ignorance of it, is disabled, as a general rule, from giving part of his property to some creditors, with a view of giving them a preference over his other creditors. But a man who is insolvent, and knows that he cannot pay all his creditors, is at liberty to prefer any of his creditors he pleases where their debts are due in actual money. He is at liberty to give the full sum of their debts to some creditors, and not to others, though he is not at liberty to give any pledge of them in security of his debt. Nor does the creditor's knowledge of his debtor's insolvency bar him from receiving payment of his debt.[1] But cash payments, like other preferences, will be set aside whenever the creditor is not merely affected with a suspicion or knowledge of his debtor's embarrassed affairs or even insolvency, but when he has a full and certain knowledge that the debtor is immediately to become openly bankrupt, and in that knowledge not only connives, but actively concerts with him a plan for diverting to himself the funds that truly belong to the whole body of creditors.[2]

Alienations Reducible at Common Law.—At common law, independently of such preferences as are struck at by the Acts 1621, cap. 18, and 1696, cap. 5, which will be noticed shortly, any preference granted by an insolvent to a favoured creditor, or any donation to a friend, or, in short, any act, such as the indorsation of a bill or delivery order, or the granting of any additional security or advantage whatever, by which the insolvent prevents or defeats a fair division of his estate among his creditors, will be set aside. In such cases the issue sent to the jury is, " Whether the said disposition was granted by the said A. B., and taken by the defender fraudulently to disappoint the rights of the creditors of the said A. B." [3] The receiver's fraud is not a necessary element in the challenge.[4] The fact that the granter is himself conscious of his own insolvency is necessary to reduce a transaction

---

[1] *Per* Lord Young in Coutts' Tr. & Doe *v.* Webster, 1886, 13 R. 1112 ; Thomas *v.* Thomson, 1865, 3 M. 358.

[2] Taylor (Jones' Tr.) *v.* Jones, 1888, 15 R. 328.

[3] Bell's Com. (M'L.'s ed.) i. 8, and ii. 182 and 197 ; Wilson *v.* Drummond, 1853, 16 D. 275 ; Dobie *v.* Macfarlane, 1854, 17 D. 97. See also M'Ewen *v.* Doig, 1828, 6 S. 889; Wilson's Trs. *v.* Raeburn and Others, 1900, 38 S.L.R. 228 ; M'Innes and Others *v.* M'Callum, 1901, 9 S.L.T. 171 (O.H.) ; Logan's Trs. *v.* Logan, 1903, 11 S.L.T. 14 (O.H.).

[4] Edmond *v.* Grant, 1853, 15 D. 703 ; Thomas *v.* Thomson, 1866, 5 M. 198 ; Lawrie's Trs. *v.* Beveridge, 1867, 6 M. 85 ; M'Cowan *v.* Wright, 15 D. 494. See also Forsyth *v.* Duncan, 1861, 1 M. 1054.

at common law.[1] Therefore, transactions in the ordinary course of business, or in implement of prior obligations, are not struck at.

The alienation sought to be reduced must be voluntary and prejudicial to the insolvent's creditors,[2] and they, or a trustee in bankruptcy, have a good title to insist on the reduction.[3] So stringent is the law, that not only is the alienation itself reducible, but a debtor who being insolvent "away puts, secretes, or conceals" his effects with intent to defraud his creditors, may be tried before the High Court of Justiciary for so doing.[4]

Deeds Challengeable under Act 1621, cap. 18.—The Court of Session, by an Act of Sederunt dated 12th July 1620, declared that, "in all actions pursued by any true creditor for recovery of his just debt, or satisfaction of his lawful action and right, they will decreet and decern all alienations, dispositions, assignations, and translations whatsoever, made by the debtor of any of his lands, teinds, reversions, actions, debts, or goods whatsoever, to any conjunct or confident person, without true, just, and necessary cause, and without a just price really paid, the same being done after the contracting of lawful debts (that is, of course, debts beyond the measure of his ability to pay)[5] from true creditors, to have been, from the beginning, and to be in all time coming, null and of no avail, force, or effect, at the instance of the true and just creditor, by way of action, exception, or reply, without further declarator." The Act 1621, cap. 18, ratified and approved the Act of Sederunt, and further provided that, where the subject alienated by the insolvent is *bonâ fide* acquired by purchase, or in satisfaction of a just and lawful debt, by a third person from such conjunct and confident person, "the right lawfully acquired by him, who was nowise partaker of the fraud, shall not be annulled in manner foresaid, but the receiver of the price of the said subject from the buyer shall be holden and obliged to make the same forthcoming, to the behoof of the bankrupt's true creditors, in payment of their lawful debts"; and it also declared that it should be sufficient proof of the fraud intended against the creditors, "if they, or any of them, shall be able to verify, by writ or oath of the party receiver of any security from the bankrupt, that the same was made without any just and necessary cause, or without any true and competent price, or that the whole or most part of the price of the lands and goods of the bankrupt, being sold by him who bought them from the bankrupt, was converted, or intended to be converted, to the bankrupt's profit and use."

---

[1] Galbraith (M'Dougall's Tr.) v. Ironside, 1914, S.C. 186.

[2] Forrest v. Robertson's Tr., 4 R. 22 ; Main v. Fleming's Trs., 8 R. 880.

[3] Bankruptcy Act, 1913, sec. 9.

[4] Clendinnen, 1875, 3 R. (Just.) 3.

[5] Gartland v. Kerr, 1632, M. 915 ; Clerk v. Stewart, 1675, M. 917 ; Ballantyne v. Dunlop, 17th February 1814, F.C.

Effect of Act.—The effect of the Act, as will be noticed, is to materially strengthen the common-law prohibition of the gratuitous alienation of their estates by insolvent debtors, and to declare that to be a substantive fraud in itself, which, prior to the Act, was merely a circumstance from which fraud might be inferred and proved.

Presumptions against Insolvent.—The result of the decisions interpreting the Act, show that where an insolvent has granted a conveyance of his goods to a conjunct and confident person, there is a presumption (first) that at the time when the debtor granted the alienation challenged he was insolvent ; and (second) that the alienation was made gratuitously.[1] The benefit of this legal presumption may be lost by *mora*,[2] and may be overcome by proof.

Conveyances Struck at.—The conveyances subject to challenge include deeds of all sorts, conveyances, assignations, contracts, obligations, bills, promissory notes,[3] discharges, and generally whatever may confer on the grantee property belonging to the debtor, or enable him to claim as a creditor in competition with the true creditors of the granter, or save him from a demand for payment of what he owes to the debtor.[4]

To bring a transaction within the scope of the Act, the following circumstances must coexist :—(1) The alienation sought to be reduced must have been made to a *conjunct or confident person*. Conjunct persons include brothers, sisters, sons, sons-in-law, uncles by consanguinity or affinity, step-sons, sisters- or brothers-in-law ; partners in business, a factor or steward, a confidential man of business, a servant or other dependant, are examples of confident persons.[5] Where a husband within sixty days of bankruptcy sold his business to his wife for an inadequate price, the transaction was reduced.[6] But where a debtor, three months before his sequestration, married, having first, with the object of defeating his creditors, entered into a marriage contract which had the result of making him insolvent, it was held in an action at the instance of his trustee, that the contract was not reducible, but the opinion was reserved as to what the effect might have been had it been proved that the wife was cognisant of the intended fraud or had it been shown that the provision made for her was exorbitant.[7]

---

[1] Dawson *v.* Thorburn, 1888, 15 R. 895, *per* Lord Rutherfurd Clark ; North British Ry. Co. *v.* White and Others, 1882, 20 S.L.R. 129 ; Bolden *v.* Ferguson, 1863, 1 M. 522 ; Wilson *v.* Drummond's Reps., 1853, 16 D. 278, *per* Lord Rutherfurd.

[2] Blackwood *v.* Hamilton's Crs., 1749, M. 904 ; Elliot *v.* Elliot, 1749, M. 905 ; Guthrie *v.* Williamson, 1711, M. 1020.

[3] Thomas *v.* Thomson, 1865, 3 M. 1160.

[4] Bell's Com. ii. 174.

[5] Edmond *v.* Grant, 1853, 15 D. 703.

[6] Tennant *v.* Miller, 1897, 4 S.L.T. 440.

[7] M'Lay *v.* M'Queen, 1899, 1 F. 804.

On the other hand, where a husband gifted his estate to his wife under cloak of making an adequate provision for her, with the result of rendering himself insolvent, it was held that the gift was reducible at the instance of the husband's trustee in sequestration.[1] Trustees under a testamentary settlement are not rendered conjunct or confident persons by the fact that the beneficiaries for whom they act fall within this category.[2] With regard to ante-nuptial trustees, the opinion has been expressed that such persons are third parties representing those who, at the time of their appointment, were not conjunct or confident to each other.[3] (2) The alienation must have been "without true, just, and necessary cause, and without a just price really paid," that is, *without an onerous consideration.*[4] The price must be just, that is, fairly adequate to the value of the subject alienated.[5] To place an alienation by an insolvent debtor outwith the scope of the Act, it is not, however, necessary that the consideration be a payment in cash. Any deed granted for a genuine and adequate consideration, pecuniary or other, or in consequence and implement of a previous specific obligation, as for example one granted in implement of a legal obligation incurred while solvent,[6] or of provisions contained in an ante-nuptial contract of marriage,[7] is free from challenge under the statute. A post-nuptial contract of marriage may be a true, just, and necessary cause, within the meaning of the statute, and as such it is not affected by the statute, except to the extent that the onus of proving it to be so is thrown upon the wife.[8] (3) The debtor must have been *insolvent* when he executed the deed, and bankrupt or insolvent at the raising of the action for setting aside the alienation. (4) The party challenging the deed must have been a creditor at the date of the alienation,[9] his debt must have had its origin prior thereto, or he must have advanced money to pay off prior creditors, in whose place he comes. A trustee in bankruptcy, under sequestration,[10] or even a trust-deed, has a sufficient title to sue under the Act, if the debt of the creditor whom he represents

---

[1] Robertson's Trs. *v.* Robertson, 1901, 3 F. 359.

[2] Young *v.* Darroch's Trs., 1835, 13 S. 305.

[3] *Per* L. J.-C. Moncreiff in Watson *v.* Grant's Trs., 1874, 1 R. 882.

[4] Grant *v.* Grant, 1748, M. 951 ; Dawson *v.* Thorburn, 1888, 15 R. 891.

[5] Hodge *v.* Morrison, 1883, 21 S.L.R. 40.

[6] Horne *v.* Hay, 1847, 9 D. 651 ; Thomas *v.* Thomson, 1866, 5 M. 198 ; Williamson *v.* Allan, 1882, 9 R. 859 ; Matthew's Tr. *v.* Matthew, 1867, 5 M. 957.

[7] Garden *v.* Stirling, 1822, 2 S. 39 ; Mackenzie *v.* Cotton's Trs., 1877, 5 R. 313. See also Dawson *v.* Thorburn, and M'Lay *v.* M'Queen, *supra.*

[8] Bell's Com. ii. 176 ; Hodge *v.* Morrison, 1883 ; Robertson's Trs. *v.* Robertson, 1901, 3 F. 359.

[9] Mansfield *v.* Stewart, 1833, 11 S. 389 ; M'Cowan *v.* Wright, 1852, 14 D. 968 ; Edmond *v.* Grant, 1853, 15 D. 703.

[10] Bankruptcy Act, 1913, sec. 9.

had its origin prior to the date of the alienation. By section 9 of the Act of 1913, the trustee's power is extended, in so far that he is entitled to set aside any deed or alienation *for behoof of the whole body of creditors*, and in so doing he is entitled to the presumption which would have been competent to any individual creditor.[1]   (5) The estate alienated must be such as might have been attached by the diligence of creditors.[2]   A challenge under the Act is competently made either by an action of reduction in the Court of Session, or by way of exception or reply to an action in the Court of Session or Sheriff Court.[3]

Deeds Challengeable under Act 1696, cap. 5.—By this Act it is declared that "all and whatsoever voluntar dispositions, assignations, or other deeds, which shall be found to be made and granted directly, or indirectly, by the foresaid dyvour or bankrupt, either at or after his becoming bankrupt,[4] or in the space of sixty days before, in favour of any of his creditors either for their satisfaction or farder security in preference to other creditors, to be void and null." The sixty days are held to have expired the moment the sixtieth day is begun.

The object of the statute is to preserve, as far as possible, equality among creditors, by restoring to the estate, for the benefit of all interested, any assets, whether heritable[5] or moveable, which by having been alienated in satisfaction or security of a prior debt within sixty days of insolvency, has disturbed the equal distribution of the insolvent's assets. It is not necessary for the purposes of the statute that there should be any want of *bonâ fides* in the alienation struck at, but only that the equality of the distribution of the insolvent's estate among his creditors has been disturbed. Thus the Act has been held to strike at bills of exchange granted by the bankrupt within the restricted period,[6] bills not yet due indorsed by the bankrupt in payment of past due furnishings,[7] a delivery order signed by the vendor in favour of the seller while the goods were still on their way to the consignee,[8] and

---

[1] Thomas *v.* Thomson, 1865, 3 M. 1160; M'Cowan *v.* Wright, 1852, 14 D. 968; Caird *v.* Key, 1857, 20 D. 187; Bolden *v.* Ferguson, 1863, 1 M. 522; Mackay's Prac. ii. 174.

[2] Bell's Com. (M'L.'s ed.) i. 52, and ii. 191; Buchanan *v.* Carrick, 1838, 16 S. 358.

[3] Bankruptcy Act, 1913, sec. 8.

[4] See Notour Bankruptcy, *infra.*

[5] Mitchell (Weir's Tr.) *v.* Mackenzie, 1868, 6 S.L.R. 107.

[6] Blaikie *v.* Wilson, 1st July 1803; Bell's Com. (M'L.'s ed.) ii. 204, note 5; Blincow's Trs. *v.* Allan & Co., 1828, 7 S. 124; 7 W. & S. 56; Mitchell *v.* Rodger, 1834, 12 S. 802; M'Cowan *v.* Wright, 1852, 14 D. 901 and 968; Ehrenbacher & Co. *v.* Kennedy, 1874, 1 R. 1131; Nicol *v.* M'Intyre, 1882, 9 R. 1097; Thomson on Bills, p. 518.

[7] Horsburgh *v.* Ramsay, 1885, 12 R. 1171.

[8] Wright *v.* Moncrieff Mitchell, 10th February 1871, 9 M. 516.

mortgages over ships.[1] In short, it may safely be stated as the law, that, under the statute, any act whatever affecting the insolvent's estate, whereby the equality of distribution is disturbed, will be set aside.[2] The question has been raised as to whether the Act applies to bankers receiving negotiable securities such as bills to be discounted or credited to the customer's account within the statutory period of challenge, with the result that the banker obtains a right of property over the securities. The question was decided in favour of the banker,[3] and the law was thus stated : " A banker is entitled in the ordinary course of his business to discount a bill either by means of cash or giving credit to the last hour previous to a person's avowed bankruptcy, provided it is done fairly and without reference to any unlawful object."

In the leading case of Taylor, noted *infra*, the following dictum was concurred in by the whole Court : " We think that by that statute the Legislature did not intend to disable persons in the predicament therein set forth from fairly paying their debts as these became payable—or from fairly and strictly performing their obligations *ad factum præstandum* as these became prestable. It is legally necessary for such obligants so to pay their debts and to perform their obligations ; and it was not the object of the statute to disable them from doing without compulsion what the law itself would compel them to do. What the Legislature intended by the statute was to disable a debtor who is in the predicament therein set forth, and unable to pay his debts, from entering spontaneously into some new transaction with a favoured creditor, wherein in lieu of—or as a substitute for—regular payment of a debt in cash, the debtor grants and the creditor receives a transference of some other funds or effects forming part of the debtor's estate."

The mere granting of a voluntary trust-deed for behoof of creditors, without a clause giving express power to reduce illegal preferences, does not give the trustee a title to reduce such preferences, as under such a conveyance the trustee is not the assignee of the creditors, but only of the insolvent debtor, from whom alone he derives his whole right and title.[4]

Transactions not Struck at by the Act.—(1) Cash payments legally exigible,[5] *i.e.* those in which the term of payment has arrived.[6] Thus cash payments made by a debtor while he is still in the administration

---

[1] Anderson *v.* Western Bank, 1859, 21 D. 230.

[2] Renton & Gray's Tr. *v.* Dickison, 1880, 7 R. 951.

[3] Blincow's Trs. *v.* Allan & Co., *supra*.

[4] Fleming's Trs. *v.* M'Hardy, 1892, 19 R. 542 ; Forbes' Tr. *v.* Forbes, 1903, 5 F. 465.

[5] Watson *v.* Young, 1826, 4 S. 507 ; Rose *v.* Falconer, 1868, 6 M. 960 ; Nicol *v.* M'Intyre, 1882, 9 R. 1097.

[6] Spiers *v.* Dunlop, 1827, 5 S. 729 ; Rose *v.* Falconer, *supra*.

of his estate, in discharge of debts justly due, are not challengeable on the ground that the debtor was or knew that he was insolvent, and that the creditor also knew or had reason to know the fact.[1] But it is not sufficient to characterise a transaction as a cash payment that money or cash has been paid to one who is a creditor, unless he be a creditor entitled at that time to demand payment, or who may be supposed *bonâ fide* to receive it in extinction of his debt as in the ordinary course of dealing.[2] Certain equivalents to cash payments have been recognised. Thus a draft or order purchased from a banker and transmitted to a creditor in another town, the debtor's cheque on his own banker, and in some cases even the indorsation and transmission to a creditor abroad of indorsed bills payable in the country where the creditor resides, have each been regarded as equivalents of cash payments. But a cheque drawn by a third party in favour of a merchant and indorsed by him within sixty days of bankruptcy to a creditor, in payment of a debt already due, has been held to be struck at by the statute as being neither a payment in cash nor a transaction in the ordinary course of business.[3] Similarly, in a case where in payment of an unsecured debt of the bankrupt's his law agents indorsed a cheque in their own favour which they had received in payment of the price of property belonging to the bankrupt to a creditor within sixty days of bankruptcy, it was held that the transaction was not a cash payment in the ordinary course of business, but an assignation, and therefore null and void.[4] (2) Transactions in the ordinary course of trade, such as payments or other operations in the course of a current account between two merchants, or between a banker and his customer, whether made in cash or by the indorsation of bills.[5] In one case a bank discounted a bill for the drawer, who informed the bank that it had been accepted for his accommodation. Before the bill matured, the drawer paid it in cash, and the bill was delivered to him. At the time the drawer was insolvent, though not to the knowledge of the bank, who had no reasonable ground for believing him to be insolvent, and became bankrupt within sixty days thereafter. It was held that in the circumstances, and looking to the fact that retiring a bill before maturity falls within the ordinary course of a banker's business, the payment was not an illegal preference within the meaning of the Act, and was not a fraudulent preference at common law.[6] But in another case a person

---

[1] Pringle's Trs. *v.* Wright, 1903, 5 F. 522, *per* Lord Kyllachy.

[2] Bell's Com. ii. 201 ; Commercial Bank *v.* Angus' Trs., 1901, 4 F. 181.

[3] Carter *v.* Johnstone, 1886, 13 R. 698. See Scott's Trs. *v.* Low & Co., 1902, 4 F. 562.

[4] Anderson's Tr. *v.* Somerville & Co. Ltd., 1899, 1 F. 90.

[5] Stewart *v.* Sir William Forbes & Co., 1791, M. 1142 ; Sievwright *v.* Hay & Co., 1913, S.C. 509.

[6] M'Laren's Tr. *v.* National Bank of Scotland, 1897, 24 R. 920.

A. signed a promissory note along with and for the accommodation of his brother B., which was discounted by a bank. Within sixty days of his bankruptcy B. caused a sale of some of his effects, and authorised the auctioneer to pay the bank the amount due on the note, which at the time had not matured. The Court held that the transaction was struck at by the Act, and ordained A. to repay to the trustee on the sequestrated estate of his brother B. the amount paid to the bank.[1] (3) *Nova debita*, or new transactions ; as where an indorsement is granted to pay goods actually furnished at the time and in exchange for the indorsed bill, since in such a case the indorsement is not given for a prior debt.[2] Where, on an advance of cash, or transference of goods, a simultaneous engagement is made to give a specific security for the advance, such security may be validly completed within the sixty days.[3] Thus where an advance was obtained from a bank on a distinct undertaking and promise that a bill of lading would be delivered in security, which was subsequently and within the sixty days indorsed and delivered to the bank, it was held that the bill was a security for a present advance, and therefore unchallengeable.[4] When the bankrupt's obligation to deliver goods in repayment of an advance is general, applicable, it may be, to a particular description of goods, but not to any specified and identified goods, that is, when the party making the advance has no control over, or right of disposal of, the goods, the entire right of disposal remaining with the bankrupt, and there being no defined or specific obligation to deliver the particular goods, the transaction would seem to be in contravention of the Act.[5] A security which is granted by the bankrupt prior to the sixty days, and which he does not voluntarily attempt to complete within the sixty days, is unchallengeable, although the creditor have done something to complete the security within the sixty days, or the debtor something which he was legally bound, and could have been compelled, to do.[6] Although a security is granted

---

[1] Craig's Trs. *v.* Craig, 1903, 10 S.L.T. 357 (O.H.).

[2] Scougal *v.* White, 1828, 6 S. 494 ; Bruce *v.* Hamilton, 1832, 10 S. 250 ; Loudon Bros. *v.* Reid & Lauder's Tr., 1877, 5 R. 293 ; Horsburgh *v.* Ramsay, 1885, 12 R. 1171.

[3] Bell's Com. (M'L.'s ed.) ii. 211, note 2 ; Bank of Scotland *v.* Stewart & Ross, 7th February 1811, F.C. ; Stiven *v.* Scott & Simpson, 1871, 9 M. 923.

[4] Cowdenbeath Coal Co. *v.* Clydesdale Bank, 1895, 22 R. 682.

[5] Gourlay *v.* Hodge, 1875, 2 R. 738 ; Moncrieff *v.* Hay, 1851, 14 D. 200 ; Stiven *v.* Scott & Simpson, 1871, 9 M. 923 ; Gourlay *v.* Mackie, 1887, 14 R. 403 ; Galbraith *v.* Price, 1923, S.L.T. 47.

[6] Lindsay *v.* Adamson & Ronaldson, 1880, 7 R. 1036 ; Moncrieff *v.* Hay, 1851, 14 D. 200 ; Inglis *v.* Mansfield, 1835, 1 S. & M'L. 203 ; Rose *v.* Falconer, 1868, 6 M. 960 ; Macfarlane *v.* Robb & Co., 1870, 9 M. 370 ; Stiven *v.* Scott & Simpson, 1871, 9 M. 923 ; Gourlay *v.* Hodge, 1875, 2 R. 738 ; Loudon Bros. *v.* Reid & Lauder's Tr., 1877, 5 R. 293 ; Taylor *v.* Farrie, 1855, 17 D. 639 ; Gibson *v.* Forbes, 1833, 11 S. 916 ; Lindsay *v.* Shields, 1862, 24 D. 821 ; Scottish Provident Institution *v.* Cohen & Co., 1888, 16 R. 112.

within the sixty days of bankruptcy, if no advances are made against the security until after its completion the security is good.[1] The Act does not apply if the security be granted by the bankrupt, not to his own creditor, but to the creditor of a third person. Thus in one case a bill was drawn by A. upon B., and indorsed by A. to C. for value. When the bill became due, C. consented to take a renewal of it, on condition that B. gave him a guarantee for certain other bills then current granted by A. to C. B. became bankrupt within sixty days after granting the guarantee, and C. claimed in his sequestration for the amount thereof. The claim was repelled by the trustee, on the ground that the guarantee was in contravention of the Act, but the Court held that, as the guarantee was not granted in satisfaction or security of a prior debt due by the bankrupt, it was not struck at by the Act.[2] Again, the Act does not apply to a sale of his property by the bankrupt, although the price paid may not have been a full price, and more might have been got, unless it can be proved that unfair practices were used for the purpose of reducing the price and benefiting the purchaser at the expense of the other creditors.[3] A security which is substituted for an already existing one in consideration that a loan granted in respect of the prior security should not be called up, is not struck at by the Act; [4] but a conveyance of property which is made in fulfilment of a promise to give security for a past loan is.[5] Again, where A. B. assigned rights in a trust-estate to C., D., and E. in security partly of a present advance, and also partly of certain sums which one of them had previously advanced and at the time of the transaction had agreed not to call up, it was held that the whole consideration constituted a *novum debitum*, and that the assignation was good.[6] In another case, where a farmer who had received an unsecured advance of £200 from a firm of auctioneers, employed them within sixty days of his bankruptcy to carry through his displenishing sale, at the same time giving them an ante-dated receipt for the £200 as being a payment " towards my displenishing sale," it was held that the transaction was struck at by the Act, and that the auctioneers were not entitled to retain £200 out of the sum realised at the sale.[7]

Effect of Annulling Preference.—Where a debtor within sixty days of bankruptcy assigns part of his estate in violation of the Act, any creditor at the date of the alienation has a title to reduce the assignation, but he has no title to recover the subject of the assignation for

---

[1] Whyte *v.* Union Bank of Scotland Ltd., 1917, S.C. 549.
[2] Ferguson *v.* Welsh, 1869, 7 M. 592.
[3] Wilson's Tr. *v.* Raeburn, 1900, 38 S.L.R. 288.
[4] Roy's Trs. *v.* Colville & Drysdale, 1903, 5 F. 769.
[5] Hill's Trs. *v.* MacGregor, 1901, 8 S.L.T. 387 (O.H.).
[6] Browne's Trs. *v.* Browne, 1902, 10 S.L.T. 57 (O.H.).
[7] Craig's Trs. *v.* Macdonald & Fraser, 1902, 4 F. 1132.

behoof of himself and the other creditors. The effect of annulling an illegal preference is simply to restore the alienated subject to the position in which it was prior to the alienation ; it becomes assets of the bankrupt's estate, and may be attached by the diligence of the creditor who has established the nullity, and also by the other creditors whose claims are prior in time to the alienation, but it does not give the creditor any right against the assignee to require payment or delivery of the subject to himself, a proceeding which would be tantamount to creating a new preference in place of the one cut down.[1]

---

[1] Cook *v.* Sinclair & Co., 1896, 23 R. 925.

CHAPTER II

PUBLIC INSOLVENCY OR NOTOUR BANKRUPTCY

WHEN a debtor in an obligation is unable to fulfil his obligation according to the terms of his undertaking, and acknowledgment of his inability to do so is made public, in manner determined by statute, the status or condition of bankruptcy has arisen, and the insolvent debtor is, in the language of the statutes, a " notour " bankrupt. Notour bankruptcy is thus simply acknowledged or public insolvency. When accompanied by certain judicial proceedings for the divestiture of the bankrupt in favour of his creditors, this public insolvency is termed sequestration.

The first statute dealing with the subject is that of 1696, cap. 5, which provided that insolvency, by which is meant present inability to meet debts due,[1] coupled with an expired charge for payment and followed by imprisonment or certain equivalents therefor, was in future to be the only competent mode of proving that a debtor was notour bankrupt. These provisions were somewhat extended by the Act 23 Geo. III. c. 18, by the Bankruptcy Act of 1856, sec. 7 (now repealed), and subsequently by the Debtors Act of 1880, sec. 6 (now repealed). Since 1835 imprisonment for debt of sums under £8. 6s. 8d. has been incompetent, and since 1880 imprisonment for debt has been altogether abolished, except in respect of debts incurred for taxes, fines, or penalties due to His Majesty, rates and assessments lawfully imposed, and sums decerned for aliment, although the sum due be under £8. 6s. 8d. The mode of constituting notour bankruptcy is now contained in the Bankruptcy (Scotland) Act, 1913, sec. 5, and may be constituted (1) by sequestration, or by the issuing of an adjudication of bankruptcy or the granting of a receiving order in England or Ireland, (2) by insolvency concurring (a) with a duly executed charge for payment, where a charge is necessary followed by the expiry of the days of charge without payment, (b) where a charge is unnecessary, that is where decree is granted against a debtor in a Small Debt Court when the debtor is personally present with the lapse without payment of the days which must elapse before poinding or imprisonment can follow on a decree or warrant for payment of a sum of money, (c) with a poinding or seizure of any of the debtor's move-

---

[1] Teenan's Trs. v. Teenan, 1886, 13 R. 833.

ables for non-payment of rates or taxes, (d) with a decree of adjudication of any part of the bankrupt's heritable estate for payment or in security, or (e) with sale of any effects belonging to the debtor under a sequestration for rent.

The notour bankruptcy of a firm or company is constituted in any of the foregoing ways, or by any of the partners being rendered notour bankrupt for a company debt.

Corporations, public companies, and corporate bodies, whose members are not individually liable for the companies' obligations, can be rendered notour bankrupt in the mode prescribed by sec. 5 of the Act of 1913. Unincorporated associations cannot be made bankrupt at all, and recourse must be had against the individual members separately.

The chief effects of notour bankruptcy arising under statute or at common law relate to (1) the invalidating of preferences,[1] (2) equalisation of diligence and *pari passu* ranking of diligence,[2] and (3) liability to sequestration.[3]

---

[1] See *ante*.   [2] See Diligence.   [3] See *infra*.

CHAPTER III

SEQUESTRATION

SEQUESTRATION was formerly a process of distribution applicable only to the bankruptcy of traders, but the remedy is now extended to all persons, without distinction, who are debtors. Formerly there were a number of statutes regulating the process, but the principal Act is now the " Bankruptcy (Scotland) Act, 1913," [1] which consolidated and amended the laws relating to bankruptcy in Scotland. This statute abolished the old process of *Cessio Bonorum*, and introduced a new process called Summary Sequestration,[2] which is applicable to the estates of debtors whose assets of every description do not in the aggregate exceed three hundred pounds in value. Sequestration may be defined as " a judicial process for rendering litigious the whole estate of a bankrupt, in order that no part of it may be carried away by a single creditor for his own benefit, but that the whole may be vested in a trustee, to be administered by him and distributed among the various creditors, in accordance with certain fixed legal rules of distribution." [3]

Who may be Sequestrated.—Sequestration of the estates of any person may be awarded in the following cases. In the case of any living debtor (which includes firms and companies other than those incorporated by Royal Charter, or under the Companies Acts) subject to the jurisdiction of the Supreme Courts of Scotland, sequestration may be awarded either (1) on the debtor's own petition, with the concurrence of a creditor or creditors, qualified as after-stated, or (2) on the petition of a creditor or creditors, qualified as after-stated. In the former case it is not necessary that the debtor be notour bankrupt or even insolvent, it being sufficient that he has the necessary consents ; whereas in the latter case the debtor must be notour bankrupt,[4] and have within a year before the date of the presentation of the petition resided, or had a dwelling-house or place of business, in Scotland. In the case of a firm besides notour bankruptcy the firm must have carried on business in Scotland within a year before the date of the presentation

---

[1] 3 & 4 Geo. V. cap. 20.
[2] See *infra.*
[3] Sinclair *v.* Edinburgh Parish Council, 1909, S.C. 1353, *per* Lord Kinnear.
[4] See Constitution of Notour Bankruptcy, *ante.*

of the petition and a partner resided or had a dwelling place or the
company had a place of business in Scotland, within the same period.
The time for the creditor to petition is limited to a period of four months
after an act of notour bankruptcy, but such bankruptcy may be constituted any number of times.[1] Sequestration of the estates of a
deceased debtor may competently be awarded where the debtor, at
the time of his death, was subject to the jurisdiction of the Supreme
Courts of Scotland, either (1) on the petition of a mandatory to whom
he had granted a mandate to apply for sequestration, or (2) on the
petition of a creditor or creditors, qualified as after-stated. Where
a creditor applies for sequestration, the petition may be presented at
any time after the debtor's death, but no sequestration can be awarded
until the expiration of six months from that date, unless the debtor
was, at the time of his death, notour bankrupt, or unless his successors
concur in the petition, or renounce the succession.

Sequestration of Firm or Company.—It is an important feature of
the Scots law of partnership that a firm or company constitutes
a separate person, distinct in law from all or any of its members.[2]
It therefore follows that a company may be sequestrated, although
all, or some, of the partners remain solvent, and *vice versâ*. In practice,
however, it rarely happens that a firm is sequestrated without the
individual partners being also included in the sequestration. If, however, the firm alone is sequestrated, while the individual partners,
or any of them, remain solvent, the creditors are entitled to demand
from the solvent partners any balance which may remain unpaid from
the partnership funds. Where two firms, although consisting of the
same partners, carry on separate and distinct businesses, the estates
of the two firms must in bankruptcy be treated as separate, provided
there is a real and perceptible distinction of trade and establishment
between them.[3]

Jurisdiction.—The jurisdiction necessary for the awarding of
sequestration is that necessary for the founding, before the Scots
Courts, of any personal action, or for the execution of diligence. It
may be established—(1) By continuous residence in Scotland. (2) By
a residence for forty days continuously in Scotland. In one case a
person, English by birth, domicile, and connection, being insolvent,
came to Scotland and had his exclusive residence there for more than
forty days. He was not a trader in any country, had no estate in
Scotland, and all his creditors, with one exception, resided out of
Scotland. The avowed object of his residence in Scotland was to have
his estate sequestrated there, and this was accordingly done, on a

---

[1] Balfour v. Pedie, 1841, 3 D. 612.
[2] See p. 61.
[3] Commercial Bank of Scotland v. Tod's Tr., 1895, 23 S.L.R. 161, *per* Lord Low.

petition presented by the bankrupt himself, with the concurrence of a creditor. The validity of the sequestration was objected to on the ground of want of jurisdiction, but the Court held that at the date of the presentation of the petition the bankrupt was subject to the jurisdiction of the Supreme Courts of Scotland.[1] The fact that the debtor possesses a domicile *of succession* in Scotland is not of itself sufficient to constitute jurisdiction against him.[2] (3) By being the owner of heritage in Scotland. In this case, where the debtor does not himself apply for sequestration, it is necessary that he should have carried on business in Scotland within a year prior to the date of the presentation of the petition.

Sequestration may be awarded by the Court of Session, or by the Sheriff of any county in which the debtor, for the year preceding the date of the petition, has resided or carried on business.[3] In the case of a deceased debtor, sequestration may be awarded by the Court of Session, or by the Sheriff of the county in which the debtor, for the year preceding his death, had resided or carried on business.[4] No sequestration can, however, be awarded by any Court after production of evidence that a sequestration has already been awarded in another Court and is still undischarged. Where a prior petition is in dependence the Court to which a subsequent petition is presented may remit such subsequent petition to the Court in which the prior petition is in dependence. Where, however, it happens that sequestration has been awarded against a debtor by the Sheriffs of two or more counties, the later sequestration or sequestrations are, on production of a certificate by the Sheriff-Clerk of the county in which the sequestration first in date was awarded, setting forth the date of such sequestration, remitted to the Sheriff of such county.[5] An appeal to the Court of Session is competent against the deliverance of a Sheriff refusing a petition for sequestration.[6]

Qualification of Petitioning or Concurring Creditors.—The petition may be at the instance, or with the concurrence, of any one or more creditors whose debt or debts together amount to not less than fifty pounds, whether such debts are liquid or illiquid, provided they are not contingent. Where a creditor who has petitioned, or concurred in petitioning, for sequestration of a debtor's estate, subsequently withdraws, becomes bankrupt, or dies, any other creditor may be sisted in his place and follow out the proceedings.

---

[1] Joel *v.* Gill, 1859, 21 D. 929. *Contrast with* Cooper *v.* Baillie, 1878, 5 R. 564.
[2] Strickland, *Petr.*, 1911, 1 S.L.T. 212, *per* Lord Ormidale.
[3] Bankruptcy Act, sec. 16.
[4] *Ibid.* sec. 16.
[5] *Ibid.* sec. 17.
[6] Marr & Son *v.* Lindsay, 1881, 8 R. 784.

Whether the petition be at the instance of the debtor with the concurrence of a creditor, or by a creditor alone, there must be produced along with it an oath in the same terms as that, afterwards explained, with reference to claims for voting, and also the account and vouchers necessary to prove the debt, otherwise the petition will be dismissed. The production of an I.O.U. is not, of itself, a sufficient voucher for petitioning for sequestration.[1]

Interim Preservation of Estate.—It is competent for the Court to which a petition for sequestration is presented, whether sequestration can forthwith be awarded or not, on special application by a creditor, either in such petition, or by a separate petition, with or without citation to other parties interested, as the Court may deem necessary, or without such special application if the Court think proper, to take immediate measures for the interim preservation of the estate. This is done either by the appointment of a Judicial Factor, who requires to find such caution as may be deemed necessary, with the powers necessary for such preservation,[2] including the power to recover debts, or by such other proceedings as may be requisite. Such interim appointments, or proceedings, are carried into immediate effect, but if they have been made or ordered by the Sheriff, they may be recalled by the Court of Session on appeal.[3] The Judicial Factor thus appointed may be called upon to account for his intromissions at the instance of any party interested.

Recall of Sequestration.[4]—The deliverance awarding sequestration is not subject to review, but the sequestration may in certain circumstances be recalled. The petition for recall must be made to the Lord Ordinary on the Bills in the Court of Session. The petition may be at the instance of (1) any debtor whose estate has been sequestrated without his consent ; (2) the successors who have not renounced the succession of any deceased debtor whose estate has been sequestrated without their consent, unless on the application of a mandatory authorised by the deceased debtor ; or (3) any creditor. The petition for recall must in the ordinary case be presented within forty days after the deliverance awarding sequestration, unless in the case of a deceased debtor when his successor was cited edictally, in which case the petition may be presented at any time before the publication of the advertisement for payment of the first dividend. An application for recall may at any time be presented during the course of the sequestration provided nine-tenths in number and value of the

---

[1] *Per* Lord Rutherfurd Clark (unreported), *in re* Goodwillie's Sequestration, 5th February 1876. See also Gascoyne *v.* Manford, 1847, 10 D. 231 ; Laidlaw *v.* Wilson, 1844, 6 D. 530 ; Aitken *v.* Stock, 1846, 8 D. 509 ; and Dyce *v.* Paterson, 1847, 9 D. 1141.

[2] Crawford *v.* Corsan, 1827, 6 S. 127 ; Malcolm, *Petr.*, 1828, 6 S. 1025.

[3] B. A., sec. 14.

[4] B. A., sec. 30.

creditors ranked on the estate apply by petition to the Lord Ordinary.[1] The effect of a recall is to leave intact transactions which have been *bonâ fide* carried through prior to its date. The proceedings in the sequestration go on notwithstanding the presentation of a petition for recall until the petition is finally disposed of.

Reduction of Sequestration.—Where the recall of a sequestration is incompetent application may be made for the reduction of an award of sequestration. A reduction, however, will only be granted in very exceptional and special circumstances.[2]

First Meeting of Creditors.—In the Interlocutor awarding sequestration of the estates of a debtor, a meeting of his creditors is appointed to be held at a specified time and place, for the election of a Trustee, or Trustees in succession. Two or more creditors may give notice to the Sheriff of the county to attend the meeting, and, on such notice being given, the Sheriff is required to attend the meeting and any adjournment of it.[3]

Creditor's Qualification to Vote.—To enable a creditor to take part in this election, it is necessary for him, or a mandatory on his behalf, to attend such meeting, and produce an oath, taken by him before a Judge Ordinary, Magistrate, Justice of the Peace, Notary Public or Commissioner for Oaths as to the verity of the debt claimed, and to produce the vouchers proving the debt referred to in the oath. The sum due under a bond of cash-credit is sufficiently vouched by production of the bond, coupled with a certificate, indorsed thereon by an official of the bank, bringing out the amount due, as provided for in the bond. The vouchers necessary for sums due on an overdrawn current account are a copy of the account, having prefixed a copy of the last docquet, and production of the cheques. It has been decided[4] in the Edinburgh Sheriff Court that this is not sufficient, the proper vouchers being, in addition to the account, the principal docquet and the bills or cheques paid by the bank. When the docquet is in the ledger, it is difficult to see how it could be produced. In cases where the claim of the bank is material, the risk of having the vote rejected might be obviated by having the account, including a copy of the docquet, certified in terms of the Bankers' Books Evidence Act, 1879.[5] Where an account does not begin with a docquet, it is not sufficiently vouched when it begins with a balance, either on the creditor or debtor side.[6] In all cases where there is not a docquet the account must go back to the first transaction on it. After having been lodged,

---

[1] B. A., sec. 31.
[2] Central Motor Engineering Co. and Others *v.* Galbraith, 1918, S.C. 755.
[3] B. A., sec. 64.
[4] Millar *v.* Romanes, 1912, 2 S.L.T. 209.
[5] See p. 3.
[6] Low *v.* Baxter, 1851, 13 D. 1349.

the vouchers may be borrowed up, and unless specially called for, the creditor or his mandatory may vote at subsequent meetings without their reproduction.[1] It is necessary that the oath be taken before a proper magistrate, who must attest the fact.[2] The creditor swearing to the verity of the debt must be put on oath by the magistrate, or other person before whom the oath is taken, and if this be not done, the oath may be rejected.[3] A creditor who makes a false statement, and swears to the verity of a debt which is not due, or makes any other false statement wilfully, is liable, at common law, to be prosecuted for perjury. Over and above this, the statute [4] provides that, " if any person shall be guilty of wilful falsehood, in any oath made in pursuance of this Act, he shall be liable to a prosecution, either at the instance of the Lord Advocate, or at the instance of the Trustee, with the concurrence of the Lord Advocate—provided that, in the latter case, the prosecution shall be authorised by a majority of the creditors present at a meeting to be called for the purpose—and such person shall, on conviction, besides the awarded punishment, forfeit to the trustee, for behoof of the creditors, his whole right, claim, and interest in, or upon, the sequestrated estate, and the same shall be distributed either under the sequestration, or, if it be closed, under a process of multiplepoinding."

When the creditor is a corporation, such as a bank, the oath is competently made by the Secretary, Manager, Cashier, or other principal officer, although such officer be not a member of the corporation. The oath of a country agent of an incorporated bank, swearing to the debt being due to the bank, has been held to be bad,[5] while the oath of the assistant manager has been held competent.[6]

Election of Trustee.—The creditors or their mandatories assembled at this meeting—and a meeting, although attended by only one duly qualified creditor, is a meeting under the Act [7]—then and there elect a person to be Trustee, or two or more persons to be Trustees in succession, in case of the non-acceptance, death, resignation, removal, or disqualification of the first-named Trustee. Where the estates sequestrated are those of a company, and of the individual partners, the meeting may elect one Trustee for all the estates, or separate Trustees on the estates of the company, and on the estates of all or each, of the individual partners, or Trustees in succession. It is not lawful to

---

[1] Woodside v. Esplin, 1847, 9 D. 1486.

[2] Hall v. Colquhoun, 1870, 9 M. 891.

[3] Blair v. North British and Mercantile Insurance Company, 1889, 16 R. 325, 947 ; 1890, 17 R. (H.L.) 76.

[4] Sec. 186.

[5] Anderson v. Monteith, 1847, 9 D. 1432 ; Campbell v. Myles, 1853, 15 D. 685.

[6] Dow & Co. v. Union Bank, 1875, 2 R. 459.

[7] Cookson v. Boyd, 1863, 2 M. 268.

elect as Trustee the bankrupt, or any person conjunct and confident [1] with him, though such persons can competently vote for the election of a Trustee, their claims, however, being closely scrutinised.[2] It is, further, unlawful to elect anyone who holds an interest opposed to the general body of creditors, or one whose residence is not within the jurisdiction of the Court of Session. It is not *per se* a sufficient reason to disqualify a competitor for the office of Trustee, (1) that he has advanced arrears of rent due by the bankrupt, and holds an assignation to the landlord's hypothec ; (2) that he has intromitted with the bankrupt's estate, as Trustee under a voluntary trust-deed executed by the bankrupt for behoof of his creditors ; or, (3) that he has acted as interim factor on the estate.[3]

Competition for Trusteeship.—In the event of a competition for the trusteeship, the Court will confirm him as Trustee who has a majority in value, even though a minority in number, of the creditors present supporting him, the reason being that the control of the administration of the estate is given to the persons having the largest interest in such estate.

Valuation of Securities.—Over and above the requisites already mentioned, the Act provides special rules as to the valuation and deduction of securities held, and only gives creditors in possession of securities a right to vote in respect of the balance, after deduction of the value of such securities. Thus if a creditor holds at the date of sequestration [4] a security for his debt over any part of the bankrupt's estate, such as a transfer to stock belonging to the bankrupt, a security over his heritage, an assignation to a policy over his life, or otherwise, he must, before voting, in his oath put a value upon such security, deduct the same from the amount of his claim, specify the balance, and vote only in respect of such balance. If the property over which the security extends be sold before the date of sequestration, he must state the free proceeds he has received, or is entitled to receive therefrom, deduct the same from his claim, and vote in respect of the balance thus brought out, without prejudice to his claim in other respects. A creditor is, however, entitled to vote in respect of the full amount of his debt, without deduction, in any question relating to the disposal or management of any estate held by him in security.[5]

---

[1] See p. 297.

[2] Anderson *v.* Guild, 14 D. 866 ; Walker's Trs. *v.* Walker, 1883, 10 R. 699.

[3] Macfarlane *v.* Grieve, 1848, 10 D. 551 ; Reid *v.* Barry, 1836, 14 S. 809 ; Colville *v.* Ledingham, 1850, 13 D. 415. See also decision in Sheriff Court, Edinburgh, by Sheriff-Substitute Rutherfurd, 31st October 1884, in H. & R. Rigg & Co.'s Sequestration.

[4] Royal Bank *v.* Millar's Trs., 1882, 9 R. 679 ; University of Glasgow *v.* Yuill's Tr., 1882, 9 R. 643.

[5] Addison *v.* Crabb, 1853, 25 Jurist, 270.

A value of some kind must be placed on whatever security is held over the estate of the bankrupt. It is not a compliance with the statute to say that the security is worthless. A nominal value will suffice, or the creditor may even value it at nothing.[1] A promissory note granted by the bankrupt is not a security,[2] though an arrestment,[3] or an inhibition,[4] is.

If the creditor hold a number of securities for the same debt, altering the previous law on the point, the Act of 1913 provides that each security must be valued separately.[5] Where the creditor holds separate securities for separate debts, the securities must be valued as against the particular debt to which they refer.[6] Where the security the creditor holds is not over the estate of the bankrupt, but has been conveyed to him by others, such as a co-obligant or an outsider, while such security requires to be stated for the information of the Trustee, its value does not require to be deducted. Similarly, a creditor of a firm consisting of more than one partner, in voting on the estates of such firm, does not require to value and deduct a security he may have received from one of the partners of the firm over his individual property, although he requires to do so in voting on the individual estates of such partner.

Valuation of Claims against Co-obligants.—Besides valuing and deducting whatever securities he may hold over the estates of a bankrupt, a creditor, for the purposes of voting, must, in his oath, put a specified value on, deduct such value from his debt, and vote in respect of the balance only of (1) the obligation of any person he may hold bound with, but liable in relief to, the bankrupt to the extent to which the bankrupt has a right of relief ; (2) any security he may hold from such obligant ; and (3) any security from which the bankrupt has a right of relief. Thus the holder of a past due bill, in voting on the estates of the drawer, must value and deduct the obligation of the acceptor, who is liable in relief to the drawer, and the effect of this, if the acceptor be good for the amount, is practically to preclude a vote altogether on such claim. But it has been held competent for the holder of such a bill to vote on the estates of the drawer for the full amount thereof without valuing the obligation of the acceptor, on his deponing in his oath " that the bill was granted for the accommodation of the bankrupt, and that the acceptor is not bound to relieve the bankrupt of the debt

---

[1] Poynter *v.* Lorimer, 1839, 1 D. 700 ; M'Ewan *v.* Cleugh, 1842, 5 D. 273 ; Hay *v.* Durham, 1850, 12 D. 676 ; Gibson *v.* Greig, 1853, 16 D. 233 ; Aitken *v.* Callender, 1848, 10 D. 1269.

[2] Boro, 1st June 1811, F.C.

[3] Woodside *v.* Esplin, 1847, 9 D. 1486 ; Gibson *v.* Greig, *supra* ; Dow *v.* Union Bank, 1875, 2 R. 459.

[4] Hay *v.* Durham, *supra* ; M'Ewan *v.* Cleugh, *supra*.

[5] Bankruptcy Act, sec. 55.

[6] Smith *v.* Borthwick, 1849, 11 D. 517.

contained in, and constituted by, the bill or any part thereof." [1]
Similarly, if a bill be current, and the drawer become bankrupt, there
can be no good vote unless the acceptor be also bankrupt or insolvent
(which fact must be deponed to by the holder), as the creditor would
require to value his security in full, there being a presumption that the
bill will be taken up by the acceptor at maturity. [2] The rule also applies
to voting upon the estates of one of the sureties in a bond of credit,
since, as the principal obligant is bound to relieve the surety, his obligation must be valued and deducted. Where several bills are held, it is
not competent for the holder to value at a slump sum the obligations
of the co-obligants thereon. He must put a specified value on the
obligation of each co-obligant. [3]

At this stage of the proceedings regard is paid only to the oath,
without reference to what may afterwards turn out, on a more thorough
investigation of evidence, to be the true state of matters. So, where
a vote was objected to on the ground that the claimant had received
payments to account of his debt which he had not credited, and had
held securities which he had not valued in his affidavit, the Court
declined to grant a diligence to have such averments proved. [4]

A fair valuation, for the purposes of voting, should be put upon
securities and claims against co-obligants, as, in order to provide a
check on creditors undervaluing their securities, the statute [5] makes
it competent (1) for the trustee, with the consent of the Commissioners,
within two months after such vote has been used at any meeting, or
in assenting to, or dissenting from, the bankrupt's composition or discharge, and (2) for a majority of the creditors (excluding the creditor
making such oath) assembled at any meeting and during such meeting,
to require from the creditor making and using such oath, a conveyance or assignation, in favour of the Trustee, of such security, obligation,
or claim, on payment of the specified value, with twenty per centum
in addition to such value, and the creditor is bound to grant the same,
but at the expense of the estate. [6] Where, however, a creditor has put
a value on such security or obligation, he may, at any time after
the lapse of twenty-one days from the date on which the claim has been
voted on and before he has been required to convey and assign as aforesaid, correct such valuation by a new oath, and deduct such new value
from his debt.

Appeal against Election of Trustee.—Although at the meeting the

---

[1] Dyce v. Paterson, 1847, 9 D. 993.
[2] Gordon v. M'Cubbin, 1851, 13 D. 1154.
[3] Bankruptcy Act, sec. 56.
[4] Dyce v. Paterson, 1847, 9 D. 993.
[5] B. A., sec. 58.
[6] Greig v. Crichton, 1853, 15 D. 742 ; Russell v. Daniel, 1868, 6 M. 648.

preses declares elected as Trustee the candidate who has the largest support in value of the creditors present, it is competent for the parties opposing his election to appeal to the Sheriff. The grounds of such appeal may be in respect of (1) the qualifications of the voters, (2) the qualifications of the candidates,[1] or (3) the irregularity of the proceedings.[2] When an appeal is to be proceeded with, a short note of objections must be lodged with the Sheriff-Clerk within four days from the date of meeting. The Sheriff thereafter hears parties *viva voce*, and gives his decision, which is final, and in no case subject to review in any Court or in any manner whatever. Since the object aimed at in declaring that the Sheriff's decision on the question of the election of the Trustee should be absolutely final and not subject to review in any way obviously was to prevent the administration of sequestrated estates being hung up by litigations between parties contending for the office of Trustee, it follows that not only in declaring the election of the Trustee but in deciding questions incidental to the election—such as, *e.g.* that the person proposed is conjunct and confident with the bankrupt or has an interest opposed to that of the general body of the creditors— the Sheriff's judgment is also final and not subject to review.[3]

Trustee's Caution.—At this meeting the creditors must [4] fix a sum for which the Trustee shall find security for his intromissions and the performance of his duties as Trustee, in accordance with the provisions of the statute, and they must also decide on the sufficiency of the caution offered. The bond of a guarantee society may be accepted.[5] The cautioner is liable for the Trustee's intromissions, even although there may have been negligence on the part of the Commissioners and creditors in superintending his transactions.[6]

Election of Commissioners.—At the meeting for the election of the Trustee, the creditors, or their mandatories, present elect three Commissioners, who may be either creditors, or mandatories of creditors, if there be so many creditors who have claimed, and if not, then as many as do claim, or their mandatories. No person is eligible as a Commissioner who is disqualified to act as Trustee,[7] and any mandatory who has been elected a Commissioner loses that office upon written intimation being sent by his constituent to the Trustee that he has recalled the mandate. The election of Commissioners proceeds in the same way

---

[1] For qualifications of Trustees, see p. 313.

[2] Yeaman *v.* Little, 1906, 8 F. 702.

[3] B. A., secs. 66 and 67 ; Grierson *v.* Ogilvy's Tr., 1908, S.C. 959, *approving* Yeaman *v.* Little, 1906, 8 F. 702 ; Farquharson *v.* Sutherland, 1888, 15 R. 759.

[4] A. B., *Petr.*, 1833, 11 S. 412 ; Bell's Com. (M'L.'s ed.) ii. 372.

[5] B. A., sec. 69.

[6] M'Taggart *v.* Watson, 1834, 12 S. 332 ; *revd.* 1 S. & M'L. 558 ; Creighton *v.* Rankin, 1838, 16 S. 447 ; 1 Rob. Ap. Cas. 131 ; Biggar *v.* Wright, 1846, 9 D. 78.

[7] B. A., sec. 72.

as the election of Trustee. Commissioners do not require to find caution, nor are they entitled to any fee for their services. Where a Commissioner declines to act, resigns, or becomes incapacitated, the Trustee calls a meeting of the creditors for the purpose of electing a new Commissioner, and such Commissioner is elected as in the case of the first elected.[1] A majority of the creditors assembled at any meeting, duly called for the purpose, may remove a Commissioner and elect another in his place.[2]

Duties of Commissioners.—The Commissioners, who have access to the sederunt book and accounts of the Trustee, and to documents of a confidential nature, superintend the proceedings of the Trustee, advise with him as to the management, recovery, and realisation of the estate where no special instructions have been given by the creditors, concur with him in submissions and transactions, and decide as to the paying, or postponing payment, of a dividend. Any one of them may make such report as he thinks proper to a general meeting of the creditors. The consent of the Commissioners is not necessary to the Trustee's general acts of management.[3] Within fourteen days after the expiration of four months from the date of sequestration, the Commissioners meet and examine the Trustee's account of his intromissions with the estate, and ascertain whether he has lodged the moneys recovered by him in bank, or not. If he has failed to do so, they debit him with a sum at the rate of twenty pounds on every hundred pounds not so lodged, and so, after that rate, on any larger or smaller sum, being not less than fifty pounds. They then audit his accounts, settle the amount of his commission, and authorise him to take credit for such commission in his accounts with the estate. They further certify by a writing under their hands, engrossed or copied in the sederunt book, the balance due to, or by, the Trustee, and declare whether any, and what part, of the net produce of the estate, after making a reasonable deduction for future contingencies, should be divided among the creditors.[4] They have power to postpone payment of a dividend, and to declare that no dividend should be paid.[5] The Commissioners have power to meet at any time, to ascertain the situation of the bankrupt estate, and may, by giving notice,[6] at any time call a meeting of the creditors. A Commissioner is not, though a creditor is, entitled to purchase any of the bankrupt estate sold publicly.[7] The Commissioners are not personally liable for damage caused to the estate by the Trustee acting according to their advice.[8]

---

[1] B. A., sec. 72. [2] B. A., sec. 73.
[3] Hamilton's Exec. *v.* Bank of Scotland, 1913, S.C. 743.
[4] B. A., sec. 121. [5] Sec. 131.
[6] Campbell *v.* M'Fadyean, 1884, 21 S.L.R. 479.
[7] B. A., sec. 116
[8] Wilson *v.* Alexander, 1803, M. 13968.

But they are liable if it can be shown that, through their wrongful actings, any one has suffered damage.[1]

The Trustee.—*Confirmation of.*—On being elected, the Trustee lodges with the Sheriff-Clerk for the due performance of his office a bond of caution, signed by him and his cautioner, for the amount of security fixed by the creditors at the first meeting. On this being done the Sheriff confirms the election, and the Sheriff-Clerk issues an Act and Warrant of Confirmation, a copy of which is immediately transmitted to the Accountant of Court, who makes an entry of the name and designation of the Trustee in the Register of Sequestrations.[2] Within twenty-one days after the confirmation of his election, the Trustee causes an Abbreviate of his confirmation to be recorded in the Registers of Abbreviates of Adjudications.[3] The effect of the Act and Warrant in the Trustee's favour is to transfer to, and vest in, him or any succeeding Trustee, for behoof of the creditors, absolutely and irredeemably as of the date of the sequestration, all right, title, and interest in the whole property of the debtor, whether heritable or moveable in which the bankrupt has a beneficial interest, whether the title be in him or in a Trustee for him to the extent of that interest. In particular, it vests the Trustee in (1) the whole moveable estate and effects of the bankrupt wherever situated, so far as attachable for debt, or capable of voluntary alienation by the bankrupt, to the same effect as if actual delivery or possession had been obtained, or intimation made at that date, subject to such preferable securities as existed at the date of the sequestration, and are not null or reducible ; (2) the whole heritable estate in Scotland, to the same effect as if a Decree of Adjudication in Implement of Sale, as well as a Decree of Adjudication for payment and in security of debt subject to no legal reversion, had been pronounced in favour of the Trustee and recorded at the date of the sequestration, and as if a poinding of the ground had then been executed, subject to such preferable securities as existed at the date of the sequestration and are not null or reducible. Such transfer and vesting has no effect on the rights of the superior, nor upon any question of succession between the heir and executor of any creditor claiming on the sequestrated estate, nor upon the rights of the creditors of the ancestor (except that the Act and Warrant operates in their favour as complete diligence). If any part of the bankrupt's estate is held under an entail, or by a title otherwise limited, the right vested in the Trustee is effectual only to the extent of the interest in the estate which the bankrupt might legally convey or the creditors attach ; (3) all real estate in England, Ireland, or in any of the British dominions, provided that, as regards freehold, copyhold, and leasehold estate, the Act and Warrant is properly registered in the Book of the Court of Bank-

---

[1] M'Taggart v. Watson, 1 S. & M'L. 553.
[2] B. A., sec. 70.   [3] B. A., sec. 75.

ruptcy for the country in which the property is situated, and likewise, that it be enrolled and recorded where, according to the laws of that country, conveyances would require registration or enrolment;[1] and (4) introducing an extension of the right of the Trustee the Act of 1913 provides[2] that "if any estate wherever situated shall, after the date of the sequestration and before the bankrupt has obtained his discharge, be acquired by him or descend or revert or come to him, the same shall *ipso jure* fall under the sequestration and the full right and interest accruing thereon to the bankrupt shall be held as transferred to and vested in the Trustee as at the date of the acquisition thereof or succession for the purposes of this Act." Accordingly now a *spes successionis* falls under the sequestration. The Trustee is entitled to insure the life of the bankrupt to cover the risk of his dying before the estate vests in the bankrupt.[3]

Duties of Trustee.—As soon as may be after his appointment, the Trustee takes possession of the bankrupt's estate and effects, and of his title-deeds, books, bills, vouchers, and other papers and documents. Thereafter he makes up an inventory of such estate and effects, and a valuation showing the estimated value and the annual revenue thereof.[4] Following upon this, his duty is to manage, realise, and recover the estate belonging to the bankrupt, and to convert it into money according to the directions given by the creditors at any meeting, or if no such directions be given, then with the advice of the Commissioners.

Lodgment of Money in Bank.—The Trustee lodges all money which he receives in such bank as the majority of the creditors in number and value at any general meeting may appoint ; and failing such appointment, in any joint-stock bank of issue in Scotland (provided that the bank be not one in which the Trustee is an acting partner, manager, or cashier), at the highest rate of interest which can be procured. It is for the Trustee, not the bank, to decide into what account the money is placed. The bank is required once a year to balance such account.[5] Where the Trustee lodges money in his official capacity, he is not liable for failure of the bank, as he is if he lodges it in his private account. If the Trustee becomes bankrupt, money lodged in his official character belongs to the estate, but money lodged in his private account belongs to his own creditors.

Penalty on Trustee Retaining Funds.—If the Trustee keeps in his hands any sum exceeding fifty pounds belonging to the estate for more than ten days, he must pay interest to the creditors at the rate of twenty pounds per centum per annum on the excess of such sum above fifty pounds, for such time as the same is in his hands beyond that period. Unless the money has been so kept from innocent causes, the Trustee is liable to be dismissed from office, on petition to the

---

[1] B. A., sec. 97. [2] B. A., sec. 98.
[3] B. A., sec. 78. [4] B. A., sec. 76.
[5] B. A., sec. 78.

Lord Ordinary or Sheriff by any creditor, and he forfeits all claim to remuneration, and is liable in expenses.[1] The fund set apart by the Commissioners for the payment of a dividend is subject to the provisions just referred to ; and it has been held that the Trustee is not entitled to withdraw from bank the amount set apart for payment of a dividend at the time at which it is payable, but only to withdraw from time to time such sums as may be required to meet the payments to the creditors as they claim their dividends.[2]

Trustee's Remuneration.—It is the duty of the Commissioners to fix the commission or fee payable to the Trustee.[3] When this has been done the Trustee is required to intimate by circular to every creditor and to the bankrupt the deliverance of the Commissioners fixing his commission or fee.[4] Charges for clerk's writings in addition to commission cannot be allowed.[5] The Trustee or any of the creditors, and the bankrupt, are each entitled, within ten days from the issue of such circular, to appeal to the Accountant of Court against the deliverance. If any of the parties be dissatisfied with the determination of the Accountant, the matter is forthwith reported to the Lord Ordinary or the Sheriff, whose decision is final.[6] A Trustee who engages in litigation renders himself personally liable to the opposite party for any costs to which the latter may be found entitled.[7]

Removal or Resignation of Trustee.—A majority in number and value of the creditors present at any meeting duly called for the purpose may remove the Trustee without giving any reason for so doing, or they may accept his resignation.[8] One-fourth of the creditors in value may at any time apply by petition to the Lord Ordinary or to the Sheriff for removal of the Trustee. After service of the petition on the Trustee and intimation in the *Gazette*, the Lord Ordinary, or the Sheriff, if satisfied that sufficient reason has been shown, such as neglect, misconduct, or malversation of duties,[9] can remove the Trustee, and appoint a meeting of the creditors to be held for devolving the estate on the Trustee next in succession, or electing a new Trustee. The Trustee may also be removed from office at the instance of any one creditor or of the Accountant of Court.[10] If the Trustee dies, resigns, is removed,

---

[1] B. A., sec. 79.

[2] Accountant in Bankruptcy in Fredy's Tr., 30th June 1864.

[3] B. A., sec. 121.

[4] B. A., sec. 122.

[5] Lindsay v. Hendrie, 1880, 7 R. 911.

[6] B. A., sec. 122.

[7] Cowie v. Murden, 1893, 20 R. (H.L.) 81.

[8] B. A., sec. 71.

[9] Bell's Com. (M'L.'s ed.) ii. 382 ; Aytoun v. M'Culloch, 1824, 3 S. 80 ; Richmond v. M'Phun, 1854, 16 D. 546 ; Brown v. Burt, 1848, 11 D. 388.

[10] B. A., secs. 157 and 158.

or remains furth of Scotland for three months consecutively at any time, any Commissioner, or any creditor, ranked, or claiming and entitled to be ranked, on the estate, may apply to the Lord Ordinary or the Sheriff for an order to hold a meeting for devolving the estate on the Trustee next in succession, or electing a new Trustee. The Lord Ordinary or the Sheriff grants warrant to hold such meeting at a certain time and place, which is advertised in the *Gazette* by the Commissioner or creditor so applying. At the meeting the creditors may devolve the estate on the Trustee next in succession, or elect a new Trustee.[1] The procedure as to the fixing of security, the lodgment of the bond, and the issuing of the Act and Warrant, is similar to that followed in the case of the first election.[2]

Examination of the Bankrupt.—Within eight days after the date of his Act and Warrant, the Trustee applies to the Sheriff to name a day for the examination of the bankrupt. A diet is fixed by the Sheriff, and notice thereof is given by the Trustee to each creditor who has lodged a claim, or who is named in the bankrupt's state of affairs.[3] The Trustee may apply to the Sheriff to order the examination of the bankrupt's wife and family, clerks, servants, factors, law agents, and others who can give information relative to his estate.[4] Creditors or other persons litigating with the Trustee cannot be examined on matters which affect their own claim. The object of the bankrupt's examination is to ascertain what his estate consists of, where it is, and what he has done with it or to affect it,[5] or, in other words, to enable the Trustee to trace property which the bankrupt may otherwise have concealed. Formerly he was not entitled, but he has now the right to inquire into collateral matters which may in certain circumstances affect the pecuniary value of a bequest to which the bankrupt is entitled. Questions directed to the investigation of the merits of a particular creditor's claim are incompetent.[5] It is in the discretion of the Trustee either to hold the examination in open Court or privately. Questions may be put by the Trustee, or the Sheriff, or a Commissioner appointed by him. With the sanction of the Sheriff, any creditor or his mandatory may attend and put questions.

---

[1] B. A., sec. 71.   [2] See *supra*.
[3] B. A., sec. 83.   [4] B. A., sec. 86.
[5] Delvoitte *v.* Baillie's Trs., 1877, 5 R. 143.

CHAPTER IV

RANKING

Nature and Requisites.—Ranking is, in all questions relative to bankrupt estates, equivalent to a discharge of the debt in so far as the estate is bound for it ; but the receipt of a dividend is not full payment in a question with the creditor, who is free to employ whatever means are competent to him for obtaining full payment of his debt from co-obligants or otherwise. To entitle a creditor to draw a dividend, he must lodge in the sequestration process, or at a meeting of creditors, or in the hands of the Trustee, an oath or affirmation, and produce such accounts and vouchers as are necessary to prove the debt therein referred to, to the effect before explained with reference to claims for voting. There is, however, this distinction between a claim for voting and one for ranking, that whereas in the former case the creditor requires only to produce *primâ facie* evidence in support of his claim, in the latter he must produce such evidence as would be sufficient to prove his debt in an ordinary action for the recovery thereof.[1] Where a creditor claims a preference for the whole or part of his debt, not only must satisfactory evidence in support of the claim be produced, but also of the creditor's right to the preference.[2] If the oath or vouchers of a creditor's claim be lost or destroyed by fire while in the hands of the Trustee, the creditor will still be entitled to draw his dividend.[3] A reference to the bankrupt's oath in support of the creditor's claim is incompetent.[4]

Where a creditor is not in possession of such accounts and vouchers as are necessary to prove his claim at the time when it requires to be lodged with a view to the participation in a dividend, he must state in his oath the cause of their non-production, and in whose hands, to the best of his knowledge, they are. An oath so sworn to entitles the creditor to have a dividend set apart for him till a reasonable time be

---

[1] Laidlaw *v.* Wilson, 1844, 6 D. 530 ; Miller *v.* Lambert, 1848, 10 D. 1419 ; Turnbull *v.* M'Naughton, 1850, 12 D. 1097.

[2] Walker *v.* Hunter, 1853, 16 D. 226.

[3] Galloway *v.* Henderson, 1849, 12 D. 394 ; Campbell *v.* M'Neille, 1856, 18 D. 843.

[4] Adam *v.* M'Lachlan, 1847, 9 D. 560 ; Thomson *v.* Duncan, 1855, 17 D. 1081.

afforded for their production, or for otherwise establishing his debt according to law.[1]

A creditor who has a claim or debt due to him at the date of sequestration is entitled to vote and rank for the accumulated sum of principal and interest up to that date, but not for any interest accruing thereafter. If the debt is not payable till after the date of sequestration, the creditor can only vote and rank for it after deduction of the interest from the date of sequestration till the due date of payment. He must further deduct any discount beyond legal interest to which his claim is liable by the usage of trade applicable to it. If, however, there is any residue of the estate after discharging the debts ranked, the creditors are entitled to claim out of such residue the full amount of the interest on their debts in terms of law. In the absence of agreement to the contrary, interest is calculated at the rate of five per cent.

Deduction of Securities for Ranking.—To enable a creditor who holds a security over any part of the bankrupt's estate (which is defined to include securities, heritable or moveable, and rights of lien, retention, or preference, and conveyances thereof, or any part thereof [2]) to be ranked in order to draw a dividend, he must, on oath, put a specified value on such security, or if required by the Trustee on each such security deduct the same from his debt, and specify the baiance. Upon the amount of such balance, and no more, he is entitled to be ranked for and to receive a dividend, without prejudice to the amount of his debt in other respects.[3] The security requiring to be deducted must, at the date of the sequestration, be part of the estate of the bankrupt ; the reason being that the creditor, by virtue of his security, has appropriated a part of the estate which, but for the security, would be divisible amongst the general body of creditors. The date of sequestration is alone looked to in determining what securities require to be deducted. Thus it has been held that, where a person who had granted a bond and disposition in security over his heritable property, subsequently sold it and thereafter became bankrupt, the bond-holder was entitled to rank on the granter's estate for the full sum in the bond, without deducting the value of the security, on the ground that at the date of the sequestration the burdened subjects did not form part of the bankrupt estate.[4] Securities received from parties independent of the bankrupt do not require to be deducted ; nor do securities received from one of the partners of a firm in security of the firm's indebtedness, although in ranking on the partner's individual estate it is necessary that they

---

[1] B. A., sec. 46 ; Taylor *v.* Drummond, 1848, 10 D. 335 ; Liston *v.* Macintosh, 1853, 15 D. 923.

[2] B. A., sec. 2.

[3] B. A., sec. 61.

[4] University of Glasgow *v.* Yuill's Tr., 1882, 9 R. 643.

should be deducted. For the information of the Trustee, all securities held are stated in the affidavit. Three cases may be referred to. In one, a bank had made advances to a firm on obtaining as security certain bonds, transferable by indorsation, belonging respectively to A. and B., two of the partners, by whom they were blank indorsed and delivered to the bank. Subsequently the firm acquired from A. his right to the bonds belonging to him. Thereafter, the firm having been sequestrated, the bank claimed to rank on their estates for the full amount due to them, without deduction of any securities. The Court held that, in so far as the bonds belonged to the firm at the date of bankruptcy, although originally belonging to A., the bank's right was a right of security over part of the bankrupt estate, and that, as a condition of ranking, they were bound to deduct the value of these securities from the amount of their debt.[1] In the second case (decided by Lord Adam as Ordinary and acquiesced in), a bank gave a cash-credit to a firm and got in security a disposition to certain heritable property, which *ex facie* of the titles was the absolute property of one of the partners, although it was afterwards contended the subjects really belonged to the firm. On the bankruptcy of the firm, the bank claimed to rank for the full sum due to them, and, though called upon by the Trustee, declined to deduct the value of their security. In an action which followed, it was held that the rights of parties fell to be determined by the terms of the cash-credit bond, which specified the particular security which the bank agreed to take and receive, and that it was immaterial whether or not the bank knew that the partner only held in trust for the firm. In his note to the judgment, Lord Adam remarked that, as the firm consented to the subjects being disponed in security by a partner as his absolute property, they, or their trustee as representing them, could not object to this agreement receiving effect, and that to do so would be to diminish the security intended to be given by all parties concerned.[2] In the third case, bills drawn by A. and accepted by B. were discounted by a bank, and delivery orders for certain parcels of whisky standing in the joint names of A. and B. were assigned to the bank in security thereof. In a letter sent with the bills, A. stated that the whisky was held on joint account by B. and himself, and that the whisky was to be held by the bank in security of that specific transaction only. On the bankruptcy of A. during the currency of the bills, the bank claimed a ranking for the whole amount thereof, without deducting the value of their security over the whisky. This claim the Trustee disallowed. On an appeal, it was held that the bank were not bound to deduct the value of the

---

[1] Royal Bank *v.* Millar & Co.'s Tr., 1882, 9 R. 679.

[2] Royal Bank *v.* Purdon, 1877, 15 S.L.R. 13. See also M'Lelland *v.* Bank of Scotland, 1857, 19 D. 574 ; British Linen Co. *v.* Gourlay, 1877, 4 R. 651.

security either at common law or under the Bankruptcy Act.[1] It is only in the case where a person claims as an ordinary creditor that he requires to value and deduct his security. Where he claims for a preference only, such as that obtained by an arrestment of the bankrupt's funds, no valuation is necessary.[2] It must, however, be kept in view that where the creditor, having valued, and deducted the value of, his security, is allowed to retain the security subjects, he does not thereby acquire a proprietary right therein ; and that although he has discharged the debtor, his right nevertheless remains a security right, entitling him to call upon the debtor at any time to accept a reconveyance of the subjects.[3]

Claims on Partnership or Company Estates.—In the case of a firm or company consisting of more than one partner, the rule before explained applies. The creditors of the firm are entitled to rank on the estates of the firm to the entire exclusion of the private creditors of the partners, and also to rank equally with the private creditors on the individual estates of the partners, after deducting the amount they are entitled to receive from the firm's estate.[4] It is the duty of the Trustee, before ranking a creditor of the firm on the estates of an individual partner, to put a valuation on his claim on the estate of the firm, deduct from the claim of the creditor such estimated value, and rank and pay to him a dividend only on the balance.[5] If the creditor is dissatisfied with the valuation put on his claim against the firm's estate, he may appeal. Where one person carries on business under a company name, on his bankruptcy no distinction is made between his private and trade creditors. They all rank equally on the funds available for division.[6] Similarly, where two or more persons carry on the same or a similar business though under different firms' names, the whole estates of the firms are massed together and divided among the creditors of the different firms without distinction. A different rule would apply if there was a real and perceptible distinction of trade and establishment between the firms. In such a case the creditors of the different firms would rank on their separate estates.[7]

Partner becoming Bankrupt while Firm Solvent.—Where a partner of a solvent firm becomes bankrupt, his creditors have a right to his share of capital and profit in the firm, but as every partner is liable for

---

[1] Brickmann's Tr. *v.* Commercial Bank of Scotland, 1911, 38 S.L.R. 766.
[2] Brown *v.* Blaikie, 1849, 11 D. 474.
[3] Clydesdale Bank, Ltd. *v.* M'Intyre, 1909, S.C. 1405, *approving* Kinmond, Luke & Co. *v.* Jas. Finlay & Co., 1904, 6 F. 564.
[4] Bell's Com. ii. 660 ; Lusk *v.* Elder, 5 D. 1279.
[5] B. A., sec. 62.
[6] Reid *v.* Chalmers, 1828, 6 S. 1120 ; Cullen *v.* Macfarlane, 1842, 4 D. 1522.
[7] Commercial Bank of Scotland *v.* Tod's Tr., 1893, 23 S.L.R. 161 (*per* Lord Low).

the whole debts of the concern, the creditors' interests in the estate of the firm can only emerge after provision is made for the payment of the whole debts of the firm. A creditor of a solvent company can have no claim on the estate of a bankrupt partner, as he would require to value the obligation of the firm, which, of necessity, would be at twenty shillings in the pound.[1]

Co-obligants.—In claims for ranking, unlike those for voting, where a creditor holds an obligant bound with, but liable in relief to, the bankrupt, he does not require to value and deduct the obligation of such party in ranking upon the bankrupt's estate. The creditor is entitled to rank, and draw a dividend, for the full sum due to him. Where the creditor holds several obligants bound for the same debt, and they all become bankrupt, he is entitled to rank on the whole estates for the full sum due to him, to the effect of receiving twenty shillings in the pound, but no more, on the total amount of his claim, deducting only payments or recoveries made before bankruptcy, but not payments or recoveries made after that date, except only the produce or value of a security over the estates of the bankrupt, held by the creditor before bankruptcy.[2] Thus, in claiming on the bankrupt estate of one obligant, the creditor must deduct the amount of a dividend previously received from the sequestrated estate of another obligant.

Bills.—Where a creditor claims on a number of bills held by him, the surplus on one bill cannot be applied in relief of the deficit on another. In one case the Royal Bank were agents at Edinburgh for the Renfrewshire Bank, which was sequestrated in 1842. Among other debts the Royal Bank claimed for eight bills which were discounted by the bankrupts, and transmitted to the Royal Bank in security of advances. After two dividends had been paid on their claim as lodged, the Royal Bank recovered from the primary obligants full payment of these eight bills over and above the dividends paid on them. They thereupon withdrew their claim for these bills, and subsequently received payment of two additional dividends and a composition on their claim as restricted. Thereafter the Renfrewshire Bank was discharged on a composition, and an action was subsequently raised by their representatives against the Royal Bank for recovery of the amount received by that bank on the eight bills over and above twenty shillings in the pound. The Royal Bank sought to place the amount received in connection with the eight

---

[1] M'Clelland v. M'Cowan, 1849, 11 D. 1168.

[2] Robertson v. Bank of Scotland, 1823, 2 S. 450 ; Mein v. Sanders, 1824, 2 S. 778 ; Farquharson v. Thomson, 1832, 10 S. 526 ; Houston's Exr. v. Spiers, 1835, 13 S. 945 ; Hamilton v. Cuthbertson, 1841, 3 D. 494 ; Royal Bank v. Commercial Bank, 1881, 8 R. 817, *vide* Lord President's opinion. See also Lord President's opinion in Royal Bank v. Saunders & Sons' Trs., 1881, 8 R. 805 ; 1882, 9 R. (H.L.) 67, L. R. 7 Ap. Cas. 366.

bills to account of their other indebtedness, but the Court held they were not entitled to do so, and that the representatives were entitled to the repayment asked.[1]

Security Bills.—Where ordinary trade bills are lodged in security of a debt, and the principal debtor becomes bankrupt, the creditor is entitled to rank upon his estate for the full amount of his claim without deduction, and thereafter to call upon the parties to the bills to make good the deficiency. In the event of the parties becoming bankrupt, the creditor is entitled, to enable him to get full payment of his debt with interest, to rank on their estates for the full sum appearing on the face of the bills, irrespective of the amount of his debt. If, however, in this way he gets more than the sum due him, he will hold the surplus as trustee for the party from whom he received the bills.[2] Where a debtor gives to his creditor a bill for a sum greater than the amount due by him to such creditor, the creditor can only rank for the true amount of his debt, and a mere cautioner who is, admittedly in the knowledge of the creditor, nothing more than a cautioner for the debt, although he may have signed the bill for a large amount, can never be liable for a larger sum than was due by the principal debtor.[3] But a holder in due course [4] of such a bill, as, for example, a bank who may have discounted it, is entitled to rank for the full sum appearing on the face of the bill.

Agent's Bills.—In England, where goods are consigned by a merchant to a factor for sale, the owner of the goods is allowed to draw on the factor for a certain proportion of the value, more or less, according to the prospects of the market ; but in Scotland, in the event of the failure of both merchant and factor, while the bills are in the circle and the goods remain unsold, the holder of the bills is entitled to rank upon both estates, in order that he may, if possible, get full payment of his claim ; the factor's estate has a lien over the goods to the extent of entire relief and indemnification ; and, lastly, the merchant's estate is entitled to the balance of the proceeds of the goods after such relief.[5] If, however, it can be shown, upon a sound construction of an agreement between the parties, that the goods were appropriated towards payment of the bills drawn against them, the agreement will receive effect, and the billholder will have a right to insist upon payment of the proceeds of the goods in the extinction of his debt.[6]

Double Ranking.—It is a general rule of bankruptcy law that the same debt cannot be twice ranked for on the same estates, either by the

---

[1] Patten *v.* Royal Bank of Scotland, 1853, 15 D. 617.

[2] Black *v.* Melrose, 1840, 2 D. 706. See also Jackson *v.* M'Iver, 1875, 2 R. 882.

[3] Jackson *v.* M'Iver, *supra.*

[4] See Bills.

[5] Royal Bank of Scotland *v.* Saunders & Sons' Trs., 1881, 8 R. 805.

[6] *Per* Lord Watson in above case.

original creditor or anyone claiming through him. Thus if a creditor claim upon the principal debtor's estate, a cautioner (as, for example, in an ordinary bond of caution, guarantee, etc.) who may have paid the difference between the creditors ranking and the amount guaranteed, cannot rank on the principal debtor's estate for the sum so paid by him.[1] Similarly, in a bond of credit, where the principal debtor becomes bankrupt, and the bank claim on his estate for the full sum due, and receive a dividend, the other obligants are not entitled, upon their paying the difference, to rank on the principal debtor's estate for the amount so paid. The same rule applies to bills. In one case, A. accepted bills for the accommodation of B., who discounted them at a bank. A. and B. having become bankrupt, the bank claimed on both estates for the full amount of the bills. A.'s trustee claimed to retain a debt due by him to B.'s estate as a security for the dividend on the bills paid by him on B.'s account to the bank, on the ground that he was entitled to be reimbursed for his loss by B. The Court held that the bank having been already ranked on B.'s estate for the full amount of the bills, A.'s trustee could not also be ranked for the same debt, and therefore was not entitled to retain the sum due to B.'s estate either in security or satisfaction.[2] Although a cautioner is not entitled to rank on the bankrupt's general funds for his loss as cautioner, yet if the cautioner holds a lien over any special fund or any security belonging to the bankrupt, his right to full indemnity therefrom will not be affected by the prior ranking of the creditor.[3] The rule as to double ranking does not, however, apply to a case where a debtor has compounded with his creditors without becoming bankrupt or being divested of his estate. In such a case the debtor's estate never belongs to his creditors or to any trustee for their behoof, and thus there never is any separation or distinction of rights and interest between the insolvent and his estate, as there is in the case of sequestration. There is no ranking of the creditors, and therefore there cannot be a double ranking. There is no payment of the debts of the creditors, but only a purchase of a discharge from these debts for a consideration stipulated for and agreed to.[4]

Re-Valuation of Securities.—When a creditor has valued and deducted a security held by him and has ranked for the balance, he is not thereby precluded from re-valuing the security in claiming for a second dividend ; but he is not entitled to an equalising dividend in respect of the difference.[5]

---

[1] See under Guarantees, *ante*, p. 291 ; Harvie's Trs. *v.* Bank of Scotland, 1885, 12 R. 1141.

[2] Anderson *v.* Mackinnon, 1876, 3 R. 608.

[3] Bell's Com. i. 347, 348 ; Jamieson *v.* Forrest, 1875, 2 R. 700.

[4] Mackinnon *v.* Monkhouse, 1881, 9 R. 393.

[5] Commercial Bank of Scotland *v.* Speedie's Trs., 1885, 13 R. 257 ; Bell's Com. (M'L.'s ed.) ii. 361.

Assignation of Securities to Trustee.—As a check upon undervaluation, the Trustee, with consent of the Commissioners, is entitled, at the expense of the estate, and on payment out of the common fund of the value specified by the creditor, without the addition of twenty per cent. as in the case of voting, to a conveyance or assignation of any security over the bankrupt's estate held by a creditor, or to reserve to the creditor the full benefit of such security.[1] Under the scheme of the Act greater latitude is given to the creditor in his valuation for voting purposes than in that for ranking, for the obvious reason that in valuing for voting the creditor may not have had time to consider the matter carefully, whereas in valuing for ranking, having had time for careful considera- tion, he is tied down to specifying the true value of his security. No creditor is, however, obliged to rank in the sequestration, and if a creditor holds security sufficient to cover his debt there is no need for him to appear in the sequestration at all, since he can realise his security and recoup himself without further trouble. The creditor is not bound to give notice to the Trustee of his intention to realise his security. But if he does appear in the sequestration it is obvious that it is to his interest to value his security at the lowest possible figure, and it is to counteract this manœuvre that the Trustee is given power to take over the security at the figure which the creditor puts upon it. The condition on which the creditor is obliged to hand over the security is upon receiving actual payment of the value from the Trustee, and a mere tender of payment is not sufficient, since a creditor may quite competently sell his security and recoup himself even after he has made his claim in the sequestration, and a mere intimation on the part of the Trustee of his intention to take over the security creates no *nexus* on it such as to prevent the creditor disposing of it if he wishes.[2] While there is no statutory limitation of the time within which a Trustee may exercise his right, he must do so within a reasonable time. Whether the Trustee takes over the security or not, the creditor is entitled to a dividend on the balance of his debt.

Claims Depending on a Contingency.—When the claim of a creditor depends upon a contingency [3] which is unascertained at the date of lodging his claim, he is not entitled to vote or draw a dividend in respect of such contingent debt. He may, however, apply to the Trustee, or to the Sheriff if the Trustee has not been elected, to put a value on such debt, and the Trustee or the Sheriff (as the case may be)

---

[1] B. A., sec. 61 ; Hunter *v.* Slack, 1860, 22 D. 1166.

[2] Maclachlan *v.* Maxwell, 1910, S.C. 87, *per* Lord President (Lord Dunedin), *ap- proving* Henderson's Tr. *v.* Auld & Guild, 1872, 10 M. 946, and *commenting on* Macdougall's Tr. *v.* Lockhart, 1903, 5 F. 905.

[3] As to what is a contingency, see Stair, i. 3, 8 ; Bell's Com. i. 315 ; Garden *v.* M'Iver, 1860, 22 D. 1190 ; Morrison *v.* Turnbull, 1832, 10 S. 259 ; Gordon *v.* M'Cubbin, 1851, 13 D. 1154.

fixes the value thereof as at the date of such valuation. On such value being fixed the creditor is entitled to vote and draw dividends in respect of such value and no more. If the contingency have happened before the debt has been valued, the creditor may vote and draw dividends in respect of the amount of the debt ; but his doing so will not be allowed to disturb any former dividends allotted to other creditors. When such application is made to the Sheriff, notice thereof must be given to the bankrupt and petitioning or concurring creditor. The judgment of the Sheriff or Trustee is subject to review, and any creditor who has claimed on the estate may appeal and be heard on any appeal.[1] Until the appeal is disposed of the creditor is entitled to vote.[2] Where the contingency of a debt is incapable of present valuation, it would seem that the Trustee's duty is to lay aside a sum sufficient to provide a dividend for the debt until the issue of the contingency.[3]

Valuation of Annuities.—No creditor, in respect of an annuity granted by the bankrupt, is entitled to vote and draw a dividend until such annuity is valued. He may apply to the Trustee, or to the Sheriff if the Trustee has not been elected, to put a value on such an annuity. The Trustee or Sheriff (as the case may be) puts a value on the annuity, paying regard in so doing to the original price given for the annuity, and deducting therefrom such diminution in the value of the annuity as shall have been caused by the lapse of time from the grant thereof to the date of sequestration. Thereafter the creditor is entitled to vote and draw dividends in respect of such value and no more. The valuation is subject to review, and the like notice must be given as in the case of contingent claims.[4]

Trustee's Adjudication on Claims.—Within fourteen days after the expiration of four months from the date of sequestration, the Trustee, where a dividend is to be paid, but in that case only,[5] must examine the oaths and grounds of debt of the various creditors, and in writing admit or reject them, or require further evidence in support thereof. For this purpose he is entitled to examine the bankrupt, creditor, or any other party, on oath, relative thereto. The Trustee may, however, where a creditor claims a preference, reject the claim as regards the preference, but admit it to an ordinary ranking,[6] or he may admit the claim only to a limited extent, or subject to a condition.[7] Where the Trustee rejects a claim in whole or in part, he must in his deliverance state the ground

---

[1] B. A., sec. 49.

[2] Watson v. Morrison, 1848, 10 D. 1414.

[3] Mackenzie v. Macpherson, 1855, 17 D. 751 ; Garden v. M'Iver, *supra*.

[4] B. A., sec. 50.

[5] Monkhouse v. Mackinnon, 1881, 8 R. 454.

[6] Forbes v. Manson, 1851, 13 D. 1272.

[7] Gibb v. Brock, 1838, 16 S. 1002 ; Ewart v. Latta, 1863, 1 Macph. 905 ; *revd.* 1865, 3 Macph. (H.L.) 36.

of such rejection.[1] Within eight days after the expiration of the above fourteen days, the Trustee gives notice, in the *Gazette* published next after the expiration of such fourteen days,[2] of the time and place of the payment of the dividend. He also notifies the same by letter addressed to each creditor (posted on, or before, the first lawful day after the said fourteen days), in which is specified the amount of the claim and proposed dividend thereon. Where he has rejected any claim, he requires to notify the same to the claimant by letter as aforesaid, which letter must contain a copy of his deliverance and specify the amount of the claim. If any creditor is dissatisfied with the decision of the Trustee, whether on his own claim or that of another creditor,[3] he may appeal against the same by a short note to the Lord Ordinary or to the Sheriff; but if no such note is lodged with, and marked by, the Bill-Chamber Clerk or Sheriff-Clerk (as the case may be) before the expiration of fourteen days from the date of the publication in the *Gazette* of the said notice, the decision of the Trustee is final and conclusive in regard to that dividend. Where a claim has been rejected, such rejection is without prejudice to any new claim being afterwards lodged in reference to future dividends, but such new claim cannot disturb prior dividends. When the Trustee once issues his deliverance, ranking a claim for a particular dividend, he cannot afterwards alter it on the ground that he has discovered the claim to be bad.[4] This does not, however, prevent him rejecting the claim, in whole or in part, for subsequent dividends.

Expenses of Appeal.—A creditor who is unsuccessful in an appeal against a Trustee's deliverance is personally liable to the Trustee in expenses. Where the creditor is successful, it is incompetent to deduct any part of the expenses awarded to him from his dividend.[5]

Time of Lodgment of Claims.—To entitle a creditor to payment of the first dividend, he must produce his oath and grounds of debt at least two months before the time fixed for the payment thereof, when the time of payment has not been accelerated, or one month before the time fixed for payment of the first dividend where such time has been accelerated.[6] If the failure of the creditor to claim has arisen from want of the statutory notice by the Trustee, the creditor may obtain interdict against the payment of the dividend.[7] Where a creditor has not already lodged his claim, to entitle him to payment of the subsequent dividends, he must produce his oath and grounds of

---

[1] B. A., sec. 123.

[2] B. A., sec. 124.

[3] Morris *v.* Connal, 1843, 5 D. 439.

[4] Hamilton *v.* Kerr, 1830, 9 S. 40.

[5] De Tastet *v.* M'Queen, 1825, 4 S. 241; Houston *v.* Duncan, 1841, 4 D. 80; Adam & Kirk *v.* Tunnock's Tr., 1866, 5 M. 40.

[6] B. A., sec. 119.

[7] As to Statutory Notice, see B. A., sec. 83.

debt at least one month before the time fixed for payment of the
dividend which he means to claim. If, however, a creditor has not
produced his oath and grounds of debt in time to share in the first
dividend, but has done so in time to share in the second dividend, he
is entitled, on the occasion of the payment of the second dividend, to
receive out of the first of the fund (if there be sufficient for that purpose)
an equalising dividend corresponding to the dividend he would have
drawn if he had claimed in time for the first dividend. The rule applies
to all subsequent dividends.

CHAPTER V

DIVISION OF THE ESTATE

THE whole estate of the bankrupt, when realised and reduced into money, is, after paying all necessary charges, including the expenses of obtaining the sequestration, the expenses of management and a commission to the Trustee, divided among those creditors who were creditors of the bankrupt at the date of sequestration, ranking on the divisible fund according to their respective rights and interests.[1]

Payment of Dividends.—Immediately on the expiration of four months from the date of the deliverance actually awarding sequestration, unless the dividend is accelerated, the Trustee makes up a statement of the whole estate of the bankrupt, of the funds recovered by him, and of the property outstanding (specifying the cause why it has not been recovered), and also an account of his intromissions, and generally of his management of the estate. Within fourteen days thereafter the Commissioners meet,[2] audit the Trustee's accounts, and declare whether any and what part of the net produce of the estate, after making a reasonable deduction for future contingencies, should be divided among the creditors. On the expiration of eight months from the date of sequestration, the Trustee again makes up a similar statement, which he requires within fourteen days thereafter to exhibit to the Commissioners, who meet, examine, and audit the same, and perform the other duties incumbent on them.[2] If there are funds for the purpose, they then direct a second dividend to be paid. Similar proceedings take place at subsequent meetings.[3]

First Dividend.—On the first lawful day after the expiration of six months from the date of the deliverance actually awarding sequestration, unless the dividend is accelerated or altered, and at a place appointed, the Trustee pays to those creditors whose claims have been admitted by him, or by the Court on appeal, according to their respective rights, the dividends allotted to them, in terms of a scheme of division, which he is bound to make up, of the funds directed by the Commissioners to be divided. The scheme of division is patent to all

---

[1] B. A., sec. 117.
[2] See Duties of Commissioners, p. 317.
[3] See Payment of Subsequent Dividends, p. 334.

concerned. The Trustee further requires to send notices to each creditor of the amount of the dividend to which he is entitled.

Subsequent Dividends.—On the first lawful day after the expiry of ten months from the date of sequestration, if there be funds available therefor, the Trustee makes payment of a second dividend to those creditors entitled thereto. The like procedure is followed, as to subsequent dividends, at similar intervals of time thereafter, in order that a dividend may be paid on the first lawful day after the expiration of every three months from the payment of the immediately preceding dividend, until the whole funds of the bankrupt are divided. As in the case of the first dividend, a scheme of division with reference to the second dividend must be prepared within eight months of the date of sequestration, and similar notices to creditors sent out. The like procedure is followed with reference to subsequent dividends.[1]

Postponement of Dividends.—The Commissioners may postpone the declaration of a dividend until the recurrence of another statutory period for the payment of a dividend, and may, if they think fit, authorise the Trustee to give a notice to that effect in the next *Edinburgh Gazette*,[2] but the Trustee does not require to send notices to creditors.

Claims under Appeal.—Where, at the time of payment of a dividend, a claim is under appeal, and in the case of contingent or other claimants not then entitled to uplift the same, the Trustee is taken bound to lodge the dividends apportioned to those claims in the bank appointed by the creditors for the lodgment of all moneys received by the Trustee, or, failing such appointment, in any joint-stock bank of issue in Scotland, in a separate account. If the money be deposited in bank, he must transfer it to a separate account in name of himself and the Commissioners, to remain there until the appeal is disposed of or the dividend becomes payable. If ultimately successful in an appeal the creditor is entitled to the interest accrued on the dividend so lodged.[3] In the event of the appeal being dismissed or abandoned, the dividend set apart goes into the funds of the estate for payment of a second or subsequent dividend, and is not divided as a supplementary dividend among those creditors ranked for the first dividend.[4]

Winding up Estate under Deed of Arrangement.—At the meeting for the election of the Trustee, or at any subsequent meeting to be called for the purpose, a majority in number and three-fourths in value of the creditors present, or represented, at such meeting, may resolve that the estate be wound up under a deed of arrangement, and that an application should be presented to the Lord Ordinary, or the

---

[1] B. A., sec. 129.
[2] B. A., sec. 131.
[3] Houston *v.* Duncan, 1841, 4 D. 80.
[4] Blair *v.* Morrison, 1844, 6 D. 705.

Sheriff, to sist procedure in the sequestration for a period not exceeding two months. If this course be resolved on it is not necessary to elect a Trustee.[1] The bankrupt or any person appointed by the meeting reports such resolution to the Lord Ordinary, or the Sheriff, within four days of the date of such resolution, and applies for a sist of the sequestration. The Lord Ordinary, or the Sheriff, may hear any party having interest, and if he find that such resolution was duly carried, and that the application is reasonable, he may grant the same.[2] In the event of such application being granted, the Lord Ordinary, or the Sheriff, may, on the application of any creditor, make such arrangement for the interim management of the estate as he may think reasonable, and if any appear to be necessary.[3] This applies, however, only where a Trustee has not yet been appointed, and does not authorise the Sheriff, where a Trustee has been appointed to supersede his administration, appointing a judicial factor.[4] If the sequestration is sisted, the creditors may, at any time within the period of sist, produce to the Lord Ordinary or Sheriff a deed of arrangement subscribed by, or by authority of a majority in number and three-fourths in value of the creditors of the bankrupt. The Lord Ordinary, or the Sheriff, may consider the same and make such intimation thereof as he may think proper, hear parties having interest, and make such inquiry as he may think necessary. If he is satisfied that the deed of arrangement has been duly entered into and executed, and is reasonable, he approves thereof, and declares the sequestration at an end. Such deed is thereafter as binding on all the creditors as if they had acceded thereto. The sequestration, however, receives full effect in so far as may be necessary for the purpose of preventing, challenging, or setting aside preferences over the estate.[5] The Act contains no provisions as to the requisites or form of a deed of arrangement, the creditors and the bankrupt being left to arrange the terms of the deed as they choose. When the sequestration is declared at an end, the creditors lose all the remedies of the statute, except those already explained with reference to the reduction of preferences, and their rights are fixed and regulated by the deed of arrangement. It is, however, quite competent to them to agree to discharge the bankrupt with or without security, or to make the discharge conditional on payment. Thus where a bankrupt bound himself to pay a composition in three instalments, at four, eight, and twelve months, and failed to pay the last instalment at the time stipulated, it was held that a creditor was entitled to sue him for his whole debt under deduction of the instalments paid.[6] If the resolution is not duly reported, or if a sist be refused, or if the deed of arrange-

---

[1] B. A., sec. 34.   [2] B. A., sec. 35.   [3] B. A., sec. 36.
[4] Brown v. Bayley's Trs., 1910, S.C. 76.   [5] B. A., sec. 37.
[6] Alexander & Austine v. Yuille, 1873, 1 R. 185.

ment is not duly lodged and approved of, the Lord Ordinary, or the Sheriff, may make all necessary orders, by appointing meetings [of creditors and otherwise, for resuming the necessary procedure in the sequestration.[1]

Discharge of Bankrupt on Composition.—Instead of having the estate of the bankrupt realised and divided among the creditors, it is competent for the creditors, with the approval of the Court, to accept an offer of composition from the bankrupt or his friends, with security for its due payment, and to reinstate him in possession of the estate. The procedure is as follows :—At the meeting for the election of Trustee,[2] the bankrupt or his friends, or, in case of his decease, his successors, and in case of a company, one or more of the partners thereof, may offer a composition to the creditors, whether they have claimed or not, on the whole debts, with security for payment of the full amount of the composition. Security for a part thereof is not sufficient. If the majority of the creditors in number and three-fourths in value,[3] present at such meeting, resolve that the offer and security be entertained for consideration, the Trustee forthwith advertises in the *Gazette* a notice that an offer of composition has been so made and entertained, and that it will be decided upon at a meeting to be held after the examination of the bankrupt. To enable the creditors to judge of the offer and security, he must further transmit by post to each of the creditors claiming on the estate, or mentioned in the bankrupt's state of affairs (where one creditor was omitted an appeal against the resolution was sustained),[4] a letter containing a notice of such resolution and of the day and hour at which, and the place where, such meeting is to be held, specifying the offer and security proposed, and giving an abstract of the state of affairs and of the valuation of the estate, so far as the same can be done. If at such meeting a majority in number and three-fourths in value of the creditors present accept such offer and security,[5] a Bond of Caution for payment of the composition, executed by the bankrupt or his successors, or the partners of a company (as the case may be), and the proposed cautioner, is forthwith lodged in the hands of the Trustee, who transmits a report of the resolution of the meeting with the Bond to the Bill-Chamber Clerk, or Sheriff-Clerk, in order that the approval of the Lord Ordinary or the Sheriff (whoever may be selected by the Trustee) may be obtained thereto. If the Lord Ordinary, or the Sheriff, after hearing any objections by creditors,[6] or by the Trustee and

---

[1] B. A., sec. 38.

[2] B. A., sec. 134.

[3] As to claims for voting and computing majorities, see *ante*, p. 311 *et seq.*

[4] Smith *v.* Chrystal, 1848, 10 D. 1474.

[5] B. A., sec. 135.

[6] Brown *v.* White, 1846, 8 D. 822 ; Scottish Provincial Assurance Co. *v.* Christie, 1859, 21 D. 333.

cautioner,[1] who are entitled to appear and oppose the application, finds that the offer with the security has been duly made, is reasonable, and has been assented to by the foresaid majority, he pronounces a deliverance approving thereof. Creditors, or the Trustee and cautioner, are entitled to state objections in respect of (1) irregularity in the proceedings ; (2) fraud and collusion between some of the parties ; (3) insufficiency of the caution ; (4) unreasonableness of the composition ; or (5) failure to pay five shillings in the pound, or to show that such failure has been due to causes for which the bankrupt cannot be justly held responsible.[2] In like manner, at the meeting held after the examination of the bankrupt,[3] or at any subsequent meeting called for the purpose by the Trustee with the consent of the Commissioners, in whose discretion the calling of the meeting is,[4] the bankrupt, or his foresaids,[5] may offer a composition to the creditors on the whole debts, with security for payment. If a majority in number and three-fourths in value of the creditors present resolve that the offer and security be entertained for consideration, the Trustee calls another meeting, to be held not less than twenty-one days thereafter, and seven days at least before such meeting he posts to the creditors a notice similar to that already referred to.[6] If at the meeting so called a majority in number and three-fourths in value of the creditors present accept the offer and security, a Bond of Caution is lodged, a report made, and the like procedure followed as in the case just mentioned.[7] Any alteration, or amendment, or variance, not of the nature of a trivial and wholly accidental correction, on the offer as originally submitted, is incompetent at the second meeting.[8] On such deliverance being pronounced, the bankrupt makes a declaration, or oath, in the form prescribed by the statute,[9] before the Lord Ordinary or the Sheriff, and such deliverance, when pronounced, operates as a complete discharge and acquittal to the bankrupt of all debts and obligations contracted by him, or for which he was liable at the date of the sequestration, reinvests him in his estate, subject to the claims of the creditors against him and the cautioner for the composition, terminates the sequestration, and exoners and discharges the Trustee.[10] When once

---

[1] Miller v. Keith, 1872, 11 M. 164 ; Ironside v. Gray, 1841, 4 D. 629 ; Lee v. Stephenson's Tr., 1883, 11 R. 26.

[2] Wallace on Bankruptcy, 189.

[3] B. A., sec. 136.

[4] Weldon v. Ferrier, 1879, 7 R. 235.

[5] *Ante*, p. 336.

[6] *Ibid.*

[7] B. A., sec. 136.

[8] Milne v. Boyack, 1845, 7 D. 888.

[9] B. A., sec. 137.

[10] *Ibid.* ; Holmes v. Reid, 1829, 7 S. 535. See also Shand v. Winton, 1848, 11 D. 162 ; Fleming v. Walker's Tr., 1876, 4 R. 112.

22

accepted, the offer cannot be recalled without cause assigned.[1] In the case of firms, the offer may be accepted from one partner and he be discharged, while as to the others it may be refused, and the sequestration allowed to go on. Neither the bankrupt, nor his successor offering the composition, nor the cautioner, is entitled to object to any debt which the bankrupt has given up in the state of his affairs as due by him, or admitted without question, being reckoned in the acceptance of the offer of composition, nor to object to any security held by any creditor, unless in the offer of composition such debt or security is stated as objected to, and notice in writing given to the creditor in right thereof.[2] Where a creditor holds a security over any part of the bankrupt's estate, he can only claim a composition on the balance of his debt after deducting such security.[3] No person who has not produced an oath as a creditor before the date of the deliverance approving of the composition, is entitled to make a demand against the cautioner after the space of two years from the date of such deliverance, but he may do so against the bankrupt and his estate.[4] After the bankrupt is discharged, the creditors' claim against him is only for the composition, and if he fail to pay the same, they can only sue him for the amount of the composition, while, if he be again sequestrated, they can only rank for the composition.[5]

Reduction of Discharge.—A composition contract, and the discharge following thereon, may be reduced and annulled, and the proceedings in the sequestration resumed, on the ground (1) that the proceedings had not been conducted in terms of the statute ; [6] (2) that preferences or payments, or collusive agreements, had been entered into for the purpose of facilitating or obtaining discharge ; [7] or (3) of wilful concealment, or defective representations, in the state of affairs and valuation of the estate, by which the creditors were prevented from properly judging of the offer made.[8] The creditors must institute their challenge as soon as the facts, upon which they base their right to annul the discharge, become known to them.

Illegal Preferences.—The policy and object of bankruptcy law are to secure to all creditors an equal distribution of a bankrupt's estate, according to their just claims and equities, and to give to the bankrupt

---

[1] Bell's Com. ii. 469 ; Ironside v. Gray, 1841, 4 D. 629 ; Lee v. Stephenson's Tr., 1883, 11 R. 26.

[2] B. A., sec. 140 ; Adam v. Wylie, 1842, 5 D. 391 ; Sillars v. Western Bank, 1850, 13 D. 431. See also Irvings v. Cliffe, 1824, 3 S. 129.

[3] M'Bride v. Stevenson, 1884, 11 R. 702.

[4] B. A., sec. 141.

[5] Saunders v. Renfrewshire Banking Co., 1827, 5 S. 565.

[6] Milne v. Boyack, 1845, 7 D. 888.

[7] As to preference, see *infra*.

[8] Stewart v. Stirling, 1836, 14 S. 989.

considerable advantages in regard to his discharge. To prevent a creditor obtaining an unjust preference for himself, by receiving a payment in excess of his share in this equal distribution, the statute contains provisions of a stringent character against both the bankrupt and the creditor participating in such arrangement, and enacts that " All preferences, gratuities, securities, payments, or other consideration, not sanctioned by this Act, granted, made, or promised, and all secret or collusive agreements and transactions, for concurring in, facilitating, or obtaining the bankrupt's discharge, either on, or without, an offer of composition, and whether the offer be accepted or not, or the discharge granted or not, shall be null and void ; and if, during the sequestration, any creditor shall have obtained any such preference, gratuity, security, payment, or other consideration or promise thereof, or entered into such secret or collusive consideration, or agreement, or transaction, the Trustee shall be entitled to retain his dividend ; and he, or any creditor ranked on the estate, may present a petition to the Lord Ordinary, or to the Sheriff, praying that such creditor shall be found to have forfeited his debt, and be ordained to pay to the Trustee double the amount of the preference, gratuity, security, payment, or other consideration given, made, or promised ; and if no cause be shown to the contrary,[1] decree shall be pronounced accordingly ; and the sums which in such case may be recovered shall, under deduction of the expenses of recovering the same, be distributed by the Trustee among the other creditors under the sequestration ; and if the sequestration shall have been closed, it shall be competent to any creditor, who shall not have received full payment of his debt, to raise a multiplepoinding in name of the person who has obtained such preference, gratuity, security, payment, or other consideration or promise, as aforesaid ; and on the value of the preference, gratuity, or security, or amount of the sum paid, or consideration obtained, being ascertained, double such value or amount, together with the amount of the debt of the colluding creditor, shall be ordered to be consigned by him, and shall be divided among the creditors who were ranked, or were entitled to be ranked, in the sequestration, and have not received full payment of their debts, and who shall lodge claims in such multiplepoinding, according to their respective rights and interests, and such multiplepoinding shall be executed in terms of law against the colluding creditor, and notice thereof at the same time be inserted in the *Gazette* ; and in the event of there being any surplus after paying the full debts of the creditors and defraying the expenses of the sequestration or other proceeding, the same shall be paid into the account of unclaimed dividends." [2]

---

[1] See Carter *v.* M'Laren, 1871, 9 M. (H.L.) 49, where the House of Lords held that these words gave the Court no discretion in pronouncing decree.

[2] B. A., sec. 150.

Every illegal preference or payment of whatever kind, whether actually made, or obtained, or promised, and whether by the bankrupt, or others directly acting on his behalf, is followed by the penal consequences provided by this section. The section was passed in the interests of commercial morality, and it is enforced without any attempt to mitigate its severity. When it has been proved that the statutory offence has been committed, the Court has no power to remit or mitigate any portion of the penalty. Collusion and secrecy are immaterial.[1]

As regards the bankrupt, if he has been personally concerned in, or cognisant of, the granting, giving, or promising of such preferences, etc., the Act provides [2] that he shall forfeit all right to a discharge and all benefits under the Act. If a discharge has been granted, it is competent for the Trustee, or any one or more of the creditors, to apply by petition to the Lord Ordinary to have such discharge annulled. On the above facts being established, the discharge is annulled accordingly.

Though a bankrupt has been discharged under a sequestration, yet, if he subsequently accept a bill for a debt which existed prior to the sequestration, he will incur liability for it, provided the transaction be not tainted by any illegal arrangement prior to the discharge.[3]

---

[1] Carter (Pendreigh's Tr.) v. M'Laren & Co., 1871, 9 M. (H.L.) 49 ; 2 L.R. Scot. Ap. Cas. 120 ; Thomas v. Sandeman, 1872, 11 M. 81.

[2] Sec. 151.

[3] Sutherland v. Mackay, 1830, 8 S. 313 ; Hunter v. Lindsay, 1835, 13 S. 390 ; Halyburton v. Rutherford, 1838, 16 S. 1235.

CHAPTER VI

DISCHARGE OF BANKRUPT AND TRUSTEE

When Competent, and how Effected.—The policy of bankruptcy law is to enable a debtor, who has given up all his estate for the benefit of his creditors, to obtain his discharge and to start business afresh, unencumbered with his previous indebtedness. The bankrupt, or when he is abroad, a mandatory on his behalf,[1] may, at the following stages in the sequestration proceedings, apply to the Lord Ordinary, or the Sheriff, to be finally discharged of all debts contracted by him before the date of sequestration. (1) At any time subsequent to the meeting held after his examination, provided every creditor who has produced an oath concurs in the petition. (2) On the expiration of six months from the date of sequestration, provided a majority in number and four-fifths in value of the creditors who have produced oaths concur in the petition. (3) On the expiration of twelve months from the date of sequestration, provided a majority in number and two-thirds in value of the creditors concur in the petition. (4) On the expiration of eighteen months from the date of sequestration, provided a majority of the creditors in number and value concur in the petition. (5) On the expiration of two years from the date of sequestration, without any consents of creditors.[2] Where a creditor has given his consent, he cannot withdraw it after the application has been presented, but he may do so before that time.[3] In each of the above cases the Lord Ordinary, or the Sheriff, orders the petition to be intimated in the *Gazette* and to each creditor, whether he has claimed or not.[4] Each creditor has a right, within twenty-one days from the date of publication of such notice, to appear and oppose the application. If there be no appearance to oppose the same, the Lord Ordinary or the Sheriff pronounces a deliverance finding the bankrupt entitled to his discharge. If appearance be made by any of the creditors or by the Trustee, the Lord Ordinary or the

---

[1] Cameron *v.* M'Nab, 28th February 1818, F.C. ; How *v.* Bank of England, 1833, 12 S. 211.

[2] B. A., sec. 143.

[3] Bell's Com. (M'L.'s ed.) ii. 445.

[4] Geddes, *Petr.*, 1840, 2 D. 833.

Sheriff judges of such objections, and may either find the bankrupt entitled to his discharge or refuse the discharge or defer the consideration of the same for such period as he may think proper, and may annex such conditions thereto as the justice of the case may require. Accordingly the Court may order the bankrupt to pay over to the Trustee a portion of his salary accruing after the date of sequestration.[1] Prior to presenting his petition, the bankrupt must obtain a report from the Trustee with regard to his conduct, stating in how far he has complied with the provisions of the Act, and, in particular, whether he has made a fair discovery and surrender of his estate, whether he has attended the diets of examination, whether he has been guilty of any collusion, and whether his bankruptcy has arisen from innocent misfortunes or losses in business, or from culpable or undue conduct.[2] The report may be given by the Trustee at any time, but cannot be demanded as a right until five months after the date of sequestration.[3] Under the Bankruptcy Act of 1856, which has now been repealed, if no creditor appeared to oppose the application, and on evidence being produced of the concurrence necessary, where such was required, the Court had no discretion, but was bound to grant the discharge craved.[4] This state of the law is now altered, and the Lord Ordinary, or the Sheriff, may refuse a discharge although two years have elapsed, and although no appearance or opposition is made by or on behalf of any of the creditors if it appears from the report of the Accountant or other sufficient evidence that the bankrupt has fraudulently concealed any part of his estate or effects or has wilfully failed to comply with any of the provisions of the Act.[5] Further, a bankrupt is not, at any time, entitled to be discharged of his debts [6] unless it be proved to the satisfaction of the Lord Ordinary, or the Sheriff, (1) that a dividend or composition of not less than five shillings in the pound has been paid out of the estate of the bankrupt, or that security for payment thereof has been found to the satisfaction of the creditors ; or (2) that the failure to pay five shillings in the pound has arisen from circumstances for which the bankrupt cannot justly be held responsible.[7] The Lord Ordinary, or the Sheriff, has power to require the bankrupt to submit such evidence as he may think necessary, in addition to the declaration made by the bankrupt [8] and the report by

---

[1] Caldwell v. Hamilton, 1918, S.C. 677.

[2] B. A., sec. 143 ; Scott v. Couper, 1872, 10 M. 626.

[3] Mather v. M'Kittrick, 1881, 8 R. 952.

[4] Millar, Petr., 1877, 5 R. 144.

[5] B. A., sec. 151.

[6] B. A., sec. 146.

[7] As to the construction of this section, see Shand, Petr., 1882, 19 S.L.R. 562 ; Wilson & Co., 1882, 20 S.L.R. 17 ; Clarke v. Crockatt, 1883, 11 R. 246 ; Boyle, Petr., 1885, 22 S.L.R. 767 ; Neilson, 1901, 3 F. 446 ; Gemmel, 1902, 4 F. 441.

[8] B. A., sec. 146 (2).

the Trustee,[1] and to allow any objecting creditor such proof as he may think right. While the judgment of the Lord Ordinary, or the Sheriff, is subject to review by the Inner House of the Court of Session, the statutory provision gives such weight to the opinion of the Lord Ordinary, or the Sheriff (as the case may be), that the Court of Appeal is not justified in altering his determination unless it is so plainly wrong that there are no reasonable grounds on which it can be supported.[2] The decision of the Inner House is, however, final.[3] In the event of a discharge being refused, the bankrupt may at any time, if his estate yield five shillings in the pound, or if he shall pay to his creditors such additional sum as will, with the dividend or composition previously paid out of his estate, make up five shillings in the pound, apply for, and obtain, his discharge in the same manner as if a dividend of five shillings had originally been paid.[4]

Firms.—In the case of a firm of two or more partners, where both the firm and individual partners are sequestrated, a discharge may be granted to the partners, as such and as individuals, or they may be discharged as partners, without being so as individuals, or *vice versâ*. One partner may be discharged without the others being discharged.

Effect of Discharge.—The deliverance awarding discharge operates as a complete discharge and acquittance to the bankrupt of all debts and obligations contracted by him or for which he was liable at the date of the sequestration [5] with the exception of any debt due to His Majesty or any debt or penalty with which he stands charged at the suit of the Crown unless the Treasury consents to such discharge.[6] The discharge does not release the bankrupt from any obligation incurred by him subsequent to the date of sequestration.[7] Neither does the discharge put an end to the sequestration [8] nor reinvest the bankrupt in his estate.[9] The discharge does not relieve cautioners and co-obligants who, at the date of the sequestration, were bound along with the bankrupt, nor does assent to a discharge deprive a creditor of his right to recourse against such obligant. A co-obligant may, at his own expense, obtain from the creditor an assignation to the debt, on payment of the amount thereof, and in virtue of the assignation he may himself claim on the estate.[10]

---

[1] B. A., sec. 143.

[2] Bell *v.* Bell's Tr., 1908, S.C. 853.

[3] B. A., sec. 146 (3).

[4] *Ibid.* sec. 146 (4).

[5] B. A., sec. 144.

[6] *Ibid.* sec. 147.

[7] Mackenzie *v.* Macpherson, 1855, 17 D. 551 ; Jackson *v.* Keil, 1862, 1 M. 48 ; Fraser *v.* Robertson, 1881, 8 R. 347.

[8] Henderson *v.* Bulley, 1849, 11 D. 1470.

[9] Buchanan *v.* M'Culloch, 1865, 4 M. 135.

[10] B. A., sec. 52 ; Ewart *v.* Latta, 1865, 3 M. (H.L.) 36.

Trustee's Discharge and Disposal of Unclaimed Dividends.—After a final division of the funds has taken place, the Trustee calls a meeting of the creditors, by advertisement in the *Gazette* and notice posted to every creditor, to consider as to an application for his discharge. At this meeting the Trustee lays before the creditors the Sederunt Book and Accounts, with a list of unclaimed dividends, and the creditors may then declare their opinion of his conduct as Trustee. The Trustee may thereafter apply to the Lord Ordinary, or the Sheriff, who, on advising the petition, with the minutes of the meeting, and hearing any creditor, may pronounce or refuse decree of exoneration and discharge.[1] A creditor may appear and oppose the discharge of the Trustee.[2] Before his discharge the Trustee must transmit the Sederunt Book to the Accountant of Court, who thereupon directs him to deposit the unclaimed dividends [3] and any unapplied balances in the same bank in which money received by him was lodged under the provisions of the Act.[4] The Trustee forthwith transfers the whole dividends not then claimed and any unapplied balances to such bank, in an account under the title of " Account of Unclaimed Dividends." A book or books is kept in the office of the Accountant of Court, entitled " The Register of Unclaimed Dividends," containing a list, alphabetically arranged, of all the creditors entitled to such unclaimed dividends, and the name of the bank in which they are deposited. This book is patent to all persons, and the deposit receipts for unclaimed dividends are kept by the Accountant. After the discharge of the Trustee, it is competent to any person, producing evidence of his right, to apply to the Accountant of Court for authority to receive any such dividend which has been deposited within seven years immediately preceding the date of such application and for which the deposit receipt is still in the custody of the Accountant, and on the Accountant being satisfied of the claimant's right a warrant is granted by him for payment of such dividend, and upon such warrant the bank pays the same with any interest accrued thereon.[5] At the expiry of seven years from the date of deposit of any unclaimed dividends or unapplied balance the Accountant of Court hands over the deposit receipt or other voucher to the King's and Lord Treasurer's Remembrancer, who can thereupon obtain payment of the amount due, principal and interest, from the bank in which the deposit was made ; the indorsation by the Remembrancer of any deposit receipt or other voucher is a sufficient warrant to a bank to pay the amount, with interest, to the said Remembrancer.[6]

---

[1] B. A., sec. 152.

[2] Hamilton's Tr. *v.* Caldwell, 1918, S.C. 190.

[3] See Appendix.

[4] See p. 319.

[5] B. A., sec. 153 (2).

[6] Court of Session Consignations (Scotland) Act, 1895, secs. 10, 11.

Prior to the Bankruptcy Acts of 1839 and 1856, there was no statutory provision for the lodgment of unclaimed dividends in bank, but it seems to have been a condition of the Trustee's obtaining his discharge that such dividends should have been consigned. In a sequestration awarded in 1820 under the Bankruptcy Act of 1814, certain unclaimed dividends were lodged in the Royal Bank. The dividends were unclaimed by the original creditor or his representatives, and in 1886 the representatives of the bankrupt brought an action against the bank for payment. The Court held that neither the bankrupt nor his representatives were entitled to the dividends.[1]

---

[1] Air *v.* Royal Bank of Scotland, 1886, 13 R. 734.

CHAPTER VII

SUMMARY SEQUESTRATION

ABOLISHING the old process of *Cessio Bonorum*, the "Bankruptcy (Scotland) Act, 1913"[1] in substitution thereof has introduced a new process known as Summary Sequestration. The law, already explained, applicable to ordinary sequestrations applies to summary sequestrations except where special provisions otherwise are made in the Act. These special provisions regulating the new process may thus be briefly summarised.

Presentation of Petition.—The petition is presented to the Sheriff of any sheriffdom within which the debtor has resided or carried on business during the year immediately preceding the date of the petition. A petition at the instance of the debtor is not competent in the Court of Session, nor is a petition in that Court competent at the instance of a creditor unless in the two following cases, viz. :—(1) Where the creditor does not know within which sheriffdom the debtor resided or carried on business during the year immediately preceding the date of the petition ; or (2) if the debtor be furth of Scotland. In these two cases the petition may be presented to the Court of Session in the Bill Chamber.

Who may Apply.—The petition may be at the instance of the debtor without the concurrence of any creditor, and in this case the debtor need not be notour bankrupt, or where the debtor is notour bankrupt and within four months after the constitution of notour bankruptcy at the instance of one creditor or two or more creditors whose claims in the aggregate amount to £10 or upwards.

When Competent.—Summary sequestration is only competent where the debtors' assets of every description do not in the aggregate exceed £300 in value. There is no provision in the statute for the winding-up of the estates of a deceased debtor by summary sequestration.

Procedure on Petition.—Where the petition is presented by a debtor he must, along with the petition, lodge with the Sheriff-Clerk a short state of his affairs subscribed by himself. Where the petition is at the instance of a creditor or creditors the first order by the Court contains an order to cite the defender to appear in court within a specified number

---

[1] B. A., sec. 174. The special provisions regarding summary sequestrations are contained in secs. 174 to 177 of the Act.

of days to show cause why sequestration of his estates should not be awarded, and also contains an order on the debtor within six days after the order is served upon him to lodge in the hands of the Sheriff-Clerk or Clerk of the Bills, as the case may be, a short state of his affairs subscribed by himself. The judge to whom the petition is presented may either order the sequestration to proceed as a summary sequestration or he may make no such order in which case the sequestration proceeds as an ordinary and not a summary sequestration.

Examination of the Bankrupt.—Instead of requiring the Trustee to present a petition to the Sheriff for the examination of the bankrupt in a summary sequestration, the Trustee applies orally to the Sheriff to fix a day for the examination of the bankrupt. Not less than seven days prior to the date fixed for the examination the Trustee must give notice to the bankrupt to attend, and he must also give notice in the *Edinburgh Gazette* and post to each creditor who has lodged a claim or who is mentioned in the bankrupt's state of affairs or is otherwise known to the Trustee, a circular, which notice and circular must intimate the Trustee's name and designation, his appointment as Trustee, the day, hour, and place fixed for the examination of the bankrupt, the period within which claims should be lodged, and a specified day, hour, and place for holding a second meeting of creditors. Creditors must lodge their oaths and claims and grounds of debt with the Trustee not less than twenty-one days before the second meeting. The Trustee is appointed at the first meeting of creditors, which is held as in an ordinary sequestration.

Dividends.—When a dividend is to be paid the Trustee must not less than fourteen days prior to the second meeting adjudicate upon the claims of creditors, admitting or rejecting them in whole or in part. The Trustee must prepare a list thereof, which is open to inspection by the bankrupt and by the creditors. Where a claim is rejected in whole or in part the Trustee must intimate the fact to the creditor ten days at least before the second meeting. Where the deliverance of the Trustee is objected to by the bankrupt or any of the creditors, the bankrupt or the objecting creditor must give notice to the Trustee and to any creditor whose claim is objected to of his intention to object thereto and of the nature and particulars of the objection by registered letter, posted three days at least before the second meeting. The Trustee then applies orally to the Sheriff to fix a day for the disposal of such objections. At the diet so fixed the Sheriff hears parties *vivâ voce*, and after such proof as he thinks fit disposes of the objections summarily and settles the ranking of the creditors so objected to. The judgment of the Sheriff is subject to appeal. At the second meeting the Trustee attends and the creditors may also attend by themselves or their mandatories. The Trustee and Commissioners may fix a date for payment of the first or final dividend, or they may postpone payment of a dividend to a date not later than three months after the date of the second meeting. Where there are appeals pending against any deliverance by the Trustee, the Trustee and Commissioners, if they find it inexpedient to fix a time to declare a dividend, may determine to declare a dividend as soon after the objections have been disposed of as in their opinion it is expedient to do so. At the second meeting, if it appear that there will be no funds for division among the creditors, the creditors shall direct the Trustee to report the fact orally to the Sheriff, and failing such direction the Trustee may then or at any subsequent period orally report to the Sheriff that there will be no funds for division, who may thereupon in writing dispense with any further procedure in the summary sequestration.

Accounts of Trustee.—Ten days at least prior to the date fixed for the payment of a dividend the Trustee's accounts with the relative vouchers must be submitted to the Commissioners for audit. The Commissioners fix the Trustee's remuneration. The decision of the Commissioners is subject to review by the Accountant of Court at the instance of the Trustee, the bankrupt, or any creditor. The law agent's account must be taxed by the auditor of the Sheriff Court previous to the meeting and produced at the meeting.

Subsequent Dividends.—Where the Trustee has funds in hand, or is about to come into possession of funds which will admit of a dividend to the creditors, it is his duty and that of the Commissioners to fix a date for the payment of the second or any subsequent dividend. The date fixed for the payment of the second or subsequent dividend is advertised in the *Edinburgh Gazette*. The Trustee must also send notice to any creditor mentioned in the debtor's state of affairs known to him who has previously failed to lodge his claim intimating the proposed dividend and stating the last day for lodging claims. Where a creditor has failed to lodge his claim in time to participate in any previous dividend or dividends, he is entitled if he lodges his claim, to participate in the new dividend, and is also entitled to an equalising dividend as well as to the new dividend upon the amount of his claim which may be sustained.

Meetings of Creditors.—The Trustee, or any creditor with the consent of the Trustee and Commissioners, or with the consent of the Commissioners alone, may at any time call a meeting of the creditors to consider and dispose of any matters to be specified in the notice calling such meeting.

Periodical Reports to the Accountant of Court.—It is the duty of the Trustee periodically to report to the Accountant of Court the then state of a summary sequestration, and specifying the following particulars :— (1) The amount of the funds recovered ; (2) the amount of the dividend or dividends paid ; (3) the amount and nature of the assets not realised ; (4) the reason or reasons which have prevented him from realising the said assets ; and (5) an estimate of the time when in his opinion these assets will be realised.

Discharge of Trustee.—Unlike in the case of an ordinary sequestration the Trustee in a summary sequestration does not require to present a

formal petition to the Sheriff for his discharge. To obtain his discharge
after the final division of the funds, or where the Sheriff has in writing
dispensed with further procedure, the Trustee may apply to the
Accountant of Court for a certificate that he is entitled to his discharge,
at the same time delivering to the Accountant the Sederunt Book and
Accounts with a list of unclaimed dividends, if any. If the Accountant
is satisfied that the Trustee is entitled to his discharge, and upon the
Trustee depositing in bank any unclaimed dividend and unapplied
balances, the Accountant issues a certificate stating that the Trustee
is entitled to his discharge. On getting this certificate the Trustee orally
reports the fact to the Sheriff, who fixes a diet for hearing any objections
which may be made to the Trustee obtaining his discharge. At least
seven days prior to the diet so fixed the Trustee publishes in the *Edinburgh
Gazette* a notice intimating the same. The bankrupt or any creditor
may appear at the diet and state objections. If no creditor appears, or
if a creditor or the bankrupt do appear, and the objections are repelled,
the Sheriff issues an interlocutor exonerating and discharging the Trustee
of all his actings and intromissions, and orders his bond of caution to be
cancelled and delivered up. The judgment of the Sheriff granting a discharge is final. If the Sheriff refuses the discharge, the Trustee may
appeal against his judgment to the Court of Session.

Discharge of Bankrupt.—The rules already explained with regard to
the discharge of a bankrupt apply to the discharge of a bankrupt in
summary sequestrations with this exception—Where the Sheriff has in
writing dispensed with further procedure in a sequestration, the bankrupt
may at any time thereafter petition the Sheriff for his discharge. The
bankrupt, however, must satisfy the Sheriff that his failure to pay five
shillings in the pound has arisen from circumstances for which he cannot
justly be held responsible.

CHAPTER VIII

WINDING-UP OF COMPANIES INCORPORATED UNDER THE COMPANIES ACTS

UNDER the Bankruptcy Act it is incompetent to sequestrate a company incorporated under the Companies Acts,[1] but such a company may be made notour bankrupt to the effect of equalising diligence [2] in terms of the Bankruptcy Act of 1913, sec. 10.[3] Such companies may be wound up in three ways, namely :—(1) By the Court, (2) voluntarily, and (3) under the supervision of the Court. The procedure in connection therewith is regulated principally by the Companies (Consolidation) Act, 1908.

1. Winding-up by the Court.—This process is known as compulsory or judicial winding-up. By " the Court," as regards Scotland, is meant the Court of Session in either Division thereof,[4] and when the Court makes a winding-up or a supervision order, or at any time thereafter, it may, if it think fit, direct that all subsequent proceedings be taken before one of the permanent Lords Ordinary, and remit to him accordingly. Thereafter such Lord Ordinary is deemed to be " the Court," and has for the purpose of the winding-up all the powers of the Court of Session. The judgments of the Lord Ordinary are subject to review,[5] and he may report to the Division of the Court any matter which may arise in the course of the winding-up.[6] A company may be wound up by the Court in any case where (a) the company has passed a special resolution resolving that the company be wound up by the Court ; (b) default is made in filing the statutory report or in holding the statutory meeting ; (c) the company does not commence its business within a year from its incorporation, or suspends its business for the space of a whole year ; (d) the members are reduced, in the case of a private company, below two, or in the case of any other company below seven ; (e) the

---

[1] Standard Property Investment Co. Ltd. *v.* Dunblane Hydropathic Co. Ltd., 1884, 12 R. 328.

[2] See Diligence.

[3] Clark, etc. *v.* Hinde, Milne & Co., 1884, 12 R. 347.

[4] Sec. 135.

[5] Sec. 181.

[6] Sec. 136.

company is unable to pay its debts ; [1] or (*f*) the Court is of opinion that it is just and equitable the company should be wound up.[2] A company is deemed to be unable to pay its debts : (*a*) whenever a creditor, by assignment or otherwise, to whom the company is indebted in a sum exceeding fifty pounds then due, has served on the company, by leaving the same at its registered office, a demand under his hands requiring the company to pay the sum so due, and the company has, for three weeks thereafter, neglected to pay the sum, or to secure or compound for it to the reasonable satisfaction of the creditor ; (*b*) whenever in Scotland—a different rule as to this applies in reference to companies registered in England and Ireland—the *induciæ* of a charge for payment on an extract decree, or extract registered bond or protest, have expired without payment being made ; or (*c*) whenever it is proved to the satisfaction of the Court that the company is unable to pay its debts.[3] In determining whether a company is unable to pay its debts the Court take into account the contingent and prospective liabilities of the company.

Application for Winding-up, and who may Apply.—The application is made by petition to the Court. It may be presented by the company, by any creditor or creditors (including any contingent or prospective creditor or creditors), by any contributory or contributories, or by all or any of these parties together or separately. A contributor is not entitled to present a petition for winding-up unless (1) either the number of members is reduced, in the case of a private company, below two, or in the case of any other company below seven ; or (2) the shares in respect of which he is a contributory, or some of them, either were originally allotted to him or have been held by him and registered in his name for at least six months during the eighteen months before the commencement of the winding-up, or have devolved on him through the death of a former holder. Every order on such petition operates in favour of all the creditors and contributories in the same manner as if it had been made upon the joint petition of a creditor and a contributor.[4] The winding-up is deemed to commence at the time of the presentation of the petition.[5]

Court may Grant Injunction and Appoint a Provisional Liquidator.— The Court may, at any time after the presentation of the petition, and before making an order for the winding-up of the company, restrain further proceedings in any action against the company, upon such terms

---

[1] M'Donnell's Trs. etc. *v.* Oregonian Railway Co., 1884, 11 R. 912.

[2] Companies Act, sec. 129. See Anglo-American Brush Electric Light Corporation *v.* Scottish Brush Electric Light and Power Co. Ltd., 1882, 9 R. 972.

[3] Sec. 130.

[4] Sec. 138.

[5] Sec. 139.

as the Court thinks fit,[1] and may also, at any time after the presentation of such petition, appoint provisionally an official Liquidator on the estates and effects of the company.[2] After the order for winding-up of a company has been made, the creditors are restrained from proceeding against the company, except by leave of the Court,[3] and subject to such terms as the Court may impose.

Effect of Order of Winding-up on Share Capital of Company Limited by Guarantee.—When an order has been made for the winding-up of a company limited by guarantee, and having a capital divided into shares, any share capital that may not have been called up is deemed to be assets of the company, and to be a debt due to the company from each member to the extent of any sums that may be unpaid on any shares held by him and payable at such times as may be appointed by the Court.[4]

Appointment of Official Liquidator.—For the purpose of conducting the proceedings in the winding-up, and performing such duties in reference thereto as the Court may impose, the Court may appoint an official Liquidator or Liquidators. Such officers may resign or be removed by the Court on due cause shown.[5] A vacancy in the office of a Liquidator appointed by the Court is filled by the Court. The duties of the Liquidator may be stated generally to be to take into his custody, or under his control, all the property and effects of the company, and to perform such duties as may be imposed upon him by the Court. The Liquidator has, with the sanction of the Court, extensive powers with regard to the raising of actions, carrying on the business of the company so far as may be necessary for the beneficial winding-up thereof, selling the property of the company by public auction or private contract, with power to transfer the whole thereof to any person or company or to sell the same in parcels, doing all acts and executing in the name and on behalf of the company all deeds, receipts, and other documents, and for that purpose to use, when necessary, the company's seal ; drawing, accepting, making, and indorsing any bill of exchange or promissory note in the name and on behalf of the company, with the same effect with respect to the liability of the company as if the bill or note had been drawn, accepted, made, or indorsed by or on behalf of the company in the course of its business ; raising on the security of the assets of the company any money requisite, and generally doing all such other things as may be necessary for winding-up the affairs of the company and distributing its assets.[6]

Collection and Application of Assets.—As soon as may be after the order of winding-up has been made, the Court settles a list of contributories, and causes the assets of the company to be collected and applied

---

[1] Sec. 140. [2] Sec. 149. [3] Sec. 87.
[4] Secs. 123 and 125. [5] Sec. 149. [6] Sec. 151.

in discharge of its liabilities.[1] The Court may fix a time or times within which creditors are to prove their debts or claims, or to be excluded from the benefit of any distribution made before these debts are proved.[2] A form of claim will be found in the Appendix.

2. Voluntary Winding-up.—A company may be wound up voluntarily (a) when the period (if any) fixed for the duration of the company by the articles expires, or the event (if any) occurs on the occurrence of which the articles provide that the company is to be dissolved, and the company in general meeting has passed a resolution requiring the company to be wound up voluntarily ; (b) the company resolves by special resolution that the company be wound up voluntarily ; or (c) the company resolves by extraordinary resolution to the effect that it is satisfactorily proved that the company cannot, by reason of its liabilities, continue its business, and that it is advisable to wind up.[3] The winding-up is deemed to commence at the time of the passing of the resolution authorising the winding-up.[4] A notice of the resolution as respects companies registered in Scotland is inserted in the *Edinburgh Gazette.*[5]

Effect on Status of Company.—From the date of the passing of the resolution, the company ceases to carry on business, except in so far as may be required for the beneficial winding-up thereof.[6]

Consequences of the Winding-up.—The property of the company is applied in satisfaction of its liabilities *pari passu.* Liquidators are appointed, and on their appointment the power of the directors ceases, except in so far as the company in general meeting, or the Liquidators, may sanction the continuance of such powers ; and without the sanction of the Court the Liquidators may exercise all the powers given to an official Liquidator. If from any cause whatever there is no Liquidator acting, the Court may, on the application of a contributory, appoint a Liquidator. The Court may, on cause shown, remove a Liquidator and appoint another Liquidator.[7] The minutes of the meeting of the company appointing Liquidators prove themselves, and no parole or other evidence is admissible to explain or contradict the terms of the Liquidator's appointment as therein set forth.[8] There is no power under the statute for staying diligence during the subsistence of a voluntary liquidation.[9] The Liquidators settle the list of contributories, make calls, and adjust the rights of contributories *inter se.* The voluntary winding-up of a company is no bar to the right of any creditor to have it wound up by the Court, if the Court is of opinion that the rights of

---

[1] Sec. 163.   [2] Sec. 169.   [3] Sec. 182.
[4] Sec. 183.   [5] Sec. 185.   [6] Sec. 184.
[7] Sec. 186.
[8] City of Glasgow Bank Liquidators, 1880, 7 R. 1196.
[9] Sdeuard v. Gardner, 1876, 3 R. 577.

such creditor will be prejudiced by a voluntary winding-up. An arrangement that the rights of all parties under the voluntary liquidation should be settled on the same footing as if there had been a winding-up by, or subject to, the supervision of the Court, is incompetent and ineffectual to give to the voluntary winding-up the incidents of a judicial winding-up, as, *e.g.* in the matter of restraint of diligence.[1]

3. Winding-up under the Supervision of the Court.—In the case of a voluntary winding-up, creditors are not debarred from proceeding against the company, and, where there is a chance of preferences being granted, recourse is had to have the winding-up continued under the supervision of the Court.[2] The petition may be presented either by the company, or by contributories or creditors, and upon such petition being presented, the Court has full power to order the voluntary winding-up to be continued, subject to the supervision of the Court, upon such terms and subject to such conditions as the Court thinks just. When such an order has been made, the Liquidators appointed to conduct the voluntary winding-up may, subject to any restrictions imposed by the Court, exercise all the powers of the Court, without its sanction or intervention, in the same manner as if the company were being wound up altogether voluntarily ; but all actions, suits, and proceedings against the company are stayed except with the permission of the Court. Where an order is made for a winding-up subject to supervision, the Court may, by the same or any subsequent order, appoint any additional Liquidator.[3] The Court can exercise all the powers which it has in a compulsory winding-up. A supervision order may be superseded by an order directing the company to be wound up compulsorily. In cases of winding-up under the supervision of the Court, all the advantages to be derived from a compulsory winding-up are secured, while the Liquidators and the company are free to conduct the winding-up without applying to the Court for its sanction. The winding-up is, as at the date of the presentation of the petition on which a supervision order is afterwards pronounced, equivalent to completed diligence, as in the case of a sequestration, and no arrestment or poinding, or poinding of the ground, within sixty days of that date is effectual, except for the current term's interest, and a year's arrears of interest.[4]

Difference between a Trustee in a Sequestration and a Liquidator.— The Trustee in a sequestration is invested in the entire estate of the bankrupt, and the bankrupt is entirely divested.[5] Liquidators, on the

---

[1] Clark *v.* Wilson, 1878, 5 R. 867.

[2] Gardner *v.* Hughes, 1883, 10 R. 1138 ; Benhar Coal Co. *v.* Turnbull, 1883, 10 R. 558 ; New Glenduffhill Co. *v.* Muir & Co., 1882, 10 R. 372.

[3] Sec. 202.

[4] Sec. 213.

[5] See *ante*, p. 318.

other hand, are not vested with the estate of the company. The estate remains in the company itself, and the Liquidators are merely the administrators of it. But they are administrators for the special purpose of dividing the estate among the creditors of the company, and if there be any balance, of dividing it among the contributories. If the estate be insolvent, then the sole purpose for which the Liquidators administer is to distribute it amongst the various creditors of the company according to their rights as creditors. The statute specially provides that the distribution is to be *pari passu*, every creditor receiving an equal share, unless of course he has a preferable security over the estate of the company or some part of it.[1]

The rules in regard to voting and ranking for payment of dividends in the case of sequestrations apply, so far as consistent with the Bankruptcy Acts, to the winding-up of joint stock companies. For this purpose, sequestration is taken to mean winding-up, Trustee to mean Liquidator, and Sheriff to mean the Court.[2]

---

[1] Clark *v.* West Calder Oil Co., 1882, 9 R. 1017 ; Gray's Tr. *v.* Benhar Coal Co., 1881, 9 R. 225.

[2] Sec. 208.

CHAPTER IX

EXTRA-JUDICIAL SETTLEMENTS WITH CREDITORS

1. Trust-Deeds

THE estates of embarrassed debtors may be realised and divided among their creditors under a private trust-deed without resort to the judicial process of sequestration. Where all the creditors are agreeable, this course is in many respects preferable to that of sequestration, as being less expensive, and as enabling the Trustee to work out and realise to advantage, as opportunity affords, a complicated estate. The creditors, however, must be unanimous, as one recalcitrant creditor may prevent the adoption of the course which the great body of creditors think best for all concerned.

Constitution of Trust.—The trust may be constituted in one of two ways, namely, either (1) by a deed, in which the purposes of the trust are specially set forth, granted by the debtor, conveying his whole estate and effects, heritable and moveable, to a Trustee for behoof of his creditors ; or (2) by an *ex facie* absolute disposition by the debtor of his whole estate and effects, heritable and moveable, in favour of a named person, qualified by a back-letter from such person, in which the purposes of the trust are set forth. The first course is preferable, as being less cumbersome. To provide against the possibility of the trust lapsing through the death of the named Trustee, it is usual to make the conveyance to the Trustee and his heirs and assignees, or to two or more Trustees in succession. Should this not be done, and the Trustee die, the creditors require to take proceedings in Court for the appointment of a new Trustee. Whichever way is agreed upon, the deed or deeds must, in order to be effectual, be executed in regular form and delivered. The Trustee's title is completed as in ordinary conveyances. It is advisable to provide in the deed that the Trustee shall act with the advice of a committee of the creditors, who are thereby enabled to exercise more control over his actings.

Effect of Trust-Deed.—A voluntary trust-deed granted by a party, insolvent but not bankrupt, for behoof of all his creditors equally, and containing no extraordinary clauses, is irrevocable by the granter, and good and available to bind non-acceding as well as acceding creditors, if the estate be reduced into the possession of the Trustee, and the debtor is not rendered bankrupt within sixty days thereafter. The Trustee in such cases does not represent the debtor, but the creditors in their just proportions, all preferences by arrestment being excluded.[1] No one creditor can, by diligence against the Trustee, create a preference over the other creditors, so as to draw more than his fair share of the trust-estate.[2] A provision in the deed for the debtor's discharge is not a condition of such an extraordinary character as to render it invalid.[3] It is not necessary, in order to give due effect to a trust-deed, that all the creditors are named therein. Those creditors who were creditors of the debtor at the date of the granting of the trust-deed are alone entitled to any advantage under it.[4] Creditors whose debts are incurred subsequent thereto have no claim against the Trustee unless there be a reversion.[5] The trust may at any time be superseded by sequestration, and upon this being done the estate is vested in the Trustee under the sequestration.[6]

Accession of Creditors to Trust-Deed.—As a trust-deed is a voluntary agreement, it follows that no creditor is bound by its terms unless he has specially assented thereto, although, as stated above, the trust-deed is irrevocable by the granter, if the estate is reduced into the possession of the Trustee, and the debtor is not rendered bankrupt within sixty days thereafter. The creditor's assent may be proved either by writing or by oath, or, in some cases, even by parole evidence. Where the creditor's assent is proved by writing or by oath, he is bound to all the conditions of the deed.[7] Where his consent is sought to be established from his actings, the most explicit proof is required before the creditor can be bound to the terms of the trust-deed. It has been held that instructions to accede to a trust-deed, given by a creditor to his agent, coupled with the fact that such agent had attended a meeting of the creditors and concurred in their measures, were sufficient to bind the creditor to the terms of the deed.[8] Lodging a claim is not sufficient to infer accession,[9] and while a creditor's accession to the terms of the trust-deed cannot be implied from the fact of his having attended a meeting of creditors, where common measures were resolved on without his having dissented,

---

[1] Nicolson v. Johnstone, 1872, 11 M. 179 ; Henderson v. Henderson's Tr., 1882, 10 R. 185 ; Lamb's Tr. v. Reid, 1883, 11 R. 26.

[2] M'Dougall v. Stevenson, 1834, 13 S. 55.

[3] Henderson v. Henderson's Tr., supra.

[4] Bell's Com. ii. 490.

[5] Marianski v. Wiseman, 1871, 9 M. 673.

[6] Lockie v. Mason, 1837, 15 S. 547 ; Campbell v. Macfarlane, 1862, 24 D. 1097 ; Nicolson v. Johnstone, supra ; Kyd v. Waterson, 1880, 7 R. 884.

[7] Gibson v. M'Donald, 1824, 3 S. 374.

[8] Wilson v. M'Vicar, 1762, M. 1214 ; Lea v. Landale, 1828, 6 S. 350.

[9] Athya v. Clydesdale Bank, 1881, 18 S.L.R. 287 ; Kyd v. Waterson, 1880, 7 R. 884.

yet such conduct, if it induce the other creditors and the debtor to rely on his concurrence, will bar him from pursuing separate diligence. In whatever way a creditor's accession is sought to be established, such accession implies (a) that perfect equality of division among the creditors according to their rights will be observed, and (b) that all the creditors will accede, because, the contract being mutual, all must be bound or none. An acceding creditor cannot resile and proceed to do diligence against the estate, from the mere fact that certain creditors who have not acceded are doing nothing.

Rights and Liabilities of Parties.—(1) *The Debtor.*—Notwithstanding the trust-deed the radical right of property remains with the debtor,[1] and he is entitled to any reversion there may be after the purposes of the trust have been satisfied, and to compel the Trustee to hold just count and reckoning with him.[2] He is entitled to see that the Trustee is carrying out the purposes of the trust, and is not impairing his reversionary interest. He can call upon the Trustee to denude on his paying the creditors. He has a right to apply for sequestration provided he obtain the necessary concurrences.[3] Should the Trustee die, resign, or become otherwise incapacitated from acting, the debtor has a right to appear and object to any new Trustee, on the ground that he is not a fit and proper person for the office. He is entitled to a complete discharge, if this has been stipulated for and agreed to ; but if there has been no such stipulation, and the creditors do not voluntarily grant him a discharge, he remains liable for the debts under deduction of the dividends paid.

(2) *The Creditors.*—Having once acceded to the trust-deed, they cannot pursue separate diligence against the estate. They have power, on the malversation of duty by the Trustee, or on his non-acceptance of office, death, or resignation, to have a successor appointed. They may, if they have power in the deed, nominate a new Trustee. They are entitled to see that the estate is realised and divided among them according to their several rights and interests. They can take proceedings for the setting aside of preferences struck at by the Acts 1621 and 1696, or by common law. They can concur in an application for sequestration. Where disputes arise among the creditors as to the division of an estate after it has been realised, very urgent cause must be shown to make an action of multiplepoinding competent. In such circumstances the proper course for acceding creditors is to raise a direct action against the Trustee for their respective dividends, and for non-acceding creditors to have the estate sequestrated.[4]

---

[1] M'Mullan *v.* Campbell, 4th March 1821 ; Barbour *v.* Bell, 1831, 9 S. 334.
[2] Ritchie *v.* M'Intosh, 1881, 8 R. 747.
[3] Thomson *v.* Broom, 1827, 5 S. 468 ; see p. 309.
[4] Kyd *v.* Waterson, 1880, 7 R. 884.

(3) *The Trustee.*—He has a right to take whatever action is necessary for the realisation of the estate,[1] and thereafter to rank the creditors, and pay them a dividend according to their rights and interests.[2] He cannot exceed the powers conferred on him by the trust-deed. He may enter into obligations, and bind the trust-estate, so far as necessary, for the due fulfilment of his office. He cannot delegate his authority, but he may appoint a factor. He has a lien over the estate for his outlay and expenses,[3] and for his remuneration provided for in the trust-deed. The Bankruptcy (Scotland) Act, 1913, for the first time makes a statutory provision for the audit of the accounts of a Trustee under a voluntary trust-deed.[4] In the case of every trust-deed granted after 1st January 1914 by an insolvent for behoof of his creditors generally where there is no provision made *in gremio* of the trust-deed for the audit of the Trustee's account and the fixing of his remuneration by a committee of the creditors, or where such committee is not appointed or does not act, the Trustee before making a final division of the estate among the creditors must submit his accounts to the Accountant of Court, who is required to audit the same and fix the amount of the Trustee's remuneration. Any Trustee who fails to observe the provisions of the section forfeits all claim to commission or other remuneration in respect of his acting as Trustee. Moneys coming into the hands of the Trustee should be lodged in bank in his official name.[5] He has a right on the termination of the trust, should he be unable to get his discharge from the creditors, to call them all in an action of multiple-poinding and exoneration in order to enforce it.[6] He cannot raise an action to reduce preferences unless specially authorised by the creditors to do so.[7] Where the debtor's estate has been sequestrated during the subsistence of the trust-deed, the Trustee under it must hand over the estate to the Trustee under the sequestration, upon payment of his outlay, expenses, and remuneration.[8]

Claims and Ranking.—It is not compulsory for creditors under trust-deeds to lodge sworn affidavits in support of their debts, a statement of claim being in most cases accepted as sufficient. Where, however, a formal claim is required, the forms appropriate to sequestrations may be altered to suit the requirements of the case.[9] An important

---

[1] Ker *v.* Graham's Tr., 1827, 6 S. 270.

[2] Mansfield *v.* Burnet, 1843, 6 D. 146 ; Globe Insurance Co. *v.* Scott's Tr., 1849, 11 D. 618 ; *affd.* 1850, 7 Bell, 296 ; 22 Jur. 625.

[3] Thomson *v.* Tough's Tr., 1880, 7 R. 1035.

[4] B. A., sec. 185.

[5] Mansfield *v.* Burnet, *supra.*

[6] Edmond *v.* Dingwall's Tr., 1860, 23 D. 21 ; Kyd *v.* Waterson, *supra.*

[7] Fleming's Trs. *v.* M'Hardy, 1892, 19 R. 542.

[8] Thomson *v.* Tough's Tr., *supra* ; Dall *v.* Drummond, 1870, 8 M. 1006.

[9] *Vide* Appendix.

feature in ranking on trust-deeds is that, apart from special stipulations in the trust-deed agreed to by the creditors, the ranking of creditors is not regulated by the rules of sequestration, but by common law. The common-law rules are :—(First), a creditor who holds personal or real securities, other than those of the bankrupt and his estate, is entitled so to use his various securities as to make them all available to the utmost extent in operating payment in full, but no more ; (Second), a creditor is entitled to rank on the estate of each bankrupt co-obligant, bound with the debtor either as joint debtor or as cautioner for the full amount of his debt, so as to operate full payment out of the combined rankings ; (Third), a creditor who has, in addition to the personal obligation of his debtor, a security over some subject not belonging to his debtor, is entitled to realise the full value of his security, and if that does not satisfy his claim, to rank on his debtor's estate for the full amount of his debt ; and (Fourth), it is important to observe, that it is immaterial that the real security is over a part of the insolvent debtor's estate. The creditor may therefore exhaust that security and rank *pari passu* with the unsecured creditors on the remainder of the insolvent's estate not merely for the balance, but for the full amount of his debt, so as to operate full payment.[1] In most trust-deeds it will be found that special provision is made that the insolvent's debts, preferable or ordinary, are to be ranked according to the principles of the bankruptcy statutes, as if the estates had been sequestrated. A non-acceding creditor is not bound by any such stipulation, nor is he bound to accede to the trust-deed as a condition of his drawing a dividend. He is entitled to his rateable share of the debtor's funds, and should he not be paid he has a direct action against the Trustee for recovery thereof.[2] Nothing more can be enforced from a non-acceding creditor than a simple receipt for the money paid, and should the debtor be afterwards in a position to pay, the creditor has a right of action against him for the balance, provided, of course, the debt has not prescribed. Where a creditor does not wish to accede to a trust-deed, his course is to merely intimate his claim to the Trustee. This entitles him to receive a dividend along with the other creditors, and does not bind him to the terms of the trust-deed.

Cautioner Bound for Creditor's Debt.—The rules already explained[3] as to the consents necessary to acceding to a trust-deed or drawing a dividend will of course be kept in view.

---

[1] See opinion of Lord President in University of Glasgow *v.* Yuill's Tr., 1882, 9 R., at p. 650.

[2] Ogilvie *v.* Taylor, 14 R. 399.

[3] See *ante*, p. 357.

2. Composition Contract

Where it is considered desirable to allow a debtor to remain in the possession of his estate and to continue to carry on his business, instead of divesting him of his estate in any of the modes already explained, the creditors may enter into an extra-judicial composition contract, to allow the debtor such time as the creditors think proper for the payment of their debts or the acceptance by them of a composition.

Effect.—The effect of every such contract must be considered with reference to its terms, but as the contract is a mutual one, and as the estate of an insolvent debtor is the common property of his creditors,[1] unless otherwise agreed upon, such a contract implies (1) that all the creditors will be treated with equality ;[2] (2) that no undue preference is granted by the debtor to any of the creditors ; and (3) that they all concur in the arrangement. Following the rule of all consensual contracts, if a material part of the contract is not fulfilled, the creditors who may have previously agreed to its terms are entitled to resile ; as they also are, if the debtor has made any wilful misrepresentation or concealment as to the true state of his affairs which it was material the creditors should know.[3]

Creditors not Bound to Accede.—A creditor cannot be compelled to accept a composition, nor can he be bound to any composition arrangement, unless he has specially consented thereto.[4]

Mode of Carrying Out.—The composition contract is usually carried out by the debtor, or some one on his behalf, offering to the creditors a sum in settlement of his debt, in one or more payments (with, usually in the latter case, a cautioner for the due payment of the last instalment), under certain specified conditions, which include a stipulation for the debtor's discharge, on bills being granted for the amount of the composition. Unlike a composition under a sequestration, if the agreed-on composition be not paid at the time when it falls due, the original debt revives,[5] and if such failure be at the second or any of the subsequent instalments, the creditor is entitled to proceed for his whole debt, under deduction of the payments received, unless at the time of agreeing to the composition he has finally discharged the debtor,[6] in which case he can only proceed for the amount

---

[1] See *ante*, p. 294.

[2] Macfarlane *v.* Nicoll, 1864, 3 M. 237 ; Bank of Scotland *v.* Faulds, 1870, 42 Jur. 557 ; Ironside *v.* Wilson, 1871, 9 S.L.R. 73.

[3] Baillie *v.* Young, 1837, 15 S. 893 ; Howden *v.* Haigh, 11 Ad. & E. 1033.

[4] Montgomerie *v.* Boswell, 1841, 4 D. 332.

[5] Paul *v.* Black, 19th December 1820, F.C. ; Horsefalls *v.* Virtue, 1826, 5 S. 36.

[6] Graham *v.* Cuthbertson, 1828, 7 S. 152.

of his composition. If the composition be not paid when due, the creditor is not bound to accept it afterwards, but where it has not been discharged, may proceed for payment of his full debt.[1]

Illegal Preferences.—It is illegal for the debtor secretly to come under an obligation to give one of his creditors a preference on condition of that creditor's accession to the composition, and payment cannot be exacted by the party to whom the preference has been given. It is not necessary that the preference should be given directly as an inducement to grant a discharge. What the law forbids is any concealed violation of the equality which the bankrupt is bound to observe towards all his creditors while he remains undischarged. Even an understanding, which never is reduced to a legal contract, to give a creditor a special benefit has been found to vitiate a discharge.[2] Proceedings for the setting aside of the preference may be taken by (1) the debtor ;[3] (2) the trustee on the sequestrated estates of the debtor, where sequestration has been awarded subsequent to the date of the preference ;[4] (3) any creditor ; or (4) the cautioner for the payment of the composition. A voluntary payment after discharge is not subject to reduction.[5] The general rules before explained apply to cautioners under composition contracts.[6]

---

[1] Woods, Parker & Co. v. Ainslie, 1860, 22 D. 723.

[2] Per Lord Justice-Clerk in Bank of Scotland v. Faulds, 1870, 42 Jur. 557.

[3] Arrol v. Montgomery, 1826, 4 S. 499.

[4] Macfarlane v. Nicoll, 1864, 3 M. 237.

[5] Macfarlane v. Nicoll, supra ; Ironside v. Wilson, 1871, 9 S.L.R. 73.

[6] See ante, p. 263. See also Scott v. Campbell, 1834, 12 S. 447 ; Clerk v. Russell, 1825, 3 S. 541 ; Freeland v. Finlayson, 1823, 2 S. 389 ; Muir v. Scott, 1825, 4 S. 252 ; Thomson v. Latta, 1863, 1 M. 913.

PART V

DILIGENCE

1. Arrestment.—Arrestment is the diligence used in order to prevent a person parting with money or moveables in his hands or under his control, belonging to a third person who is in the position of debtor to the person using the arrestment, until the arrester's debt is paid or provided for, or while the arrestment remains in force. The party in whose hands an arrestment is lodged is called the arrestee, the party using the arrestment the arrester, and the party against whom the arrestment is used the common debtor. An arrestment in the hands of the debtor himself, or of his servant, or anyone who is a mere custodier for him, or of his factor, is invalid.[1] An arrestment in the hands of a person as " agent " of a particular bank is inept and ineffectual to attach funds due by the bank to a depositor.[2] Such funds must be arrested in the hands of the bank. In the case of *Skardon (John Dunn's Executor) against The Canada Investment and Agency Company Ltd.*, February 1898 (not reported), Lord Kyllachy decided, and his judgment was acquiesced in, that an arrestment in the hands of the officials at the head office of a Scottish bank was effectual to attach money at the bank's office in London. Where funds are arrested in the hands of trustees, the arrestment must be used in the hands of each person acting under the trust-deed. Arrestments are preferable according to their dates.

Arrestments are of four kinds, namely, those used (1) in execution, (2) on the dependence of an action, (3) on a warrant obtained on a liquid document of debt such as a bond or bill, and (4) to found jurisdiction.

1. *Arrestments in execution* proceed upon an extract decree of the books of a competent Court; on an extract from the books of Council and Session of a duly recorded bond or obligation; on an extract registered protest of a bill of exchange or promissory note; upon

---

[1] Trowsdale's Tr. *v.* Forcett Ry. Co., 1870, 9 M. 88 ; 43 J. 51. See as to arrestment by a creditor in his own hands under sec. 3 of the Mercantile Law Amendment Act, 1856.

[2] Graham *v.* Macfarlane & Co., 1869, 7 M. 640 ; 41 J. 332.

special letters of arrestment; or on a warrant contained in letters of horning.

2. *Arrestments on the dependence of an action* proceed on a warrant to arrest contained in the summons or petition in the action, in letters of arrestment, or in a precept of arrestment obtained in the Inferior Courts. If the warrant to cite the defender to appear in the action is not served upon him within twenty days after the date of the arrestment, or if the summons or petition be not called in Court within twenty days thereafter, or, when the Court is in vacation, on the first sederunt day thereafter, the arrestment falls.[1] The arrestment does not fall *eo ipso* by a judgment of the Court of Session in favour of the defender, but remains effectual in case the pursuer is successful in an appeal to the House of Lords.[2]

3. *On Warrant on Liquid Document of Debt.*—Where a creditor holds a liquid document of debt, such as a bond, or bill not yet due, and can show that his debtor is *vergens ad inopiam* (that is, bordering on insolvency), he can, on application to the Court, obtain a warrant, upon which arrestments can at once be used. It is essential to the granting of such a warrant that the debtor be *vergens ad inopiam*, and to entitle him to the warrant the creditor must aver this fact.

4. *Arrestments ad Fundandam Jurisdictionem.*—Perhaps the most unsatisfactory of all arrestments for banks to deal with are those to found jurisdiction. The object of such an arrestment is to subject a foreigner, who would not otherwise be so amenable, to the jurisdiction of the Scots Courts in an action about to be raised against him. The arrestment proceeds either on a warrant granted by the Sheriff, or on what are called letters of arrestment, passing the Signet on a warrant obtained at the Bill Chamber. The smallness of the sum arrested is no competent objection to the foundation of jurisdiction. In one case £1. 8s. 6d. was held enough,[3] and in another 9s. 3d.[4] But jurisdiction is not constituted by arresting plans and documents, of no mercantile value, in the hands of the debtor's agent in Scotland.[5] Some money belonging to the debtor must be arrested.[6] The main point for consideration is whether, after such an arrestment has been used, a bank would be entitled to refuse payment of a sum at the credit of the person against whom such arrestments had been used; or, in other words, whether such a *nexus* has been placed on the money as to

---

[1] 1 & 2 Vict. cap. 114, secs. 16, 17.

[2] Johnstone *v.* Jeudwine, 23rd January 1813, 17 F.C. 110; Haddington *v.* Richardson, 8th March 1822, 1 S. 387 (N.E. 362); 2 S. App. 406. See as to Prescription of Arrestments, p. 367.

[3] Shaw *v.* Dow & Dobie, 1869, 7 M. 449; 41 J. 246.

[4] Ross *v.* Ross, 1878, 5 R. 1013.

[5] Trowsdale's Tr. *v.* Forcett Ry. Co., 1870, 9 M. 88; 43 J. 51.

[6] Murray *v.* Wallace, Marrs & Co., 1914, S.C. 114.

prevent the bank parting with it. The point is not free from difficulty, and although frequently alluded to by the Court, has not yet been authoritatively decided. There has been a considerable divergence of opinion among the Judges on the subject. As matters at present stand, it will be prudent for banks not to part with the money except under judicial authority, or upon receipt of a letter from the arresting creditor consenting to the bank parting with the money. Should the bank's customer insist upon immediate payment, it would seem [1] that the bank would be entitled to raise an action of multiplepoinding, calling both the arrester and their customer, and thus leave the Court to determine the question. It will be found in practice, however, that an arrestment to found jurisdiction is usually, if not invariably, followed by an arrestment on the dependence of an action, for the purpose of raising which the arrestment to found jurisdiction was used. [2]

The subjects of arrestment consist in the whole personal debts or moveables in the hands of a third party or of his servant, or of anyone who is a custodier for him, for which, as debtor, the arrestee is accountable to the common debtor. Among the subjects liable to arrestment may be mentioned the following :—A debtor's interest in a deceased's estate, provided his interest is to be paid to him in cash or other moveable subject ; rents, interest, and annuities on the expiry of the term day on which they are payable ; wages of labourers, farm servants, manufacturers, artificers, and workpeople, so far as they are in excess of one pound per week ; [3] the interest held by a debtor in a mutual insurance company under a policy payable at his death, the arrestment on which does not fall by another termly payment of premium falling due after the date of arrestment ; [4] the subject of a pending lawsuit ; arrears of alimentary funds ; and ships,[5] which are rendered available as a source of payment, not by an action of furthcoming, but by a process of sale.

Among the subjects not liable to arrestment may be mentioned : funds secured heritably ; debts due on bills and the bills themselves ; goods or money specially appropriated ; alimentary funds ; fees, pensions, and salaries payable by the Crown ; debts, the term of payment of which has not arrived or which are contingent, unless upon the ground

---

[1] On the authority of Malone & M'Gibbon v. Caledonian Ry. Co., *infra*.

[2] For authorities, see Cameron v. Chapman, 1838, 16 S. 907 ; Matthew v. Fawns, 4 D. 1242 ; 14 Jur. 398 ; White v. Spottiswoode, 1846, 8 D. 952 ; 18 Jur. 479 ; Lindsay v. London and North-Western Ry. Co., 1855, 18 D. 62 ; 28 Jur. 17 ; Trowsdale's Tr. v. Forcett Ry. Co., 1870, 9 M. 88 ; Carlberg, etc. v. Borjesson, etc., 1877, 5 R. 188 ; Metzenburg v. Highland Ry. Co., 7 M. 919 ; 41 J. 522 ; North British Ry. Co. v. White and Others, 9 R. 97 ; Malone & M'Gibbon v. Caledonian Ry. Co., 1884, 11 R. 853.

[3] 33 & 34 Vict. cap. 63.

[4] Bankhardt's Trs. v. Scottish Amicable Society and Duncan, 1871, 9 M. 443.

[5] Clark v. Loos, 1853, 15 D. 756 ; Bell v. Gow, 1862, 1 M. 183.

that the debtor is *vergens ad inopiam*, or other similar ground ; [1] and goods left with a bank for safe custody.

Effect of Arrestment.—The purpose of arrestment, whether in security or execution (with the exception of that used in order to found jurisdiction), is to attach such a sum in the hands of the arrestee as will suffice to pay the debt of the arrester, principal, interest, and expenses. In the schedule of arrestment the arrester usually specifies a certain sum, the words " less or more " being added after the sum named to meet any contingency. When funds are arrested " less or more " the arrester should be very cautious in parting with them without judicial authority, or the consent of the arresting creditor, as practically these words have the effect of stopping payment by the arrestee of whatever sums he holds. The common debtor's remedy is to apply for loosing of the arrestment. [2]

Effect of Bankruptcy of Common Debtor on Funds Arrested.—Where prior to the date of the bankruptcy of a debtor, funds belonging to him have been effectually attached by arrestment, the Trustee on the debtor's estate is, notwithstanding the arrestment, entitled to uplift the money and discharge the debtor of the bankrupt. But the right of the Trustee in such circumstances is subject to such preferable securities as existed at the date of the sequestration, and are not null or reducible. Hence, although the Trustee is entitled to uplift the money, the position of the arresting creditor is not prejudiced, for if his arrestment is valid his claim to be preferably ranked in the sequestration will be sustained. [3]

Loosing of the arrestment will be granted by the Court on caution being found that the funds will be made furthcoming to the arrester. Where the funds arrested are greater than the amount due to the arrester, the Court will restrict the amount of the caution to be found ; and where the arrestment can be shown to have been used oppressively, the Court may recall it, without caution, and may even subject the arrester in damages. [4]

Action of Furthcoming.—The *nexus* imposed by an arrestment does not of itself operate as a transference of the debt or subject to the arrestee, nor does it entitle the arrestee to pay over the funds arrested. To complete the arrester's right, and to make the arrestment available, it is necessary for him either to raise an action of furthcoming, to which are called the arrestee and common debtor, or to get a letter from the common debtor addressed to the arrestee consenting to the arrested funds being paid over. Until an extract decree of furth-

---

[1] Symington *v.* Symington, 1875, 3 R. 205 ; Smith *v.* Cameron, 1879, 6 R. 1107.

[2] As to the effect of arrestment used within sixty days of sequestration, see Equalisation of Diligence.

[3] Gordon *v.* Miller, 1842, 4 D. 352.

[4] Ritchie *v.* Maclachlan, etc., 1870, 8 M. 815.

coming, or a letter from the common debtor is delivered to him, the arrestee is not in safety to part with the arrested subjects. The objects of an action of furthcoming are : (1) to ascertain the amount of the debt due by the arrestee to the common debtor, or, where goods have been arrested, the present extent of the subjects ; and (2) to have the arrestee decerned to pay the fund to the arrester, or so much of it as will pay his debt, or, where goods have been arrested, to authorise a sale and payment out of the proceeds. Questions as to the validity of arrestments can only be tried in an action of furthcoming.[1] Thus in such an action it is competent for the common debtor to prove that he is not the debtor of the arrester, in which case the action falls to be dismissed, and for the arrestee to prove that he is not the debtor of the common debtor, that he has a lien over the property arrested, that the arrestment is informal, or that there are competing claims for the money. When there are competing claims, the proper course for the arrestee to adopt is to raise an action of multiplepoinding and allow the Court to divide the arrested subjects among the various claimants according to their respective rights and interests. An arresting creditor must take his debtor's interest subject to all charges and modifications to which it is subject in the debtor's own hands.[2] It is the duty of the arrestee, if he have any funds in his hands belonging or owing to the common debtor, to give a correct statement of the amount. It is for the interest of the arrestee to see that the action of furthcoming is not informal, as if he pay over the funds on a decree pronounced in an action, which afterwards turns out to have been informal, and to which he has not lodged an objection, he will not be protected from having to pay the amount a second time to the original creditor.

Prescription of Arrestments.—Arrestments in execution prescribe in three years from their dates ; and arrestments used upon a future or contingent debt, or on the dependence of an action, prescribe in three years from the time the debt becomes due, the contingency is purified, or decree in the action is pronounced, unless during the said period of three years the arrestments are pursued and insisted on.[3] Under the Small Debt Act,[4] which deals with cases of twenty pounds[5] and under, it is provided that all arrestments laid or under authority of that Act cease and determine on the expiry of three months from the date of the arrestment. Arrestments may be renewed, but in any

---

[1] Vincent *v.* Chalmers & Co.'s Tr., 1877, 5 R. 43 ; *approved* in Barclay, Curle & Co. Ltd. *v.* Sir James Laing & Co. Ltd., 1908, S.C. 82, *per* Lord President (Lord Dunedin).

[2] Chambers' Trs. *v.* Smiths, 1877, 5 R. 97 ; *revd.* 1878, 5 R. (H.L.) 151.

[3] Personal Diligence Act, 1838, 1 & 2 Vict. cap. 114, sec. 22.

[4] 1 Vict. cap. 41, sec. 6.

[5] Sheriff Courts (Scotland) Act, 1907, sec. 42.

question of preference the date of the renewal, and not of the original arrestment, is the criterion.

Interruption of Prescription.—The prescription may be interrupted either by the arrester raising an action of furthcoming or a multiple-poinding, or appearing in such a process raised by some one else within the prescriptive period.[1] Although the arrested funds are not payable till the death of an annuitant, it is competent for the arrester to interrupt the course of prescription by raising an action of furthcoming concluding for payment upon that event.[2]

2. Poinding.—Poinding is of two kinds—real and personal—which are quite distinct in their nature and effect.

1. *Personal Poinding* is the ordinary diligence by which any creditor may attach, and thereafter sell, his debtor's moveables for payment of his debt. It is incompetent to poind horses or oxen, or the implements used in husbandry, during the season of agricultural labour if the debtor has other effects ; [3] and it is also incompetent to poind goods in which the debtor is only joint owner [4] or in which he has only a qualified or temporary interest.[5] The fact that goods belonging to the debtor are in the creditor's possession does not prevent their being poinded.[6] The question has been raised, but not decided, whether bank notes or money in a man's pocket can be lawfully poinded.[7] In poindings at the instance of the Crown the Sheriff has power to attach the debtor's " whole moveable effects without exception, including bank notes, money, bonds, bills, crop stocking, and implements of husbandry of all kinds." [8]

Warrants to poind are contained in extract decrees and deeds or protests registered in the books of the Supreme or Inferior Courts, in virtue of which it is lawful, on the expiry of the days of charge, to poind the moveable effects of the debtor to an extent sufficient to cover the creditor's debt, with interest and expenses. An officer who is proceeding with a poinding must, if required, before the poinding is completed, conjoin in the poinding any creditor of the debtor who exhibits and delivers to him a warrant to poind, so as to entitle such creditor to participate in any benefit to be derived from the poinding. The poinding must be reported within eight days (or thereafter only on cause shown) to the Sheriff, who grants warrant to sell the poinded articles by public roup at a specified place and time, being not sooner than eight, nor later than twenty days after the publication of the sale.

---

[1] Jameson *v.* Sharp, 1887, 14 R. 643 ; Thomas *v.* Stiven, 1868, 6 M. 777.

[2] Jameson *v.* Sharp, *supra.*

[3] Erskine, iii. 6, 22.

[4] Fleming *v.* Twaddle, 1828, 7 S. 92.

[5] Scott *v.* Price, 1837, 15 S. 916.

[6] Lochhead *v.* Graham, 1883, 11 R. 201.

[7] Alexander *v.* M'Lay, 1826, 4 S. 439.

[8] 19 & 20 Vict. cap. 56, sec. 32.

The manner of the publication is contained in the warrant, and the sale must be carried out in terms of the Personal Diligence Act, 1838. At the sale the poinded articles are offered at upset prices, being not less than the appraised value. If there be no offer to purchase, the articles are delivered over to the poinding creditor at their appraised value. The sale or delivery is reported to the Sheriff within eight days and thereafter approved of by him, the creditor's debt, interest, and expenses being ordered to be paid. Until this is done the diligence is not legally completed. The poinder, or any other creditor, may purchase the articles exposed for sale. Any person who unlawfully intromits with, or carries off, the poinded effects, is liable, on summary complaint to the Sheriff of the county where the effects were poinded, or where he is domiciled, to be imprisoned until he restore the effects or pay double the appraised value.[1] A poinding is preferable to a prior arrestment.

2. *Real Poinding, or Poinding of the Ground.*—This poinding is competent to a superior for his feu-duties and casualties to an annual renter for the arrears of his interest, to a heritable creditor, such as a creditor in a bond and disposition in security, or bond of credit and disposition in security, and generally to all creditors in debts which constitute a real burden or lien on land.[2] A creditor who, under a bond and disposition in security, has obtained a decree of maills and duties is not in such possession of the lands as proprietor as to render it incompetent for him to bring an action of poinding of the ground,[3] but a superior who has divested himself of his superiority in favour of a third party has no title to sue an action of poinding of the ground for recovery of arrears of feu-duties due prior to his divestiture.[4] The diligence is usually resorted to when, by miscalculation or emerging circumstances, the value of the heritable subject proves, or is likely to prove, inadequate to cover the heritable debt.[5] The diligence is competent in security for interest current but not yet due, but payment cannot be demanded till the stipulated term arrives.[6] The theory on which poindings of the ground proceed is that the pursuer has a real right in the lands, and, by virtue of that right, has a title to the moveables upon the ground as accessory thereto, so long as no completed alienation of them, voluntary or judicial, has been effected.[7] In a question between the creditor and

---

[1] Personal Diligence Act, 1838, sec. 30 ; Brown *v.* Hewitt, 1849, 11 D. 1083.

[2] As to a creditor in an *ex facie* absolute disposition, see p. 214 *et seq.*

[3] Henderson *v.* Wallace and Others, 1874, 2 R. 272.

[4] Scottish Heritages Co. Ltd. *v.* North British Property Co. Ltd., 1885, 12 R. 550.

[5] See opinion of Lord Deas in Royal Bank *v.* Bain, 1877, 4 R. 985.

[6] Stewart *v.* Gibson's Tr., 1880, 8 R. 270.

[7] Thomson *v.* Scoular, 1882, 9 R. 430.

the owner of the ground, the latter's moveables on the ground are attachable to the full amount of the debt with interest, and the moveables of
tenants or occupants to the extent of the rents due by them or current
at the time.[1]

In a competition between a heritable creditor and a Trustee on the
sequestrated estates of the proprietor of the ground, or a Liquidator
under the Companies Act,[2] the creditor, provided he has not carried into
execution a poinding of the ground by sale sixty days before the
sequestration, or liquidation, is only entitled to poind the ground to
the extent of interest on the debt for the then current half-yearly term
and for arrears for one year immediately preceding such term.

The diligence commences by summons if before the Supreme Court,
or by petition if in the Sheriff Court, and contains no personal conclusion,
but only concludes for execution against moveables. The service of the
summons or petition attaches without further procedure the moveables
then upon the ground, gives to the heritable creditor a preference over
them,[3] and interpels the heritable proprietor from allowing others to
acquire a right over them. The creditor, however, has no claim over
moveables which have been removed prior to the date of the service of
the petition.[4]

Priority of Creditors inter se.—A superior for his feu-duties is preferable to all other creditors. Creditors holding *debita fundi* are preferable,
not according to the priority of their poindings, but according to the
priority of their real rights.[5] There is no equalising of poindings of
the ground by bankruptcy, as in ordinary poindings.

Equalisation of Diligence.—(1) *In Notour Bankruptcy.*—Arrestments
and personal poindings used within sixty days prior to the constitution
of notour bankruptcy, or within four months thereafter, rank *pari
passu* as if they had all been used of the same date. If the arrestments
are used on the dependence of an action, or on an illiquid document of
debt, they must be followed up without undue delay. Any creditor
judicially producing in a process, such as in a furthcoming or multiplepoinding, relative to the subject of such arrestment or poinding liquid
grounds of debt, *i.e.* a probative writ, bond, or bill or decree, for payment
within such period, is entitled to rank as if he had executed an arrestment or a poinding. In the event of the first or any subsequent
arrester obtaining a decree of furthcoming and preference, and thereafter recovering payment, or a poinding creditor carrying through a
sale, such creditor is accountable for the sum so recovered to those who,

---

[1] Brown *v.* Scott, 1859, 22 D. 273.
[2] Companies Act, 1908, sec. 213.
[3] Urquhart *v.* Macleod's Tr., 1883, 10 R. 991.
[4] Lyons *v.* Anderson, 1880, 8 R. 24.
[5] Bell *v.* Cadell, 1831, 10 S. 100 ; Campbell's Trs. *v.* Paul, 1835, 13 S. 237.

by virtue of the foregoing provisions, are eventually found to have a right to a ranking *pari passu* thereon, and is liable to an action at their instance for payment to them proportionally after allowing out of the fund the expense of recovering the same.[1] If any arrestments are used attaching the same effects after the period of four months subsequent to the bankruptcy, such arrestments do not compete with those used within the said periods prior or subsequent thereto, but rank with each other on any reversion of the fund attached according to law and practice.[2]

(2) *In Sequestration.*—No arrestment or poinding of the funds or effects of the bankrupt, executed on or after the sixtieth day prior to the sequestration, is effectual, and such funds or effects, or the proceeds of such effects, must be made forthcoming to the Trustee. Any arrester or poinder who is thus deprived of the benefit of his diligence is entitled to a preference out of such funds or effects for the expenses *bonâ fide* incurred by him in such diligence.[3] But while arrestments used within the sixty days are ineffectual to create a preference in favour of the arresting creditor, they are effectual to impose a *nexus* on the funds, to the effect of prohibiting the arrestee from parting with them to the prejudice of the Trustee, to whom they are transferred by the sequestration.[4]

3. Inhibition.—An inhibition is a writ passing under the Signet prohibiting a debtor from alienating, or otherwise affecting, his heritable estate, to the prejudice of the creditor inhibiting. Inhibition may be used in security either of debts already due or of future debts. The diligence proceeds upon an extract decree—except those obtained in the Sheriff Small Debt Court [5]—or liquid document of debt, recorded or unrecorded, or upon a signeted summons or process depending in the Court of Session, or upon a process depending in the Sheriff Court. To render inhibition on the dependence competent, the summons must have pecuniary conclusions other than those for expenses.[6] Inhibition for a debt not yet due is competent only when the debtor is *vergens ad inopiam*, the risk of averring which the inhibiter must take upon himself.[7] The form of letters of inhibition is regulated by the Titles to Land Consolidation Act, 1868.[8]

When completed, an inhibition strikes at all voluntary alienations of, and all diligence done against, the debtor's heritable estate for debts

---

[1] Gallacher *v.* Ballantine, 1876, 13 S.L.R. 496.

[2] Bankruptcy Act, 1913, sec. 10.

[3] Bankruptcy Act, 1913, sec. 104.

[4] Mackenzie *v.* Campbell, 1894, 21 R. 904.

[5] Lamont *v.* Lorimer, 1867, 6 M. 84.

[6] Weir *v.* Otto, 1870, 8 M. 1070 ; Burns *v.* Burns, 1879, 7 R. 355.

[7] Dove *v.* Henderson, 1865, 3 M. 339 ; Symington *v.* Symington, 1875, 3 R. 205.

[8] 31 & 32 Vict. cap. 101, secs. 156, 157.

contracted subsequent (but not prior [1]) to the date of the inhibition.[2] An inhibition has no force or effect as against any lands acquired by the person or persons against whom such inhibition is used after the date of recording such inhibition, or of the previous notice thereof prescribed by the Act,[3] except such lands as were at the date of registration destined to the person inhibited by a deed of entail or other similar indefeasible title.[4]

The diligence is personal to the party inhibited, and strikes against the debtor only. Thus if he die, his heir will not be affected by the prohibition unless it be renewed against him. The diligence confers no active right on the creditor using it, and in order to obtain such a right he must follow up the inhibition with an adjudication. An inhibition followed by adjudication gives the inhibiting creditor an available preference over all the creditors whose debts were contracted subsequent to the execution of the inhibition. Creditors whose debts were incurred prior to the date of the inhibition are not prejudiced thereby, but if such creditors do not secure a *pari passu* ranking by adjudging, within a year and a day of the inhibiting and adjudging creditor, he excludes them, in virtue not of his inhibition but of his adjudication.

Inhibitions prescribe in five years, but may be renewed.[5] Inhibitions may be withdrawn by a voluntary discharge by the creditor or an order of Court recalling them. Where inhibitions are used on the dependence of an action, it is competent for the Lord Ordinary to recall or restrict them on or without caution, as may appear just. His judgment is subject to review by the Inner House.

4. Adjudication is the diligence by which land and other heritable subjects are attached in satisfaction of debt. The subjects which may be adjudged are heritable estate, in its most extensive signification, including not only feudal rights, but all rights or interests affecting or connected with land, such as heritable bonds and real securities, and personal rights to land, stocks of any chartered bank where the diligence of arrestment is excluded, and the like. The action of adjudication in payment proceeds on a decree or liquid document of debt not prescribed or not contingent. The decree in the action of adjudication supplies in law the want of a voluntary conveyance from the debtor. The decree is extracted with an abbreviate, and is recorded in the Register of Abbreviates of Adjudications within sixty days after the date of the decree. The right acquired by the creditor under the decree is not

---

[1] Livingstone *v.* M'Farlane, 1842, 5 D. 1.
[2] Baird & Brown *v.* Stirrat's Tr., 1872, 10 M. 414. As to effect of inhibition on bond of credit and disposition in security, see p. 214.
[3] 31 & 32 Vict. cap. 101, secs. 156, 157.
[4] *Ibid.*
[5] 37 & 38 Vict. cap. 94, sec. 42.

absolute, as it may, in the case of a general adjudication, be redeemed by the debtor within ten years. If the right to redeem be not exercised, the creditor on the lapse of the ten years may raise in the Court of Session an action of Declarator of Expiry of the Legal, the decree in which converts the redeemable security into an absolute and irredeemable right of property. A charter of adjudication and infeftment, followed by forty years' possession, forms a good irredeemable title without a declarator of expiry of the legal. The right which an adjudger has, during the legal and before declarator, is not a right of property. The adjudication is not a transference of the property in the lands, but is only a *pignus prætorium*, a step of diligence, which only creates a security for debt.[1]

Any creditor who can produce instruction of his debt with a summons of adjudication libelled and signeted at the expiration of twenty days from the calling of the summons in the first adjudication, is conjoined by the Court in one and the same adjudication, and any creditor who obtains decree in an action of adjudication within a year and a day from the date of decree in the first effectual adjudication, is entitled to share equally with the first adjudger. Adjudications, after the expiration of the year and day, are preferred upon the residue of the estate according to the dates of recording the abbreviates. Sequestration under the Bankruptcy Acts [2] is equivalent to a decree of adjudication of the heritable estates of the bankrupt, and when the sequestration is dated within a year and a day of any effectual adjudication the estate is disposed of under the sequestration. A winding-up under the Companies Act has the same effect.[3]

The diligence of adjudication is also competent to a creditor whose claim is contingent, future, or uncertain in amount, if the debtor be *vergens ad inopiam*, or if the creditor be in danger of losing his debt by other creditors adjudging a year and a day before him. Unlike adjudication in payment, adjudication in security is not founded on statute, but has been introduced and sanctioned by the Court from equitable considerations. Hence such an adjudication subsists merely as a security, has no legal, and may be redeemed at any time.

Note on Bank's Responsibility in Respect of its Name Appearing on a Prospectus

Questions frequently arise regarding the liability of those whose names appear on a prospectus of a company to persons who apply for shares or debenture stock, relying on the statements contained in the

---

[1] Hill *v.* Hill, 1871, 10 M. 3.
[2] See Sequestration, *ante.*
[3] Companies Act, 1908, sec. 213.

prospectus which ultimately turn out to be untrue. The question was dealt with in the Directors' Liability Act of 1890. That Act has been repealed, and the point under consideration is now regulated by section 84 of the Companies (Consolidation) Act of 1908. So far as material to a banker, the statutory law on the subject is as follows :—" Where a prospectus invites persons to subscribe for shares in or debentures of a company, every person who is a director of the company at the time of the issue of the prospectus, and every person who has authorised the naming of him and is named in the prospectus as a director or as having agreed to become a director either immediately or after an interval of time, and every promoter of the company, and every person who has authorised the issue of the prospectus, is liable to pay compensation to all persons who subscribe for any shares or debentures on the faith of the prospectus for the loss or damage they may have sustained by reason of any untrue statement therein, or in any report or memorandum appearing on the face thereof, or by reference incorporated therein or issued therewith, unless it is proved—(a) With respect to every untrue statement not purporting to be made on the authority of an expert, or of a public official document or statement, that he had reasonable ground to believe, and did up to the time of the allotment of the shares or debentures, as the case may be, believe, that the statement was true ; and (b) with respect to every untrue statement purporting to be a statement by or contained in what purports to be a copy of or extract from a report or valuation of an expert, that it fairly represented the statement, or was a correct and fair copy of or extract from the report or valuation : Provided that the director, person named as director, promoter, or person who authorised the issue of the prospectus, is liable to pay compensation as aforesaid if it is proved that he had no reasonable ground to believe that the person making the statement, report, or valuation was competent to make it ; and (c) with respect to every untrue statement purporting to be a statement made by an official person or contained in what purports to be a copy of or extract from a public official document, that it was a correct and fair representation of the statement or copy of or extract from the document." In deciding whether statements in a prospectus are untrue or not within the meaning of the Act, the sense which they convey to those who read them must be looked to, and not the sense intended by the issuers thereof. Almost invariably the name of a bank appears on the prospectus of a proposed public company as the bankers of the concern, and not unfrequently such prospectuses are submitted to the bank in draft before being issued to the public. It is important that the above section should be kept in view by bankers, as the words " every person who has authorised " in the section may, under certain circumstances, be interpreted to include bankers who have permitted their names to appear on the prospectus. The position and possible liability of the bank in any particular case must necessarily depend upon the actual course taken by the bank in connection with the preparation and issue of the prospectus. The mere fact that the bank's name appears on the prospectus cannot establish liability, as, whatever may be the meaning of the words " has authorised," it is plain that knowledge and consent, at least, on the part of the bank are essential elements. Nor, it is thought, would the statute render the bank liable, if the acts of the bank were limited to receiving from the company, as their agents for circulation, copies of the prospectus after it had been prepared by the company, and giving such copies out to customers or the public. The bank would run the risk of bringing themselves within the statute if they in any way altered, interfered with, or expressed their approval of the material parts of the prospectus, such, for example, as set out the purpose for which the company had been formed, or described the property acquired or to be acquired by it. But the bank might properly, and without incurring any liability, suggest or make an alteration in, or addition to, the phraseology of the draft which referred to themselves as bankers, as, for instance, with reference to the manner in which the bank's name appeared in the prospectus. To avoid risk, a bank should hold aloof from taking any part in the preparation or approval of the prospectus.

APPENDIX

APPENDIX I

TABLE SHOWING DISTRIBUTION OF MOVEABLE ESTATE OF PERSONS [1] DYING INTESTATE

Note.—By the Intestate Husband's Estate (Scotland) Act, 1911, the procedure under which is regulated by the Intestate Husband's Estate Act, 1919, the heritable and moveable estate of every man who dies intestate domiciled in Scotland, leaving a widow but no lawful issue, where the net value of such estate taken together does not exceed £500, goes absolutely and exclusively to the widow. Where the heritable and moveable estate together exceed £500 the widow is first entitled to the £500 with interest at four per cent. from the date of the death of the intestate until payment and on the balance of the moveable estate to her share as in the succeeding table.

If Intestate die leaving	Distribution of Estate among Representatives.
I. *Husband dying*	*survived by Wife and Children.*
1. Wife and child or children	The estate is divided into three parts. One-third falls to the widow as *jus relictæ*; one-third to the child or children as *legitim*; the remaining third, or *dead's part*, to the child or children as *next of kin*.
2. Wife, child or children, and issue of predeceasing child or children	One-third to widow as *jus relictæ*; one-third to surviving child or children as *legitim*; and the remaining third, or *dead's part*, between the surviving child or children, *per capita*,[2] and the issue of predeceased child or children *per stirpes*.[3]
3. Wife and issue of predeceased child or children	One-half to widow as *jus relictæ*; and half to such grandchildren *per capita* as *next of kin*.

[1] In the case of intestacy, illegitimate children do not succeed to their father and mother. When an illegitimate child dies intestate and leaves neither wife nor children, his estate falls to the Crown.

[2] *I.e.* by the head. Where an estate is divided *per capita*, it is divided into as many shares as there are children.

[3] *I.e.* by descent, through a parent. In such cases the share which would have fallen to a deceased parent if alive, is divided equally among his or her children.

If Intestate die leaving	Distribution of Estate among Representatives.
4. Wife and husband's children by two or more marriages	One-third to widow as *jus relictæ*; one-third to whole children as *legitim*, and the remaining third, or *dead's part*, to them as *next of kin*.
5. Wife and husband's children, and children of wife by former marriage	One-third to widow as *jus relictæ*; one-third to husband's children as *legitim*, and one-third to them as *next of kin*. The widow's children by former marriage have no share in the intestate's succession.
II. *Husband dying*	*survived by Wife only.*
6. Wife without children -	One-half to widow as *jus relictæ*; the other half, or *dead's part*, to the intestate's *next of kin*. (See Note, p. 379.)
III. *Husband dying*	*predeceased by Wife, leaving Children.*
7. Child or children only -	Whole estate to such child or children in equal shares; one-half as *legitim*, and the other, or *dead's part*, as *next of kin*.
8. Child or children, and issue of predeceasing child or children	One-half to child or children as *legitim*, and the other half, or *dead's part*, between such child or children *per capita*, and the issue of predeceased child or children *per stirpes*, as *next of kin*.
9. Issue of predeceasing child or children	Whole estate to such child or children equally *per capita*, as *next of kin*.
10. Husband's children by two or more marriages	Whole estate to such children equally, one-half as *legitim*, and the other half, or *dead's part*, as *next of kin*.
11. Husband's children and wife's children by former marriage	Whole estate to intestate's children equally, half as *legitim*, and the other half as *next of kin*. The wife's children by former marriage have no share in the intestate's succession.
IV. *Husband dying predeceased by Husband*	*ceased by Wife without Issue, or Wife dying without Issue; or a person dying unmarried.*
12. Father only, or 13. Father and mother only - - -	Half to father by sec. 3, Moveable Succession Act, 1855, and the remaining half by common law.
14. Mother only - - -	By Intestate Moveable Succession Act, 1919, the mother has now the same rights as father. See 12.
15. Father, mother, and brothers $\frac{and}{or}$ sisters 16. Father, and brothers $\frac{and}{or}$ sisters - -	Half to father under sec. 3, Moveable Succession Act, 1855, and the remaining half to brothers $\frac{and}{or}$ sisters equally.

If Intestate die leaving	Distribution of Estate among Representatives.
17. Mother, and brothers and/or sisters	One-half to mother under Act of 1919, and the remaining half to brothers and/or sisters equally.
18. Father, mother, brothers, and/or sisters, and issue of predeceased brothers and/or sisters 19. Father, brothers and/or sisters, and issue of predeceased brothers and/or sisters - -	Half to father under sec. 3, Moveable Succession Act, 1855, and half between brothers and/or sisters *per capita*, and such issue *per stirpes*.
20. Mother, brothers and/or sisters, and issue of predeceased brothers and/or sisters	One-half to mother under Act of 1919, and the remaining half between such brothers and/or sisters *per capita*, and such issue *per stirpes*.
21. Father, mother, and issue of predeceased brothers and/or sisters 22. Father and issue of predeceased brothers and/or sisters - -	Half to father under sec. 3, Moveable Succession Act, 1855, and half to such children equally.
23. Mother and issue of predeceased brothers and/or sisters	One-half to mother under Act of 1919, and the remaining half to such children equally.
24. Father, mother, children and grandchildren of predeceased brothers and/or sisters 25. Father, children, and grandchildren of predeceased brothers and/or sisters - - -	Half to father under sec. 3, Moveable Succession Act, 1855, and the remaining half between such children *per capita*, and such grandchildren *per stirpes*.
26. Mother, children, and grandchildren of predeceased brothers and/or sisters	One-half to mother under Act of 1919, and the remaining half between such children *per capita*, and such grandchildren *per stirpes*.
27. Brothers and/or sisters only	Whole estate is divided among them equally.
28. Brothers and/or sisters and issue of predeceased brothers and/or sisters	Estate divided between brothers and/or sisters who take *per capita*, and such issue who take *per stirpes*.
29. Brothers and/or sisters and the issue of predeceased brothers' and/or sisters' deceased children	Estate divided between such brothers and/or sisters who share *per capita*, and such children who share *per stirpes*, the shares to which their respective parents would have been entitled had they survived the intestate.

If Intestate die leaving	Distribution of Estate among Representatives.
30. Brothers and/or sisters, the issue of predeceased brothers and/or sisters, and the issue of predeceased brothers' and/or sisters' deceased children	Estate divided between brothers and sisters who take *per capita*, the issue of predeceased brothers and sisters who take *per stirpes*, and the issue of predeceased brothers' and sisters' deceased children who take *per stirpes*, the shares to which their respective parents would have been entitled had they survived the intestate.
31. Issue of predeceased brothers and/or sisters	
32. Issue of predeceased brothers' and/or sisters' deceased children	Estate divided among such issue equally.
33. Issue of predeceased brothers and/or sisters, issue of predeceased brothers' and/or sisters' deceased children	Estate divided between nephews and nieces who take *per capita*, and grand-nephews and nieces who take *per stirpes*.
34. Brothers and/or sisters german, and brothers and/or sisters consanguinean	Estate divided between brothers and sisters german equally. Among collaterals, relatives of the full blood exclude those of the half blood in the same line of succession.
35. Brothers and/or sisters consanguinean, and brothers and/or sisters uterine	Estate divided among brothers and sisters consanguinean equally.
36. Brothers and/or sisters consanguinean, and uncles or aunts	Estate divided among brothers and sisters equally.
37. Brothers and/or sisters uterine, and uncles or aunts	One-half to brothers or sisters uterine equally, under sec. 5, Moveable Succession Act, 1855, and the remaining half to uncles or aunts equally.
38. Brothers and/or sisters uterine, the issue of predeceased brothers and/or sisters uterine, and uncles or aunts	One-half among brothers or sisters uterine who take *per capita*, and the issue of predeceased brothers or sisters uterine who take *per stirpes*, under sec. 5, Moveable Succession Act, 1855, and the remaining half to uncles or aunts equally.
39. Father and brothers and/or sisters, consanguinean and uterine	One-half to father under sec. 3, Moveable Succession Act, 1855, and the remaining half to brothers or sisters consanguinean.

If Intestate die leaving	Distribution of Estate among Representatives.
40. Mother and brothers and/or sisters, consanguinean and uterine	One-half to mother under Act of 1919, and the remaining half to brothers or sisters consanguinean.
41. Father, mother, and uncles and/or aunts -	
42. Father and uncles and/or aunts - - -	Whole estate to father, by common law.
43. Father and issue of predeceased uncles and/or aunts - - -	
44. Mother and uncles and/or aunts - - -	
45. Mother, uncles and/or aunts and issue of predeceased uncles or aunts - - -	One-half to mother under Act of 1919, and the remaining half to uncles or aunts, the issue of predeceased uncles or aunts being excluded from participation.
46. Mother and issue of predeceased uncles and/or aunts	One-half to mother under Act of 1919, and the remaining half to such issue equally *per capita*.
47. Issue of predeceased brothers' and/or sisters' deceased children, and issue of predeceased uncles and/or aunts	Whole estate among the issue of brothers' or sisters' deceased children equally.
48. Issue of predeceased brothers' and/or sisters' deceased children's children, and brothers and/or sisters consanguinean	Whole estate among such issue equally to the exclusion of the half blood.
49. Issue of predeceased uncles and/or aunts, and issue of predeceased uncles' and/or aunts' children	Whole estate among the issue of predeceased uncles or aunts. No representation is admitted among collaterals after the descendants of brothers or sisters.
50. Uncles and/or aunts and children of great-uncles and/or aunts	Whole estate among uncles or aunts equally.
51. Great-uncles' and/or aunts' children, and issue of predeceased uncles and/or aunts	Whole estate among such issue equally.
52. Grandfather and uncles and/or aunts	Whole estate among uncles or aunts equally. When a person dies without leaving descendants or collaterals, or the descendants of collaterals, the father succeeds at common law; and failing the father, *his* collaterals succeed, then the descendants of his collaterals, then failing them the remoter ascendants take.

If Intestate die leaving	Distribution of Estate among Representatives.
53. Grandfather and uncles $\frac{and}{or}$ aunts consanguinean	Whole estate to uncles or aunts consanguinean equally.
54. Grandfather, grand-mother, and great-uncles $\frac{and}{or}$ aunts	Whole estate to grandfather.
55. Grandfather, grand-mother, and mother	One-half to mother under Act of 1919, and the remaining half to grandfather.

V. *Wife dying survived by Husband and Children, by Husband without Children, predeceased by Husband leaving Children, where the Wife has separate estate of her own.*

Sec. 6 of the Married Women's Property Act, 1881, provides that the husband of any woman who may die domiciled in Scotland shall take by operation of law the same share and interest in her moveable estate which is taken by a widow in her deceased husband's moveable estate according to the law and practice of Scotland, and subject always to the same rules of law in relation to the nature and amount of such share and interest, and the exclusion, discharge, and satisfaction thereof.[1]

Sec. 7 provides that the children of any woman who may die domiciled in Scotland shall have the same right of legitim in regard to her moveable estate which they have according to the law and practice of Scotland in regard to the moveable estate of their deceased father, subject always to the same rules of law in relation to the character and extent of the said right, and to the exclusion, discharge, or satisfaction thereof as the case may be.[2]

VI. *Wife dying predeceased by Husband without Children ; or a Woman dying unmarried.*

The succession falls to be divided among her own relatives in the same manner as the husband's falls to be divided among his relatives, as detailed in Section IV.

---

[1] Poë v. Paterson, 1883, 10 R. (H.L.) 73, decided that the application of this section was not restricted to marriages contracted after the passing of the Act.

[2] Miller v. Galbraith's Trs., 1886, 13 R. 764, decided that under this section a woman cannot discharge a claim for legitim without her husband's consent. This is now altered by the Married Women's Property (Scotland) Act, 1920, under which a married woman can discharge her claim to legitim without the consent of her husband.

APPENDIX II

STAMP DUTIES

1. BILLS OF EXCHANGE (excepting promissory notes) drawn, or paid, or negotiated in the United Kingdom.

> Payable on demand at sight or on presentation, or within three days after date or sight, or in which no time for payment is expressed - - - - - - - 2d.
> (But as regards promissory notes, see PROMISSORY NOTES.)

> This stamp may be either impressed or adhesive, but must not be on a twopenny bill stamp, such as the stamp used for a bill not exceeding five pounds, drawn at a currency. If the bill be presented for payment unstamped, the agent must affix and cancel a stamp before paying it. He should, however, deduct the price of the stamp from the amount to be paid.

> Payable at a currency. The following *ad valorem* duties, viz.—

> If drawn otherwise than on demand (and promissory notes whether drawn on demand or at a currency) :—

Not exceeding £5	-	-	-	-	-	2d.
Exceeding £5 and not exceeding £10	-	-	-	2d.
,, £10 ,, £25	-	-	-	3d.
,, £25 ,, £50	-	-	-	6d.
,, £50 ,, £75	-	-	-	9d.
,, £75 ,, £100	-	-	-	1s.
And for every additional £100, or fractional part of £100	-	-	-	-	-	1s.

> The *ad valorem* duties payable on bills of exchange and promissory notes, drawn or made, or purporting to be drawn or made, out of, but negotiated in, the United Kingdom, are to be denoted by adhesive stamps. Such stamp must be put on the bill or note and cancelled before it is presented for payment, indorsed, transferred, or in any manner negotiated or paid. As to the cancellation of these, see *post*.

> In the case of bills drawn in sets, the full duty must be paid upon one, and the others of the set will go free.

2. BILLS OR DRAFTS by Accountant-General of Chancery in England or Ireland, or drawn by the Lords Commissioners of the Admiralty, or by any person under their authority, upon and payable by the Accountant-General of Navy, or on "form prescribed by public authority," for army pay, or other army allowances - - - Free of duty.

25

385

3. BONDS OF CREDIT are liable to mortgage duty as under :—

    Not exceeding £10 - - - - - 3d.
    Exceeding £10 and not exceeding £25 - - - 8d.
      ,,   £25   ,,   £50 - - - 1s. 3d.
      ,,   £50   ,,   £100 - - - 2s. 6d.
    Thereafter at the rate of 1s. 3d. for every £50 up to £300.
    In bonds exceeding £300 the duty is at the rate of 2s. 6d. for every £100 or fractional part of £100.

4. CALLS—RECEIPTS FOR. (See RECEIPTS.)

5. CHEQUES payable to bearer or order on demand - - - 2d.

    If presented for payment unstamped, a stamp must be affixed, cancelled, and charged in the same way as with bills of exchange payable on demand, No. 1.

6. CONSIGNATION RECEIPTS - - - - - - 2d.

    Note.—Consignation receipts for funds held under order of Court, or under any other arrangement, or on which interest is directed to be paid periodically to a liferenter, etc., require a twopenny stamp (to be cancelled, in the case of an adhesive stamp, by the proper party [1]) before the issuing of the receipt. This is over and above the stamp required when the receipt is discharged.

7. COUPONS, if issued with any security. (See also WARRANT FOR INTEREST.)

    Where a coupon can be cut off, and is simply delivered upon payment, without requiring to be signed, no receipt stamp is necessary. But where the holder of the coupon does, or has to. sign the coupon, the stamp required is - - - - - - 2d.

8. DEBIT VOUCHERS.

    For sums advised from the branches or from correspondents—
    (1) When *placed to accounts* of customers - Free of duty.
    (2) When *paid* to the party - - - - 2d.

9. DELIVERY ORDER, entitling person therein named, or holder, to delivery of goods, of the value of 40s. or upwards, lying in any dock, port, or warehouse, or on any wharf (adhesive stamp sufficient) - - 1d.

    (This duty was repealed by the Finance Act, 1905.) (See WARRANT FOR GOODS.)

10. DEPOSIT RECEIPTS. When payable (1) to the party from whom the money has been received, (2) issued in the names of two or more persons, to be drawn by any or either or the survivor, and (3) in the names of two persons, in terms of the Titles to Land (Consolidation) Act, 1868, for behoof of the party or parties having best right thereto, are not now chargeable with duty on issue. Until recently, deposit receipts framed in terms of (2) and (3) were charged with a duty of one penny on issue.

    Every deposit receipt when paid must be discharged upon a twopenny stamp. The forms supplied to branches have the requisite stamps impressed upon them.

---

[1] See No. 24.

11. DISCHARGES.

For sums due under lost documents ; and

For small sums due to parties deceased when confirmation is not exhibited.

These documents, in addition to the discharge, always contain a guarantee against loss being sustained by the bank through making payment. The stamp required is 8d.—twopence for the discharge and sixpence for the guarantee.

12. DIVIDENDS ON GOVERNMENT FUNDS, BANK OF ENGLAND STOCK, OR OTHER STOCKS. (See MANDATES and RECEIPTS.)

13. DRAFTS OR ORDERS, payable to bearer or to order on demand, whether drawn by, or on, a banker, or not   -   -   -   -   2d.

14. GUARANTEES. A letter of guarantee requires a stamp of -   -   6d.

15. INTEREST WARRANTS. (See WARRANTS.)

16. LETTERS OF CREDIT on the bank's foreign correspondents   -   2d.

17. LETTER OR POWER OF ATTORNEY, for drawing and indorsing bills, indorsing deposit receipts, etc. -   -   -   -   -   10s.

18. MANDATES.

To uplift dividends. A mandate in the form of an order, request, or direction by the owner of any stock, addressed to any company, or to any officer thereof, or to any bank, to pay dividends or interest arising from such stock to any person therein named, requires no stamp. If not so expressed and addressed, and made for the receipt of one payment only, the stamp is 1s. In any other case   -   5s.

To operate on current accounts. A mandate addressed to the bank, and authorising some one to operate on the granter's account, has been adjudged not to require a stamp. But a mandate in any other form, either to operate on an account, or to draw or indorse bills, must be stamped with -   -   -   -   -   -   10s.

To accept transfers of bank stock. Such mandates are liable in a duty of -   -   -   -   -   -   -   -   10s.

19. PROCURATION. (See MANDATES and LETTER OR POWER OF ATTORNEY.)

20. PROMISSORY NOTES, whether payable on demand or at a currency. Same *ad valorem* duties as BILLS OF EXCHANGE.

21. RECEIPTS.

For or upon payment of £2 or upwards -   -   -   -   2d.

Consignation Receipts. See above (No. 6).

For Lodgments on current or cash accounts, if merely filled up with the title of the account, and with no other narrative or addition whatever -   -   -   -   -   Free of duty.

For Calls on Shares. Where there is a perforation between the allotment letter and the receipt form -   -   -   -   2d.

21. RECEIPTS—*continued*.

In cases where there is no such perforation and the form is entire, no duty is payable.

For Receipts of a payment either in full or to account, written upon a bill of exchange or promissory note   -   -   -   -   2d.

Deposit Receipts. See above (No. 10).

By Accountant-General of the Navy as such   -   -

By any Agent, " for money imprested to him on account of the Pay of the Army"   -   -   -   -   -

To the Admiralty or Army Pay Office, for Navy, or Army, or Pensions   -   -   -   -   -

For the consideration money, for the purchase of any share in any of the Government or Parliamentary stocks or funds, or in stock of the East India Company, or in the stocks and funds of the Secretary of State in Council of India, or of the Governor and Company of the Bank of England, or of the Bank of Ireland, or for any dividend paid on any share of the said stocks or funds respectively   -   } Free of duty.

Upon any Bill or Note of the Governor and Company of the Bank of England or the Bank of Ireland -   -   -

For Drawback or Bounty upon the exportation of any goods or merchandise from the United Kingdom -   -   -

Acknowledging receipt of Bill or Promissory Note, to be presented for acceptance or payment, free of duty. Do. do. in any other case   -   -   -   -   -   -   -   -   2d.

22. WARRANT FOR GOODS,[1] being evidence of person therein named, or holder, to the property in any goods lying in any dock, port, or warehouse, or on any wharf (adhesive stamp sufficient)   -   3d.

Exemptions—

   (1) Any document given by an inland carrier, acknowledging receipt of goods conveyed by him.
   (2) A weight note issued with a duly stamped warrant, and relating solely to the same goods.

23. WARRANTS FOR INTEREST, if issued with any security, and payable without indorsation by holder   -   -   -   - Free of duty.
Do., if indorsed or requiring to be indorsed   -   -   -   2d.

24. STAMPS IMPRESSED AND ADHESIVE.—As to affixing and cancelling them.

As already mentioned, the *ad valorem* stamp or stamps on bills of exchange or promissory notes, drawn or made, or purporting to be drawn or made, out of, but negotiated in, the United Kingdom, *must be adhesive*. The stamps on bills of exchange or promissory notes drawn or granted within the United Kingdom *must be impressed*, except bill stamps payable on demand, which may be adhesive (see p. 385). In the case of all other kinds of vouchers

---

[1] As to interpretation of phrase "Warrant for Goods," see Commissioners of Inland Revenue *v.* Distillers' Co. Ltd., 1899, 1 F. 737.

24. Stamps Impressed and Adhesive—*continued*.

referred to in this table which require a twopence stamp, it may be either impressed or adhesive, and may be either a receipt or draft stamp ; but impressed stamps are always preferable as not requiring cancellation.

In all cases the stamp or stamps must appear on the face of the document.

Adhesive stamps must be cancelled as follows :—

In the case of a bill, cheque, draft, or letter of credit payable on demand, by the drawer or granter, before delivering it out of his hand, by writing across the stamp his (or his firm's) name or initials, with the true date of such cancellation. Where there is more than one adhesive stamp on the one document, all the stamps must be separately cancelled in the above manner.

In the case of a receipt, it must be so cancelled by the granter before delivering it out of his hands.

Note.—As already mentioned, deposit receipts have always an impressed stamp for their discharge.

In the case of bills or promissory notes made and granted out of, but negotiated in, the United Kingdom, adhesive stamp or stamps of sufficient amount must be affixed ; and when such bills or notes are drawn in a set, the stamp or stamps must be affixed to one bill of the set, and must be cancelled (or bear to be cancelled) by the holder, or by a previous holder, *in the United Kingdom*, by writing his (or his firm's) name or initials, with the true date of such writing, across the stamp. In the event of the stamp or stamps not being so cancelled before coming into the bank's hands, they must be cancelled by the bank.

FORMS REFERRED TO IN PART I

Affidavit under Bankers' Books Evidence Act

(Copy Account)

At Edinburgh the
day of   19 .
In presence of *A. B.*   one of His
Majesty's Justices of the Peace for the County of Edinburgh.
Compeared *C. D.*   of   ,
Edinburgh, who, being solemnly sworn and examined, Depones that the
foregoing is a copy of the account kept in the ledger of the said Bank at
their branch in   , in name of   , from the
day of   until the   day of   , when the said
account was closed (or as the case may be) : That the said ledger was at the
time when the entries in the said account were made one of the ordinary
books of the Bank, and the said entries were made in the usual and ordinary
course of business, and that the said ledger is now in the custody of the
Bank ; Depones also that he has examined the foregoing Copy Account with
the original and found it correct : All which is truth, as the deponent
shall answer to God.

C. D.
A. B., J.P.

Guarantee to Bank in respect of Bills sent Abroad for Collection

To the
Bank of

Gentlemen,—With reference to any bills, promissory notes, or other documents, payable out of the United Kingdom, which from time to time may
be discounted by you for (me *or* us) or which (I *or* we) may lodge with you
for collection, (I *or* we) hereby undertake and agree that (my *or* our) liability
to you in respect of such bills or other documents shall continue not
only during their currency and until final payment, but also during the
currency of any bills or letters of credit which you may receive from your
agents or correspondents in remittance of the proceeds thereof.

(I *or* we) guarantee to you due payment of such remittance bills or letters
of credit which you may discount to (me *or* us), or on which you may make
(me *or* us) advances.

Further, (I *or* we) agree and undertake to free and relieve you from
liability for the intromissions of the agents or correspondents to whom you
may send such bills or other documents for negotiation, and it is of course
understood that you are not responsible for any documents lost in transmission.—Yours truly,

6d. Stamp.

DISCHARGE AND GUARANTEE FOR LOST DEPOSIT RECEIPT [1]

To the
      (*Designation of Bank.*)

Gentlemen,—I, *A. B.*, residing at   , considering that I have lost or mislaid a Deposit Receipt, " No.   ," dated the day of   Nineteen hundred and   , granted for you at your office in   , in my name for payment to me of the sum of   sterling : And whereas you have, notwithstanding the want of said document, made payment to me of the said sum of   sterling, and   of interest due thereon to the date of delivery hereof : Therefore I, the said *A. B.*, and I, *C. D.*, residing at   , hereby oblige ourselves and our successors whatever, all conjunctly and severally, to guarantee and defend and relieve you from all and any claim, question, and expense which may be raised against or incurred by you in reference to the said Deposit Receipt, which we oblige ourselves to deliver to you if and when found.—In witness whereof.

GUARANTEE BY BANK WHO CASH A CHEQUE TO BANK ON WHICH CHEQUE DRAWN, IN RESPECT OF PAYMENT BY LATTER WHEN CHEQUE LOST IN TRANSMISSION THROUGH POST OFFICE.

                              Edinburgh,   19 .

Gentlemen,—In respect you have agreed to pay to us (*or to as the case may be*) the sum contained in a cheque for £   , drawn on you by   in favour of   , dated   and indorsed by him, and which has been lost in the course of transmission through the Post Office, we hereby undertake to guarantee and defend and relieve you and the said   from all and any claim, question, and expense which may be raised against or incurred by you or them in consequence of your having so paid to us the amount of the said cheque, and whether altered in any way or not, the original of which we oblige ourselves to deliver up cancelled if found.—We are, Sirs, your obedient servants.

     To the
          (*Designation of Bank to whom granted.*)

                                    6d. Stamp.

GUARANTEE TAKEN FROM CUSTOMER BY BANK WHO CASH CHEQUE IN RESPECT OF THEIR GUARANTEE TO BANK ON WHOM CHEQUE DRAWN

                                 (*Place and date.*)

Gentlemen,—With reference to the guarantee granted by you at our request in favour of the (*designation of Bank*) we hereby undertake to guarantee, and defend and relieve you from all and any claim, question, and expense which may be raised against or incurred by you in consequence of your having granted the said guarantee.—We are, your obedient servants.

     To the
          (*Designation of Bank.*)

                                    6d. Stamp.

---

[1] The phraseology of this form may be altered to suit the case of a draft or dividend warrant. The form is liable to a stamp duty of 8d.—6d. in respect of the guarantee, and 2d. as receipt stamp.

COMMUNICATIONS APPROVING OF BANK ACCOUNT IN LIEU OF DOCQUET
OF LEDGER

Bank

(*Place*)   19 .

Sir,—I beg to send you herewith Statement of your Account with the
Bank at this office for the year ending   December last,
showing a balance at that date of   due
the Bank. Please examine the same, and, if found correct, be so good as
to fill up the annexed letter and return it to me at your earliest convenience.
—I am, yours faithfully.

19 .

To the   Bank
Sirs,—   have received Statement of   Account with the
Bank at your office for the year ending   December last, showing
a balance at that date of   due   the
Bank, which   have examined and hereby acknowledge to be correct.
Please send the cheques passed by   on the account to that date.
—Yours faithfully.

Bank

(*Place*)   19 .

Sir,—I beg to acknowledge receipt of your letter of
and now send herewith the vouchers passed by you on your account with
this Bank, of which you have approved. Please acknowledge receipt on the
accompanying form.—I am, yours faithfully.

19 .

Sirs,—   beg to acknowledge receipt of your letter of
and of the cheques on   account with you for the year
ending   .—Yours faithfully.
To the   Bank.

CONSIGNATION RECEIPT IN TERMS OF THE TITLES TO LAND
CONSOLIDATION ACT, 1868

Bank of

19 .

£110. 4s. 11d.
Received for the Bank of   from *A. B.*, Writer to the Signet,
Edinburgh, and *C. D.*, merchant, 150 George Street, Edinburgh, the sum
of One hundred and ten pounds four shillings and eleven pence sterling,
being surplus of the price, stated to be of £2500, of the subjects in Constitution Street, Leith, sold by the said *A. B.* to the said *C. D.*, by disposition
dated 25th, and recorded in the Division of the General Register of Sasines
applicable to the County of Edinburgh 26th, both days of April 1913, under
powers of sale contained in a bond and disposition in security granted in
favour of the said *A. B.* by *E. F.*, Chartered Accountant in Edinburgh,
dated 1st and recorded in said Division of the General Register of Sasines
3rd, both days of June 1889, after deducting the debt, stated to be of £500
sterling, secured, with interest due thereon and penalties incurred and whole
expenses attending the sale, and also after paying all the prior incumbrances
and expenses of discharging the same ; such sum being consigned for behoof

of the party or parties having best right thereto in terms of the Titles to Land Consolidation (Scotland) Act, 1868.

CONSIGNATION RECEIPT IN A SUSPENSION [1]

Bank of

19 .

£1000 stg.

Received for the   Bank, on behalf of the Accountant of Court and his successors in office, from *A. B.*, Esquire, Clerk of the Bills in the Bill Chamber, Court of Session, the sum of One thousand pounds sterling, stated to be the amount offered by the complainers, and upon consignation of which the Lord Ordinary officiating on the Bills, by Interlocutor dated the   day of   , passed the Note of Suspension at the instance of Messrs. *H. G. & Co.*, merchants in Leith, and *C. D.* and others, the trustees of the deceased   , and which sum is deposited with us to abide the orders of Court in said Suspension.

CONSIGNATION RECEIPT FOR MONEY LODGED BY RAILWAY COMPANY TO MEET TENANT'S CLAIM FOR LAND TAKEN FOR PROPOSED RAILWAY

Bank

Edinburgh,   19 .

£750 stg.

Received for the   Bank from the Railway Company (first) the sum of £244. 5s. 1d. sterling, stated to be the amount to be due and payable by the said Railway Company to *A. B.*, farmer, M., near Perth, on the footing that he is a yearly tenant of certain lands in the Parish of Y. and County of Perth occupied by him, and that for and in respect of his said interest in the said lands taken for the purposes of the construction of the said Railway, and as the amount of compensation to be made by the said Railway Company to him in respect thereof, and also in respect of all damage sustained and to be sustained by him by reason of the exercise by the said Railway Company of the powers conferred upon them by their Act of Parliament and Acts incorporated therewith; together with the sum of £5. 14s. 11d. sterling, being the interest at 5 per cent. on said sum from   to this date; (second) the sum of £491. 3s. 4d. sterling, which with the said sum of £244. 5s. 1d., amounting together to £741. 3s. 4d. sterling, is stated to be the amount to be due and payable by the said Railway Company to the said *A. B.*, on the footing that he is lessee of the said lands under a lease terminating at Whitsunday 1914, for and in respect of his said last-mentioned interest in the said lands taken for the construction of the said Railway as aforesaid, and as the amount of compensation foresaid, and also in respect of all damage sustained and to be sustained by him as aforesaid; together with the sum of £8. 16s. 8d. sterling, being the interest at 5 per cent. on the said sum of £491. 3s. 4d. from   foresaid to this date, which whole sums amount together to £750 sterling : Declaring that in the event of the said *A. B.* failing to take competent proceedings within three months from this date to instruct his pretended right of lessee foresaid until Whitsunday 1914, and notify the same to the said Bank, the said sums of

---

[1] This form may be altered to suit consignation in the Sheriff Court, the words " Sheriff Clerk of the County of   " being substituted for " Accountant of Court."

£491. 3s. 4d. and £8. 16s. 8d., and all interest thereon, shall be payable to and upliftable by Messrs. *C. D. & Co.*, W.S., Edinburgh, agents for the said Railway Company : Further, declaring that the other sums of £244. 5s. 1d. and £5. 14s. 11d., together with all interest thereon, shall be unliftable by the said *C. D. & Co.*, agents foresaid, and Messrs. *E. & H.*, Writers, Glasgow, agents of the said *A. B.*, upon their joint indorsation.

CONSIGNATION RECEIPT FOR MONEY LODGED TO MEET AN EXPECTANCY UNDER AN ENTAIL

                                                          Bank
                                    Edinburgh,   19 .

£320 stg.

Received for the   Bank from *A. B.*, Esquire of L., in the County of Forfar, the sum of Three hundred and twenty pounds sterling, said to be the value in money of the expectancy or interest of *C. D.* (brother of the said *A. B.*), presently residing with his mother, Mrs *E. B.*, widow of the deceased *G. B.*, Esquire of L., at No. 150 Atholl Crescent, Edinburgh, in certain entailed lands and others in and around the Burgh of O., which sum has been placed to the credit of an account opened in the name of the said *C. D.*, and is to be payable to him after he attains majority.

CONSIGNATION RECEIPT FOR MONEY LODGED IN RESPECT OF LANDS PURCHASED

                                                          Bank
                                    Glasgow,   19 .

£10,000 stg.

Received for the   Bank from *A. B.*, Esquire of M., in the County of Lanark, the sum of Ten thousand pounds sterling, stated to be the agreed-on price of the lands and estate of X., in the County of Dumfries, consigned by him in terms of the second article of a Minute of Agreement entered into between him and *C. D.*, Esquire of X. and Y., in the said county, executed in duplicate, and dated 12th, 15th, and 20th February 1913, which sum shall, as provided in the said Minute, be repayable upon the joint indorsation of Messrs. *E. F. & Co.*, W.S., and Messrs. *G. & H.*, W.S., both of Edinburgh.

CONSIGNATION RECEIPT FOR MONEY LODGED TO AWAIT ORDERS OF COURT

                                                          Bank
                                    Edinburgh,   19 .

£5500 stg.

Received for the   Bank, on behalf of the Accountant of Court and his successors in office, from *A. B.*, Esquire of G., in the County of Fife, the sum of Five thousand five hundred pounds sterling, stated to be the purchase price of the mansion-house and estate of H., parts of the entailed lands and estate of K. and others, in the County of Midlothian, purchased by him from *C. D.*, Esquire of K., under an order approving of a Minute of Agreement to sell the said lands of H. and others, and authorising the sale thereof, obtained by the said *C. D.* under a petition at his instance, and which sum is now consigned subject to the orders of the Court of Session in the said petition in terms of an Interlocutor by the Lord Ordinary (Lord Hunter) officiating on the Bills, dated   19 .

CONSIGNATION RECEIPT FOR MONEY LODGED IN TERMS OF THE LANDS CLAUSES CONSOLIDATION ACT, 1845

Bank of
Edinburgh,   19 .

£500 stg.

Received for the Bank of   from the Railway Company the sum of Five hundred pounds sterling, which has been placed to the credit of an account opened in the name of *A. B.*, tenant of the farm of G., in the County of Midlothian, the party interested as tenant in certain lands situated in the parish of H. and County of Midlothian, required by the said Railway Company for the purposes of their Act, extending to 92·321 acres imperial measure, and numbered 30, 31, and 32 upon the Parliamentary plan of the said Railway, and which sum is stated to be the balance of the value of the said lands as ascertained by *C. D.*, valuator appointed for that purpose by the Board of Trade, and which is now deposited in the said Bank of   at the head office in Edinburgh, by way of security for payment by the said Railway Company of the interest upon the compensation determined to be due to the party interested as aforesaid as tenant in the said lands, under sections 84 and 85 of the Lands Clauses Consolidation (Scotland) Act, 1845, and other Acts relating to the said Company : Declaring that the said deposit is to remain subject to the control and disposition of the Court of Session in terms of Interlocutor of Lord Hunter (Ordinary), dated   19 .

CHEQUE BY EXECUTORS FOR SUM STANDING AT THE CREDIT OF DECEASED PERSON ON CURRENT ACCOUNT

(*Place and date.*)

To the Agent of
          The   (*designation of Bank*).
     On demand pay to   or Bearer the sum of £   , and debit the account of the deceased *A. B.* (*giving designation*) therewith.

C. D.,
E. F.,
Executors of the said *A. B.*, conform to
confirmation by the Sheriff of the
County of   , dated the
day of   19 .

Indorsation on Deposit Receipt by Executors where Receipt in name of Deceased Person

A. B.,
C. D.,
Executors of the within *E. F.*, conform to
confirmation in our favour by the
Sheriff of the County of   ,
dated the   day of   19 .

DISCHARGE BY EXECUTORS FOR SUM STANDING AT THE CREDIT OF A DECEASED PERSON ON CURRENT ACCOUNT

We, *A. B.*, residing at   , and *C. G.*, residing at   , the executors of the deceased *M. B.*   , who died at   on the   , conform to confirmation by the Sheriff of the County of   , dated the   day of   Nineteen hundred and   : Grant us to have received from (*designation of Bank*) the sum of   sterling, being the whole money accountable by the said (*designation of Bank*) on Current Deposit Account kept with them at their office in   , in name of the said   as at the day of   Nineteen hundred and   , the date of death (as also the sum of   of interest due thereon to the date of delivery hereof) ; of which sums now paid to   and of the said Current Deposit Account, and of all claims competent thereon, we hereby exoner and simpliciter discharge the said (*designation of Bank*) for ever : And we hereby oblige ourselves and our successors whatever to make forth-coming to the said (*designation of Bank*) the foresaid testament   whensoever and as oftensoever as required.—In witness whereof.

DISCHARGE BY EXECUTORS FOR SUM DUE UNDER A DEPOSIT RECEIPT IN NAME OF A DECEASED PERSON

We, *A. B.*, residing at   , and *G. C.*, residing at   , the executors of the deceased *M. B.*   , who died at   on the   , conform to confirmation by the Sheriff of the County of   , dated the   day of   Nineteen hundred and   : Grant us to have received from (*designation of Bank*) the sum of   sterling of principal and   of interest due thereon, contained in and due by a Deposit Receipt " No.   ," dated the   day of   Nineteen hundred and   , granted for the said (*designation of Bank*) at their office in .   in name of the said   now deceased, and the sum in which Deposit Receipt is duly confirmed in the said confirmation : of which sum so paid to us and of the said Deposit Receipt, and of all claims competent thereon, we hereby exoner and simpliciter discharge the said (*designation of Bank*) for ever ; and we have herewith delivered up to the said (*designation of Bank*) the foresaid Deposit Receipt ; and we oblige ourselves and our successors to make forth-coming to the said (*designation of Bank*) the foresaid confirmation   whensoever and as oftensoever as required.—In witness whereof.

DISCHARGE BY REPRESENTATIVES OF A DECEASED PERSON, CONTAINING A GUARANTEE BY A THIRD PARTY WHERE CONFIRMATION IS DISPENSED WITH.[1]

We, *A. B.*, residing at   , and *C. G.*, residing at   , being the (*describe relationship to deceased*) and whole (*or as the case may be*)

---

[1] This form may be altered to suit the case of the amount due being on current account.

representatives and next of kin of the deceased *M. B.*   , who died
at   on the   : Grant us to have received from the
(*designation of Bank*) the sum of   sterling of principal, and
          of interest due thereon, contained in and due by a Deposit Receipt
" No   ," dated the   day of   , granted
for the said (*designation of Bank*) at their office in   , in name of
the said deceased   , of which sums now paid to us, and of the said
Deposit Receipt itself, and of all claims competent thereon, we hereby exoner
and impliciter discharge the said (*designation of Bank*) for ever ; and we,
the whole granters hereof foresaid, and I, *L. M.* (*designation and address*)
hereby bind and oblige ourselves and our heirs, executors, and successors
whatever, all conjunctly and severally, to defend, relieve, and skaithless
keep the said   from all claims, questions, loss, costs, and charges
which may be raised against them, or incurred by them, because of, or in
relation to, the said Deposit Receipt, which is herewith delivered up to the
said (*designation of Bank*) : And we, the whole granters hereof, excepting
me the said *L. M.*   bind and oblige ourselves whenever required
by the said (*designation of Bank*) to complete our title or the title of such
of the next of kin as may be preferred to the office as executor to the said
deceased   , and exhibit confirmation thereof expede before
the proper Court.—In witness whereof.

Form of Docquet by Notary Public, Justice of the Peace, or Parish Minister, where Granter of Deed Cannot Write

By authority of the above-named and designed *A. B.*, who declares that
he cannot write, on account of sickness and bodily weakness [*or never having
been taught, or otherwise as the case may be*], I, *C. D.* (*design him*), Notary
Public [*or Justice of Peace for the County of* (*name it*), *or as regards wills or
other testamentary writings executed by a parish minister as Notary Public in his
own parish*, minister of the parish of (*name it*)], subscribe these presents for
him, he having authorised me for that purpose, and the same having been
previously read over to him, all in presence of the witnesses before named
and designed, who subscribe this docquet in testimony of their having heard
[*or seen*] authority given to me as aforesaid, and heard these presents read
over to the said *A. B.*

(Signed)	*C. D.*, Notary Public.
E. F., witness.	*or* Justice of the Peace.
G. H., witness.	*or* Parish Minister.

Form of Docquet used when Deeds are Executed according to both the English and Scottish Forms

In witness whereof.

(*Testing clause in ordinary form.*)

Signed, sealed, and delivered by the said *A. B.* before
    and in presence of—
C. D., Merchant, 170 George Street, Edinburgh, witness.   *A. B.*   Seal.
E. F., Solicitor, 131 Bernard Street, Leith, witness.

MINUTE OF MEETING OF DIRECTORS OF INCORPORATED COMPANY AUTHORISING OVERDRAFT AND PLEDGING UNCALLED CAPITAL IN SECURITY

At   the

day of   19 .

At a meeting of

, incorporated

under the Companies Acts.

Present—

The Company having resolved to avail themselves of the borrowing powers contained in the Memorandum and Articles of Association of the Company, and considering that the   Bank have agreed to grant to the Company certain banking accommodation on an overdrawn current account in their name, the amount of which is not to exceed at any time the sum of £   and interest, and which account is to be operated upon by cheques signed by   or in such other manner as the Directors shall from time to time appoint, hereby bind and oblige the said Company to pay to the   Bank all sums which are or may be due in any manner of way to the said   Bank from the said Company : And the Company further bind and impledge the whole funds, property, assets, and effects of the Company, heritable and moveable, in security to the said   Bank of payment of whatever sums may be due to them in any manner of way as aforesaid. The Company also hereby impledge to the said   Bank the uncalled capital of the said payable by the shareholders ; and they bind and oblige themselves, when required by the said   Bank, to call up from the shareholders the uncalled capital, and to make payment of the amount thereof to the said   Bank so far as necessary for repayment to them of the whole sums, principal and interest, which may be due to them at the time : The Company further impledge themselves not to call up any of the uncalled capital without first obtaining the consent in writing of the said Bank : And the Company further declare and bind themselves and their successors that any account or certificate signed by the cashier of the said Bank, or by any agent or accountant in the service of the Bank, shall sufficiently constitute and ascertain the amount which may at any time be due to the Bank as aforesaid.

EXTRACT MINUTE OF MEETING OF PARISH COUNCIL AUTHORISING OVERDRAFT TO MEET CURRENT EXPENDITURE [1]

Excerpt Minute of Meeting of the Parish Council of   held on   .

Present—

The Board resolved to avail themselves of the borrowing powers contained in the 89th section of the Poor Law (Scotland) Act, 1845, and transferred to them by the 22nd section of the Local Government (Scotland) Act, 1894, and directed their chairman to apply to the agent for the   Bank at   for permission to overdraw their General Parish Fund Account, on the security of the Assessment still due and unrecovered, which Assessment they pledged and hereby pledge to the said Bank ; the overdraft not to exceed at any time the sum of

---

[1] This form may be altered to suit the case of an overdraft by a County Council.

pounds, and the cheques on the account to be signed by and
, two members of the Council, and countersigned by the Clerk, in terms of section 35 of the said Local Government Act.

The Council also directed the Clerk to prepare for the information of the Bank a certificate, showing the amount of Assessment for the current year, and the amount due and unrecovered at this date.

Extracted from the Minutes of Meeting of the Parish Council of
By me,

Form of Certificate

I hereby certify that the Assessment imposed by the Parish Council of for the year from to is at the rate of per £, and is estimated to amount in all to not less than pounds; and further, that of that Assessment is due and unrecovered at this date.

A. B., Clerk.

MINUTE OF MEETING OF EDUCATION AUTHORITY AUTHORISING OVERDRAFT

At the
day of
At a meeting of the Education Authority of the Parish
of .

Present—

The Chairman submitted to the meeting a statement of the probable income and expenditure for the year from
to , showing the estimated total income for the period to be .

The Chairman also stated that the Education rate would not be received till , while the expenses of the Authority have to be provided for in the meantime, and that it was desirable to effect arrangements for that purpose. The Authority therefore authorised, and do hereby authorise, the treasurer to open a current account with the
at , to be operated on by and to overdraw the same, so as not to exceed at any time the sum of
; and the Authority hereby bind themselves to apply the school fund and the school rate in repayment to the of all sums which may be due upon the said account, and interest thereon at the Bank's usual rate for such advances; and they agreed, and hereby agree, that the amount which may at any time be due shall be sufficiently constituted and ascertained by a certificate under the hands of any agent or accountant in the service of the said Bank.

Extracted from the Minutes of Meeting of the Education Authority of the parish of .
By me,

FORMS RELATING TO PART II

INLAND BILL OF EXCHANGE

Edinburgh, 1st January 1923.

£50.

Three months after date pay to me or my order the sum of Fifty pounds, value received.

Messrs. Peter Jones & Co. JOHN SMITH.

FOREIGN BILL

Bombay, 1st January 1923.

£50.

One month after sight of this first of exchange (second and third unpaid) pay to the order of Messrs. Jones & Co. Fifty pounds for value received, and charge the same to account of Messrs. Brown & Co. against your letter of Credit, No. 2.

To Mr. William Walker. PETER SMYTH.

BILL PAYABLE BY INSTALMENTS

(Place and date.)

£100.

By equal instalments at three, six, and nine months after date, pay to me or my order (within the   Bank here) the sum of One hundred pounds, value received.

To *C. D.* *A. B.*

BILL HAVING TWO OR MORE ACCEPTORS

(Place and date.)

£100.

Conjointly and severally, three months after date, pay to me or my order (within the   Bank here) the sum of One hundred pounds, value received.

BILLS IN A SET

(Place and date.)

£50.

At usance (*or* at two or more usances) pay this my first [1] bill of exchange (second and third of the same tenour and date not paid) to *A. B.* or his

---

[1] The phraseology of the other bills of the set differs from the above only in that they are respectively called " second " or " third " bill of exchange, and in stating " first and third " as to the one and " first and second " as to the other " of the same tenour and date not being paid."

order within the   Bank Fifty pounds sterling at the
current exchange, value received from him, and place the same to account
as per advice (*or* without further advice from   ).

(Signed)	*C. D.*
(Accepted)	*E. F.*

To *E. F.*
     Address.

PROMISSORY NOTE

(Place and date.)

£50.
     On demand (*or* three months after date, etc.) I promise to pay to *A. B.*
or order (with interest at   per cent. till payment) the sum of Fifty
pounds, value received.

CHEQUE

(Place and date.)

To the   Bank.
     Pay to   or order (*or* bearer) the sum of
£   .   *A. B.*

CHEQUE BY TWO OR MORE GRANTERS [1]

(Place and date.)

To the   Bank.
     Pay to us or order the sum of £   , and charge the same to an
account in our names jointly and severally.
£   .   *A. B.*
                                                              C. D.

NOTICES OF DISHONOUR

1. *To Drawer*

(Place and date.)

To Peter Smyth.
     Take notice that a bill for £   drawn by you under date the
                    on   , and payable at   ,
has been dishonoured by non-payment [2] (*or* non-acceptance), and that you
are held responsible therefor.   (Signed)   *J. S.*

2. *To Indorser*

     Take notice that a bill for £   drawn by   under date
the   on   , and payable at   ,
and which bears your indorsement, has been dishonoured by non-acceptance [2] (*or* non-payment), and that you are held responsible therefor.
                                             (Signed)   *J. S.*

---

[1] This form will be found of service where a loan is granted to two or more
persons, and where the cheque is the only document of debt the Bank are to receive.
The account should be headed with the name of the drawers and the words " jointly
and severally " added.

[2] In the case of a foreign bill add " and protested " if it have been noted or
protested.

26

3. *To Drawer of Partial Acceptance*

Take notice that a bill for £   drawn by you under date the   on   has been accepted by him for £ only, and that you are held responsible for the balance and expenses.

(Signed)   J. S.

PROTEST OF BILL OR PROMISSORY NOTE FOR NON-PAYMENT OR NON-ACCEPTANCE

{ Rules as to Presentment.   Bills of Exchange Act, sec. 45.
  Place of Protest, *ib*. sec. 51.
  Contents of Protest, *ib*. sec. 51.

(Here copy the Bill or Promissory Note protested.)

On the   day of   in the year of our Lord One thousand nine hundred and   , I, *A. B.*, of the city of   , in the County of   , in that part of the United Kingdom called Scotland, Notary Public, by royal authority duly admitted, allowed, and sworn, at the request of the holder of a certain original Bill of Exchange (*or* Promissory Note), a copy of which is above written, did, at   (*proceed to*) the place of payment specified in the said Bill of Exchange (*or* Promissory) Note),

or

a. The address of the drawee (*or acceptor*) of the said Bill of Exchange (*or maker of the said Promissory Note*).
b. The place of business of the drawee (*or acceptor*) of the said Bill of Exchange (*or maker of the said Promissory Note*).
c. The ordinary residence of the drawee (*or acceptor*) of the said Bill of Exchange (*or maker of the said Promissory Note*), because his (*her, their*) place of business was not known [*or because*   he   has (*have*) *no place of business*].
d. The place where the drawee (*or acceptor*) of the said Bill of Exchange (*or maker of the said Promissory Note*) was found.
e. The last known place of business (*or residence*) of the drawee (*or acceptor*) of said Bill of Exchange (*or maker of the said Promissory Note*).

demand payment (*or* acceptance) of the said Bill of Exchange (*or* Promissory Note) from   , to which demand he made answer

or

and after the exercise of reasonable diligence no person authorised to pay or refuse payment (*or* acceptance) of the said Bill of Exchange (*or* Promissory Note) could be found there.

Wherefore I, at request foresaid, did at said place, and on said date, duly protest, and do hereby protest, the said Bill of Exchange (*or* Promissory Note) as well against the drawer [*or* acceptor *or* (maker)] *and indorsers thereof*, and as against all others whom it doth or may concern, jointly and severally, *for non-payment of the contents and* for (*exchange, re-exchange*) interest, damages, and expenses (*or for non-acceptance*), as accords, before and in presence of witnesses specially called to the premises.

Act of Honour

Thereafter the same day, in presence of me, Notary Public, appeared *H. F.*, merchant in Glasgow, who offered to pay the contents of said bill to the said *X. Y.*, the holder thereof, for honour and on account of *J. K.*, indorser (*or as the case may be*), and having paid the same accordingly, he protested that said drawer (and acceptors if *the bill has been accepted*) and indorsers, prior to the said *X. Y.* and the said *J. K.*, should remain liable, jointly and severally, to him in like manner as they had been to the said holder. In presence of, etc., as above.

Form of Protest to be Used when the Services of a Notary cannot be obtained

Know all men that I, *A. B.*, householder of   , in the County of   , in the United Kingdom, at the request of *C. D.*, there being no Notary Public available, did on the   day of   19 , at   , demand payment (*or* acceptance) of the Bill of Exchange hereunder written from *E. F.*, to which demand he made answer (*state answer, if any*), wherefore I now, in the presence of *G. H.* and *J. K.*, do protest the said Bill of Exchange.

(Signed)   A. B.

G. H.⎫
J. K.⎭ witnesses.

N.B.—A copy of the Bill itself with its indorsations should be annexed.

Protest of Bill left for Acceptance, but Delivery refused where Bill one of a Set

(*Copy Bill and Indorsations*)

At Glasgow, in the County of Lanark, in that part of the United Kingdom of Great Britain and Ireland called Scotland, on the day of   , in the year of our Lord One thousand   , at the request made to me by or on behalf of *A. B. & Co.*, Bankers, London, the holders of the second Bill of Exchange, of which the above is a true copy, I,   , Notary Public, by royal authority duly admitted, allowed, and sworn, presented the second Bill of Exchange at the place of business, No. 10 St. Vincent Place, Glasgow, of the above-named *C. D. & Co.*, merchants there, and demanded delivery of the first of exchange of said Bill, which first of exchange had previously been sent to them for their acceptance, when I received for answer that the said first of exchange could not be delivered up (*here state answer given*).

Therefore I, the said Notary Public, at the request aforesaid, protested, as I do hereby protest, the said Bill of Exchange, not only against the above-named and designed *C. D. & Co.* for want of delivery of the first of exchange thereof, but also against the above-named drawers and indorsers thereof for recourse, and against all concerned, for all exchange, re-exchange, interest, costs, damages, and expenses suffered, or to be suffered, for want of delivery of the said first of exchange, and for remedy at law.

Thus done and protested at Glasgow aforesaid, before and in presence of *A. B.* and *C. D.*, witnesses to the premises, specially called and required.

Form of Protest for Non-Delivery where there is only one Copy of Bill

At   , in the County of   , in that part of the United Kingdom of Great Britain and Ireland called Scotland, on the
day of   , in the year   , before
me   , Notary Public, by royal authority duly admitted, allowed, and sworn, appeared   , who declared that on the   day of   he left for acceptance, agreeably to usage and custom, with   , a Bill of Exchange dated the   day of   , drawn by
on the said   , for the sum of   ,
and that the said   had repeatedly sent to get back the said Bill accepted or unaccepted, but without success, wherefore he required me to demand delivery thereof, accepted or unaccepted, and in default to protest in conformity, whereupon I passed to the place of business of the said   and demanded delivery thereof, when I received for answer (*here state answer*). Wherefore I, the said Notary Public, at the request aforesaid, have protested, etc. etc., as in preceding form.

Protest in Case of Need

(Copy Bill and Indorsations, including the Reference in Case of Need)

At Glasgow, in the County of Lanark, in that part of the United Kingdom of Great Britain and Ireland called Scotland, on the
day of   , in the year of our Lord One thousand   ,
at the request made to me by or on behalf of   ,
the   of the original Bill of Exchange, of which the above is a true copy, I,   , Notary Public, by royal authority duly admitted, allowed, and sworn, presented the said Bill of Exchange at the place of business No. 15 Argyle Street, Glasgow, of the above-named *A. B. & Co.*, fruit merchants there, upon whom the same is drawn, and demanded acceptance thereof, when I received for answer that the same could not be accepted ; thereafter I presented the said Bill of Exchange at the Bank of Scotland, St. Vincent Place, Glasgow, in terms of the reference in case of need on said Bill of Exchange, and demanded acceptance, when I received for answer that the same could not be accepted.

Therefore I, the said Notary Public, at the request aforesaid, protested, as I do hereby protest, the said Bill of Exchange not only against the above-named and designed *A. B. & Co.* for want of acceptance thereof, but also against the above-named drawers and indorsers thereof for recourse, and against all concerned, for all exchange, re-exchange, interest, costs, damages, and expenses suffered, or to be suffered, for want of acceptance of the said Bill of Exchange, and for remedy at law.

This done and protested at Glasgow aforesaid, before and in presence of   witnesses to the premises, specially called and required.

Note.—A bill presented to referee in case of need must be accompanied by a Protest against the Drawee or Acceptor as the case may be.

Protest of Cheque

(*Copy Cheque*)

At Glasgow, the   day of   , in the year Nineteen hundred and   , the principal cheque or order above copied was at the desire and request of   , the indorsees and holders thereof, duly and lawfully presented by me, Notary Public, to the Agent of the Bank of Scotland, Glasgow, requesting him to pay the same, or to give a fiat to the teller of said Bank for payment thereof, which he refused to do, saying that the Bank had no funds to meet the said cheque or order ; therefore I, the said Notary Public, protested, as I do hereby protest, the said cheque or order not only against the above-named   (*here add designation*), the granter thereof, for non-payment of said cheque or order, but also against the above-named payee and indorsers thereof for recourse, and against all concerned, for all exchange, re-exchange, interest, costs, damages, and expenses as accords of law, before and in presence of *A. B.* and *C. D.*, witnesses to the premises, specially called and required.

FORMS RELATING TO PART III

To the   Bank.

1. I, the undersigned, hereby declare that I have deposited with you the documents mentioned in the schedule hereto, for the purpose of securing the payment of the moneys hereinafter mentioned, and intended to be hereby secured, and I, as beneficial owner, charge in your favour all my present and future estate, and interest, both legal and equitable, in all the hereditaments and other property to which the said documents or any of them relate, including all trade and other fixtures which now are, or which at any time or times may be in, upon, or about the said hereditaments or property, or any part thereof, with the payment to you of all the said moneys.

2. The moneys intended to be hereby secured shall include all moneys which now are, or which at any time or times hereafter may become, due or owing, or may be accruing due to you from me, either alone or jointly with any other person or persons on any account or liability whatsoever, and whether in my character of principal debtor to you, or guarantor, or surety, or otherwise howsoever, and shall also include all commission and other charges and interest in account with quarterly rests, according to your course of business, interest being computed day by day at one per cent. per annum above the Bank of England rate of the same day, but never below five per cent. per annum, or at such other rate as may be specially agreed ; and shall also include all costs, charges, and expenses which you may pay or incur in stamping this or any other document deposited with you, or in perfecting this present security, or in enforcing or obtaining payment of the said moneys, or in paying any rent, rates, taxes, or other outgoings in respect of insuring, repairing, maintaining, or completing any buildings, or in managing or realising any hereditaments or other property to which any of the said deposited documents relate, and all other costs and expenses which may be incurred by you in respect of the premises, together with interest at the rate aforesaid on all sums so expended by you from the date of their being expended until payment thereof : And I further agree that you may insure any buildings included in this security for any amount you may think necessary.

3. I hereby agree to pay off all such moneys, costs, charges, and expenses at such time as may be agreed upon with you, or, in default thereof, upon demand in writing addressed and sent to me or my legal personal representatives (if any), at my address for the time being in your books.

4. I further agree that you may exercise all such powers and remedies as you would have had, or would hereafter have, if section 17 of the Conveyancing and Law of Property Act, 1881, had not been enacted, and also that you may exercise all powers and remedies conferred on mortgagees by the

Conveyancing and Law of Property Act, 1881, in manner as if section 20 of that statute had not been enacted, and that (in the event of my becoming a bankrupt within the meaning of the Conveyancing and Law of Property Act, 1881, or assigning any part of my property for the benefit of my creditors generally) notwithstanding that the moneys intended to be secured hereby, or any of them, may not be then actually due and payable, but only accruing due, or that the liability hereunder may be future or contingent, and that I and all other necessary parties (if any) will, on any demand for this purpose, and at my cost, execute and deliver any deed or deeds which may be necessary or proper in order to convey the legal estate in the property sold to the purchaser or purchasers thereof, or to reconvey to the mortgagor any property submortgaged by me to you, and to secure the due registration of any such conveyance or reconveyance : And I further agree that I and all other necessary parties (if any) will, on any demand for this purpose, and at my own cost, execute and deliver to you, or to such person or persons as your general or principal manager for the time being may appoint, such legal or other mortgage or mortgages of the premises hereby charged, or any of them, for further securing the payment of the said moneys and interest hereby secured, and also any memorial for registration thereof, as you or such general or principal manager may require, and that every such mortgage shall be prepared by your solicitors at my expense, and shall contain such covenants, powers, and provisions, and be in such form as your solicitors shall think proper : And I hereby irrevocably appoint   ,
your present general manager, or other your general or principal manager for the time being, to be my attorney, for me, and in my name, and on my behalf, and as my act and deed, or otherwise, to sign, seal, and deliver, and otherwise perfect any such deed or deeds, memorial or memorials, or other assurance or assurances, and to do every such act as may be required or deemed proper on any sale of any of the said premises, or in giving any legal mortgage thereof, and in order to vest in any purchaser or mortgagee (including yourselves) the legal estate, and all or any estate and interest in the said premises, and also in my name to grant any such lease or leases as mortgagors or mortgagees in possession are, under section 18 of the Conveyancing and Law of Property Act, 1881, empowered to grant.

Any demand to be made to me hereunder shall be sufficiently made, if made in writing and addressed and sent by post to me, or in case of my death to my legal personal representatives (if any), at my address for the time being in your books, and notwithstanding that you may have had notice of any disposition or other dealing by me, or my heirs, or my legal personal representatives, of or with any of the premises hereby charged.

5. I declare that the said hereditaments and property and premises are free of all charges and encumbrances, saving only as may appear by the said documents, and I hereby agree not to create any further charge or encumbrance upon them without your consent thereto in writing first obtained.

Dated the   day of   19 .

Signed, sealed, and delivered
    in the presence of

(*For Schedule see succeeding page.*)

The Schedule to be Signed by Mortgagor

The schedule within referred to :—

Date of Deed.	Parties to Deed.		Particulars.

Another Form of the Preceding

Memorandum of Agreement made this   day of
    One thousand   , between
                                                    (hereinafter
        called the Mortgagor) of the one part, and the
                            (hereinafter called the Bank) of the
    other part.

It is agreed that, in consideration of any overdraft already granted or hereafter to be granted to the mortgagor by the Bank, the document specified in the schedule hereto (which the mortgagor has deposited with the Bank) shall be held by the Bank as an equitable security for the payment by the mortgagor to the Bank of all moneys which now are, or which at any time hereafter may become, due from the mortgagor to the Bank, either alone or jointly with any other person or persons in account current with the Bank, or which may at any time hereafter, while the said deeds shall continue in the possession of the Bank, be advanced by the Bank to the mortgagor, together with interest thereon until payment at the rate from time to time charged by the Bank on cash accounts in Scotland.

The mortgagor charges the property to which the said documents relate with the payment to the Bank of all such moneys and interest, and agrees at the request of the Bank, but at the cost of the mortgagor, to execute to the Bank a legal mortgage by demise of the said property, with such powers and provisions as the Bank may require for further securing the payment of the said moneys and interest.

It is also agreed that the Bank, their successors and assigns, shall have all the powers conferred on mortgagees by sections 19 to 24 of the Conveyancing and Law of Property Act, 1881, as though this agreement were a mortgage by deed, and that the mortgagor, and all persons deriving title under him, shall upon any such sale under such powers execute and do such assurances and things for vesting the property sold in the purchaser as shall be required by the person selling.

As witness the hand of the said   the day and year first above written.

The Schedule.

DELIVERY ORDER

To   ....19 .

Please deliver to the Bank of   or their order
(*description of goods*)   marked as
under

(*Signature*)
(*Date*)
marked thus.....................................

ACKNOWLEDGMENT BY STOREKEEPER OF ABOVE

To   ....19 .

Gentlemen,—Referring to the delivery order, of which the annexed is a copy, (I *or* we) have now to state that (I *or* we) hold the therein specified on your account, free from all right of lien, excepting to the extent of what may be due to (me *or* us) for warehouse rent thereof.— Your obedient servant.

SCHEDULES TO TRANSMISSION OF MOVEABLE PROPERTY (SCOTLAND) ACT, 1862

Schedule A.—Where Assignation granted by Separate Deed

I, *A. B.*, in consideration of, etc. (*or otherwise as the case may be*), do hereby assign to *C. D.* and his heirs or assignees (*or otherwise as the case may be*) the bond (*or other deed, describing it*) granted by *E. F.*, dated, etc., by which (*here specify the nature of the deed, and specify also any connecting title and any circumstances requiring to be stated in regard to the nature and extent of the right acquired*). —In witness whereof (*insert Testing Clause in usual form*).

Schedule B.—Where Assignation Indorsed upon Bond or other Deed

I, *A. B.*, in consideration of, etc. (*or otherwise as the case may be*), do hereby assign to *C. D.* and his heirs or assignees (*or otherwise as the case may be*) the foregoing (*or within written*) bond (*or other writ or deed, describing it*) granted in my favour (*or otherwise as the case may be, specifying any connecting title and any circumstances requiring to be stated in regard to the nature and extent of the right assigned*).—In witness whereof (*insert Testing Clause in usual form*).

Schedule C.—Certificate by Notary Public

I, *A.*   , of the city of   , Notary Public, do hereby attest and declare that upon the   day of   , and between the hours of   and   , I duly intimated to *B.* (*here describe the party*) the within written assignation (*or otherwise as the case may be*), or an assignation granted by (*here describe it*), and that by delivering to the said *A.* personally (*or otherwise*) by leaving for the said *A.* within his dwelling-house at E., in the hands of (*here describe the party*), a full copy thereof (*or if a partial copy, here quote the portion of the deed which has been delivered*) to be given to him : All of which was done in the presence of *C.* and *D.* (*here name and describe the two witnesses*), who subscribe this attestation along with me.—In witness whereof (*insert Testing Clause in usual form*). To be subscribed by the party and the two witnesses.

ASSIGNATION TO POLICY OF LIFE ASSURANCE, CONTAINING AN OBLIGATION BY A THIRD PARTY TO SEE PREMIUMS PAID [1]

(*See as to Stamp Duties, ante,* POLICIES OF INSURANCE)

I, *E. P. M.*, residing at   , do hereby for certain good and onerous causes and considerations, assign unto   and to their assignees a Policy of Insurance, No.   , for the sum of   , dated   , over my life by the   Company, together with the said assured sum of   , and all bonus additions accrued or that may accrue thereon, and my whole right, title, and interest therein, with full power to the said   and their foresaids to sell, in such manner as they may see fit, and that either by public roup or private bargain, with or without advertisement or notice to me, or to assign, or surrender the same at pleasure, to uplift and recover the proceeds thereof, and generally to do everything in relation to the said Policy of Assurance and sums therein contained which I could have done before granting hereof : And we, the said *E. P. M.* and *C. G.*, residing at   , do hereby bind and oblige ourselves, our heirs, executors, and successors whomsoever, all conjunctly and severally, unto the said and their foresaids, that we shall pay or cause to be paid to the said   regularly as it falls due the annual premium of   payable in respect of the said Policy, and that on or before the   next, and in each succeeding year thereafter during the life of me the said *E. P. M.*, and also such other or additional premium or premiums as may become due and payable in respect of the said Policy in order to keep the same in force : And we, the said *E. P. M.* and *C. G.*, also bind and oblige ourselves and our foresaids to deliver to the said   the receipts for the said premiums or additional premiums within ten days next after they respectively become payable : And in case we shall at any time fail or neglect to pay the said premiums, and deliver the receipts for the same to the said   , then it shall be competent to them to pay the same, but without any obligation on them to do so : And we further bind and oblige ourselves and our foresaids to reimburse and pay to the said   all and every such sum or sums as shall have been so paid by them, with interest thereon at such rates as may be charged by them on overdrafts from time to time from the respective times of advance till pay-

---

[1] This form may be used whether the assignation be granted by the holder of the account, by a member of a firm in security of his firm's indebtedness, or by a third party on behalf of a customer.

ment, and all expenses which they may sustain or incur in consequence of any such neglect or failure on our part : And declaring hereby that the whole sums which may become due by us to the said
under and in virtue of the obligations herein contained shall be sufficiently constituted and ascertained by a certificate under the hands of any agent or accountant in their service. And I, the said *E. P. M.*, have herewith delivered to the said   the foresaid Policy of Assurance : And we both consent to the registration hereof and of the said certificate for preservation and execution.—In witness whereof.

NOTICE OF INTIMATION OF ASSIGNATION

To the
        at their (*name of office*).

    Take notice that by

has assigned to the   and their assignees a
Policy of Assurance for the sum of   sterling, dated the
        day of   , and marked No.   , granted by
you over his life, together with the said assured sum of   sterling, and all bonuses and additions accrued or that may accrue thereon, and his whole right, title, and interest therein ; with full power to the said
            and their foresaids to sell, assign, or surrender the same at pleasure, to uplift and recover the proceeds thereof, and to grant discharges therefor, and generally to do everything in relation to the said Policy of Assurance and sums therein contained which he could have done before granting the said Assignation.
                    Dated at   this
                    day of   Nineteen hundred and   .

EXPLANATORY LETTER BY A MEMBER OF A FIRM WHO HAS ASSIGNED A POLICY IN SECURITY OF A FIRM'S INDEBTEDNESS

Note.—This form may be altered to suit the case of a third party who has assigned a Policy in security of a customer's indebtedness.

    I, *M. B.*, residing at   , considering that by assignation granted by me in your favour of even date herewith, I assigned to you a Policy of Insurance over my life for the sum of   , dated the   day of   , and marked No.   by the
Company, and which Policy is intended to be a security to you as aftermentioned : Therefore I do hereby agree that you are to hold the said Policy of Insurance and sums therein contained in security of all and whatever sum or sums which are or may at any time become due by me, or by *C. D. & Co.*, carrying on business at   , of which firm I am a partner, with or without any other partners, dissolution of copartnery or change therein to you in any manner of way, with interest on such sums severally from the respective dates of advance till payment, and to apply the proceeds thereof in such manner as may be most convenient to you ; but on repayment of all such sum or sums and interest before the sale or surrender of the said Policy you shall be bound to reconvey the same to me, at my expense ; and it is hereby declared that the foresaid assignation is granted over and above and without prejudice to any other securities

or remedies which you the said   have or may acquire for the general obligations or any particular obligation by me or my said firm of *C. D. & Co.* or their foresaids, to you in any manner of way.—In witness whereof.

Form of Retrocession of Policy of Life Assurance

Stamp 10s.

We   , considering that the purpose for which the Policy of Assurance aftermentioned was assigned to and held by us has now been served, and that we have been asked to grant a retrocession of the same : Therefore we do hereby retrocess, repone, and restore   , his heirs, executors, and assignees, in and to his own right and place in the Policy of Assurance on his life, No.   , granted by the in his favour for the sum of   , dated   , assigned to us by assignation granted by the said   in our favour, dated   , and duly intimated to the said on the   day of   in the year 19   ; together with the sums thereby assured, and all bonuses and additions thereto past and future, and that to the effect the said   may uplift, discharge, and convey the same as freely in all respects as he might have done before the said assignation in our favour was granted : And we have delivered to the said   the foresaid Policy of Assurance and the said assignation, to be used by him and his foresaids as their own proper writs and evidents in all time coming.—In witness whereof.

Intimation to Insurance Company of Retrocession

To the   Insurance Company
          at their Head Office in

Take notice, that by retrocession dated the   day of   , the   Bank   have retrocessed, reponed, and restored   , his heirs, executors, and assignees, in and to his own right and place in the Policy of Assurance granted by you over his life for the sum of   , dated the   day of   , and numbered   , together with the said assured sum and all bonuses and additions thereto, past and future, and that to the effect the said   may uplift, discharge, and convey the same as freely in all respects as he might have done before the said assignation thereof by him in favour of the said   was granted.

Dated at   this   day of

(Signature.)

Transfer of Shares in Company registered under Companies Acts to Bank's Nominees

I, *E. P. M.*, residing at   , in consideration of the sum of five shillings paid to me by *A. B.* and *C. D.*, hereinafter called the said transferees, do hereby bargain, sell, assign, and transfer to the said transferees, and the survivor of them   of and in the undertaking called   To hold unto the said transferees, and the survivor of them, and their or his executors, administrators, and assigns, subject to the several conditions on which I held the same immediately before the execution hereof; and we, the said transferees, do hereby agree to accept and take the said shares subject to the conditions foresaid.—In witness whereof, *or* As witness our hands and seals this day of in the year of our Lord One thousand nine hundred and .

Signed, sealed, and delivered by the above-named *E. P. M.* } *E. P. M.*   Seal.
in the presence of—

| Do. | do. | *A. B.* | Seal. |
| Do. | do. | *C. D.* | Seal. |

Transfer of Debenture

I, *A. B.*, for certain good and onerous causes and considerations, do hereby assign and transfer to the Governor and Company of the Bank of Scotland, incorporated by Act of Parliament, and to their assignees, a Debenture, No. , dated and sealed the day of , granted by for the sum of £ to me, the said *A. B.*, repayable on and the interest due thereon, and all the moneys thereby secured, and all the right and interest competent to me therein.—In witness whereof.

Explanatory Letter following upon Transfer of Stocks, Shares, or Securities

To the Bank.

It is hereby agreed that all Stocks, Shares, and Securities of any description which have already been or may hereafter be handed or assigned and transferred to you or into the names of your nominees, or lodged or deposited with you in any manner of way by or on account of....................................

....

....

(all hereinafter referred to as "the said securities"), as well as all relative interest and dividends (including bonuses) accrued and to accrue thereon, are and shall be held by you in security and for payment to you of all sums which are now or that may hereafter become due to you by....................

....

....

whether on cash account, overdraft, bills, or otherwise as principal debtor, co-obligant, cautioner or guarantor for any other person or persons or otherwise in any manner of way with interest from the date or dates of advance till payment: And in the event of failing to repay any such sums when called upon by you to do so, or to maintain such margin as may be required by you, it is understood and agreed that you shall have full power to sell or realise at your discretion the said securities or any of them at any time and in such way or manner as you may think proper, and undertake to grant any transfers, conveyances, or other writings necessary for carrying said sales into effect: Further, it is understood and agreed that in the case of all or any of the said securities particularly identified by specific numbers and/or otherwise, you shall not be under any obligation to retain or to account for or reconvey to the said securities bearing the specific numbers and/or other particular identification of those handed or assigned or transferred or lodged or deposited as aforesaid.

Dated this day of nineteen hundred and

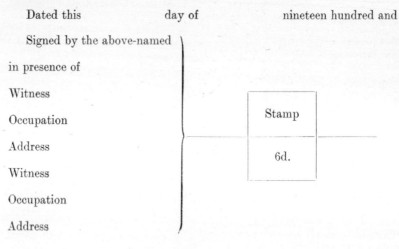

Signed by the above-named

in presence of

Witness

Occupation

Address

Witness

Occupation

Address

Stamp

6d.

LETTER PLEDGING BEARER BONDS IN SECURITY

To the Bank.

Gentlemen,—I hereby lodge with you the following bonds (*or otherwise as the case may be*), namely : (*here describe bonds*), to be held by you in security of any sums due, or that may become due by me to you in any manner of way : And I authorise you to sell or realise the said bonds, or any of them, at any time, and to apply the proceeds in payment of any sums that may be due as aforesaid, with interest thereon, from the date or dates of advance : And I further agree, whenever called upon by you, to grant at my expense any necessary assignations, of which you shall be the judges, in your favour of the said bonds or any of them. Further, it is understood and agreed that in the case of all or any of the said bonds particularly identified by specific numbers and/or otherwise, you shall not be under any obligation to retain or to account for or return to me the said bonds bearing the specific numbers and/or other particular identification of those handed or lodged as aforesaid. —Your obedient servant.

ANOTHER FORM OF ABOVE

To the Bank.

Gentlemen,—In consideration of your allowing me from time to time to overdraw my account with you, I hereby authorise you to hold as collateral security for such overdrafts and interest, the securities which I have deposited or may deposit with you from time to time, whether in security of advances or for safe custody : And I authorise you in your discretion to sell or realise the said securities, or any of them, at any time, and in such manner as you think proper, and to apply the proceeds in or towards payment of any sums that may be due by me to you. Further, it is understood and agreed that in the case of all or any of the said securities particularly identified by specific numbers and/or otherwise, you shall not be under any obligation to retain or to account for or reconvey to me the said securities bearing the specific numbers and/or other particular identification of those handed or assigned or transferred or lodged or deposited as aforesaid.—In witness whereof.

Letter of Postponement

To the   Bank.

Gentlemen,—We   considering that   are indebted to us by way of sums advanced to them on loan amounting to £   , and that we have agreed to postpone our claim upon them in respect of such loans and of any further loans which we may make to them in the future to your claim upon them in respect of their obligations to you ; therefore we do hereby agree and declare that the said loans made by us to the said   and any loans which we may hereafter make to them, and all sums of principal and interest due and to become due thereon shall be postponed to your claim upon them, and that we shall not without your consent first had in writing be entitled to recover or take payment of or security for any part of such loans by us until all sums of principal and interest due or to become due to you by the said   in any manner of way shall have been paid in full ; provided always that in the event of the bankruptcy or (liquidation) of the said   we shall be entitled to claim and rank on their estate in respect of the said loans made to them by us subject to the obligation which we hereby undertake to assign to you or at your option to account to you for all dividends to be received by us therefrom until full and final payment of your debt as aforesaid.—In witness whereof.

Trust Letter as to Sale of Produce

To   Bank.   (*Place and date.*)

Gentlemen,—I/We have to acknowledge receipt of invoice, Bill of Lading, and Copy of Insurance Policy representing :—

....

I/We receive the above as agent for and on your account, and I/we undertake to hold the Goods when received, and their proceeds when sold in that capacity. I/We further undertake to keep this transaction separate from any other, and to remit you direct the entire net proceeds as realised, while we undertake to sell the said goods for not less than the sum of £   . I/We undertake upon demand forthwith to return the goods to you, or, if not in my/our hands, the value thereof.

I/We undertake to cover the goods by insurance against fire and to hold the policy or policies on your behalf.—Yours faithfully.

Narrative of Mortgage of a Ship to secure an Account Current granted in favour of a Bank

Fill in on the print the particulars of the ship as in the bill of sale, and proceed :—

Whereas I, *A. B.*, carrying on business at   , have an account current with the   Bank, incorporated by Act of Parliament, Edinburgh, kept in their books in my name, to the debit of which they shall be entitled to place all sums which are or may be due by me to the said   Bank in any manner of way, whether drawn out in my name, or liable on me by any drafts, orders, bills, promissory notes, indorsements, receipts, bonds, letters, procurations, guarantees, documents, or legal construction whatever, and the amount due on which account shall be payable on demand, with interest on the sums which may be due on the said account severally, at the rate of five per cent., or at such higher rate as shall be charged by the said   Bank on overdrafts on current accounts for the time : And whereas the amount of principal and interest at any time due on said account shall be sufficiently constituted and ascertained by an account or certificate under the hands of any agent or accountant in the service of the said   Bank : Now, etc., as in print.

(Where the mortgage is granted by an incorporated or joint-stock company, or by two more individuals, the form will be altered to suit the circumstances.)

Narrative of Mortgage of a Ship granted in Favour of Bank's Nominees

Fill in on the print the particulars of the vessel as in bill of sale, and proceed :—

Whereas there is an account current between   and   , manager, and   , sub-manager in Glasgow of the   Bank, incorporated by Act of Parliament, and further advances are intended to be made by the said and   , and the amount of principal and interest which may at any time be due on such account current is to be fixed and ascertained by a stated account made up and certified by the manager, sub-manager, or accountant of said Bank, at their principal office in Glasgow, interest being charged at the rate current for the time being on overdrawn accounts, but never at a less rate than five per cent., and the amount so fixed and ascertained is to be repayable at the principal office in Glasgow of said Bank at the expiration of one month from the date when a copy of such stated and certified account shall be posted in the General Post Office, Glasgow, addressed to the said   at his last known address : Now, etc., as in print, the blanks being of course duly filled in.

Explanatory Letter with reference to the foregoing Mortgage

Stamp 6d.

We,   , manager, and   , sub-manager in Glasgow of   Bank of   , incorporated by Act of Parliament, considering that there has been executed and delivered to us a mortgage, dated   , granted by   in our favour over sixty-fourth shares held by him in the sailing-ship   of Glasgow : Now we do hereby confess and declare that the said mortgage is held by us, and was granted in security of the payment of all sums for which the said   is or may become liable to the said Bank of   , incorporated by Act of Parliament, on open account, overdraft, or otherwise, and of all bills or notes or other obligations upon which the name of the said   appears discounted, or to be discounted, or otherwise held by the Bank and generally of all sums which the said   shall at any time be owing, or in any way liable for, to the said Bank, with all interest which may be chargeable at the overdraft rates current from time to time, but never at a less rate than five per cent., and all expenses incurred or to be incurred by the Bank, and of all sums which the Bank may advance by way of premiums of insurance or otherwise : Declaring that, on repayment and satisfaction thereof, interest and all charges and expenses, and all sums that may be advanced by way of premiums of insurance, with interest thereon, we shall, at the expense of the said   , discharge the said mortgage : Declaring that the said   shall keep the said shares in said ship always insured to the extent, at least, of the balance due to the Bank on outstanding or current obligations of his, and deliver the policy or policies duly indorsed to us or to the said Bank ; and failing the said   doing so, we or the said Bank shall have power to insure the same to that extent, and to debit the premiums in the said   's account current with said Bank : Declaring also that should the balance due to the Bank not be repaid on demand, or should the said   fail to pay any bill or promissory note or part thereof when due, or to keep the said shares in said ship insured as aforesaid, then we shall have the right to exercise the powers of sale conferred on us by said mortgage, either by public roup or private bargain, but always on giving to the registered owner or owners of said shares in said ship one month's notice in writing through the post-office to his or their last known address, and shall account to the registered owner or owners of said shares for the proceeds after payment of the whole sums due to the Bank, and all expenses : And declaring that a certificate under the hand of the manager, sub-manager, or accountant of the said Bank for the time being at their principal office in Glasgow, shall be sufficient to ascertain and constitute the balance due to the Bank at any time : And I the said   agree to the above conditions.—In witness whereof.

FORM OF ASSIGNMENT TO BE INDORSED ON MARINE POLICIES OF ASSURANCE

I, *A. B.*, of, etc., hereby assign unto *C. D.*, etc., his executors, administrators, and assigns, the within Policy of Assurance on the ship, freight, and the goods therein carried (*or* on ship or freight or goods, *as the case may be*).—In witness whereof.

LETTER FROM CAUTIONERS CONSENTING TO BANK ACCEDING TO TRUST-DEED

To the   Bank.

Gentlemen,—With reference to our letter of guarantee (*or otherwise, as the case may be*) for   to you, dated   on account of   , we hereby consent to your acceding to any trust-deed which may be granted by the said   , and we agree that you may at any time or times at your discretion grant to   , or to any drawers, acceptors, or indorsers of bills of exchange or promissory notes received by you from   , or on which   may be liable to you, any time or other indulgence, and compound with them or with the said drawers, acceptors, or indorsers respectively without discharging the liability of us or either of us.—Your obedient servants.

Bond of Credit in Name of Individual, with Individuals as Co-obligants

We, etc., having obtained a credit of   pounds sterling with the   , on cash account in name of me the said   , do therefore hereby bind and oblige ourselves, our heirs, executors, and successors whatsoever, all conjunctly and severally, to pay to the   or to their assignees, on demand, all such sums, not exceeding   pounds sterling, as are or shall be due to the said   from me the said   , whether drawn out on said cash account by me, or liable on me by any drafts, orders, bills, promissory notes, indorsements, receipts, bonds, letters, procurations, guarantees, documents, or legal construction whatever, with interest on such sums severally at the rate of five per cent., or at such other higher rate as shall be charged by the said   on cash accounts for the time,—the said   being hereby allowed to fix the rate of interest from time to time without notice given,—from the date or dates of advance until payment ; and with   pounds sterling of liquidate penalty, or for costs and charges ; which cash account may be kept at any office of the said Bank, and may be debited with any sums such as aforesaid whensoever by the said Bank, without losing any right or remedy of law on bills or otherwise : And any account or certificate signed by the cashier of the said Bank, or by any accountant in the said Bank, or by the manager or sub-manager, or agent, or accountant for the office where the said cash account may then or before be kept, shall ascertain, specify, and constitute the sums or balances of principal and interest to be due hereon as aforesaid, and shall warrant hereon all executorials of law for such sums or balances and interest, and for the liquidate penalty aforesaid, whereof no suspension shall pass but on consignation only : And all costs of discharges and conveyances hereof shall be borne by us and our foresaids jointly and severally : And we consent to the registration hereof, and of the said account or certificate, for preservation and execution.—In witness whereof, etc.

Bond of Credit in Name of an Individual, with a Firm and Partners as Co-obligants

We, etc., having obtained a credit of   pounds sterling with the   on cash account in name of me the said   , do therefore hereby bind and oblige ourselves, our heirs, executors, and successors whatsoever, and all copartneries under said firm of   , present and future, comprehending any of us or of our foresaids, with or without any other partners, and notwithstanding any deaths, retirements, substitutions, or additions of partners, dissolution of copartnery, or change therein, all conjunctly and severally, to pay to the   , or to their assignees, on demand, all such sums, not exceeding   pounds sterling, as are or shall be due to the said   from me the said   , whether drawn out on said cash account by me, or liable on me by any drafts, orders, bills, promissory notes, indorsements, receipts, bonds, letters, procurations, guarantees, documents, or legal construction what-ever, with interest on such sums severally at the rate of five per cent., or at such other higher rate as shall be charged by the said   on cash accounts for the time,—the said   being hereby allowed to fix the rate of interest from time to time without notice given,— from the date or dates of advance until payment, and with pounds sterling of liquidate penalty, or for costs and charges ; which cash account may be kept at any office of the said Bank, and may be debited with any sums such as aforesaid whensoever by the said Bank, without losing any right or remedy of law on bills, or otherwise : And any account of certificate signed by the cashier of the said Bank, or by any accountant in the said Bank, or by the manager, or sub-manager, or agent, or accountant for the office where the said cash account may then or before be kept, shall ascertain, specify, and constitute the sums or balances of principal and interest to be due hereon as aforesaid, and shall warrant hereon all executorials of law for such sums or balances and interest and for the liquidate penalty aforesaid, whereof no suspension shall pass but on consignation only : And all costs of discharges and conveyances hereof shall be borne by us and our foresaids jointly and severally : And we consent to the registration hereof, and of the said account or certificate, for preserva-tion and execution.—In witness whereof, etc.

Bond of Credit where Account to be in Name of a Firm

We, etc., having obtained a credit of   pounds sterling with the   on cash account in name of us, the said   , do therefore hereby bind and oblige ourselves, our heirs, executors, and successors whatsoever, and all copartneries under said firm of   , present and future, comprehending any of us or of our foresaids, with or without any other partners, and notwithstanding any deaths, retirements, substitutions, or additions of partners, dissolution of copartnery, or change therein, all conjunctly and severally, to pay to the   or to their assignees, on demand, all such sums, not exceeding   pounds sterling, as are or shall be due to the said   from any copartnery, persons, or person under firm aforesaid, now or hereafter, of whomsoever constituted, comprehending any of us or our foresaids, or any partners or successors with or to any of us in said firm, or survivor thereof, and whether drawn out on said cash account by such copartnery, persons, or person, or liable on such copartnery, persons, or person by any drafts, orders, bills, promissory notes, indorsements, receipts, bonds, letters, procurations, guarantees, documents, or legal construction whatever, with interest on such sums severally at the rate of five per cent., or at such other higher rate as shall be charged by the said   on cash accounts for

the time,—the said   being hereby allowed to fix the
rate of interest from time to time without notice given,—from the date or
dates of advance until payment, and with   pounds sterling of
liquidate penalty, or for costs and charges; which cash account may be
kept at any office of the said Bank, and may be debited with any sums such
as aforesaid whensoever by the said Bank, without losing any right or remedy
of law on bills, or otherwise: And any account or certificate signed by the
cashier of the said Bank, or by any accountant in the said Bank, or by
the manager, or sub-manager, or agent, or accountant for the office where the
said cash account may then or before be kept, shall ascertain, specify, and
constitute the sums or balances of principal and interest to be due hereon
as aforesaid, and shall warrant hereon all executorials of law for such sums
or balances and interest, and for the liquidate penalty aforesaid, whereof
no suspension shall pass but on consignation only: And all costs of discharges
and conveyances hereof shall be borne by us and our foresaids jointly and
severally: And we consent to the registration hereof, and of the said
account or certificate, for preservation and execution.—In witness
whereof, etc.

Bond of Credit containing Assignation to Policy of Life Assurance

   We,   , having obtained a credit of £
sterling with   on cash account to be kept in their
books in name of me, the said   , do therefore hereby bind
and oblige ourselves, our heirs, executors, and successors whatsoever, all
conjunctly and severally, to pay to   , or to their assignees,
on demand, all such sums, not exceeding £   sterling, as are or shall
be due to the said   from me, the said   ,
whether drawn out on said cash account by me, or liable on me by any
drafts, orders, bills, promissory notes, indorsements, receipts, bonds,
letters, procurations, guarantees, documents, or legal construction whatever, with interest on such sums severally at the rate of five per cent., or
at such other higher rate as shall be charged by the said
on cash accounts for the time,—the said   being hereby
allowed to fix the rate of interest from time to time without notice given,
—from the date or dates of advance until payment, and with £
sterling of liquidate penalty, or for costs and charges; which cash account
may be kept at any office of the said Bank, and may be debited with any
sums such as aforesaid whensoever by the said Bank, without losing any
right or remedy of law on bills, or otherwise: And in security of the
personal obligation before written, I, the said   , do
hereby assign, convey, and make over to the said   and
to their assignees, a Policy of Assurance for the sum of £   sterling,
dated the   day of   , and marked No.   , over
the life of me, the said   , by the   , together
with the said assured sum of £   sterling, and all bonus additions
accrued or that may accrue thereon, and my whole right, title, and interest
therein; with full power to the said   and their foresaids
to sell in such manner as they may see fit, with or without advertisement
or notice to me, and that either by public roup or private bargain, or to
assign or surrender the said Policy of Assurance at pleasure, to uplift and

recover the proceeds thereof, and to grant discharges therefor, and generally to do everything in relation to the said Policy of Assurance and sums therein contained which I could have done before granting hereof, all without warning or consulting us, the parties hereto, or any of us, it being hereby declared that all discharges or conveyances or other deeds necessary to be granted, or procedure to be adopted by the said

in relation to the said Policy of Assurance, or sums to become due in terms thereof, shall be good, valid, and sufficient without being consented to or concurred in by us, or any of us : And we, the said

hereby bind and oblige ourselves and our foresaids, conjunctly and severally, unto the said   to pay or cause to be paid to the said   regularly as it falls due, the annual premium of £   sterling, payable in respect of the said Policy of Assurance, or such other annual premium as shall become payable thereon, and that on or before the   day of   next, and in each succeeding year thereafter during the life of me, the said   ,

and also to pay or cause to be paid whatever additional premium or premiums may become due and payable in respect of the said Policy of Assurance in order to keep the same in force : And further, we bind and oblige ourselves and our foresaids, jointly and severally, to deliver to the said   or their foresaids the receipts for the said premiums or additional premiums within ten days next after they respectively become payable ; and in case we shall at any time fail or neglect to pay the said premiums or additional premiums, and deliver the receipts for the same to the said   or their foresaids, then it shall be competent to them to pay the same, but without any obligation on them to do so : And we further bind and oblige ourselves and our foresaids, conjunctly and severally, to reimburse and repay to the said   or their foresaids, all and every such sum or sums as shall have been so paid by them, with interest at the rate foresaid, from the respective times of advance till payment, and all expenses which they may sustain or incur in consequence of any such neglect or failure on our part : And any account or certificate signed by the cashier of the said Bank, or by any accountant in the said Bank, or by any manager, or sub-manager, or agent, or accountant for the office where the said cash account may then or before be kept, shall specify and constitute the sums or balances of principal and interest to be due hereon as aforesaid, and also such sums of premiums or additional premiums that may be paid by the said   , with the interest due thereon and the expenses incurred as aforesaid ; and shall also warrant hereon all executorials of law therefor, whereof no suspension shall pass but on consignation only : And all costs of discharges or conveyances hereof shall be borne by us and our foresaids jointly and severally : And we, the said   , have herewith delivered up to the said   the said Policy of Assurance : And we all consent to the registration hereof, and of the said account or certificate, for preservation and execution.—In witness whereof, etc.

GUARANTEE IN SUPPORT OF BOND OF CREDIT

To the   Bank.

Gentlemen,—I (or we) hereby (jointly and severally) guarantee you full and final payment of all sums of principal, interest, and expenses which are or may at any time become due to you under and in virtue of a bond of

credit granted by   in your favour for a cash account
in name of   for   , and corresponding interest and
penalties dated   . This guarantee is to remain in force
until recalled by me or my (*or* us or our) heirs or executors in writing.—
In witness whereof.

LETTER BY SURVIVING OBLIGANTS UNDER BOND OF CREDIT, REQUESTING
    THE RELIEF OF THE EXECUTORS OF A DECEASED OBLIGANT FROM
    THE OBLIGATIONS UNDERTAKEN BY HIM

To the   Bank.

Gentlemen,—We (*here specify surviving obligants*), considering that we
are obligants along with the now deceased   for a cash
account kept with you in name of me the said   for a credit of
                  , under and in virtue of a bond of credit granted by us and
the said deceased   to you, dated   : And
considering that we are desirous that the executors of the said deceased
                  should be relieved entirely from the obligations undertaken by
him in the said bond of credit, and that you have at our request agreed
to relieve them accordingly, therefore we hereby desire you to free and
relieve the said executors of the said deceased   of and from
the whole obligations undertaken by him under the said bond of credit :
And we hereby declare that the said bond of credit shall continue binding
and effectual upon us.—In witness whereof, etc.

LETTER BY BANK RELIEVING EXECUTORS OF DECEASED OBLIGANT
            UNDER BOND OF CREDIT

To the Executors of the deceased

Gentlemen,—On behalf of the   I beg to
inform you that at the request of (*here specify surviving obligants*), they have
agreed to relieve you from the obligations undertaken by the said
in the bond of credit (*here specify bond*), under reservation of the Bank's
claim upon the other obligants under the bond which is still to continue
binding and effectual upon them, and you are hereby relieved accordingly.
—Your obedient servant.

RECEIPT TO BE INDORSED ON BOND OF CREDIT WHEN PAID BY AN
    OBLIGANT AND CONTAINING AN UNDERTAKING TO ASSIGN BOND

                                        Bank
                            Edinburgh,   19 .

Received from the within mentioned
in equal proportions (*or as the case may be*), the sum of £   , being
the amount of principal and interest due to us under the within bond of
credit, which we undertake to assign to them, if and when required, at their
expense, to the extent of the sums paid by them respectively, in order that
they may operate whatever relief is competent to them.

Assignation by Bank of Bond of Credit in favour of an Obligant who has paid same

We,   , considering that by the bond of credit after mentioned (*here specify obligants*), bound and obliged themselves, their heirs, executors, and successors whatsoever, all conjunctly and severally, to pay to us, or our assignees, on demand, all such sums, not exceeding £   sterling, as were or should be due to us from the said   on a credit of that amount with us on cash account in his name, with interest on such sums severally at the rate of five per cent., or at such other higher rate as should be charged by us on cash account for the time until payment : And whereas the said   has made payment of the sum of £   sterling of principal contained in and due under the said bond of credit, together with the sum of £   of interest due thereon, conform to stated account indorsed on the said bond, and certified as therein provided, and signed as relative hereto, and of which sums we hereby acknowledge receipt and discharge the said   : And now, seeing that the said   has requested us to do so, and it is reasonable we should grant these presents in his favour, so that he may operate whatever relief is competent to him in the premises : Therefore we do hereby assign to the said   , his executors, administrators, and assignees, the bond of credit above referred to, dated   , granted by the said   , with the whole clauses and obligements in our favour therein contained, to the end that he the said   and his foresaid may, in respect of the foresaid payment by him to us of the said sums of £   of principal and £   of interest due thereon, operate his relief against the other granters of the said bond of credit : And we have herewith delivered up to the said   the foresaid bond of credit, with relative stated account indorsed thereon, to be used by our assignee and his foresaids as their own proper writs and evidents in all time coming : And we consent to registration hereof for preservation and execution. —In witness whereof.

Short Form of Guarantee

(Place and date.)

To the

Gentlemen,—   hereby guarantee due payment of all sums for which Messrs.   are or may become liable to you ; the amount payable under this guarantee not to exceed   pounds, with interest from the date of advance.

This guarantee is to remain in force until recalled by   in writing, and is not to be affected by any changes in the partnership of the above firm of Messrs.

—Gentlemen, your most obedient servant.

Form of Guarantee by one or more Parties to a Bank

To the

Gentlemen,—I (*or we, as the case may be*)   hereby (jointly and severally) guarantee you due payment of all sums for which   is (*or are*) or may become liable to you ; the amount which I (*or we*) am (*or are*) to be bound to pay under this guarantee not to exceed pounds sterling, with interest from the date or dates of advance : I (*or* we) agree that you shall be entitled to make calls on me (*or* us, *or* each of us, *or* any of us, *or* us or each or any of us, *as the case may be*) from time to time, in respect of my (*or* our) said guarantee, for such sums as you may fix : And I (*or* we) further declare that you may at any time or times at your discretion grant to the said   , or to any drawers, acceptors, or indorsers of bills of exchange or promissory notes, received by you from   , or on which   may be liable to you, any time or other indulgence, and compound with   or with the said drawers, acceptors, or indorsers respectively, without discharging or satisfying my liability (*or* the liability of us, or   of us) ; and that this guarantee shall apply to and secure any ultimate balance of the sums that shall remain due to you, after applying any dividends, compositions, and payments which you may receive : And it is further declared that this guarantee is to remain in force until recalled by me (*or* us) or by my (*or* our) heirs or executors in writing, and shall be without prejudice to any other securities or remedies which you have or may acquire for the general obligations or any particular obligation of the said   , and is not to be affected by any changes in the partnership of the said firm of   ; *and particularly is granted as an additional obligation by   and without prejudice to obligation under   granted by   in your favour for £ on account of the said   , dated   .*—In witness whereof, etc.

Guarantee without any Pecuniary Limit

To the

Gentlemen,—I (*or* we)   hereby (jointly and severally) guarantee you due payment of any advances made and which may hereafter be made to A. B. (*design*), whether by way of overdrafts, or by bills, promissory notes, cash orders, or other obligations discounted and held, or to be discounted and held, by you ; and I (*or* we) dispense with any necessity for intimation being made to me (*or* us) of the dishonour of any or all of said bills, promissory notes, cash orders, or other obligations, and declare that the claim under this guarantee shall be sufficiently ascertained by an account made out from the books of the bank, and certified by the accountant or other officer thereof, and the balance appearing due thereon shall be exigible from me (*or* us) at any time upon a demand being made therefor, and without the necessity of enforcing payment from the parties to said bills, promissory notes, cash orders, or other obligations, and generally to transact with the said A. B. in the same manner as if he were the only party bound or liable, without thereby impairing or affecting the liability of me the said   (*or* of us the said   ). —In witness whereof.

Another Form of Guarantee

To the

Gentlemen,—I (*or* we)   do hereby (jointly and severally) guarantee you full and final payment of all sums advanced or that may be advanced by you on drafts or orders passed or to be passed upon an account kept or to be kept in your books in name of (*or, in case of bills*, of all bills, promissory notes, and other negotiable documents, discounted or held, or which may be discounted or held, by you, on which   are or may be obligants) : But providing and declaring that my (*or* our) liability under this guarantee shall be and is hereby limited to the principal sum of £   , with interest at such rate as may from time to time be charged by you : And further providing and declaring that this guarantee shall be a continuing obligation until specially recalled in writing. [*In cases of advances to a firm, add,* and shall remain binding on me (*or* us) notwithstanding any change that may take place in the constitution or partnership of the said firm of   .]—In witness whereof.

ANOTHER FORM OF GUARANTEE

We, etc., guarantee to the   payment of all sums which now are, or may at any time or times be, due to the said Bank upon the account current or cash account kept or to be kept in the name of   in the books of the said Bank at   , with interest on the sums due on the said account from the date or dates of advance till repaid, at the rate or rates charged by the Bank for the time on cash-credit accounts, the Bank being entitled to place to the debit of the said account not only all sums drawn out of the account upon drafts or orders signed by   , but also all or any other debts or liabilities of the said   to the said Bank of any description now due or incurred, or which may hereafter be due or incurred, by   : Declaring always that our liability under this guarantee shall be limited and restricted to the sum of   , with interest at the rates foresaid on the Bank's advances to that extent from the date or respective dates of the advance till payment : But with that limitation this is intended and shall be held to be a continuing guarantee for any sum or balance which may at any time be due upon the said account, and interest thereon as aforesaid, till the same shall be recalled by us or our heirs or representatives.

Signed by   at   , this   day of   Nineteen hundred and   , in presence of us.

GUARANTEE FOR DISCOUNTS

To the   Bank.

Gentlemen,—I hereby guarantee you due payment of all bills and promissory notes which you may now or hereafter hold binding on   , the amount which I am to be bound to pay under this guarantee not to exceed £   sterling and interest : I agree that, without prejudice to your right to demand payment of the whole sums hereby guaranteed, you shall also be entitled to make calls on me from time to time in respect of this guarantee for such sums as you may fix : And I further declare that you may at any time or times at your discretion grant to the said   , or to any drawers, acceptors, or indorsers of bills of exchange or promissory notes received by you from him or on which he may be liable to you, any time or other indulgence, and compound with him or with the said drawers, acceptors, or indorsers respectively without discharging or satisfying my liability, and that this guarantee shall apply to

and secure any ultimate balance that may at any time become due to you :
And it is further declared that this guarantee is to remain in force until
recalled by me or my heirs or executors in writing, and shall be without
prejudice to any other securities or remedies which you have or may acquire
for the general obligations or any particular obligation of the said   .
[*Where for firm, add*, and is not to be affected by any changes in the partnership of the said firm of   .]—In witness whereof.

Discharge and Guarantee in respect of Payment of Destroyed Bank Note

Stamp 8d.

To the   Bank.

Gentlemen,—I, *A. B.* (*designation and address*), considering that on
              I inadvertently mislaid or destroyed a bank note
for £   , number   , issued by you : And considering that
you have at my request agreed to pay me the said sum of £   on
these presents being granted : And now seeing that you have accordingly
made payment to me of the said sum of £   , of which I hereby
acknowledge the receipt : Therefore I, the said *A. B.*, and I, *C. D.* (*designation
and address*), do hereby bind and oblige ourselves, our heirs, executors, and
successors whatsoever, all conjunctly and severally, to defend, relieve, and
skaithless keep you the said   Bank from all claim and question
in relation to the said note, and of all loss and expense which may be
incurred by you in connection therewith in any manner of way.—In witness
whereof.

FORMS FOR VOTING AND RANKING IN SEQUESTRATIONS

FORM OF AFFIDAVIT

At Glasgow the   day of
19 . In presence of   , one of His
Majesty's Justices of the Peace for the County of

Compeared *A. B.*, cashier, and one of the principal officers, and in name and for behoof of the   Bank   (*or otherwise as the case may be*), who, being solemnly sworn and interrogated, depones that (*here fill in name and designation of bankrupt as in sequestration proceedings*) was at the date of the sequestration of his estates on
and still is justly indebted and resting owing to the said
Bank   the sum of   , being the amount brought out in the annexed state of debt, and conform to the grounds of debt therein specified, and relative vouchers thereof, which state is signed by the deponent as relative hereto, and is held as engrossed herein ;— *a* Depones that no part of said debt has been paid or compensated to the said   Bank   , and that they hold no persons bound for the said debt other than the bankrupt, and no security for the same *b* : All which is truth, as the deponent shall answer to God.

VARIATIONS IN FORM OF AFFIDAVIT

For from *a* to *b* substitute—

Depones that no part of said debt has been paid or compensated to the said   Bank (except the sums received to account since the date of sequestration, as specified in the Appendix to the said state of debt), and that they hold no persons bound for the same other than the bankrupts and the other persons mentioned in said state.

Depones that in security of said debt the said   Bank hold the securities specified in the Appendix to said state, which Appendix is here referred to and is held as engrossed herein, and that they hold no other security for the said debt.

Further, and with a view to voting on the individual (*or* company) estate (*as the case may be*) of the said   , the deponent hereby values the several and respective bills (*or* the security of right of pledge for said debt over a quantity of goods placed in the said   Bank's custody by the said   on the   *or*, the security of the house and pertinents, *or otherwise, as the case may be*) specified in the note

of securities forming the   head of said Appendix at the
respective sums there stated, amounting together to the sum of   ,
and he values the obligations of the parties liable in relief to the said
               , and bound on the several and respective bills specified and
contained in the said Appendix under the   head thereof, at the
several and respective sums there mentioned, amounting *in cumulo* to
                  , which two last-mentioned sums, amounting together to
the sum of   , being deducted from the foresaid sum of   ,
leaves a balance of   , for which the deponent claims a right
to vote on the estate (*or* the company estate, *as the case may be*) of the
said   .

And with a view to voting on the individual estate of the said   ,
a partner of the said firm of   , the deponent hereby values the
security held by the said Bank against his estate as specified in the said
Appendix under the   head thereof at the sum of   ,
and the deponent values the claim of the said   Bank against
the estate of the said company at the sum of   , and the
claim of the said   Bank on the estate of   , the
other individual partner of said company, at the sum of   ,
amounting, said three last-mentioned sums, to   , which, being
deducted from the foresaid sum of   , leaves a balance of
                  , for which the deponent claims a right to vote in all
matters relating to the individual estate of the said   ; and in
like manner the deponent, in claiming to vote on the individual estate of
the said   , hereby values the claim of the said
against the said company at the sum of   , and the claim of the
said (creditor) against the estate of the said   at the sum of
               , which two sums, amounting together to   , being
deducted from the foresaid sum of   , leaves a balance of   ,
for which the deponent claims a right to vote in all matters relating to the
individual estate of the said   .

Further, the deponent claims to be ranked on the said company estate,
with a view to drawing a dividend for the foresaid sum of   ,
under deduction of   , the value of the foresaid securities over
their estate, which sum being so deducted, leaves a balance of   ,
and he claims to be ranked on the estate of the said   with a
view to drawing a dividend for the foresaid sum of   , under
deduction of the foresaid sum of   , the value of the foresaid
security over his estates, which, being so deducted, leaves a balance of
                , and he claims to be ranked on the estate of the said
for the foresaid sum of   .

MANDATE TO VOTE IN SEQUESTRATION

                                                     (*Place and date.*)

Sir,—I hereby authorise you to attend, act, and vote at all meetings
in the sequestration of   , with all the powers which belong
to   .

Your obedient servant.

To *A. B.*   (*Address.*)
Whom failing,
    C. D.

EXAMPLE OF STATE OF DEBT ANNEXED TO AFFIDAVIT

STATE OF DEBT due to the   Bank by *A. B. & Co.*, merchants, 201 North Bridge, Edinburgh, and *A. B.*, merchant there, the sole partner of the said firm, as such partner and as an individual, as at the date of the Sequestration of their Estates, 15th March 1894.

I. Principal sum due to the said Bank on current account kept at their head office in Edinburgh in name of the said *A. B. & Co.*, as per copy of account from and including the last docquet and relative vouchers herewith produced   -   -   -   -   -   £782 19 9
     Add interest to date   -   -   -   -   -   -   8 5 6

II. On bill drawn by *C. D. & Co.*, Aberdeen, upon and accepted by the said *A. B. & Co.*, and indorsed to the said   Bank by the drawers, dated 2nd January 1894, at six months' date, and due 5th July 1894   -   -   -   -   - £203 9 6
     Deduct rebate of interest -   -   -   3 2 3
                               200 7 3

III. On the following bills drawn by the said *A. B. & Co.*, upon and accepted by the said *C. D. & Co.*, and indorsed to the said Bank by the drawers, viz. :—
    (1) Bill dated 1st September 1893, at six months' date, and due 4th March 1894 -   - £200 0 0
         Add noting and charges   -   -   0 11 6
         Add interest to date of seques-
            tration   -   -   -   -   -   0 6 0
                               200 17 6

    (2) Bill dated 1st September 1893, at six months' date, and due 4th March 1894 -   - £277 14 5
         Add noting and charges   -   -   0 15 5
                             £278 9 10
       Add interest to date of seques-
          tration   -   -   -   -   -   0 8 4
                               278 18 2

IV. On the following bills drawn by the said *C. D. & Co.*, indorsed by them to the said *A. B. & Co.*, by whom indorsed to the said   Bank, viz. :—
    (1) Acceptance by *E. F. & Co.*, Ayr, dated 25th October 1893, at four months' date, and due 28th February 1894   -   -   - £200 0 0
         Add notarial expenses -   -   -   0 18 5
                             £200 18 5
       Add interest to date of seques-
          tration   -   -   -   -   -   0 8 9
                               201 7 2

                     Carry forward -   -   - £1672 15 4

Brought forward -   -   -   £1672 15 4

(2) Acceptance by *G. H.*, merchant, Liverpool,
dated 1st October 1893, at six months' date,
and due 4th April 1894 -   -   - £194 12 11
Deduct rebate of interest -   -   0 10 8
                                                    ——————
                                                                        194 2 3

V. Bill drawn by the said *A. B. & Co.* upon and accepted
by *L. M. & Co.*, 80 Constitution Street, Greenock,
and indorsed to the said   Bank by
the drawers, dated 3rd December 1886, at six
months' date, and due 6th June 1887   - £700 0 0
Add notarial expenses -   -   -   -   1 13 9

1887.   £701 13 9
Oct.   6. Interest to date   -   -   - £11 14 0
 ,,   ,, Paid to account   -   -   -   -   - 400 0 0
                                                    ——————
                                                                   £301 13 9
1888.
June 28. Interest to date   -   - £10 17 9
 ,,   ,, Paid to account -   -   -   -   - 38 15 6
                                                    ——————
                                                                   £262 18 3
1890.
Aug. 13. Interest to date   -   - £27 15 0
 ,,   ,, Paid to account -   -   -   -   - 190 9 6
                                                    ——————
                                                                   £72 8 9

Interest to date of sequestration -   -   -   - £9 3 7
Add interest -   -   -   -   - 59 10 4
                                                    ——————
                                                                        131 19 1
                                                                    ——————
                                                                   £1998 16 8

Note.—The said Bank of   hold in security of the overdraft, forming item No. I. of the foregoing state of debt (*or* " in
security of the said debt," *or otherwise as the case may be*), the following bills drawn by the said *A. B. & Co.*, viz. :—

(1) Bill accepted by *O. P.*, merchant, Montrose,
dated 1st January 1893, at six months'
date -   -   -   -   -   - £300 0 0
(2) Bill accepted by *X. Y.*, commission
agent, Dundee, dated 7th December
1893, at three months' date -   - 222 12 8
                                                    ——————
                                                                   £522 12 8

or

The said   Bank hold in security for the above debt letter of
guarantee by *A. C.*, solicitor, Perth, for £500, dated 21st June 1890.

or

The said   Bank hold in security for the above debt :—
  (1) Certificate for £1000, Caledonian Railway ordinary stock.
  (2) Promissory note for £500 by *G. H.*, merchant in Aberdeen, and
      E. C., shipbroker, Dundee.

or

The said   Bank hold in security for the above debt :—
  Assignation by *A. C.* in favour of the Bank of Policy No. 63503, *p.*
    £1000 by the Life Association of Scotland, dated 1st February
    1860, over his life, with explanatory letter agreeing that the said
    Policy shall be held in security   (*or as the case may be*).

Appendix

Amount of debt as before   -   -   -   -   -   -   £1998 16   8
Deduct with a view to voting, the following valuations :—

I. *Securities held by the Bank*—

  (1) Acceptance by *O. P.* for -   £300   0   0 £150   0   0
  (2) Acceptance by *X. Y.* for -   222 12   8   12   0   0
                                                  ————————————
                                                   £162   0   0

II. Valuation of the obligations of parties liable in
    relief to the said *A. B. & Co.*—

  (1) *C. D. & Co.*, acceptors of bills Nos. 1
      and 2, forming item No. III., and
      of bills Nos. 1 and 2, forming item No.
      IV. in said state   -   - £450   0   0
  (2) *E. F. & Co.*, acceptors of
      bill No. 1 under item No.
      IV. in said state   -   -   60   0   0
  (3) *G. H.*, acceptor of bill No. 2
      under item No. IV. in
      said state   -   -   -   80   0   0
  (4) *L. M. & Co.*, acceptors of
      bill forming item No. V.   5   0   0
                                 —————————— 595   0   0
                                            ————————————
                                                 757   0   0

Amount for which the said   Bank claim to
  vote in the sequestration of the said *A. B. & Co.* -   -   £1241 16   8

Form of Deposit Receipt for Unclaimed Dividends

(*Place and date.*)

£

  Received for   Bank on behalf of the Accountant of
Court and his successors in office from *A. B.*, Trustee on the sequestrated
estate of *C. D.*, the sum of   , being the amount of dividends
unclaimed in this sequestration, conform to list annexed, which is carried
to the " account of unclaimed dividends " in the books of the Bank in terms
of the Bankruptcy (Scotland) Act, 1913, sec. 153.

(*Signature of Bank Officer.*)

List of Unclaimed Dividends referred to in the Foregoing Receipt

Names and Designations of Creditors entitled to Dividends.	Amount of Claims.	Particulars of Dividends.	Amount Deposited.
A. B., merchant in			

Claim under a Trust-Deed

At   the
day of   Nineteen hundred
and   years.
     In presence of   , Esquire, one
of His Majesty's Justices of Peace for the County of   .

I,
do solemnly and sincerely declare that
on the
the date on which   executed a trust-deed for behoof of
     creditors, and still   justly indebted and resting
owing to
the sum of
according to an account indorsed hereon, which is docqueted and subscribed
by me as relative hereto ; and I make this solemn declaration, conscientiously
believing the same to be true, and by virtue of the provisions of an Act
made and passed in the fifth and sixth years of the reign of His late Majesty
King William the Fourth, entitled " An Act to repeal an Act of the
" present Session of Parliament, entituled ' An Act for the more effectual
" abolition of oaths and affirmations taken and made in various departments
" of the State, and to substitute declarations in lieu thereof ; and for the
" more entire suppression of voluntary and extra-judicial oaths and affidavits,
" and to make other provisions for the abolition of unnecessary oaths.' "

       *   *
_____   _____
   The Magistrate signs above.   The Declarant signs above.

FORM OF ACCESSION BY CREDITOR TO TRUST-DEED

19 .

Sir,—

hereby accede to the trust-deed
above referred to, executed
for behoof of   creditors, and empower
to sign the deed of accession to said trust on   behalf.—
Yours respectfully,

*

The Creditor, or, if a Company, the Firm, signs above.

FORM OF AFFIDAVIT FOR RANKING IN THE LIQUIDATION OF A LIMITED COMPANY

At Edinburgh, the
day of   19 .
In presence of
one of His Majesty's Justices of the Peace for the County
of   .

Compeared *A. B.*, cashier, and one of the principal officers, and in name
and for behoof of the   Bank (*or otherwise as the case may be*),
who, being solemnly sworn and interrogated, depones that the
Company Limited was at the date of the liquidation of its estates, and still
is, justly indebted and resting owing the said   the sum of
£   , conform to the state of debt which is annexed and signed
as relative hereto, and held to form part of this affidavit : Depones that no
part of said sum has been paid or compensated to the said
and that no security is held for the same (*or otherwise as the case may be*) :
Depones further, that no other person than the said company and the other
persons mentioned in the said state of debt is bound for the said debt, and
that there is no co-obligant bound in relief to the company (*or otherwise
as the case may be*) : All of which is truth, as the deponent shall answer to
God.

Note.—The state of debt annexed is similar in form to that used in the case of a
sequestration.

MISCELLANEOUS FORMS

MANDATE TO OPERATE ON CURRENT ACCOUNT, INCLUDING THE INDORSATION OF CHEQUES [1]

(Place and date.)

To the

Gentlemen,—I hereby request you to honour all cheques drawn on my account by Mr.   , or cheques signed or indorsed for me by him.   This authority to subsist until recalled in writing.—I am, your most obedient servant.

MANDATE TO OPERATE ON CURRENT ACCOUNT, INCLUDING POWER TO OVERDRAW SAME [2]

(Place and date.)

To the

Gentlemen,—I hereby request you to honour all cheques or drafts drawn on my account kept at your head office at Edinburgh, which may be signed by my clerk   for me, and that even though your honouring the said cheques or drafts should have the effect of overdrawing said account, but so as not to exceed at any time the sum of £   .
This authority to subsist until recalled by me in writing.—I am, gentlemen, your obedient servant.

PROCURATION

To the   Bank.

Gentlemen,—We   , carrying on business under the firm of   , and we, the said   , do hereby nominate, constitute, and appoint   to be our procurator and attorney for the purpose and to the effect aftermentioned ; giving, granting, and committing unto him full power, warrant and authority to grant and subscribe receipts, discharges, and vouchers of every kind, for and in the name of us the said   , and also to draw, accept, indorse, and discharge for us, and in our name, all bills, promissory notes, cheques, or other obligations, and generally to grant and subscribe, on our behalf, all writings or documents of every other kind whatsoever : Declaring that all documents or writings subscribed for us, the said

---

[1] This mandate does not cover overdrafts.

[2] The above two forms of mandate have been adjudged by the Revenue Authorities as exempt from Stamp duty.

by the said   , shall be
equally valid and binding on us, the whole granters hereof, as if the same
had been subscribed by us or by any of us; and that this authority shall
remain in force until recalled by us in writing; and that it shall not be
affected by any changes which may take place in the partners of the said
firm of   .—In
witness whereof, etc.

FACTORY AND COMMISSION CONFERRING EXTENSIVE POWERS ON ATTORNEY

I,   , considering that I am about to go
abroad, and that I intend to be absent from the United Kingdom for an
indefinite period, and that it is proper that I should appoint a person or
persons to manage my affairs there during my absence, and having confidence in the fidelity, ability, and integrity of
and   , I do hereby nominate, constitute, and
appoint the said   and   , jointly and
severally, and the survivor of them, to be my factors or factor, commissioners
or commissioner, and attorneys or attorney, and I hereby give, grant, and
commit to the said   and
jointly or either of them, and the survivor of them, full power, warrant, and
commission for me and in my name to ask, demand, receive, pursue for, and
discharge, assign, or convey all and sundry debts and sums of money, interest
and dividends, and others whatsoever due and addebted to me, or
which may become due and resting owing to me by or upon bond, bill,
account, mortgage, debenture, or otherwise, together with all sums of money,
funds, estate, legacies, or provisions to which I am entitled to have already
succeeded to or to which I may hereafter become entitled or succeed, to sell,
assign, transfer, convey, and discharge all stocks, moneys, shares, or securities
which may at present or at any future time belong to me or stand in my
name, to grant all assignations, transfers, discharges, or other writings whatsoever that may be necessary for any or all of these purposes, to invest or
lay out in such stocks, shares, securities, mortgages, bonds, debentures, or
other manner of way which they may in their discretion think proper, all
or any sums of money belonging to me which may come into their hands in
any manner of way, and to grant and accept all such transfers, deeds, or
other writings whatsoever (whether involving personal liability on my part
or on their part or not) as they may consider necessary for the purposes
of such investments, to institute all actions at law which they may think
necessary to vindicate my rights, and to defend me in any suit, action,
or process which may be brought against me, and for these purposes to
employ such advocates, procurators, and others as they may think fit to
appoint, and transact any doubtful debts and claims which may be due or
owing to me or which may lie against me, to enter into submissions on my
behalf, to employ law agents when necessary or to act themselves in such
capacity, and apply the interests, dividends, and other moneys coming into
their hands in payment of any accounts and debts which may be due; and
generally I hereby give and commit to the said   and
jointly and severally, and the survivor of them, as full power to manage and
intromit with my whole estate in the United Kingdom, and the whole
income, interest, and proceeds thereof, as I could do myself if personally

present : Declaring always that all transfers, assignations, receipts, discharges, conveyances, and other deeds and writings whatsoever granted by the said   and   , or either of them, to, or accepted by them from, whatsoever person or persons, and all actings or deeds done or granted by them or either of them in execution of these presents, shall be equally valid and binding as if granted, done, or accepted by myself : Declaring also that this factory shall subsist until recalled in writing by me, providing always that the said   and   shall be bound and obliged, as by acceptance hereof they bind and oblige themselves, their heirs, executors, and successors, to hold just count and reckoning with me, my heirs, executors, or assignees, for their intromissions under and in virtue hereof, and to make payment to me of whatever balance shall be due by them after deduction of all payments made by them to me or on my behalf, and all necessary charges and expenses : And I consent to the registration hereof for preservation and execution.—In witness whereof.

EXPLANATORY LETTER WITH REFERENCE TO LOANS ON STOCKS, ETC.

19 . .

To the   Bank.

Gentlemen,—With reference to any advances of cash which you have made or may make to (me *or* us) from time to time, and to the stocks or other securities which you may hold for such advances, it is understood and agreed between you and (me *or* us), as follows :—

1. That (I *or* we) shall at all times maintain a margin at least   per cent. above the sum at (my *or* our) debit, calculating the value of the securities at the market price of the day ; and if at any time the margin fall below that value, (I *or* we) shall be bound forthwith either to increase the security or reduce the advances to a corresponding extent.

2. That (I *or* we) shall be allowed to exchange the securities held from (me *or* us) as aforesaid, or any of them, for other securities to your satisfaction of equal value which (I *or* we) shall deliver to you in their place.

3. That in the event of (my *or* our) failing to increase the security, or to reduce the debt as above provided, or, in the event of (my *or* our) failing to repay the said advances and interest due thereon when required, you shall be entitled, on your giving (me *or* us) notice by letter sent to (my *or* our) usual address through the post-office, to sell and dispose of the securities held from (me *or* us) without further notice, and to apply the proceeds in reduction or extinction of the Bank's claims on (me *or* us).

4. It is understood and agreed that in the case of all or any of the said securities particularly identified by specific numbers and/or otherwise you shall not be under any obligation to retain or to account for or recover to me the said securities bearing the specific numbers and/or other particular identification of those handed or assigned or transferred or lodged or deposited as aforesaid.—In witness whereof.

GENERAL INDEX

INDEX OF FORMS

Printed in Great Britain at THE DARIEN PRESS, *Edinburgh*